NICK KRAUSER
BALLS DEEP

BALLS DEEP
FROM JILTED LOVER TO LADY KILLER

NICK KRAUSER

Balls Deep, Volume 1 of the Nick Krauser memoir, Second Edition.

© Copyright: Nick Krauser 2014/2019.

The right of Nick Krauser to be identied as author of this Work has been asserted by him in accordance with sections 77 and 78 of the Copyright, Designs and Patents Act 1988.

All rights reserved. No part of this publication may be reproduced, stored in retrieval system, copied in any form or by any means, electronic, mechanical, photocopying, recording or otherwise transmitted without written permission from the author. You must not circulate this book in any format.

www.krauserpua.com

CONTENTS

		Acknowledgements	4
		Introduction	6
1	—	Infant Terrible	14
2	—	Painted Into A Corner	26
3	—	Video Nasty	38
4	—	Mayfair	50
5	—	Schooldaze	58
6	—	College	68
7	—	University	78
8	—	London Calling	90
9	—	Shuttle Japan	108
10	—	Soup Kitchen	120
11	—	Kickboxing	134
12	—	Leaving Japan	148
13	—	Married Life	160
14	—	The Journey Begins	178
15	—	Somali Pirates	204
16	—	The Daygame Grind	216
17	—	Nigerian Nurse	240
18	—	A Romanian Immigrant	256
19	—	Unplugging	272
20	—	Great Giana Sisters	284
21	—	Thai Girls Are Tigers	306
22	—	Yet More Grinding	320
23	—	Crusader King	338
24	—	D Day Landings	358
25	—	Reconquista	372
26	—	Lithuania	382
27	—	Turkish Delights	408
28	—	Black Mamba	430
29	—	Baltic Campaign	456
30	—	Last Exit to Camden	474
31	—	Pornalikes	494
32	—	Dutch Uncle	506
33	—	Euro Jaunts	520
34	—	Old Wine, New Bottles	538
35	—	Wizard and Oz	550
36	—	Master of the Universe	562
37	—	Operation Barbarossa	586
38	—	Depraved	614
39	—	Living The Dream	638
40	—	The Summit	656
		Epilogue	676

ACKNOWLEDGEMENTS

If I'd known how much time and effort I'd eventually sink into writing my memoir, I'd have never had the courage to begin. Fortunately, many people helped me along the way. Suzanne was instrumental in putting together the first edition manuscript, using my blog posts and dictated audio files. From her work, I was able to expand and rewrite what became the final published book in 2014. Reader feedback and encouragement of that first effort spurred me on to continue with additional memoir volumes and, ultimately, to completely re-write *Balls Deep* for this second edition.

Davorin returns with a new cover design and interior graphics, as does Cristian, colourising his original girl caricature art. I thank Alexey for his new layout design. Edward and Sofija provided chapter-by-chapter feedback upon test-reading my updated manuscript. I give additional thanks to those readers kind enough to review the first edition, often with helpful constructive criticism.

This second edition is considerably changed from the first. The opening thirteen chapters are entirely new, recapping my pre-Game life (the first edition jumped in to Game within a few pages of chapter one). Though I have kept all the original player stories, I have extensively rewritten every one of them to flesh out additional details, improve the literary presentation, smooth out the chronological sequencing, and to update my analysis of events in light of an additional five years of hindsight and Game experience. All told, this book is seventy thousand words larger than the first edition and, in my opinion, a more engaging and instructive narrative. Hopefully, returning readers will agree.

INTRODUCTION

This is a memoir primarily about my banging a lot of hot young women, one hundred and sixty of them in total. At least that appears to be the memoir's focus, initially: "look at me, I'm a player!" To write such a book *without* coming across as an insufferable show-off is well beyond my literary ability. So I faced a conundrum. On the one hand are factors leading me towards arrogance. I'm a man who broke through the limits nature intended for me and vastly outperformed reasonable expectations in the Sexual Market Place. I owe my notoriety to this fact and, chances are, you're holding this book in your hands right now because that intrigues you. Probably, you assume that my travelling the world chasing skirt for nine years has furnished me with many good stories. Funny stories, squalid stories, dramatic stories....

Yes, it did.

You wouldn't believe how many stories a man can collect when he seeks adventure and figures out a means to find it. When asked "what is a really long novel?" most people think of Tolstoy's epic *War And Peace*. Just the first four volumes of my story alone exceed Tolstoy's word-count by quite a margin. And there's a lot that I left out. So yes, I have plenty of stories.

Most of you have a reason to pick up this memoir that is over and above its mere entertainment value. You want to know *how I did it*. How does an average-looking, middle-aged man successfully seduce over a hundred and sixty hot young women without paying for it? Perhaps you have ambitions to pull off a similar feat yourself. What I achieved was statistically rare, but not special. Nature has prepared us all for it. That potential is buried deep if only we know where to look and how to tease it out. Each and every man among us carries within his DNA the burden of responsibility to pass it on to the next generation. Every single one of us is the current version of a DNA strain honed through a million years of evolution to be a winner.

Yes, that's right. Every single man reading this book is the latest incarnation in a long line of winners.

Of course, so is each of the other three billion men on the planet, so let's not think of ourselves as unicorns just yet! The struggles of our ancestors secured our existence in this present generation, and now it's our responsibility to win this round and to successfully reproduce. Like it or not, we are embroiled in a Darwinian struggle for survival and replication and... it's a dirty low-down fight. Our popular culture tends to put a clean romantic gloss onto this struggle, promoting themes of love, soulmates, honour, and perhaps even chivalry. The reality on the streets, in the bars, and in the bedroom is often squalid, dishonest, and shocking. Just pick up a women's gossip magazine and read the relationship pages. It's a war-zone out there! They do say "all is fair in love and war."

This brings me to 'the other hand', and the factors that lead me *away* from arrogance.

Most men are dupes. Like most such men, I preferred to believe the Disney fairytale version of relations between men and women. I wasn't a hopeless romantic like the saps from a Hollywood romantic comedy. I knew women were not all sugar and spice, and that men were neither the pigs feminists slandered them as, nor the heroic gallants of classical fiction. Nonetheless, I identified with the general thrust of social harmony as taught to me first by my parents, then by my school, and later through popular culture generally. I truly believed in the white-picket-fence respectability of the suburban family. It's how I grew up. My parents are still married as I write these words, and my older brother is also married with two children, a mortgage and his own business. Before discovering Game, I had a steady, high-paying professional job at a prestigious bank. I'd worked hard at school and university to graduate with distinction, then worked even harder in the office to secure my career and with it my financial position. By the age of thirty-one I was happily married to a sweet Japanese girl one year younger than myself. It was what was expected of me, and I was happy to fulfil my role. That was how I planned to shoulder my burden of responsibility and do right by my ancestors who'd struggled under far more perilous conditions than I.

I felt like I'd succeeded in life.

And then things went wrong, badly wrong, towards the end of 2008.

My marriage turned sour, my wife left me, and I quickly lost all interest in my job. It was a bad time. I was consumed by a confusing swirl of emotions: shock at the suddenness of separation, heartbreak at the disappearance of our loving connection, and also the shame of failure. I was the only person in the history of my family to have gotten divorced. It stung my pride, too. All of life's meaning drained away. I'd had a future with purpose and now, suddenly, I had nothing. For three months I moped around. I couldn't sleep, couldn't eat, and took no joy from life. At work I was an imposter in my own body. As I approached my thirty-fourth birthday I was single and completely lost. I had no idea how to find a new girlfriend. The rest of my life stretched out ahead of me as a sexually-barren wasteland.

I was crushed.

It was an overreaction.

When you're at the centre of a storm it feels all-consuming and you lack perspective. The reality was that only one part of my life had changed, my marriage. Admittedly, that was the single most emotionally significant part of my life, and the foundation of my future, but it was still only *one* thing. I remained healthy, gainfully employed, and financially comfortable.

My desperation was purely emotional, but desperation it was.

Those three months were by far the worst of my life.

I felt utterly hopeless so on my birthday I decided to treat myself. I banged an escort in her High Street Kensington apartment. She was a twenty-four year old Hungarian brunette and pretty damn hot. I returned home afterwards and calculated how many times a month I could afford the £150 in-call cost of such escorts and then checked several such websites to see if the girls were hot enough to attract me. I seriously budgeted it. I needed some kind of physical intimacy with women. Escorting was the only way I knew to get sex with women I found sexually attractive.

I certainly didn't know how to date beautiful young women.

Ugh! I shiver at the thought now.

For three months of my life I was an abject loser. I'd allowed my divorce to hit me far harder than it should have. Fortunately, I was unwilling to remain a loser forever. As the shock receded, I resolved to do whatever it took to get back on my feet, brush myself off, and figure out a new plan. It was at this low ebb that I recalled the existence of the 'Seduction Community', a world-wide group of men (connected through Internet forums) who claimed to have discovered a secret code to picking up women and having sex with them. I'd first read about them a few years earlier, not paying much attention to it. I needed to believe something and appeared to have no better options. So, I gave 'Game' a try.

Incredibly, it worked. Most men fail at the Game, but I actually succeeded (eventually!).

I'd found a new path to replace the earlier route that had so suddenly evaporated before my eyes. I embarked upon the 'Player's Journey', which is not unlike the Hero's Journey of epic fiction but with less monsters to slay and far more shagging. By the end of it, nine years later, I'd learned far more about women and about myself than I ever dreamed possible. All of my preconceptions would be smashed and my entire world-view rebuilt from the ground up. As you sit reading these words it probably sounds far-fetched, so let me ease you into the story one chapter at a time. Almost everything I thought I knew was wrong. I wrote these books so they show, through examples, how I stumbled upon the truth of male-female attraction. And to share my hard-won knowledge.

These books are, at first blush, about the women I met along the way. We players always start out thinking we are in the Game in order to seduce women. So, you'll read about *a lot* of women. As my story progresses you'll see me develop from my lowest ebb following my divorce, a sexless, hopeless fool who didn't understand women, felt uncomfortable in new social situations, and couldn't even get a kiss for six months. By the end of this first volume, I'd transformed into a man who was having sex with nineteen-year-old students in pub restrooms in the middle of the day an hour after meeting them. As I sat writing this introduction for the first edition, just two hours earlier, I had "notched" (had sex for the first time with) a nineteen-year-old fashion model from Serbia on our second date.

And it was fucking awesome.

(You can read that story in volume four, *Adventure Sex*).

So, inevitably, I'll come across as an insufferable braggart in places. I apologise for that in advance. There's no other way to write about banging over a hundred and sixty hot young women. But to balance the highs, I've also tried to share the darker sides of my story. This Player's Journey has been an emotional roller-coaster where, for the first few years, I was unhappy far more than I was happy. I'll relate to you the anxiety, self-doubt, and sense of isolation I felt for months on end as I knuckled down and tried to get good at seducing women. I'll write about my failures; and there were a lot of them.

It quickly became apparent that my true problem was never really my lack of success with women. That was merely a symptom of a more general malaise. I had some personality issues that needed to be fixed. To successfully seduce women I needed to work on myself too. I got into the Game in order to seduce women but the Player's Journey is really about seducing yourself. Hence while this memoir is ostensibly a collection of stories about chasing skirt, it's really about deep-level identity change. It's about a man realising he is deeply flawed and then trying his best to become a better man. I just tended to push all that self-improvement stuff into the background so I could get on with chasing skirt.

This volume is the first of seven. It begins with my childhood, where I provide context to my story and offer a window into embryonic personality traits (good and bad) that would bloom in adult life and come to dominate my skirt-chasing days. The Game part of the story begins in 2009, chapter fourteen, when I made my fateful decision to become a 'pick up artist'. If you bought this book only for the skirt-chasing stories, feel free to skip ahead to that chapter. From there, it covers the first two years of my Player's Journey. It shares my experience of beginning the most difficult journey of my life and, by the end of this volume, reaching a level beyond what most wannabe players ever attain. Many of my readers will be dipping their toes into these waters for the first time, wondering if they too could become a professional seducer. I'll do my best to guide them through those tough early stages where most of the feedback from girls is failure, and the path is littered with landmines and wild goose chases.

I hope you enjoy reading my story. I certainly enjoyed living it.

Nick Krauser

Belgrade, October 2018

The end of a journey

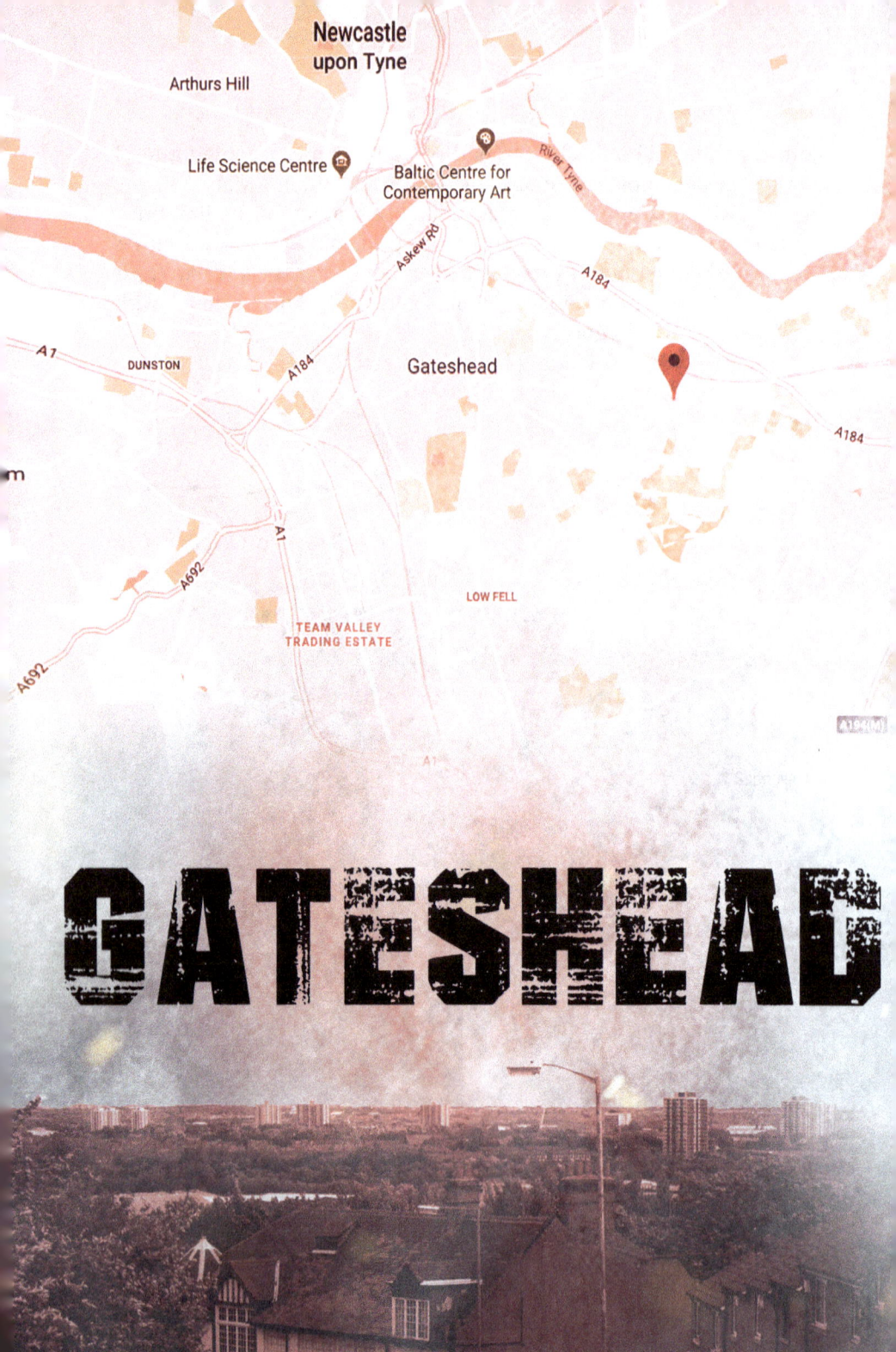

CHAPTER 01

INFANT TERRIBLE

CHAPTER 1

INFANT TERRIBLE

My earliest memory is of standing in the bathroom in my parents' council house screaming my head off because I had tonsillitis. Strangely, that memory is stored visually from a third-person perspective. The images, just a split second of action not unlike a short gif from an internet meme, are viewed not through my own eyes but from side-on about five metres away, to the left of three-year old me.

There I am, standing defiant on the small faux-wool light blue rug, facing the bath, screeching until I'm red-faced. Also in the picture is a small sink and bathroom mirror, and the shower curtain. My parents are there, presumably, but I can't see them.

My next memory comes from the hospital. I'd caught tonsillitis so frequently that the NHS doctors recommended having the pesky appendages removed. My mother explained it to me that tonsils were an unnecessary nuisance and I'd be better off without them. I never thought to question why, if they weren't needed, that nature would equip me with them in the first place. Then again, I believed in Santa Claus back then, so I wasn't of fully rational mind.

I was an overnight patient because I required a general anaesthetic to put me to sleep before the operation. The only part of the process that stayed with me is when I lay on the operating table and the nurse leant over me to apply a black plastic cup over my nose and mouth. I remember the shape vividly: the cup was shaped like a cricket player's groin protector and had a soft dark grey rubber ribbing around the edges to soften its touch to the patient's face.

The smell was awful. No doubt worse than an actual cricket player's crotch.

"Count to ten with me," the nurse told me, "one... two.... three... four...."

And there that memory ends. I never did forget the smell.

In fact, for months afterwards I'd have nightmares about it, waking up in the middle of the night panicking that I was dying. Three-year old me didn't have a concept of death but I did understand oblivion because I'd experienced it by dint of the general anaesthetic. So that brings me to my third memory of childhood: lying in bed under my Star Wars blanket (this was only a year after the blockbuster movie's initial cinema release) in the dark, hyperventilating and hoping my mum or dad would come and calm me down. If my thrashing and moaning didn't wake them, I'd sneak into their bed at night.

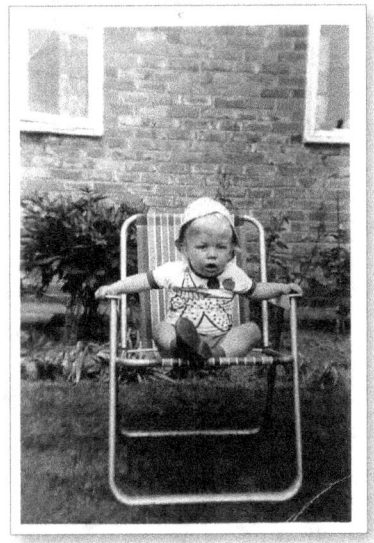

The earliest existing photo of me

I don't want to give the impression my childhood was traumatic because it wasn't. Nonetheless, it's notable that my three earliest memories involve a temper tantrum thrown due to pain, being gassed unconscious by a nurse, and then waking up bathed in sweat after nightmares about it.

Around the same time, I remember sitting in the bath with a big yellow plastic ring on my head like the brim of a hat. Or like a huge pineapple slice. This was to allow my hair to be washed without water running into my ears and damaging the grommets doctors had placed there. These are small temporary tubes placed into a child's eardrums to treat recurring ear infections and 'glue ear'. Apparently I was almost deaf for six months, at the critical time when I was learning to speak. My mother later explained that the grommets probably didn't help but the infections cleared up eventually.

Unfortunately, I'd been left with a stutter.

The solution to that was sending me to a speech therapist, something I have absolutely no recollection of. The therapist fixed my stutter and I've never had a problem with it since. An added bonus of therapy was I was taught to speak by professionals from the very beginning. They taught me vocal projection and I've had a booming voice ever since. Aside from occasionally annoying people in public places or being overheard when I don't intend to be, this has been very helpful. Few things dominate a social situation like verbally blasting everybody so hard that their hair stands on end. It would be extremely useful in later years when I began chasing women.

My parents were of modest background. My dad was locally born in Gateshead as the middle of three children. His two sisters left home as soon as they could, apparently because my grandfather on that side was a tyrant. They worked their entire adult lives in Ibiza, starting as tour reps when cheap air travel first became available to the masses and the Spanish island began its run as a major tourist destination. I'd see them every few months when they'd return with gifts for my brother and I. One time, they brought us a pair of blunderbuss replica guns that I loved. I think I still have mine in a box in the attic somewhere.

My dad grew up in a delightful council house on a model estate. There were three bedrooms, a lounge, a dining room, a shed, and in addition to the small front garden there was a massive back garden where, thirty years later, my brother and I would play every Sunday when we visited our paternal grandparents. Readers younger than myself probably can't imagine how idyllic the North of England was in the 1970s because it's since been utterly destroyed. My grandfather, Sidney, was a lazy cantankerous bureaucrat who sat on his ass all day in a government job (according to my dad) while my grandmother, Ruth, was a full-time housewife. Despite such modest means, they lived in a lovely house, on a lovely estate resplendent with grassy knolls and tree-lined streets, with lovely neighbours and tonnes of kids playing around.

This is the kind of life that, as a successful finance professional in London, I couldn't hope to afford for myself in the 21st Century. As this memoir develops, we'll get into when I realised this, what

I consider to be the reasons, and how I responded. The realisation that my country had been stolen from me is pivotal to how my story plays out.

My mother was an only child, born on the English south coast near Gosport. Her mother and father, my grandparents, met through a pen-pal letter exchange programme in the Army during World War Two. My granddad, Jack, was stationed in North Africa with Montgomery and my grandma, Elsie, exchanged letters with him without having met and they married on his return.

Theirs was a harsher upbringing than on my paternal side. Elsie suffered severe tuberculosis during the war and spent two years convalescing in a hospital bed, unable to go outside. Though Jack never saw battle, his post-war work in the local NEI Parsons chemical plant was strenuous and he eventually contracted a serious disease that almost killed him. My great grandfather, Elsie's dad, was trapped in a collapsed coal mine in his mid-forties and his back broken by falling rocks. He died soon after. I never met him.

Elsie and Jack relocated to Gateshead in the North East of England when my mother was still a toddler. This was the golden era of incredible council housing so, like Sidney and Ruth, they were given a nice house at an affordable rent. This was on a brand new model housing project called the Ellen Wilkinson Estate, apparently the largest such project in all of Western Europe at the time. The estate is all owner-occupiers now but it's still beautiful in 2018: rolling grass hills, pretty red-brick semi-detached houses with gardens front and back, and a peaceful vibe. Even now, when visiting my parents, I'll take a walk through the estate where I spent most of my childhood.

My father had a normal, unremarkable upbringing. He went to the local comprehensive school, joined the cross-country running club, and like most working class boys left aged sixteen and went down the Job Centre to see what the government would give him. In my dad's case, he was offered a choice of four jobs. He quit the first after a month, went back to the Job Centre, and was immediately offered a role in the local depot of a big brewery. He worked there for twenty-five years until being made redundant in his early forties and retiring to the life of leisure he enjoys to this day.

My mother's parents put her through a top quality private school called Dame Ellen's. This is because my grandfather Jack placed great importance on education and wanted his family to be upwardly mobile. The tuition fees didn't cost anything like they would now but it was still a major drain on the family budget. My mother graduated with good scores and then worked as first a barmaid and then in the local tax office, until marrying my father and becoming a housewife. She later went to Newcastle University as a mature student (around thirty years of age), added two Masters degrees, then got a job as a psychologist at precisely the time the National Health Service was massively expanding its spending in that area.

After a registry office wedding when my dad was twenty three and my mum twenty, they moved into a council flat above a shop in a rough part of Gateshead. In 2018, "rough" would mean tattooed welfare louts dealing drugs to children, hundreds of hostile burkha-clad Muslim immigrants, rampant knife and gun crime from third-generation Africans, and likely Pakistani child-rape gangs. Rough in 1972 meant the neighbours smoked indoors and perhaps their son would steal clothes from your washing line.

Like I said, readers of later generations likely cannot believe how idyllic England used to be.

School photo with my older brother Lee

My brother, Lee, was born in 1973 and then, two years later, your humble narrator entered the world in 1975. Soon afterwards, the council gave my parents a bigger, better house on the same housing estate as my maternal grandparents. This was an outstanding piece of luck because I got to grow up in a great house tucked into a quiet back lane, directly opposite the recreation field of the best school in the district. My brother and I went to that school.

It's in the bathroom of that modest but delightful council

house that I had my tonsillitis-induced temper tantrum that I remember so well.

At the time, I believed my childhood to be blissful. There's no doubt some element of rose-tinted glasses looking back at it, but I was certainly spared most of the usual problems that can mess up a child. My parents rarely fought and never once separated. There was no tragedy in my family until my teenage years when my granddad Jack became very ill. None of my friends died, nobody got molested by priests, nobody drank or took drugs, and though money was often tight we were never forced out of the comfortable upper-working class pattern of life.

We didn't have a foreign holiday until going to Paris when I was eleven. I often wore hand-me-down clothes when my brother grew out of them. That's about the extent of privation we endured as kids. My parents were blessed to come of age at the easiest time in the history of the world to be parents and, to their credit, they didn't mess it up. There were parenting problems and mistakes, which I'll relate in due course, but this must be balanced against the knowledge that they side-stepped all of the important landmines in parenting.

I can only hope I'll be as lucky when it's my turn to be a father.

My infant school was excellent. I could walk there over the school field in just a few minutes. There were just three classes, one for each year group, with about twenty kids in each. I quickly stood out as the smartest kid, causing the teachers to keep an eye on my potential. I loved being there and tore through the work as fast as I could. By the third and final year I'd seamlessly accepted the reality that I was smarter than everyone else I knew. Sometimes I'd say things that seemed outrageously arrogant but didn't intend it that way. I just said what I thought to be the case.

One day our teacher announced we'd begin rehearsing for the annual school play, called Hasebu. It was the story of a young boy from Hawaii and that's all I remember of it. The teacher picked my best friend Neil for the title role as he was smart, charming, and extremely outgoing. This seemed an obvious choice to me and, not realising how presumptuous it was, I told the teacher, "Yes, that's the right decision."

The main supporting role, Hasebu's younger brother, was given to a boy I didn't like much, George. He was a bit dim and unengaging. I approached the teacher after the assembly hall announcement.

"Excuse me, miss. You should give Hasebu's brother's part to me. I'm much better than George."

Needless to say, George kept the part. He was unable to par-lay it into a big break in show-business but he did have the satisfaction, a few weeks later, of delivering dozens of lines to an assembly hall full of proud parents while I stood at the back of the stage dressed as a palm tree, waving a big leaf made out of green paper and a kitchen roll tube.

By my final year, aged almost seven, I'd become a disciplinary problem. I continued to study hard but I'd finish my assignments twice as quickly as the rest of the class. At first I'd sit at my desk tapping my fingers and scribbling Garfield The Cat pictures on my exercise book. Eventually I'd get bored and look for anything to entertain my fertile young mind.

I was sent to the head mistress quite often. The first time I remember, it was for lifting up a girl's skirt and laughing. Another time I drew naughty pictures on the blackboard when the teacher had stepped outside the room. It didn't get serious until I got into an argument with my friend Scott. Let's go into that because it gives a window into my personality.

Scott lived a few streets over from me, a place called Redemarsh that was between my area of the estate (Creslow) and my grandma's (Chilcrosse). Of the three, Redemarsh was considered a bit 'poor'. It was one long street on a steep incline, following the old railway lines from an abandoned (and long since demolished) coal mine. On one side was the tree-lined road and front gardens which were often quite dark due to the canopy of tree cover. On the other side of Redemarsh were the back gardens and then a long row of single-car garages. Between the garages and the gardens was an uninterrupted tangle of grass and weeds three metres wide that went the whole length of the hill. Don't ask me why we considered Redemarsh 'poor' as it clearly wasn't. Still, that's how petty rivalries are when you spend your whole lives as kids playing within a few square kilometres.

"My mum says Redemarsh is full of povs," I taunted Scott. I didn't realise it then, of course, but my mother was a terrible snob and really had said words to that effect. We were playing soldiers on the school field before tea time. There was no-one else about.

"No it's not!" screamed Scott, unexpectedly taking it to heart. His family had a few money troubles I was oblivious to.

"Yes it is. It's where people live when they've got no money and can't buy nice things."

So Scott punched me on the nose, drawing blood. Seeing the blood dribble out of my nose shocked him and he back-peddled immediately, "Sorry! I didn't mean to bust your nose."

We ended up fighting. It was trivial kid's stuff and Scott got the better of it. I went home with a bloody nose and mussed-up hair. I didn't even listen when my mother was shouting at me for getting into trouble. All my thoughts were devoted to figuring out how to get Scott back. By the next morning I had a plan. Class went as normal then as we all packed up for the afternoon, I pretended to fiddle with my bag as an excuse to stay behind until the class, including the teacher, had all left the room. Then I stole a pair of scissors from the teacher's desk and hid them outside under the food waste bins by the canteen. I fell asleep feeling excited at my developing plan of revenge.

The following day I walked the alternate route to school, down a back lane rather than across the field. This was so I could intercept my friend Paul who lived there and walk in to school with him. We were joined by Neil. As we approached the main entrance, I unfurled the next phase of my plan.

"I saw Scott stealing scissors off the teacher's desk," I stated authoritatively.

Paul and Neil were scandalised. "Really?" they both cooed, wide-eyed. It seemed impossible anyone would do something so *naughty*.

"Yes. He hid them, I think."

"Where?" they said, looking around at the bushes and drainpipes. I'd convinced them. Time for the killer blow.

"I don't know. He had them in his hand when he walked over there," I said, pointing at the waste bins, "but not after."

Predictably, Paul and Neil rushed over to the bins and triumphantly 'discovered' the scissors then ran off to tell the teacher.

I stayed in the background not knowing there was a phrase to describe the trick I'd done: cat's paw.

Scott was soon hauled into the teacher's room and accused of theft. Quite naturally, he denied it. He was then taken to the headmistress and sweated until he broke down and admitted it after all. Then his parents were brought in and were no doubt humiliated by the news their son was a thief. I saw all this happening around me but didn't pay attention. I hadn't thought of any consequences beyond getting Paul and Neil to tell on him. I'd inadvertently unleashed the remorseless steamroller of school justice.

Luckily for Scott, and less so for me, the teachers began to smell a rat. I don't know how they got suspicious but I was hauled into the headmistress's office and questioned. I denied everything but she had a trick up her sleeve. Scott was brought in and we were led into the empty assembly hall.

"Stand here," she said.

Scott and I looked at each other confused. He still didn't suspect me. On reflection, I suppose he should thank me for giving him an early Kaftka-esque experience that may fortify him for the challenges of adult life.

"I am going to call in Mrs Evans. She has a special power," said the headmistress.

We stood there, in the centre of an empty assembly hall, two very confused seven year old boys. The headmistress gave us a knowing look and delivered her clever kill-shot. "Mrs Evans is a mind reader. When you tell a lie, she can see the word 'lie' on your forehead."

Guess which one of us went red and started sweating.

Now that I was busted, the teachers were aghast. Not only had I stolen some scissors, which is a bit naughty, but I'd had the foresight and cupidity to frame another boy for the crime. I'd even manipulated two other boys into acting as my cat's paw. The staff knew I was smart but this worried them. So, my parents were brought in and I was sat next to them in the teacher's office while the headmistress outlined the whole sordid story.

My parents consented to having the school psychologist brought in to assess me.

I don't remember anything about the assessment except being given an IQ test which, my mum said years later, scored me at 135. "Don't get big-headed, they aren't accurate at that age or at those extremes" she said when relating it back to me. I tested around 135 again a few years later in junior school, so who knows?

Not a bad lad

The psychologist delivered his report, the essence of which was "Nick isn't a bad lad but if he gets bored he'll make trouble to entertain himself, and if he feels someone has crossed him he'll want revenge." I dare say I haven't changed in either regard. The school quickly worked out a strategy to deal with me: they created a Special Study class for the three smartest kids, me and two girls. If we finished our work early, we'd be pulled out of the regular class and taken to the library for Special Studies. This involved sitting on the floor reading library books, mostly. I remember a multi-book series about three pirates, dressed in blue, red, and green respectively. I really enjoyed that one. The placebo special class kept me out of trouble and when, the following year, I moved over to the junior school next door those teachers had been tipped off and maintained the ruse.

A pleasant side consequence of all this is I developed an extremely strong emotional bond to studying and reading books. It made me 'special' and I thoroughly enjoyed it. I was now a model student.

GATESHEAD

CHAPTER 02

PAINTED INTO A CORNER

CHAPTER 2

PAINTED INTO A CORNER

The first girl I ever kissed was called Jean and she was the school tramp.

It took another few years before she earned that reputation, finally dropping out of school aged fourteen to have a baby. She was my girlfriend in the third year of junior school, when I was ten. We held hands a few times, went to the after school film club together, and kissed a bit. I think the relationship lasted two weeks. Jean was a pretty girl. Tall, strong-featured, and with long blonde hair. She wouldn't be the last girl I failed to sleep with although given our age and experience, that's probably a good thing.

The first time I saw a girl's pussy was also in the third year, but it wasn't Jean's. That honour belonged to a pretty little brunette called Leslie. We were sitting in class together around a table. Neil, whose nickname was Beefy because his older brother liked beef flavoured crisps, myself, and two girls: Leslie and Joanne. For some reason the conversation turned towards dares so Neil and I got our dicks out under the table. Being pre-pubescent, there wasn't much to see. The girls reciprocated but it was hard to see anything due to the viewing angle craning our necks to look without being too obvious to the teacher, the girl's school uniforms, and the briefest seconds that the whole thing lasted. It didn't make a strong impression on me.

I'd been friends with Neil for five years now, a lifetime for young kids. His parents were landlords at *The Deuchar's Arm*s pub at the bottom of my grandma's street. I lived a few minutes walk from there so it was no surprise we became friends though I can't remember how it began. His family lived in spacious rooms above the pub. We'd hang out there or in the massive enclosed courtyard stacked with empty plastic crates from beer bottle deliveries. Neil was a good lad and deservedly popular. His family, unfortunately, were extremely fat. Neil stayed in shape until his late teens and then succumbed to the family curse, though by then we'd long since grown apart.

Let me recall a few memories of Neil and I.

By the first year of junior school, aged seven, we were already known as jokers, like a double act. One day, we showed up for school wearing skirts we'd borrowed from the girls. Nowadays, that would have meddlesome Leftists declaring us gender-fluid and trying to get us onto hormone cocktails and into reassignment surgery. Back in 1982 it meant the whole class had a great laugh and the teacher let us continue the joke until first playtime before telling us to change into trousers.

Our school had an annual art competition. All kids in the school would paint a picture to be pinned to the walls of the cafeteria, arranged by grade. There would be a couple of hundred pictures in all, brightening up the space. It was quite an eagerly anticipated event. The first year, I started work on a painting of the seaside as viewed from land, looking out over the water. There were cliffs on either side and a large solitary rock thirty metres high in the middle. It was inspired by Marsden Rock, a local tourist spot my parents had driven us to that summer.

During art class, I painted away. It was coming on well. Neil came over, paint streaked all over his face and hands, to take a look at at.

"That's good, that," he said. "Where is it?"

"Marsden Rock."

"Oh yeah, I've heard of it. Never been."

That lunch time, we all filed into the cafeteria to eat school dinners (in the North of England, 'dinner' is when you have lunch, and 'tea' is when you have dinner). The fourth year (top year) kids had already finished their paintings and most had been stapled to the wall that morning. All of us young 'uns stared open-mouthed at the kaleidoscope of colour. The paintings seemed to be done with impossible levels of skill. It was natural to be in awe of what older kids could do. I finished my plate of pie, chips and cabbage, then walked back and forth like I was in an art gallery.

One picture caught my eye as by far the best. It was of a surfer catching a wave, painted in vibrant colours and minute detail. We had art class again two days later to finish our paintings. I binned my cliff-side work and started afresh painting a surfer. Then in the next period we were sent into the cafeteria to put up our work. Having changed course so late, my painting was a rush job, but I liked it and took some pride when the teacher came over with the staple gun and stuck it to the wall.

"Nice picture," she said.

"I know. I'm gonna win," I replied, confidently, then walked over to where I saw Neil standing holding his painting close to his chest.

"What did you paint?" I asked.

"Just wait and see" he replied, with a cunning smile.

The teacher stapled a few more student efforts to the wall and soon worked her way around to Neil, taking his painting and stapling it up. For a half minute she was standing in the way, her body obscuring my view. Then she turned around, congratulated Neil on an excellent effort, and walked off. I finally saw Neil's picture. It was Marsden Rock, a direct copy of my first try.

"You copied me!" I squawked.

"Yeah I know. I couldn't think of anything."

By the end of the week the whole student body's pictures were on the wall and we were led directly from morning assembly to the cafeteria for a judgement ceremony. Three teachers made serious faces and a show of deliberation before pinning colourful little rosettes to the top three pictures per grade. Not surprisingly, the fourth year kid's surfer picture took his grade's first prize. It was by far the best.

Neil's painting took first prize for the first years. He came over with a huge grin, carrying a brand new set of watercolour paints in a tin casing with a nice folding cover. I don't remember if I called him a bastard, being seven years old, but that's what I thought.

I'm not sure which emotion I felt strongest: outrage at Neil taking what I saw as my prize and watercolours; disappointment at not winning what I assumed was a sure thing; or foolhardy for binning a good original submission in favour of a rushed copy of an older kid's work.

I settled for outrage. I strode over to the judge's table.

"You got the wrong winner. Neil copied my painting."

Some eyebrows were raised. They indulged me with a few questions.

"Show us your painting," they asked and I took them to my shitty surfer picture. "Okay, now show us Neil's."

As I walked them over to his landscape scene I began to realise the flaw in my complaint. The head judge was the headmaster, a kind man we called Mr Scott. He had another episode of eyebrow raising.

"Nick, you painted a surfer and Neil painted a shoreline. They are completely different ideas."

"B....b....b...but." This wasn't my stutter returning whilst *in extremis*. I was hurt. Butt hurt. "I painted Marsden Rock first. I painted it and Neil copied it."

Mr Scott found Neil sitting on a table merrily swinging his legs, listening to the rest of the class congratulate him, and called him over. Neil showed up with a big smile like the most harmless puppy who ever lived.

"Neil, Nick says you copied him."

"No I didn't."

"You haven't even been to Marsden Rock!" I exclaimed, suddenly remembering the damning evidence that would decide the case conclusively in my favour.

"Yes I have. I went last week with my mam and dad."

Despite occasional clashes like this, Neil and I remained best friends until the second year of comprehensive school when he was forced to transfer because his parents took a job running the Conservative Club in the countryside town of Haltwhistle. Aside from an interest in creative writing and art, my main hobby in junior school was football and I was goalkeeper for our school team.

That's me on the far left

My parents adopted a rescue dog from an animal shelter a year before my brother was born. Angel was a mongrel, a mix of Labrador with something else, with a shiny black coat. Like all family dogs, she was fiercely protective of the children so when my brother and I played in the back street or school field, she'd sit and watch alertly. When we walked, she'd circle us in a protective orbit.

I loved Angel and those early experiences made me a dog lover for life.

As I was finishing junior school, Angel was getting old in dog years and her health failed. The old energetic Angel we knew suddenly became apathetic, lying around all day. One afternoon when I was playing in the back street with the other kids, I saw my dad coming up the street carrying Angel in his arms, rocking her like a baby.

It looked funny, so I started laughing.

My dad came closer and I noticed a very sad expression on his face, the strongest emotion I've ever seen him show. There were tears welled up in his eyes and even as an uncomprehending child my intuition immediately made me realise things were badly wrong. I ran up to him and asked what was going on.

"It's Angel. She collapsed on our walk. Her legs have gone."

I followed him into the house and we stayed all evening with her. My dad laid her on the sofa, which she wasn't usually allowed on, as a small treat to raise her mood. She was shivering and softly moaning. I didn't know what to do except stroke her coat and say nice things. My brother and I wanted to stay up all night but we were finally sent to bed before midnight.

The next day, while we were at school, my parents took Angel to the vet, who recommended she be put down. It was the saddest day of my childhood. Dogs are unique amongst animals in the emotional bond they make with humans and I believe the only two normal circumstances where its acceptable for a man to cry is when either his dog or his laptop dies.

Perhaps in reaction to the sad death of our family dog, my parents never did get another. Instead they became obsessive cat owners. My mother would go up to the local animal shelter at Eighton Banks and bring home abandoned cats, usually while still kittens. We'd have five of them at any one time and over the next twenty years there'd be a rotation to keep the numbers up when cats went missing or died. By the time I went to university I'd confuse the names of the new cats with old ones.

I never liked cats.

They were okay to have around, and as a kid I liked how cute the kittens were. Generally, I enjoyed the animation of living creatures around me. It made things more interesting, and I'd happily have a cat fall asleep in my lap while I watched television or read a book. But I never cared for them. I felt instinctively that they were predators who simply used us for free food and lodging. So to me it was a fair-weather friendship between the cats and I. To this day I yearn to own a few dogs. The close bond between man and dog is the single biggest element I missed from spending my adulthood living in a number of cities dotted across the world. I don't trust any man who dislikes dogs and I'm turned to rage much easier when I see a dog mistreated than a human.

It was around this time I became vegetarian. At the time I thought I'd made the decision myself, but with the benefit of hindsight I think it was at parental urging.

Although my brother and I didn't want for anything important as children, one thing we never had were proper holidays. Our family couldn't afford them. My parents were frugal, having grown up when post-war rationing was still in effect, so it wasn't as if they squandered money. We were a single-income household until I was into my teens. My dad worked overtime where he could get it, sometimes night shifts, and had long lie-ins on Saturday morning to recover. Our house in Creslow was newly and sturdily built but we didn't have much in it beyond essentials. The furniture was mostly a patchwork of hand-me-downs or charity shop stock. Our first television was a rental, from a company called Rediffusion and we changed the channel by turning a dial on the set.

I didn't care about any of that. As a kid, you just acclimatise to the environment. Even now as an adult, I don't much care for the fancy things in life and don't seek to clutter up my living quarters with expensive furniture and gadgets.

My parents wanted Lee and I to have an appreciation for our country in general and the North East region in particular. As soon as we got a family car, the first being a battered second hand red Ford Estate, they took us on drives through the countryside. We'd go to Alnick Castle, the lighthouse of Seaburn, the museum in Barnard Castle, and the preserved Victorian-era village of Beamish. When that car wore out we got a brown Ford Capri. I remember the front doors were both stuffed with crumpled newspaper to make up for missing upholstery. Our first new car was a blue Lada Estate. I didn't think anything unusual in my parents buying a Russian car in the 1980s, at the height of the Cold War. They told us it was the best value, and unusually cheap. Perhaps it was my first inkling that my dad was a socialist.

As Lee and I grew older and my dad got promoted to depot supervisor at work, our family trips took us further across the British Isles. My dad has nerdy hobbies and at that time had just developed what would become a lifetime interest in narrow gauge railways. All the best such railways are in the rural north of Wales, so we had some holidays there. We'd drive down the motorways, turn off into Wales, and then wind through the mountains until we found places with funny names that sold locally-baked mint cake. Budgets must've been tight because I only ever remember sleeping in tents on campsites. It doesn't bother me at all that we didn't stay in hotels.

Lee and I quite enjoyed the adventure of pitching tents and laying in sleeping bags with a camping light. We never slept well, especially one time a storm blew and we stayed up all night holding onto tent poles to stop it blowing away. But to us it was an adventure. We'd read *The Hardy Boys* books in school and figured this was our slice of that.

I think we only did two Welsh trips, but it feels like more. One day we drove into a small farming town on market day. All the local animal farmers had driven their livestock into the auction ground and we were treated to the spectacle of live auctions. It was bewildering to watch the rapid turnover of livestock and the bizarre language of the auctioneers. I don't mean Welsh, though that too is a bizarre language, I mean the language of the farm auction trade. Eye-opening.

My mother was strongly affected by the farmyard squalor. Being a bookish (and snobbish) city woman, she looked down on these coarse countryfolk who smelled like horse manure.

"It's disgusting," she said, pinning her nose for effect. "And it's unconscionable what they are doing to the animals."

"What are they doing to the animals?" I asked.

"They are selling them to the abattoirs," put in my dad. "Can you see them getting loaded onto carts over there? They are going off to get slaughtered."

My blood froze. That was the first time I'd made the connection between the cute farmyard animals of kid's hour TV cartoons and the meat that was served up on my plate at the dining table. Don't judge me harshly, I was only ten.

"We shouldn't support this," my mother continued. "We should become vegetarian."

I knew that meant not eating meat. It got me thinking. At that time my mother enjoyed making chilli con carne from beef mince, kidney beans, and onion. I really disliked it and thus at least once a week there'd be a showdown at dinner when I refused to finish it.

"If I go vegetarian, does it mean I don't have to eat chilli con carne?" I asked.

"Yes."

"Okay, I want to be vegetarian too."

That would be a foolish move for a growing boy but I'd come to realise that one failing my parents did have was to be completely clueless about food. It wouldn't even dawn on me for years to come. I didn't eat my first pizza until I was twelve and for many years Lee and I would eat McCain's Microchips which were awful junk food french fries that were cooked in a microwave and then lathered in salt. When I ate packed lunches at school, my mother would send me in with a tupperware tub containing: one white bun, with margarine and a slice of processed cheese; one Mars bar; one packet of Capri Sun sugared orange drink. It wasn't until I was married to a very good cook that I began to appreciate just how important nutrition (and flavour) is.

Many a time playing here

Messing around in school playground

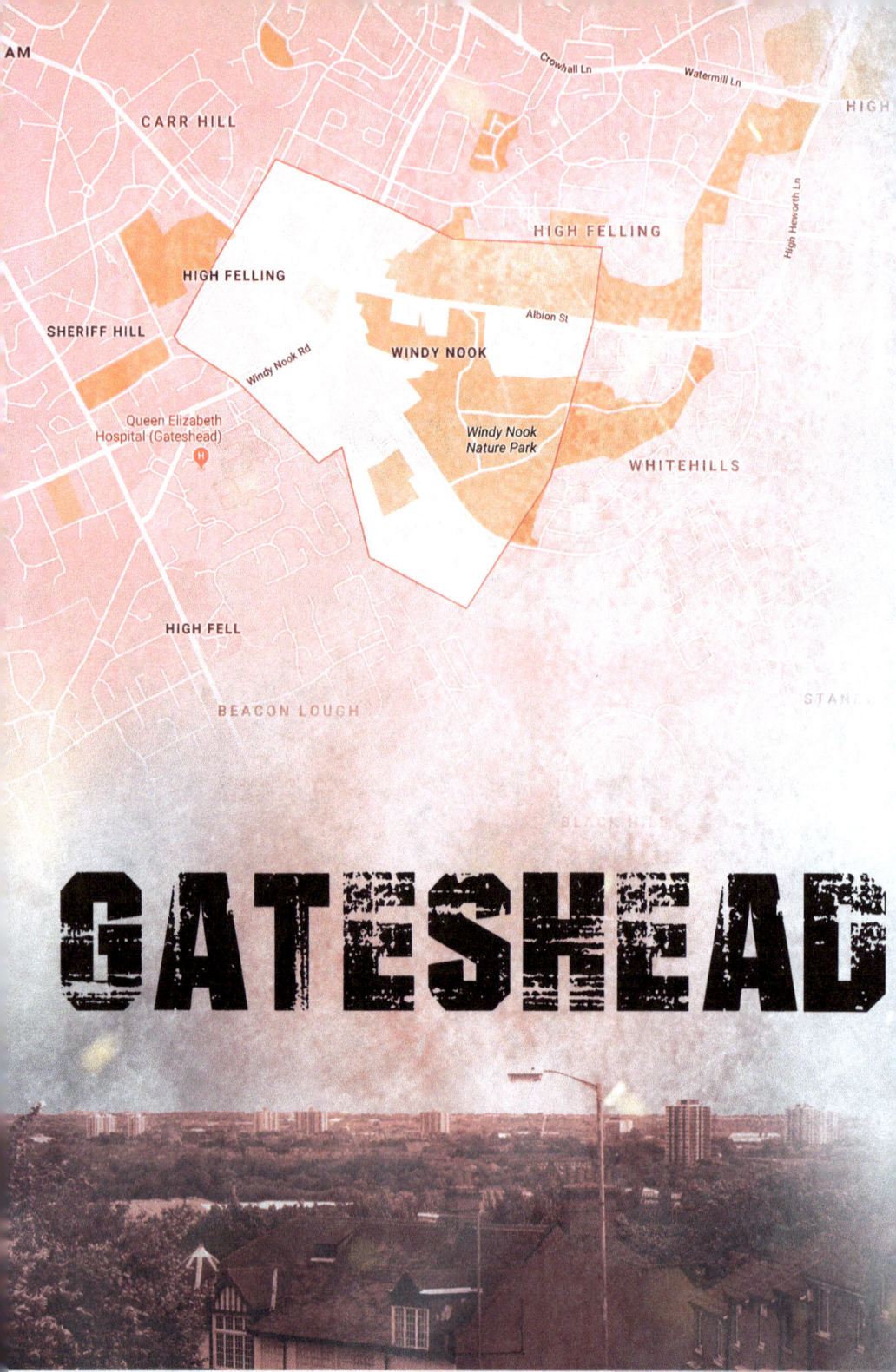

CHAPTER 03

VIDEO NASTY

CHAPTER 3

VIDEO NASTY

It was around the time that Neil was pulled out of school by his parents, when I was twelve, that I first started to show signs of weirdness. If I was to blame anyone but myself, I'd blame Satan. Or more specifically, the heavy metal music through which he speaks.

My brother was still lightly into the BMX trick riding scene we'd competed in a few years earlier. The fashion there had moved into 'street' and 'dirt' riding as the boys involved grew older. Magazines imported from the USA such as *Homeboy* showed cool older lads riding massive dirt jumps and concrete ramps in abandoned water drainage run-offs. They'd wear t-shirts of bands like Black Flag or Metallica. Lee drifted into thrash metal and reading weekly magazines such as Metal Force and Kerrang.

"Nick, Anthrax are playing at the City Hall next month. Me and Spugsy are going," he said one morning.

Spugsy was his best friend from school who I looked up to because of his quick irreverent wit. Last time I'd seen him he wore a black denim jacket with lots of band's logo badges pinned to his collar and a Stormtroopers Of Death t-shirt underneath.

"Who are Anthrax?"

"A thrash metal band. My dad said he'll take us. Are you coming?"

So in November 1987 I went to my first ever live gig, aged twelve. I loved it. It was the height of the thrash metal fashion and over the next six months I saw all four of the big bands: Metallica, Slayer and Megadeth being the others. The gigs made a big impression on me as I stood in the stalls and copied the older kids who were banging their raised fists into the air in time with the music.

Nowadays, I suspect the only time I'd ever repeat that motion as an adult would be to Sieg Heil in public to wind up some progressives.

There were some literal head-bangers in the Anthrax crowd, leaning out from the balcony above, thrashing their heads fast enough to loosen them from their necks. Newcastle City Hall was a fully seated venue, still looking every bit the old theatre it used to be. I wouldn't see my first 'mosh pit' until I attended smaller shows at independent venues a year later.

I quickly became a metaller, growing my hair and matching ripped blue jeans with a black leather motorcycle jacket my mum bought for me. Once a week I'd take my pocket money into the city centre and browse the record shops before eventually buying a 12" vinyl album. There was a lively social scene centred on a small grassy area in Old Eldon Square where all the metallers would hang out on a Saturday afternoon. I loved it. I'd found a new tribe and felt awfully grown up. The natural outcome of this was I looked less and less to my school friends for my weekend socialising while at the same time I began dressing differently to them all.

There's an old English phrase "in for a penny, in for a pound" to describe the feeling that if you're tempted to dip your toe in the water, you might as well just dive right in. Similarly, we say "might as well hang for a sheep as a lamb" to mean if you are already irrevocably committed to a plan of action, you should go all the way. I'm like that. I don't do half measures.

I got so into metal that the dark lyrics began to appeal to me and I soon sought out Black Metal music which, coincidently, had been invented by a Newcastle band called Venom with their landmark 1981 album of the same name. Perhaps it was a teenage boy thing, but I found the 'dark side' titillating. I began listening to hardcore bands like Celtic Frost, Dark Angel and Deicide who abandoned the family-friendly image of light-hearted pranksters that Anthrax promoted. Deicide claimed to be avowed Satanists and the singer, Glenn Benton, caused a stir branding an inverted crucifix into his forehead. At no point did I take any of it seriously. It was just like watching horror movies. Fun and nothing more.

You know how when 'activist' women under thirty-five want attention they always find a pretext to get their tits out in public? Black metal's Satanism was just the equivalent attention-seeking from white American farm boys.

One of my new metal friends, a boy called Chris who was three years older than me and lived in a nearby mining village, was an obsessive collector of horror movies. That too rubbed off on me. I soon began collecting them on VHS tape. This was the pre-internet era so it was quite a challenge to do so. Nowadays you can just google a director's filmography and pick a movie to google further. You'll be offered a range of options from officially re-released and remastered DVDs for sale, and pirated versions thereof on download sites. For example, you could download the entire oeuvre of cult Italian director Lucio Fulci in one evening, all perfect quality.

In the late 1980s it was a different world.

When I was collecting, we tape-traded by finding like-minded men advertising in classified pages of monthly horror fan magazines and then exchanged photocopied film lists. Each time a movie was copied it degenerated in audio-visual fidelity because of the analogue VHS dubbing procedure so we'd list our movies by 'generation' of dub since the original tape. It took months, even years, to build up a good collection. Every week the postman brought me a big parcel full of chunky VHS tapes and I'd excitedly watch the new movies, log them accurately on my growing list, then file them on a bookcase in my bedroom.

My parents appeared bemused but were laissez faire about it all and doubtless didn't really know I was watching R-rated movies.

The movies were usually crap, but that didn't matter. It was the collectors spirit that appealed to me. On my father's side the family were all slightly afflicted by Asperger's syndrome, a condition that makes people anti-social and prone to obsessive list-making and collecting. My dad expressed it by filling ring binders with photos of buses from around the UK, all carefully logged according to their operating firms. He'd buy speciality guide books from bus spotting fan publishers then drive for hours to a small town so that he could stake out the bus depot and photograph rare buses for his collection.

By comparison, my horror movie collection hobby seems almost sane.

I took great pleasure in watching my collection grow and the task of compiling and curating my 'list' relaxed me. Before long it was in strict alphabetical order and every listed movie had information on its most well-known title, the title on my version, alternate titles, running time, year of production, director, running time, subtitle language, generation quality, and notes on how heavily censored it was. I've always wanted my thought to be precise and organised. This was reflected in my collecting.

`Obviously that made me want them more`

Fun though the curation process was (my own virtual allotment to potter around on) the real satisfaction came from seeking out rare copies of movies and getting my hands on them. I had pen-pals in New Zealand, Finland, and Italy who had access to releases unavailable in most of Europe. This was a time of heavy censorship in the UK, only six years after the 'video nasties' moral panic in the newspapers that led to the government creating the BBFC age-classification rating system, heavy cuts to movies showing gore or sex, and the outright banning of 82 movies by the Director Of Public Prosecutions.

Even 18-rated slasher flicks had most of the explicit violence cut out of them for UK release. Some, such as *Hollywood Chainsaw Hookers*, even had their titles censored (in this case, removing 'chainsaw'). Nowadays ghoulish kids can watch torture porn movies like *Hostel* or *The Strangers* on their mobile phones or even watch real-life Mexican cartel beheading and dismemberment murder videos. I certainly don't recommend that, by the way. Once time when I was in my late thirties curiosity got the better of me and I watched such a 'snuff' movie on the internet. It was one cartel's sicarios killing a rival cartel's sicario they'd captured. The violence was appalling and my mood was disturbed for days afterwards, even though the victim was an evil bastard who likely deserved it. I wished I could unwatch it. When I watched horror movies as a kid, it was tame stuff and I had no desire to see the real thing.

As I keep saying, it was a different world back then. The UK still had a functioning culture and the authorities still tried to keep things sane. The lawlessness and depravity of the current era had yet to materialise.

Anyway, back to my collection.

Those 82 movies banned by the DPP became known as the 'video nasties list' by collectors and my first priority was to own copies of them all. Original commercial VHS tapes were out of the question because the rarest of them, movies like the Nazi death camp schlock *The Beast In Heat*, sold for £250 (in the unlikely event you could even track down a willing seller). That was six month's pocket money. I'd scour car boot sales and second hand shops for elusive 'original' VHS tapes and something would always pop up. I was especially proud of my rarer video nasties original tapes such as *Gestapo's Last Orgy* and *Anthropaphagous The Beast*.

I'd figured out that Finland was a good country for movies because they'd always release the fully uncut English language version with Finnish subtitles. That made Finnish tapes both desirable and watchable. Italy was great because it was the originating country of over half of the best movies due to peculiarities of its film industry. There were many highly-sought-after directors whose minor movies weren't even released outside of Italy. I got lucky in striking up a trading relationship with a middle-aged enthusiast called Simone

Romano who was a regular specialist contributor to fan magazines such as *Video Watchdog*. He had literally thousands of movies on his list including all the rare Italian-language only gems that couldn't be found elsewhere.

I focus on my tape trading here to convey several points that are relevant to my later womanizing. Firstly, I have the soul of a collector. I liked scouring the globe for rare movies that I could acquire and add to my list. That attitude resurfaced later in my chasing of skirt around the world. Just as movie collectors obsess over and compare their lists, womanizers obsess over and compare their notch counts and latest conquests. The girls find themselves broken down analytically for discussion by age, country, hotness, sexual chastity and so on in a way not dissimilar to a movie being listed by a collector.

Second, I don't do things by halves. When I began collecting movies, it consumed me. I spent hours ferreting out original tapes, compiling data for my list, and watching the movies themselves. They were frequently terrible too, but it didn't matter. If the title was cool (e.g. *Doctor Butcher MD* or *Cannibal Holocaust*) I had to watch it. Likewise if it was rare, from a director I collected, or had an odd premise (e.g. *Emanuelle And The Last Cannibals*).

Third, I was attracted to the transgressive nature both of horror/exploitation movies in themselves and also the illegal importation thereof. The government tried to crack down on it, banning movies and examining packages at customs. My friend Moy had his house raided by customs agents seeking to confiscate his entire collection. Luckily for him, a few months prior I'd persuaded him to store his videos in a different location to his postal address used for trading. They raided his mum's house while his collection was at his dad's, where he lived.

A rare upside to his being from a broken family.

Though I never took the movies seriously (to me it was just silly splatter) there were some awkward moments from people who thought I did. The first of which involved my English teacher, a Mr Boardman.

To understand Mr Boardman, I have to describe him. He was a recently qualified teacher who was still in his late twenties when he started at my school. A slight, somewhat effeminate man he dressed like a hippy with tattered brown slacks, a checked shirt that looked like a table cloth, and a thin woolly cardigan. He also had an afro to rival a 1970s Michael Jackson, though he was white and it was just naturally very curly hair. There was probably not a boy in my comprehensive school who couldn't beat him in a fight. Despite all this he was probably the most popular teacher in the school and remains in my all-time top three favourites. I was in his class in my second year, then again for the final two years. There were many reasons why we all liked him. Though quietly-spoken he'd be strict and never shout. Naughty kids were warned first time and then ejected from the class the second time. I got sent out a few times and it was always without ceremony or rancour. I'd find myself sitting alone for half an hour until the recess bell, bored out of my mind and without even the story of a confrontation to show for it. As a consequence, we were rarely naughty in Mr Boardman's class. He also had a genuine affection for teaching English literature that showed through. He had what Nicolas Nassim Taleb would later call 'soul in the game'.

I sat at the front of his class with my new best friend Derrick. When not wisecracking, we were good students. One week we were set a homework assignment to write a short story about a hero rescuing a hostage. Perhaps the teacher expected something like St George liberating a maiden from a castle tower, or Mario rescuing Princess Peach from Bowser. I, however, had just bought Dark Angel's new album and its extremely verbose lyrics about psycho-sexual sadism had impressed me in a superficial manner. It wasn't the content so much as the ridiculous long words the lyricist had used. I wanted to use them.

So, given the vocabulary list was all about psycho-sexual sadism, that's what my story had to be. I concocted a short action tale about a swordsman breaking into the Spanish Inquisition's torture chambers to rescue a hot bird. I thought I'd been quite clever. Mr Boardman worried I had something wrong with me.

Admittedly, the week before I'd read Ramsey Campbell's *The Face That Must Die*, a horror novel about a closest gay who expresses his denial and self-loathing by hunting down and killing outed homosexuals. That's not usual reading for a kid and I was oblivious to its adult themes, thinking it was just another horror novel to read. I'd read some Stephen King and Shaun Hutson and heard Campbell was a writer to try. However, add that to my recent short story and it got me 'referred upstairs'.

After the next school parent-teacher evening, my dad came into my bedroom and announced he wanted to see what kind of trash I was watching. He picked a video tape at random from my shelving, which now contained a few hundred of them. It would've been helpful if fate had guided his hand to *Monty Python's Life Of Brian* or even *A Nightmare On Elm Street 3*. No such luck for me. He chose *Ilsa: Harem Keeper Of The Oil Sheiks*, the third in a quartet of women's prison exploitation movies from the 1970s starring the large-breasted Dyanne Thorne as a sadistic lesbian commandant. The movies were about as racy as was possible without being actual porn or snuff.

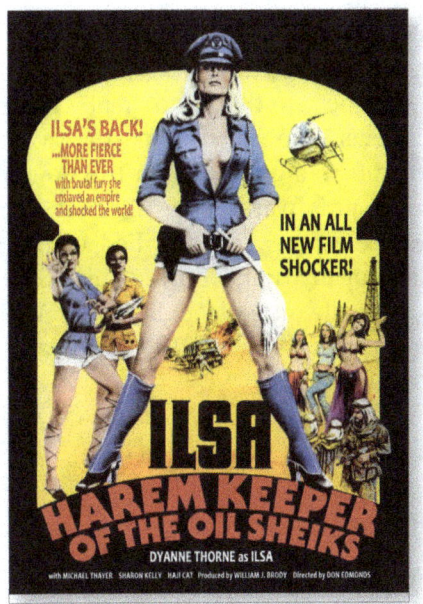

Frankly, I can't see what the problem was

My dad watched it and wasn't at all impressed with what was going on under his roof. For a few anxious days it looked like I'd have to trash my entire collection but fortunately my parents cooled off.

Another awkward moment came the next year with a girl from the grade below me called Lynne. She was a buxom blonde chick of medium looks who had told her friends she fancied me. Word got around and I had a date with her where we met at the school field and walked around a bit before hanging out in my bedroom. I think I was fourteen at the time. My lack of social acuity should already be quite clear to you, and that same cluelessness leaked into how I talked to girls.

We sat down on my bed and Lynne asked, "what shall we do?"

"Let's watch a movie," I said. I had a TV and video recorder in my room. So far so good.

"That sounds great!" she cooed and shuffled alongside me. "What are we going to watch?"

"Have you seen *Zombie Flesh Eaters*?"

I dare say that even after that, it was still 'on'. I mean, not to the extent of having sex because that didn't really go on in my school in that grade. Almost everyone I knew was still a virgin, both girls and boys. It's not like stuff was going on 'on the down low' either. Word got around and the girls were all terrified of being labelled sluts, whereas the boys were just plain terrified of the girls. But I think I should've at least got my hands up her shirt. She had great tits.

Sadly, I wasn't really interested in girls. We kissed a bit and I didn't press the issue. A week later I decided girls were stupid and I didn't want a girlfriend.

Slayer were the wrong role models

Who wouldn't like it?

Still pissing about

CHAPTER 04

MAYFAIR

CHAPTER 4

MAYFAIR

Let's skip forward a couple of years to my first sexual experience. I was now sixteen years old and had blonde hair halfway down to my ass. I'd been learning to play guitar at weekly lessons and joined my brother's metal band *Malevolence*. That had me on guitar, Lee on bass, and then an older lad called Lindsay on drums. Unfortunately our singer, Mickey, was a lazy unreliable weirdo who never showed up for the evening practices in our school's art room. If I remember correctly we just played a few Led Zeppelin covers and never had a gig.

The popular local venue for metal gigs was the Newcastle Mayfair club, another former theatre. It has long since been knocked down and replaced by a cinema complex. But when I was sixteen it was a gig venue mid-week and a metal-heads nightclub on weekends. My parents had let me drink in pubs since I was fifteen but wouldn't let me stay out past last orders, before midnight. My brother, now eighteen, would go clubbing and come back around 3am steaming drunk.

"Have you heard Sepultura are touring next month?" asked Chris, my horror-mad friend who had recently taken Mickey's place in the band. Though we were getting increasingly into anarchist punk rock (and our band had renamed itself *Decontrol* to reflect this) we both still liked the Brazilian thrash metal act.

"Brilliant! I'm going."

When the day of the gig came around Chris let on that he'd met an out-of-town girl, Sophie, at another gig the previous week and she was coming all the way from Keswick on the West coast just to see him and Sepultura.

The legendary local rock club

"I reckon I'm in," he grinned, rubbing his hands in his studded leather metal-head gloves. "My folks said she can sleep in our living room."

I wished him luck and that evening Sophie showed up with her best friend in tow. That friend was a very pretty sixteen year old brunette called Leanne, also visiting from Keswick. I fancied her but my mind was on Sepultura so I only made brief small talk. The gig was good and we drank a few beers in plastic glasses served at the Mayfair bar. By the time the gig finished at midnight we were all a bit drunk and Leanne jumped me. Chris went off on the last bus to his village with Sophie and I found myself alone with Leanne. I hadn't planned any of it. We walked through the centre of town and soon realised we'd missed the last buses home.

"Where are you staying?" I asked.

"I don't know. With you, I guess. Is that okay?"

"It is with me but I'll check with my dad. I have to call anyway to get a lift. The taxis are too expensive."

Note this wasn't me being tight. I was still a kid living on pocket money, all of which I'd spent on the concert ticket and beer. I'd expected to walk home, a one-hour journey I sometimes made after a night out. I called my dad from a payphone and he sleepily agreed to come over.

"It's okay," I told Leanne, hanging up. "He'll be half an hour."

The centre of town was quiet as this was before the laws changed to allow twenty-four hour liquor licenses. All pubs closed by 11pm and only a small number of nightclubs could stay open until 2am. However, it was mid-week. There were just a few stragglers here and there. We were standing next to the flagship Fenwick's department store, the Newcastle equivalent to Selfridges or Maceys.

As expected when two sixteen year olds are alone, drunk, and pulsing with hormones, we started kissing. I walked Leanne into the back alley leading to the tradesman's entrance for Fenwick's. It was cluttered with packing crates, some bins, and litter. Being one of the few dark alleyways in the vicinity, it's where drunks went to urinate so it smelled bad too. Leanne sat on a step below a locked door and let me pull her jeans off. I got my dick out. I'd never expected to get laid but I made a habit of keeping a condom in my wallet just because the older lads I'd started drinking with told me I should. It appeared Leanne was keen to fuck and I was about to lose my virginity.

Behind a department store, at midnight, after a metal concert. How very rock'n'roll.

Sadly, the sex was terrible because I came almost immediately. Somehow I hadn't expected a vagina to be so warm and tight. It had never crossed my mind as I'd only ever seen one in photos or movies. My mind hadn't connected the dots. Leanne didn't seem to mind, being very understanding. My dad picked us up soon after.

Once home, we drank a pint glass of water each in the kitchen then I told my dad I was going to walk around our housing estate to show Leanne the area. The family had moved a kilometre up the bank from the first house in Creslow and we were now next to some large wildly-wooded fields.

"Can't it wait until tomorrow?" he asked, not really caring as he'd resigned himself to staying up an hour or so to set up Leanne's bedding on the couch and making our supper.

Leanne and I went for a walk and she wanted to fuck again, in the long grass, but I felt too ashamed at being so bad the first time. I was secretly elated that I'd lost my virginity, and to a hot girl at that, but I was feeling a familiar set of conflicting emotions around her. For all my desire and horniness to get laid was set an opposing desire of wishing not to get involved. We messed around a bit and then went back home and to sleep, on separate floors of the house.

The next morning I went downstairs in my dressing gown for breakfast. Leanne was already awake, sitting on a plastic chair in the back garden talking to my mother. It was nine AM. As I looked at her, I felt a mild distaste that I didn't understand. Considering that I did, in fact, like her. I went into the kitchen and boiled the kettle, tipped a teaspoon of instant coffee granules into my cup, and stirred in the hot water. I was trying to nail down why I was uncomfortable with the girl in my house and why my first thought was to wonder when she would take her bus back to Keswick.

I took my coffee out into the garden and sat on a step. It was still the summer holidays from school and the sky was a clear bright blue. Our garden was long and narrow, ending in a garage. The head-height wall around the fringe made it feel satisfyingly private.

My mother was talking, not stopping to give Leanne or myself a chance to reply. "Yes, so the big red car out front there is Willie's (my dad). It's an old import from America. A Chevrolet Malibu. It's a gas guzzler which I don't like because we have to think of the environment, don't we? I'm trying to get the family to recycle but nobody listens. Willie hasn't driven his car for a month though because some of the local joyriders smashed the back window and you can't easily get replacements for such an old car."

Leanne nodded and convincingly feigned interest. If the number of people-hours wasted on feigning interest in my mother's monologues was redirected into public works, you could probably build another Westminster Abbey. I don't think she's ever realised most people are indulging her out of politeness (or fear).

"We've started shopping at the Co-Op because they do a good line in eco-friendly brands," she continued, not pausing for breath. "It's a bit of a drive up to Wrekington to the nearest shop but I think it's worth it. We all have to do our bit you know. Oh you're up Nick! Good morning sleepy-head. Leanne was just telling me she's staying on Tyneside all week with her friend. Whatshername?"

"Sophie."

"Yes, staying with Sophie. That's nice isn't it Nick? You'll have to show her around of course. If you want we can drive down to

Beamish or to the seaside at South Shields. Have you ever seen South Shields, Leanne? No? It's beautiful. There's a long flat beach stretching for miles and then sand dunes, and an amusement park. The town centre is picturesque. You really should tell Nick to take you down there. We used to go as a family every summer so the boys could play in the sea."

I realised what was bothering me. My mother had just demonstrated it to me in vivid terms: I detested the burden of responsibility which came from getting emotionally involved with a girl. I'd only just shagged her the night before, about ten seconds of fun on my side and likely none on hers, and already my mother was planning how I'd devote the entire week to my new 'girlfriend'. I felt a pressing need to squirm out of the strait-jacket before the buckles were all clamped down. I went back into the house and telephoned Moy, one of my best friends who lived two miles down the bank in Pelaw. He was the horror movie collector who I mentioned was raided by Her Majesty's Customs and Excise.

Behind here

"Moy, can you do me a favour? There's a girl here, from Keswick, who needs somewhere to stay for a week and I can't put her up at my house. Is there any chance you can?"

"Who is it?"

"She's called Leanne. Our age. She's nice."

"Hang on, I have to ask my dad."

Moy's father was a long distance truck driver who hauled goods from the North East of England all the way into Belgium and

Germany. He was frequently away a week at a time. That meant Moy was often on his own in the house and over time his dad had come to trust him with guests. He came back on the phone a minute later.

"Yeah, no problem."

Later that morning I explained to Leanne that I'd arranged a place to stay and she seemed fine about being dropped off at Moy's, a boy she'd never met, in Pelaw, a place she'd never been. I then avoided her most of the week, until she was taking the bus home. Looking back on this incident, every element of it surprises me: my callousness, Moy's generosity, and the ease with with Leanne adapted to it. I saw her once that week where we made out a bit and she seemed just fine with it.

This would be a pattern for me over the next few years. I'd position girls at arm's length so that I wasn't obligated towards them but still got occasional jollies. It cost me many opportunities for sex but I was certain in my core, absolutely certain, that the very last thing I wanted was a girlfriend.

There were so many more important things in my life, it seemed.

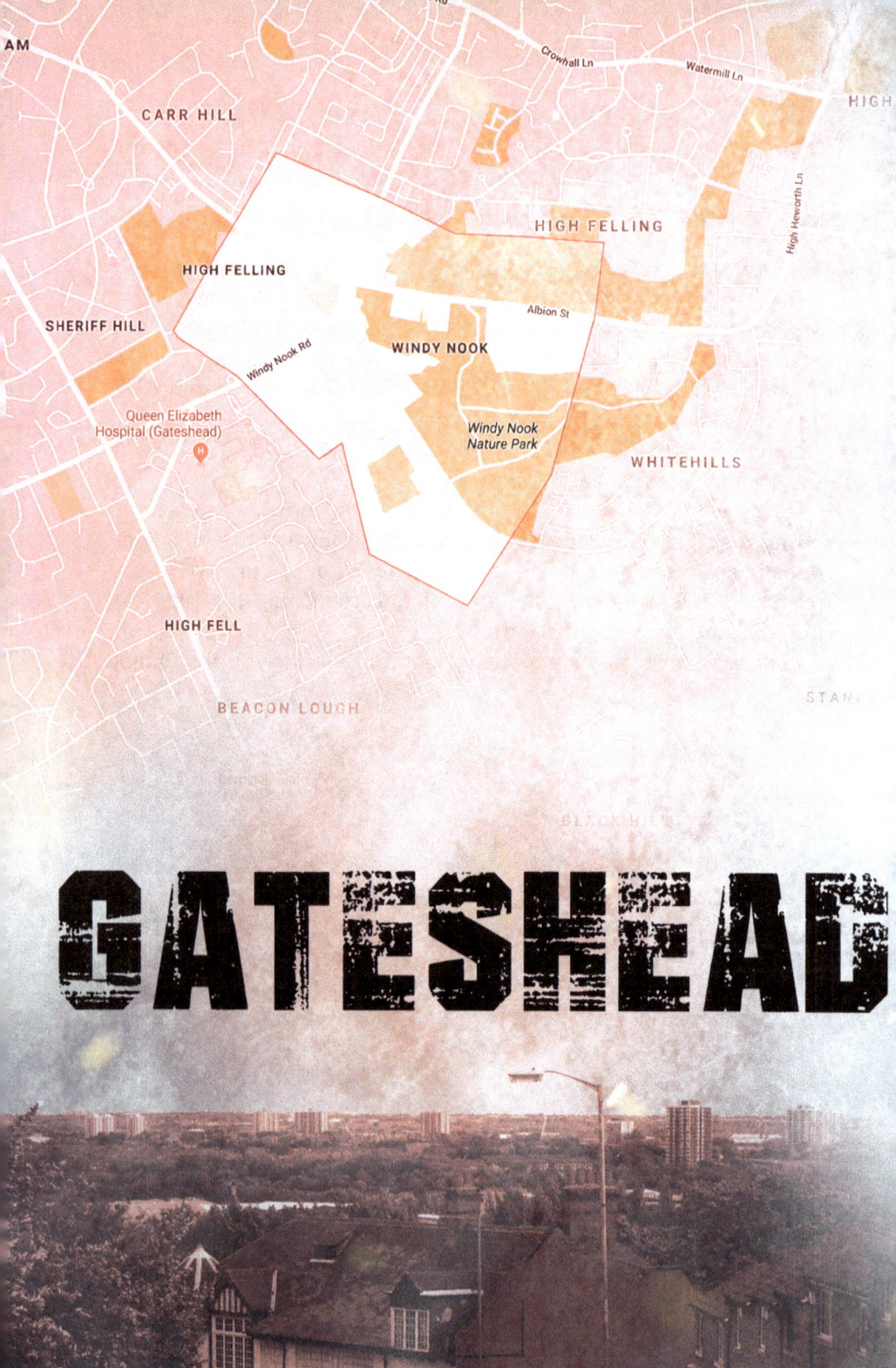

CHAPTER 05

SCHOOLDAZE

CHAPTER 5

SCHOOLDAZE

I graduated comprehensive school that summer. In England at that time the school-leaving exams were called the General Certificate of Secondary Education (or, 'GCSEs') that all sixteen year-olds took. They were introduced only a couple of years earlier, to replace the old O-levels. It represented an obvious dumbing down of the English education system. The GCSEs were calibrated so that passes from grade A down to C were equivalent to the simple 'pass' grade in O-levels. However, pupils could now score even lower, an F grade, and still get a GCSE pass.

My brother was a work-shy teenager, his work ethic having been destroyed by the poor comprehensive school my parents had allowed him to go to. After the excellent infant and junior schools, at eleven years old Lee had a choice: Heworth Grange was an excellent school with a high reputation and solid track record on school-leavers exam passes, or Highfield which was an awful school but was closer to home and thus where all his friends were going.

My parents let him choose, so he went to Highfield. They let me do the same. It was a terrible mistake and it amazes me my parents could be so negligent at such a pivotal moment in our development. I don't know why it happened. Was their's a misplaced proletarian consciousness that the children of good socialists should be sent to a school with incompetent teachers and naughty kids? Was it a parental principle of granting children autonomy to make their own decisions and thus develop the skills to succeed in later life? Was it rather that they were oblivious to the far-reaching consequences of sending their children to the worst school in the district?

Believe me, Highfield was the worst. When school league tables were published each year (a practice not introduced until my final year there) Highfield came bottom in the entire district, except for the special schools. Lee found out the hard way and came back with some lurid stories in his first year.

There was the metalwork teacher who was a literal alcoholic. He turned up drunk for class and frequently threw things at pupils. He was eventually fired for hitting a boy with a metal stool and cutting his head open. The history teacher was a fawning pervert to the girls but would harshly discipline boys. His favourite punishments were to give ten raps of his wooden ruler onto the knuckles if you rested your elbows on the table, and to make you rewrite your entire exercise book if you made a spelling mistake. Lee also told me that first years were often 'thrown over the wall' by older kids, referring to a two-storey concrete wall that separated the two levels of land upon which the school was built. I was hearing these stories when I was nine and cannot vouch for their accuracy. Kids do like telling tales. By the time I went to Highfield I saw no such misbehaviour but it was still a shockingly bad school, which rubbed off on me. My first direct experience of this was the night before my first day there.

"Nick, come have a look at this!" said Lee one evening, shouting at me from his bedroom. I went next door and saw him knelt on the bed looking out of the window in fascination. "Look!" He pointed out in the distance. There was a big fire, the flames lighting up the dark sky with a red glow.

I jumped up onto the bed next to him and strained my eyes.
"What is it?"
"I don't know, but that's where Highfield school is."

The next day, on being given an introductory tour of the school, we walked past the smouldering embers of 'East Block', a building composed of three classrooms. One room was smoke-blackened and the roof had fallen in, totally destroyed. Luckily the fire brigade had arrived in time to save the rest of the building and it was reopened within the week, just closing off the one damaged area.

A few days later police arrested one of my fellow first years for having set the fire.

The teachers weren't the ogres that legend had painted them but at least a third of them should've been fired and furthermore sued for back-earnings. Our Religious Education teacher Mr Roper didn't even make a pretence of teaching. At the beginning of our one-hour class he would write a short quotation from The Bible onto the blackboard then tell us to copy it out until the recess bell rang. Then he sat at the front, his feet up on the desk, and read his newspaper. Every fourth or fifth lesson he'd hand out prints of line-art depicting Bible scenes and tell us to colour them in.

Once I was knocked almost unconscious in Art class. I very much enjoyed drawing and had a fair talent for it. I'd become interested in Judge Dredd comic books and moved on to Marvel superheroes. Todd McFarlane was just building his name for work on The Amazing Spiderman, and I also liked Brian Bolland's depiction of Dredd. So, I tried to imitate their style and drew lots of comic pictures. I even bought *How To Draw Comics The Marvel Way* and studied it at home.

My second year Art teacher, Mr Daniels, was very popular with the girls even though he didn't play up to them. Looking back now as a game-aware adult I can see why. He was in his late thirties and husky in masculine fashion. He had the hair and fashion of the popular TV character Lovejoy, that hair long enough to suggest rebellion but not so much as to be effeminate. Mr Daniels couldn't help but like me due to my passion for art but, like all the other teachers, he became frequently exasperated by my occasional shows of arrogance, disobedience, and back-chat.

One class, Neil and I were at a high table drawing and joking on with the two girls who always sat with us, Lindsay and Maxine. We were loud and after several failed attempts to shush us, Mr Daniels came over to do so emphatically.

"Shut up or I'll knock your heads together," he said, then walked off.

A few minutes later we were making noise again. Mr Daniels came back, "Right! You two, stand up!" Neil and I stood, smirking. Mr Daniels stood almost between us and gestured us to turn and face each other. Then he stretched his arms out from his sides so as to gently rest a hand on the back of each of our heads.

"On the count of five, I'm going to knock your heads together."

The whole class had stopped to watch. Neither Neil nor I knew what was going on. Was he joking? I had no idea what to do, so I just stood there feeling awkward, a sense of foreboding that I was about to be publicly humiliated but didn't know how and thus couldn't take countermeasures.

"One...." Mr Daniels called out, looking around at the class like a stage magician addressing his crowd. The other kids were transfixed. A hush fell over the room.

"Two.... Three..." I looked at Neil and he at me. We were equally confused.

"Four....."

"Five!"

I felt a slight push on the back of my head from Mr Daniels' hand, more gesture than shove. It wasn't anywhere near hard enough to put me off balance and my head only moved an inch or so. Quite unexpectedly, Neil headbutted me full in the face.

I stumbled back, dizzy, and would've fallen to the floor if the teacher hadn't grabbed hold of my collar. Stars danced in my eyes and my forehead really hurt, where Neil's head made contact just above my nose. Luckily, he hadn't actually hit my nose or mouth. He too was dazed, leaning over the table moaning in pain. After a few seconds I recovered my senses and looked at Mr Daniels. He was deathly pale, like he could already see the unemployment office looming ahead. The other pupils were aghast, whispering amongst themselves.

"What did you headbutt me for you idiot?" I shouted at Neil, who was the focus of my anger.

He tried to laugh it off, because people were watching, but later apologised in private saying he hadn't expected Mr Daniels to push the back of his head and he'd only meant to pretend to hit me, to put on a show. I think he was telling the truth. If not, he'd really miscalculated because he was hurt more than me. I have quite a thick head.

Mr Daniels was rather obsequious towards us for a week or so and then, when he realised we hadn't complained of the incident and didn't seem to bear a grudge, he seemed to develop a new respect for us. The truth is that as soon as my head stopped hurting, about an hour later, I wasn't bothered in the slightest. It was just a daft story and I didn't even tell my parents.

Although I was the best student in the school at every subject, and by a very wide margin, I didn't do so well in my final GCSE examinations. The syllabus was covered in the fourth and fifth years at the school and that coincided with my entry into punk rock music and anarchist ideology. Suddenly all the bands I liked and respected were telling me to 'fuck the system', and the older punks I hung out with were all on welfare, drinking cheap cider all day. This wasn't conducive to studying hard and I slacked off. My sense of academic pride meant I still did all my homework and aced the term tests, but there was a perceptible slip in my results.

There were two additional structural issues. It wasn't possible to choose electives in both French and German, though I and other students wanted to do both. The head of German, a nice man called Mr Walmsley, offered to teach the German GCSE syllabus after school for an hour a time, twice a week. Eight students did so and it should've gone fine, but after the first year I began to regret my decision and didn't study hard (though I never missed class). We also had a maths problem. Unlike the other subjects, the maths GCSE had three levels of exam and pupils elected which of them to take. Advanced level would be scored from A to C, or fail. Intermediate was D to F, and Basic was just F. Despite government propaganda to the contrary, everyone knew that any pass grade below C was effectively a 'fail'. The head of Maths brought us together six months before the exams and announced to the class that they hadn't taught *any* of the advanced syllabus.

Yes, my school was that bad.

There was an outcry and, after parental petitioning, one of the maths teachers was strong-armed into cramming all of the additional content into a twice-weekly after school session. So, including the German, I was doing four extra hours a week plus associated homework.

If you, the reader, were lucky enough to study at a good school you likely think this isn't a big deal because after-hours clubs are common. There was no such culture of learning at Highfield. Some of my best friends would instead entertain themselves each evening by 'TWOCing'. That's the street slang for 'taking without owner's consent', which meant stealing cars for pleasure rides. For several years there were police chases on the main roads near our house. At least once a month an abandoned car was set alight on the school field.

One morning I came to school and a former good friend since infant school, Peter, pulled me to one side. "We were going to steal your parent's car last night but I talked them out of it. You owe me one." Somebody did steal it a month later, quite likely Peter himself.

It was during the GSCEs period that two girls left school to have children and a few of the bad lads were expelled. Two such incidents I saw for myself.

In one case, a fight had been organised between the toughest lad in Highfield, called George, and the toughest in Heworth, called Danny. As it happened, the *real* toughest lad in our school was my new best friend Derrick but he was an exceptionally nice boy who never fought. The issue had been settled six months earlier when George tried to pick a fight with him to establish the top dog and Derrick, far bigger and stronger than the rest of us, had literally picked him up and thrown him away over a fence. Not wishing to get involved in such nonsense, Derrick allowed George to reframe the situation and set himself up as the guv'nor.

I already knew Danny slightly because in junior school I'd been goalkeeper for 'blue' team on Sports Day and in the final against 'red' team I'd saved the key penalty kick which Danny had taken. Back then he'd just been slightly coarse, but as kids age the naughtiness rises in severity.

George and Danny were set to meet on a field equidistant between the two schools. Word went around and likely a hundred kids from each arrived to cheer on their own fighter. Everyone being white, it was a civilised affair with a spirit of fair play between the two rival crowds and there were no side-beefs being fought. The fight itself was a dud. Danny came out strong, punched himself out fast, and then was exhausted as George punched and threw him around. Something must've snapped inside Danny's mind, because he broke off and bent over to rummage in his coat, which was piled on the grass. He came back brandishing a screwdriver. George's eyes popped out of his head and he ran off. Nobody got stabbed but the story later told to teachers by the grasses likely exaggerated the incident and, seeing as George had been skating on thin ice for years, it was enough to get him expelled.

Another day, our form group was walking back from morning assembly. One boy, Richard, was quiet and had been among the smallest in class but he'd hit puberty first and by now looked adult. He'd gotten into an argument with a bad lad, Dean. As we crossed the playground, Dean suddenly rushed over and cold-cocked Richard on the back of the head, knocking him over. He then grabbed his hoodie with one hand and pummelled him with his other. It was shocking enough in its violence, more like a real adult fight than kid's stuff. Even worse, Dean wore two big sovereign rings which opened up several gashes and closed one of Richard's eyes with swelling.

There were about two hundred witnesses so, unsurprisingly, Dean was expelled soon after.

When the year's lessons ended and the GCSE exams began, I had the most horrible luck. I caught the 'flu. The first five or six exams were fine but on the day I had French and History exams I had to leave the examination hall (with teacher escort to prevent cheating) for ten minutes each time to vomit in the toilets. I felt awful and fuzzy-minded, unable to concentrate on the questions. The next day I had the German speaking and listening test, delivered one-to-one by Mr Walmsley to all students. I kept sneezing and couldn't think straight. I remember Mr Walmsely staring imploringly at me to do better but exam rules didn't allow him to break script.

Looking back, I'm shocked at the behaviour of my parents and the teachers. At no point did anyone pull me to one side and explain that there is a procedure for sick students and I was thus entitled to re-sit the exams. Instead, I got a C in French and History, and a D in German. I'd been predicted easy As.

I dare say I still haven't forgiven them for that. As an adult, I take responsibility for my mistakes but in this case I was a sixteen year old kid with no idea how the system worked. I just took my lumps and accepted the consequences.

Already socialising outside school

But not yet pro social

Starting to meet girls

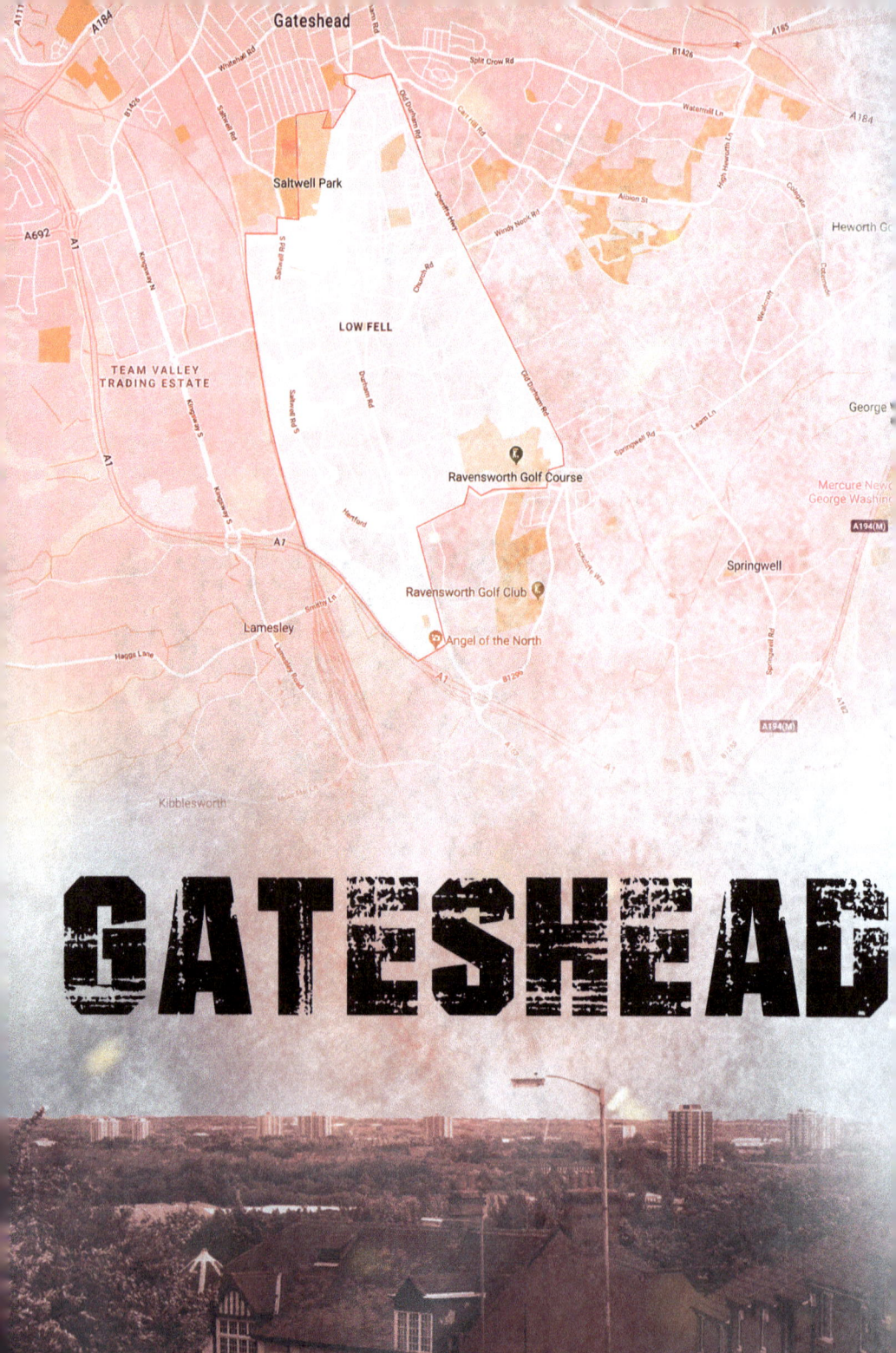

CHAPTER 06

COLLEGE

CHAPTER 6
COLLEGE

I was surprisingly popular with girls in the two years between school and university, much more so than prior years. I was studying my A-levels at the local Gateshead College, which was a dreary place. In keeping with the pattern of my education, I chose that venue because it was easiest. The main campus was a half hour walk from home, and the secondary campus where I did half my lectures was closer still. It never occurred to me to research which of the local colleges was *best*.

Nor did that occur to my parents either, it would seem.

I had little interest in the dull college social scene. There weren't many students and they mostly struck me as weird. Think of student life as portrayed in teen movies such as *American Pie* with its beautiful campus, lively parties, and cute girls. Gateshead College was nothing like that. There'd be a dozen of us in class, and at lunch time we'd sit in the canteen and talk. Other groups we didn't know sat in their own cliques too. That was it.

My social life was entirely rooted in the local punk rock scene, which had a large cross-over with the metal scene. On Friday evening I'd get the bus into town, stopping off at an off license to put a four-pack of beer in my small canvas rucksack (which was covered in punk patches and paint). Then I'd meet my friends inside The Broken Doll pub. After an hour there we moved to The Dog And Parrot, then down to the quayside to The Barley Mow. That would be around nine-thirty, when my main punk friends would arrive.

Those punks were a group based in nearby Cramlington, a small town that was more like a single huge council housing estate. A girl called Joanne would usually drive a battered old mini-van containing the rest of the gang: Geeky, a short but extremely muscular Scotsman; Johnny, a dreadlocked oddball; a couple of quiet wallflowers called Danny and Frank, plus the girls Phillipa, Claire, and Anna. Being the only punk kids in their area, they were pretty tight. Before long I was playing guitar in a band with Geeky, Johnny, and a lad who lived near me called Whitey. We called ourselves *Rigor Tortoise*.

Technically, I was in two bands now. We'd started playing gigs in pubs and clubs for the small but lively punk/metal scene. I'd also begun writing and publishing a small fanzine called *All Talk No Action* which did written interviews with bands, music reviews, and

Band practice for Rigor Tortoise

(embarrassingly naïve) political polemics. I did four issues in total, printed at a community printing project in the shifty Scotswood area of Newcastle where all the drug dealers and gangsters lived. By the final issue I was selling 250 copies, hawked at gigs or through underground 'distro' lists circulated by other punks. I liked producing my own little magazine, having acquired the taste when Lee, Spugsy and I did a couple issues of *Psycho Moomin Zine*, a childish BMX fanzine we sold at competitions back when we were riding.

Eagle-eyed readers will see this as the antecedent to my later PUA blog and Sigma Wolf publishing house. In that sense, I never grew up.

It was at The Barley Mow, at around ten pm, that I would cold approach girls. Usually I was a little drunk by then and being a seventeen year old with raging hormones, I found myself drawn to all the student girls in the bar. It was popular with the alternative kids at the local university and polytechnic college, so they were usually a couple of years older than me. There were two large indoor rooms and then a fantastic beer garden overlooking the River Tyne, which is beautiful at night.

I'd developed a little system for pick-up.

My friends and I would roll in as a group of ten, making a noise and dressed in very obvious punk fashion. We didn't go for the mohican-and-safety-pins style of the first wave punks (think Sex Pistols) but rather the grunge look of combat pants, Doctor Marten boots, and long green German army coats or leather biker jackets. I still had my long blonde metaller hair. We'd all squeeze into an A-frame wooden bench/table and drink. By then the beer garden would be buzzing with revellers.

I'd come up with a wheeze. I bought a small teddy bear and dressed him with camouflage trousers, a green vest with a circle-A anarchy symbol drawn in marker pen, a safety pin in his ear, and then shaved and dyed a black mohican on his little furry head. I then hung him around my neck with a boot lace. My inspiration had been Johnny, who wore a big plastic lobster around his neck and I'd noticed people always asked him about it. Spotting a student girl I liked, I'd approach. "Hello. This is Punky Bear and he wants to meet you."

It was extremely rare not to end up in conversation. Now, looking back with my knowledge of seduction, I realised I had so many elements aligned in my favour.

Rare surviving image of Punky Bear

Age-match with girls I'm opening. *Check.*
Light-hearted party mood. *Check.*
Sense of all being members of same widely-construed alternative scene. *Check.*
Visibly with lots of friends having fun. *Check.*
Bold enough to open. *Check.*
Unusual conversation starter. *Check.*

There was also something intangible working in my favour; I was brimming with conviction. Seventeen-year-old me knew exactly where he wanted to go in life and was doing it. All I wanted then was to play in my bands, pass my A-levels, and go drinking with friends. It was clear that I enjoyed my life and that sense of grounded-ness gave me a strongly positive vibe that girls liked. Additionally, I'd built a coherent (if dumb) world-view that I passionately believed in and had no shortage of faith in my own awesomeness.

I'd kiss a girl most weekends and if The Barley Mow didn't provide, we all had last orders down the road at The Egypt Cottage which was more cliquey and pretentious but was also full of university girls. There were also regular house parties, at least one a fortnight, because my older punk friends had a couple of shared houses in the Fenham area of Newcastle, the rent paid by the taxpayer.

Another route to meeting women was the Tyneside Hunt Saboteurs Association.

When getting into the second wave of UK anarchist punk rock, I'd taken it seriously. I read the lyrics, the fanzines, and pamphlets. I wanted to develop a world-view and they gave me one that seemed plausible. My brother Lee was also drawn into it and set up one of hundreds of one-man 'distro' operations where he'd take literature wholesale from small publishers, typically five to ten copies per title, and then circulate his stock list to subscribers. So whereas my bedroom was full of horror videos (which I'd now lost interest in) his was stacked with anarchist literature from Freedom Press and other small publishers. I treated it as my personal library, knocking on his door to borrow a copy of Peter Kropotkin's *Memoirs Of A Revolutionist* or Alexander Berkman's *ABC Of Anarchism.*

I felt like I was seeing the world in a completely different way. The mainstream media looked like capitalist propaganda to me and I was being 'woke' before woke was a thing. I followed the argument where it appeared to lead and, oblivious to my reasoning errors, became a vegan, a half-hearted animal rights activist, and an anarchist revolutionary.

I don't do things by halves.

Most of my friends just liked the music and fashion, and let the lyrics wash over them. That said, about a third of them also put their money where their mouth is and became vegans and activists. We heard about the 'hunt sabs' who would drive into the countryside and disrupt fox hunts. I went perhaps a dozen times in total before I soured on the experience. In that time, I pulled three girls in the hunt sab minivan. Once I explain how, the pick-up artist principles fall into place.

We'd all meet at the Newcaslte Central Station at 6am on Saturday morning. Graeme, the designated driver, would arrive with the sab van. By then eight to twelve of us would be standing around in the cold. Usually at least two or three were new to me, either first-timers or irregulars. For whatever reason, at least one would be a university girl introduced through the university animal rights club. At least half the time they were fairly hot.

We'd introduce ourselves and then spend the next ten hours in the van, sitting facing each other on wooden bench seats. Sometimes we were out in the field 'sabbing', other times standing around sharing coffee from Thermos flasks or eating a packed lunch. Several hours were spent driving. The upshot of which was I had a captive audience. The three senior guys claimed the upholstered front seats and were thus taken out of the game. I was usually the main talker, and joker, leading all the conversations. At least half of the time, I'd see the new girl take a shine to me. Then it was a simple matter of asking for her phone number when we were dropped off at Central Station in the evening, or to go straight to the pub.

Of the three girls I pulled that way, a Cheshire-born polytechnic student called Joanne was the hottest. Memories fade over time but my impression is that nowadays I'd rate her an eight. She was tall, leggy, sported a great ass, and flowing brown-ginger hair to her waist. We went on three dates, made out, and I felt her tits but lacked the follow-through to fuck her. She was nineteen to my seventeen, so perhaps I was a little intimidated. After our second date, I was

Rigor Tortoise playing a gig in South Shields. Nick, Frank, Danny

sitting at home watching television when my mother commented, "Nick, shouldn't you have a girlfriend?"

I hadn't brought any girls home since Leanne a year earlier and never talked about them. All the action I had, none of which went as far as actual sex, was in bars or at house parties. To my parents, I probably looked like an involuntary celibate. In contrast, Lee was in a series of three consecutive long relationships and his girlfriends were always visiting.

Naturally my parents didn't suggest *how* I'd find a girlfriend. The only woman my dad ever shagged was my mother, and that wasn't a very smart move given how querulous she is. So, he was in no position to advise.

"I'll see what I can do," I replied, then brought Joanne back the next day.

By coincidence, the next two weekends I pulled a girl each who wanted to date me, so I also brought home Sally, a polytechnic art student with red hair and big tits, and Kirsten, a really hot graphic design student. I failed to fuck both but that was due to my appalling lack of escalation and comfort skills, rather than lack of desire on their part.

"Is that alright, then?" I asked my mother when I got back from putting Kirsten on the bus home. "I tried to find some girlfriends."

I should've been getting laid a lot in the two years between school and university but it just wasn't in me. I wasn't especially good-looking because my total lack of athleticism, naturally slim frame, and stupid vegan diet meant I weighed just sixty kilograms and some of that was my growing beer belly. I also dressed terribly, in the punk style. My skinniness did, however, give me chiselled facial features and my youthful exuberance got me off to a good start.

Attraction wasn't the problem.

```
             Decontrol playing
              The Irish Club
```

It's not as though I was going to the coolest nightclubs and swooping on the super-fly girls, mind. My feeding ground was alternative university pubs where the girls peaked at sevens, and an eight was extremely rare. But still, young, attractive girls. This was before England became fat and I didn't waste time on chubbies. If pick-up artist Nick Krauser was to coach seventeen-year old me, he'd have spotted the problems immediately.

"Go to the gym and put on some muscle, you spaghetti-armed faggot," he'd say. "Once you've put on five kilograms of lean muscle mass I'll take you shopping. We'll throw out all that punk crap and get you proper clothes. You can keep the biker jacket, that's cool. But everything else must go, including your girly faggot long hair."

Not that I'd have listened to the advice. Since I was a toddler, I'd always figured I knew best.

"Your biggest problem is comfort," Old Me would tell Young Me. "All these girls hang around you, interested, and they are waiting for you to take the next step, of building a connection and getting to know the real them. Instead, you keep them at a distance and talk superficially about hobbies and politics." This is what led to my 100% drop-off rate within a few weeks of meeting any one girl. I remained the one-dimensional joker I'd been on the first night. "And your escalation is terrible. You don't even try to fuck them. You have them in your room, on the bed, and you just kiss them a bit and expect them to take their own clothes off."

For all this, I did get laid two more times before going to university. The first time I met a sixteen year old metal chick in the Mayfair club on a Saturday night. We were soon in a dark corner making out. I walked her outside at 2am to St James Park, the actual park beside the football stadium of the same name. Nobody was around so I banged her on the grass by the lake. We never swapped numbers.

The other time was a fifteen-year old called Christiane who I met in The Barely Mow. We had a date the next day, a Saturday afternoon, in the same pub. I decided I didn't fancy her much. She had a trim curvy body but something just didn't appeal. I considered her a bit.... scraggly faced. So after the second drink, I was trying to find an excuse to leave. This is what I hit on.

"Look, Christiane. You're a nice girl and quite pretty, but I don't want a girlfriend. I could take you home and just fuck you, but that wouldn't really be fair on you, would it?"

She put her drink down, looked me in the eyes and said, "I think you should take me home and fuck me."

So I did.

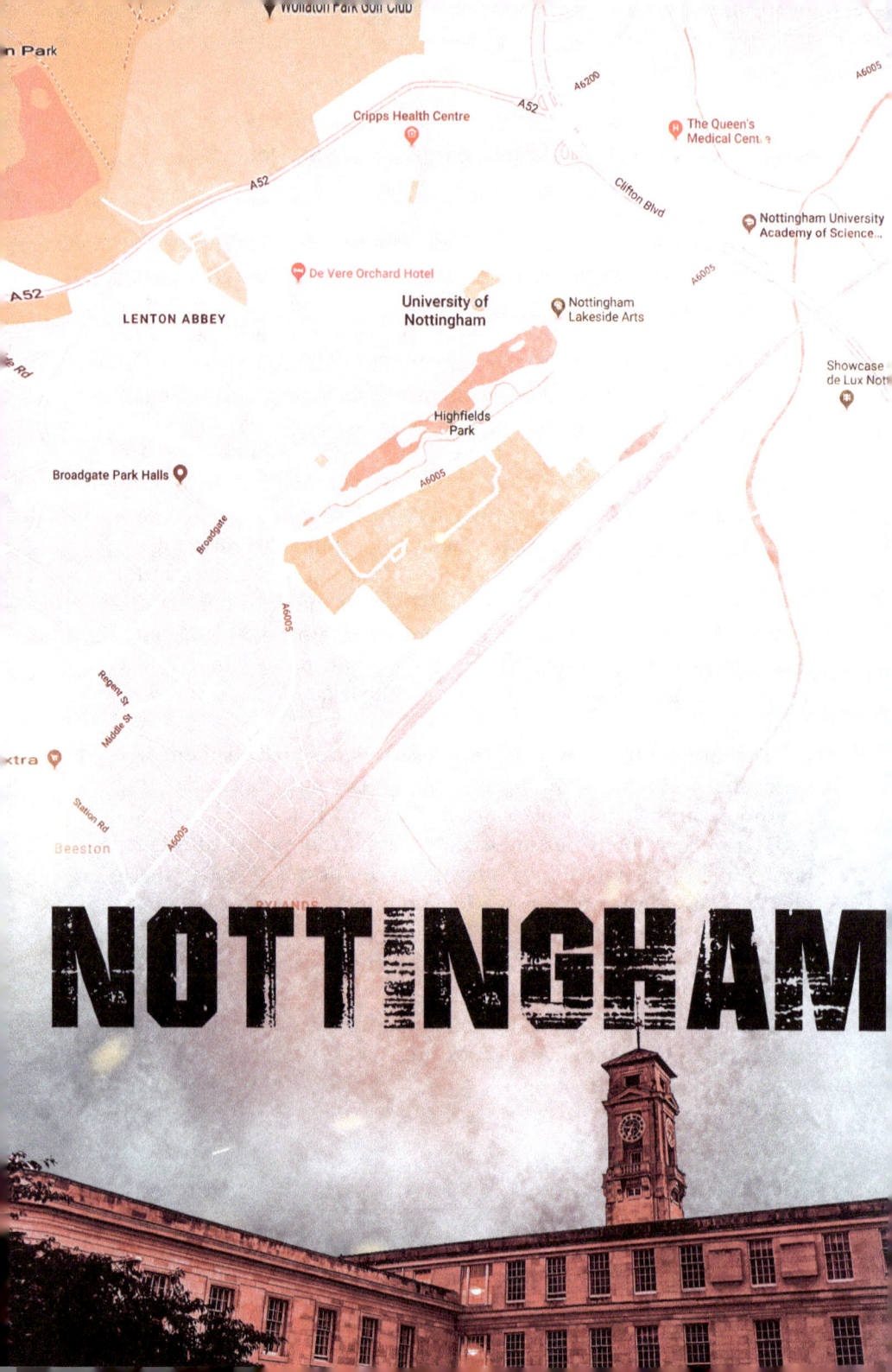

CHAPTER 07

UNIVERSITY

CHAPTER 7

UNIVERSITY

My first impression of the University Of Nottingham was that it embodied every dream I'd ever fostered of university as a seat of higher learning. The campus was set deep inside grounds resembling a park, with long lawns, fields and copses of trees everywhere. Fourteen student dormitories dotted the fringe of the campus. My own, Ancaster Hall, was on the side bordering the quaint old Beeston village. The main academic and administrative buildings were in the centre, overlooked by the modern and menacing library. It was like Harry Potter without the wizards. The centrepiece of it all was the Student Union building, gifted to the university by Jesse Boot in the 1920s, with a large lake fronting it.

I saw this all for the first time when my dad drove me down for an open day, after the Faculty of Social Sciences had sent me an offer, conditional upon my achieving grades of two Bs and a C in my A-Levels. As the staff walked us around the campus I kept thinking, *I have to get in here.* There were still a couple of months remaining before my exams so upon returning to Gateshead I cracked open my books and, foregoing my earlier slacker attitude, studied like a man possessed. I passed, getting two As and a B.

Teaching began in early October. Two semesters were split across three ten-week terms. I threw myself headlong into both the intellectual and social life of the university. Most nights we'd hang out in the bar on the ground floor of our dormitory, but often sorties were arranged to check out other dormitory bars and once in a while we'd try to get a drink in all fourteen of them. Following such nights I usually woke up with assorted scrapes and bruises from unknown drinking injuries.

All the new Ancaster students had arrived the same day for check-in and orientation. We mingled around the entrance and inner courtyard, waiting in line to be assigned a room and given our keys. It was clear that barely anyone knew any other, which was good as it encouraged openness in meeting new people. That evening all two hundred Ancaster Hall students joined a big party in the ground floor bar and began the nervous business of making new friends. I was slightly unnerved by how many posh southern accents I heard, and at least a dozen from thickly-set boys in rugby shirts. For the past three years I'd read much anarchist literature bemoaning Britain's class system, and I read the monthly newspaper Class War which cheerfully stirred up resentment of the working

Exactly how a university ought to look

classes against those above them in the social hierarchy. Though processing this intellectually, the class divide had seemed illusory to me, as far removed from my day-to-day life as the differences between the Whigs and the Tories on the 1700s, or even the Spartans and the Trojans. Standing in the university bar with a pint of John Smith's bitter, chatting to a dozen wide-eyed eighteen-year-old fellow students, was the first time I actually felt the class system as an emotional beast. I talked and acted like a rough uneducated northerner while almost all students around me were lager-drinking soft southern puffs.

I felt like an outsider but it didn't bother me in the slightest. It never has. I like to be a stranger in strange lands. Or, if you prefer, a wolf among the sheep. That night I felt more like a sheep amongst wolves.

"What's this German army shirt you're wearing?" asked a skinny kid with hair down to his shoulders, a style popular amongst the indie kids of the day. He looked like Jarvis Cocker, the singer of then-popular Brit Pop band Pulp. "Are you a Nazi?"

I could tell he was joking, just thinking of an interesting gambit to break the ice.

"Nah, quite the opposite. It's punk rock."

He introduced himself as Paul, from the suburbs in East London, and studying biology. Our conversation moved on to music and his interest in The Smiths and Pulp. The evening was a drunken blur and we ended up in a small party in the room next to mine. That was Charlie's room, a middle-class lad from Kent who looked like he'd eventually grow up to become Hugh Grant and star in a romantic comedy. Charlie was studying economics and, as we were next door neighbours, I'd get to know him well.

It thrilled me to go to lectures because everything seemed so important and serious. My college in Gateshead seemed, and indeed was, small-time by comparison. My faculty had only eight hours lectures per week, which I took as encouragement to slack off and drink beer. By the end of the first semester I had quite a beer belly even though the rest of my body was skinny due to my vegan diet and lack of exercise. Fun though it was, my complacent first semester ended with a series of three jarring shocks in quick succession.

First, my two upper front teeth developed extreme sensitivity to cold liquids. Any time I drank fruit juice or cold water there'd be a stinging pain making me gasp. I went to the university dentist who informed me the enamel on both had worn down to expose the softer dentine underneath. They operated on me to attach artificial veneers. I felt uncomfortable under the dentist's drill so I asked them how long the veneers would last, hoping I'd not need to return to the dentist chair any time soon.

"Five, maybe ten years," she replied. As a matter of fact, I still have them now, undamaged, almost twenty-five years later. That's quality English craftsmanship, I do say. After the treatment I called home and spoke to my mother. I became quite angry.

"I'm not surprised you needed them," she said, matter-of-factly. "That vegan diet of yours, you don't get any protein or calcium. And then drinking all that orange juice was going to wear down your weakened tooth enamel."

I almost spluttered down the phone, and needed to collect my wits for a moment. "What? It never occurred to you to tell me I was destroying my teeth? I'm eighteen years old and already I've got these plastic covers on my two front teeth. You knew it was going to happen and never warned me?"

"How do they look?"

"Fine, you can't tell it's not my own enamel."

"Well, what's the problem then? All the rest of your teeth are fine."

My first year rooms at Ancaster Hall

Indeed they were, but that wasn't the point. I was becoming increasingly aware that my mum and dad's approach to parenting could be summed up as 'abandon them to their fate'. The only reason I was making this phone call from the top-ten University of Nottingham rather than some shitty third-rate polytechnic was through good luck. They hadn't given me any help or direction in my choosing and applying to university, aside from a drive down for the open day. I quit veganism that day, which wasn't hard because it was terribly restrictive for a fussy eater like myself. I was tired of telling the Pakis in the local pizza shop to remove the cheese topping from my order. I remained vegetarian, as that was easy.

The second jarring shock was when a fat girl called Joanne tried to seduce me. She was best friends with a different girl, a posh chick from East Anglia who studied economics and talked like a character from a Jane Austen novel, called Amanda. I'd made out with Amanda in the first week of term after a party in Ancaster bar and spent the night in her room, but she'd been so drunk I elected not to fuck her. *I was a gentleman.*

Perhaps I should have, because she never gave me another chance after that, restricting our merry-making to make-outs and a little hands-up-the-shirt action.

Joanne was a second year student in the Russian Studies department and had recently returned from a three-month exchange trip to Minsk, Belarus. It had deeply scarred her and she now didn't want any more contact with the Former Soviet Union, which naturally sapped her of motivation in her studies. I liked Joanne — in a friend-zone sense — but she was chubby, with skin like a shaved cat. She got drunk one night and tried to lure me to her room, which I declined. Though I didn't break etiquette, I was thinking to myself, "how dare this fat chick try to make me fuck her." It played on my mind throughout the following day. What gave her the idea she had a chance? One year ago I'd been dating some hot girls, including Hot Joanne. I wasn't about to date Not-Hot Joanne. Something was up, because Amanda aside, I wasn't attracting much female attention at university. Perhaps I'd lost my mojo.

My third shock came in the reception area of the Faculty Of Social Studies when I went to check the noticeboard for my first semester exam results. Pinned up by the secretary's window was a leader-board of scores for each exam. My eyes scanned the top of each list but I couldn't find my name. *Surely there's some mistake,* I thought.

I found my name midway down the list, hardly befitting my self-image as the smartest kid in class. For one exam, "Conflict And Controversy In Contemporary Britain", I'd scored forty-eight of a possible hundred, which is arguably lower than what you'd expect from an Amazon pygmy pulled out of a mud hut to sit the exam using only his bongo drums. I resolved there and then to spend more time in the library. By the second semester I was once more a model student, shaking off the torpor that my seven years at Highfield Comprehensive and later Gateshead College had dulled me with. I wasn't so interested in beating the other students as I was with making good use of what I considered my academic promise. I was in a centre of higher learning, with good professors and an amazing library. I really ought to take advantage of it.

My faculty allowed me to take half of my study modules outside the department, so I took some in the faculties of psychology and philosophy. I also persuaded professors to let me sit in on additional lessons, just to maximise my own learning. One of my friends in Ancaster Hall, a theology student from Birmingham called Mat, was equally keen to haunt the library so we began coordinating our study sessions and meeting up for coffee breaks in the ground floor library cafe. The staff in my faculty were quite astonished by the change in attitude. I remember one assessment on my end-of-year report card; "Nick is challenging, committed, and rather intense."

While good for academic learning, those same character traits were less helpful socially.

I got into the habit of debating everyone who showed an interest in doing so. This wasn't so weird as it may sound. I didn't go around bothering people who were enjoying a quiet drink. Many students were into the debating spirit so I took part, arguing with Christians, Young Conservatives, Marxists, Feminists and anyone else I could find to butt heads with me. I got rather enthused by it, totally believing in Enlightenment ideals about the 'battleground of ideas'.

Charlie knocked on my bedroom door early one evening. "Nick, Dave and I are going over to Hugh Stuart Hall bar tonight. Some of the economics lads have invited us out clubbing in the city centre. We're gonna chat up girls. Are you coming?"

"Nah, mate. The Christian Society is having an open night in the common room. I'm going down to argue with them," I replied.

You'd think that specialising in aggravating my fellow students would be a bad strategy for increasing my popularity, and you'd be right. That said, I rarely went too far and most people enjoyed butting heads. While I was never one of the 'cool kids' in Ancaster, I had plenty of friends and was never at a loss for people to hang out with. It piqued the interest of a couple of girls too.

One evening in the second term, I was standing by the bar chatting to Paul. We were now good friends as we were both academically proud and into bullshit niche music. He was also of similar social class to myself, which made him below the university average. Perhaps that exaggerates things a little, as University of Nottingham was hardly an elite networking club like Eton or Hogwarts. There were plenty of working class kids around who'd gained admittance the same way I had, through good exam results. One such kid had just come up and approached me. It was Emily, a pretty blonde from a village outside Coventry. Emily always wore tight blue jeans and a tasselled black leather jacket. She belonged in the crowd at a Guns'n'Roses concert.

"I heard you're not vegan any more," she said. We barely knew each other, so it hadn't been me who'd told her.

"Correct."

"Why were you vegan in the first place?"

"Moral reasons. I saw a meat market in Wales when I was a kid and turned vegetarian. Later, I reasoned that all animal products are intimately tied up to the profits of the meat industry, so I swore off them."

She nodded silently, processing the new information before responding. "So what changed to make you give it up?"

"It knackered my front teeth. I need to drink milk to be healthy."

"So you're still vegetarian?"

"Yes. There are additional environmental reasons why eating meat is morally wrong. It takes approximately ten times as much land to graze cattle for beef as it does to grow soy beans for the same amount of protein and calories. It's simply inefficient and contributes towards deforestation and third world hunger."

As an eighteen-year-old I didn't have my later knowledge of the estrogenic effect of soy. The emergent phenomena of the 'soyboy' Leftist progressive wouldn't become visible for another twenty years. As a teenage Leftist, I actually gave a shit about third world hunger too, gay as that seems now. Emily nodded silently again, now looking me up and down. Then she replied.

"What if the farmers tied up the cattle? If they don't walk around so much, they don't need all that space."

I laughed aloud. What a stupid thing to say! Then I realised she was joking and suddenly I liked her. She joined Paul and I for the rest of the evening until he needed to shuffle off to his room around ten pm. The bar was quite empty now and Emily and I were standing in the vestibule. I had a bottle of Newcastle Brown Ale in my hand and felt drunk. Emily looked increasingly pretty and seemed very keen to linger around me. Somehow, I don't know how, we began talking about sex. I think I'd said something rude about her fashion, like how her tight jeans made her ass look fat. They didn't. She had a great ass.

"You'll never get near this ass," she retorted, tartily.

"That's fine, I don't want to fuck you."

"I'll bet your dick is tiny."

"I'll get it out right here in the bar and prove it's not."

"You don't have the courage," she said, her eyes flashing with animation. She was clearly relishing the challenge. I looked around and decided it wasn't wise to follow through. Too many people.

"You'd be too scared to look, anyway," I countered.

"No I wouldn't."

"Right, I'll get it out in my room. Then you look, and you'll have to admit my dick isn't tiny."

"Okay."

We walked up to my room and were fucking within two minutes of closing the door. I'd fuck Emily on-and-off over the entirely of my three years at Nottingham and she visited me in Gateshead once while I was studying my Masters degree locally. That time, I banged her in the woods at the end of my parent's street when we got off a night bus home after drinking in town.

One time in the Ancaster bar, Paul asked Emily, "why do you like Nick?"

"Animal attraction," she replied simply. I liked that.

Animal attraction is taking hold

I only banged six girls in Nottingham, and in the final year Emily punched me in the face and almost broke my nose. That was at Pieces nightclub in the city centre on a student night. I can't remember what I said to anger her, but she sucked me off later the same night in the alleyway outside her house so it wasn't all bad.

The last girl I banged at university was on the day I received my final degree results. It was a nerve-wracking day because by then I'd spent the whole course working hard, writing essays, and trying very hard to score a First Class degree pass, the top possible classification. The results for everyone in the Faculty would be pinned up on the ground floor noticeboard so all morning students were hanging around, nervously waiting. By the time my department announced the scores, I'd expended all my anxiety so I was stoic in reading the lists. This time my name was at the top of them all, which I rather liked. The faculty head called us into the main lecture theatre for a goodbye-and-thank-you speech and then thanked me specially by name, for being the top student. The entire auditorium, teachers and students alike, gave me a standing ovation. Nice.

My course-mates had arranged a pub crawl through nearby pubs dotted along the outer edge of the campus so I joined them. I was buzzing with happiness, having achieved my primary goal in going to university. I'd taken full advantage of the learning opportunity, and additionally had a First Class pass to prove it.

As the night drew to a close I realised one of the girls was hanging around me. Claire was a chubby English girl with long silky brown hair and a pretty face. She was likeable in every way except the significant blubber around her thighs and ass. I conjectured that if we ever fell overboard in the Arctic circle, she'd likely survive the cold waters many hours longer than I. Still, I was drunk and she was

Results day for my university degree

making it obvious she fancied me. At last orders, she sneaked me outside the pub.

"Let's go to your place," she said. "But don't let Barry see us leaving together." Barry was a shaven-headed socialist course-mate a couple of years older than me. He looked like a limp-wristed hairdresser and though we got on fine, it never crossed my mind he was interested in women.

"He likes girls?" I asked, incredulous.

"He likes me. He's been trying to sleep with me for three years."

Frankly, Claire didn't strike me as the calibre of girl who could inspire a monk to give up his vows, much less inspire a homosexual to give up bum-sex with street puffs. Still, the world moves in strange ways. We rushed off down the street and around a corner, then walked more leisurely until reaching my house.

I still didn't have smooth escalation skills. My main strategy to move a girl from 'interested' to 'naked and having sex' was to either pick an argument with her, or wait until she jumped me. Claire required neither. We sat on the sofa drinking cans of beer and then fell onto each other. I banged her up in my room and halfway through we fell off the end of the bed, landing with a heavy thud on the floor. Tim was living in the room downstairs so he banged angrily on the ceiling and shouted at us to keep quiet.

I was sad to leave Nottingham, having had such a good time. Looking back, there were many ways in which I'd squandered my opportunity to make the most of it, but for a dumb teenager who'd felt greatly out of place for the first term, things had turned out fine. I'd look back on it as the best three years of my life.

Until I went to Japan, that is. But we'll get to that.

Claire, shortly before boozing

CHAPTER 08

LONDON CALLING

CHAPTER 8

LONDON CALLING

The first time I ever thought about getting a job was immediately upon graduating university. I intended to study a Masters Degree and needed to pay the tuition fees. I tried to get an Economic & Social Research Council scholarship to study at Lancaster University but those few placements are as oversubscribed with applicants as is a hot girl's favour in a nightclub. They turned me down. I'd have to 'self fund' and that meant living at home and going to a local university for the one-year course. Luckily, the North East has a pair of good universities and the course I wanted to do at Durham University cost just two thousand pounds in fees.

Earning those two thousand pounds was more difficult than I anticipated.

I walked into a few recruitment agencies in Newcastle City Centre to find a summer job. I was focused on an academic career and nothing would stand in my way. Due to my excellent academic credentials — coming top of my faculty just two weeks earlier — I felt my resume was good. The first agency paired me with a morbidly obese middle-aged woman who sported a severe short haircut and thick bottle glasses. She waved me into her office, waved me again to sit, then perused my resume. Then she looked up at me over the tops of her spectacles.

"You haven't listed any work experience here."

Surely there was some mistake. I did a one week placement at a comic shop, Timeslip, when I was fifteen and then a week in the local tax office the following year. It was the school work experience program and on my resume. I explained this. She was unimpressed.

"Have you done any paid work?"

"I had a paper round when I was twelve."

"Okay, no matter," she continued, smiling kindly. "Let's talk about your skills. What are you good at?"

"I've read extensively in sociology, psychology, politics, philosophy, and economics."

That didn't move her either. She gave me a wan smile and pulled a sheaf of papers from a cardboard manilla folder. Licking her thumb, she flicked through them for a minute, finding two pages that she pulled out. She laid them side-by-side and swivelled the pages around so I could read them. They were job advertisements. I read off the headline to each.

"Packing Assistant, Peter Vasallo's Frozen Foods. Sorting Assistant, Post Office."

It looked like my grandiose dreams of leaving an intellectual stamp upon the canon of Western thought would have to wait another year at least. I did leave a stamp on something that summer: I chose the packing assistant role and spent a week stamping the best-before date onto several thousand packets of frozen fish. It was the most depressing week of my life and I vowed to never work in a factory again. In my later career, nothing would motivate me more through the tough times than the memory of standing in the corner of a freezing cold warehouse, stamping dates onto cardboard packaging for eight hours straight. It terrified me to think that could be my future.

To add insult to injury, when I was finally paid, the benefits office reduced my unemployment benefit by exactly the amount I'd earned. Calculated net, I'd literally worked for nothing. That engendered my sympathy for the so-called 'welfare trap', having now been ensnared by it. Unemployment benefit in England was 'means tested', meaning claimants only received it if they had nothing, and if they earned anything the benefit was correspondingly reduced. It's the most perverse incentive imaginable, encouraging people to avoid working and instead throw themselves upon government largesse. Like I said earlier, the People's Republic Of Northern Britain was a despondent communist hellhole. In despair, I explained to my parents that I couldn't possibly earn my tuition fees because the work

I was offered was so low-paid and irregular that I could save maybe five pounds a week after benefit deductions. Fortunately, my parents decided to pay my tuition fees, thus rescuing my fledging academic career. I thoroughly enjoyed my year at Durham University.

The second time I thought about a job was a year later, just before submitting my Masters thesis, two months before graduation. It was the 'milk round' season in which blue chip employers send their graduate recruitment teams to the careers fairs of each of the top ten to twenty universities. I'd completely ignored the milk round at Nottingham the previous year. Suitably chastened by my week printing best-before dates onto frozen fish packets, it was a mistake I wasn't about to make a second time. Rather than chasing jobs, at the milk rounds the jobs were coming to me. Graduate jobs. Real jobs.

Sadly, my job-related skills were no more advanced than the prior year and a week packing frozen fish hadn't prepared me well for the boardroom. I didn't even know what job I wanted to do. So I spent a few afternoons in the university careers office reading up on all the guidance literature. It wasn't very helpful but I remembered my old dormitory room mate Charlie explaining the year before that he'd found an excellent job in finance. I looked into that and it seemed alright. Secure, lucrative, professional, and reasonably high status.

Unfortunately, I knew nothing about finance.

My ambition overruled my ignorance so when the first day of milk round came, I went to the student union hall. It was filled with a hundred small kiosks, each holding a couple of be-suited recruiters and their corporate marketing videos showing on small television screens. I located the booths of all six of the Big Six consulting firms (mergers and bankruptcy have since reduced that to Big Four) and filled in an application form. Each promised to give a screening interview the next day if they liked my application.

Astonishingly, four of the six offered an interview. I had them all the same day, each taking a half hour. It was formulaic, sitting me across a desk in a small room to run through my resume and ask simple questions. Before all that I'd sat a generic aptitude test (verbal, mathematical, visuospatial reasoning and so on, like an IQ test) which I knew I'd aced, the results of which were shared with all four recruitment teams. They must've liked me because three offered me second interviews at company offices.

One of those second interviews went really well. I was sent a train ticket and hotel voucher to spend two nights in London, which made me feel adult. I put on a cheap ill-fitting suit I'd bought the previous week and suffered two days of multiple interviews, group tasks, and more aptitude tests. Then I took a train to Nottingham to meet my undergraduate thesis supervisor, a nice man called Dr Christian Heath who was the very image of a distinguished English professor. He looked like he'd be friends with C.S. Lewis and J.R.R. Tolkien. We had a long talk about my intention to study for a PhD under his supervision, funded by the ESRC.

"Nick, I would be happy to supervise you. I think you have wonderful potential as an academic but, frankly, I don't think you want to do it. It's clear from this conversation that you don't really know what you want to study. Look, a PhD is a very long, lonely journey. It will take five years, mostly on your own in the library. Even with funding, it's a Spartan life. You have to really want it. My recommendation is this: get a job, in the real non-academic world. See how you find it. If you want to come back in a couple of years and do the PhD, I'll be more than happy to supervise you."

I sensed he was right, but it was a big change of plans to give up on academia. I wouldn't just be giving up intellectual advancement. I'd also be bidding a permanent adieu to tweed jackets, flannel trousers, and pipe-smoking. Clearly, I'd have to think carefully about that. One can't be rash, can one? Back in the North East I called the Business School at my university and secured an appointment with one of the professors there. He listened to my case.

"Nick, PhDs are a qualification to prove you can research. That's the skill they demonstrate. You have told me you want to find out more about the world. PhDs don't do that. You get a very deep but also very narrow specialism. I agree with what your supervisor said. You need to have an intense interest in the subject matter, something you don't possess right now."

I walked out of that meeting decided that I should indeed get a real job first. Luckily, the very next morning I received a letter containing a formal job offer from one of the Big Six consulting firms. I accepted.

I'd already submitted my Masters thesis so there were a few weeks to kill before work in London began. I went on holiday to Tenerife with my Japanese girlfriend, Reiko, a fellow student on my Masters course. Then my dad drove me down to London, where I'd lined up a shared house with two other lads also joining the same company to do the same apprenticeship, in different business units. My corporate life had begun.

To say I struggled to adapt is an understatement. I knew nothing about accounting, finance, or business. They'd only hired me because in 1997 there was a financial boom so after hiring all the appropriately-qualified candidates, companies were filling vacancies with literally anyone with a good score from a good university. Thus I'd lucked into a fantastic job that I was totally unqualified for. Sadly, I didn't feel lucky. It was the hardest I'd worked in my life and I'd started from a position way behind my peers, all of whom were intelligent high-achievers with relevant degrees. At my first year-end assessment my department manager almost fired me. By the middle of the second year I'd found my feet and by the third and final year I was pretty good at my job. I still hated it, though. The stress was unbelievable because I was doing a difficult professional job, constant commuting, and in addition I bore a study load equivalent to a university degree. Luckily, I passed all my exams and earned my professional license.

Socially, life was considerably more upbeat. I was in the Big Smoke, reacquainted with my best friends from university. We went out drinking every weekend. Tim and Yasin shared a house with three other lads in Wimbledon, south-west London, so usually we met up there. We'd hit a bar, then finish the night drinking cans of beer while playing Tekken 3 on the Playstation at their house. Every other Saturday we'd meet at The Moon Under The Water pub on Charing Cross Road (now renamed as a Lloyds Bar) so that Paul and his friends from East London could join us.

Friday nights were often work drinks. The training system in my profession was highly organised such that my company had well over a hundred young graduates joining at the same time as I, to do exactly the same job. We were all mixed into one cohort to do our orientation, exams, and technical training together. It created camaraderie from the first day at work, a two-week bookkeeping course we attended at The Financial Training Company in Angel, Islington.

Did I say stressful? Failure in the course-ending exam meant immediate dismissal. Two hopeful apprentices were fired that first month. The threat of dismissal hung over our heads the entire three years, with the first year being most perilous. At least in the latter two years, you had a chance to resit an exam before being fired (though if you'd failed more than one..... immediate dismissal).

I enjoyed being around smart motivated people. It was so alien compared to my loutish school friends and the lazy welfare-scrounging Newcastle punks I'd stayed in touch with during university. The professionalism of my qualified office colleagues rubbed off on me. Strangely, the manager I looked up to most was the one I disliked most. He was called Will, an English public-school alumni who was five years ahead of me in his career. He was job leader on a few projects I did and every time we worked together he was a tough task master with a peremptory, almost rude, manner. That's why I didn't like him. That and also him catching me skiving a few times. What I admired, however, was his exceptionally organised mind and his mastery of the fundamentals. He was extremely good at his job.

I admire competence, so I suffered his moods and learned as much as I could.

My sex life in London was good enough that I didn't worry about it. I'd broken up with Reiko because she was returning to Tokyo at the end of her course and now I lived in London. My parting gift was to write her entire dissertation the weekend before leaving Durham, as she was hopelessly out of her depth in both English and knowledge of sociology so unable to write it herself. I briefly dated another Japanese girl, Hiroko, who worked in a sushi takeaway in Chinatown by Leicester Square station. Our romance lasted three dates, but that was long enough to fuck her.

I didn't suspect it at the time, but I wasn't to sleep with another English girl for many years. In fact, my girl diet was to become entirely Japanese, so much so I'm surprised my own eyes didn't become slanty. Though we were often out drinking, my friends and

I never cold-approached. What had seemed normal throughout university now seemed somehow weird. It was as if the moment I'd been handed my degree certificate, the Chancellor had secretly sucked out my mojo in payment. My mild interest in Japan had strengthened considerably now that I'd banged two of its women. I started learning the language from a textbook and taking an interest in their culture.

There was a big shop in Piccadilly called The Japan Centre. I'd bought my textbook in the bookshop there and also bought the occasional instant noodles and rice from the small supermarket in the basement. One time, I saw a noticeboard by the cashier. It was full of small personal ads — rooms to let, language tuition and so on. I saw one card from a man offering free language exchange.

An idea formed. I placed my own advertisement.

I met a dozen girls through language exchange, of which I banged two. One was a young girl called Hiroko who'd worked in an Osaka convenience store for a year to save up money to study in London. The other, Rena, was in her mid-twenties and I dated her for six months. Another Japanese girl, Chigusa, saw me reading my Japanese textbook on the Underground and she opened me. She was a shy bank clerk who I banged for a couple of months. It seemed there was a never-ending train of Japanese girls visiting London and I met enough of them that I never needed look elsewhere.

The two girls I knew best were two I didn't actually shag. Kaori and her friend Mayumi answered my advertisement in The Japan Centre and it was clear it wasn't 'on' so I accepted the friend-zone. We met for coffee twice a week after my work and became real friends for two years. We even had a trip to Amsterdam together. One evening Mayumi, who worked at All Nippon Airlines, had news.

"Nick, one of my work colleagues has a daughter coming to study in London. She's a flute player entering music school. Would you meet her for language exchange?"

I certainly would.

A week later Mayumi and I sat in the basement of a Caffe Nero in Piccadilly waiting for the girl, Miwako, to arrive. I didn't know what to expect. It turned out she was a very pretty twenty-two year old with spritely energy. I liked her from the first moment. The feeling was clearly mutual as Miwako barely spoke to Mayumi and spent our initial meeting overwhelming me with smiles before asking when we can next meet.

I banged her the next meeting.

Dating Miwako was eye-opening even though we were never close. It was the first time I'd experienced the uniquely girly energy popular in Japan, often called '*genki*'. Miwako's eyes were always bright with mischief and she'd hop and dance around. That probably makes her sound retarded but it was actually very sweet, and always within the boundaries of propriety. She made English girls look sullen and withdrawn by comparison. It was my first experience with hyper-femininity and I loved it.

Miwako shortly before the banging

I didn't love *her*, by the way. She was a bit of a retard.

For a couple of months I had a pretty, energetic girlfriend who complimented me perfectly. Sadly, she was always at music school or practising, so we only met once a week. Miwako was equally entertaining in bed and quite liked to dress up. I'd bought a Japanese schoolgirl outfit for a dress-up experience with Reiko and still had it lying around at the bottom of my closet so Miwako was pleased to wear it. Halfway through banging her I noticed a big dried cum stain on the dress, as I'd forgotten to wash it since Chigusa was last at my house. Oops.

My single most treasured memory of Miwako was when she woke me up one Sunday morning by giving me a blow job. In itself, that's nice but not special. However, she kept stopping to stare at me with an excitable grin before going back to work. I was bemused as to why, but it was endearing. We finally broke up when I expressed my dissatisfaction with only meeting once a week. I think it was a communication error due to her poor English, but the relationship had a casual air about it so I doubt it would've lasted much longer regardless. We were basically fuck buddies.

Sometimes small accidents or seemingly insignificant decisions change the course of your life. Once such series of events occurred in November of 1999, soon after my second year anniversary of London life. By now I'd grown accustomed to my work, had passed my second set of exams, and enjoyed a reasonable reputation in my office. It was Friday night and unseasonably nice weather. I stood outside Brown's wine bar by the Bank of England with my university friends Tim, Yasin, and Warren. We were surrounded by other blue-shirted office drones sipping over-priced lager, all of us laughing and chatting. I felt good. I felt like I belonged in London, now more comfortable as a young professional than considering myself an academic on sabbatical. I knew I'd never do that PhD and silently thanked my two professors for their good advice.

"Shall we go to Soho?" asked Warren. "I've got a card for Stringfellows, expensed from work." Warren was the rich one of our group, a high-flying equities analyst as the financial bubble approached its peak before the Dotcom crash. He'd often entertain clients at London's most famous strip club and he'd now wangled a personal card.

I didn't like strip clubs. Paul and I had gone to a couple in Amsterdam a few years earlier and been unimpressed. What's the point of looking at a naked girl if you can't fuck her? That's like going to a restaurant and not eating the food.

"Maybe later," I put in. "But lets drink more first."

"Old Street. We can walk from here. I know a few good bars," said Tim and that settled it.

We had one more in Brown's then Tim led us towards a pleasant old man's pub on a corner at a busy Old Street intersection. Black cabs and red buses whizzed past as we waited impatiently for a green light to cross. Warren had been drinking all afternoon since a business lunch and was considerably more inebriated than Tim, Yasin, and I. He was getting impatient, prodding the button on the pedestrian crossing, as if it would make the light turn green faster.

"Bastards" he muttered under his breath, then walked across the road forcing cars to brake lest they run him down.

We pushed open the main door and approached the bar. It was a pleasant joint, the rustic Tudor-age decor belying the clientele of modern office professionals drinking therein. Warren squeezed clumsily between two punters and called the barman. He wasn't aggressive, but it was rather rude, and the barman took offence, showing distaste in his expression.

"Over here, good man! Three pints of your finest ale," called Warren.

I didn't think it insolent but the barman did. He threw us out.

"Bastard" commented my rich friend. There was another traditional English pub visible a stone's throw away so we went there. Tim and I insisted we wait outside five minutes until Warren sobered up a little, then we insisted further he drink only a Coke. He called us bastards, but good-naturedly this time.

Tim found a slot machine by the door and put in a few pounds while I collected the drinks and brought them over. I rested his atop the machine then sipped mine as I watched his fortunes change with the flashing of the machine's lights. Luck favoured him and he hit the £20 jackpot.

"Fucking brill!" he exclaimed and theatrically punched the 'collect' button. The machine coughed out twenty beautiful gold coins into the tray. At that very moment the pub door opened and three Japanese girls walked in. My eye caught the middle girl. She was very pretty. The girls walked on to stand at the bar, looking a little intimidated by all the English men.

"I'd love to shag her" I said, indicating with a tilt of my pint glass.

"Which one?"

"Middle one with pig tails."

"Ooooh fucking hell she's a bit of alright," said Warren, his eyes still bleary. "Proper tight arse she has. You should give it a go."

By now I was enveloped in a pleasant fog from three pints. Not drunk, but not quite myself either. I had a buzz on my brain. So I did something I'd not done since late night in the student nightclubs of Nottingham. I walked up to a girl I didn't know, tapped her on the shoulder, and hit on her.

"*Suimasen*" I said, which is Japanese for 'excuse me'. I blabbed some poor Japanese then switched to English. I have no idea what we talked about but, incredibly, it worked. We must've been talking a while because Tim came up and tapped me on the arm.

"Drink up, mate. We're moving on."

Tim knew nothing about pulling women but this was nonetheless sound advice so as not to overstay my welcome. I took the girl's number. "What's your name again?" I knew it was something difficult to pronounce.

"Ioe."

"Ee-you-i?"

"Ioe."

"You-oh-eh? That sounds like a card game."

"No, Ioe. Eeee like eagle. Oh like slow. And eh like egg."

"Ee-yor-e? That's the name of the donkey from Winnie The Pooh. Why would your parents call you that?"

I'd have never teased her so hard if I'd not been drunk and confused but it seemed my good luck knew no limits that night. The only reason we'd even met was because Warren had gotten us thrown out of the previous bar. Ioe was really pretty too. Easily the prettiest girl I could remember showing interest in me since my college days with Joanne and Kirsten; neither of whom I'd banged.

It proved difficult to arrange the first date. Ioe was at dance school training for a professional career and totally consumed by it. She flaked the first two date appointments, texting me a few hours in advance that her class schedule had changed. I started thinking it would be a repeat of the run-around I'd gotten with Miwako, the flute player. The third time we agreed to meet at Tottenham Court Road station at 6pm, right after I finished work.

I had a terrible day in the office. My manager wanted me to stay late and I risked his wrath in order to leave on time for the date. Worse, the Underground had delays and my train was held up in a tunnel for ten minutes, making my one-way commute forty minutes in total under the London streets. I was five minutes late and Ioe wasn't there.

I called her and she didn't pick up. I waited another ten minutes. She called back.

"Sorry! I was in class, it's just finished!" she wailed.

"Why are you in class? You were supposed to meet me fifteen minutes ago."

"I tried to call but your phone didn't connect. My schedule changed last minute. I'm sorry."

"That's no good. You should've missed the class and kept your appointment."

"Sorry! I'm free now. I'll come now. I'll be twenty minutes."

"I'll wait fifteen. Hurry up."

Then I hung up on her.

It would appear my good luck still hadn't run out because Ioe did in fact show up and she looked fantastic. My first thought was, *oh my god she's beautiful.* How didn't I notice that in the bar the week prior? My second thought was, *holy shit you nearly binned her over a missed phone call.* The date went really well because Ioe liked me from the very first moment. She later told me her friend had taken her out that night in Old Street specifically to try to find her an English boyfriend, which explains why they'd maintained a discreet distance while I was hitting on her.

We met for dinner on the second date a few days later, then she came to my house in Tooting Bec to cook sushi for the third date. After food, we started making out on the sofa. Ioe suddenly broke off and rushed to the bathroom. *Oh dear,* I thought, *this is where she gets cold feet.*

She came back into the room five minutes later and tentatively handed me a condom. I led her upstairs. She was literally shaking as she lay naked on my bed, waiting for me to poke my dick into her. I never did ask her why. Was it nervousness about the act of sex generally, or a worry I'd be disappointed with her, or something different entirely? Now that I write these words, I wish I knew. Anyway, the important thing is that I banged her and thoroughly enjoyed it.

That's what really matters here.

At first I had no special interest in Ioe. She was hot, I liked fucking her, and I saw no reason to stop doing so, but she didn't immediately seize my attention like Miwako had. After a couple of months I started to like her more and we ended up dating for the whole of my last year in London and I introduced her to my friends early on.

By mid-2000 I was coming to the end of my finance training contract and looking towards the next career step. There were three paths to choose from. Option One was to remain at the company and be immediately promoted to junior manager. My salary would double but the real attraction was the increased professional training and experience I'd get. Nobody joined a Big Six firm for the money. They were all about the career development.

On holiday in Gran Canaria
with Ioe

Should I wish to chase money — that is, Option Two — the fad at that time was to enter equities analysis. I could earn at least £50 an hour, an eye-watering sum to me then, to write reports on the past, present and (hopefully) future performance of stocks. The front office was where the big money was and I knew from Warren how that life was.

Option Three was to bin it all. I'd have my professional license and three years of top-tier experience so it was entirely feasible to take a sabbatical. Go away, do something fun, and come back to the finance industry a year later. Given that I was exhausted and stressed out, this last option was far and away the most appealing. To that end, I'd begun applying for jobs to teach English in Japan. I'd been accepted onto the Japan English Teaching programme ('JET') in which the government hires native English speakers to team-teach in high schools around Japan. The salary was equal to my current finance salary (though far below what I could earn if I hung around in London, post-qualification). I accepted the JET job though I didn't yet know where they'd send me.

I was hoping for Tokyo or Osaka.

At no point did Ioe enter into this decision, even though she was a Tokyo native and reaching the end of her own dancing course soon and thus likely to return to Japan around the same time I was set to go there. I'd decided I wanted to live in Japan for my own reasons, and that was that.

One Friday night I tried explaining my plans to my friends. We were in a fancy Slug And Lettuce wine bar on the South Bank of the river, near Shad Thames. It's an upmarket redeveloped docklands popular with those City professionals who could stomach the then-£250 per week rent for a small apartment. Tim had just moved there with his girlfriend Wendy. He was in the bar now, along with Paul and Yasin.

"So you don't know where in Japan you'll go and yet you're accepting the job?" asked Yasin, incredulous. To him, I was some kind of wild-man, as brave as Neil Armstrong flying to the moon.

"Yep."

"What about Ioe?" asked Paul.

"What about her?"

"What does she think about it?" he asked.

"Who cares? Japan is full of hot Jap lasses. I'll easily find a new one. I'll be as happy as a dog with two dicks over there."

Paul's eyes bulged and he gripped his pint glass tightly, almost crushing it in his hands. Tim noticed and looked down, seeing Paul's hand shaking as if he was deciding to glass me. Tim rested a hand softly on his forearm. "He's just fucking with you. Chill out. You know what Nick's like for provoking people."

"He shouldn't talk that way about her," Paul rasped, through gritted teeth.

"Fucking hell, pal," I joked. "I'm the one banging her, not you."

That got his hands shaking again and it was the moment I realised Paul was in love with my girlfriend. Snippets of past encounters flashed through my mind. Paul had been extremely polite and deferential towards Ioe since the moment they'd met. It all made sense now. I decided to do the decent thing and apologise.

"Sorry Paul, I didn't mean to wind you up. It's just that last night Ioe was around at my house. I handcuffed her to the bedpost, did her from behind, and then came on her face. She loved it. I'm hoping all Jap birds are that dirty."

Oops!

That wasn't an effective apology, though it was an accurate description of my previous evening's entertainment. Nonetheless, Paul regained his composure and we carried on as before. To Paul's credit, as I spent the night mulling over this new revelation, I couldn't recall a single time when Paul had actually hit on Ioe. He'd been the perfect gentleman, admiring her from a polite distance. I resolved not to wind him up any further.

I resigned my job, giving thirty day's notice, timed so that I'd meet the minimum criteria to qualify for my professional license: three year's work experience. I couldn't afford to linger because my new teaching job was starting just a week after I left my firm and if I missed that window, I'd need to wait another year. It was cutting it fine. The same evening, I returned home to find a welcome pack from the JET scheme, including a formal letter informing me where I'd be sent to teach.

I ripped it open with keen anticipation. I was about to find out where I'd spend the next year of my life. Tokyo or Osaka?

Neither.

Iheya-son, Okinawa. I had no idea where that was.

I pulled out my atlas and examined the map of Japan. It took several minutes to find Iheya-son. Starting with my finger on Tokyo, I dragged it across the page covering two thousand kilometres to the south, to Okinawa's prefectural capital Naha. From there my finger followed a line north up the island, representing a motorway, to Nago. From there, the road north wound through jungles and mountains to a small ferry port called Untenko. From there, my finger traced a path across the sea to the tiny island of Iheya. Further research informed me that Iheya-son was an island village with a population of two thousand souls (if Japanese people even *had* souls, I wasn't yet sure). Iheya's primary industries were fishing and the seaweed used in sushi rolls. I closed the atlas and dropped it on my coffee table with a thud. I then walked out into my back garden in a daze.

I wasn't going to Tokyo, or Osaka. I wasn't even going to a small provincial city.

I was going to spend the next twelve months living in a tiny Japanese fishing village isolated from the whole world. Well, you wanted to get away from the stress and bustle of central London, I told myself. This is literally as far away from that as it is possibly to be.

A very long way from home

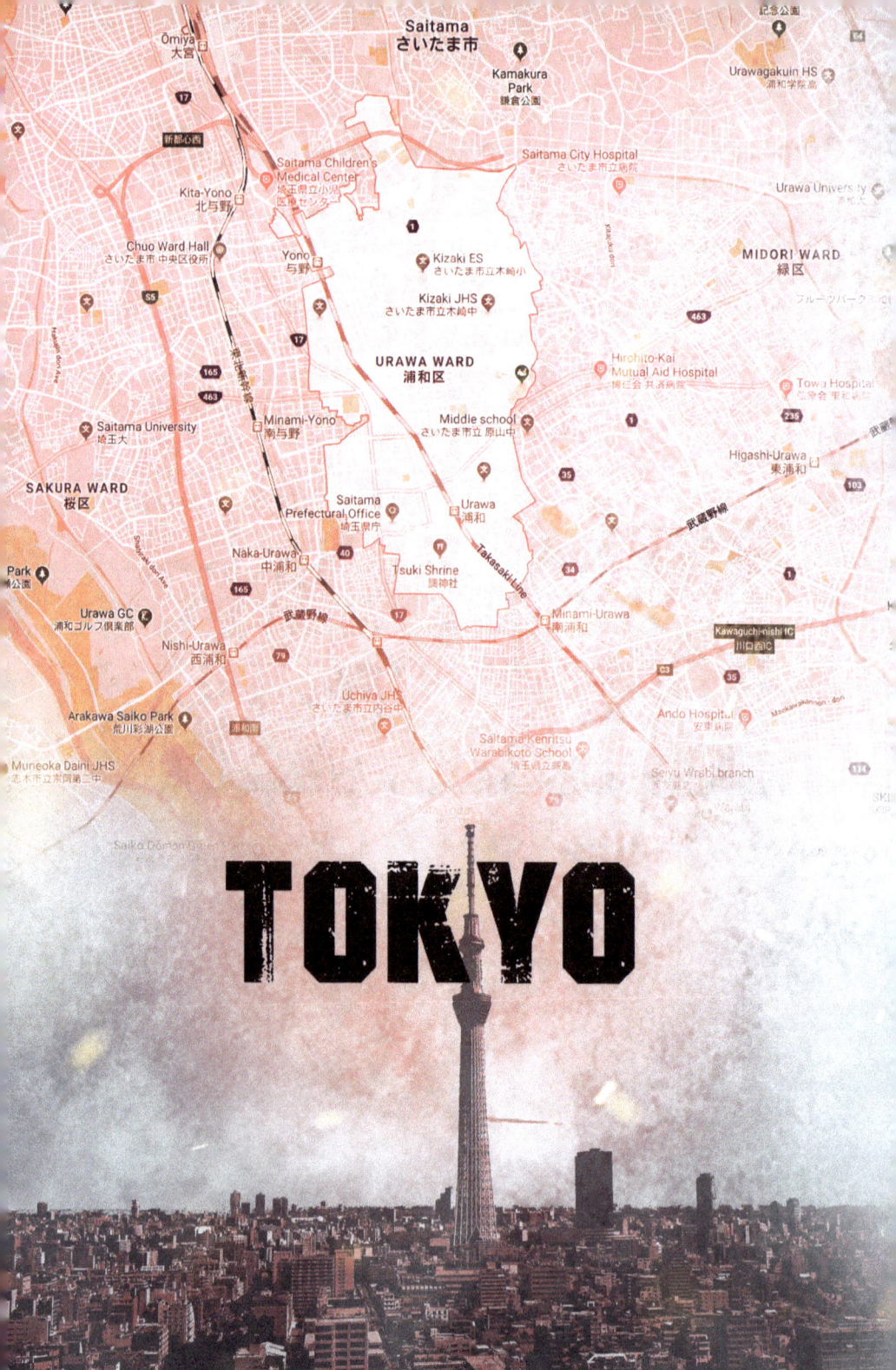

CHAPTER 09

SHUTTLE JAPAN

CHAPTER 9

SHUTTLE JAPAN

As you'd expect, living on an isolated tropical island for a year wasn't particularly exciting. I took weekend trips to the main Okinawan island every fortnight to see my fellow JET friends. The change of environment did me the world of good, shaking off the fast pace of big city life. Towards the end of the year, I banged a hot eighteen-year-old slapper with big tits, Ryoko, who I pulled from a small nightclub on the seventh floor of a building overlooking the main crossing of Kokusaidori, the centre of Naha. Aside from that I focused mainly on my teaching, reading, and newfound focus on fitness training. I also completed every Sega Dreamcast game ever released. I had lots of free time. If you want a more lively account of living on a tropical island, try *Robinson Crusoe*.

At least the main island of Okinawa was lively

So, let's skip forward a year to when I returned home to Gateshead to relax a couple of months, then flew to Tokyo to try to establish myself there.

I arrived in Tokyo in December 2001 on a ninety-day tourist visa with my accumulated savings from working in London and Okinawa, which amounted to maybe five thousand pounds. Stepping off the plane and into the arrivals lobby of Narita airport, I was excited but nervous. My plan was simple; look for a job so that I could get a working visa and live there indefinitely. I had no desire to return to the UK. The psychological trauma of working so hard for three years in finance still sent a shudder down my spine. I knew that wasn't what I wanted in life, to slave away in an office in high pressure work. With the passage of time, I'd develop some perspective and come to appreciate that work apprenticeship periods are always stressful, and that I'd grown in resilience from the experience. But for now, it was too close in my memory. The stark contrast between island life in Okinawa and Central London business life exaggerated my feeling of aversion at living in the UK.

Tokyo was the promised land. A bustling mega-city utterly alien and refreshing because of it. Once more I was a stranger in a strange land. My trajectory since leaving home for university had been to move progressively further away from Newcastle and into progressively busier madcap environments: from a Nottingham campus, to a London financial centre, and now to literally the other side of the world.

Standing in Narita airport with just one suitcase, looking around, the feeling was reinforced. Deep in my core I knew I was doing the right thing. I dragged my case to the airport shuttle train, a typically advanced-tech Japanese affair, and rode it to the terminus at Ueno on the east side of Tokyo. Ioe was waiting by the exit barriers. I'd visited her in Tokyo a couple of times while based in Okinawa and she'd been to see me too. Our relationship had survived the logistical difficulties.

She came running over in her platform shoes and mini-skirt, beaming with happiness. "*O-kaeri!*" she giggled, welcoming me to what I hoped was my new home. The twelve hour flight had knocked me for a loop so I let her take me to a nearby Doutor coffee shop, a national franchise. I settled into a chair and let the waitress bring my an americano and a toasted cheese sandwich.

"You are so brave!" said Ioe. "Coming to Japan with no job, no working visa, and no plan."

Put like that, I suspected I was more foolish than brave. Perhaps I should've thought it through.

I had arranged, via a message board, to stay with a fellow teacher on the JET program for the first month. He was an American called Tim, in his mid-twenties and into photography. We would get on well and chat a lot. He gave me a few tips on where to find job advertisements. His apartment was a small boxy place run by the private letting company Leo Palace, and he'd set up a mattress for me on the tiny mezzanine bunk that was accessible by some folding ladders. The downside was location. He lived in Tsuruse, a small city an hour's train ride north of Tokyo proper. It soon grated, to keep commuting in when I wanted to hang out with Ioe, but Tsuruse had all the usual amenities and most importantly an internet cafe where I would look for work.

I'd make the long trip to South-West Tokyo three times a week to stay over with Ioe. Having already gotten to know her mother and sister pretty well from my earlier visits, it was a simple arrangement. We ate lunch together in the compact dining room and then Ioe and I would go out to my favourite Starbucks by Jiyugaoka train station to chill for an hour or two. It was there that I'd read the classifieds section of *The Japan Times*, where most English teaching jobs were advertised. Then I'd take the train north to my rooms to sleep, or stay over with Ioe at her mum's house.

It was December and that was a problem. I'd blithely assumed work would be easy to find but almost every legit outfit required a valid working visa, which I didn't have. Worse still, the job I wanted most was teaching in junior or senior high school, like I'd done in Okinawa. However, the Japanese academic year begins in April and schools recruit once annually. Looking back that's obvious but it hadn't occurred to me. The JET scheme I'd joined for Okinawa was scheduled to match the English academic year beginning in September. Thus I'd returned to Gateshead then, deciding I was ready to go again in December, simply headed to Tokyo.

Yet again, I'd assumed the world would arrange itself according to my convenience.

The only places recruiting all-year around were the commercial *eikaiwa* (English conversation) schools of which the two biggest, Nova and Geos, recruited exclusively overseas. So, I had to step down a level and tap up the smaller outfits. It was discouraging, watching a few weeks fly by, my savings and visa days dwindling, while getting exclusively bad news on the job front. On the plus side, every other aspect of Tokyo life was great. I was greatly enjoying my time with Ioe, loved absorbing the city atmosphere, and also began to attend all the mixed martial arts fight shows that were on every week or so.

I finally found a job in Takagi's English Club in Urawa City. It was the next city south of Omori on the train line ending in Ikebukero. The job wasn't an especially good deal but it was all I could find. Takagi's was run by an old Japanese man of the same name. He'd bought a big single storey house and converted the lounge/dining area into a classroom with tables and chairs. The other rooms, off-limits to students, were converted into teacher bedrooms. The deal was we each taught twelve hours a week and received room and board in exchange. Mr Takagi claimed that by not paying a salary to teachers we weren't in breach of visa restrictions. Naturally, I didn't press him on this point.

I expected to hate the job, having taken it out of desperation, so was nicely surprised that I settled in within a week. There were six teachers, all in their twenties. Damian and Sylvester were black Americans with opposite body types. Damian was reed thin with a Chris Rock look whereas Sylvester had played high school football (the version only Americans play, not the proper one with the World Cup) and was jacked. I got on really well with both men and when I unpacked my Sega Dreamcast games console things got even better. There was a sofa and TV at one end of the classroom so after each day's teaching ended at nine, Takagi would lock the front door and go home. We'd put NFL2K on the Dreamcast and play versus mode multiplayer all evening.

There was also a young Canadian tech nerd called Albert and two girls: a blonde Pole called Julia and a Brit called Sarah. The social atmosphere was excellent, like being back in a student house, and just what an introvert like me needed to stop getting into my head over my uncertain future. Takagi forbid overnight guests but it was easy to sneak them in against his rules. I spent two months at Takagi's and enjoyed it all. Teaching was a chore because it was one-to-one and thus more intimate and high-pressure than I'd like, but three four-hour sessions passed quickly and the students were all office workers or retirees with a passion for the language.

Around February, finally, the job market came alive as recruitment for the coming academic year began. Whereas the JET scheme sourced teachers outside of the major Tokyo-Osaka nexus, within those two cities the jobs were run by private agencies contracted with schools. JET paid 300,000 yen per month, which anchored the market rate. The jobs I saw in classifieds and forums were quoting 220k to 275k which suited me fine. A young adult can live comfortably on that.

My first interview was way out in the north west, at literally the end of a train line in Yori, well past Tsuruse. You couldn't conceivably call it part of the Tokyo urban sprawl as, looking out of the train window, I saw many rice fields and small forests breaking it up. It felt like countryside and upon stepping out of the station I noticed there was too much sky. In central Tokyo you are surrounded by high-rise buildings, which were absent here. I walked across the station's car park and into a small office clutching my resume. It was a tiny operation, just two men: the owner, a big fat Japanese guy called Akihiro and his young Canadian flunky Sam. Right from the beginning I felt like I was being pitched a scam. I could feel the wool scratch my eyeballs as Akihiro attempted to draw it over my eyes.

He read my resume aloud (he already had a copy by email) and asked about my teaching experience in Okinawa. Nodding his head he muttered, "Yes, one year on JET. We can sell that." He then gave me a long allegorical story he claimed to be true about a former teacher who'd signed a contract with him but tried to lure students away into his own new English teaching business. Akihiro assured me he'd crushed the traitor, though he implied it was done legally, thank God.

Obviously they wanted me because within five minutes they began outlining a job in a junior high school in Nishi-Kawagoe, itself way out from Central Tokyo but less so than Yori. It was looking likely that my dream of living in Tokyo-proper had been crushed and, the salary being on the low-end at 210k yen per month, didn't please me either. Still, they were offering me a real job to teach in a Japanese junior high school including support for a one-year working visa. It could be a lot worse.

Actually, it *was* a lot worse.

"We need you to interview with the Kawagoe education board before we can confirm. Can you make it tomorrow?"

"Yes."

"Okay, come back here at 9am and we'll drive you there."

Something didn't smell right but it was my only option so the next morning I put on my suit and got the early train out to Yori. Akihiro drove us to the meeting in his big SUV, keeping a constant monologue of the rights and wrongs of Japanese interview etiquette. He was more nervous than I. We parked up outside a large government building and then I sat in the waiting room while Akihiro went off to talk to the receptionist.

"Just wait, ten minutes maximum" he reassured me.

Nothing happened for half an hour, until a grey-haired Japanese man in an ill-fitting navy blue suit popped his head out from a door, gave me a quick once-over, then closed it again. Fifteen minutes after that we left. I hadn't said a word to anybody. Akihiro began making excuses as he drove us to a sushi restaurant.

"Let's get a big lunch. My treat!"

It was obvious the whole interview process had been a scam. Akihiro was pitching for a contract with the Kawagoe education board and had brought me along as proof he had native-English speaking teachers on his books. There was no job, or at least if there was his outfit had not yet been given the contract for it. I'd been cheated.

"Don't worry, we'll make sure the interview is set up next week. There was a communication error and they couldn't do it today," he said.

My social calibration and worldliness was far below the level I have now, but even blissfully ignorant twenty-five year old me knew I was being bullshitted. I didn't go back to Yori.

I had a similarly unproductive second job interview, this time with Interac, then the big player in the Tokyo high-school teaching market. I'd noticed they advertised in *The Japanese Times* every Monday and on all the forums. My one year's JET experience secured me an interview that I then messed up through my overwrought nerves.

The face-to-face segment was easy enough but the four interviewees had to each present a five minute demo lesson to the room. I'd already been discouraged to hear all three of the other candidates had working holiday visas that would let them slide comfortably and legally into work without any bureaucratic wrangling. The demo lesson requirement blind-sided me and my nerves were already taut because I had three weeks left on my tourist visa and no other leads. An annoying Canadian guy went first, doing a brash high-energy demonstration that was a lot better than I could manage. During my demo I paced back and forth nervously and couldn't bring the class alive.

"Your demonstration was not so good," the head interviewer told me afterwards in the debrief. "You walk so aggressively it would scare the children."

"I was nervous. I didn't know a demonstration was required so I hadn't prepared."

"Yes, we understand. We don't tell candidates until the interview day. But unfortunately, we cannot accept your application."

I was despondent. I sat still on the train ride back to Urawa, staring blankly at the floor. I sleep-walked through a four-hour session of teaching at Takagi's and then locked myself in my room and wouldn't come out when Damian and Sylvester invited me for a drink. Ioe called me on my mobile, asking hopefully for news of the interview.

"Terrible. I didn't get it."

"Oh, I'm sorry. Don't give up! You'll get a job."

"Where? I don't know who else is recruiting. That was the last chance. I've got three weeks left and my money is getting low."

The phone went silent several seconds, then Ioe chirped with forced optimism, "Come over here tomorrow. I'll cook your favourite ramen and we can rent a movie. We can still have fun." I appreciated

Returning to Okinawa had started to look appealing

the sentiment but I slept horribly and was exhausted the next morning.

I was saved at the last by a stroke of extraordinary good luck. Just a couple of days later I found a small classified advert from a new agency called Sagan Speak, the first time I'd seen them advertise. They offered the usual deal, of teaching in a junior high school but with two big differences: the salary quoted was a mighty 300k yen, right at the top of the scale for that work, and they claimed to specialise in central Tokyo. But more importantly, when I emailed my resume they got back to me the same day and set up an interview the day after that.

I had a lifeline.

Sagan Speak was run my two English brothers in their late-twenties, of which the fatter older one clearly had a background in sales. It seems they'd only recently set themselves up so at first I was wary, should they be a fly-by-night scam. However, the fat lad, Gary told me, "we have just signed a deal to supply two teachers to a school in Ogikubo in West Tokyo. It's a private junior high, an escalator school to the famous Nihon Daigaku university. Everything is rushed and the principal wants to fill the position immediately. He was very specific that the teachers must be English, highly educated, and professional."

I was English, highly educated and professional. If their fourth stipulation had been 'querulous cunt' I'd have had it locked down.

Gary continued, "we've got a girl lined up for interview tomorrow, a Cambridge graduate. I'll call and try to get you in at the same time."

Unlike Akihiro in Yori, Gary didn't come off as a slimeball. Also unlike Akihiro, he already had the contract signed and it was just a case of presenting some potential teachers to get the school's approval. Sagan Speak had a pressing problem to which I was a potential solution. Obviously, I agreed to the interview.

That interview was a mere rubber-stamping exercise. The girl, Emma, and I were led into the principal's office together with the whole English department of six teachers. We were all introduced and within minutes we were approved. Formal confirmation didn't come until the next morning but as I left the room, the head of English, a big hearty man called Mr Takayama shook my hand and said, "we look forward to working with you." Words can't convey my relief. My dumb plan hadn't just worked out. It had worked out *blindingly* well. Not only was I to teach in a prestigious private junior high school, but it was in a great part of Tokyo, and the salary was top-end. Even my work visa was fast-tracked. I'd achieved my wildest dreams.

I had started my new life in Tokyo.

My old shack in Okinawa

Summer camp on the Island

With the lads in Naha

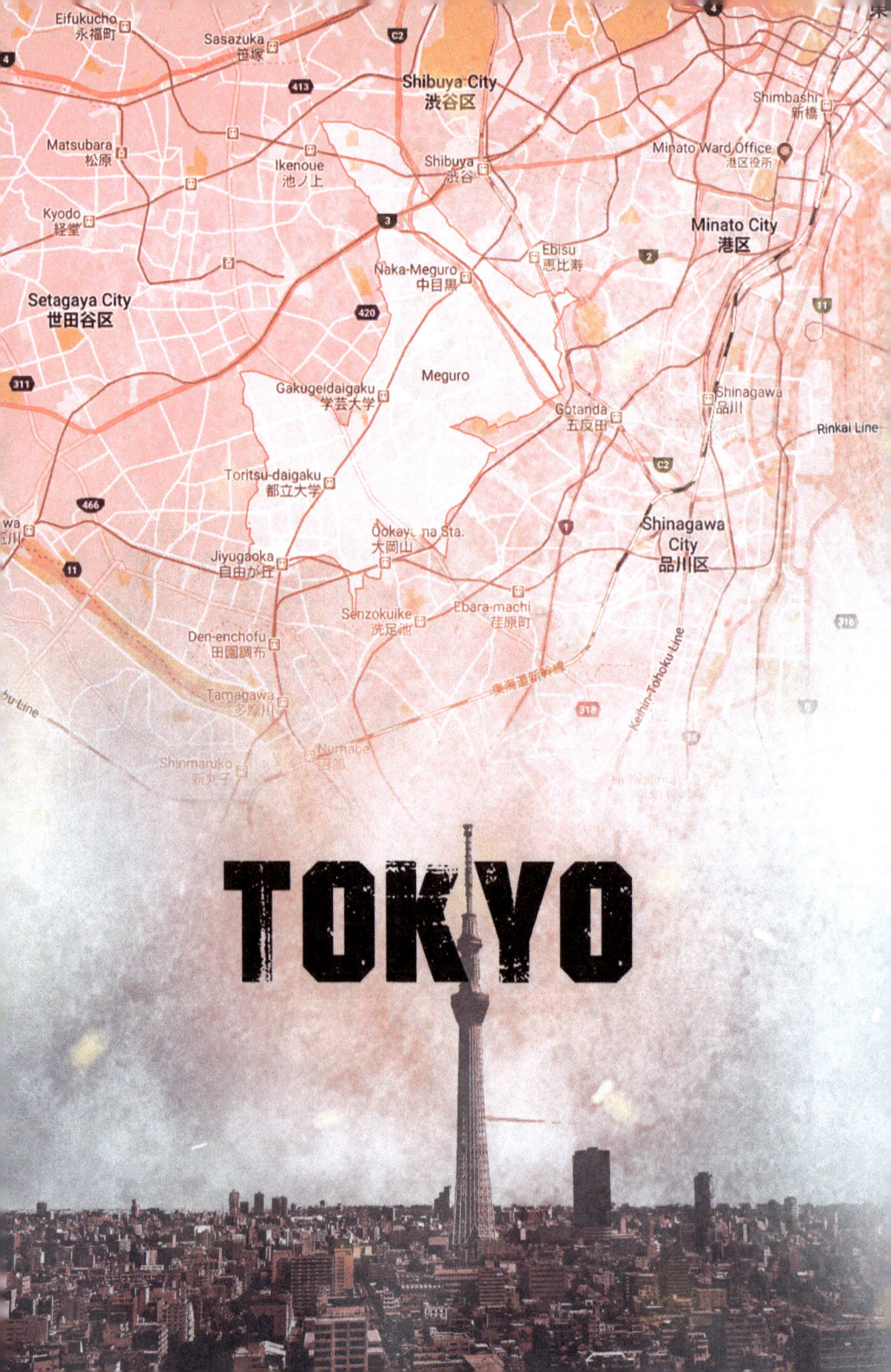

CHAPTER 10

SOUP KITCHEN

CHAPTER 10

SOUP KITCHEN

Like any red-blooded male, I like the sight of hot naked females. The first dirty pictures I remember seeing were in the imported American biker magazine *Superbike* that my dad used to read. He was into American muscle cars first, then the gas-guzzling Cadillacs and Lincolns, before drifting into Harley Davidson fandom. Such magazines tended to drape naked models over the bikes for photo shoots, and I liked it. I was probably twelve years old, and girls were no longer icky.

Kids today can't understand how it is to live in a world without freely-available hardcore pornography. There's something sweet and innocent about such a world. When it's literally impossible to get porn on demand, you simply turn your attention to other things, such as talking to real girls in your school. Or playing football. Or video games. Nowadays it takes mere moments browsing the internet on your smartphone to find stuff so hardcore that literally nobody in my school would've ever seen anything like it.

We kids of the 1980s built our dirty magazine collections by keeping our eyes peeled when walking across fields. Once in a while some older man would have thrown away his softcore porno magazine under a bush. If we were lucky, we found it rain ruined the paper. It puzzled me why softcore porn always turned up in hedgerows and under bushes. Finally I reached a surmise: the prior owner was too embarrassed to put it in the bin lest the binmen find it and word went around that he was a perv.

By the time I went to university, England's indecency laws were relaxed and it was possible to buy hardcore magazines made by the Private publishing company, at least theoretically. Practically, they were only available from licensed sex shops in Soho, London. They cost thirty pounds, which in 1993 was a lot of money. *Sonic The Hedgehog* on the Sega Megadrive retailed at just five pounds more. Always trying to figure out a dodge, my university housemates agreed it was best to import them from Amsterdam on our upcoming weekend away, mid-way through our second year. We bought a dozen issues of Private, Pirate, Sex, and Triple X magazine then divided them up amongst the three of us; Paul, Tim, and myself. We did this to minimise the risk of catastrophic loss should one of us get searched coming back through Customs. Fortunately every magazine survived the trip and we dumped them into the 'porn box' that was left out on the stairs for public use.

That porn box was my first experiment with communism, and I soon found out I was giving capital according to my ability while the others took liberally according to their need. Sadly, the life lesson didn't sink in until much later.

A drink, drugs, and porn trip to Amsterdaam with Joe and Paul

I didn't realise it at the time but Private magazine (and its three sister publications) would greatly shape my taste in women. Being from Newcastle, where every girl over twenty is ugly, I didn't acquire any specific tastes from real life. Some girls such as Leanne were pretty, some weren't, and that was that. When I started looking at Private magazine in 1993 it was shortly after the economic collapse of the Soviet Union and times were tough for its residents. Contemporary newspapers were full of stories about malnutrition, out-of-control crime, and the eventual rise of gangster capitalism under Boris Yeltsin's incompetent drunken reign.

The upside of this economic chaos was many pretty Eastern-Bloc women were willing to sell themselves for sex.

Private magazine hired French creep Pierre Woodman as their talent scout and he soon set up a recruitment network out of Budapest, with occasional forays into countries such as Latvia, Czech Republic, and eventually Russia itself. He'd place advertisements or get previously-hired girls to spread word of mouth. Then he'd fly into town for a week or so and line up a dozen or more 'castings'. Being a creepy piece of shit, Pierre filmed the castings with a camera hidden in his bag and seventy such recordings have been officially released on the internet. In one, with a Hungarian girl called Yasmin who would become his 'bottom bitch' recruiter, you can actually hear her getting suspicious about being filmed and Woodman making weaselly denials as he fiddles with the camera. Pierre paid the girls a fee for showing up (and to arrange their blood test a few days in advance) and a larger fee if they had sex there and then. Many girls did so.

I believe he was paying around $500 for a 'full casting', which was an absolute fortune at the time for broke-ass former-communist students and waitresses. Imagine what $500 would buy you in Venezuela right now, as I write in 2018. So, Pierre Woodman recruited a lot of girls and got Private magazine to pay for his own use of what were, effectively, prostitutes.

Private got a good deal because suddenly the quality of their models shot up from mediocre French and Swedish slags to really hot Slavs. Many only made a couple of scenes and then quit the business. It was a solid two-point quality jump and made Private far and away the best hardcore magazine and video publisher. As a young kid, used to English girls around me and on television, these painted-up Slavic tarts looked like perfect tens to me. Even with my later higher standards, looking back at the videos now on

Pornhub's retro portal, some girls look like an eights, and there were many, many sevens. Now that the former-Soviet Union countries have functioning economies and living wages for young women, the quality in porn has nose-dived back down to scraggly fives and sixes. The porno talent pool nowadays is mostly narcissistic tattooed psychopaths in Los Angeles or busted-up strippers in Budapest. I can quite do without that, thank you very much.

So, from around the age of eighteen and on well into my twenties, the agreed gold standard for 'hot naked birds' were the Slavs of Private magazine. I think it made a much larger impression upon me than I credited at the time. It must have, because since graduating with my bachelor's degree, I've never dated an English woman (with a couple of minor lapses, as you'll see later).

I started to become interested in Japanese girls after dating a Nagoya-born girl on my Master's course, Reiko, when I was twenty-one and that interest continued in London as you've seen. Once I moved to Okinawa in 2000, I had access to Japanese porn which was quite eye-opening in comparison to the European stuff I was accustomed to. The Japanese are both more creative and more OCD than Europeans and this is reflected in their porn by the insane scenarios they conjure up and the tendency of all their movies to be ordered into numbered series that feature exactly the same formula from one video to the next, swapping out only the actress for variety.

One such Japanese company was called Shuttle Japan, a small indie firm based in central Tokyo who lay claim to having invented the 'bukkake' genre. Smartphone owning kids are no doubt well aware of it, but in (then) 2000 it was still just a weird Japanese niche. The first one I saw, on VHS video tape, was an oddly hypnotic experience.

Picture the scene.

There's a small Japanese office space the size of a regular double-room in a hotel. Filing cabinets and desks have been moved to clear a space in the middle upon which a firm mattress has been placed. Lying on that mattress, masturbating, is a cute but slightly grotty Japanese bird dressed in a sexy spy costume. Seven men, clearly friends with each other, surround her, dressed only in identical white speedos, cheap dark sunglasses and bad eighties hairstyles. After finishing up with her masturbation, the girl then sucks off each guy in turn (heavily pixelated due to local indecency laws forbidding the display of genitals) and then one of them bangs her a while. Finally, they all cum on her face. Shuttle Japan did a series of these low-budget movies and they must've sold okay because they returned soon afterwards with the vastly more ambitious *Bukkake Festival* series. The girls were hotter, the costumes more fantastic, and somehow they'd gotten up to seventy men into the room to cum on the actress's face at the end. Thus was born the porn genre of 'bukkake'.

All this happened in the mid- to late-nineties so by the time I arrived in Japan several other bigger companies, such as WAAP, Moodyz and Soft On Demand, had hopped onto the bandwagon and the 'bukkake wars' began, with each company upping the ante. You're probably wondering why I bother to go into a long history of such a sordid topic, especially as I wasn't particularly enamoured by the genre. I didn't dislike it, but I found it odd.

Let me explain.

I was quite curious about all forms of Japanese weirdness. The country has a reputation for it, after all. When visiting Ioe in Tokyo, from Okinawa, in late 2000 I decided to pay a visit to the Shuttle Japan shop, tucked away on the fifth floor of an office building near Meguro station and impossible to find without the aid of a small map published on their website. It was tiny, filled with shelves to store all the VHS titles on sale, and a small counter where the sales clerk sat reading manga. Production memorabilia was pinned in every free space, such as photos from on-set, signed by the actresses, and a couple of mannequins dressed in the actual costumes worn (hopefully, after being washed with good detergent). Think of it like the memorabilia on the walls of Hard Rock Cafe, if you will. I had a look around, bought a VHS video tape for the eye-watering price of 10,000 yen (one day's salary at my school), and left. I didn't consider returning until a couple of years later, when I lived in Tokyo. It was then that I was idly browsing the Shuttle Japan website and, able to read Japanese fairly well, I noticed a casting call:

Soup Men wanted for filming.

That's the industry term for the stunt cocks in bukkake movies. I think it may be a derogatory term, but I'm not sure. *Hmmmmm, that's how they find the men,* I thought. I'd assumed it was all done by word of mouth between friends:

"Hey, Masahiro. Do you want to cum on a hot girl's face this weekend?"

"Sure."

"Okay, come over to the studio at noon on Saturday. If any of your mates are up for it, have them come along too."

But no, this was Japan so things were considerably more formal. Shuttle Japan paid minimum wage, quoted at 5,000 yen for a couple of hours work. So, theoretically, if you filmed two movies you'd earn enough to buy a video souvenir of one of them. The idea played in my mind as I taught my lessons in junior high school at Nichidai and then again when I was in Jiyugaoka banging Ioe at her mum's house. Ioe had let me cum on her face since the very beginning in London, and liked costumes too, so that got me thinking. Curiosity gnawed at me. Call it 'confirmation bias' but I now seemed to see the word *bukkake* everywhere I went in Tokyo.

The term was originally used to describe a type of ramen noddles, and only later stolen and adopted by the pornographers. So when I ate in fast food restaurants I'd see 'bukkake ramen' written on the menu board. I'd see 'bukkake' in foot-high letters on advertising boards outside shops, or on television in the commercials for the larger restaurant chains.

Bukkake. Bukkake. Bukkake.

By the weekend, I'd cracked. *Right, I'm having a closer look at this*, I decided and checked the internet to confirm the Shuttle Japan shop was still at the same place in Meguro. It was. I took an early train, bought a coffee and sandwich in the Dotour coffee shop by the station. I began to experience second thoughts, lingering at my table and eventually ordering a second coffee.

"You can't not check it out," I told myself. "You're in the world's capital of weirdness and this is as weird as it gets. You have a moral duty, as an Englishman abroad. If Marco Polo can check out the Chinese court and report back to Europe, you can follow in his footsteps and explore your only little secret corner of Asia."

The chubby nerd sitting at the cash register of the fifth-floor Shuttle Japan store was quite surprised that a *gaijin* was not only enquiring into the casting call, but doing so in the Japanese language. He had to remove his thick glasses, rub them on his Doraemon t-shirt, then squint at me to be sure I was real. He was unfailingly polite and dug out a registration form, which I signed. It was more detailed than I expected and laid out the terms: address of the studio, my daily rate, and a number of disclaimers stating that my registration didn't require the actress to engage in any sexual acts with me. It wasn't clear to me if I was now a registered porn actor, or merely some kind of understudy. They took my phone number and email address. "Don't call us, we'll call you," he said and ushered me out.

I decided not to mention it to my girlfriend. Two weeks passed. I forgot about it.

Then, one day after teaching class, as I returned to my desk in the teacher's room I saw my phone flashing to indicate unread text messages. I flipped it open and the inbox menu said I had an SMS from an unknown number. Clicking onto that, I saw a wall of Japanese text. Another junk mail, I thought, and scrolled down to the menu option to delete the message.

Suddenly, I stopped.

Hidden in the body of the text were the *katakana* letters spelling the name Shuttle Japan. I read the message again, more carefully. Show up that Saturday lunchtime, it read, to provide my services in Shuttle Japan's continued efforts in creating exportable cultural artefacts. I had been offered my first porno shoot.

I closed the phone rapidly, lest one of the Japanese teachers happen to walk behind me and read it over my shoulder. My breath came quickly and shallow. Should I do this? Wouldn't it be weird to roll up at a film studio as the lone foreigner surrounded by maybe a hundred Jap perverts, almost all of whom would know exactly what's going on while I was clearly playing it by ear. I'd watched spy movies where winging it in places you don't belong always got you stabbed or shot. I doubted porn carried the same risks, but what if the Japs all ganged up on me to play a practical joke? Perhaps "bum-rape the foreigner" was a parlour game in the Tokyo underworld: how would I know otherwise?

There were also moral issues. For starters, did it constitute cheating on my girlfriend? We'd been together almost three years now and though we'd never made any explicit commitments to each other, we'd clearly drifted into exclusive-partners territory. Would dumping my cum onto a professional actress, who didn't even know my name, be cheating? Was it immoral?

I'd need to think about it.

Twenty seconds later, I'd finished thinking about it. I was gonna do it.

It felt odd waking up on Saturday morning knowing I had a porn shoot coming. I felt nervous from the beginning, more for the social awkwardness of being the sole foreigner in an underground meet-up than from the thought of being in a porno *per se*. The trance held during my shower and while riding my mountain bike to Fujimigaoka metro station. I arrived early at the appointed station and sat in Doutor sipping coffee. My mind refused to settle. Finally, it was time to check in at the studio.

The map directions took me on a good five-minute walk into a residential district of narrow streets, high walls, and the usual random mish-mash of individual houses and apartment blocks each built to a completely different design. At a corner stood one such building, six stories high, red brick, and very narrow. A handful of nerds stood outside smoking cigarettes. All wore glasses and a couple wore the white face masks usually used in public situations to avoid spreading germs. I realised that in this case the men were hiding their identities. How silly! Didn't they know all Japs look the same? Of the six men, three were rail-thin and the other three obese.

I entered the lobby.

The staircase wound upwards and I followed it to the third floor where two employees sat in the hallway on plastic chairs behind a folding table. One looked at me and I noticed he had a sheaf of papers in front of him that looked like a register. I signed in. He gave me a slightly surprised look, at me being foreign, but said nothing about it. He waved me in to a large waiting room strewn with other men sitting or lying on the tatami mats that covered the floor. Some were in small groups chatting while others preferred to be alone, reading books or checking their phones. I found a quiet corner and waited.

Half an hour later the ushers left their desk and came in to give a rules speech. They began by outlining the day's schedule, namely that the actress had just finished a scene and the crew were setting up cameras in the main room for the bukkake scene. Shooting was expected to resume in twenty minutes. They then explained, with gestures, how we were to approach the actress and be mindful of the cameras. There was a ticket system by which after we'd shot our muck we would immediately walk to an intern who'd hand us a ticket as proof of, I dunno, 'delivery'? At the close of filming we'd exchange the ticket for payment.

If we wished, he said, we could rejoin the queue, do it all again and get paid double.

The two organisers instructed us to strip to our shreddies and then disappeared upstairs. After initial excitement, the hub-bub of mutterings in our room subsided. I went back to reading my book and about thirty minutes later the ushers returned to announce our scene would begin. *What happens now?* I wondered

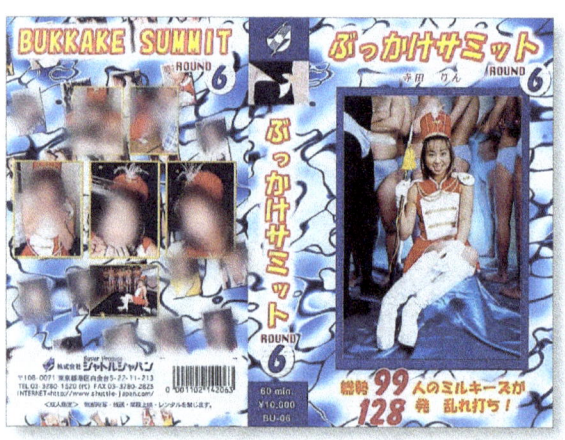

```
This kind of depravity
```

It took mere seconds to find out.

There was a mad scramble for the door as all the men raced up the stairs, in their underwear, to get to the front of a queue beginning inside the top floor studio where the actress and crew waited patiently. It was as if someone had shouted 'fire' in a crowded theatre. Not wishing to rush into god-knows-what, I found myself near the back of the queue. It snaked down the stairs two whole floors. Then I waited. I heard someone shout "*hajime!*" upstairs, meaning 'begin'. Every minute or so the whole group would shuffle up one step each. It felt like waiting to board a Ryanair flight.

By the time I reached the top, I'd been standing in my shreddies on a cool air-conditioned staircase for nearly fifteen minutes. Many of the similarly almost-naked Japs around me had spent that time with their hands down their pants maintaining a chubby in preparation. Several times I wondered why I hadn't stayed in bed. Before long, I was in the studio. It was packed.

In the centre of the room, on a large plain rug, sat a pretty girl who was already dripping in cum. A camera man squatted on his haunches in front of her and his 'grip' followed him around, managing the cables, as he moved his shoulder-mounted camera to better angles. There was also a still-photographer snapping off photos. Six more crew stood off to one side working jobs I couldn't figure out. Another woman sat on a folding chair surrounded by small brushes, jars, and tins. I guess she was the make-up artist. There were a dozen Japs in speedos lined up on the left, this being the head of the queue. They took turns to run up to the girl, cum on her face, then run off behind the cameraman to collect a ticket, then disappear downstairs. Each time this happened, the line inched forwards.

Before long I was at the front of the queue. I felt like I was about to jump out of an aeroplane. To my surprise, I was no longer overawed. I'd had no difficulty getting a boner upon entering the room, as the girl was quite hot and squeaked in simulated ecstasy. I was indifferent to everyone watching me. Perhaps they couldn't even see me properly, them having slanty eyes and all. When my moment came I strode up, came on the right side of her face slightly to above her eye.

"Ah.... *atatakai!*" she gasped in what I take was her 'sexy voice'. Her utterance translated as 'pleasantly hot'.

Then I walked off, took my ticket, and went downstairs. Plenty of men had rejoined the queue but I returned to the staging area, put my clothes back on, and read my book. Ten minutes later an employee sat back at the desk to begin paying off the actors. This time I was near the front of the queue, quite keen to get out of there. I got my 5,000 yen in crisp new banknotes and stepped out into the fresh afternoon air. It wasn't yet three o'clock.

What a very odd experience.

Each month for the rest of the year I received additional text messages calling me to further video shoots. I answered the call the second and fifth times. The third and fourth times, I was back in England for the school holidays. First of these callbacks, the actress was a skinny girl who was well into the action, and the second time it was a hot chick with big fake breasts. I was near the front of the queue that time, waiting in the studio before filming began so as she gazed curiously around the room her eyes stopped on me as she did a double-take noticing I was a foreigner.

After that, I lost interest in my burgeoning porno career. I'd gone to satisfy my curiosity and log an interesting story, but it was a boring experience. There was an hour of travel, two hours waiting around, and then a couple of minutes entertainment. It was completely lacking in sexual thrills, and of course none of it mean anything in terms of seduction. Shuttle Japan must've curated their master list of active participants because after skipping a couple of shootings, the messages stopped and I never thought to contact them again. If you're interested, the movies I was in are from the *Bukkake Drinker* series, numbers six, seven, and ten featuring Erika Ando, Momoko Tabata and Tomomi Ayukawa respectively. You can find them on porn sites.

Don't worry, my dick is pixelated out. Even girls I've banged wouldn't recognise it.

On holiday in Phi Phi

My first MMA gym in Omiya

Thailand with the missus

CHAPTER 11

KICKBOXING

CHAPTER 11

KICKBOXING

In 2002, Ioe and I went on holiday to Phi Phi island off the coast of Phuket, Thailand. It was a fantastic two weeks. We rented a beautiful beach cottage and spent the time idling in chairs on our porch, walking along the golden beach, or sitting in bars by the port eating food and watching pirated movies on the big televisions there. It remains one of the nicest holidays I've ever had, and when I get a serious girlfriend again I fully intend to recapture that kind of magic by travelling to pleasant destinations such as scuba in the Maldives, or a safari in Kenya.

Travelling with the lads to chase skirt was something I'd come to greatly enjoy over the following years, but it's a completely different experience to travelling *with* the skirt: Old Town centres of capital cities rather than isolated beaches, and considerably more drinking and stress.

While lying in a hammock in the shade of a Thai palm tree, itself in the shadow of a large cliff looming over the beach, I read a lot of books. I'd stumbled across a second-hand bookshop in Kichijoji, back in Tokyo, run by an elderly American couple. I had stocked up there on my English-language paperbacks for my trip. Being Americans, and most ex-pats in Tokyo also being yanks, the selection of books differed from my British literary taste. The shelves were stacked with cowboy westerns and Tom Clancy-style adventurist military novels. The autobiographies tended to be by people I'd never heard of, famous only in the US.

There was one book whose subject I did recognise. It was the official WWE autobiography of Kurt Angle, the former Olympic wrestling champ who was then the most skilled worker in the whole of professional wrestling. I'd been watching WWE on satellite TV since my time in Okinawa in 2000 so I was well-informed on the WWE 'Attitude' era in which pro-wrestling was big business. I liked watching Kurt. He was hilarious on the microphone and astonishingly talented in-ring. I bought the book and read it in Phi Phi.

It inspired me.

Young Kurt had trained fanatically, setting his mind on Olympic gold. The book outlined more than just his training and diet regime, though. It showed his outright obsession with success. He won his trial for the US Olympic team in dramatic fashion, countering a match-ending throw by twisting awkwardly and landing on his neck, breaking two discs. He subsequently scored a pin and went to the Olympic games with his neck still broken. Somehow, he won two gold medals. It seemed rather stupid of him to sacrifice his future health for glory (Kurt's WWE career was cut short by recurring neck problems), but I couldn't help be inspired by his dedication.

Ioe sat at a table doodling with a pen, drawing cartoon rabbits on her handmade postcards she'd send to family and friends from the post office by the Phi Phi island harbour. I finished the book and shut it theatrically.

"I'm going to have kickboxing fights," I declared.

"Ooooooh! Are you sure?" she asked. Girls are usually both scared and excited by men fighting, in equal measure.

"I've been training martial arts for six years now and never competed in real full-contact competition. I'm twenty-five years old. I really ought to test myself out. I want to get punched hard in the face and see how I feel. If I wait too long, I'll get old and miss my chance."

Ioe's eye's sparkled. She always loved it when I talked decisively about my plans, no matter how trite they might be. This was, for a change, an exciting plan. "How will you do it?"

"My gym in Kichijoji recently started a new professional show. It's small-hall kickboxing, called R.I.S.E. They have the pro fights in the evening but they rent the hall all day and run amateur bouts in the afternoon. I'll do one of them."

"Ooooooh! Good luck!" she cooed.

A great holiday in Phi Phi

Back in Tokyo, after the holiday, I resumed training three times a week at my gym, Crosspoint. It was a small outfit, run out of the basement of a building sandwiched between a ramen shop and an apartment block in the entertainment quarter of the town. The Muay Thai classes were taught by a Thai national, former Lumpinee champion Ramba 'M-16' Somdet who had fought on Japanese kickboxing shows since the early nineties and eventually married a Japanese women. He now lived permanently in Tokyo. His classes were from 8pm to 10pm so after showering up and leaving class I'd usually have to weave my way through drunken businessmen staggering out of the nearby hostess clubs.

Somdet was a cheerful lunatic brimming with physical charisma and thus extremely likeable. His teaching style was highly technical and he seemed to have a great time hanging about the gym. He'd always have a couple of Thai pros help him out on what I gathered was a short working-holiday system. Friends or gym-mates from back home visited Japan as tourists for thirty days and were hire off-the-books to help coach, covering the lads' costs. There was an ever-refreshing rotation of Thai pro fighters coaching at the gym. It was win-win all around.

Crosspoint was run by a former Japanese champ, one Mr. Genki Yamaguchi, who was around thirty years old when I joined the gym and still in fighting shape though retired. He was a very nice guy and though I tended not to speak much in the gym, I was favourably impressed with him as a man. He was conscientious, friendly, and took real care of his fighters, whose careers he managed. The R.I.S.E. promotion was his brainchild. Ex-fighters always want to stay involved. The smell and sound of the fight gym never wears off. Even now, any time I step into a boxing gym it feels like putting on a pair of favourite old slippers.

Yamaguchi had been All Japan Kickboxing lightweight champion several years earlier. His title reign ended when the promotion's match-maker flew in Somdet as his next challenger. The crazy Thai thoroughly dismantled him inside one round, a video of which is easy to find on YouTube. Rather than get pissy about it, Yamaguchi hired Somdet to be head coach for the Thai-rules classes while Yamaguchi himself taught the Japanese-rules classes.

On my first day back at Crosspoint I pulled Yamaguchi to one side and asked him when the next R.I.S.E. show was to be held. It was six weeks away.

"Do you do?" he asked.

"Yes, I do."

Saying those words sent a thrill through my body right down to my toes. I was committed to a real fight. Even if I subsequently became scared and wanted to bottle out later, there was no way I could walk up to Yamaguchi and say, "actually, sorry, but I'm a frightened little faggot who might cry if he's punched so please cancel my fight."

Nope, that would be humiliation. It would also be doing my opponent a disservice after he'd spent weeks preparing for the match, and would dishonour my gym in the eyes of that rival gym.

I was committed. It felt good. I had a goal.

I re-read sections of the Kurt Angle book to get me fired up. The first issue was weight. I walked around at 75kg but the fight was at 73kg. That's not much weight to cut but I'd never tried it before. I knew from my reading of boxing magazines and books that I needed to be out doing roadwork, running slowly for six miles or so each time, taking little shuffle steps to protect my joints, and to tuck my head in to build the muscle memory to keep my chin down when tired. Roadwork is what gives a fighter 'legs'. Without it, they go leaden within a couple of rounds and you can't move around freely. I began jogging three times a week, every other day, around my neighbourhood in Ogikubo and went to kickboxing class the other three nights. Sunday was a rest day.

The coaching staff paid extra attention to the students who'd signed up to fight, eight of us. I felt special. Though a long way below the professionals who trained afternoons, I was a step above the casuals who did the evening classes. I was going to fight. I was *serious*.

Two weeks out from the day of the fight, Yamaguchi posted up a paper showing the match making. My name was up there with a "vs" alongside a Japanese name whose *kanji* I couldn't read. I had no clue who my opponent was, but trusted the amateur network system. Yamaguchi would've carefully discussed match-making with the other R.I.S.E.-affiliated gyms to ensure there were no mismatches. At an amateur level it was a friendly rivalry between gyms.

I liked seeing my name next to a "vs".

Nonetheless, now that I had a specific named opponent things suddenly felt real. I was no longer fighting an abstract concept, but a real man who had strengths, weaknesses, and had trained specifically to beat me up. I'd now be introduced to the most difficult aspect of fighting: the adrenal release. Those of you who've

With Mirko Cro Cop
backstage at Pride

fought, or at least competed in a contact sport such as rugby, will know what I mean. It's like waiting for an extremely important exam, where passing wins you something you desperately want, and failing keeps it beyond your grasp. Add to that, in kickboxing failure gets you beaten up in public.

Training camp in Kamakura

From that day forward, I suffered a slow steady release of adrenalin. My sleep was disturbed and while teaching class at Nichidai my concentration would dissolve. I continued training as hard as ever but became increasingly agitated outside the gym. The stress reminded me of London, when studying for my professional exams before leaving for Okinawa. My loss of appetite made the weight cut an foregone conclusion.

The two days before the fight I barely slept at all. Intellectually I looked forward to competing but my body rebelled. Doubts crept in. What would I do when punched? In sparring we never attacked full power and if you accidentally clocked someone hard, you'd step back, apologise, and let them recover. In a real match, that's the time to move in for the kill. I dredged my memory for any event in my past where I'd been punched hard in the jaw. I came up blank.

I'd had a football blasted into my face in the school playground when I was nine. I'd been dragged off a six-foot high stack of crash mats in the school gymnasium and landed on my head when twelve.

I'd also had a couple of childish fights that same year, but it was kid's stuff and nobody hit hard. There was a genuine mystery to be solved: what would I do if someone socked me hard on the chin and didn't let up? Added to this were my concerns over the spectators. I'd be perhaps the only foreigner in a hall full of Japs, most of whom were from rival gyms and thus not on Team Nick. Crosspoint would support me but I had a duty to not embarrass them by being a pussy. Lastly, Ioe was coming to support me. The very worst outcome would be to get knocked unconscious in front of my girlfriend. That could snuff out her attraction for me. Worse still, what if I somehow lacked courage and acted like a pussy? The last thing I wanted was to be the patsy in someone else's highlight reel video.

The day of the fight came. It was held in Gold's Gym in south-central Tokyo. Ioe had stayed over at my apartment and we took an early train because weigh-ins were at 11am. We walked up to the 2nd floor gym together and already several dozen men were milling around, a combination of amateur fighters, their cornermen, and the event organisers. A table was set up next to the door and a scale next to it. One of the young professionals from our gym was helping out, recording everyone's weight. I stripped to my boxer shorts and joined the short queue behind a half dozen Jap lads also in their underwear. It gave me flashbacks to the porno filming at Shuttle Japan's studio, but fortunately none of the other lads had their hands down their pants tugging themselves. When I reached the front, I gave my name, stepped on the scales, and had my weight registered at 72.5kg, half a kilo under the limit.

My stress-based weight loss program had been a success.

I dressed and took Ioe to a nearby cafe. Gold's Gym buzzed with an electric energy of rising stress which I'd rather not absorb. Finally allowed to eat after a 24-hour pre-weigh-in fast, I tucked into a cheese toastie and cafe latte. Then sleep overwhelmed me. It was only just past noon but my eye-lids drooped and my head nodded. It didn't worry me because I'd read an interview with former world heavyweight boxing champion Lennox Lewis who claimed he always slept the afternoon of a fight.

Ioe seemed more excited than I. A strange calm had come over me as my body shut down to conserve energy. By contrast, her eyes sparkled and her movements were jerky and agitated. She was having fun, like a young child on her way to the zoo. My fight was eighth on the card so I went back into Gold's Gym when the earlier fights were already underway. I found a quiet spot on the mats, away from the ring, and wrapped my hands and stretched off. I shadow-boxed a few rounds and hit the heavy bag a little. One of our gym's best MMA fighters, former Shooto lightweight champ Naoya Uematsu, came over and gave me a few minutes on the pads and a pep talk.

Suddenly my name was called by an organiser. The nerves came flooding back.

Amateur fights are run like an assembly line so I sat on a chair outside the red corner while 14oz gloves were fitted. The fight before mine was still going on inside the ring. Those lads soon came out and I stepped through the ropes to take their place. I heard Ioe shout "*Gambatte!*" which translates directly as "try your best" but is used idiomatically to mean "good luck!"

The moment I turned to face my opponent I was struck by a keen awareness of new physical and psychological sensations. I'd seen hundreds of real fights as a spectator, from a third person perspective outside the ring, and of course I'd been in a ring many times for sparring. This was different. I felt the soft canvas under my bare feet as real as it's ever felt. There was nothing between myself and my opponent, whose name I still didn't know. There were perhaps six metres between opposing corners but it felt like inches. There was nothing and nobody to keep him off me, except my own fists and smarts. I was truly alone.

The referee called us to ring centre, ran through the rules, then had us touch gloves. I felt no animosity to my opponent and I detected none from him. Still, when the bell went and I walked over to meet him, the first thing he did was wing a massive haymaker at my head. I slipped it and moved off to the side, feeling my blood rush. The fight was on.

Do you have nightmares where you are trying to run from danger but your legs don't work properly, and you run the speed of a baby crawling? That's how round one felt. My skills deserted me. I'd expected to establish a jab, circle around to my right side (I'm southpaw), and begin working in low kicks as I tried to figure out my opponent's patterns and predilections, to exploit later. What actually happened is the first time he threw a straight right hand punch I slipped to the outside and his glove caught on the right-hand side of my headgear, jerking my head backwards. I'd been unprepared for the fact that headgear both made my head heavier (and thus it moves slower in slipping) and also widens the contact area due to the padded material protruding outwards. Like wearing a crash helmet.

So, I got hit with a shot that I'd have slipped if unencumbered by head gear. The impact spun my head a little, disoriented me, and his follow-up left hook hit me on the nose. I stepped back to safety, resolving to take the next straight punch on my gloves rather than slip it.

Emboldened, my mysterious opponent came on with an identical straight-right-left-hook combo. I rested my finger tips on my forehead and turned the gloves inwards in anticipation. This cupping motion dissipates a punch's power. I covered up thus, ready to let his shots bounce harmlessly off my guard, like I'd done a thousand times in sparring. Instead his right hand crashed through the middle and onto my chin. Stars exploded in my head and my legs wobbled, fortunately for only brief seconds before my head cleared. The headgear had betrayed me again, this time because the padding around my forehead had expanded the gap between my gloves, giving sufficient room for a fist to squeeze between.

Things weren't going well. I could feel a trickle of blood from my nose.

I was fully defensive that first round. I could hear the opposing corner cheering and egging on their fighter, while Ioe's voice drifted over shouting, "Don't hit my boyfriend!" I ended the round backed up against the ropes. My opponent fired off a jab, cross, hook, low kick combo that I fully blocked and then when I raised my left leg to check another low kick he swept underneath it, kicking my standing leg from underneath me and dropping me heavily onto my arse. I was embarrassed rather than hurt. The bell went and I walked back to my corner.

Uematsu was my cornerman and he sprayed water down my neck and encouraged me. "Don't worry, it's normal. You are hard puncher. Throw your hard punches!"

Mid-way through the interval, as my breath settled down and my lungs stopped heaving, I had a moment of clarity. *I was enjoying this!* I didn't mind that I'd taken a few solid shots. I was in a fight and I wanted to sock this other lad on the jaw. By God, I was going to hit the bastard!

I came out for the second round full of enthusiasm. We touched gloves again and then when my opponent threw a half-hearted right mid-kick, I rocked back so it sailed past. His foot swiped empty air and touched down to the mat off-balance. I stepped in and whacked him hard on the chin with a solid left. I felt the impact buzz up my arm to my shoulder. He wobbled and backed off. For most of the round I chased him around the ring landing the occasional hard

Fucking come here, pal!

punch. To his credit he sometimes stood his ground and gave as good as he got. What seemed like only moments after the round began, it ended. I'd been completely lost in the flow of fighting.

It was only a two round fight. The judges scored a win for my opponent, which seemed about fair. We touched gloves again and I returned to my corner. Though from my perspective, the fight was a pivotal moment in my twenty-five years of life, to the R.I.S.E. organisers I was simply number eight on a docket of twenty fights that day. Guy number nine was ready to step into the ring to take my place. I was hustled to a chair and two of the Crosspoint pros

Getting my breath back post-fight

stripped me of the headgear and gloves.

"Good fight Nick!" said Uematsu, patting me on the shoulder, then turned to corner our next guy.

Ioe had been flitting around behind my team and now that I was alone she sprang over and sat on the chair next to me. Her eyes glittered and a dopey smile lit up her face. She looked like she was high on cocaine.

"You are so cool!" she gushed. She couldn't keep her hands off me, running them up and down my shoulders and arms which still glistened with sweat. I couldn't believe how tired I was. It was only two rounds of fighting but I was more exhausted than after sparring ten. Adrenalin kills you.

I stumbled off to the shower and stood under the hot spray. The numbness in my limbs abated and my body once more felt lived in. The pain in my ribs and nose reduced, suggesting I hadn't been hit especially hard after all. All that remained were the endorphins pulsing through my veins.

I felt fantastic. It is, literally, the best I've ever felt in my life before or since.

I had the satisfaction of knowing I wasn't a pussy, I'd publicly displayed my courage, and I was high on the human body's natural drug. Prior to this moment I'd always thought fighting was something scary that boxers did as a means to an end. Now I understood why so many said they fought for fun. I couldn't imagine any feeling in life as good as this. I wanted to fight more.

Fifteen minutes later I was fully dressed and back in the main hall of Gold's Gym. To a curious stranger I looked the same as when I'd entered at 11am to weigh in, but internally I was a changed man.

My opponent stood to one side chatting with his team. He was a lanky guy of university age. When he saw me approach he broke into a broad smile and came a few steps forwards to meet me. We exchanged thanks for the fight and complimented each other, me in broken Japanese and then in English which Ioe translated.

"Halfway through the first round, you hit me with a great right hand," I said. "It made me dizzy."

He laughed and said something to Ioe, who put it into English. "He said he was dizzy every time you hit him."

We laughed, had a bro hug — no homo — then I said goodbye to Uematsu and Yamaguchi. We went home. The moment I shut the door inside my apartment, Ioe dropped to her knees and sucked me off. Girls do get excited by men fighting.

CHAPTER 12

LEAVING JAPAN

CHAPTER 12

LEAVING JAPAN

I had four more fights over the following twelve months until I decided to stop competing and simply train. The primary reason was realising I wasn't especially good at it. I won two, lost two, and drew one which is okay but this wasn't a high level of competition. Five fights was enough to answer the important question of, "do you have the balls to fight?" (yes) and also the more speculative "would you be successful in a professional fight career?" (no). It didn't help that in the last three fights I injured my left hand by bouncing it off the thick skulls of my opponents.

Competitive fighting was physically punishing. I didn't need to prove myself a hard-ass, and likely couldn't have should I have so wished. It was sufficient to expunge that vague feeling of potential cowardice that I'd harboured since little Scott from Redemarsh had bust my nose in infant school. Every boy wonders if he's destined to become courageous or cowardly. I'd always suspected I was below average in physical bravery yet now I had objective, and welcome, proof that I was actually significantly above average. That was enough. I could leave the higher levels of manliness to real fighters, like my role models Harry Greb, Igor Vovchanchyn, or Henry Armstrong. I'd be content to watch and admire them from afar. My newly-acquired fighting experience had given me a taste of the ring, which helped me better relate to their accomplishments.

I taught two academic years at Nichidai school before they fired me and my then co-teacher, an Australian girl called Elke. The Head of English explained she wished to refresh the teaching stock. We were novelty teachers hired by an agency, rather than legitimate employees with real careers covered by Japanese employment law. Their freedom to swap out teachers was part of the service Nichidai had paid Sagan Speak for. Though entirely reasonable, the shock of the "we're letting you go" call rattled me nonetheless. It was the first time I'd been fired from anything.

It was a blessing in disguise.

While I'd thoroughly enjoyed my first year teaching in Tokyo, I'd become unsettled and aimless during my second. Teaching English in Japan is a dead-end job, a cool foreign adventure in your twenties but loserdom from your thirties onwards. I'd already stretched out the experience a year longer than I should have, three years in all including Okinawa. I'd been treading water to avoiding returning to the finance career I'd found so tough in London. Getting fired made the decision for me, a splash of cold water to shake me out of my comfort zone. I resolved *not* to get a new English teaching job, even though my resume would've made it easy to do so.

I enrolled in a Japanese language school in Kichijoji while I looked for a finance job in Tokyo. It quickly became apparent that I'd need two more years of solid study to reach the language proficiency required to work professionally in Japan (as opposed to an English-speaking ex-pat job). So I binned that goal and opted for a new plan: I'd return to Newcastle to start a three month temp job (in finance) that precisely covered one academic term in Japan. I'd save money and then spend it by returning to Kichijoji Language School for the following term. I did this twice, flipping between Newcastle and Tokyo in three-month stints. The first time I worked at a housing association assessing its subsidiaries, and then the second job was at a government department. In total I worked six months and studied nine.

It was good for me. My path back into the financial industry was greased and the big black mark from my resume removed, that having resulted from being 'out' of the industry longer than I'd ever been 'in'. Two recent lines on my resume and two good references made me employable again. My thoughts then turned to resuming my career in London, where the real opportunities were. Frankly, I realised Japan is not somewhere for a foreigner to make his life. You are always an honoured guest, but never considered one of them.

I support national isolationism like that, as it keeps Japan Japanese. Sadly, it was to my personal detriment in this case.

More than just my own future hung upon my career decision. I'd been dating Ioe five years and we were in a serious relationship. It hadn't been discussed but we both recognised it as a *de facto* exclusive deal. I thought about my romantic situation logically, and I was introspective to better understand my emotions.

Was I in love with her?

I wasn't really sure. Unquestionably, I felt kinder towards Ioe than any other girl I'd ever met. I genuinely cared about her future and felt bad anytime she was upset. However, I wasn't seeing the rainbows and unicorns that Hollywood movies called love. Was this it? Was this what love feels like? Weren't people supposed to just *know*? I certainly didn't know. Perhaps I'm incapable of passionate blood-boiling love, I considered. My family were always rather cold and though my parents often said "I love you" it seemed to me a strangely muted expression of emotion and they'd never insist I say it back. Now that I thought about it, I don't think I'd ever told my parents I loved them. I wasn't even sure if I did.

The end result of these ruminations was that I knew I felt a stronger attachment towards Ioe than I did to my close family, and considering that my positive disposition towards them *must* be love, then what I felt for Ioe must, logically, be my own personal experience of romantic love. Now that I write it, I question whether this was a sound basis upon which to build a marriage. Perhaps this was my first inkling it wouldn't last.

Clearly I wasn't a romantic idealist. My plan of action was to sound out the logistics: would Ioe be willing to relocate to England upon marriage? I broached the subject indirectly as we drank coffee in the business district one afternoon. I'd been to an English-language jobs fair that had finally convinced me I wouldn't be getting a real job in Tokyo. I still wore my suit, from the screening interviews I'd attended there.

"My Japanese isn't good enough to work here," I lamented, truthfully. "The level three exam I passed isn't high enough. They all demand level two and I'm at least a year from that. Also, the jobs just aren't very good."

"Oh, that's too bad."
"It will be much easier to get a good job in London."

Ioe knew this, but didn't like to be reminded. She loved London but her dancing career had taken off in Japan. It wasn't something that could be packed up into a suitcase and taken elsewhere. She'd been preparing for just this career since she was a ten-year old ballerina. It didn't feel fair to ask her to give it up now, aged twenty-eight, when she was finally living her childhood dream.

Doutor Coffee after another disappointing career meeting

"I don't see how this can work," I continued. "I can't get a real job here, and I'm not willing to be a loser English teacher my whole life. I have to return to London. If you come great, but if you can't we have to break up."

Ioe's face seemed to crumble, making her eyes even more slanty than usual. She began bubbling. "No, don't say that! I know it, but don't say it!" She cried for five minutes, sobbing with her head on my shoulder. "I will follow you," she sniffed.

That was the answer I was hoping for because it cleared the only path to a future together. I firmly believe it's the woman's role to fit herself around the man's life, but such things can't be forced. Women must believe it themselves and genuinely want it. Ioe had told me she was such a woman. The logistics were agreed.

I felt a surge of relief. There had been no Plan B.

Over the next few weeks my mindset became entirely forward-looking. Japan was now in my rear-view mirror even though I still lived there and had two months left of the current study term at the language school. Life was fantastically pleasurable. Five mornings a week I'd cycle from my apartment to the bicycle park by the language school. I ate breakfast in Cafe Excelsior (a Starbucks clone) while finishing the previous day's homework, then I went to class. We finished at noon and then I ate lunch in Kichijoji centre, usually at Hanamaru ramen bar. I'd return home for a nap and then, depending upon the day, either go to kickboxing training at Crosspoint or have Ioe come over and shag her. I also played lots of video games on my Playstation 2 and PC. About once a week I attended a fight show and wrote a report for a UK martial arts magazine, a side-gig I had on as a dodge to get free ringside tickets.

It was a pleasant life, but without forward motion. It was that sense of treading water which had caused my ennui in my final year at Nichidai. When I'm not swimming forwards, I'm drowning. Now I finally had a sense of what my future held, back in England.

I decided to marry Ioe.

She'd told me about a popular tourist spot in the North of the main Honshu island, called Nikko. It's an old medieval capital in the mountains, surrounding a big lake. A hundred years ago, the European nations built small embassies there, which they still used as holiday retreats for diplomats.

"You can go hiking in the mountains. And there are bears and monkeys!" she enthused.

"Monkeys? Great, count me in."

It was also a spa town, called *'onsen'* in Japanese to mean hot springs. That sounded great so I suggested we have a long weekend there. It was now late 2005 and I had recently turned thirty. My whole adulthood, I'd fostered the vague feeling that I shouldn't marry before thirty. That sentiment now looked remarkably prescient.

We took the bullet train north and checked into a small pension guest-house tucked halfway up a hillside, barely visible through the trees from the road. It felt like somewhere legendary samurai wanderer Miyamoto Musashi may have stayed before a deadly duel. The wrinkly old couple running the place had probably been born back then, to look at them. We checked into a spacious tatami-matted room on the second floor and then went for an early-evening stroll. It was still sunny.

I was nervous. I'd already resolved to propose and now my guts churned. I'd be committing myself to an irreversible change, a turning point beyond which my life became serious. I couldn't help visualising myself in a large room, full of doors, and all but one of those doors were being locked and bolted shut, never to reopen.

I was surrendering my freedom.

It felt like the right thing to do, and didn't trouble me unduly, but I definitely felt that whatever I gained through marriage would be offset somewhat by a tangible loss in my freedom. My stomach

Travelling north in Nikko

tightened like it had before my first kickboxing match and I was equally nervous. It never crossed my mind Ioe may actually reject my proposal because I knew she was deeply in love with me. The tension came from the realisation my life would irrevocably change.

We were now on the main road, three hundred metres from the big lake. A few hikers and tourists clustered outside a waterfront restaurant in the distance but we were otherwise alone. I looked at Ioe as she skipped merrily down the road ahead of me. She was lively and excited to be on a trip with me. She wore light training shoes, green fatigues cut to mid-calf, and a red vest. Her movements were graceful, as you'd expect from a professional dancer.

As I looked, I asked myself a question: Will you be happy if, from this moment forwards, this is the only woman you ever shag?

I conjured up memories of shagging Ioe, the highlight reel from hundreds of bedroom experiences. She was a beautiful girl, with a tight athletic body and pretty face. Her disposition fitted mine as an astonishingly complimentary counter-balance. She was also fantastic in bed.

Yes, I think I'd be quite happy with that.

The last doubt was erased from my mind. I knew for sure I wanted to marry her and what I'd lose in juvenile freedoms I'd gain many times over in mature companionship. I called her over and pointed out some steps leading down into a valley towards a viewing platform. Across the valley, a large waterfall burst from the cliff side hundreds of feet above. A tourist couple was already at the platform so I made light conversation until they moved on and left us alone.

Ioe turned, giving me an odd look. She knew something was up, but didn't know what. Perhaps she thought I intended to throw her over the metal rail. I'd certainly never hinted about marriage before. It was time to take the plunge. "Ioe, I didn't just bring you here for a holiday," I began, my voice suddenly tight with tension. "I brought you here because I have something important to say."

She bit her lip and listened intently, still showing little suspicion of what I intended to say.

"The thing is... I no longer want you to be my girlfriend."

I left a meaningful pause and watched the realisation sink in. *He's dumping me!* Her face began to crumble again and she muttered "no, no" softly, in denial of the bad news. I'd fully intended to give her a little scare, to better contrast the good news. I'd underestimated how hard it would hit her, so I quickly rushed on.

"I don't want you to be my girlfriend because," and now I took both her hands and looked into her eyes, "because I love you and I want you to be my wife. Will you marry me?"

I got to watch in glorious technicolour clarity as the good news hit home and she bounced from the depths of despair to the height of joy. Her eyes came alive and she hugged me tight, pressing her face against my chest.

"Yes, yes! I'll marry you" she whimpered. We kissed, and then as an elderly couple mounted the platform we asked them to take a picture of us.

We ate at a restaurant and then had sex in the tatami room, before sharing a hot-springs bath in the ground floor public bathing area that connected to the garden. The same words kept spinning in my mind, right until I finally dropped off to sleep a couple of hours later: *this is your life now.*

I was happy with my decision.

We married a few months later. The first ceremony was in Roppongi, Tokyo at a specialised modern wedding venue with

Enjoying the hot baths

a chapel and banquet hall. My parents flew over for it and my mother gave a short speech in English. A few of my Tokyo friends came too. Mostly, it was Ioe's family, friends, and work colleagues. The choreographer of her dance company created a special piece that the other dancers performed while we watched from the high table. The whole evening flew by and I barely remember the details, except that I enjoyed it. A small group of us had an after party, Ioe's best friends and dance company, where I got roaring drunk and fortunately didn't embarrass myself.

The second ceremony was a couple of months later in England, to accommodate my side of the guest list to whom it was too much of an ask to expect to fly to Japan. I hired the function rooms of a handsomely refurbished castle, Lumley. After the ceremony, the lads all hurried down their dinner so we could go next door and watch the England vs Portugal match at the World Cup. England lost on penalties. That too was a lovely evening and the after-party wound down in the castle library bar where we all sat in leather easy chairs by a log fire, sipping whiskey. At closing time, Ioe and I went up to the master bedroom, furnished in old Elizabethan style, and I banged her on the four poster bed then passed out.

                    Happily married
                in Japan and England

It took a few months for logistics to fully work themselves out. Although Ioe had decided to give up her place at the dance company, there were two scheduled world tours she wanted to finish as her send off. I was supportive of that, as I wanted her to eke out as much as she could from her dream job before settling down to be my new wife. We'd eventually have two delayed honeymoons in the early part of 2007. First was a week in Tunisia catching a good off-season all-inclusive deal at a hotel by the beach, followed by an even better holiday in Anatolia, Turkey where we stayed in a delightful hotel run by the architect who'd designed it. But for now, she was wrapping up her Japan life.

I found a six-week contract working in the finance department of a big London company and by the time Ioe had tied up her loose ends in Tokyo and was ready to come join me, the contract had been extended to what would eventually be almost a year. My friend Derrick, who you'll remember was my best friend towards the end of high school, rented me his girlfriend's flat in Kennington, South London at a mates-rate and I took great pleasure in cleaning it up and preparing it for Ioe's arrival.

Finally, the big day came, when she'd move to London permanently.

I met Ioe at Heathrow Airport and, as she wheeled her suitcase into the Arrivals lobby, she caught my eye and I saw her face light up. She rushed over, gave me a hug, and we took the underground into Central London and to our first home together. She stood uncertainly outside the building, taking it all in. Our flat was on the ground floor of a 1890s block with Victorian arches and ornate windows. There were several such blocks, housing several hundred people. It looked nice, by London standards.

"Wait a minute, let's do this properly" I said, setting her suitcase to one side and pulling my house keys out of my pocket so they'd be in my hand. Then I reached over and scooped her up in my arms. "I believe the husband should carry his woman over the threshold."

Ioe giggled and cooed, as she always did when I picked her up, and we stepped indoors to begin our married life.

CHAPTER 13

MARRIED LIFE

CHAPTER 13

MARRIED LIFE

The first two years of marriage were blissful. We'd agreed Ioe would quit her career and become a housewife but we both wanted to ensure she wouldn't feel trapped or isolated at home. She had plenty of friends still in London from her study year in 1999, plus she'd long since gotten to know my old university friends: Yasin, Tim, Paul and others. Still, I was acutely aware that she'd given up performing to come to London and that she'd want something productive to do while I was at work earning the family's crust.

She expressed an interest in returning to dance school, as a hobbyist, and in perfecting her English. Those struck me as ideal activities. So she found a dance school she liked in North London called *The Place* which offered classes every day, including afternoon classes for professionals (a system not unlike Crosspoint in Kichijoji). That fit in well with her morning classes at Callan English School on Oxford Street. She had her schedule and I was enthusiastic in my support, including paying for it all.

My vision of a happy marriage was to be welcomed home from work by a happy wife and a delicious hot meal. Ioe shared that vision and this arrangement worked out well for two years.

After a year at my contract job, as a special-cases consultant in a large media enterprise, I realised I was spinning my wheels again, learning nothing. That familiar ennui, of treading water, crept up on me. Worse, I felt I was failing to live up to my potential. My three years training in London had been world-class, something I could've built on to launch a successful corporate career. I'd instead hopped on a flight to Okinawa the moment I got my professional license. Had I squandered four years chasing thrills and adventure? My colleagues in the same training cohort were now mid-career with high-paying jobs and positions of responsibility. Now, back in London, I was dicking around in a large audit room with a dozen young Australian and South African contractors. We took full advantage of poor managerial supervision in a media company that pissed away money on us. Not only was I failing to advance my career, I was losing what little work ethic I'd built.

I was married. I needed to knuckle down and get back into a top-tier corporation. Low salaries and casual work were okay when I was farting around in Tokyo but now I had to think of buying a house, raising a family, and giving my future children a role model. I began looking for a new job.

Moving up in class was harder than moving down, I found. No surprise there.

Christmas back in Newcastle

It was easy to get recruitment agents to meet me, but the first few roles they offered were in finance departments of medium-sized companies in retail, fashion, and manufacturing. That didn't appeal to me. This was in 2006, the financial bubble, when banking and hedge funds were the 'cool' place to be. I considered a man of my academic credentials and professional training belonged in an investment bank such as Morgan Stanley, or a global name like Deutsche Bank.

Sadly, those institutions didn't seem to agree with me.

I approached my nominal manager in the media firm, a friendly Irishman called Brian. He was officially in charge of our team but worked in a different room and had no real connection to us. Rather, he signed our time-sheets and was more interested in being friends and playing on our five-a-side football team than he was with providing genuine supervision.

"What's up mate?" he asked, minimising his internet browser and then swinging around in his chair. Like us, he did almost no productive work.

"Can I change my official job title? Can you authorise it?"

He'd never been asked this question before. He thought about it. Our situation on this hastily-assembled team was fluid and no-one had a defined role. We were just called 'auditors' or 'royalties administrator', neither of which correctly described our work.

"Yes, I think I can. So long as it doesn't change your hourly rate."

"Great, what title could I have?"

"What do you want? I'll sign off whatever you need." It took me a moment to realise he was serious. I had free reign to choose my job title.

"Lord of Audit."

"Sure. Just let me make a note of it."

It seemed too easy, so I wanted to check. "Just to be clear, if a recruiter or Human Resources spod come checking up on me, that's my formal job title I'll have on the official record here?"

"Yep. And I'll confirm it in writing or over the phone if they ask. Don't worry mate, everyone here is trying to leave and get a proper job. I'll help you out."

A couple of days later, I sent my updated resume to another recruitment agency. Within an hour they called. A young man named Max introduced himself with some high falutin' title such as Senior Talent Placement Executive. He sounded like a syrupy-voiced snake oil salesman, but no more so than any other recruitment agent. After a few minutes working through my background he stopped suddenly. I could hear a pencil tapping a desk.

"Lord of Audit?" he said, with a disbelieving tone. "Do I have this correct?"

"Yes."

"What is a *Lord* of Audit? So far as I'm aware, there are Lords of a manor, and of 'the Rings', and of course Westminster has a house full of Lords for the sober discussion and ratification of legislation sent by Parliament. But I believe this is my first time encountering a Lord of Audit."

I gulped. What seemed funny in Brian's office now seemed rather silly over the telephone to a stranger whose cooperation I needed if I was to ever find a good job.

"It's exactly the same as a Senior Auditor. Our team has an odd naming convention. Something to do with a famous alumni of the firm, I believe." I'd made that up, of course.

"Oh, I see. Would you mind if I strike though 'Lord of' and replace it with 'Senior'? Would that be a problem for you?"

"No, not at all."

The rest of the call went smoothly and he said he'd call back that afternoon. I sensed he already had me in mind as a potential fit for a job that had come in. After a month of job-search frustration, I was to be offered an unexpected lifeline.

He called back that afternoon.

"Hey Nick, this is Max again. Is it a good time to talk?"

I looked around the audit room where my best buddy Bruce was shadow-boxing in front of the wall. He was a surfer from Cape Town who'd recently begun training with me at the company gym in lunchtimes. I'd taught him some boxing and Brazilian Ju Jitsu. Usually we had two-hour lunches: one hour to train and one hour to eat and relax. The audit room was at the end of a long corridor so we had over a minute's warning when the 'Big Boss' manager, Susan, was coming. She rarely did because she had no interest at all in our work and, being grotesquely overweight, she never left her office. Nobody was held accountable for our work nor our cost centre. Susan counter-signed our time-sheets and ignored us. So we pissed around all day, still not quite believing we were getting paid £25 per hour to do absolutely nothing.

"Yes, I can talk." I put my feet up on my desk. If I'd had a cigar, I'd have lit it.

"An unusual opportunity has opened up. There's a big American investment bank which is hiring for their London business assurance team. The team covers all non-US business, so the role involves frequent foreign travel."

"That's fine" I said. I'd have swept floors and served coffee to work in a prestigious financial institution, so long as my job title was something professional.

"Here is what is unusual. The Head of Global Audit, a man named Amir, is specifically seeking candidates who are finance professionals but who lack experience in banking. You specialised in media and telecommunications firms, according to your resume, yes?"

"Yes." That was partially true. That had been the division which hired me but my department had mostly put me on clients in aerospace, infrastructure, and retail.

"It's a very competitive market for experienced candidates, so the Head has decided to go outside the expected talent pool to get equal aptitude on a lower budget." That suggested the salary would be below industry average, but I didn't care. It was a way in. I could always move sideways later if I felt under-compensated. I agreed for my resume to be sent on, and a week later I was invited to interview.

Ioe was sitting at the breakfast table looking up in awe at me, full of pride at having me as her husband. I was wearing a suit for the first time since the wedding. My current job had a casual dress code.

"Are you nervous?" she asked.

"Yes. This is probably my only shot at getting into banking. I'm amazed they are considering me because I know nothing about the industry."

She stood up and straightened my tie, kissed me on the cheek, and called "*gambatte ne!*" to wish me good luck as I walked to the Underground station and then on to The City for the interview. The bank's offices were a massive seven-storey brick and glass behemoth that covered half of the city block. I walked through revolving doors and presented myself at reception. It was years since I'd been in such an imposing building. The receptionist gave me a clip-on pass and instructed me to sit on one of two expensive-looking black leather reclining chairs by a low glass table. A few minutes later, a young English lad of about twenty-eight stepped out of the elevator and came to greet me.

"Nick? Hi, I'm Toby. I'm on Amir's team. Let me take you up to the interview suite."

The experience lasted less than an hour. I had a screening interview with a lady from Human Resources who seemed mostly interested in why I'd not had a real job in four years. She seemed to imply I didn't belong in a fine institution such as hers. Then I was interviewed by the deputy head of Business Assurance, a middle-aged Englishman called Graham who I liked. He was well-spoken, well-educated, and looked like a rugby enthusiast. Finally, I was taken to Amir's office for a short chat and to shake hands with the six members of the team.

All of them were around my age and professional background, with experience outside of banking. Every one seemed intelligent and dedicated. I decided then that I definitely wanted to work there. Luckily, Amir and Graham were favourably impressed with me and a week later I had a second interview. That was really tough but I acquitted myself well. I felt like I had the job.

Two days later Max contacted me again, while I was at work. It was now November 2006.

"I'm afraid Amir has decided to go with the other short-listed candidate. He's got more banking experience than you."

I hung up the phone and shouted "Fuck!" at the wall.

Everyone else in the audit room looked up. We were all job-hunting now so this kind of thing happened a couple of times per week with different people on the team. I was desperately disappointed because Amir had created a dynamic, professional environment that I very much wanted to be a part of. If they'd hired me, I'd have learned a lot not just about banking but also the art of consulting. It had been a lifeline. Sadly, I'd pissed away my potential in Japan and now that I was married and committed to excelling in my finance career, it seemed no-one would give me a chance to prove what I was capable of. I felt dejected for a week. Ioe was sympathetic and eased the pressure.

"Don't worry. You already have a good job. I believe in you. You'll get what you want eventually, you always do. I'm happy with whatever you choose."

A month after that interview, Max called me up.

"Nick, I've heard from Amir this morning. They didn't go ahead with the other candidate after all. He instructed me to offer you the role. Are you still interested?"

I was. Max laid out the terms for a standard employment contract. It was the most money I'd earned in my life and hovered around the industry average. We agreed I'd start in the third week of 2007. Finally, I was back in the saddle in a promising corporate career. In the break between jobs, in early January, Ioe and I finally squeezed in our delayed honeymoon to Tunisia and Turkey.

A delayed honeymoon in Turkey

Upon entering the banking world, I worked ten hour days and came home mentally exhausted but satisfied that I was learning new things. My work ethic had been rescued and I thrived in the strict professional atmosphere Amir had created. By the second year, my job had gotten easier as I became acclimated to it, but things were ominous at home. Ioe had grown tired of her routine studying English and dancing, having quit both schools. She now wanted an office job.

"We don't need the money," I argued. "I earn way more than we need, so we can save a lot to put towards buying a house."

This was at the peak of the UK housing bubble so all young professionals were frightened at missing the chance to 'get onto the housing ladder'. I'd investigated the housing market but hadn't yet come to the conclusion that buying in London was madness.

"But I'm not doing anything now. I want a job. I need to be useful," she retorted.

"You are useful. You're a great housewife and a fantastic cook. If you want to do more, then find a hobby and I'll support you."

I really didn't want a working wife. It struck me as a terrible idea because the housework would get neglected, or worse I'd have to add my share of it to my responsibilities after finishing an exhausting day at the office. Worse, I'd come home every evening to an exhausted wife. Surely that would create problems. I sensed the comfortable bliss of our home coming under strain but Ioe was insistent and I felt it would be tyrannical to deny her.

It was a big mistake.

Ioe found a job in the London call centre of a Japanese airline. At first she was excited by the new experience, new work friends, and the sense of being useful outside the home. Her salary was only £15,000 annually, less than a quarter of mine. As expected, I lost a good housewife without us gaining anything important in financial security. Ioe loved it because we agreed I'd cancel the weekly entertainment and household allowance and she contributed to the bills proportionately to her lower salary. Except for the biggest bill, that is, the rent, which I paid in full. The rest of her earnings she was free to spend on herself.

Now, don't get the impression she splurged all that money on shoes and handbags. Ioe was a down-to-earth prudent girl who disliked conspicuous consumption. Nevertheless, she could easily triple her weekly spending, buy herself nice things, and feel awfully independent while still saving a tidy sum each week. It was a false independence, as it relied entirely on my paying the real costs of our London life, but she *felt* self-sufficient.

I still bore the entire responsibility for our financial security, which I now resented because I'd lost an important pillar of a happy home life: of having a clean, pleasant refuge to retreat to after a hard day's work, and a happy wife to meet me at the door with a smile. Increasingly, Ioe was put onto shift work that started before I awoke, or finished late at night. We could only snatch brief hours together mid-week and though we had the whole weekends together, we'd be tired and irritable. Increasingly, I was sent onto business trips for a week or two at a time. It would've been nice to schedule time together and go out on dates but we rarely seemed to manage it.

We visited Newcastle a couple of times in 2007 and 2008 in order to view houses for sale. London was prohibitively expensive. The flat we lived in, a musty old building in a shit part of town, was valued at £280,000 in the local estate agent's window. In normal times in normal countries, couples can expect to pay three-to-five times annual earnings for a house. Any more than that is asking for trouble, and eventual mortgage default and repossession. So despite being in a two-income family and me having a highly-paid job, we could only barely afford to buy a shitty flat.

Our upstairs neighbour lived rent free. He was an African immigrant who spoke no English, and had been given a council-owned home simply because he was African. It was extremely galling to have a lazy bum living for free in an apartment identical to mine, which cost me £1,100 per month in rent and which I couldn't afford to buy. It was observations such as this that led me to peruse right-wing blogs, as these were the only places that discussed such problems openly. All the establishment media thought what London needed was *more* lazy third-worlders and even higher taxes so we could give them more free stuff. To say otherwise was to be called a racist and a Nazi.

So, we couldn't afford London and, frankly, it's a horrible place to raise a family anyway. Ioe agreed, reluctantly, that we should live in Newcastle but the two times we looked at houses she was visibly unenthusiastic. The houses themselves were vastly superior to anything we could find in London, as were the neighbourhoods, but it wasn't 'hip'. They lacked London's sense of dynamism, of being in the centre of the world. That didn't bother me because all my entertainment involved books, television, or boxing gyms, which you can find in any city. Ioe liked to be out at restaurants, shows, and events so Newcastle felt to her like living in a cave in the forest by comparison.

By the time Ioe had been at the call centre for six months the atmosphere in our house was at an all-time low. We'd begun arguing for the first time in eight years. Usually something trivial set it off, but it was clear that something was fundamentally wrong between us. I guessed Ioe would eventually refuse to relocate to Newcastle, and she was still stalling for time before starting a family.

"We've been married two years now. We should be planning for our first child," I said.

"Yes, I know but I want one more summer as a girl, before I become a mother."

That seemed eminently reasonable and I supposed one more year didn't mean much when our future likely had fifty or sixty of them remaining. By this second year she'd become eligible for a permanent resident status in the UK so we began that application. Unlike her marriage visa that needed to be reissued periodically, this new status was a single one-time approval.

By late 2008, as a combination of all these changes, I'd begun to feel cheated. I'd fulfilled my end of the marriage bargain to advance my career, make us financially secure, and to devote myself to the duties of a husband. I'd supported Ioe in her choices. So far, however, she was indicating that she didn't want to be a housewife, didn't want children any time soon, and didn't want to leave London. That was a long way from the girl who'd gushed, "I'll follow you anywhere."

As this memoir's narrative progresses, you'll see I became gradually more aware of my share of the blame for our failing marriage. My blind spots and ego issues hid it from me at the time. I was pretty sure it was all her fault.

One night, we lay on separate sides of the bed, several inches of space between us. We still had sex about once a week, and there were still many moments of tenderness and joy, but they were increasingly subsumed beneath a heavy atmosphere of coldness and resentment. I didn't even want to fuck her any more, doing it only because I felt it was my duty to not neglect her. I'm sure she felt similarly, so our shagging was less enjoyable that prior years.

"Ioe, I no longer enjoy being married to you," I said, which was true. We needed to admit that something was badly wrong and then try to fix it. Right now, life was intolerable. We were both badly stressed at work and coming home to a cold, unwelcoming home life. Ioe sobbed quietly next to me. She didn't have any answers either.

With the benefit of hindsight, there was nothing sudden about our separation. I should've seen it coming, picking up on little signals here and there. I was too absorbed in my own dissatisfaction, trying to understand how things had gone sour so suddenly. My department underwent a major restructuring so work become considerably more stressful and that distracted me further. It never crossed my mind to divorce my wife. For me our troubles were a problem to understand and then fix. I just didn't yet know how to do so.

Ioe booked a two-week trip back to Tokyo over the New Year, to visit family. It had been planned for months. We had quite a big argument a few days before she left.

"We've been married nearly three years," I said. "We should be starting a family."

"I told you, I'm not quite ready!"

"Will you ever be ready? What's the point of having a wife who doesn't want children, and who doesn't want to live with me?"

"I do want to live with you!" she wailed, her eyes blazing in defiance, "but not with you telling me what to do all the time!"

"Don't paint me as some kind of tyrant. I've bent over backwards to let you have independence. I barely ask for anything from you."

"You were against me getting a job!"

"Yes, and I was right. Look at how you've changed. Always stressed, always out of the house, and now always giving me back-chat. You aren't the same girl I married. The last thing I want is a feminist wife."

"I'm not a feminist! But you can't tell me what to do!"

"For fuck's sake. For our whole relationship, I was the boss. You never had a problem with that in eight years. Now suddenly that's a problem?"

"Yes, you're the boss but you're not a good boss!" she cried out, her eyes shining with tears not quite shed.

I was both confused and furious, so I left the house and walked around the block a few times to cool off. This was outright rebellion in my own home. Ioe wouldn't provide a single logical reason to support her claim that I was doing things badly. Instead, she'd dredge up things I'd said in jest years ago as if they'd been serious and that I was now to be held accountable for such jokes today. It infuriated me to see my wife lying to my face, spinning sophistry, to justify her own acting out. It made me cold to her. I despise liars, especially those brash enough to lie to your face when you both know the truth.

Ioe was not, by female standards, a dishonest person. To fix things, I should've been looking towards the emotion that was inspiring her rebellion and dealing with that. She was like a ship's first mate telling the captain she no longer trusted his captaincy. That was the root of her rebellion. She had doubts about tying herself to a man who was recently losing his mojo. A baby would make our tie irrevocable and we knew the matter was fast coming to a head. Ioe was thirty-two years old, which is ancient in woman years. It felt desperately unfair, as there were real-world reasons why I'd lost my mojo. I was under incredible stress at work. Having Ioe act up at home felt like betrayal, like there was no safe harbour in which I could relax and recuperate. It was grinding me down. She should have been supporting me through the bad times, as I tried my best to keep us financially secure.

I enjoyed Christmas alone, with Ioe in Tokyo. The oppressive pall that made my house feel gloomy was lifted. I had two weeks to organise my mind and potter around the house without marriage issues disturbing every waking moment. The stress dissipated, reduced to a manageable level. I assumed Ioe's mother would talk some sense into her and I looked forward to us sitting down to rationally work out a solution to our crisis.

Ioe returned on the second week of January, 2009. On the appointed day, I didn't receive her expected phone call from Heathrow, nor was she back at our flat that evening. Perhaps her flight was delayed, or I'd written the wrong date into my diary? The next afternoon she telephoned while I was in a meeting. I excused myself and sat in the stairwell, nervous. I knew something was badly wrong.

"I'm back in London. I stayed at Andrea's house last night. Can we meet after your work and talk?"

I felt my stomach drop. I couldn't formulate it into words, but my body knew what my mind wouldn't contemplate. "Okay, I'll be done by six."

"Let's meet outside your office. We can go to the bar next door."

As you can imagine, I couldn't concentrate at work. I stared vacantly at my screen for a few hours, fobbed off my colleagues if they tried to make conversation, and then watched the clock tick down to six. Even now, nearly ten years later, the image of her walking towards me down the cobbled street alongside my office is burned into my mind. She was timid and excessively polite, as though trying to control a swirl of contradictory emotions by squeezing them into the straitjacket of social decorum. We sat down at the back of a pub.

"I need space," she said simply.

"You just had two weeks of space, in Japan."

"I know, and I spent a long time talking things through with my mother and sister."

Ioe's parents had gotten divorced when she was in elementary school. Her mother kept the big house in a lovely area, and both children, while her father made do with a tiny rented flat. Despite this unequal outcome, Ioe took her mother's side and barely saw her father. That should've been a red flag from the beginning of our relationship, but I tended to underestimate such things.

"What did your mother say?"

"She just wants me to be happy."

That seemed eminently understandable, but it contradicted my own view of marriage as a solemn contract. Our marriage vows had included the standard lines: to have and to hold, from this day forward, for better for worse, for richer for poorer, in sickness and in health, to love and to cherish, till death do us part. I took the vows seriously. I was now to find that Ioe's concept of marriage was rather more modern, that when you fall out of love you are no longer bound by your promises. Marriage to her was more like a job you quit when it no longer forwards your career.

I'm being too harsh on her, I realise. I write this to explain how I felt at the time, rather than how I feel now with the benefit of considerable reflection and a better understanding of myself and of women.

Ioe continued, "I need more time. I need to keep thinking this over. It's not a good idea that I come back to the flat yet."

I was against a trial separation and did everything I could to convince her to return with me but she was resolute. After finishing our drinks we said goodbye. There was still a strong emotional bond between us but it was no longer a pure romantic love. I walked across Blackfriars bridge looking at the dark evening sky and the twinkle of coloured lights reflecting in the water. My steps were hurried and I kept shaking my head and clenching my fists.

"No, no, no" I repeated over and over, as if my denying reality with words would somehow change it. There is a psychological model called Kubler-Ross which outlines five stages, denial, anger, bargaining, depression and acceptance as a part of the framework that makes up our learning to live with deep loss. I was grieving the loss of love and entering the first stage: denial.

I barely remember the next few days. For every minute of every day I felt like I was recovering from electric shock therapy. My body tingled and my blood ran cold. My sense of propriety and professional self-respect forced me to keep showing up at work. Everyone in the office could tell something was wrong but I didn't elaborate and they never asked, though concern showed in their faces. I remained in denial for about a week, convinced Ioe would soon come home. She called a couple of times, and we shared a few emails.

The absolute low point

Clearly, the separation was very tough on her too. I wasn't the only one of us mourning the loss of something very special in my life. We met again to talk and she was constantly on the verge of tears. It appeared that she still hadn't made up her mind so I kept trying to make the case that we should fix the problem rather than abandon the marriage. Two weeks after the first separation, I was sent to Japan on a business trip with my boss Amir, and my colleagues Magda, a Polish girl, and Teo, a Singaporean man. It felt oddly ironic to be returning to Tokyo so soon after Ioe had left it, to be within touching distance of her family, who I'd met for dinner last time I'd had a work trip there. I suffer jet lag badly so every day for a week I'd be unable to sleep at night and then drop off mid-afternoon in the office. Lying in a hotel bed alone, on the other side of the world, while unable to sleep is depressing at the best of times. This was not the best of times. Ioe and I sent each other 'good morning' and 'good evening' messages each day but I knew she was simply being polite.

I returned to London in mid-February and we met again. Ioe brought the divorce filing she intended to submit to the Tokyo authorities to formally dissolve our marriage. We had a drink in a wine bar by St Paul's Cathedral.

"What will you do?" I asked.

"My permanent residence visa was approved, so I will stay in London for now."

That was another of the red flags I'd ignored. It dawned on me Ioe had been considering divorce a good bit earlier than I'd realised, as she was now financially independent with her job, and no longer need the marriage to legally remain in the UK. Such timing seemed awfully coincidental. I felt like I'd been played.

I indicated the envelope containing the divorce papers, on the table between us. "I need a week to think about it. I'll probably sign, as you seem adamant and thus there's no point refusing. But I repeat I think this is a terrible mistake. What we had once, we can have again. The moment I sign these, it's all over. I too need a point at which I consider it final. Signing the papers is that point."

Ioe nodded, like a judge pronouncing the death penalty on a defendant she'd once loved. "A week is fine."

That was the moment I finally accepted the inevitable. I won't go so far as to say I felt better, but at least the uncertainty was lifted. I would no longer try to fix things. So I entered the next stage of divorce: withdrawal symptoms and loss of hope. I imagine it's how junkies experience cold turkey when coming off heroin. It was a primarily physical pain. Love is an addictive drug with a strong physiological component. My body now began weaning itself of off Ioe.

It took a month for the physical symptoms to abate.

All of this was a surprise to me. I'd have never believed divorce could be so traumatic. Ours wasn't even a complicated divorce. We had no children, no shared assets, only a handful of shared friends, and Ioe made it clear she wasn't interested in stealing my money through the divorce courts. She wanted a clean break and for us to both be let down gently.

If nothing else, at least I'd finally answered an important question: Yes, what I'd felt for Ioe had indeed been love.

Here my new path began; single, uncertain, and broken. I felt like a glass vase had been shattered and now rattled around inside me. It knocked me very low and I would take a long time to recover.

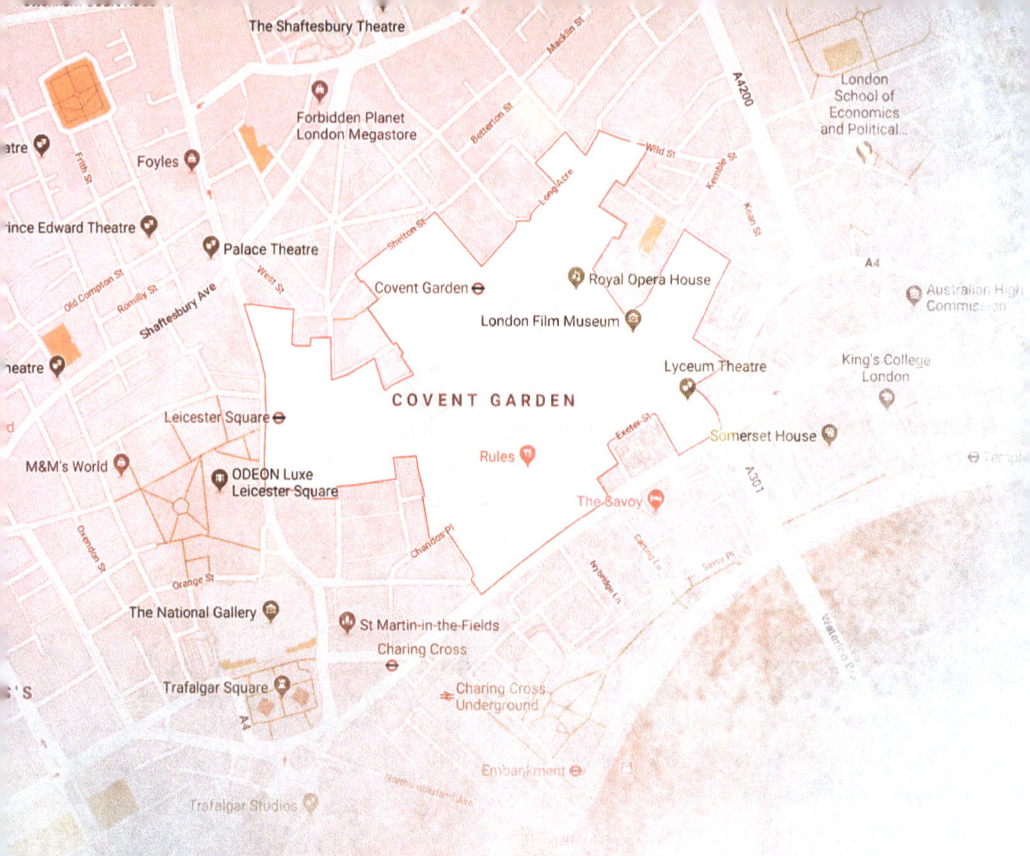
The Shaftesbury Theatre
Forbidden Planet
London Megastore
Foyles
Palace Theatre
Covent Garden
Royal Opera House
London Film Museum
London
School of
Economics
and Political...
Lyceum Theatre
King's College
London
COVENT GARDEN
Leicester Square
M&M's World
ODEON Luxe
Leicester Square
Rules
Somerset House
The Savoy
The National Gallery
St Martin-in-the-Fields
Charing Cross
Trafalgar Square
Charing Cross
Underground
Embankment
Trafalgar Studios
Shaftesbury Ave
Long Acre
Wild St
A4200
A301
A4

LONDON

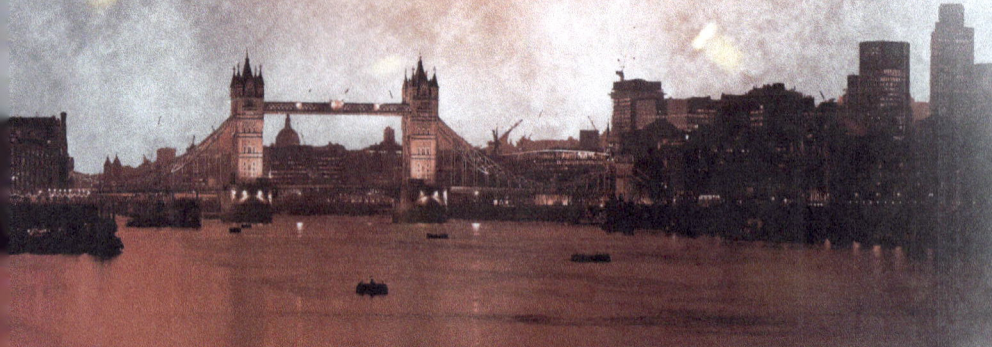

CHAPTER 14

THE JOURNEY BEGINS

CHAPTER 14

THE JOURNEY BEGINS

During that month of withdrawal I moped around the house each evening. A few times I went out to meet Tim and Yasin. They tried to console me but were even more clueless with women than myself, and unable to offer practical help anyway. So we got drunk together and they patiently listened to me spew out all my heartache and confusion. I must've sounded like such a drama-queen but, to be fair, it was the worst month of my life so I was entitled to a little indulgence from my best friends. I played lots of video games, and jogged around Kennington Park every evening to burn off my nervous energy.

I found myself sleeping twelve hours a day. When asleep, I didn't feel sad. I didn't enjoy waking up in the morning because that meant dealing with reality and I still had no idea what I'd do with myself for the rest of my life. Things couldn't go on like this, with me moping around full of bitterness and self-pity. I wasn't that type of man and deep down I knew I was acting like a temperamental little bitch.

One evening I lay on my sofa, Xbox360 controller in my hand as I played *Battlefield Bad Company*. I'm a video game nerd and a sucker for first person shooter games so this should've been a perfect evening's distraction. I couldn't enjoy it at all. Everything seemed so dull and pointless. My life seemed dull and pointless. I turned the game off, shut my eyes, and began serious introspection. What was so wrong? Why was I so unhappy? Okay, so I'd just gotten divorced but this horrible feeling hinted at deeper issues. I thought of my university friend, Tony, who had gotten divorced six years earlier and never remarried, or even had a girlfriend, since. He'd forsworn women entirely (which didn't take much grit as he was hopeless with them anyway) and dedicated himself to scuba diving. He travelled the world diving in wrecks, caves, and other interesting environments. His passion for adventure had replaced his desire for female intimacy. I knew intuitively that I couldn't do likewise. I'd always had hobbies but they'd have to run parallel to my interest in women, not replace it. Tony had given up. I'd never quit anything in my life.

Introspecting, I recalled my attempts so far to rebuild after divorce.

I wanted a new girlfriend. I wanted sex. I wanted companionship. But how could I find it? After signing the divorce papers, I'd asked Toby about dating. He sat opposite me in the office. We were good friends and he'd been the first work colleague I'd told about my divorce.

"How did you meet your bird?" I asked.

"I'm no good with women, so take this advice with a pinch of salt," he said, modestly. Toby was a nice guy in both the positive and negative senses of the label. "I signed up to Match.com and we swapped a few messages before meeting on a date."

"That's all?"

"Yeah."

His girlfriend wasn't a hotty but she was reasonably pretty, a year younger than him, and they'd been together a year. I saw no reason why that wouldn't work for me. It's not like Toby was a lady-killer. As I write these words, Toby is married with two young girls. I follow his Instagram and they look happy.

"So internet dating actually works? There are normal women on it, not crazies?"

"It worked out all right for me."

I couldn't think of a better option so I created a profile on Match.com. I abandoned that experiment within a fortnight when I realised it was impossible to get matches with women I liked. I had one date with a mid-thirties English woman who turned out to be rather fatter than her profile pictures had suggested.

Perhaps I hadn't been smart enough. I was attempting to compete with a wide-open field that must include thousands of men taller, younger, richer, and better-looking than me. Why didn't I leverage my old "in" of Japan? I spoke passable Japanese and had always done okay with Jap girls. I found a niche online dating site called JapanCupid.com and messaged every single pretty girl on there who listed her location as London. There were only half a dozen of them. I also messaged girls who didn't post a profile picture because that was the only way to boost my first message count into double figures. The pretty girls ignored me but I got replies from a few of the unknowns. That led to three uncomfortable dates with post-thirty girls who I didn't fancy.

Online dating wasn't working for me. I needed something different. Perhaps salsa dancing?

There was a group called City Salsa who met in a wine bar close to my office. Every week after work was the beginners class, followed by the later intermediate class. I signed up and paid my fiver on the door, attended by a good-looking Cuban dude who turned out to be the head teacher. The class was in the basement, taking advantage of the bar's big dance floor. It was a shabby experience, as if a singles night was set to music. Beaten down as I was at this point in my life, I was far from the lowest of this particular barrel's dregs. Most of the men looked so much like paedophiles on community release that I found my eyes drifting to their ankles to check for an electronic monitoring tag. The women were all chubby office girls at-or-around thirty years old.

There were two exceptions, a pair of twins. They looked South-East Asian and were rather hot, solid sevens by my later quality measure. Partners changed during the course of the class, so I got to dance awkwardly with both girls. It went nowhere, but it was the last time I'd have my hands on a hot girl for quite a few months to come. I quickly realised that I had no love nor talent for salsa. The dancing itself was as awkward as the losers who did it. I was only temporarily a loser, at a passing low-point in my life, and I felt that staying involved in salsa risked making my loserdom permanent. The three coaches were cool, lithe, athletic black men, but when they danced they looked homosexual. I'm sure they did great picking up chubby white chicks in the class but it confirmed to me that salsa is just odd.

Like Star Trek and My Little Pony.

Salsa was out and thus I was out of options. It was at this point that I'd turned off *Battlefield Bad Company* and began ruminating. How on earth was I going to find a girlfriend?

This is the moment I turned to Game.

I cast my mind back to a book I'd read some six or so years earlier called *The Lay Guide*, written by a man calling himself Tony Clink. I'd been browsing the book section of HMV music store in Piccadilly. They stocked edgy paperbacks: rock star biographies, Hunter S Thompson diaries, and true crime books. *The Lay Guide* had been tucked in amongst them and I'd picked it up, attracted by the cartoon cover art depicting a suave man in office dress who had a hot woman draped over his shoulders. The back cover blurb spoke of a secret system to seducing women and how a man adept in it could sleep with a different girl every night of the week.

"A different girl every night of the week?" I repeated under my breath, "That sounds rather unlikely."

I didn't believe it for a moment but the book intrigued me. I'd only recently finished reading Doyle Brunsen's *Super System*, a treasure trove of underground knowledge on how to play poker. I'd developed a literary interest in claims of 'secret systems' so I was curious what Tony Clink had to say for himself. I bought the book and read it in one weekend, fascinated. True to the back cover's blurb, *The Lay Guide* was a step-by-step guide to picking up women. That's not to say I believed Clink had cracked any kind of code, but I read it and compared his advice against my own small database of successes and failures. I came away with an overall favourable impression, thinking, "I can see that working."

Who wouldn't choose this as a reliable source of information?

But, of course, I was at that time in love with my soon-to-be wife, Ioe. My job was already done. I didn't need that Game stuff and I rapidly forgot the specifics of Tony Clink's advice. "I don't need to be told how to pick up girls," I told myself, haughtily. "I know how to do that already."

My more recent experiments with internet dating and salsa had conclusively proven to me that I'd been wrong in my estimation. I didn't know how to pick up girls and I did in fact need someone to show me how. Over the previous two months my ego had been relentlessly bowled over, crushed, and stamped into the dirt. I was temporarily humble and open to a change in direction. For my whole life I've never been good at taking a telling, and resented the idea that I may be incompetent or wrong in something. But now a brief window of opportunity had opened. I was receptive to change. I had the beginner's mindset and was ready to begin at the ground floor.

So as I laid back on the sofa with my eyes closed my introspection turned into idle speculation. Could I become a pick up artist like Tony Clink? Could I walk into a bar and leave with a fistful of hot girls' phone numbers then get them out on dates the following week? It didn't seem very likely for an average-looking thirty-four year old man. How was I going to compete with all the good-looking guys, the rich guys, the young guys? Last time I'd been to a nightclub I'd felt completely out of place. I'd felt old, and it seemed like everyone else was having more fun than me.

Nah. No chance.

Banging lots of hot girls like some kind of modern day Errol Flynn was definitely out of reach. But what about more modest goals? I didn't need to etch my name into player folklore. I just wanted a nice girlfriend. She didn't need to be a cheerleader, or actress, or catwalk model. A pretty girl in her late-twenties would be fine. Maybe she would fill the empty void in my life and I could go back to what I'd been doing before Ioe had left me.

As will become obvious soon enough, that mindset was all wrong. Life had presented me with a difficult problem and I wanted an easy solution. I was reluctant to change anything significant in my life, my habits, or my character. I was refusing to learn the main lesson of Ioe leaving: that something was a bit wrong with me. We'll get to that as the memoir progresses. I avoided learning that lesson for a long time.

Everyone avoids it, at first. So, I don't judge myself harshly.

Four days later the brown cardboard Amazon package thumped onto my doormat, and I had a fresh copy of *The Lay Guide*. I read it on the toilet at work. This time around my interest was no longer mere idle curiosity. Game was a potential lifeline to solve my life's problems. I devoured every page. Before finishing the book I'd already become increasingly determined to give Tony Clink's advice a try. I'm pretty earnest when I commit myself to a new hobby, and Game was to become a hobby. For the previous two years my hobby had been global economics and I'd been obsessional in reading blogs and dozens of dry academic books until I'd cracked the code and figured out how the economy works. I had accepted then that I was a clueless beginner and was willing to humble myself and start from the basics. I would apply the same approach to learning Game.

The Lay Guide explained to me there are three places to pick up girls, each requiring its own type of game. Bar Game was, as the name suggests, about talking to girls in social venues in the evening such as pubs and bars. This is mostly a verbal game in which you impress her with your witty repartee and use knowledge of group dynamics to manipulate yourself into a strong position from which to collect phone numbers. Club Game is mostly about getting physical with girls on or near the dance floor and then sexually escalating them until they are horny and ready to leave with you. I hadn't done that since I was in Okinawa, and I'd only pulled it off once there with Ryoko, and a couple of times at university. I doubted I'd ever be able to learn club game. Lastly was Daygame. That involved meeting girls during the daytime in coffee shops and on the street, striking up a conversation, and then taking a phone number.

What all three types of Game shared in common was an emphasis on 'cold approach'. That meant stepping up to a girl you've never met and introducing yourself. All three methods went into extreme detail on how to do this so as to maximise your chances of a favourable reception. It didn't seem like such a big deal to me.

"Going up to birds and saying hello? How hard can that be?"

How little I knew!

I'd eventually experiment with all three types but, as you'll see, I quickly gravitated to daygame. After finishing with Tony Clink I went back through the book and wrote out my own flashcards of his salient points. He gave suggestions for further reading which I supplemented with internet searches. I moved on to the next books on my list, the most famous of which is *The Mystery Method* by Erik Von Markovich (better known by his PUA name Mystery). I still swear by this tremendously misunderstood book. It is the foundational text in Game and I'd refer back to it for years to come. Unlike most newcomers, I didn't go through a long "theory phase" of consuming dozens of books and instructional videos before actually going out and talking to girls. Right from the beginning I knew that excessive study was really a form of avoidance: a way to delay the anxiety a man feels before approaching a girl he doesn't know. Instead, I read *The Lay Guide*, *The Mystery Method* and Neil Strauss' famous memoir *The Game*. Within a fortnight of deciding to learn Game, I was already itching to hit the streets.

The VH1 television show

My big day was to be Wednesday, 20th May, 2009. I had a day off work so this was when I'd decided to begin daygame. I took the underground into town from Kennington to Covent Garden and my hands shook. My skin was clammy and my heart thumped in my chest. It was a gloriously sunny day with happy tourists milling around the marketplace, yet I was shitting myself because so much was at stake. I'd foolishly built it up in my mind into my one chance, my Last Chance Saloon for happiness with women. If I couldn't make Game work, I was fucked. And not in the good penis-in-vagina way.

I remember the day as if it was yesterday.

When I stepped out of the Underground station I felt like I'd walked into an invisible wall. I stood still in the centre of the cobbled street leading down to the Covent Garden market. It was busy and lots of pedestrians brushed past me, including some pretty girls. I felt immobilised. It was impossible to take steps towards a girl to approach her.

How odd.

I walked down the gentle incline towards the historic market building and then along a side-street towards The Strand. My mind was fogged, like I'd been sniffing glue. Eventually I recognised the blue and black livery of Caffe Nero so I went inside, ordered a coffee, and tried to understand what had happened. Surely I should've been talking to girls by now?

I settled into a large leather sofa chair by the door and rummaged in my over-the-shoulder courier bag for my *The Mystery Method* hardback and ran my finger down the contents page. The book detailed concepts that were new to me such as 'survival and replication value', 'indirect openers', 'the three-second rule', and other such technical terms. My mind reeled with the sheer amount of new information. Mystery's underlying world-view, that states women are an abundant resource that you pro-actively hunt for, was alien to me. Finally I found the section I wanted, that was relevant to my odd experience of being unable to act: Approach Anxiety. Mystery had borrowed the term from sales training to describe the gut-churning sense of dread deep in your stomach that you feel once the idea of talking to a new girl moves from idle possibility to immediate probability. "AA", as it is commonly abbreviated to, and I were to become intimate bedfellows over the next few years.

Okay, now I understood the problem. I snapped the book closed and resolved to get back onto the street. Mystery's solution to AA is 'the three-second rule' which requires you to open a girl within three seconds of seeing her. The rationale is it will force action before AA takes hold.

I stayed in the comfy sofa-chair much longer than I needed to as little demons whispered in my ears, giving me reasons to give up and go home. Nonetheless, I finally roused myself and began my walk through the market towards Neal Street. It felt like taking the field for a football match. Several hot girls walked past and I did nothing. No-one had explained to me how to approach a moving target. Time stretched on. I spent twenty minutes with my hands in my pockets, beating myself up for not approaching. Perhaps I should find a less intimidating environment, I considered, and walked into a retro clothing shop. There was a Japanese girl browsing a rail of trousers. Great! I really liked Japanese girls at this point, more so than any nationality. I also had a lingering belief that speaking Japanese would impress them, giving me an "in".

I looked around for a prop to use in an indirect opener. I picked up a shirt, took a deep breath, and walked over to her.

"Hey. Do you think this shirt suits me?"

She smiled and told me it looked nice.

I kept talking. Well, perhaps babbling is a more accurate verb. My mind was blank, my heart pounded, and my hands seemed to shake. This was it! I was actually talking to a hot girl I'd just "opened"! A few minutes of jibber-jabber dribbled out of my mouth and this Japanese girl hadn't yet given me the brush off. Now I remembered I was supposed to do 'kino', meaning to make some light physical contact. The PUA books told me this would sub-communicate to girls that I was hitting on them.

"I lived in Tokyo for a while."

"Oh, that's my home town," she enthused.

"Do you know Kichijoji? Here, give me your hand a moment and I'll show you," I said and then used my finger to trace a map on her palm. It turned out she knew the area. It was too much to hope I'd get to the end of the chat without putting my foot in it.

"Look, let's get a coffee sometime," I said.

She paused a second, looking carefully at me.

"Oh, no thank you. I'm very busy. Bye."

This Japanese girl had declined my offer but I didn't feel at all dejected. Quite the contrary, I glowed with excitement. I'd just approached a random girl, struck up a conversation, and had a pleasant experience. Perhaps I could do this pick-up thing!

I wanted to build on this tiny sliver of momentum so my first thought was to find *another* retro clothing shop, thinking if it had worked in one maybe it would in the next. I wandered fifty yards down Neal Street and into Rockit, tucked in a cobbled back alley across from the Diesel flagship store. Dusty Springfield's voice lilted over the air as the speakers pushed out *I Only Want to be With You*. At a circular clothes rail by the back wall there was an okay-looking English girl rummaging through the surplus German army coats. I hastily grabbed a Hawaiian shirt and blundered over to her.

"Hey. Do you think this shirt suits me?"

"Um, yeah."

"I'm going to a hula-themed party next weekend so wondered if this is right for it."

"It's fine."

The girl give a timid smile and turned away. I put the shirt back on the rain and noticed my hands were sweating and trembling like a Parkinson's sufferer. I felt my lips pulled back in a rictus grin and I imagined my head like a skull-faced bogeyman from a horror movie. I'd probably terrified the poor girl.

Whatever, I was on a roll!

Adrenalin flushed my veins and distorted all sense of perspective. I was elated that I had spoken to two girls without traumatic incident. Deep down I'd worried they might tell me to fuck off, or even call the store manager to have me ejected for harassment. It's a silly thought, but approach anxiety warps your mind. Having approached two girls in clothes shops I felt emboldened to branch out. Could I approach a girl in a *different type of shop?*

Woah, easy there tiger! Let's not get ahead of ourselves.

I walked down to The Strand and popped into Dixons electronic shop. There was an American girl looking at some SLR cameras under a glass case. I walked up from behind her (usually a no-no, but I was socially clueless at this point in my life). I tried to be casual.

"What you thinking of buying?"

She jumped, visibly shocked. Then she calmed down and replied, "Uh, that one."

At first she looked at me like I was a mugger, startled by the abruptness of my approach. Then she calmed, realising I was just a harmless fool, and dismissed me from her mind and turned back to the camera display. I stood there a few moments, absorbing the shame of being a man of so little presence that she'd sized me up in moments and lost interest. I shuffled out of Dixons and crossed the road, walking down towards Embankment and the river. A really hot Malaysian girl was coming up the street towards me. I stepped across her path and gestured.

"Are you someone I should get to know?" I ventured.

"No."

She kept walking.

Even now, years later, I cringe as I write that. This episode conveys just how low my social intelligence was in 2009. At heart, daygame is a test of how socially normal you are. No matter how slick your lines they must be overlaid onto a foundation of sound social skills. Girls sniff out weirdos in a heartbeat, which has proved the undoing of many a hapless new daygamer. At this point, I was that hapless daygamer. Fortunately, my social intelligence was so low that I didn't realise just how low it was. I was filled with a beginner's overestimation of how quickly he can "get it". That delusional overconfidence would serve me well in powering through the daily grind and endless rejections that were to come. If I'd been more socially savvy I'd have probably felt the embarrassment more acutely and abandoned the 'pick up artist' project as an impossible dream. It was not in my reality to stop random girls in the street, interest them, and then get a phone number.

I approached only those four girls that day. I didn't get any phone numbers and only one of the girls had allowed herself to be drawn into a short conversation. That didn't matter to me. What did matter is I'd controlled the one thing that can be controlled, my own behaviour.

I'd started.

Another week of work passed. My evenings at home were still miserable but the whirlwind trauma of divorce was mostly behind me. Hope for the future had rekindled. While my body was physically present in team meetings and PowerPoint presentations, my brain was elsewhere, turning over the latest information to be gleaned from my instructional books and the PUA blogs I'd found on the Internet. A whole new world had opened up in front of me. There were actually men on the Internet who wrote journals detailing their attempts to seduce women! It was like discovering forbidden knowledge, akin to dusting off a copy the *Necronomicon* recovered from an Egyptian pharaoh's tomb. Perhaps I, too, could learn these mystical incantations that will make women feel uncontrollable attraction towards me.

"Nick!" barked my manager and my mind snapped back to the job. "Nick, have you cleared review points six and nine from the work papers?" I muttered an unfocused reply and began plotting my next daygame session. At meeting's end, I snuck away with *The Mystery Method* for a furtive read on the toilet. The weekend soon came.

On the toilet, yesterday

In the early days, I could remember each individual daygame session in detail. I'd log them on an Excel spreadsheet, listing each approach. My second effort was on June 1st. I was now loitering in St James Park as summer arrived. I wandered around the park looking for girls sitting alone. I floundered for a while, nerves shaking my limbs, so I sat in a deck chair reading a detective novel. It was tempting to stay there, approach anxiety rearing its ugly head to sap my energy, but with force of effort I made myself talk to girls.

The first was a cute brunette sitting on the grass with her little lapdog. I walked over and stroked him, going to my haunches so that I wasn't towering over her.

"Your dog is cute. What breed is he?"

"Thank you. She's a chihuahua"

Although she was socially polite, I detected not the slightest flicker of interest from her. I kept making small talk but felt nervous and could feel my throat constrict from the self-imposed pressure. The conversation stuttered and died after two minutes. It became unbearable and I found an excuse to eject before my ego got battered by rejection. She didn't dismiss me, I just bailed. My legs were still shaking.

Next, I saw a colourfully-dressed girl sitting on the grass reading *The Economist*.

"Hi. What's that you're reading?"

She responded pleasantly in a French accent and we chatted. I was so nervous I wittered on aimlessly about the magazine, France, and then asked mundane questions. There was no rhythm or purpose to my conversation and I tried too hard to fill the spaces. She didn't flinch when I sat down, which was a good sign, but I had no idea where to take the interaction. What do you do once a girl is talking? I hadn't gotten that far in my Game studies. The French girl continue to chat but I felt out of my depth and contrived to eject at the earliest opportunity.

"Anyway, I need to go. It was nice meeting you."

"Okay, have a nice afternoon!"

That was it. Two conversations and I was physically spent. The anxiety had drained me. My legs felt weaker than they used to after a two hour kickboxing session at Crosspoint. Who would've thought daygame could be an extreme sport?

The next day I wanted to try walking around Soho. This is the entertainment district in Central London, packed with trendy cafes, bars, pubs, and all manner of media offices. I'd noted it tended to have pretty women walking around. I was off work and I started strong. Immediately upon boarding the Northbound train at Kennington I saw a hot Asian sat listening to her iPod and writing into a paperback Sudoku book. A random man sat next to her, and as I didn't want to risk being rejected in front of him, I bottled out of approaching her. So much for the three-second rule. Luckily, she changed trains at the same station as me, Embankment. I planned my exit to step onto the escalator slightly ahead of her, so I could turn over my shoulder and open casually.

"Hey, I've always wanted to know, is Sudoku really Japanese?"

"Um, I'm Korean."

"*Pangapsumnida.*"

She smiled at that so, emboldened, I continued, "Yeah, it's just I used to live in Japan, and I never saw them play Sudoku. I think it's probably one of those things they say is 'big in Japan' because they know nobody is gonna prove them wrong."

We chatted, she got the same train connection as me and, as she sat down, indicated for me to sit with her. Famed PUA Mystery seemed to be speaking in my mind: 'affect disinterest, my son'. So I stayed standing next to her, not giving her my full body language. I struggled a bit for conversation, and I knew I had to get off in two stops. Things felt strained. Fake.

"I'm getting off in a minute. If I wanna see you again what do I do?"

She didn't seem too convinced. "Um, take my number."

We swapped about thirty texts over the next week but I couldn't get her out on a date. Re-reading those texts now with the benefit of hindsight I realise my text game was awful. Nevertheless it was another victory story, my first ever daygame "number close", despite how little a phone number actually signifies. I was making small incremental moves towards my goal of being the kind of man who picks up hot girls on the street. Flush with the rush of my illusory success, I found another four Japanese girls that afternoon and asked each about sudoku. One pair of tourists in a cafe hooked well and chatted, but I was lacking direction and ran out of steam again.

I returned home and took stock of my progress.

I was pleased with myself for hitting the streets and making things happen, no matter how incompetently. There was a pleasure from taking action and bringing my sex life under (the illusion of) control. It would've been easy to just stay home and play the latest *Call of Duty*, yet, here I was stalking the streets in a constant battle against my own approach anxiety and negative self-talk, and eventually getting some work done. That said, I knew I was clueless. It was time to find someone better than me to give me direct training. So I opened my laptop and searched the Internet for a PUA 'boot camp'.

"A boot camp?" you say. "What's that?"

The 'boot camp' structure was another of Mystery's innovations, bringing it over from the more established world of cold-calling sales training. Way back in 2001, Mystery had moved out from Canada to Los Angeles to hit on the local women. To cover his rent and feed his ego he began teaching other men his new pick-up system. In that era, instructional events in the Seduction Community were always seminars held in hotel conference rooms. They looked more like business presentations. A guru would pace around on a stage, talk into a microphone, and scrawl things on a whiteboard. That was all! No evidence. No demonstrations. No interactivity.

The students were expected to accept the instructors at face value without the slightest shred of proof that they were any better with women than the eager young men in the audience. With no barriers to entry, the Seduction Community was awash with outrageous charlatanry. Instructors such as David De Angelo, Vin DiCarlo, Carlos Xuma, and Hypnotica made money hand-over-fist without ever proving their bona fides. Mystery's great innovation was to conduct his instructional events "in field" by going to real bars and hitting on real women in unscripted encounters, providing a live demonstration both of his method and also his pick-up skills. He called it a "boot camp" and it was a revolution for the Seduction Community. They were typically held over a weekend. The early evening would be devoted to lectures and then everyone would head out to the bars for the in-field practice. Mystery's wingmen would help out as "approach coaches", encouraging students past their approach anxiety and into set. The West Coast of the USA became a hive of pick-up coaching activity and a number of new companies sprang up, all offering these boot camps.

I wanted to take one.

In my naïveté, I projected mythical levels of "mad skills" onto professional instructors and desperately hoped just a little of their awesomeness would rub off on me. I searched Google for the big-name PUA companies, names such as Real Social Dynamics, Love Systems, and Venusian Arts. Their listed tuition prices brought me crashing back to earth. Jesus Christ! £2,000 for a weekend?

I mean, I wanted to get better with women. But... £2,000? That was two months of savings to piss away in a single weekend.

Lest I come across cheap, it wasn't the sum of money that bothered me in itself. If I was guaranteed success with beautiful young women, or at least measurable improvement, I'd have happily handed over my credit card, date of birth, and mother's maiden name. The pick-up gurus were welcome to empty my life savings so long as I got to tap top-quality ass. I didn't lack desire. Rather,

I doubted my ability to survive a boot camp weekend without suffering a mental breakdown. They'd push me hard. Would I stand up to it? I was still feeling rather fragile. If I buckled under pressure I'd be squandering the money with only myself to blame. Wasn't there some way to test the waters first, at lower risk? A way to dip my toe in the shallowest end of the kiddie pool. I looked for the cheapest local boot camp that I could find, telling myself I'd just show up, no pressure, see what happened and, if it was okay, I'd spend the big money on the premium coaches later. Now that I'm an experienced instructor myself, I see this half-assed attitude all the time. People are always half-assing the important decisions, and so was I.

I was stupid, but I was also lucky.

Only a handful of companies offered live events in London that year. The premium names would fly in a couple of instructors every month or so, like old-time barnstormers, but charged well north of £1,000 for the privilege. The local big fish was a company called *PUA Training* who seemed to have the slickest overall package. The sticking point was their £800 price tag, and the online photo directory of their instructors looked like a rogue's gallery of chancers, buffoons, and fruitcakes. A level below this were the 'indies', just small groups of friends with makeshift websites. *PUA Method* were charging £300, which was within my budget, but I didn't like their site.

The marketing is all terribly cringe

I turned to the product reviews sub-forum of a popular PUA messaging board and posted a question: is there a reputable company offering boot camps in London for men on a tight budget? An anonymous commentator suggested *Sarge School*. A couple of other London forum guys gave them positive reviews and when checking out their amateurish website, I thought they looked cool in the photos. My search was concluded: I'd found depths sufficiently shallow to dip my toe into. It was poor decision-making exemplified but little did I know how much it would subsequently affect my life.

Sarge School's next "beginners" boot camp was scheduled for July, a month away. I completed their online application form including a free-form notes field asking about my age, background, and current success (or lack of it) with women. I answered honestly.

The following afternoon I was sat at my desk in the office reviewing a colleague's work papers. A half-eaten Pret A Manger tuna sandwich and fresh steaming coffee were close at hand. I saw a new mail appear in my inbox from someone calling himself Jimmy Jambone. The words *Sarge School* were in the title. Oh, that was quick. I clicked it open, thrilled that a pick-up guru was communicating directly to me.

"Hey Nick. Thanks for your inquiry and booking. It's great that you're taking positive action on this path. We'll send out a detailed email in the week before the boot camp giving you all the necessary information. But for now, feel free to ask any questions. JJ."

Jimmy Jambone was so cool he signed his mails "JJ". God, the girls must *love* him!

I felt the status differential between us starkly. I was too scared to ask anything in case I annoyed the *Sarge School* coaches and wasn't allowed to take the boot camp. I felt like a man caught in a river flood looking up at the rescue helicopter, stretching out a hand to my rescuer. Determined not to let myself down on the fast-approaching boot camp weekend, I studied my books *extra* hard and read the *Sarge School* site from top to bottom. Two days before the fateful July day, Jimmy emailed meet-up instructions couched in secretive tones. We were to meet outside Borough underground station on Friday evening, whereupon an instructor would collect us and take us to the hush-hush seminar venue.

It was all thrillingly secretive.

I slipped out of work early while my boss was in a meeting, slinking out of a side door, so I could get home in time to shower and change for the big night. Borough station was a short walk from my house as, unbeknownst to me, Jimmy also lived in Kennington and liked to organise meet-ups at his own convenience. I arrived at the Underground station to find four nervous men stood in a furtive-eyed huddle. That would be the other students.

I introduced myself. There was a Polish guy, an Italian, a Scot, and a white-Zimbabwean called Steve. The latter would be my first wing over the next couple of months until he ended up in a serious three-year relationship. We chatted excitedly, and then the instructor arrived.

"Hey lads, are you here for the boot camp?" he asked.

Johnny Wisdom was a confident young man in his mid-twenties. Nicely dressed, a deep cool voice, and light brown hair brushed back behind his ears like an Argentine footballer. He shook our hands and led us away to a nearby pub in the English style but with a Thai food menu. It was here we'd have a couple of hours' classroom teaching before the in-field session began. A sense of adventure hung in the air, like anything could happen and probably would. Johnny put us at ease with a mix of light chit-chat and a few probing personal questions. He spoke with genuine warmth and interest. Another of my preconceptions about Game was being dispelled.

I'd assumed the men who are good with women were all aloof arrogant swine, as this is how movies portrayed them, and Mystery himself put on lofty airs and graces in the videos I'd seen of him. I assumed the Sarge School team would lord it over me, impossibly far above my own weak position. Johnny was quite the opposite. When he spoke he turned his body fully towards me, looked into my eyes, and oozed understanding and rapport. This is how good seducers are. They make you feel good about yourself in a very authentic way. They aren't "playing" you. This is crucially important when talking to girls because not only do they usually need to feel comfortable around you, but they are also extremely good at sniffing out inauthentic and fake behaviour.

The old pub was empty but for the Sarge School team playing pool and chilling at the bar. Seven guys in all and every single one of them exuded an aura of coolness. I was encountering a real live "rat pack", a group of men who had actively worked upon their value and knew how to support and reinforce one another. This was not the clueless ill-coordinated rabble that I called my own friends. It was a class apart and I was already sold. Whatever they had, I wanted it for myself too and was prepared to work hard to get it. They waved us in and then a charismatic black Londoner called Diamond led us to the function room.

I scanned the faces but Jimmy Jambone himself wasn't there. I'd have recognised him from his picture on the website. He looked like Liam Gallagher, the lead singer of Oasis.

Diamond was a tall slim man who looked a little like the actor Will Smith. He gave a talk on the basics of Game, including how to begin conversation in a bar by using an "opinion opener." That's as simple as it sounds: you ask girls for their opinion on an interesting topic. At the time Sarge School was using this unremarkable opener: "My friend is going to take his girl on a trip to propose. He's wondering where to go. Which is more romantic, Paris or New York?"

There's no magic to it. It's just an ice-breaker. If the girls want to chat they'll run with it. And if not, no big deal. They can give a curt answer and you can eject without feeling bad. Remember, I was in a bad way at this time, just five months after the love of my life had walked out on me. I was still broken inside, lacked any kind of self-confidence, and was easily overawed in social situations. Diamond went around the students in turn asking them what they wanted from Game and women. When it came to my turn I was almost choking up with emotion when I replied.

"I think if a woman gets to know me, she'll love me. I just don't know how to get her that far."

Diamond winced involuntarily. Perhaps he coughed up and swallowed down some of his own vomit. I still hadn't recovered my old confidence and the self-pity must've emanated from me in waves. "Don't worry mate, we'll get that handled," he reassured and swiftly turned to the next student. Then he continued outlining basic game theory. After two hours, they ordered taxis to take us up to Piccadilly Circus.

It was a warm breezy evening. We huddled up under the famous neon signs at the roundabout. It was half past nine and the streets buzzed with revellers.

"Right lads, we're going to do warm-up sets outside. Simple stuff, just stick to the New York opener. Don't push anything hard. It'll loosen you up. Here look, I'll show you."

A couple of Spaniards were tottering past on high heels. Diamond stood in front and chatted to them. They giggled a bit, answered, and after a minute he let them go.

"Now we've given each of you an approach coach. Nick, you're with me tonight." The other lads each got assigned one of the Sarge School team. I immediately opened a pair of Italians and Diamond joined me to share the burden of conversation. The girls liked it, though clearly Diamond was the star of the show. We chatted several minutes before they excused themselves to go off to a club. One of the other instructors came up to me. He was about my age but better-looking and in good shape. He had a short masculine beard, brown hair styled carefully like a fashion model, and was immaculately dressed in a manner that was casual but organised. I recognised him from the Sarge School website. It was Tony T.

"Good set, Nick. The girls liked you. That might've been a same day lay."

I doubt he was serious, as it's usual for approach coaches to exaggerate all positives. Their role is to make you approach, so positivity is far more valuable than realism. I trusted Tony's opinion implicitly and was buoyed by it. Another half hour passed until all the students had done a few warm-ups, then we went into nearby Jewel Bar.

Diamond kept an eye on me all night, encouraging me, giving feedback, and demonstrating on girls. He seemed so impossibly cool and friendly. I felt a warm glow of gratitude that he so expertly guided me through what I'd feared would be a stressful evening. I ended the evening with the number of a Moroccan-English girl I'd found sitting with her friend at the end of the bar. We swapped texts but she never came out on a date. Around midnight our energy flagged. The instructors let us go home with an admonition to sleep well and meet up at London Bridge Station at noon the next day for the day game session.

"You did great, buddy," said Diamond, clapping me on the shoulder. "Johnny is taking the daygame session tomorrow afternoon. You'll be in good hands."

I bought a slice of pizza from a Turkish kebab stall then took a train home. I pulled off all my clothes and collapsed on the bed, fast asleep within moments. Life is full of bifurcation points, moments when you're at a fork in the road (wittingly or unwittingly). The smallest accident or slightest whim decides which direction you take and yet that radically changes the course of your life. Picking up *The Lay Guide* had been the first. Choosing *Sarge School* was the second. The first decision rested on a whim (I'd almost bought *Killing Pablo* instead) and the second upon a chance recommendation by an anonymous forum member I never did meet. Moments before I drifted into blissful sleep, I reflected that I still didn't know this Jimmy Jambone character. He had started to take on a mythical quality, like Fu Manchu or The Candyman. The other coaches spoke of him in tones of quiet respect. Who was this shadowy figure who led Sarge School?

I slept like the elder God Cthuhlu, my mind lost amid aeons of unimaginable, unfathomable time and space. Such gods are awoken from eternal cosmic slumber by the long-forgotten, jealously-guarded rituals of sea-dwelling occultists. In my case, a simple alarm clock sufficed. At ten am I leapt out of bed. The second day of boot camp would prove pivotal as it would introduce me to a workable method of daygame. Johnny's style was simple but direct. Had I been left to aimlessly wander parks asking girls what they were reading ("going indirect" in the jargon) I'd have likely given up on day game within a month or two. Saturday with Johnny gave me a better way.

I rushed through my morning shower and breakfast with a spring in my step then arrived on time at London Bridge station to meet Johnny and.... Jimmy.

"Alright mate, I'm Jimmy," he said, shaking my hand. Then he passed the reins over to Johnny to lead the session. They both looked tense, like something was going on that I wasn't aware of. We began walking around the tourist-thronged South Bank by the river, and outside the station proper.

"No hot birds," said Jimmy. "It's tear gas, this is."

Johnny flashed him a look I couldn't understand. "We'll find something. This place is usually good."

After half an hour, Johnny spotted a pretty blonde dragging her suitcase to a bus stop. He walked over to her and said something we couldn't hear. Jimmy leant back against a lamppost, arms folded, watching intently like a cricket umpire. We students were watching Johnny from a distance thinking, "Is this really happening?" The girl tapped something into Johnny's phone and he sauntered back, grinning.

"Yep, number close," he said, more to Jimmy than to us.

"Nice one," he replied.

We were dumbfounded. It was like witnessing a magic trick.

Months later, Johnny would confide to me that he'd been extremely nervous in that demonstration set because he'd only joined Sarge School the previous week. It was his first coaching gig for them. Jimmy was on hand to check out his game and report back to the team if he was good enough to pass probation.

"How'd you do that?" I asked Johnny.

"I wanted you lads to see a set before I explained the method. Let's huddle up and I'll explain daygame opening." He pulled us to one side down a quiet street and taught us the basic direct approach. "First thing is let the girl walk past so she's a few metres in front of you. This is so you have time to get a good look at her. Catch up with a playful jog, then when you draw alongside let her catch you in her peripheral vision. That's very important so as not to startle her."

Jimmy nodded approval. Johnny continued.

"Circle in front, so you're blocking her path from a few feet away. Smile, so you're not threatening. Usually the girl will stop. If she doesn't, just let her go. Then say, "Hi. I just saw you walk by, and I knew I'd be kicking myself if I didn't come over and talk to you. You're gorgeous." Wait a bit, for it to sink in. Then, lean back looking all inscrutable, like this."

Johnny leant back, folded his arms, and raised an eyebrow. Jimmy was doing that already, looking inscrutable, but for entirely different reasons.

"Then you say, "so.... who *are* you?"" Johnny finished.

If I hadn't just seen it successfully employed with the girl at the bus stop, I wouldn't have believed it. There seemed so much wrong with it when compared to what I thought I knew about women. Several questions leaped into my mind. You can just interrupt women who are going about their day? You can tell her, right off the bat, that you think she's attractive? Girls will just give up their phone number after a few minutes? And this is done... sober? With people walking past all the time?

Johnny answered affirmatively to all of them.

We poor students had difficulty adjusting. We still felt like having watched a magic show, but only now the magician was explaining the trick. I still had so many mental barriers that I couldn't quite take it in, even though I'd already tried a few days talking to girls in parks and shops. When Johnny turned to me to check my understanding, I told him, "I find it difficult to open a moving target. It feels like they have their stuff to do and I'm just interrupting, getting in their way".

His response really stuck with me. "That's tough to answer because it's not even in my reality. I'm offering them the value, the opportunity to know me."

This was a major shift in thinking. In the community we call it a "reframe", a way of replacing a given interpretation of a situation with a new interpretation that is more favourable for you. From an early age boys are constantly drilled with variations of the same message: they must *earn* the right to a girl's intimacy. In contrast, girls are taught to feel entitled to men pandering to them. England in 2009 was a feminist's paradise (which made it a nightmarish hellhole for men). Culture backed them up.

It's the knight who risks life and limb to rescue the damsel in distress. The prince must win over the princess. The man must put the roof over the family's head. The men fight and die in wars to protect the women. If a little boy cries because he can't handle the pressure of life, he's told to "man up" and "pull his weight" whereas the crying little girl is indulged. This is the cultural expression of harsh biological fact: men are expendable and thus men give, women receive. It's the extravagant privilege of being born female. This seemed desperately unfair to me at the time, a single lonely man working his ass off in a career and having only an empty apartment to return to.

I wished I could internalise Johnny's belief in his own intrinsic value as a man. I'd have some reprogramming to do.

"Daygame is mostly about creating the opportunity for a conversation to happen," he continued in his pep talk. "Some girls are going to like you, but if you don't open then you don't find out. You have to be in it to win it."

Johnny's method was based upon "flipping stones", finding out which girls like you immediately based on a quick once-over. By approaching confidently and decisively, girls would be more inclined to receive your pass. That's something of a numbers game. It's an order of magnitude more difficult to turn around a girl who is initially uninterested, but we'll get to that as the book (and my own daygame skill) develops.

That Saturday afternoon in London Bridge, Johnny and Jimmy pushed me into six "sets" (new interactions with girls). I didn't get any phone numbers but only one interaction was a painful rejection: a fast-moving blonde girl gave me an "eye roll" blowout that stung. My lack of confidence and clumsiness of execution hamstrung me, but I didn't care. I found myself overly interrogating the poor girls with rapid-fire questions so much so that one actually asked if it was an interview. The last two girls showed me engagement rings but smiled at my approach.

It was all over by two pm.

"Come on lads, I think you've all earned a pint of England's finest ale," said Jimmy. He ushered us into a traditional pub outside the market. As we walked indoors he hung back with Johnny, whispering in low tones. I noticed Johnny nod and smile, then visibly relax. I think Jimmy had told him he'd passed the test.

We crowded around a table, excitedly telling our little war stories of the afternoon. We glowed with manic energy, like having been shot at and missed. I felt comfortable, temporarily at peace. I'd ended the session feeling *I can do this*. I could jump in front of moving girls and open. I'd continue to practice night game, including that very night when Sarge School took us to the bar district in Old Street, but the seeds were sown for my daygame journey.

CHAPTER 15

SOMALI PIRATES

CHAPTER 15

SOMALI PIRATES

I wasn't expecting the player's journey to be such a lonely one, in the beginning at least. Perhaps that's symptomatic of life generally. Since we first sit giggling and cooing on our mother's knee, we are lulled into the comforting fantasy that others genuinely care about us. Some reckon a mother's love for her child is the only genuine selflessly unconditional love in the world. I've seen plenty of cases where even that is a fantasy. The only person who will consistently put your own interests front and centre is yourself. Not surprising, really. It's a harsh realisation nonetheless and most of us spend a lifetime avoiding it. I had numerous experiences reinforcing this message, such as the feeling of solitude upon stepping into the boxing ring, and again when wandering through Covent Garden looking for girls. Committing myself to a project to become 'good with women' was turning out to be a frequently lonely path, ironically so considering the amount of fresh social contact it involves.

Though I'd entered the Seduction Community via reading books and browsing the internet, I couldn't shake the feeling that I was the only person trying this "game thing" and that I must be weird. It would hit me hard while on the streets. I'd be scanning the crowd for women, making small on-the-fly decisions on where to walk, what side of the street to stay on, whether to stop for coffee, and so on. The world would appear to zone out, like I was the last man on earth and everyone around me was a hologram running on an endless loop created by a lost long-dead civilisation.

Of course, this was silly. A self-induced illusion. The streets were full of well-rounded individuals. Boyfriends shopping for birthday presents for their girl, best friends sharing a beer while watching the rugby on television, or a grandfather baby-sitting the grandkids. I was surrounded by a rich tapestry of human connection. Nonetheless, at this point in my life, I couldn't help but feel apart from it all by the nature of my goals. I'd tried telling my friends, one night in a City of London pub after work.

"Have you heard of Game?" I asked speculatively. "The idea that there's a system for meeting women that can be learned."

"Is that where people wear furry hats and do magic tricks in bars?" said Tim, no doubt thinking of Mystery who had been known to do both such things. He'd briefly had a TV show called *The Pick Up Artist*.

"Well, yes and no. That's just one guy. I've been reading the textbooks about it and they give advice on body language, opening lines, and how to move things forwards. It looks interesting."

My friends scoffed.

"Bullshit," said Ian, "all you need is a bit of charisma and then crack on to the birds. All that system stuff is nonsense."

I decided to wait a few more weeks before letting on that I was now a 'gamer'. I hadn't yet told my workmates, though we were a close-knit group so I probably would eventually. For now, I was committed to learning, but still wildly uncertain whether it would be worth the trouble. It would be embarrassing for me to come out with a grandiose declaration I was a player only to subsequently fail to bang any girls. So I accepted that most of the time I'd be alone in this journey, be it walking the streets or pouring over the instructional materials.

In August 2009, not long after my first Sarge School boot camp, I was still only beginning to come to terms with this position. I was thoroughly immersed in my new hobby and had already zoned out at work, physically present but mentally absent. My work had transformed from a source of progression and self-esteem to merely that thing to be finished as soon as possible in order to get back to browsing the latest Game blog posts and watching instructional DVDs. There was a vast library of material to consume and I worried I'd never get abreast of it all. Imagine going to juggling school and on day one you're expected to keep six balls in the air. Overwhelming but also exciting. For the first time in my life I felt like I had a real shot at dating hot girls. Once I've taken a bite out of something I lock on as relentlessly as a terrier.

My plan to mitigate the solitude of the journey was to find a wingman. I'd exchanged numbers with the Zimbabwean lad Steve at the boot camp. A Dutch lad I'd met through a shared interest in martial arts, Devak, also expressed an interest in night game. The problem was both men were rank beginners like myself. What I really needed was to find experienced players I could learn from. The Sarge School guys were hired coaches, so I couldn't expect them to hang out with me. I reached the somewhat naïve conclusion that it would be a good idea to go in search of these people via an "underground" community of Pick Up Artists called *The London Seduction Society*. These men met online in "lairs" to discuss the game and their supposed conquests of women. I assumed that, as it was an exclusive Members Only club, they would be master seducers. This is where the top players congregated to share tips.

You couldn't simply browse the LSS. It was members only. The homepage displayed an online contact form with a series of demographic questions and a space to explain your motivation and why they should accept your application. I crafted my responses carefully, lest they be unimpressed. What if they said no? I could miss out on a once-in-a-lifetime opportunity to learn from London's greatest womanisers.

Two days later an email notified me I was granted permission to browse the LSS message board. I spent a week or so reading forum threads to get a feel for the place. It was bewildering. Sub-forums for Game theory, field reports (after-action reports of talking to girls), product reviews, and an off-topic board mostly about football and politics. Of most interest to me was the meet-ups sub-forum. Members would post requests and availability for wingmen in different cities across the UK.

There were a couple of members in London looking for daygame wings. The most promising-sounding had the online handle of Diego Armando, the real name of the Argentine superstar footballer Maradonna. He explained he'd been daygaming six months and hinted at great success, implying he already had the most hallowed of all Game possessions: a 'harem' of women. I jumped on his request immediately, not wishing to risk another beginner cutting the queue ahead of me in what I presumed must be a busy schedule for Diego. I sent him a direct message explaining my background and my limited qualifications of having approached about sixty girls so far. I didn't hear from him for a couple of days but then, while nodding off during an interminable conference call at the office, my phone vibrated. There was a text message from Diego asking if I wanted to meet. I agreed.

The next evening after work I stood outside Liverpool Street train station watching the rush hour commuters fly past on their way back to the tree-lined suburban streets of Essex. Diego had suggested we meet outside Burger King at the main entrance. I cast my eyes around, trying to decide who the coolest man was, as I knew players were cool. Diego hadn't given me his description. I only now released this was an inconvenient omission.

A tall muscular guy stood by a rubbish bin, smoking. He was a few inches taller than myself, with a light tan and tasteful clothes. He wore a beige wool cardigan over a thin grey t-shirt, and high quality blue jeans. His movements were laconic and purposeful, just as I imagined James Dean or Clark Gable would move should they be found smoking outside a Burger King. I walked towards him but a few seconds before I got there, he looked up at me. I hesitated. Then I realised he was looking past me, over my shoulder. A moment later a pretty girl came rushing past and gave him a hug. They exchanged greetings, he kissed her, and they walked off together.

I shrugged. Evidently not Diego.

There was a skinny shaven-headed Mediterranean guy standing next to him, clad in a cheap grey polyester suit like a mobile phone salesman. He now caught my eye and smiled.

"Are you Nick?" he said. "I'm Diego."

Thus was shattered my first illusion about The London Seduction Society. He was a dork.

We began opening girls around the station. Nothing went anywhere. Most were rushing from one place to another and few were pretty. I did get the number of a twenty-year old Spanish brunette called Irati. Before long Diego and I gave up the street and tried a nearby wine bar. It was a pretentious place, where the wine is "reassuringly expensive" and it's impossible to visualise any of the food dishes merely from reading their menu descriptions. Groups of work colleagues stood around unwinding over a beer or two before their trains home. There were a lot of office girls, hence our presence. They weren't hot, but I wasn't too demanding in my standards.

"Excuse me, I've got a question," I said to a trio of girls near the bar. I'd positioned myself side-on and opened by turning my head to look over my shoulder, exactly as Mystery recommended. "My friend is going to propose to his girlfriend and has asked me which city is more romantic, Paris or New York. What do you think?"

The girls thought about it and gave conflicting answers. They were happy to chat so we continued on a little while, one girl expanding upon her recent business trip to Paris on the Eurostar train. Diego waited until the conversation was rolling, the set has "hooked", in the Game parlance, and then joined us. He seemed overly excitable, talking over the top of me and moving with awkward jerking gestures. I sensed the girls pause, as if reconsidering the wisdom of talking to us. Conversation stopped suddenly, like a YouTube video buffering. I waited expectantly to see how the more experienced Diego would pick up the ball.

He pulled a deck of playing cards out of his back pocket. "Girls, pick a card," he said, fanning them out. I stood slack-jawed in shock.

"You really just happened to have a deck of cards in your back pocket?" asked one girl, laughing at him and, by extension, at me. I groaned inwardly.

This was my introduction into the delusional and downright odd world of pick-up forums. Diego was slavishly emulating Mystery, who was by trade a magician before he got into the game. Mystery was the star of a reality show on VH1 called *The Pickup Artist* and generally considered the father of the seduction community. The key difference between Diego and Mystery is the latter was an actual magician by trade. Diego was a mobile phone salesman working in the Balham branch of Carphone Warehouse. The girls rapidly lost interest and left. Nothing went right and my ill-fated partnership with Diego died that night.

I put this episode down to bad luck, an aberration. A week later I met another LSS guy from the meet-up sub-forum, a Belfast native called Paddy. He was a good guy, in his late twenties, and I liked him. He always looked intense, I'm not sure why considering the Irish Republic Army had long since abandoned their war on England, but he turned out to be fun to hang out with. Paddy and I decided to go out one night to a Shoreditch indie bar called Cargo, a really "hip" place with a noisy dance floor, beer garden, and bar area. The beer garden was great on warm summer nights, crowded with university students and hipster chicks. By the time my friends Steve and Devak joined us we were a pint to the good and soaking up the weekend atmosphere.

Cargo beer garden

We began making the rounds, walking through each room looking for likely girls. As I came back out into the beer garden I spotted two young black girls. It turned out they were Somali sisters, maybe eighteen and nineteen years old respectively. The younger one was built nice with a big ass and big tits. Her hair was long and she was pretty. Her sister less so. Paddy had gone on ahead and already turned a corner, so I start talking to the girls solo.

"Hey ladies. You look like trouble," I said.

"Oh, we're more trouble than you'd think," replied the pretty one, called Hibaq.

Her sister, Haweeyo, gave us both encouraging looks but seemed to know immediately that it was her sister I was interested in. I could tell Hibaq liked me. She was making eye contact and giggling at everything I said, so when Steve came over to help out I suggested we go down the street to another bar called *The Elbow Room* to play pool. PUAs have jargon for everything normal people use everyday words for, and this technique is called the "bounce." It's an early test of the girl's compliance to your leadership and also a demonstration of that ability to lead. If the girl is willing to follow you, she's likely interested.

The Elbow Room had a pleasant 70's retro vibe and a few pool tables.

Pool gave us plenty of excuses for casual touch. Steve and I helped the girls adjust their pool cues, line up shots and so on, allowing a touch of hands or soft, brief pressing together of bodies. This was hardly any more advanced than the seduction techniques seen in a high school disco, really. Hibaq let me kiss her but, perhaps because of my hesitation and lack of assertiveness, she got away that night. I did get her number, and we texted for a while, but I could never get her to commit to a date. After a few weeks it died off.

A month later, Paddy and I were back in Cargo as it was rapidly becoming my favourite nightgame venue due to its open-plan that encouraged mingling, an easy-going atmosphere, and music that didn't reduce us to shouting at each other in monosyllables. It was popular with students so there was decent talent.

The bar area filled up on weekends and we found a spot at the end of a long table, just behind the four-deep crush of revellers ordering drinks. A drunken girl walked towards Paddy and smiled. He instinctively put his hand out; I think originally to shake hers. She took his hand, he pulled her in and started making out with her in a single smooth moment. At this point, Hibaq was the only girl I'd kissed in the nine months since Ioe's trip to Japan. And here was Paddy making out bar centre with a girl he hadn't even met. They broke free and she went on to the toilets. Paddy never saw her again, but I thought it was amazing.

I asked him, "How did you do that?"

He grinned. "I don't know, I just pulled her in for a kiss and it worked."

He was proud of himself, and I was pretty impressed as well. It seems like a small thing now but this was the stage of wide-eyed wonder newbie players can go through. Remember the context: I was thirty-four years old, had never been especially good with women, and I believed whatever window of opportunity I may have once had to pick up hot young women had since slammed shut. Even in my university years that would've been a memorable event, if not quite so impressive. What optimism I possessed was fuelled by the PUA propaganda rather than recent direct personal experience of success.

We headed into the beer garden. Sitting at a table near the back, tucked into a corner, were two familiar faces: Hibaq and Haweeyo. They looked up, their eyes attracted by the motion of us walking out of the door. Hibaq shot me a guilty look, perhaps thinking I'd be mad at her for not replying to my texts. I played along, giving her a parody angry look and wagging my finger at her.

"I knew you were trouble," I admonished. She giggled. Game on.

Paddy and I went sat at their table and chatted for a while. The ease with which we were received suggested Hibaq was still interested so I wanted to isolate her a little, to better monopolise her attention. I turned her away from her sister so that although they sat back-to-back, they were psychologically separated and thus Paddy and I could run two independent conversations. It relieved some of the pressure on Hibaq of having her sister know what she was up to with me.

I pulled her up onto my lap. She was giggly and a little bit drunk. Her thighs were over mine with her lower legs dangling between. The left side of her ass was hanging off the side of my left thigh. I could reach up and grab a handful of ass with my left hand, which is exactly what I did do. The rest of the bar seemed to fade away and I was in a bubble with Hibaq, intensely aware of her perfume and the smell of her shampoo. Wishing to press this situation for maximum advantage I put my face close to hers and dirty talked into her ear. She was regaled in seductive tones about how great her tits looked and the risk of them being taken out right there and mauled in the beer garden.

"I'm going to put your nipples in my mouth and roll my tongue around them until they are rock hard," I said.

"I think they are rock hard already," she giggled, and squirmed her ass on my lap.

As you'll recall, I have strong vocal projection following my sessions with a speech therapist in early childhood. Thus I talked rather louder than I intended. I happened to look up at Paddy and he was laughing. Pretty much half the bar was in on my conversation. Haweeyo sat with her back to us, pretending she hadn't heard a word so as not to embarrass her sister but she writhed uncomfortably at my frequent verbal embellishments.

"I'm so horny" said Hibaq, breathing heavily in my ear. I slipped my hand from her ass to up her skirt from behind. I started fingering her through her panties and along the side where it was skin-to-skin. She draped an arm around my shoulder and squeezed my muscles as she got hotter.

I said, "Let's get out of here."

"I can't. I have to go home with my sister. We live with my parents, I can't stay out."

There was no feasible place to have sex in the bar without getting busted and thrown out. I'd already checked. It seemed that first Game lay may yet elude me.

"How about you suck my cock outside?"

"Okay."

I took her hand and we walked along to the entrance. It was a large glass door with a bouncer standing next to the girl taking admission fees. Paddy and I had arrived before ten o'clock when Cargo was free entry. Now it was close to midnight and they were charging a cover of ten pounds.

"Can you give me a hand stamp to come back," I said, rolling up my jacket sleeve. The doorman shook his head and the girl ignored me completely.

"If you go out, you have to pay to come back in," he said.

"Come on, we're just going to be five minutes, have a really quick smoke and come back in."

Hibaq was holding my hand and leaning against me, her eyes on fire. The doorman couldn't have failed to know he was cock-blocking me but didn't give a shit. If I could just get Hibaq out in the side alley for the blow job, I could probably spin her around and fuck her right there. What a story that would be: banging a nineteen-year-old large-breasted Somali next to the recycling bins and fire escapes in the alleyway behind a bar.

But no, nothing doing.

As I was to learn many times over in the subsequent years, fast lays live or die on momentum and if you come to a screeching halt it's probably lost forever. I should've boldly walked her out, had sex, then figured out the re-entry issue when it arose. Quite likely she'd have gotten into a taxi home with me. At worst, I could've telephoned Paddy to bring Haweeyo out to meet us in another bar later. None of these solutions occurred to me when I needed them. Instead we walked back to the beer garden and an hour later I went home alone. Hibaq and I texted on and off for a while.

One evening she messaged: "Do you want to fuck?"

I replied, "Yes. Kennington station, thirty minutes. Bring your biggest smile." She arrived dressed really nice in a tight skirt and flimsy vest showing lots of cleavage. I walked her directly to my apartment and fucked her on the sofa in the lounge, scoring my first lay.

No.

That's what I *should* have done. What I actually did was reply, "What? Now?"

That reply leaked weak conviction. I waited half an hour and she didn't reply so I called her. I could hear her sister talking in the background. They were giggling. "My sister grabbed my phone and messaged you. Sorry!" said Hibaq. I didn't believe her, I'd just failed a test. I never saw her again.

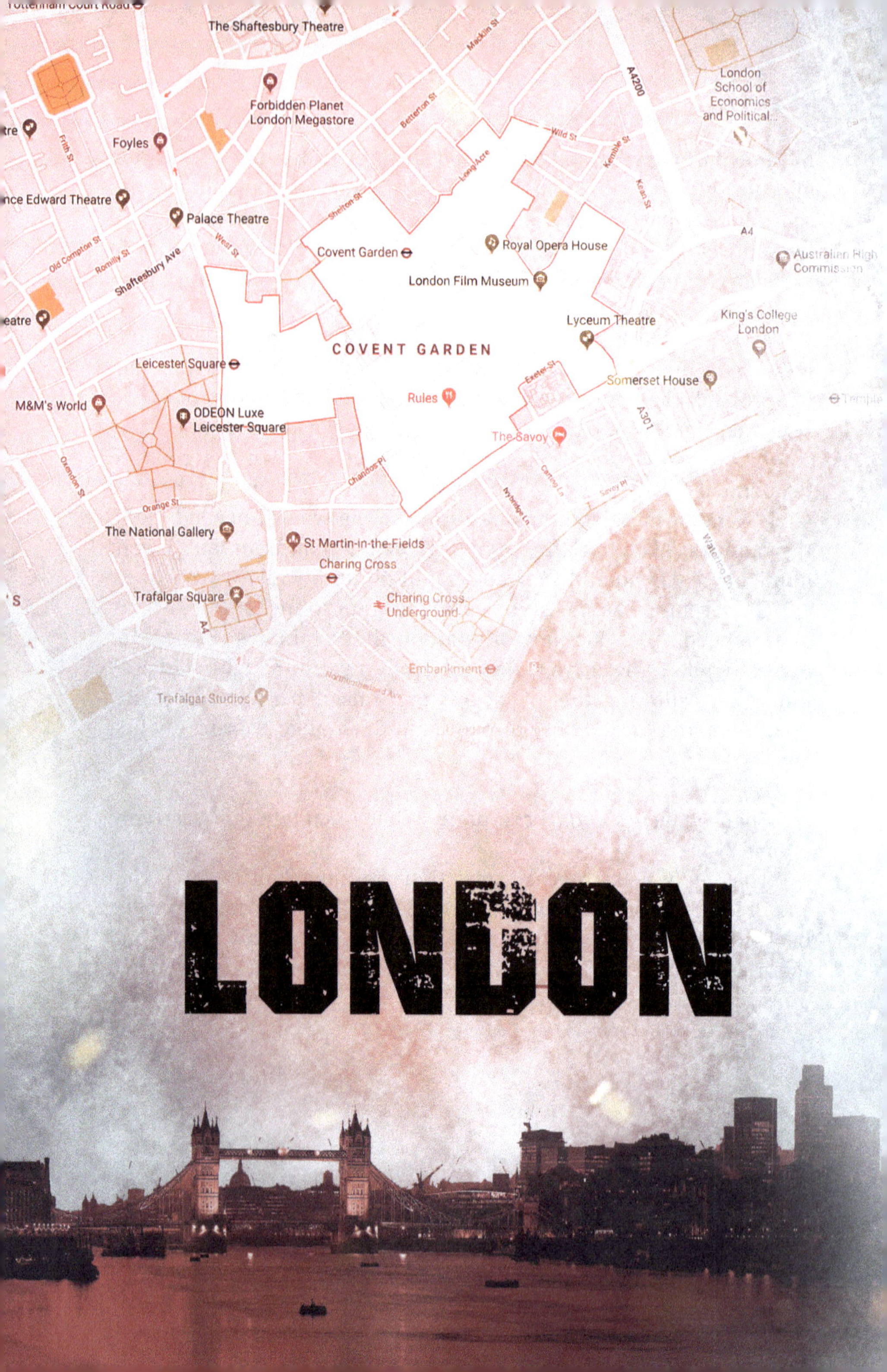
The Shaftesbury Theatre
Forbidden Planet London Megastore
Foyles
Frith St
Macklin St
Betterton St
A4200
London School of Economics and Political...
Wild St
Kemble St
Long Acre
Shelton St
Kean St
Palace Theatre
West St
Old Compton St
Romilly St
Shaftesbury Ave
Covent Garden
Royal Opera House
London Film Museum
A4
Australian High Commission
Lyceum Theatre
King's College London
COVENT GARDEN
Leicester Square
Exeter St
Somerset House
M&M's World
Rules
ODEON Luxe Leicester Square
A301
The Savoy
Chandos Pl
Carting Ln
Nyhridge Ln
Savoy Pl
Oxendon St
Orange St
The National Gallery
St Martin-in-the-Fields
Charing Cross
Waterloo Br
Trafalgar Square
Charing Cross Underground
Embankment
Northumberland Ave
Trafalgar Studios
LONDON

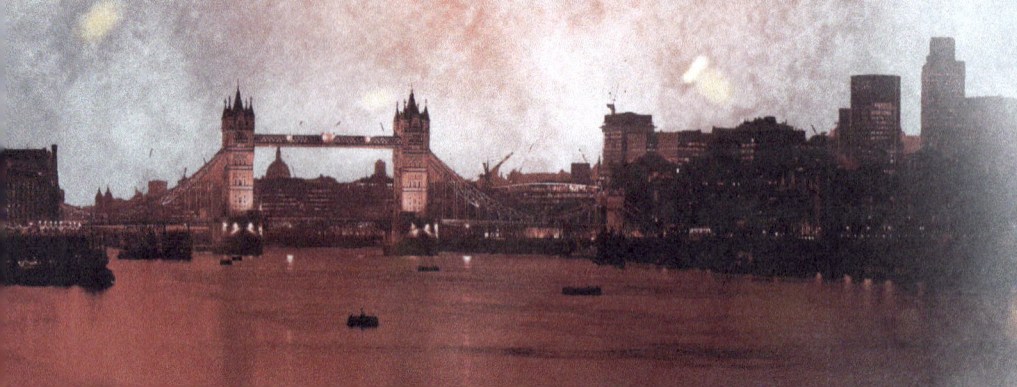

CHAPTER 16

THE DAYGAME GRIND

CHAPTER 16

THE DAYGAME GRIND

When recounting stories it is natural to focus upon the successes, explaining them in detail, and to compress all the boring periods of failure. That's good story-telling. When out in the pub with your friends, it's how to share anecdotes. When the topic is pick-up, this compression can spawn a few misleading consequences. First, it can seem as if the teller is getting laid like gang-busters, fighting the girls off with a shitty stick. Second, the listener can become insanely jealous at the thought everyone is getting laid more than him.

Modern psychologists have coined a term for the emotional pain people suffer if they believe they are missing a trick: Fear Of Missing Out ('FOMO'). Marketers know this and will press your emotional buttons mercilessly. They'll show you a housewife making thousands of pounds every day from her laptop through affiliate marketing, or an average office worker becoming a secret millionaire by investing in crypto-currency. Here is a guy who lost twenty kilos and has a six pack, so why aren't *you* ripped and shredded?

To believe the Internet is to believe everyone is living the high life, except you.

You're the sucker.

Having whet your appetite and preyed upon your insecurity at being the one sucker who doesn't 'get it', the marketer then clears an easy path to success for you, if you'll just sign up to this one-time-only offer (that is closing soon.... tick tock.... tick tock....). Pretty much every spam email that lands in your inbox is based on this psychological quirk, of waving the carrot of simple solutions under your nose. They promise the 'one easy step' to lose weight/get a bigger dick/make your first million/bang hot chicks. Usually their story is that the marketer himself has discovered some kind of new underground secret that "they" (the powers-that-be) don't want you to know and the marketer himself isn't quite sure he should even accept your application to give him your money.

In the case of pick-up, the slimy marketers are *almost* right, but for the wrong reasons.

Most men really are missing a trick with women. There really is a "secret system", and the powers-that-be really don't want you to know it. The part where the PUA marketers tell a fat whopping lie is about it being *one easy step*. It's more accurate to call it several years of pain and struggle. There are no short cuts. We'll expand on this struggle as the book progresses.

But first, let's consider what philosophers of informal logic call the 'availability fallacy.' This is the name of a reasoning error in which we tend to attach higher priority in our deliberations to information readily available to us than to that which is less available. It is usually paired with the 'salience bias' in which information that is vivid, arresting, or emotionally compelling will loom larger in our reasoning process than that which is boring. This is why many people believe terrorism or school shootings are statistically more significant causes of death than falling down stairs or choking on gum. As it relates to pick-up, we tend to over-estimate the frequency of the victory stories people parade in online forums. Failure stories are less interesting, and much harder to find.

FOMO. Availability fallacy. Salience bias.

Combine those three psychological quirks and a naïve beginner can develop a picture of Game that isn't just wildly inaccurate, but is also emotionally painful to face when he isn't having much success himself. I was susceptible to this in reading pick-up forums. If it helps, I'll tell you right now that in the two years of game covered by this volume of my story, I failed with over two thousand women. You'll likely forget that fact before the end of this chapter, unless I hammer it home. As yet, success was thin on the ground. Don't get the impression I would be slaying right-and-left with wild abandon, knocking over girls like bowling pins. For the average-looking man,

Game is a grind. Failure is the base state and successes are rare blips that we cream off the top to form our personal War Stories anthology.

I hit the streets every weekend throughout the summer and autumn of 2009, practising the same direct opener time after time. I'd have liked to mix things up but couldn't find anything better in the Community material and I didn't yet trust myself to competently create my own openers. In any given session I'd talk to between five and twenty girls, taking a couple of numbers and perhaps having an instant date. Sometimes I'd get girls out on dates that would go nowhere.

For example the Spanish girl I met at Liverpool Street, Irati, came out a few times. We had coffee and a beer on the first date but I couldn't get into a position to try to kiss her. A few days later she invited me to walk around Regents Park. By the third date she came out to another pub and I finally kissed her. Somehow I even got her back to my apartment. She found an old 'burusera' Japanese girls school uniform in my wardrobe that Ioe had worn for fancy dress a few times. Irati put it on and skipped around the apartment but every time I grabbed hold of her she'd coquettishly slip from my grasp. She stayed overnight and twice I made out with her in bed and tried to fuck her, but both times she resisted. Confused, I didn't know whether to be more dominant, or to go cold as punishment for her games-playing, or to playfully redirect her and try again later. I never did fuck her.

It was frustrating.

By September I hadn't been laid for eight consecutive months and I'd only kissed two girls. I'd spoken to almost four hundred of them and had a dozen or so dates. It was always the same pattern: They'd turn up to the date keen and then gradually lose interest in direct proportion to how well they got to know me. They'd never seem to be in the correct position for me to go for a kiss and, if I ever tried to bridge the gap, I'd get artfully rebuffed. I pored over forums, books, and instructional videos for answers but couldn't get anything to work.

I thought the problem was with the material and my inadequate mastery of it. I hadn't yet dug deeper into why my results were so underwhelming. Even blind chance should've yielded more success than I was experiencing.

To be fair, there was no good instructional material out there for dates. To the extent that PUA literature gave direct practical advice, it was focused entirely on the initial meeting in the bar or night club. Once you had a girl's phone number you were left to flounder with just a few simple high-level principles as a guide. *The Mystery Method* divided dating up into three stages of Comfort, being in the location you met the girl (C-1), in a date location (C-2), and then at the location you intend to bang her (C-3). It didn't tell you much about what you were supposed to do in each place. That's all changed now, and there's some excellent "date game" material that breaks everything down to micro-level actionable advice. However, in 2009 it was all rubbish and I felt like a rudderless ship.

A1 - OPEN	C1 - CONVERSATION	S1 - FOREPLAY
A2 - FEMALE-TO-MALE INTEREST	C2 - CONNECTION	S2 - LMR
A3 - MALE-TO-FEMALE INTEREST	C3 - INTIMACY	S3 - SEX

ATTRACT			COMFORT			SEDUCE		
A1	A2	A3	C1	C2	C3	S1	S2	S3

The Mystery Method model

My biggest problem, though, was not with the paucity of good advice but rather with my own ineptitude. My confidence was still shot to pieces and I no longer felt like an attractive man. It seemed strange that my divorce would knock me so low for so long, which confirmed in my mind that there were deeper issues only now surfacing. Really, I wasn't in any kind of fit state to be subjecting myself to the pressures of cold-approach pick-up. Nonetheless, I plodded forward, one foot in front of the other. Quitting was unthinkable.

I went on dates thinking I still needed to convince girls to like me, rather than assuming that their presence on the dates already confirmed some attraction. My lack of self-belief would slowly seep out over time, turning the girls off. Broken pieces jangled inside, the after-effects of divorce. Nonetheless, I was impatient to get laid so I kept reading and, eventually, I stumbled upon a blog post which provided a novel solution to my problem of 'escalation'.

It was called the *Apocalypse Opener*.

The writer swore that his was a fool proof method to get laid so long as I did it correctly and with enough girls. Eventually one girl will bite, he assured his readers. I wasn't lacking dedication nor the willingness to try new ideas, no matter how retarded. And believe me, this is a retarded method.

So, how does one employ the Apocalypse Opener?

Approach any girl and follow this simple dialogue pattern:

"Hi, I'm Nick."

"Hi, I'm Girl A," she'll reply.

"What are you up to now?"

"Blah blah, whatever."

Which then sets you up for the (supposedly) killer finish, "would you like to come home with me?"

The key to making it work, according to this anonymous PUA blogger whose madcap advice I was about to follow, is in the boldness of execution. Look the girl dead in the eye and hold your fucking ground. She'll be taken aback and then scrutinise you briefly, alert for any wavering or indecision. And then, sometimes, she'll just agree to follow you home.

Or so he promised.

I liked it.

The escalation was to be done right up front, from the opener, before you've had time to think it through long enough to get nervous. Those readers who have experience with girls, or even just basic social acuity, can likely envision how well the theory translates to the real world. I lacked that acuity, so I was hyped to run up and down Covent Garden trying it out.

Like most pick-up advice, the Apocalypse Opener is best understood as only the beginning of a partially-completed sentence. The instructor says something like, "this really works" when the full sentence written out would be: "This really works... if you're already the sort of man who gets laid quite easily." I wasn't such a man so I tried the Apocalypse Opener twenty times and didn't get laid. Really, what did I expect? I did, however, have one highly memorable encounter, with a sexy Greek ballerina I met walking outside the National Portrait Gallery in Charing Cross.

It was September 5th, a Saturday afternoon, and my mother was visiting London. She was overstaying after a work conference and kept her hotel room near Leicester Square an additional two nights. We met for lunch near Shaftesbury Avenue and for the first time in months my mother raised the topic of my love life.

"Do you see anything of Ioe these days?" she asked.

"No. We met once after I signed the papers in March but it was just to clear up a bit of admin and she gave me a copy of the official divorce notice from the Japanese registry."

"So she went back to Japan?"

"No, she's in London, still working at the airline. I got a letter from Paul last week."

"Paul? The lad you lived with at university."

"Yes. I didn't see him much since I came back from Japan. He got divorced from that bi-polar Dutch girl and then lived in a Buddhist commune in Bethnal Green for a couple of years. He just dropped out of contact with the rest of us. Only Yasin ever saw him, because they go way back to primary school together."

Paul and I had been best friends in the second and third years at university and he'd been one of our social circle in London following graduation, as described earlier. Most of us had office jobs but he tried to run his own graphic design agency with an attached art gallery. The latter closed but he still made his living working design contracts for London councils. He'd already suffered two terribly disheartening experiences with girls. He'd first been engaged to a hot girl at the tail end of university but she cheated on him two months before the wedding then dumped him. His second fiancée, a mentally ill Dutch girl, had unravelled quickly leading to their divorce. Since his spiritual turn, he stayed clear of women and old friends.

"Oh, I see," said my mum. "How's he getting on?"

"I can't remember if I told you, but he's been in love with Ioe since I first met her in 1999. He didn't try it on or anything but we all knew it, including Ioe herself."

"No, you never mentioned it. How odd."

"He always dated small slim girls, so that probably had something to do with it. He was popular with girls at university. They liked his Jarvis Cocker indie look and he's pretty funny with a few beers in him."

"So why did he write to you?" asked my mum, no doubt starting to piece together the puzzle I was patiently laying before her piece by piece.

"Well, he didn't hang around after our divorce. I think he felt his ship had finally come in so he got with Ioe. He wrote me a polite letter saying he and Ioe have begun a serious relationship and he hopes it's not a problem for me."

"Is it?"

"No. I'd have been bothered about it a few months ago, but it doesn't mean anything now."

This wasn't entirely true as I was still quite sensitive on the topic, but didn't want to worry my mother by letting her know how broken I still felt. I'd come to suspect Ioe had struck up contact with Paul before the end of our marriage, after she mentally checked out of our relationship, but I had no evidence either way and saw no reason to ask now. It wouldn't have made a difference, because the critical fact was that our marriage had broken down due to its own internal problems.

Was I gutted that my former university best friend was now, thirteen years later, dating my ex-wife? Conversely, did I look down on him for taking my washed-up sloppy seconds after I'd already done such filthy things to her while she was still young and hot? It really depended which mood you caught me in, so I suppose both were true. Fortunately, my mother never thought to ask.

"What a bitch," said my mum. "I always thought she was needy, but jumping in with the nearest man as soon as she's alone is just.... desperate." I didn't think of it that way, and still don't, but I liked to hear it nonetheless. Thanks mum. "Do you have a new girlfriend?"

"No, but I'm starting to look for one. I've begun chatting up girls again, in bars and coffee shops but nothing solid has materialised as yet."

"Oh good, you need to get back in the saddle."

After lunch, she went off sight-seeing while I met up with an Indian man called Sai who had been winging with me recently. He taught the daygame portion of *PUA Training* boot camps. I wanted to squeeze in an hour's street work. The very first girl I stopped was the aforementioned Greek dancer. Eugenia had shoulder-length brown hair, slim muscular legs, and wore denim shorts. I got in front of her and prepared to unleash the apocalypse.

"Hi! I had to stop you. You're gorgeous."

She smiled, muttered thanks.

"What are you up to now?"

"A bit of shopping."

Deep breath, gut check and...... pull the trigger! "Would you like to come home with me?"

Eugenia smiled, taken aback. For a moment she just blinked, and stared.

"No."

"Um... okay. Is that coffee from Pret?" I asked, looking down at a cup in her hand. It was. "Cool. I normally go to Starbucks myself. I like the daily roast though, to be honest, if I'm gonna spend a long time in a cafe I normally do Caffè Nero because they have those lovely distressed leather sofas." Then I prattled on a while in this vein.

Eugenia took it all in her stride. "Come and walk with me," she suggested and we headed down to Trafalgar Square. She was pleasant, asking what possessed me to be so bold, and do I do this much. Though I withheld the sheer scale of my approaching (and subsequent failure-rate) I wanted to be honest.

"I'm a direct person. When a man approaches a woman it's always based on a sexual dynamic. I see no reason to try to sneak in under her radar."

"You could perhaps approach it in a more roundabout manner, though."

"Yeah, I suppose, but that's not me. Give me some feedback then. How did you feel when I said that?"

She smiled again. "It was kinda shocking... but cool."

Eugenia was probably still on the fence at this moment. She was intrigued by me and appeared to feel some attraction. The question was whether I could build on the strong introduction or would let my house of cards collapse yet again. Ever the motor-mouth, I overdid the honesty angle, "It looked simple but there's a lot going on there. When a man stops a woman he's got to demonstrate value without scaring her or being creepy. It could've sounded really weird, but instead I was just putting the option out there. I wasn't trying to persuade you to have sex. I put it out there as non-needy. I like sex, but I don't need it."

I did need it, so perhaps my honesty had limits after all.

We swapped numbers and after she walked off she called me two minutes later to check that she had the right number stored. She briefly mentioned a boyfriend, in passing, and that she lived in Covent Garden, and soon rang off. I'd planned to meet Sai in Tiger Tiger nightclub later that evening. Eugenia and I swapped texts the rest of the day:

"You're still thinking about it," I wrote.

"A little! Doesn't happen often in London!"

"But all the time in Greece? I'm at Tiger Tiger."

"Yea, Greece is a little bit different. I've just hopped into the bath..."

"Bath texting? You're weird"

"Thanks... multi-tasking? lol. ur in a bar with ur mate and ur texting... that's equally weird. lol"

"Make sure you soap yourself properly."

"Thanks for the tip, couldn't have done it without u. lol"

"I'm helpful like that."

My house of cards still stood but I wasn't sure how to move things ahead. I tried to comprehend the subtext of this interaction, looking for guidance. Girls have a dual mating strategy that is commonly summarised as "Alpha-fucks/Beta-bucks". This means they pursue both high quality male DNA from hot men and also long-term protection and provision from nice guys. Ideally the same man would supply both, but in practice nobody is kidding themselves. This dual strategy is what gives the player his way in. My 'apocalypse' proposition to Eugenia had identified me as the consequence-free adventure sex guy, potentially at least, and she was showing herself amenable to a secret liaison. She felt the usual trepidation and cautiousness before proceeding, and hadn't yet ascertained if I really was *that guy*.

I left it for the week and then on Thursday a hot Colombian girl stood me up on an early evening date. Disappointed by the rejection, I searched my phone for active leads. I called Eugenia. She picked up right away and after a five minute chat she invited me to Bar Salsa saying her male friend was teaching there but she wasn't dancing, so why didn't I join her for a drink? I should've agreed but I didn't have the confidence to enter her territory and still hold my frame. Remembering my awkward salsa experiences earlier in the year, I envisioned myself being tooled by more charismatic men who knew everyone in the class. I'd be excluded from the conversations she had with her friends and God knows what other silly social nightmares.

Outside Tiger Tiger

It was a mistake. I should've thrown myself into the mix to see what happened.

I went to Cargo the following evening and fell into a late-night text exchange with Eugenia. This time I tried to follow PUA text game advice. I considered my interactions with girls to be practical learning opportunities. Uppermost on my mind that evening was a maxim I'd read from a blog called *Roissy In D.C.* The writer advised sending only those text messages which you'd be comfortable having appear on a jumbotron screen in front of the whole world. Meaning, if you're ashamed of people seeing your text game, it must be weak.

So, with Roissy in mind, I wrote simply, "Old Street tonight."

"I'm off to the cinema tonight but could meet up later if ur around, " she replied.

My heart leapt with excitement but I admonished myself not to show it. I showed the message to Devak, who stood next to me drinking beer. He nodded approvingly as I wrote, "Yeah, that's a plan. Text me when you're done."

"OK."

Later she was done and messaged, "would you like to meet in Covent Garden or is it too late for you?"

It was 11pm. I called her up. She was back at her apartment, chilling. I said I'd be finished with my friends at midnight and then I'd call to arrange to go over to her place. Midnight came, I called and she didn't pick up. I tried again and still the phone rang off. Getting desperate I texted, "hey" to no response.

Fuck.

At 11am the next morning, far too late to be useful to man or beast, she replied, "Hey Nick — I'm so sorry about last night! I fell asleep in front of the tv, didn't realise how tired I was."

Shakespeare's *Julius Caesar*, in a speech by Brutus in Act IV, gives a beautiful conception of game: "There is a tide in the affairs of men, which taken at the flood leads on to fortune..." Whereas the nice guy is omnipresent with his provision of attention and resources (Eugenia was living with her boyfriend) the girl's adventure needs rise and fall like the tide- and specifically with her monthly ovulation window. She'll only have a tiny window within which motive, method, and opportunity are aligned to sneak out for adventure sex. As a player you need to be alert for that and take her at the flood. I lacked the wherewithal to pull it off. I should've given some spurious reason to declare myself available at 11pm and then gone straight over to Eugenia's place. Instead I'd dithered and given bad luck an opportunity to intervene.

I'd missed my chance. Again.

Though I'd failed to capitalise on late-night momentum, Eugenia hadn't completely dropped off the hook. She still liked me. We arranged a date for later in the afternoon. I was already in town, sitting in Caffè Nero off Covent Garden reading Ayn Rand's *The Fountainhead*, a book Real Social Dynamics recommended to improve my mindset. I wanted to meet Eugenia while in a relaxed self-amused state. Dates felt like sitting a maths exam and I always needed to micro-manage my mood so as not to let girls know how anxious and timid I really felt.

Eugenia arrived and we sat outside in the sun. I was leaning back, trying to show "alpha" body language. We connected instantly. I really liked this girl. She was smart, self-assured, and much prettier than I had first realised. It turned out she was a model and had recently begun posing naked for artists. She was also a dancer. We chatted a lot, and I kept with the authentic honesty, something I'd been focused on lately. This was during the period of my voracious reading of all things seduction and psychological, so I'd also gotten a book on speed-reading people. We discussed that and Eugenia really lit up when I outlined her character according to the book's personality model.

"Let's walk to St James' Park" she suggested, so off we went.

I knew I ought to be introducing natural touching, to create a man-woman vibe, but nothing felt at all natural about it. Rather, I fell back on 'kino' advice I'd read in the PUA books. I began with her upper arm, pulling her in with my arm around her shoulders, and later around her waist. She pleasantly stayed comfortably close but didn't respond by putting her arms around me, which is usually a bad sign. Again this was something of a calibration error from me. It's generally a bad idea for the "secret sex" guy to be touching his girl in public, that's exposing her to the risk of being caught, and undermining the whole secret society vibe. Except for fleeting moments to spike her energy levels, touching should be restricted to private environments.

That said, it was equally possible she had already decided to friend-zone me and her resistance to reciprocating my touch was for that reason rather than any fear of being busted.

I ended up talking about my interest in social dynamics and about the alpha/beta/omega male hierarchy, and sexual chemistry. She was going along with it all. I teased a bit, we joked. It felt very, very pleasant. I felt totally relaxed as if there was no judging between us, and I wasn't trying to make a big deal out of the meeting. Sadly, that was part of the problem. I'd fallen into a trap that catches almost every beginner, that of explicitly telling a girl about Game techniques in the hope she'll be impressed with your knowledge. Seduction is like sausages. Diners don't want to know how they are made. They just wish to enjoy the delicious taste of the final product.

I was unwittingly collapsing my own house of cards.

This experience would be the beginnings of a flavour I'd later add to my pick-ups successfully, but being considerably more subtle about it. I was trying to be as authentic and radically honest as possible, even overtly discussing the nature of male-female interactions. Done properly, we call it "breaking the fourth wall", after Berthol Brecht's theorising about the relationship between theatre performers and their audience. Experienced players can escalate a girl by openly telling her they're seducing her. However, beginners like myself will only get themselves into a tangle.

Three hours in, we were sitting outside another cafe when I fumbled a key test. I tried to pull Eugenia in and she resisted. She put down her sandwich, looked me in the eye and said, "You know I have a boyfriend?"

Ah!, I thought. I've read a good answer to this on the Internet! I held her gaze and with a low even voice replied, "I don't care."

The effect wasn't what I'd hoped. She took a few bites of her sandwich then told me, "Well I do. It's his flat I live in. I just don't want to mislead you."

I tried to keep a brave face, but I was crushed. I'd thought I was in. This was a beautiful, smart girl, a dancer, and the very first thing I'd said to her was a proposition for sex. I'd been friend-zoned from the Apocalypse Opener... just let that sink in for a moment.

I'd had my chance and blown it, so there was no one to blame but myself. Eugenia had asked me to walk with her a minute after my opening proposition, she'd invited me out to a bar, she'd invited me to her home late at night while her boyfriend was out (but fell asleep, so at least that failure wasn't so much my fault), and then accepted another date to walk around the park. She wanted adventure, sounded me out as a potential partner in crime, and I'd come up short. I'd even misread her final test about the boyfriend. Even at that late point in the interaction if I'd had a stronger sense of entitlement and stronger escalation skills I could've taken control and gotten back on track.

The grind continued all through September.

I took a week off work so as to spend ten straight days daygaming, ten sets a day minimum. There'd been too much half-assing so I told myself I needed 'massive action'. There was a constant battle between my stated objectives and my emotional state which could leave me exhausted before I'd even found a girl to approach. Deep in my gut churned a sickening dread at being blown out by a procession of girls and perhaps of peering into the abyss, that I'd never get good at this. Eugenia had inadvertently knocked my confidence. To fight it, I wrangled every scrap of my willpower to overrule my reticence and force myself onto the streets. So every day that week of vacation, I followed the same ritual, trying to impose the illusion of control onto the scenario.

I'd begin in the same Caffè Nero, on a street corner between The Strand and Covent Garden. My routine began gently, to ease myself into the task ahead. Usually I sat on the big brown leather sofa at the back of the room, watching RSD's *The Blueprint Decoded* instructional videos on my laptop. In time, the words of speaker Owen Cook would lift up my spirits and eventually the combined forces of my sexual desire and my desperation overcame the countervailing forces of anxiety and lethargy.

F-18 fighter pilot level game

The first day of my mini-sabbatical was Monday, September 14th. My mind was full of big plans and motivational self-talk. *No excuses*, I told myself, *I'm going to turbocharge my statistics on total approaches*. It didn't matter how I felt, or if my wings were busy, I'd go solo and just plough through the headwinds. Received wisdom in the community is you are a beginner until you've cold-approached one thousand girls. You need a certain amount of face-time in front of pretty girls just before your hands stop shaking. It can take hundreds of interactions before you are calm enough to see what signals the girl is giving you. I was at the four hundred mark and very impatient to improve. Having a full-time job restricted my daygame to weekends so the solution seemed obvious: take time off work.

That Monday, it was still not quite lunch time and Covent Garden was deserted. Until the streets perked up, it didn't feel like avoidance to stay in my chair. Finally, I stepped outside and almost bumped into a hot Belgian dancer. I opened weakly, but she still stopped and chatted. She was in a hurry to get to the Pineapple Studio for a dance class. I knew something about that, because Ioe had often trained there, so I rambled on about dance, contemporary dance, how my dancer-ex had a careless grace in her movements from all the dancing. Blah, blah, blah. The Belgian wasn't interested, and my attempt to take her number led to an awkward refusal.

It only took me a few minutes to shrug that off, and then I saw a dusky Mediterranean girl walking through the market. She stopped briefly but either didn't speak English or was seriously unimpressed with me. She smiled, waved her hand dismissively, and disappeared without a word. Next I approached an English girl carrying shopping boxes. She didn't stop, but smiled, thanked me, and said she was late getting back to work. A fourth girl stopped but the conversation petered out fast.

I could feel the physiological effect of the daygame. Damn. My forehead actually felt tight, such was my poor state. The skin was too tight for the size of my skull. I've since learned this feeling is a way to recognise when I'm pulling the "creepy face" caused by poor state.

I persevered.

On Shaftesbury Avenue, just past Forbidden Planet comic store, an Asian girl came towards me. She was young and had just started her first day as an intern in a fashion magazine. We chatted a bit. I was too talky and too outcome dependent, but she didn't seem to care. She checked the text she was writing as I approached, so I told her off for not paying attention. She giggled and twirled her hair. I made a mental note to self: set arbitrary boundaries and playfully tell a girl off for breaching them. She gave me her number but never replied to my texts.

I got myself blown out a few more times on Oxford Street before a hot English girl gave me her Facebook details. It was weird because the whole time I was thinking she wanted to excuse herself, and

I was struggling and talking into the space, yet it was five minutes or more in conversation and after getting her Facebook I kept her another few minutes talking about her Geography Uni course she was about to start. It didn't go anywhere but I was increasingly realising girls often enjoy chatting even when it requires them to artfully deflect your sexual advances. As a man, that seemed like an alien attitude. I couldn't imagine talking to a female stranger I wasn't attracted to. Surely that's just a waste of everybody's time?

It's common for beginners to think the length of the interaction is directly related to how strong the resulting contact details will be. This isn't correct. Ultimately, a player is trying to create a particular emotional impression upon the girl while also ticking off checkboxes marking particular signals she needs to give him to show she is both available and into him. If you accomplish that in two minutes the number will be stronger than if you dither around chatting for twenty minutes but fail to accomplish it. So while advanced daygamers can quickly take solid numbers (or eject when one isn't forthcoming) it's common to see beginners getting dragged into overly-long socially polite conversations that go nowhere.

That was me, in this case, talking forever with a girl who wasn't interested.

My last approach of the day was a gloriously pleasant failure. I opened a hot Lithuanian at the top of Carnaby Street, on the corner of the famous Liberty department store. She was ambling around aimlessly, which I took as a generalised invitation to any man bold enough to try it on. My forehead still felt tight and I could swear I was developing a fever. My vibe was horrible but I was determined to press on and grind out all ten sets I'd promised myself. I'd already done nine.

The Lithuanian stopped, smiled, hair twirled, and indulged me for ten minutes. Although I'd opened quite strongly, I could sense the interaction derailing like a runaway train. I continued to lose my confidence entirely of my own accord, unrelated to her reactions which were actually quite positive. It became a self-fulfilling prophecy as I told myself I was making a hash of it, which piled more pressure on me and thus caused mounting problems. The girl's face began to take on a sympathetic cast, like she was watching a lame dog try to chase a rabbit. Finally, she put me down, humanely.

"I have to go now, it was nice talking to you," she said.
"Let's go out sometime for.... I dunno.. coffee. Or tea. Or a drink."
"I don't want to exchange details."

Fair enough, on that performance she really shouldn't have. Smart girl.

The first day of my daygame sabbatical resulted in my talking to ten girls, which had netted me two worthless contact details. Neither of those two girls replied to me. For the next nine days I'd analyse my work and write extensive notes to summarise my learning points. Self-diagnosis is a crucial skill for seducers because no-one else is going to help you. Quoting my notes verbatim, this is what I felt I'd learned:

I felt crap but took right action anyway. Good work.

Even with shit state I still had good enough fundamentals to get one decent number.

I didn't worry too much opening sets. The poor state was once in-set. Only a few months ago I wouldn't even open five sets when in good state.

While in set I knew consciously all the mistakes I was making, even as I couldn't stop making them. The biggest one was outcome dependence. I really wanted to get numbers and was worried the girls would walk away and leave me feeling shit.

Lesson learned. Back out tomorrow.

The week of my game sabbatical was also when *The London Seduction Society* held a seminar at Tower Bridge called "game for men over thirty-five". It was organised by a older gentleman called Curran. As he described it in his forum post announcing the talk, it seemed perfectly pitched to me. Amusingly, I was so lacking in entitlement that I worried I'd be refused entry because at the time I was thirty-four and thus a year too young. I emailed Curran a few days before to ask if it was okay to come. As if they'd check my passport and throw me out!

The event was held in an upstairs function room of a pub by the famous Tower Bridge over the river, on a Saturday afternoon. On my walk along the South Bank of the river from Waterloo I approached three girls and all three gave me their phone number, including a very attractive French student on her way to dance school. "Three in three," I told myself, proud of a meaningless statistic. It did put me in a tangibly better mood for the talk.

About thirty older gentleman packed the pews, several rows of folding metal chairs, while a short ginger guy called London Playboy gave a talk.

"I'm thirty-three, ginger, and ugly," he said. Having not seen his birth certificate I couldn't verify the first point, but the others were self-evident. "And yet, I often date girls in their twenties. Let me tell you about my first Game experience with a younger girl." He then related a story about opening a nineteen-year-old PR tout in Leicester Square one evening, an English girl he banged a week later.

"It blew my mind. I was lying in bed with her afterwards thinking how odd it was to have a pretty teenage girl cuddled up to me. We call these 'reference experiences'. They are examples, facts, from your own life that gradually convince your subconscious that such things can happen, and are natural. Right now you don't have any, but you will."

The recurring theme throughout London Playboy's talk was *nothing is ever a big deal*. An older man is expected to be emotionally stable, and sure of himself. Don't let anything rattle you. It doesn't matter if a girl gives you stinky-face on the opener, doesn't reply to texts, or stands you up on a date. Nothing is ever a big deal. Just keep moving forward with your life plan.

Next on was the event organiser Curran. He was a muscular brown man, probably British-Indian I thought, dressed tastefully like a poster model of M&S but with a couple of rings and a pendant that hinted at bad-boy. He looked cool and projected the gravitas I lacked and desperately wanted. I don't remember anything from his talk, except that it was reassuring. Perhaps I wasn't so crazy to try to chase girls in their youthful sexual primes. In an unusual twist of fate, I'd next see Curran nine years later — 2018 — when he was my daygame client in Belgrade, Serbia. Shortly after his LSS talk, he got into a long term relationship and contacted me years later when wanting to get back into the game.

The third and final speaker was a thirty-year old lanky Scotsman called Colin who had a good reputation on the LSS forum writing under the online pseudonym of Skeletor. People often called him the "Yoda" of game because his posts were packed with detail, practical advice, and wisdom. At the time I was very impressed with his presentation about identity and how to change it. He worked with a licensed clinical psychologist and together they'd developed a pick-up system called *The Harmony Model*. I tried to get pally with him afterwards on his smoke-break but there was a ring of eager older gents two-deep around him that I couldn't penetrate.

I was still just another chump, and no-one paid any particular attention to me that afternoon.

Fortunately, I wasn't completely ignored by other experienced players. Two months after the Sarge School boot camp, I signed up for their 'advanced' program. The schedule was the same as before, early evening seminars on Friday and Saturday before hitting the bars, but the material was more involved and assumed more prior experience. This time it was held at a small private members bar in Covent Garden called *Crazy Bear*. The two talks I remember best were Tony T on masculine and feminine polarity, and Ace, a young Polish university student, on what he called "douchebag game". That meant being a playfully entertaining asshole. Both talks impressed me favourably and I wondered if there was any end to the breadth and depth of Game theory. We walked to Jewel Bar in Piccadilly again, doing warm up sets on the way. I must've shown some improvement from last time because Jimmy commented favourably on my street stops.

Drawing into Jewel Bar, there were three other lads waiting for us. Perry and Diamond I recognised from the beginners boot camp but the third guy was new. He was a thickly-set chubby Australian called Mick. He looked like a rugby centre who'd rediscovered a hearty appetite which, ironically, wasn't far from the truth. Jimmy went up to him and at first I thought they were good friends.

"Hey Mick, you fat Aussie cunt," he said. "Keep an eye on this bald Geordie bastard, will you?" and winked at me. I felt oddly special, being sufficiently important for Jimmy to playfully insult me. Mick and I shook hands.

"Have you known Jimmy long?" I asked.

"Not really. I did a Sarge School boot camp a month ago. We got on, so he invited me to this one to help approach coach."

After the second day of boot camp, Jimmy invited both of us to the after party with the other coaches at another private members bar in Soho called *Milk & Honey*. I felt like I was being initiated into an underground society. The ground floor bar was dark and shiny with booths to hold a dozen people each. Mostly I listened as the Sarge School lads cracked on with each other. They were friendly to me but I didn't have anything in common I felt comfortable talking about.

The next week, Jimmy emailed me asking if I wanted to join them the next weekend in Old Street for some drinking and skirt-chasing. I eagerly accepted. It gradually became clear that Jimmy was a leader of men and always had an eye towards recruiting new lads for his group. That Saturday afternoon I was in Covent Garden for daygame and bumped into Johnny coaching a student so we had a short chat. I didn't realise it at the time but word had gotten around Sarge School that I was very dedicated to Game, so they kept an eye on me from afar.

That night we all went drinking in Old Street and did some sets together. Tony made out with some girl who literally walked up to him and draped her arms around him before he'd spoken.

"Doesn't he need to open?" I asked, incredulous, to Mick who was standing next to me.

"It's bizarre. He just oozes masculinity. I've seen it happen a couple of times now, while us jokers are running around asking who wants to go to Paris or New York."

At the end of the night Jimmy suggested we get a taxi home together, as we both lived in Kennington. While sitting on a bench in Old Street waiting for the minicab, he waxed lyrically about Game. "I used to bang a lot of birds at university but it was crude stuff. I just took my gang into the student union pub, acted like a dick, and then looked around to see if any girls liked me. This Game stuff is different. It's controlled. It's artful. When I read *The Mystery Method* it blew me away. It was what I'd been looking for all those years, a studied, controllable system to chase after the top levels of skirt."

I nodded, soaking it all up.

"That's what I'm in it for," he added. "Top draw tottie. I've banged enough normal birds."

Jimmy gradually drew me into the Sarge School social circle, as he did Mick and the Aussie's good-looking young flatmate Lee. As November approached, he included me on an email chain with the team about a mooted trip to Malaga in the south of Spain.

"We should be expanding our horizons, lads. Chasing skirt in London is all well and good but what we need is a holiday. I bought my dad a flat in Malaga and it's empty right now. Let's all pile into it for a week, drink port, eat tapas, and chase the Spanish talent."

I couldn't believe I was getting invited. I *never* got invited to cool stuff, because I wasn't cool. Never in my life had I seen a gang as cool as Jimmy's Sarge School and now they wanted me to join them on the type of trip of which legends are made? Unbelievable. I walked into my bosses office and submitted a holiday request which was approved the same day. We all booked flights to Malaga.

Walking down Malaga high street
with my new friends

It was a great holiday. We travelled out to Gatwick airport together, started drinking in the airport bar, and then continued in a seaside bar under a hot Spanish sun while we waited for the local train from Malaga central to the suburb we were staying in. The Sarge School guys treated Mick, Lee and I as one of the gang — sometimes painfully so, as we were the butt of many jokes. For example, I showed Johnny my new business card. He took it, looked at it, then dismissively tossed it to the floor to rapturous applause.

"Lol, has Ace been teaching you Douchebag Game?" said Tony. It took me a while to get used to the ribbing, though it was all good-natured. I was still a bit fragile and simply didn't feel as cool as the others.

We spent several days touring the small tapas bars, usually on Jimmy's personal recommendations, then spent a few hours on or around the main pedestrian street chasing skirt or drinking in bars. Despite the season, it was wonderfully warm by the Mediterranean. I did lots of sets and quite impressed the lads with my improvement, though it was still clumsy stuff. On the last day, back in the apartment, Jimmy broke out a special bottle of port and made a big show of bringing his laptop in, setting it on a shelf.

"Lads, big announcement time." he said. We hushed and I got the feeling everyone knew what was going on, except for me, Mick and Lee. Jimmy opened his web browser and typed in the url of the Sarge School website, which was still a simple DIY site. He clicked the tab for "team."

Celebrating my initiation into Sarge School

I saw my photo there, mid-way down the list of coaches. Written next to it was "Nick Krauser, daygame." I looked over at Johnny and he nodded, as I realised he'd been instrumental in recommending me to the group. Mick and Lee were equally pleased to see themselves listed.

"After considerable thought," continued Jimmy, "and much discussion amongst the team, we have decided to lower our standards so far that these useless dickheads," and he swept his hand in a wide arc to encompass the new lads, "are now on the team. Welcome to Sarge School."

Tony poured a tot of the port into the lined-up glasses and handed them around. We raised the glasses for a toast and necked them. I'd been accepted into the fold.

I was awfully happy.

CHAPTER 17

NIGERIAN NURSE

My feet ached. I'd been walking around Central London for hours.

The inner lining of my brown biker boots had ripped away. A small curtain of loose fabric had folded over and was pressing uncomfortably against my ankle. The heel of my left boot was asymmetrically worn down after many weeks pounding the streets. I stepped on a loose paving slab and the rainwater pooled underneath splashed up as it wobbled underfoot, flooding my boot.

By way of reaction, I accessed that part of my brain which stores a man's accumulated vocabulary, mentally seeking the perfect words to express my frustration, as eloquently as my post-graduate education could furnish.

"Cunt!" I said.

These are the trivial annoyances of winter daygame. I wiggled my toes inside my newly-wetted sock. Prowling busy shopping streets to pick up beautiful women gets tougher when the weather turns. I'd been out four consecutive days through wind, rain, and snow. It was beginning to wear on me.

Covent Garden was wet and dreary. Now that I'd been daygaming half the year, and posting field reports on the LSS forum, I'd acquired a minor local notoriety. You could count the number of London daygamers on the fingers of one hand, so the LSS's rising opinion of me was based less upon my daygame ability than it was on the fact I was one of the few men even attempting it. Several forum members sent me direct messages asking if I would coach them. Having not yet been laid at all, I couldn't claim any special qualifications as coach. However, in the land of the subhuman, the half-man is king. At least I didn't charge money for it.

Today I had an enthusiastic young university student in tow. He was skinny, nerdy, socially awkward with an unkempt shock of black hair combed unconvincingly over a thinning crown. The kind of man you'd expect gets laid maybe once a year maximum, with a girl he'd rather not show off to his friends. He was upbeat and anxious to learn, so I was happy taking him around for free. I'd opened nearly one thousand girls by now and was at least getting some dates, so by the low standards of the LSS loser's club, I was a star. Sadly, the rest of the world wasn't so admiring.

A cold gust of wind froze me to my marrow. I pulled up the collar of my fur-lined flight jacket and pulled my woolly hat down to my eyebrows. I jammed my numbed hands deep into my pockets. It was December 30th. 2009. A cold, damp typically wintry London day, with New Year just around the corner. Christmas decorations still cluttered store windows, long streams of golden tinsel framing displays of snowmen and reindeer. As dusk approached, the fairy lights adorning lampposts and street signs twinkled in the deeply reddening sky. Everywhere I turned people were milling, jostling, and scurrying for that last sale item. Some rushed purposefully to and from their destinations as others strolled along dreamily, shopping the stores with their eyes, or watching as the street performers put on a show for their pleasure and tips. Lovers strolled hand-in-hand and looked at the sights. Japanese tourists with comically oversized cameras took pictures of everything.

This seasonal fauna of street life passed me by in a blur. My attention was focused on the fold of cotton pressing awkwardly against my ankle, creating a blister, and my wet socks. I wondered whether I should find a bench where I could take off my boots and readjust. Little things loom large when daygaming due to the high pressure of the activity.

Eight months and one thousand sets had sold me on daygame even though tangible results weren't as yet forthcoming. I loved that there was an art to meeting a girl in a public place and getting her number, perhaps taking her for a coffee there and then. For most men cold approach is a strange, intimidating but fantastically

Winter in Covent Garden

liberating experience; imagine walking around the streets scanning for pretty girls and then, when you see one, you just walk up and make a conversation from nothing. Make her laugh, make her curious, and hopefully bang her a few days or weeks later. For a man conditioned that bars, nightclubs, and Internet dating sites are the only places to meet women this is an eye-opening thought.

Any girl. Anywhere. Any time.

If only I could perfect that "bang her a few days or weeks later" bit.

The early stages of seduction were working out just fine by now. Though I'd yet to get laid, I'd developed some basic competence in drawing girls into conversation and getting phone numbers. Sometimes the girls would even come on a date, and a few times I'd kissed them and even almost banged them. I had reasons to be hopeful, that if I persevered I'd put the final pieces into place in the seduction jigsaw. As we are wont to do when New Year approaches, I took stock of my progress. Was I headed in the right direction? I'd initially promised myself a six-month commitment to Game: to see if it worked and, specifically, if I could learn it.

So how was it working out?

I thought back to Tony Clink's *The Lay Guide*. A gaudy red book with cover art of a slick lounge-lizard guy surrounded by beautiful women. Tony had promised me a secret system to meet and attract women, sleeping with different girls every week. So far I hadn't slept with any. Yet I had stored up a hundred reference experiences of pretty young women showing happiness, animation, and sometimes even sexual attraction when talking to me. I no longer doubted I was on the right track. Better than that, I was getting outside to walk around, see London, and had made a few interesting new friends. It felt like I was taking action.

As my student and I strolled through the busy streets of Covent Garden, talking to a girl here and there, I heard a voice flutter in the wind behind me. A sweet, feminine, melodic voice seemed to tinkle like water in a mountain stream. It was so sweet and uplifting. I turned to look and behind me walked a pretty young black girl. She was wearing a set of headphones, singing along with her music. I smiled and turned back to my student, and almost at once wondered what I was waiting for. I couldn't ignore this opportunity. Today I may be the coach, but I was still in the game for myself, and she looked like someone that I'd rather like to get acquainted with, on a horizontal and naked basis.

Turning back, I motioned her to take off the headphones. She gave me a wide-eyed inquisitive look but obediently took the buds out her ears and returned my smile.

"Did you really just start singing in the street?" I said.

She smiled again and giggled. "Yeah, I like this song."

Her brown eyes were large and her long hair hung in curls to her shoulders. She looked to be in her mid-twenties. I would find out later that she was twenty-six. My eyes scanned up and down. Decent height, full breasts, wide hips, quite possibly a good ass. A little chubby but she'd do.

"People may think you're crazy," I challenged. "The only people I see singing to themselves are Scottish lunatics carrying cans of Special Brew."

It was easy. She was in a great mood and she liked me. My student stood off quietly to watch me work, absorbing what he could. I teased a little and she laughed. The spark of attraction crackled like electricity. Something undefinable in her eyes and manner telegraphed, "I want this man." Back then, I was terrible at picking up on such signals but she was throwing them out so strongly that this time I couldn't fail to notice.

"I have to get back to my friend there," I told her, "but let me take your number and we can have a drink sometime."

That is how I met Rakiya, a young medical student of Nigerian descent born and bred in South London. Her number safely stored in my phone, I bid her goodbye and strolled away, re-joining my student with a smile on my face. Perhaps this curvy minx would be the one to finally end my year-long dry spell, and allow me to complete the whole daygame process from beginning to end for the first time.

The next morning I woke up to New Year's Eve and was immediately hit with mild depression. I still lived in my grotty one-bedroom flat in Kennington, a rundown area that felt more like Lagos or Kingston than the land of my forefathers. My housing estate had been built in the 1890s and probably never updated since. There were metal security bars welded across all ground floor windows due to the crime problem. Any time I read about a fatal stabbing or shooting in the London paper it was a fair bet to be nearby. The only reason normal working people lived there is it was cheap for such a central location. I could walk to my banking job in just thirty minutes. Never underestimate the squalor of London living conditions. Despite earning a salary close to £85k per year, the punitive taxation, mass immigration, bureaucratic incompetence and creeping socialism of London life meant I lived in a shithole. Any empty shit-hole, now that my wife had left. I paid £1,100 per month for this dubious privilege.

Although I'd recently been inducted into a new social circle with Sarge School, and now hung out with Jimmy and Johnny on weekends, this was far from the best time in my life. I'd work like a dog fifty hours a week, have seventy percent of my earnings stolen from me by a treasonous government, all so that I could live in a squalid damp flat and sleep in the bed that I'd shared with my wife less than a year earlier. And I still wasn't getting laid.

"Is this all there is?" I asked myself.

I'd worked hard at school, graduated University top of my faculty, gone straight into a high-pressure high-achievement professional apprenticeship and then risen up the corporate ladder through dedication, talent, and a little good luck. Yet here I was, almost thirty-five years old, single, and living next door to a work-shy African family who had exactly the same apartment as me but paid with welfare cheques funded by taxes stolen from me. This while I paid the full market rate. Just a week earlier the council had replaced the windows of every apartment *except* those of the people who actually paid their own rent. So as winter approached, the immigrant invaders had new double-glazing whereas I had draughty single-glazing.

I sometimes felt like I understood why the Hutus had massacred the Tutsis in Rwanda.

It was a kick in the teeth and I could feel myself disassociating more from regular society. The player's journey is alienating because of its rejection of the old "Disney myth" view of male-female behaviour. I was also becoming politically alienated. Already right-wing, my reading of Ayn Rand shifted me increasingly towards contempt and opposition to the Left. My country had gone badly wrong. It wasn't the England of my childhood. I'd done everything society asked of me and done it well. Yet here I was, living in squalor, alone, with no idea where it had all gone wrong. Dark thoughts filled my mind. The only faint hope was this secret system of Game. Looking back now, it sounds silly to have been so pessimistic but having your heart broken and then enduring a twelve-month dry spell will do that to a man. Its from this deep abyss that my obsession sprang, the driving energy that would eventually turn my life around.

I spent all morning mired in black depression. I drank filter coffee and played video games. New Year's celebrations have always bored me. Being introverted, the idea of being at a party or club where it was standing room only was not enchanting in the least. Neither were the obnoxious mark-ups on bar cover fees and drinks. Having resolved to stay home all day, I was surprised to get text messages from Jimmy and Lee inviting me out to Shoreditch. I was keen to cement relations with them. They were the "cool guys" and I wanted to be a part of their group. The longer I hung out with them, the more I could learn. Sarge School had thrown me a lifeline.

"Come round the flat," said Jimmy, "then we'll get a cab to *The Last Days of Decadence*. They have a retro night going on which sounds great."

Shoreditch is renowned for its party scene, frequented by a diverse demographic of hipster twats. Last Days styling was a throwback to the Roaring 20s prohibition era. From the stained glass windows to the cherry wood bars it was an exercise in old school indulgence, like a bar from the TV show *Boardwalk Empire*. They encouraged retro evening formal dress. After a few stiff whiskeys you'd feel transported back in time, the perfect atmosphere for ringing in the New Year.

I sent Rakiya a feeler text to see where I was at with her. The flake rate with game shocked me, the number of girls who will happily give up a phone number then never reply to messages. Even now, when I'm pretty good and know how to solidify a number, I still expect well over half the girls to flake. Back then it was closer to ninety percent so even though the energy and sparkle with Rakiya had been good, I wasn't expecting much.

"Hey Jimmy. I just met this Nigerian girl. She's cute and sexy but looks like one of those sex perverts you warned me about. Should I date her?" I wrote.

Rakiya understood the joke and responded almost immediately. "Hahaha, you should be careful! I recommend you run away from her."

We pinged a few messages quickly and my spirits rose. So many recent interactions had been a waste of time but this one stuck. Rakiya was keen. She lived quite close to me. A few hours passed, and as I was showering, my phone vibrated. Wiping my hands dry on the towel, I reached out from the shower cubicle and checked my messages.

"What are you doing tonight?" she asked.

Score!

Not only was she fishing for a date invitation (an extremely strong sign of interest for a girl, due to them usually taking a passive role) but she was trying to spend New Year's Eve with me. That's one of the few get-drunk-and-damn-the-consequences nights of the year. I was almost shaking in anticipation. I replied something or other and she called. After some quick chit-chat I told her about the evening plans for Shoreditch.

"That sounds like a lot of fun," she told me.

"I think it will be. Why don't you join us?"

"I'd love that," she said. I could tell by the sound of her voice that she was excited.

"Great!" I told her. We arranged to meet up near the Imperial War Museum an hour later, then I scrambled to get ready.

Jimmy lived just a couple of minutes' walk away from me, also in a squalid little room flat with his Polish mate and fellow Sarge School coach Perry. It was funny to see how these seasoned players really lived. Jimmy and Perry spent most of their free time sitting around in their boxer shorts watching DVDs on their laptops. It was as if they activated a different persona when walking out the door. We had a can of beer each, then I popped out to collect Rakiya. She was all smiles and warm energy. I took her to Jimmy's then we all got a cab into town.

With Rakiya, Tony and Jimmy

Last Days was predictably jam-packed. As promised, it was indeed like stepping into the 1920s—if that era had been popular with obese binge-drinking girls sporting trashy tattoos, that is. It's jarring to see a chubby foul-mouthed English woman swilling cocktails while dressed like Marlene Dietrich. British culture was a festering sore rotting through a once-great nation. At least the music was good. Rakiya was dolled up in a yellow dress and with her dark hair and skin she looked very cute in it. Like a big sexy banana. I'd noticed she was a bit chubby, but her smile and her youthfulness were nice and it was so long since I'd gotten laid I wasn't being too selective. Unless you counted a quickie with a prostitute in Prague five years earlier, I'd never banged a black girl.

Game is great for satisfying sexual curiosity.

We shuffled through the Last Days crowd until finding the rest of the team. Jimmy had been seeing a famous songwriter and well-connected producer in the US. Betty was blonde and slim but pushing forty and pretty haggard from all the booze and cigarettes. Not really a catch, you might say, but Jimmy wanted to get his band signed while I got the impression that Betty was using him for the bad boy sex. Jimmy was an above-average looking thirty-one year old man. Imagine Liam Gallagher, the wild and moronic frontman of Oasis, and then turn the volume down a little. Jimmy was astute, talented, but also slothfully lazy and not willing to put out the effort to reach his full potential.

Mick, the Australian raconteur, was waiting for us at the bar. Though we'd only hung out a few times, I'd noticed in Malaga that he was gifted with the ability and wit to tell a story that would have the entire room spell-bound. He was the life of the party. He'd held down a wide variety of jobs in his twenty-eight years of life ranging from a croupier on a cruise ship, a ski instructor, to faking his resume to land an accounting contract. That gave him fodder for quite a few of his tales. He was extroverted and very good with the ladies.

The grand old man of Sarge School, Tony T, was also there. Despite him being my age he appeared far more solid and wise that I, principally due to his excellent body language and mannerisms. We all looked up to him because of his experience and deep knowledge of the crimson arts. He'd been a Salsa performer and railed over three hundred women. Even now he was in great shape and projected a solid masculine presence.

An hour passed and whiskey flowed. A burlesque dancer was cavorting across the small raised stage wiggling her hips and showing skin. By the time I finished my third whiskey her breasts had been freed from their velvet prison and she was dancing the Charlestone. I was walking Rakiya down to the basement bar when Mick came over and grabbed me.

"Nick, do me a favour. I want you to use your pre-selection to help me pick up one of these girls."

What is pre-selection?, you ask.

When women see a man out with a pretty girl, they look at him differently than if he was alone or with only male friends. Deep in their hindbrain women use cognitive short-cuts to assess a man's sexual market value and one such rule of thumb is: *since he was able to score this pretty young chick there must be something about him, something she sees but that I'm missing out on.* Thus, one great way to make women interested in you is to be seen with a pretty girl on your arm. We call this "pre-selection." You'll notice that every boy-band uses the same principle in their music videos in order to impress their teenage fans.

Mick continued, "I'm going over to talk to those girls". He nodded his head towards a group of three young things standing against the bar. "Wait for me to open, then walk past with Rakiya and say to the girls, 'Be careful of this guy here, he gets laid like a rock star.'"

I agreed, thinking of it as helping out a friend while continuing my learning process. Each time that evening that I saw Mick with a girl I went over and gave him this verbal pat on the back. More whiskey blurred my mind. Things were going great, swapping stories with the Sarge School gang, drinking, lots of ribaldry. Mick was copping off with some girl in a dark corner while Rakiya was pressed up against me all night, coming on to me. I'd already kissed her.

The basement had its own bar near the dance floor and raised stage. The toilets were to the side of the stairs and, as we were coming down again, I saw Mick. He was coming out of the women's bathroom with a giggling girl close behind. She scurried off with a guilty expression, and Mick stopped when he saw me.

"I can't believe it! I just got a blow job in the toilets," then he grinned broadly and said, "Cheers for the help!"

Things had grown increasingly surreal. This was an entirely new type of experience to me. Most of my adult life I'd lived from one day at the office to the next, going home to my monogamous relationship. Here I was tonight at one of the hottest parties in the city with the coolest group of men and hanging out with a relatively hot twenty-six year old. As I watched Mick make the rounds, kissing first one girl and then the next I was filled with a renewed desire to jump on the opportunity Game had given me.

This is what and where I wanted to be right now. No more boring office life for me.

Night laboured into early morning, Betty suggested another party, at CentrePoint, a tall office complex built on the former site of a gallows with a spectacular view from the 33rd. floor bar. It was a private member's club at that time, although I believe that has changed in years since. Betty was able to get our names on the guest list and the rumour was that Beyoncé was hosting an after party. I have no idea if that was floated as a joke. Feeling star-struck, I was having a hard time believing that this could be my life. Two years prior on New Year, I'd gone up to the roof of my apartment building with a cup of coffee and watched the fireworks with my wife. Then we'd gone back down and watched TV. I hadn't even changed out of my slippers. This was a different life.

As it turned out Jimmy and Betty were so lazy and disorganized that by the time we got to CentrePoint it was 3am. If Beyoncé ever had been in the building, she certainly wasn't now. I looked under the tables and behind the curtains just in case. The party was wrapping up. Staff were stacking chairs and mopping the floor. We had time for one drink and that was it before they told us to drink up.

Rakiya was hanging tightly onto my arm, giggling at any little thing and as buzzed as I was I knew it looked extremely promising. She'd not given me any trouble all night, never called her friends, never tried to take me to different bars. She'd been pleasant undemanding company and simply let the night unfold ahead of her. We made our way along a quiet corridor right outside of the bar and started making out. It got pretty passionate and seedy as I pushed her up against a wall and started grabbing at her tits. My dick was hard and pressing up against her and she reached down and grabbed me through my pants. As things got more heated, a bouncer came along and moved us on.

"Hey kids, none of that here," the muscled-up, nicely-dressed doorman told us, putting the brakes on my moves. I had to think fast. It was crunch time. No more bars, no more stalling. Time to pull the trigger. *But how?* I thought. *How will I get her home now?*

A confident man would simply say, "let's get out of here." I wasn't confident and tended to overthink everything, according to what the textbooks had told me. The game plan then called for "extraction", meaning to take the girl to a sex location. It was nearly ten years since I'd last done that successfully. I didn't know what I was doing, but I knew that it had been a year since I'd had sex and I wanted to bang Rakiya. I looked at her big ass and imagined slapping it as I rammed my dick into her. I looked at her dark brown skin and wondered how she'd look with my cum splashed all over it. I was so horny I would've fucked the Queen Mother.

The Tube ran all night on New Year so I walked her to Tottenham Court Road station, stopping to make out and feel her up along the way. We got the Northern line south to my place. I thought, *this is really going to happen. I'm going to be banging this twenty-six year old girl less than an hour from now.* But then the train stopped at Embankment, two stations before mine, and Rakiya motioned to leave. I got a sinking feeling.

"Wait, where are you going? Come back."

"I have to change trains here to get home," she said. I was getting anxious again. What do I do now?

"Just come on to my place and have a drink."

"No, no, I have to get home," she said.

I hadn't expected drama at such a late juncture. I thought back to what I'd been taught at the boot camp. Rakiya was displaying "anti-slut defence". That's when the girl wants to have sex, but she feels guilty about it and wants the man to take the responsibility for moving it forward. She'll throw up all kinds of obstacles so as not to feel easy. The crucial point, I remembered, is she is hoping the man will find a way to brush aside those objections so she can get the sex and still feel good about it afterwards.

"It's okay, we'll just have a quick drink and then you can go. We're not going to have sex," I said.

That did the trick. She stepped back onto the Tube just before the doors closed. I was shocked and impressed with myself. It seems silly and trivial but this was a big thrill for me, being able to see the labours of my education come to fruition. We got off the tube at Kennington and were soon in my place. I was going to get laid. Finally.

I poured Rakiya a drink in the lounge, as promised. She never finished it. We were both drunk and still hot and bothered from our earlier groping session. I started kissing her and, within minutes, dragged her into my bedroom. She let it happen without resistance. She was as ready to fuck as I was. It was dark, and I didn't turn on the lights. I fumbled with my mp3 player for soft jazz and the mood turned seductive as I slipped off her yellow dress and tossed it to the floor then dropped my pants right next to it. She slid down my body while I reclined back on the bed and, as I watched her sucking my dick, I almost still couldn't believe it was happening. I looked down and could see her dark skin and big eyes looking up at me with her big fake tits bouncing around as she sucked on my dick and I thought, *Damn! This is really happening. I'm really going to get to fuck her!*

Sex was good. That much was guaranteed by how many months I'd waited. It was the first new girl I'd had sex with in almost ten years, so I think I was entitled to a little overreaction. We both enjoyed it but then things got weird afterwards. Or more accurately, I got weird.

As we lay together afterwards, I felt an intense need to "qualify". Qualifying is more pick up jargon. It means demonstrating to someone the reasons why they should like you. On a first date the man typically looks at the woman as being higher sexual market value than himself. She's the "prize", so to speak, and he needs to convince her that he is deserving of her intimacy. So, he'll talk about how successful or rich he is, brag about his car, watch, or job responsibilities: anything to make her believe he is worthy. Showing off, basically. We call that 'qualifying'. I was overwhelmed by the need to prove my worthiness to Rakiya even though I'd already fucked her. It's not logical. So I did something weird and embarrassing.

I reached under the bed and pulled out a large A2 manilla envelope. It held my resume, diplomas from my Bachelor's and Master's programs, certificates and commendations from employers, and both work and academic references. It was a package that I put together in order to obtain a job, or supply proof to Human Resources for a background check when taking a job offer.

I began showing this to her.

Rakiya was polite and attentive, but I know that she had to be thinking, "what is wrong with this guy? Why is he showing me these certificates five minutes after we had sex, at 4am? This is just weird."

She would have been right, of course. It was bizarre. I still doubted myself to the point of not seeing my own value. Qualifying to a woman is always bad for seduction. It puts her in a place of looking down on you, judging. Women don't want to be on a pedestal. They want to look up to and admire the man who is fucking them. It reassures them they've made the right choice and caught a high value man. It's much better, for both of you, to make the woman qualify to you.

Poor Rakiya got an icky feeling that maybe she'd slept with a man lower value than she'd presumed. Well, no harm done. It's only sex. I'd gotten my notch and finally broke my duck with Game. Rakiya spent the night and left late next morning. I never saw her again, and I'm not sure to this day if it was due to my peculiar behaviour, or if it was that she never really saw our connection as being more than a one-night stand. Either way, as I stood in my kitchen and poured my coffee that morning, I was smiling. I had a helacious hangover and my balls were aching from finally being relieved of their "blue-ball" state, but the smile on my face lingered throughout the day.

I had finally gotten laid. I had completed the process of meeting a stranger and then having sex with her soon after, for the first time in ten years. It had become real to me.

CHAPTER 18

A ROMANIAN IMMIGRANT

CHAPTER 18

A ROMANIAN IMMIGRANT

My daygame journey continued. I was undeterred, undaunted, unwavering and also a little unhinged. Getting laid that one time had showed me it was possible and, just as importantly, it was possible *for me*. It didn't seem to matter that I'd needed to approach a thousand girls before one of them finally let me put my dick inside her. Just knowing it was possible at all was enough.

I knew I was still broken inside. I knew my social skills sucked. I didn't expect great results. Nobody expects an average-looking thirty-four year-old man to have sex with hot young women unless he has something extra-special about him. There were no statistics to determine the probabilities and approach-to-lay ratios for something like that. If you see a blind bear juggling six chainsaws it would seem crazy to criticise him any time he dropped one. Just seeing the big furry fella keep them airborne a few seconds is a major out-of-this-world achievement. That's how I felt getting laid in my state of mind, at my age.

Objectively speaking, it wasn't such a big deal. That it felt as such to me was a function of my accumulated limiting beliefs and the low point I'd reached in life.

As the years wore on I'd come to realise, retrospectively, that my willingness to enter Game with a humble 'empty mind' was precisely the right attitude to have. Men who come in full of bluster and self-deceit about how awesome they already are, expecting fast results, are the men who drop out quickly. Traipsing the streets in all weather, constantly psyching yourself up to approach strangers and then constantly getting blown out is hard work. Prior to my divorce I'd achieved a lot in life. Yet daygame was many orders of magnitude harder than everything else I'd done in my life combined.

The reason is that daygame cuts right to the core. It addresses your SMV and ego directly, without grey areas. Without buffers.

Daygame forces you to evaluate every single part of your life. Your identity, your ego, your looks, your fashion, your lifestyle, your interests, everything. Every time you walk up to a hot girl and hit on her she will give you immediate instinctive feedback about your value. Unlike friends and family, she won't sugar coat it. Most girls are polite and well-meaning in their overt behaviours but your ego still bristles at every rejection. I was getting told the same message dozens of times every single week, by precisely the girls whose opinion mattered to me: *you aren't good enough for me*. That's a brutal amount of ego death and most men simply can't handle it.

Don't get the idea I enjoyed rejection. I simply didn't have any better options.

So, I was lucky with my attitude. I already knew I sucked. I considered myself at rock bottom and at the beginning of a journey to rebuild myself. Rejection stung but it didn't change my worldview nor did it shake my conviction to master this art.

After shooting my cum all over Rakiya's fake breasts on New Year's Day I didn't get laid again at all in January. The weather was starting to turn miserably cold. Snow and ice on the ground made walking as treacherous as a Pakistani London mayor. Cars skidded across black ice. I stepped carefully between puddles and snow drifts. I wasn't looking for an ice princess here; I wanted warm, willing flesh. It was time to improvise. Where in winter can I find pretty girls in a warm environment?

The shopping mall.

Westfield is a gigantic modern mall at Sheperd's Bush in West London. There's a part of the mall called "The Village", the more expensive area with over forty name-brand stores such as Louis Vutton and Tiffany's and a champagne bar called Searcy's. They also have a middle class section and a food court—a typical highend English mall. I went in with a plan to daygame for a couple of hours. If I spoke to ten girls I'd allow myself to claim success and go home happy. I didn't care whether I got any solid phone numbers. Rakiya had boosted my self-confidence. The trickle comes before the flood. My job was to keep practising until the skill set became second nature. Like artillery gradually zeroing in on a targeted bunker, my interactions were slowly improving and getting ever closer to good game.

The mall presented a few wrinkles not present in the streets, primary among them being it is private property and thus you can be, legally, thrown out. We have a concept in game called "the spotlight effect" when you believe everyone is watching you. This anxiety welled up in me as I stepped into Westfield. I thought everyone was looking at me and thinking, "what is this sleazy character up to?" They would point me out to one of the mall security officers and have me thrown out, I imagined.

Nowadays I scoff at the idea. Most shoppers are walking around the mall thinking about their own problems, needs, and desires. Over there is a middle-aged woman worried her husband will be mad about the new dress she just spent too much money on. She's carrying a big Debenhams bag and can't help visualising how the dress inside will make her look. That mum at the counter of Miss Sixty with her daughter is paying for a dress that she knows the girl will love to wear to the dance, but her father will hate because it's too short, and he already doesn't like her boyfriend. That normal guy in blue jeans and baseball jersey is wondering if he should duck into the toilet to scratch his itchy balls or if anyone would notice him doing it right out in the open. The bottom line is most people don't care what anyone else is doing. To convince yourself of this, spend a few minutes looking around. Sit on a bench and people-watch. See how wrapped up people are in their own thoughts.

On the rare occasion someone did see me approach a girl, the men looked on approvingly as if to say, "I wish I had the balls to do that," and the women, "I wish more men would approach me like that." Those weren't rationalisations I'd read in books but spring from my own direct experience. I've had men watch my sets while sat on stools outside a pub and then raise their glasses to me when I successfully take a number.

I didn't feel this way in January 2010. I felt creepy. Shuffling off home, tail between my legs, was never an option if I wanted to get good at this. Not just good, I wanted the hot girls that Tony Clink had promised me. My previous life achievements had convinced me that any time I turn my mind to a problem, I will find the solution, eventually. White hot fire of motivation burned inside me. Damn the consequences (real or imagined). I approached my first girl.

It was a quick conversation that didn't result in a number, but it broke the seal, and I was immediately warmed up. Nine more girls to go. Ten coins rattled in my left trouser pocket and with minor ceremony I moved one over to my right pocket. Each approach earned me the right to transfer a coin, and an instant date would allow me to move them all. I wasn't going home until the jingle of ten coins came from my right side. Confidence was what I needed, I told myself, not self-doubt. We daygamers have dozens of such tricks in our attempts to wrangle our brains into letting us overcome approach anxiety.

Now I stood in a big open plaza near Starbucks. I cast my eyes around, my gaze drawn to the shapes of pretty women among the crowd and zooming in on any which caught my eye. There weren't many sets. Half the patrons were men and most of the girls were with boyfriends or in small groups. Finding a hot young girl walking by herself requires sifting a lot of chaff to find the wheat. Finally, after ten minutes scanning all angles of approach to the plaza, I spotted a leggy girl coming out of Tommy Hilfilger. She had perfect proportions. It seemed each of her steps covered a continent, more of a stride than a walk and she moved with a graceful poise. She was dressed tastefully to show her figure but not too obviously. Later, I would come to refer to such girls as 'greyhounds', a type common in Eastern Europe. They are generally tall, curvy, intelligent, and well educated. Many of them have financial independence from following a career.

My feet were already moving to catch up before my conscious mind informed them to commence the chase. Once I got in front of her to get a good look at her face, I was slightly deflated. From ten metres away she looked amazing. From up close she looked like something made up to look amazing from ten metres away.

As good as she had looked from a distance with long brown hair and a sexy body, her face was merely pretty. She smiled as I said hello and I noted her teeth were small. They were clean, straight and looked well taken care of, but were considerably shorter than the norm, giving her a slightly strange look. Her nose was also slightly crooked, looking like it had been broken at some point in the past (I'd later discover she'd took a spiked volleyball full in the face in a competitive match at high school). These were all trivialities, however. She wasn't perfect, but she was still a fine young filly.

I stopped her with the same opening line that I'd been using lately, "Can I just tell you something?" After a thousand sets, this no longer seemed strange. We were in the middle of a public place, after all. She knew she was safe and quite probably liked the look of me. "Hi," I went on when I saw that I had her attention. "I was just over there and I saw you walking by. I thought to myself that if I didn't come over and talk to you I'd be kicking myself later. I think you're absolutely gorgeous."

"Thank you," she replied and, importantly, did not walk away. Great.

My communication style remained mechanical, all of my attention sucked up just in concentrating on delivering the material and fighting back the anxiety I felt. I wasn't yet able to detect the subtle signals in a girl's eyes, smile, and body language to know if she liked me. It was enough that she was standing still and listening to me. Perhaps she thought I was brave for approaching her so boldly. My stomach churned and my feet were numb from nerves. Like a duck gliding gracefully across the water while its feet thrash furiously under the surface, I was putting on a front.

We started chatting, her in a cute dusky accent.

"I'm from Romania," she said.

"That explains why you sound like Dracula. I can see your eyes drifting to my neck." She laughed, so I kept at it. "I'd avoid that store over there, it sells garlic."

She laughed again, more to indicate her pleasure with the interaction than with the calibre of my humour. I accused her of being a gypsy then brought the energy down a notch so we could converse normally. She introduced herself as Luminita, a twenty-eight year old office girl. After five minutes, I felt this might be an opportunity to transfer all my coins to my right trouser pocket in one fell swoop.

"Why don't we go right over there to Starbucks and get a coffee?" She was up for it. "Yeah sure, that would be nice."

We got our coffees and sat down at a table. If anything I was jumpier than her. This was maybe my fifth 'instant date' as I'd only recently begun experimenting with the concept. I wasn't sure what to talk about, so I started explaining the book I was reading, *Man of Steel and Velvet* by Aubrey Andelin. It is a 1970s relationship guide Tony T had recommended at the 'advanced' boot camp. Andelin focused on masculinity and how in order for a man to be at his best he must combine leadership and dominance (steel) with emotional connection and empathy (velvet).

After several minutes I realised that I was rather droning on a bit. These were new ideas to me, stirring something in my soul that society had never taught me, but I didn't want to come across as evangelical. Luminita continued to smile and listen but now I wondered if perhaps I'd been too clumsy and ruined the momentum. It's easy to second-guess yourself when inexperienced. I hadn't yet developed the intuition that would tell me, "Don't worry, you're right on track."

We reached the bottom of our coffees in a quarter hour. "Well, I suppose I should get back to the shopping I came here to do today," she said. "You can walk along with me if you like."

We looked in a few stores. I was proud of myself for getting this far, but at the same time struggling with the next step— Tony Clink advised I should begin touching a girl by now, to avoid the friend zone. We were passing a video game store.

"Hey, come here I want you to see this game," I said, taking her hand. I didn't care about the game, it was just an excuse to grab her hand and lead her. She allowed it. There is a natural progression of touch, casual, appropriate, and respectful in the beginning but moving towards increasingly intimate touch. We still held hands as we went around the corner to a jelly-bean kiosk. All of the seats were shaped like moped seats, each a different vibrant colour. Sitting with our knees touching, we shared a bag of jelly-beans and chatted for another half hour. What was an entertaining date to Luminita felt like a maths exam to me. It seemed like she was really in to me. Finally, I stood up and said, "I better be getting home now."

"Yes, I should get back to my shopping," she said with a laugh.

I hadn't gotten very far. We swapped numbers, and before I left we shared a very light kiss. She walked off. As I watched her ass sway side-to-side I put my hand in my trouser pocket to transfer all nine coins to the right. I found that my dick was hard. Evidently, I wanted this girl.

The warm glow of satisfaction followed me home. I'd accomplished something. My game must be improving significantly, I thought. If I banged Luminita she would be the third-hottest girl I'd ever poked. First was ex-wife Ioe, who aged twenty-three when we met had been a part-time model in addition to her dancing. She'd been way above my normal fodder. There'd also been an eighteen-year old busty Japanese girl, Ryoko, I'd picked up in an Okinawan nightclub ten years earlier while I was shit-faced drunk. That was still my "you gotta hear this" anecdote I'd trot out any time I was swapping war stories with other men.

It wasn't even particularly impressive. Sure Ryoko had massive firm tits, a pretty face, and was only eighteen years old. And, yes, I'd first banged her in a children's park at midnight and banged her the second time behind a huge rock during a late-night beach party. That's what made it a good story. Rather less impressive is that I was only twenty-four at the time (a mere six-year age gap), that she picked me up rather than vice versa, and she was a raging slut who gave me my one and only ever sexually transmitted disease.

Would Luminita take her rightful podium place and win her bronze medal?

I took her out for coffee again, a few days later, and we went for a couple of beers the week after that. We went from light kissing to making out, but still no sex. She was positioning me to be her new boyfriend and didn't want to rush things. I came to notice some of her odd habits. She was obsessive about her lips and applied balm to them after each time kissed. The smell of cherry lip balm lingered on me over the next few weeks.

On the third date she drove to my flat, picking me up in her compulsively clean red Mini. It was the first time I'd seen anything of her life and it confirmed my emerging theory that she was a little OCD. She parked up and we took a Tube to town for a couple of drinks then as she came back to collect her car I finally managed to get her into my bedroom. Heavy petting and passionate kissing ensured but she still refused to have sex and left shortly thereafter.

Yep, she wanted this to be a relationship.

An actual girlfriend,
with tits and everything

Our fourth date was in a Chinese restaurant near my house, on Walworth Road. I was treating the dates as practice so each time I'd prepare some different technique or gambit I'd picked up from the PUA literature and experiment with it. This date, I was trying Neuro-Linguistic Programming. I'd watched a seminar video by Ross Jeffries called *Make Women Hot* in which he had female volunteers sit on stage and used conversation patterns loaded with subliminal sexual words to turn the women on. It seemed to work. I needed something to get Luminita over the hump and into bed, so I decided to try it out.

I sat across from Luminita in the restaurant as I spooned Singapore fried rice into my bowl. I began talking in a low sexual voice, making strong eye contact, and telling her to take deep breaths. She played along, curious at my little game. I began to describe the sights, smells, and other sensations of the environment in vivid detail. Weird stuff, but she liked the diversion. By the time we are sipping green tea and asking for the bill I wondered if I'd successfully made *this* woman hot.

Not hot enough, evidently. She didn't come inside my flat, and we didn't have sex.

Finally the fifth date rolled around, about a month after our first meeting in Westfield. It went smoothly. Since that jelly-bean idate, I'd turned thirty-five years old, and since the Chinese restaurant date Luminita had decided it was time to fuck. I'm not sure I had much to do with her decision. She came to my place, spent the night, and I banged her. The sex was mediocre. She had no particular skill or enthusiasm. She wouldn't give a blow job, didn't make much noise, and generally seemed either unable or unwilling to let herself go. I suppose that's what happens when you're in the boyfriend box; a girl doesn't want you to think she's overly wanton lest it reflect badly on her. Though mildly disappointed, I commiserated myself that I was fucking a hot twenty-eight year old girl, the third-hottest I'd ever poked. It had taken me five dates to get there, but there I was. Life was improving.

I'd now been through the meet-to-lay process twice. Any more of this and Tony Clink might start to feel owed a beer by way of a thank you.

Luminita and I continued to date. We did things normal couples do like the cinema and taking a day trip out to Leeds Castle in Kent. I was a 'boyfriend' for a couple of months and it had a cleansing effect on my palate after spending most of the previous year on my own. Over time the spark I was looking for didn't quite happen.

At no point had I stopped my weekly grind of approaching new girls.

For one thing, the masculine-to-feminine polarity was missing between us. Luminita was of a forceful mind, probably related to her career as an office manager leading a team of twenty staff, though which was cause and which was effect wasn't clear to me. Every day she needed to show drive, discipline, responsibility, and other masculine traits. Success in her career was alienating her from her feminine core, or so the Internet told me. I wanted a feminine girl because that energy felt perfectly complimentary to my own. I was reminded of the best times with Miwako and Ioe. By comparison there was something cold about dates and sex with Luminita.

I liked her, but she didn't fulfil me. I'd learn from this and begin to focus my attention on strongly feminine girls and thus bias myself towards girls in vocations which encouraged feminine traits, such as students, waitresses, and dancers. I'd avoid career girls.

I remained bitter about life. It takes a man two years minimum to emotionally recover from divorce and I was only one year in.

In Milk & Honey's Red Room with Luminita. Fashion still terrible!

Not only that but I was submitting to a gruelling emotional roller-coaster on the streets and avidly devouring whatever reading matter I could get my hands on. My whole life was undergoing a deliberate and thorough upheaval where I questioned everything I'd previously believed. This included reading about men's rights. There is a corner of the Internet where men get together to discuss issues of concern to them, without pandering to female readers. It is now called the Manosphere and contains a few discernible subgroups:

PUA: These are the men dedicating to solving the puzzle of how to have sex with many women. I identified closely to this group because I'd set myself the target of becoming a PUA.

MRA: There is a burgeoning political movement to address inequities in the legal, political, and social spheres that discriminate against men. Men's Right's Activists focus on that.

MGTOW: This stands for Men Go Their Own Way and represents the men who have decided to disengage from normal mainstream life (career, mortgage, family, women) and forge ahead alone.

Each subgroup fascinated me. I was primarily concerned with getting laid, but the emotional trauma of divorce had caused me to re-evaluate everything. Deep down, I felt betrayed. I wasn't happy and didn't quite know why because the problems ran deeper than simply not getting laid. Why did I feel cheated out of life? Why did I have this splinter in my brain, constantly niggling me that the world isn't how I'd been taught it was? Reading the Manosphere felt like accessing forbidden knowledge. I read avidly.

One popular website called *The Spearhead*, written by men's rights activists, contained stories of men cheated or robbed by their horrible exes. It was a passionately angry site. Why were women always the ones who seemed to walk away from a relationship or divorce with everything, and the man was left to pick up the pieces? I gravitated towards this site because its anger spoke to the anger in me. It told me what I wanted to hear; life isn't fair and I'm being screwed. Most middle-aged men will pass through an anger stage but that's all it is, a stage. When a man has his eyes opened to the reality of the sexual market place, be it through unexpected divorce (like me) or perhaps a lifetime of grinding celibacy, there is an emotional process he will go through. Psychologists use the Kubler-Ross model to describe it, as I briefly touched upon in an earlier chapter. It was initially developed to explain the emotions patients feel following a diagnosis of terminal illness.

First comes *Denial*. Most men believe in the Disney fantasy they have been sold all their lives. The entirely of mainstream media and socialisation presents this sanitised view of how the world works and how men meet women. When closely examined, it's actually a completely feminine-centric world view in which female needs have come to be seen as the normal, default position (for example, that women should keep the children in a divorce). Men don't recognise their invisible prison and can't conceive of how life would look if they were free. Denial is the emotion driving men to say "daygame doesn't work" and to shout down attempts to discuss sexism against men.

Second is *Anger*. Usually it takes a traumatic experience to shake a man out of fem-centrism, such as a bad divorce. Once he overcomes denial and takes the mental leap to dispel his own illusions, he begins to see the world closer to how it really is. His natural reaction is anger: "I have been lied to all these years! My parents, my teachers, my representatives, my friends... all of them have pulled the wool over my eyes!" He feels grief for the life he could've had. He will also get angry at the sheer amount of work he sees ahead of him to reorganise his life, such as by learning to seduce women. I find the MRAs and MGTOWs rarely leave this stage of the Kubler-Ross model.

If they do, they arrive at *Bargaining*. Now he wants to negotiate a solution that doesn't involve much effort or change on his part: "I don't need the smoking hot turbo-girls, just give me a few tips so I can get a plain girlfriend." These are the men who fall prey to the magic pill marketing of dating advice, of one special trick to solve all your problems. As you've seen, I'd reached this stage within a few months of my own trauma.

Fourth is *Depression*. You realise there is no easy solution and the pretty lies have all died (Roissy's blog used the tag-line, "where pretty lies perish"). The man becomes aware of the true nature of the sexual market place and how incredibly difficult it is to be a winner. All the old sources of meaning in his life have collapsed under scrutiny. He no longer believes in his old political causes, or moral framework, or view of how men and women interact. A new code has yet to replace it, so life seems grey and pointless. If a man fails to take action, he'll spend the rest of his days here.

Finally a man reaches *Acceptance*, He lets go of the past, conceptually and emotionally, so as to shift his mind to dealing with reality on a daily basis without illusion. A new sense of meaning builds itself and he begins to realise life can be pretty damn good after all. I wasn't there yet. I was still full of anger and reading Manosphere websites fanned the flames.

One particular evening stands out.

Luminita and I sat in Pizza Express looking out over the South Bank of the River Thames. We could see the Tower Bridge and the Tower of London off to the right, and my office straight ahead. Darkness blanketed the city and colour lights twinkled reflections in the water. I was probably eating the pepperoni pizza, my favourite there. For some reason I decided that this romantic date would be a good time to bring up the topic of men's rights activism. I started out talking about how unfair the world is to a man, and how a divorced woman will usually walk away with everything he has, including his children. I recited statistics about how nearly all workplace injuries and deaths are suffered by men, how men get longer prison sentences than women for the same crimes, and many other examples of society-wide injustice against men. I built up quite a head of steam. It turned into a rant and when I had finally stopped talking my pizza was cold.

The South Bank view at night

Luminita looked at me strangely and said, "You're still quite angry, aren't you?"

"Yes," I said. "Yes, I am."

I hadn't even consciously recognised the anger. Evidently, I still had considerable pent up bitterness towards women that I needed to work through.

The next weekend my old university buddy Tim invited me to his house in Essex for a dinner party. He, Yasin, Warren, and Tony (not Tony T, but my scuba-diving university friend) were all there. Except for Tony, their long-standing girlfriends also came. I brought Luminita. It was a pleasant meal in a small conservatory but I found myself biting my tongue constantly. The girls would ramble on with empty platitudes and I seemed to find fem-centric bullshit in almost every utterance- whether it was actually there or not. All four men nodded and cowered like whipped dogs before these mediocre mouthy women. I actually quite liked Yasin's girlfriend Lucina, a traditional Slovak who was almost Alt-Right in comparison to the others, but even she was heavily masculinised by her career in the bullshit discipline of Human Resources. I ate my pasta, clinked glasses on toasts, and felt utterly alienated from this way of life.

It was a pleasant spring afternoon so Luminita and I went for a walk in a nearby forest before she drove us back into Central London.

"What's up?" she asked, applying more balm to her lips.

"I'm no longer the same person I was when I was friends with these people. They are talking about football, pension plans, IKEA furniture and..... it's all bullshit."

"What's wrong with that? It's a Sunday afternoon dinner party. That's how people talk."

"I hated it. It's so banal. So undemanding. I can't just smile and nod while they talk about so-and-so from the office who did such-and-such and isn't it so terrible. They are sleep-walking through life with the office, cable television, and the shitty Marxist rags that pass for newspapers."

Not long after that, our relationship petered out. There were no fights, no tears, no breakup; just a mutual decision that it was over, and we were both finished. We walked away with our dignity intact, hopefully to move onward and upward. Two years later I ran into Luminita near the Greenwich tunnel. I was on a date with a new Turkish girl and Luminita was on her way home from work. We stopped and chatted for a few minutes and then just went on our way. The spark was gone. I didn't even fancy her any more.

I began to see my old friends less and less. We had almost nothing in common.

CHAPTER 19

UNPLUGGING

CHAPTER 19

UNPLUGGING

"The rabbit-hole went straight on like a tunnel for some way, and then dipped suddenly down, so suddenly that Alice had not a moment to think about stopping herself before she found herself falling down a very deep well.

Either the well was very deep, or she fell very slowly, for she had plenty of time as she went down to look about her and to wonder what was going to happen next. First, she tried to look down and make out what she was coming to, but it was too dark to see anything;

Down, down, down. Would the fall never come to an end! `I wonder how many miles I've fallen by this time?' she said aloud. `I must be getting somewhere near the centre of the earth. Let me see: that would be four thousand miles down, I think--'

Alice In Wonderland, Lewis Carroll

Every single person I know who has committed themselves to the Game long enough to achieve success ended up tumbling down the rabbit hole like Alice. Each man first found himself in a state of dissatisfaction with his life, of which the most pressing symptom was a lack of good sex. So, he naturally tried to address that first. The brain being lazy, he tried to do so while suffering the minimum possible change to his habits. Ideally, he'd sit on the sofa watching *Game of Thrones* and then just pop out to the shops to get a pint of milk and a few hot girls' phone numbers. There'd be no disruption to his comfort zone.

This is, of course, magical thinking.

The harsh reality is that a man's failure with girls is symptomatic of a wider failure with life. Girls judge men quickly, delivering their verdict on whether he is worth knowing. That judgement functions akin to a final assessment of the man's way of living. When you have your shit together, love your life, stay in shape, follow worthwhile pursuits, and *only then* go approach a woman she will almost certainly respond well. Girls are hard-wired to scan you and then feel, on an instinctive emotional level, if you're confident and competent. They naturally admire well-developed men.

It happens fast. Micro-seconds.

Judgement works both ways. If a girl eats well, exercises, takes care over her fashion, make up, and grooming, develops a friendly feminine character and then puts herself in front of men, those men will check her out. A man instinctively recognises female value, based on a complex subconscious process honed over a million years of evolution. The result of this sophisticated evaluation is elevated into his consciousness elegantly:

"I'd bang her!" he resolves.

The marketing message of the Seduction Community (the 'one easy step') is bullshit but it draws in curious men. Beginners will scour forums, books, and YouTube for easy answers, such as the best openers, or good routines to perform on a date. It becomes quickly apparent that these tricks don't really work. Gimmicks seldom do. The lustre of Game as a magical system fades further with every failed approach.

I'd reached that point. Although I'd blundered my way into some entertaining situations and even gotten laid a few times, I was a long way from the success Tony Clink had promised me. I started to suspect the problem wasn't simply the routines I was using but was likely something deeper. The Seduction Community is really the self-help community in disguise. When a man realises there are no easy answers and he begins to look deeper, new questions emerge:

What is my value?
How can I improve it?
What do I really want in life?

Awkwardly trying to find my
new place in the world

When I began, in 2009, the Seduction Community was undergoing a major paradigm shift in how top coaches conceived of dating. What had originally begun as a "get laid now" set of routines and tactics had morphed into a voyage of personal discovery and self-reflection heavily influenced by mysticism and Eastern philosophy. This change was best exemplified by RSD's *The Blueprint Decoded*, a thirty-hour seminar product presented by a Canadian called Owen Cook (his fancy PUA name was Tyler Durden). His presentation was notable in that it contained almost no specific advice on what to say to a girl. His goal was to encourage 'deep level identity change' in his audience by stripping away the superficial bullshit in what you say and do, in order to begin reorganising how you think.

Mindset was paramount. In the jargon, PUAs call it 'inner game'. This term was inspired by W. Timothy Gallwey's seminal book *The Inner Game Of Tennis*. Gallwey proposed that there are two different games of tennis being played at the same time. The 'outer game' is played against your opponent and is won by mastering fitness, balance, timing, and of course the portfolio of shots used in the sport. The 'inner game' is played within your mind, and its principal obstacles are self-doubt and anxiety. Gallwey's revolutionary thinking, built on a foundation of Zen and humanistic psychology, was really a primer on how to get out of your own way to let your best tennis emerge.

The parallels to Game are obvious. It's not enough to practice opening, attraction, comfort, escalation, and all the other 'outer game' techniques. No matter how adept a player may be in such things, he is likely holding himself back due to internally-created success barriers. Additionally, if his technique is too slick girls will smell a rat.

I thoroughly enjoyed *The Blueprint Decoded*. I loaded the audio files onto my mp3 player and listened to it all during a one-week business trip in Edinburgh. Every evening after dinner with Toby and Magda, I retired to my room in The Sheraton Grand Hotel and let Owen Cook rewire my mind. By the time I reached the end of his course I felt like I'd been on a fantastical journey not unlike Alice in Wonderland.

I could think of six impossible things before breakfast.

Around the same time I discovered *Roissy In DC*'s blog.

This was a new bifurcation point and it's difficult to fully convey the influence Roissy had on my intellectual development, and indeed on the whole Seduction Community and manosphere. Roissy was the pen-name of a late-thirties office professional who picked up girls in down-town Washington DC. His blog seamlessly blended field reports of how he interacted with girls with social commentary and game theory. He revolutionised the field by integrating sociology, perfectly channelling a brand of cheerful nihilism as he navigated a collapsing social system. Roissy fiddled while Rome burned.

As an aside, he was one of the first public figures to openly predict Donald Trump's election win in November 2016. Roissy predicted it in mid-2015, soon after Trump announced his candidacy.

Roissy's blog contained the most influential material I'd ever read. Sat in my office cubicle as the autumn skies greyed, I devoured his blog from beginning to end, sometimes skipping meetings at work to finish posts. On the one hand, he spoke to my anger that our once proud Western civilisation was committing suicide with ill-fated experiments in socialism, feminism, and multi-culturalism. On the other, he peeled back the curtain on an entirely new and forbidden knowledge–that of the Sexual Market Place. His insight was penetrating and absolutely hilarious. Reading Roissy's old posts now is a little like listening to *The Beatles*. Their paradigm-shifting artistry has become so integrated into the "new normal" that it's difficult to appreciate how revolutionary it was at the time. Concepts, techniques, and mindsets that Roissy pioneered are now simply 'received wisdom' in the community and most newbies wouldn't even know his blog as the source. Roissy has retired with his anonymity intact but should he be reading this, I extend him an open invitation for a night out on the town where I'll keep him liquored up with his drink of choice.

Learning all this, I was faced with the thorny question of how to integrate the knowledge.

I can't go back to yesterday, I thought, because I was a different person then. I'd swallowed the Red Pill. My attempts to understand my failure with women and my general dissatisfaction with life led me to peel back the curtain on how society really works. None of this had been taught in my university. I felt like I'd been lied to about women for thirty-four years.

What else had they been lying to me about?

Come to think of it, who was 'they'?

As noted earlier, the Kubler-Ross model of grief lays out five emotional stages. Denial was long past me, and the final stage of Acceptance still a distant outline on the horizon. I was somewhere in Anger, Bargaining and Depression. Perhaps all three of them wrapped up into one shit sandwich that stuck in my throat. I'd begun to realise this in late 2009, when I still wasn't getting laid. My discussion with Luminita had demonstrated I still had work to do if I was to become the man I wanted to be. My inner game wasn't so strong. It was changing at a slothful pace, far slower than my outer game.

I figured out a three-part plan that would keep me moving forwards while I worked on my inner game in the background. First, I'd make a clean intellectual break with the mindsets that held me back, those links that kept me tethered to the Matrix. Second, I'd continue ridding myself of bad habits and sources of negative

```
In Milk & Honey
with two girls
I never did bang
```

energy so that nothing in the real world would slow my progress. Third, I wanted to make some lifestyle changes. A stressful corporate career was kryptonite to my vibe because every day it sucked my energy and lulled me back into a value system I now considered bankrupt.

So, I'd first put my house in order, and free myself to keep on pushing ahead with my inner game. The following notes, which I wrote in late 2009, give a sample of how I tried to accomplish the intellectual break:

"I have begun a process of re-ordering my affairs, so I can live the life that makes me happy rather than the one that society expects of me. There is only one person in the whole of this world who has my personal well-being as their single over-riding objective. That's me.

Over the past ten years I've been willing to take ballsy decisions to live how I want. I studied a degree I liked purely because I liked it then gutted out my professional qualification period in London before quitting on the first available day to live on a tropical island for a year. I spent three years doing an essentially part-time job, so I could enjoy living in Tokyo and pursue my kickboxing and writing. Life was good back then. Liberated, satisfied, always cheerful. Only when I became serious about marriage did I plug back into the matrix: full time career, accumulate savings, be respectable.

I bought into the picket-fence image of respectability. I really wanted a good wife, a nice house, clean linen, two kids, and to be a pillar of the community. I really did. No more. I simply don't want that–it was a trained response inculcated into me over thirty years of socialisation. Feminism destroyed it.

This is what I want. It's the *Krauser Manifesto*.

- My free time is my own. I want as much of it as possible.
- My money is my own. No person or organisation has any claim to it.
- I will pursue those things that interest me, and those alone.
- I will allow no-one to bleed value from me.
- I will feel pride in living the manifesto. No person can shame me for it.

So what does this mean? How can it be operationally defined? This is what I plan to do as I make my first leap: Starve the beast.

I will reduce my work week from five days/forty-five hours to three days/twenty-four hours. This gives me four days a week to live my life. Time is my most precious resource, and I'll never be granted more than this one life. I've calculated I need to work about 1.5 days to cover my bills as they currently stand, another half day to buy beer and entertainment. The third day is to continue to accrue savings. We are truly a blessed cohort of human history that beta male civilisation has engineered so much capital accumulation that three days of moderate labour provides for all material needs.

An added benefit of my 'partial-John Galt' is to minimise my financial support to the state complex that lives parasitically from the value I create, the femo-marxist beast that steals what I earned with the sweat from my brow and funnels it to a horde of mooching and looting enemies: the public sector layabouts, Diversity Outreach Coordinators, civil servants, welfare queens, etc.

As a strong, resourceful, self-concerned man I don't need much money. I'd live in a tent if I could keep the PlayStation 3 dry. Modern society has become a sophisticated mechanism for putting straight white men to work and then transferring the wealth they create to everyone else who is not straight, white, and male. I'm withdrawing as much of that economic surplus as I can without compromising my own quality of life. It's 'going Galt'—one step at a time.

I'm against Cultural Marxism.

The carrot and stick that keeps law-abiding tax-paying men in line cannot control me. I do not want a promotion. I do not want a Ferrari. I do not want membership to an exclusive golf club.

I do not seek the approval of my neighbours, nor the quasi-approval of the opinion leaders in the media. I am deaf to the shaming of the office feminists and unmoved by the veiled contempt of the manginas who worship them. While I remain fervently pro-capitalist, I do not care to accumulate the accoutrements of a consumer society except where they please me.

I will submit to only those negative sanctions to which society will not permit me to escape. Thus, I'll still have to pay taxes, I'll still have to turn up to work at 9am, and I'll still refrain from kicking feminists in the cunt when there are witnesses around. What I will not do is cooperate in society's soft oppression because I refuse to weave the ropes that bind me.

What does this mean in my day-to-day life?

I don't fear unemployment and thus the ultimate threat a company can hold over me. Through a careful understanding of global economics and a sound frugal lifestyle, I have amassed sufficient cash that I can easily live the next ten years without earning a penny more. It's not an extravagant sum, but I have no extravagant tastes. My boss holds no sway over me—there is no mortgage payment to meet, no wife to keep. Thus, I will work the way I want as a free individual. I think my professional standards are high enough to keep the boss happy, but if not we simply go our separate ways.

There'll be no work stress. I don't identify with my job. An unreasonable deadline will not be met. An unreasonably early business flight will not be caught. Office politics will pass me by. I seek to impress no-one but my inner alpha.

I'll confront misandry and cultural Marxism everywhere I find it. If some femtard in the bar/café/office pulls out an offensively misandrist comment I'll identify it as such and challenge them. The pussy cartel doesn't scare me and their typical levers of power don't move me.

I won't be frittering away my cash on nonsense and status goods. Initially, I'll have to downshift to keep costs down but I'll soon learn where to pick up value.

Oh yeah, I'm going to actively seek out feminists and ruin their day. These people are the enemy of all I hold dear about Western civilisation and a personal enemy to me. I feel liberated from all social censure. The only limits on my behaviour are those that I set myself, to live by my own code.

Don't get me wrong: I am not an egoist. I do not wish to become a cunt. Quite the opposite: I seek to strip away the rotten façade of social nicety that one must adopt to glide smoothly through the matrix. I seek authenticity.

This is how I envision my life five years from now: This is still a work in progress. Not all my ducks are in a row and I might need to rejig things. Not everything has been agreed. Here's the current plan:

- *Monday to Wednesday:* Go to work, earn my keep, maintain marketable job skills.
- *Thursday:* A day of leisure. Sleep late, then pursue my hobbies with no guilt and no urge to move my life forwards.
- *Friday:* Attend to my side businesses, move forwards in my projects and life goals.
- *Saturday:* Social circle, shopping, chilling.
- *Sunday:* Dating the LTR, keep the approach numbers up.

Most people walk the treadmill till they're sixty then wonder where their life went. I'd initially planned to retire by forty. Now I don't even need the concept of retirement because my whole life will be tailored to my own personal satisfaction.

Wish me luck fellas."

Quite a strident and militant mind set, no?

Things turned out quite differently to plan, as you'll see. My weekly routine turned out to be far easier, far more fun and took far less than five years to achieve. However, the main difference that I couldn't yet see was that rather than cling to my anger and weaponise it, I'd shed it and make peace with the world. As I started getting laid, mixing with better people, and living a life of freedom, I'd learn to chill out. Although my manifesto was inaccurate in predicting the course of my near future, what it succeeded in marvellously was in giving me the impetus to yank myself out of my comfort zone. It takes a strong explosion of intent to break free of your chains.

One that got away

Failing to enjoy Entourage Game

In Malaga with the lads

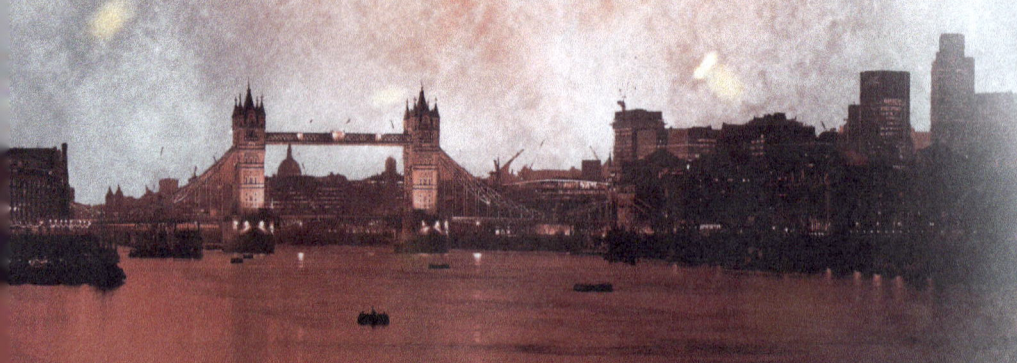

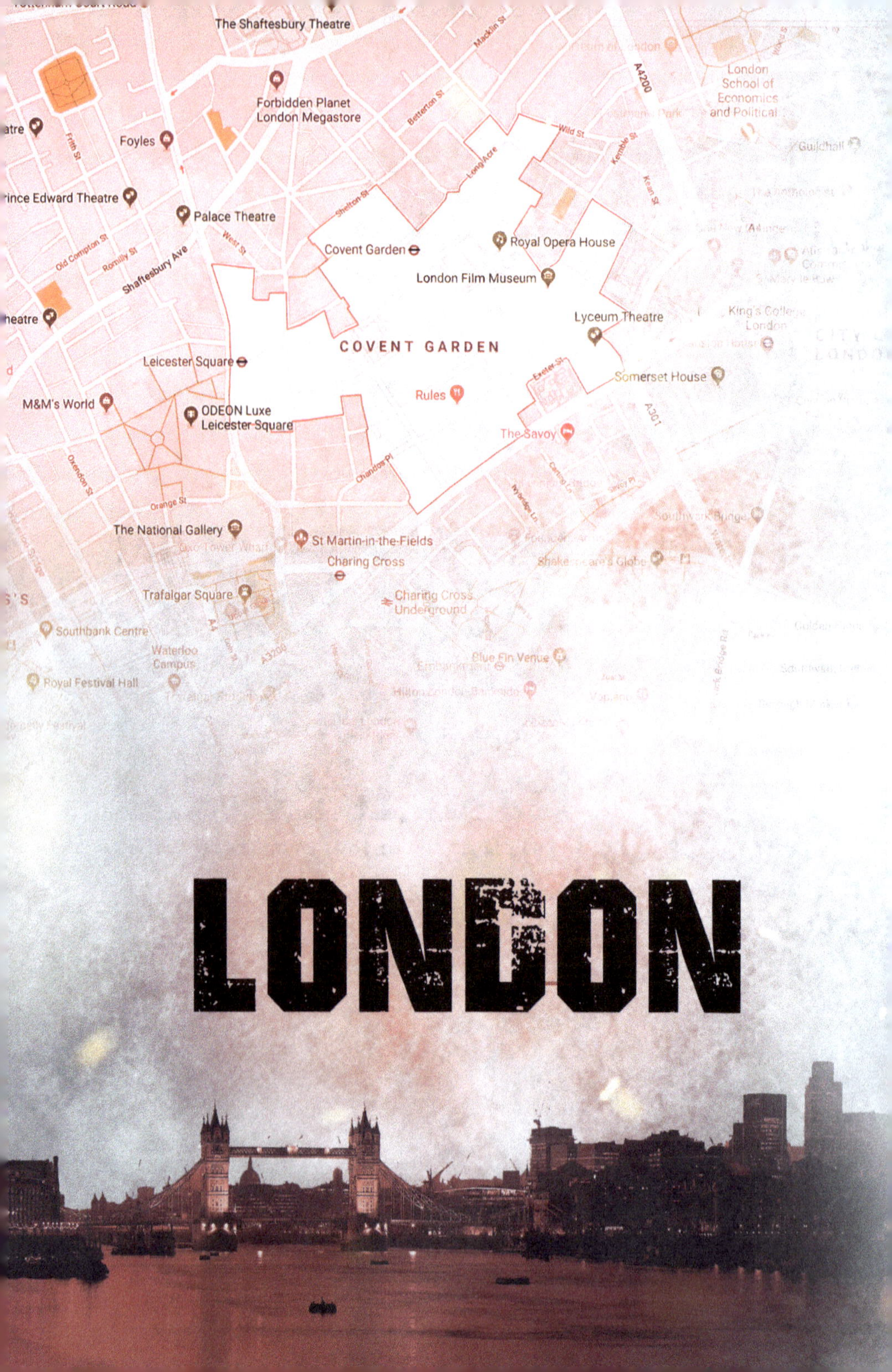
The Shaftesbury Theatre
Forbidden Planet London Megastore
Foyles
Palace Theatre
Macklin St
Betterton St
Long Acre
Shelton St
Wild St
Kemble St
Kean St
A4200
London School of Economics and Political
Guildhall
Frith St
Old Compton St
Romilly St
Shaftesbury Ave
West St
Covent Garden
Royal Opera House
London Film Museum
Lyceum Theatre
King's College London
COVENT GARDEN
Leicester Square
M&M's World
ODEON Luxe Leicester Square
Rules
Exeter St
Somerset House
A301
The Savoy
Chandos Pl
Oxendon St
Orange St
The National Gallery
St Martin-in-the-Fields
Charing Cross
Shakespeare's Globe
Southwark Bridge
Trafalgar Square
Charing Cross Underground
Southbank Centre
Waterloo Campus
A4
A3200
Blue Fin Venue
Royal Festival Hall
LONDON

CHAPTER 20

GREAT GIANA SISTERS

CHAPTER 20

GREAT GIANA SISTERS

F or all my high falutin' dreams, the reality of Game is Sisyphean. Every morning you must push the metaphorical boulder up the hill, just to watch it tumble down the other side. I'd still only been laid twice despite approaching almost one-thousand women. I think flashers exposing themselves in public parks have a better success ratio than that. There were all kinds of weaknesses in my game, both technical flaws in what I was doing but also deep identity problems that required serious introspection to identify. I was attempting to use daygame to fix these problems, like an outdoor therapy session.

But what were these inner game issues?

I thought back to my school years, after my best friend Neil had transferred away. I'd soon drifted into heavy metal music, and then punk and fringe anarchist politics. At the time, this had seemed like my own choice, following my interests. But was it? Had that been the case I could've easily drifted into something cool yet I'd ended up in precisely the type of sub-culture that serves as a dumping ground for society's misfits. That occurred to me following an off-handed comment my brother Lee had said over the phone.

"Have you noticed that Goths are always the fattest girl and the skinniest boy in the school?"

I mulled that over.

At university I'd spent dozens of hours a week in the library- a solitary pursuit- and though I'd go out with friends three or four times a week I knew I wasn't one of the cool kids. While in London I'd mostly hung out with the same university friends and it was only after meeting the *Sarge School* gang that I realised how uncool my friends were by comparison. So I posed myself a difficult question: Had I been the real author of my life's choices? Or had I followed the path of least resistance as society steered me into my natural position in the social hierarchy?

If the latter was the case, then all kinds of unpleasant new follow-up questions came to mind. Clearly, I wasn't as awesome as I'd believed. Now that I thought about it, perhaps I just wasn't a very likeable person. Sure, I had many positive traits, such as honesty, intelligence, creativity, resourcefulness, perseverance, politeness, and fierce loyalty. Balanced against this, however, were some rather sharp edges and woeful shortcomings.

The main problem was I just wasn't *cool*. I wasn't sexually attractive.

I wanted to do something about that, so I tore a sheet of paper from my notepad and brainstormed my personal failings. It was a thoroughly unpleasant process but I felt like I was grasping the nettle by my hand. It needed to be done. Two hours and two cups of coffee later, I'd whittled the list down to what I believed were the main character traits holding me back:

- bitterness;
- a sense that society owed me more than I was currently getting;
- an inability to read subtle social cues;
- self-righteousness;
- an overbearing nature;
- a lack of confidence that people would like me;
- saying things as I think them, rather than filtering out the weird ideas;
- a tendency to retreat into solitude even when not feeling introverted.

Looking down at the list, I felt the urge to crumple it up and toss it aside. Do you know those horror movies where kids in an old cabin hear the rattle of chains from the basement below? Someone always says, "let's go down and see what it is." That's how it felt contemplating turning my mind inwards to assess my deep-rooted inner game issues: like opening a trapdoor into a dark basement. What monsters lurked below? In the movies, the bold kid's curiosity is rewarded by his getting violently murdered. I knew that because I'd watched hundreds of them on VHS tape in my teens. I wasn't overly keen to suffer a similar fate with my ego, if only symbolically. Still, I knew it must be done. I wanted to get good at Game.

The daygame grind was the crucible in which I worked on these issues. Every time I went up to a girl and introduced myself, she would scan me and give immediate instinctive feedback on my vibe. Some would roll their eyes or show disgust as if smelling vomit, though fortunately they were a tiny minority of girls. Others showed mild curiosity, and some even lit up in eager anticipation. I tended to like those latter girls the most, of course.

As the conversations progressed, girls would see more dimensions to my character and thus feed back on it with ever greater accuracy. That wasn't necessarily a good thing. I quickly divined a pattern that predicted how a girl would react: the more excessively friendly I was–that is to say, the less of a sexual threat I presented–the more enthusiastic her response. There was a subtle, unspoken negotiation. My role was to pour in gentle compliments and chatty vibes along with a tacit promise that I wouldn't try too hard to fuck her. In return, she smiled, chatted and made me feel better about myself.

You can see the broken inner game written into my face

This is a great way to learn social skills, but utterly useless in getting laid. Without sexual intent, there is no sex.

Slowly, ominously, I came to appreciate the sheer scale of my problem and thus the amount of work ahead of me to fix it. The hot girls were treating me like a puppy, to be patted on the head but kept at a distance in case he tried humping their leg. To a neutral observer it looked like I was chatting her up: she'd laugh, smile, chat, and often give up her phone number. The reality was I was no closer to dating her than if she'd been a hologram behind a glass shield. I was not the kind of cool sophisticated man that women naturally want to sleep with. Not even close. My social development had been retarded somewhere in my teens and now I needed to catch up. Daygame was my intensive social-skills immersion workshop. It wasn't merely a way to get laid. Daygame was the tool to correct fundamental flaws in my character. My in-field experiences would generate feedback that I could use to spot patterns, from which I could infer root causes. Further sessions on the street would allow me to test those emerging hypotheses and practise ways to overcome them.

I embraced the grind.

In the first half of 2010 I was relentless, going out at least twice a week and racking up the stats. While I didn't get laid again until I met Luminita, I did have some great times.

Since returning from Malaga as an official *Sarge School* coach, Johnny had recruited me to help him teach the daygame session of the now-monthly boot camps. I introduced him to my main wing, a Brazilian man a few years younger than me called Fernando. Business was promising. Typically we'd have five or six students each time, paying £300 for the weekend. More experienced lads like Jimmy and Tony would handle the nightgame but they were happy to turn over the daygame to the little team of Johnny, Fernando and myself. At the time, daygame was still a novelty act that few in the PUA community took seriously.

We'd found a cool pub on Neal Street in Covent Garden which let us use the upstairs function room for free. I owned a small blue Samsung laptop that hooked up to the flat screen TV on the wall so we could deliver presentations before the infield session. Johnny went first with an inner game talk on courage and anxiety, then I went next with a basic how-to guide for opening. Later we added in Sunday daygame sessions in which Fernando gave a talk on date escalation. After the talks, usually around 2pm, we assigned an instructor to two students each and then took them onto the streets to hit on girls.

One boot camp in March 2010 was especially memorable.

For the first hour of Saturday afternoon, I had a young Asian lad who was new to the sport. Boot camps have an upbeat energy of their own which temporarily lifts student's mental state and helps them into set. My guy was making the usual technical mistakes but I wasn't having any trouble getting him to talk to girls. After one such mistake I pulled him to one side to offer advice.

"She almost stopped to talk, I could see the tiny stutter in her walk. But as she hadn't stopped entirely, you turned your feet to face her and started following. That nearly always makes them blow you out. Keep your feet planted and just turn your body, hold eye contact, and finish your opener. It's counter-intuitive but if she senses you won't follow, she's more likely to stop."

A pretty girl happened to walk past.

"Look, watch," I said, and demonstrated the point I'd just made. I opened. She kept walking. I planted my feet and turned my body while I continued to finish speaking my opener. She stopped, hooked, and after a few minutes chat she gave me her Facebook details. This was Mystery's original insight into teaching technique while in-field: immediately after explaining a theoretical point you can demonstrate it live, and then have the student practice it himself.

I'd been daygaming less than a year, so my own technique was still raw. Teaching was helping me clarify things by forcing me to think them through. I'd see students make common mistakes, then I'd need to find a way to explain it and craft a solution. However the main reason I enjoyed teaching was because I felt like one of the cool kids, working with Johnny, Fernando, Jimmy, Mick and the others. It gave a focus to the weekend and a structure to my own journey into self development. It was about more than getting laid. I was helping other men out, and came to believe I was helping the girls too, by giving them more options from which to choose.

The first hour ended and we all huddled up to take a short break and reassign partners. I passed the Asian lad on to Johnny and took a husky young English guy for the second hour.

"I want to try chatting up birds in shops," he said.

"Right then, let's give it a go. The main thing is the geometry of the open. Don't go running up and getting in front of them. Just approach from the side, give a light tap on the upper arm, and then do the same opener."

Covent Garden is full of precisely the kind of clothing and accessories shops that draw in girls of the early-twenties demographic. We tried H&M first, where I demonstrated a low-energy opener on a girl from Wisconsin. We chatted a while then she explained she had a boyfriend and excused herself. My student, James, was still a little nervous due to all the shoppers milling around so he asked me to do another demonstration. I moved on to a pair of young women from British Guyana, of all places. They happened to be laughing as we walked past so I used that.

"Girls. I was just walking past and I had to say you've got such a nice laugh."

One of them, the prettiest, gave me a coy smile and I felt an immediate strong hook point. The vibe was playful and I brought James in to make it a group chat. That gave him a better view of the conversation. I noticed the Wisconsin girl glaring over a clothes rail at me. I guess I'd ruined her Hollywood moment.

We took the Guyana girls to a retro clothes store around the corner to help them with an 80s party they were attending that night. It turned out my target girl, nick-named U.V. for reasons I can't recall, was living in London whereas the cousin was visiting from Holland for the weekend. They wanted to keep shopping and sightseeing so I figured that could turn into a big time-sink for us. Time to bail out.

"This is as far as we go, because we've got some stuff to do. Look, you're weird, but I like you. Give me your number, and I'll give you a call when I've got some time," I said.

She complied and then James and I went back onto the streets. Our vibe in the shop had been playful and teasing so I continued in that vein when texting U.V. later. Here's a literal transcription:

Me: Good fun meeting you today. I hope you got some nutty 80s gear for the party.
Her: Indeed it was. Hope you have a smashing night.
Me: (next day) Wedding party was today, right? Hope you girls didn't cause trouble…

Her: Oh dear! Close. It was last night and it was a smashing evening. I guess you're done with the more important things in life to grace me with a text?
Me: Hold it there, tiger! I'm clearing my diary later this week just for you. I'd feel bad about pulling you away from your nice friend when you're supposed to be showing her around. :)
Her: That may have awfully mean. It's my cheekiness. :) she actually headed back home today. how is your mate?
Me: Cool. Get some sleep and we'll continue this foolishness later… Night night.
Her: Bonne nuit!
Me: Konbanwa! Wednesday evening is good for me. Are you fun on Wednesdays?
Her: Hola! On Sunday's and Wednesday's I am awfully cheeky.
Me: Guten abend! Ok, Wednesday it is. Don't get too cheeky. I don't know you well enough to spank you.
Her: Bonjour! You are quite right. I'll be on my best behaviour if you are. A bientot!
Me: Ohayo! We'll meet 8pm in front of Top Shop. That good for you?
Her: Aloha! See you there. Enjoy the sunshine today. Cheers!

It was pretty obvious she liked me and was excited by the whole scenario. I'd been experimenting with being more "bad boy" in my texting so I was teasing and pushing her as best as I could. Perhaps it was try-hard. I tend to tone that down nowadays. Nonetheless, I was excited. She was a cute petite jungle girl with a great bubbly energy. I really wanted to shag her.

My life was consumed by daygame. Even on the day of the eventual date, I'd been out with Fernando hitting on girls for an hour beforehand. I only did a few approaches including a long chat with an incredibly feminine and buxom Persian girl who told me she was in a committed relationship, so I didn't bother asking for her number. There was also a nice Vietnamese girl who gave me her Facebook details but said she was on her way to meet her boyfriend. Good experiences but nothing overly memorable.

Guyana girl was early. She never did give me her real name as initially, when I took her number, I'd put her in my phone as Crazy

Guyana Girl and she let me run with that. She later said her nickname was U.V. Immediately upon U.V. arriving I launched a gamey routine Mick had taught me. I offered her my arm (she took it) and we went towards the first bar.

"Now I realise this is a date but that doesn't mean you can just kiss me. I need trust and connection first. I'm not just a piece of meat."

She gave me a long, obvious look up-and-down, smiled and replied, "You're a prime slice of sirloin." That was a huge signal, of course.

Dating the great Guyana girl

I smirked and replied, "I'll take that as a compliment, but I'll be watching you."

The vibe was fantastic and it was totally on. We were soon in *Milk & Honey* member's bar for my fifth time in a week (and she was the fifth different girl–the receptionist was wondering who the hell I was). My first escalation was to pull her in to read the menu and she shuffled up alongside me. I waited an hour to kiss her and there the dam broke. She climbed all over me, horny as an Arab in a goat farm. I thought, "what's the alpha thing to do?" so I settled into some strong body language like I was sitting on a throne while she wrapped herself all over me, snuggling her face into my neck like a cat and squeezing my nearest leg between her thighs.

I put her hand on my dick and she purred.

"I'm not coming back to your place, though" she said. Sadly, I couldn't persuasively explain why that was an error of judgement on her part. I did try. Not too hard, mind, because it was going so well I figured nothing could go wrong. *I'll definitely be shagging her next time*, I reasoned with confidence. I decided to dirty talk her.

"This is the part where you put your hand on my dick again."

She did so, giggling, "I'm a lady, you know."

"Next time we meet we are fucking. I'm gonna bring you into my house, pick you up, and carry you over my shoulder. I'll slap your arse, obviously". I slapped her ass for emphasis. "That's a nice arse, I think I'm gonna like it. Then I'll throw you onto my bed and rip your clothes off. Then... while you're naked... on my bed... I'll go and make a cup of tea."

I'd pinched that routine from Jimmy.

U.V. squirmed and moaned, massaging my dick through my jeans. I continued, "I'm gonna feel your tits in a minute." She giggled more. "No. I changed my mind. I'm gonna feel them in five seconds. 5...4... 3... 2... 1..."

She pushed her breasts into me, and I mashed them up a bit.

"Sorted. I'll be doing that again soon."

This was happening in an open lounge, but a fairly dark and discreet one. I pulled her outside and we made out heavily in some alleyways. While I was fingering her near Carnaby Street I wondered if perhaps I shouldn't try to fuck her right there in the open air. There weren't many people around and it was dark. I decided it was better to play it safe. Horny though U.V. indisputably was, public sex was a big ask.

As I thought about it, U.V. gripped my shoulders and pressed her face into my chest. My phone vibrated so I pulled it out with my free hand, holding it behind U.V.'s back so as to see the screen. It was a message from Luminita.

"I have a free day tomorrow! Shall we meet?"

"OK" I replied, and put the phone back.

U.V. moaned and bit the leather of my jacket lapel. Time to end this. I pulled my hand out of her panties, wiped it clean on her sleeve, and told her that was all she was getting and don't be greedy.

As we kissed at the tube station I told her to send me a text when she was home so I knew she got back safe. She did. She was going abroad on holiday for the next week. I took the train home feeling rather proud of myself for doing so well on the date with such a pretty girl. However, a seasoned player would be shaking his head in disapproval. I'd created a window of opportunity and not pushed for the lay when U.V. was there for the taking. I'd see her two more times, including once in Kennington near where I lived, but never quite get it right. She would tell me she got short of breath due to the excitement of meeting me, and she'd eventually straddle me on my sofa at home while I fingered her, but I never got the notch.

The U.V. experience was representative of that phase in my life. I was having amazing adventures that reinforced my belief that Game was effective, but I consistently lost girls I should've banged.

May 16, 2010 would be another near miss. It was a Sunday afternoon and I was meeting Johnny to talk a little business, after some cheeky daygame before it got dark. The first girl I tried was a Romanian on her way to work near the Strand. She was in a big rush but the planted feet and solid stare did for her and she chatted for five minutes. I felt like I couldn't hold her long enough to get a solid number so I settled for her Facebook details. We messaged a little over the next few weeks but I couldn't get her out on a date. Before long I was back in Covent Garden. That spring a public art project placed colourful statues of elephants all around central London. I was using it as an opener, testing an indirect style. I did the, "Can you take a picture of me with this elephant?" opener with a nearby tourist, a twenty-two year old German girl.

She lit up and chatted, so we fell into conversation. The vibe was great. Cristiane was on a long weekend by herself and itching for excitement. I bounced her to take more photos and then to a French cafe I'd recently found. Johnny was with me at the time so he came along, as I felt it would look odd to abandon my friend so soon. After an hour or so building comfort and rapport in the cafe Johnny made himself scarce and I took Cristiane for an alcoholic drink. This was a notable step into different territory, moving from a polite social encounter to something less deniably sexual. Recently I'd been trying to sleep with girls the same day that I met them, without any breaks in between. We call this a Same Day Lay, or "SDL". It's very difficult to pull off and relies upon a lot of luck. Seeing as I wasn't even getting laid the slow way, you can imagine how well the fast way was working out for me. I didn't care, I just wanted to see how far I could push things. You don't know how fast you can take a corner until you crash the car a few times.

In this case there was nothing to lose because Cristiane was going back to Germany the following Monday evening. We had a drink in the Sherlock Holmes pub nearby, standing by the bar.

"I just broke up with my boyfriend," she said. "He lived with me at my flat but now he's moved out."

She clearly wanted excitement but wasn't quite comfortable. I talked a little about how society judges women too much and other prattle designed to help her rationalise taking a leap of faith. She seemed to think I was super smart but I didn't want to fall into the trap of getting

On an instant date
with Cristiane

overly intellectual, or worse, dad-like with her. We had another drink at another pub and were now arm-in-arm, though she hung on only loosely. We talked more, I tried a few NLP routines to heat her up (remembering that *Make Women Hot* video) and then we kissed. Easy. She was all over me but refused to come home. I guess she'd been out since 8am so even if her objection was more related to being tired and sweaty, I couldn't blame her. We kissed goodbye at the station.

"Let's meet tomorrow," she suggested.

"Yes".

The next evening, her last in London, we kissed on the hello and she threw her arms around my neck. I shrugged her off with a hammed-up exasperation and walked her arm-in-arm to the pub. She hung on tightly the whole way and this, coupled with the mere fact she came out at all knowing what I wanted, meant it was on. I wanted to make her wait for a proper kiss and play around a bit, experimenting with making her chase: leaning back and making her lean in to me, getting her to qualify, etc. It seemed to intensify her attraction, just like the PUA books had told me it would.

We moved on to *Milk & Honey* and sat on a sofa in a quiet corner. We kissed, I repeated the same posture tricks as with U.V., and let Cristiane climb all over me. I could feel her breathing deeply and pushing herself into me passionately. So much so I was embarrassed every time the waiters walked past.

"Let's get out of here," I said.

"Where do we go?"

"My place."

"No, I can't."

"It's not far."

"No. We will not have sex tonight, sorry."

I'd half-expected that, such was the trend of my recent experience. This time I'd prepared an answer. I bit her ear and growled into it, "Let's agree now that we won't have sex tonight, no matter how tempted we get."

I didn't mean a word of it, of course. The idea was to disarm her concerns about where things were leading so that when I verbally escalated, she wouldn't block me. I was hoping she'd eventually reconsider her decision. For most of the next hour we talked about all of the sexual things we "wouldn't be doing tonight." Her mood grew crazy-hot, and her eyes sparkled. She couldn't keep her hands off my dick, to the point of snaking them down the front of my trousers without any lead from me. Usually when a girl grabs your dick unbidden, she's ready to fuck. I went for the extraction again.

"C'mon, I'll make you those cocktails. Nothing is gonna happen because we've already agreed we're not fucking."

Again she resisted. "No. Not tonight."

"Look at me. Don't you trust me?"

She whimpered, "I don't trust myself" then threw herself onto me again.

Damn it was frustrating. I racked my mind for sage advice from wise men. Wasn't there a famous line about how if Muhammad won't go to the mountain, then the mountain must come to Muhammad? Well, I didn't like Muslims so that advice was out. I remember something about leading horses to water and making them drink. Finally, I could articulate the principle I'd been groping for.

> *If the girl won't come to the sex location, you must make the current location the sex location.*

There! That's almost poetic.

We were in Bradley's Spanish Bar and there were two rarely-frequented alleyways outside. I took Cristiane outside and before long we were in one of them, in a dark doorway making out. She was horny but simply would not escalate to skin-on-skin contact. I tried putting my hand down her pants but she swatted it away the first ten times so I gave up before the eleventh. Cristiane was obviously absolutely gagging for it, so I was flummoxed. I tried to rip her trousers off right there. I figured it's better to be a pushy arsehole than a wimpy beta (to paraphrase an aphorism I'd read on Roissy's blog). When I tried unzipping her, she refused.

"You're just trying to get me hot so I change my mind."

Well, yes. But instead of admitting it I said, "No. I'm giving you are preview of what you'll get next time we meet."

"You sound sure we'll be fucking," she gasped.

"Because we will and you know it."

She was squirming. She put her hands down my trousers to grab my dick, then pushed her crotch against it. Soft moans escaped from her lips and her knees were wobbling. I growled into her ear, "I'm showing you that I go after what I want."

"That's for sure!" she gasped.

After about an hour, it was clear this lady wasn't for turning so I put her on the train home. I'd tried everything and couldn't get her over the hump. While my balls ached, I tucked this night away in my mind as a nice reference experience. I was a mid-thirties man and I'd just met a pretty twenty-two year old tourist in the street and come within a whisker of fucking her the next day.

Nice.

The spreadsheet of my first 250 approaches had columns tracking every data point that might conceivably be relevant in an analysis: the girl, her hotness, where we met, what I said, how good it went and so on. If you're struggling to approach, that's a good idea to enforce personal accountability, rather like how when dieting it's helpful to use scales and calorie counting to force oneself to face reality. After a while it becomes a burden because you invariably approach according to the spreadsheet rather than according to the girl and your mood. It's tempting to make the Game into a game. By 2010, I'd stopped logging everything. I'd write up a short diary of the memorable sets to fix them in my mind, but that was all. By May, I'd handed in my notice at work and was doing jury service that finished by 4pm. I was no longer limited to weekend daygame, or late evening when tired from work. I decided to track ten days of opens, which I've summarised below. I've retained the nerdy "HB" scale then used on PUA forums to rate girls from one to ten.

Meeting girls wasn't the problem

Monday 17th May
HB6 Dutch backpacker. Ten minute chat, she wouldn't give me a number.
HB6 Romania volleyballer. Instant date for coffee, took number, never saw her again.
HB7 Chinese tourist. Took a number, set up date, and then she flaked.
HB8 Bulgarian. Took a number, didn't go anywhere.

Tuesday 18th May
No approaches

Wednesday 19th May
HB7 Polish. Five minute chat, and she said she had a boyfriend. Didn't ask for number.
HB7 Finland. Good chat and idate but didn't see her again.
HB7 American black girl. Ten minute chat, and she was married.
HB7 Bengal. She didn't hook, so just a brief thirty-second chat.
HB7 Turkish 2-set. Five minute chat but nothing doing.
HB8 French actress. Ten minute chat, number close. Some texting but didn't get her on a date.
HB6 British 2-set. Ten minute chat, and they refused to give a number.
HB9 Brazilian. Didn't hook, just brief compliment.

Thursday 20th May
HB6 British in summer dress, five minute chat and didn't ask for number.
HB6 British burlesque, ten minute chat but didn't fancy her much so didn't ask for number.
HB7 German student, ten minute chat, she refused number.
HB9 Hungarian waitress, five minute chat, she refused number. This one stung because physically she was my ideal woman.
HB7 British seventeen year old, ten minute chat but didn't go anywhere.
HB6 German artist. A good chat and number but no date.
HB8 Dark haired Brit. Didn't hook.

Friday 21st May
HB7 Brazilian photographer. Ten minute chat, then she refused number.
HB9 Italian tourist. Ten minute chat, on her way to meeting boyfriend.
+ five more sets that didn't go anywhere

Saturday 22nd May
No approaches

Sunday 23rd May

HB6 Venezuelan with massive tits. Took her for idate and had a few dates but failed to escalate and didn't even kiss her.
HB6 Chinese student. Didn't go anywhere.
HB5 Brit long legs. I ran away when I got a good look at her face.
HB8 Pony tail. She didn't stop, just brushed me off and kept walking.
HB7 Lancaster student. Ten minute chat and refused to give her number.
HB4 China. Hooked but I ran a mile when I saw her teeth.
HB5 Japan. Five minute chat that didn't go anywhere.
HB7 French student. Five minute chat to nowhere.
HB6 Italian barrista. Ten minute chat to nowhere.
HB7 Dark hair. Didn't stop.

Monday 24th May
No approaches

Tuesday 25th May

HB9 Persia 2-set. Ten minute chat, number close but date was a failure.
HB9 Greek synchronised swimmer. Ten minute chat, she wouldn't give a number.
HB9 French dancer. Five minute chat, she wouldn't give a number.

Wednesday 26th May

HB8 Indian big tits. Instant date, number close. Date went nowhere.

Looking at that list now a few things come to mind. First, that I really was dedicated. In ten days I only skipped three despite never-ending struggles with approach anxiety and a lack of conviction that I'd ever succeed. I was wandering London solo, except weekends when Fernando was available to join me. Second, there were days when I'd be walking the streets for hours and only do a few sets. Partly this is because London doesn't have many pretty girls but mainly it shows how volatile my moods were. Sometimes things went well and I was on a roll. Other times, I shuffled around with my hands in my pockets feeling the weight of the whole world on my shoulders.

My best daygame wing, Fernando

Summer approached and the weather guaranteed the streets were now full of girls ambling around with nothing better to do. My consistent work on the streets generated leads so I was having a date almost every day, cycling girls in and out. I'd get some numbers, set up dates, make a mess of the dates, lose the girls, then start pushing the boulder back up hill like a modern-day Sisyphus. It was exhausting but also exhilarating. For the first time in my life I had some measure of control over my sex life. Each passing week I would iron out a minor flaw or add a new trick to my arsenal. I became progressively calmer and this allowed me to try new things and incorporate feedback. The street was my laboratory and I was excited to see what would happen next. There were some stubborn sticking points that kept sinking my interactions (particularly my inability to physically escalate) but I could see light at the end of the tunnel. I was full of optimism, and this dragged me through the relentless rejections and frustrations.

During the period summarised above, I also went on a bunch of dates and idates. Let's recap a few of them.

Monday was the Romanian volleyball player. Summer had brung its scorching hot weather, and I was loving it. I was over on Neal Street and saw a tall girl looking at a Google Maps printout while standing next to one of the charity elephant statues. I tried a situational opener.

"Hey, I have to ask. Is that a map of elephants?"

She laughed, "No, I start a job tomorrow. I am a barmaid."

"Your accent is nice. It reminds me of the female assassins the KGB sends after James Bond."

She was keen to chat so on the ten minute mark I bounced her to a nearby cafe. Facially, she wasn't especially pretty but she was tall, leggy, and curvy. Certainly worth doing from behind. The instant date lasted about ninety minutes and it was okay, but I struggled to maintain and build sexual tension. I could feel energy leaking out of the interaction, like air from a punctured tire. I took her number and moved on to other girls.

Nothing happened that Tuesday, as clear from the "no approaches" in my list above. I went out solo and for some reason I just couldn't get going. I couldn't remember the last time I'd failed to open even one girl so this felt like a big setback. There seemed to be no girls hot enough to inspire me and my own independent sources of inspiration had run dry. So I walked around feeling miserable and then went home beating myself up for my failure.

I bounced back on Wednesday. Walking along South Bank by the river, I saw a leggy girl dressed like she'd come out of the stables. It wasn't actual equestrian dress but rather fashionable clothes nonetheless that looked remarkably like horse-riding garb.

"Hi. Where did you park your horse?" I said. She liked that.

For the first five minutes, Heidi from Finland was very flighty but then settled. We walked across Embankment Bridge together then drank take-out coffee while we sat on the grass by Trafalgar Square. The rapport was excellent, as usual. Heidi fully opened up to me, sharing her hopes and dreams, but again I couldn't create sexual tension. I walked her along St James' Park to feed the ducks, took her number, and let her go. I knew I'd never hear from her again.

I found a German artist on Thursday. I'd already done my allocation of sets for the day when I met Fernando as he was just starting, him having finished work after my jury duty. We were chatting near Covent Garden market when I saw a cute little square-head sitting on some low steps drawing a picture of a building. I asked what she was drawing and she was very friendly. I teased her for a while then bounced her to a nearby pub. After a pint there we went on to *Milk & Honey*. The conversation was great and she tried hard to keep it going but she rebuffed all of my escalation, claiming a boyfriend. I enjoyed the date, but it was going nowhere.

The street was giving me clear feedback: *you're always getting friend-zoned.*

Nothing memorable happened on Friday and then on Saturday I met Luminita. I'd not seen her for a few weeks since she came round to pick up her cardigan. She'd left that when she'd stormed out the house after an argument. She had wanted to go to the park but I was busy fighting a three-headed hydra end-of-level boss in *Ninja Blade* and, as there was no in-game save function, going outside was clearly out of the question.

Fernando and Johnny were teaching a student on Sunday, so I rolled up to help out. It was a glorious day, and I was on fire. There was a fantastic vibe everywhere we went. About my fourth approach I hooked a timid little Chinese throwabout and I was actually surprised when I successfully bounced her to a cafe. Such timid little kittens normally bolted on me. We sat in the piazza eating ice creams. She carelessly mentioned a boyfriend but didn't seem to care much about him. After half an hour I took her number and send her packing.

On the evening I had my second date with U.V., the little Guyanan minx. That went great, and I thought I was going to shag her when we got the tube back to my place and bought a bottle of wine, but she suddenly became anxious outside of my house. We redirected to a nearby pub where I verbally escalated her then literally picked her up over my shoulder, spanked her arse, and carried her to the local park for some making out. She agreed to come inside my apartment, refused sex, but after some jollies I sent her home with a smile on her face.

Monday rolled around and I was headed along the South Bank expecting to do normal daygame when a girl I'd met the prior year, a very hot Chinese-Australian half-caste called Jackie, rang up and invited me to a park.

There was a never ending series of instant dates

We met up early afternoon in Camden and walked to Primrose Hill via a pub. We bantered from the off but I had the same old mental blocks about escalating. A month earlier, I'd written off Jackie as a dead-end but as we'd said goodbye outside the Underground station I'd tried to kiss her anyway and she'd kissed me back. Then she got busy with a family trip and the attraction momentum died. Or so I'd thought.

Jackie and I had a great time around Camden. She was the absolute best arm candy: almost six foot, catwalk-leggy, and wearing immodest short shorts and a flimsy top. As we walked through Camden with her clutching my arm, literally every man stared at her with barely-suppressed envy. We chilled in the park, and she stripped down to her bikini. There was lots of flirting, and I kissed her again.

Yet I couldn't make myself escalate.

There was a mental wall as formidable as the Krak De Chavaliers. I never felt I could push further than kissing. My timidity must have struck Jackie as weak but I knew I've never been a timid man. Something else — not timidity — was preventing me from following through in my desires. If I'd gone for it with Jackie I'm sure I could have shagged her. God knows, I wanted to. All the subtle signals were present, plus the rather less-subtle signal of her stretching out in a bikini next to me, but I was too insecure to follow through. I didn't trust my calibration, either.

My mind threw out all manner of ridiculous reasons why she might behave as she did *without* wanting sex. Perhaps she's working on her tan. Perhaps her friends cancelled and she was bored sitting at home. Perhaps.......

Perhaps there was something badly wrong with my inner game.

So that's a taster for how my daygame journey looked as the first anniversary of my first ever cold approach rolled around. Over one thousand approaches, two notches with unremarkable girls, but many, many positive interactions that fuelled my desire to keep pushing the boulder up the hill week after week. I was no longer the tired introverted shut-in with only a few old friends and no female company that I'd been a year earlier. I was constantly outside in the sunshine, meeting new girls every week, having dates, kissing, having near misses and rolling with a new group of friends. Despite the lack of sex, daygame had given me hope.

CHAPTER 21

THAI GIRLS ARE TIGERS

Luminita and I stopped seeing each other in early May, 2010. That was also when I began my unbroken streak of getting laid with one new girl each and every calendar month for a year. There'd be many failed efforts too, but the trickle was finally threatening to become a flood.

Fernando and I walked around London Bridge, experimenting with a new location, one gorgeous Sunday afternoon. There is a very nice indoor market under the old Victorian-era railway bridge where one can buy all types of speciality foods such as local cheeses, scones, and there's a beer shop selling a vast assortment of bottled micro-brewery ales. As I age the finer things in life please me more, seeing someone find a niche and then run with it, creating something different to the usual mass-market products. Being next to the river, the market views are lovely.

"Might be some decent skirt at the market," I'd suggested to Fernando. "When I did the boot camp last year, it was okay. Since then I've been daygaming further along the South Bank and it's full of tourists."

We ambled around, weaving amongst the shoppers while scanning the crowd for girls. The market itself didn't seem very amenable for the classic street-stop approach. Most of the girls were in groups and it felt weird to stand next to a girl at a market stall and start hitting on her. "The girls dress like in Brazil. Look at all the skin on show!" enthused Fernando. The blazing sunshine had brought out all the short skirts and denim cut-offs.

"Aye, but there's nothing going on here. Let's get on the edge of the market and try the street."

Having failed to get going under the bridge, we struck out onto the busy main street by the Underground station where hopefully there'd be fast footfall and less social pressure. That's where I saw Tasanee, a twenty-two year old law student from Bangkok. At first glance I noticed only denim shorts, so tight as to look spray-painted on, and gorgeous sun-bronzed legs. Long straight brown hair flowed as she walked, lighter brown highlights catching the sun. I let her stride past to take an eyeful of her ass. A single emotion bubbled up from my chest and filled my mind, forcing out all other thoughts. I was experiencing a moment of metaphysical clarity.

"I want that."

I felt a deep visceral need in me, what I call a 'DNA-tug'. It's that inexplicably strong attraction felt in every fibre of your being, like your blood is bubbling and skin tingling. Yes, Tasanee was very pretty, but no more so than many other young women. Something specific in the combination of her hair, smile, walk, and her colouring filled me with an irresistible motion-towards, what famous philosopher Immanuel Kant called an "inclination". My feet were already moving.

I hurried over to catch her, almost tripping over myself as I did. When I got in front she stopped and looked up at me. I started with my usual line, telling her that I couldn't let her go by without stopping her to tell her how gorgeous she was. Tasanee smiled shyly. I was still slow in picking up subtle signals, but I wasn't without any instincts at all. Red lights flashed Defcon 5 in my head, a buzzer sounded, and perhaps fireworks exploded in the sky. This young woman really fancied me, I could sense it.

She too felt a Kantian inclination. Who was I to critique her pure reason?

Tasanee was giggly. When she smiled her cheeks dimpled and curved like a hamster. I often compare girls to different animals when I tease them, based on their physical appearances. Girls with long skinny legs are giraffes. Short girls with big cheeks are squirrels or hamsters.

"You look like a hamster," I told her. "I like it."

Yes, Kant would've approved of that.

Now she was cooing and blushing, lighting up the street with deliciously warm feminine energy. We talked for five or ten minutes, silly talk with me teasing her, and Tasanee letting me know a little about herself. I checked out her legs and ass quite openly.

"This is why I like summer. All the girls in shorts with tanned legs," I told her.

I took her number and returned to Fernando, who was propped up against a wall waiting for me. Then we continued our stroll. Tasanee came back the same way ten minutes later, talking on the phone, and gave a wave.

Our text messaging flowed quickly and easily, showing her high interest level and competent English. Three days later we agreed to meet in London Bridge again, at precisely the same spot outside the Underground where we'd first met. As I walked along Borough Road towards the date my mind spun from excitement. I'd been on fifty dates over the past year, maybe more, and I usually ended up disappointed. Sometimes the girl would be keen and I'd mess it up. Other times, she was just milking me for attention and didn't even consider it to be a date. It was painful enough absorbing rejection after rejection on the street. When I did find a girl who seemed keen and gave out her number, I couldn't help my hopes rising at the prospect of banging her. Many would flake over texting, as you'd expect. Finally, I'd have some girls who got as far as agreeing a time and place for a date. Some wouldn't even show up.

Men bear the searching costs of dating. We have to investment heavily up front just to make things happen. Girls can't appreciate the emotional roller coaster the man has endured before she's even shown up for the date. The same girl who may be polite and conscientious on a date with a man drawn from her social circle may exhibit 'princess behaviours' with a stranger she's only known for five minutes on the street. Many expect to be entertained and feel entitled to back out at any moment at the slightest whim.

I knew, because I'd been on the sharp end of it plenty. A thousand approaches, a couple hundred phone numbers, several dozen dates, and so far only two lays. I was seeing a different side to male-female relations. This is how my thoughts ran as I walked to meet Tasanee, trying to keep my spirits high and not let my thoughts drift to the "this will be just another waste of time and effort" abyss.

I understand that girls too have frustrations in dating, but those weren't salient in my mind.

I arrived early, five minutes before six. It was still light outside, and warm. Every element of my dating strategy was under review, trying to learn from more experienced men. How should I stand so that I look cool and not too keen? Should I pretend to check my phone or is it okay to watch for her coming? Many of the things I take for granted now had to be mechanically learned back then. I no longer trusted my natural inclinations. I hoisted myself up onto a low railing and sat watching the taxis and the buses come and go as all the busy people left work. A few minutes passed, then I saw the silhouette of a curvy little girl coming to the top of the escalator inside the station. The crowd cleared a little and she walked into the light. It was indeed Tasanee. She was chuntering away on her phone, head down, taking a call as she showed up for our date. She saw me, waved a greeting, then paced back and forth on the pavement continuing her conversation. That was somewhat offensive to me. I found it rude, but I didn't know what to do about it, so I just continued my traffic- and people-watching until she was done. It took fully five minutes before she hung up.

She smiled and said, "I'm sorry about that, I got called from Thailand."

I didn't detect any princess vibe, so I couldn't stay mad. False alarm. We exchanged pleasantries then walked off to a pub across the road. She fell into step beside me. That little phone episode had tripped a switch in me, reminding me of bad experiences being tooled on dates that go nowhere. Fortunately, the vibe was back on track.

The first pub was packed inside, not surprising for a Wednesday evening outside a major rail interchange. The sun was out so we took our pint glasses onto the street and propped ourselves against a pub window. Conversation flowed easily and within a few minutes we'd left the typical first-date awkwardness behind and were building rapport. I dropped a few teases in, told some stories, and let her tell me her hopes and dreams. My whole body buzzed with sheer pleasure. I cast my eyes over the river to see little tug-boats struggling against the tide, then took in the old Victorian architecture around me. *Life isn't all that bad*, I thought. Here I was in the greatest city on earth, a warm summer day, I hadn't even been to work in a month, and now I had this sweet little Thai hamster sharing a drink and giggling at my jokes.

Tasanee was very sincere about our meeting. It was indeed a date. There was no tooling or friend-zone bullshit. She was interested in me and wanted to see if I would move along towards something romantic. We bought our second pint at the next pub along, closer to the river. It had a low wall outside literally over the river so we sat there. If I reached down with one hand at high tide I could touch the water.

Tasanee still giggled at everything I said, no matter how bland. That's a girl's universal signal meaning 'I like this, please continue'. I could've probably read the bookmakers odds from the middle pages of *The Racing Post* and still made her giggle. Now that the date was going well I became nervous. It looked increasingly like I could kiss her, and thus that I could escalate. Counter-intuitively, the very fact the date was going well was what worried me—I now had something to lose, and thus risked feel bad about myself if I squandered an opportunity. My escalation was still awful.

Perhaps, I thought, I should just throw her into the river, go home, and play video games. Save myself the rigmarole. It would be less stressful.

My nerves expressed themselves by making me brag about my awesomeness. I was trying too hard, qualifying to her. I told Tasanee about taking a sabbatical from my job at the age of twenty-five and doing a four year stint in Japan. I also rattled on about boxing and martial arts, my extensive business travelling. Basically, summarising the first fifteen chapters of this book but without any of the bad stuff. I grasped at anything and everything to make her interested in me, which was silly because she was obviously already sold on me. I wanted more affirmation of it. I really, really wanted to bang her.

As we sat there on the wall in this beautiful spot, me flapping my gums over something silly, I scooted over close so that she could hear me, and I realized we were sitting thigh-to-thigh. I felt a thrill course through my bloodstream, a visceral reaction to being within intimate distance to a girl I wanted to bang. Voices in my head bounced around saying, "I'm touching her thigh, I'm touching her thigh." It was crazy how clumsy I was being at this with this cute little Thai girl. I think teenage girls at a pop concert have more self control.

Tasanee paced me with her beer, so I told her to slow it down. "I don't want you getting drunk and causing trouble." She giggled yet again. She told me later she'd been as nervous as me, hence the fast drinking.

The sun set and a chill came across the water. Birds flapped their wings and took off, evidently thinking of warmer winds elsewhere. We took our drinks inside and found a table. We sat in a small dusty room with bare wooden floorboards and panelling, furnished to maintain a maritime air. Running up the side wall was an open staircase to the bathrooms on the first floor. Nobody else was in the room but the sounds of merry-making from the main bar drifted through the open communicating door. I had to kiss Tasanee soon. The way she was pushed against me, and stealing sly glances at my lips told me the window of opportunity was open. This was the moment I usually messed up my dates, waiting too long for a right moment.

There is never a right moment.

Tasanee liked me and I knew it, but I was still nervous, thinking of all the previous dates where the girls had recoiled, or deftly rebuffed me. I'd gone home many times distraught at yet another failure.

"Excuse me a minute," she said, and walked up the stairs to the toilet. I watched her go, my eyes fixed on her ass. For the five minutes she was in the bathroom, I thought about how many times I had screwed this up and how many missed opportunities there had been. I looked up as I heard her footsteps on the wooden stairs to see Tasanee return, cautiously descending, grabbing the bannister, careful not to catch her high heels and take a tumble. I drank in her lithe shape and shiny long hair, drawing conviction from my sexual desire. I stood up, intercepted her at the bottom of the staircase, grabbed her hands, lifted up her chin, and kissed her. She loved it.

Given permission to kiss, Tasanee jumped. *Yes! I'm kissing a twenty-two year old Thai girl!* I thought. Confidence flushed through my body as though I'd snorted a line of cocaine. My blood pumped with the vitality of a thousand warriors. Had that been in reserve the whole time? I'd have rather appreciated such confidence making a show on all those earlier dates, I thought. Then I wisely chose not to overthink things any longer. I finished my drink, Tasanee was almost finished with hers.

I looked at her and said, "What's your favourite drink?"

She giggled and said, "Gin and Tonic."

"Okay, I'm going to make you one."

"Right now?"

"Yes," I told her, "I have to send you home early, so it has to be now."

"Okay then."

My house was within walking distance, a twenty minute stroll, but I was wary of losing momentum on a long walk. Now that I recount this story, it was obviously already a done deal. Tasanee was willing the whole way, hoping I'd lead her forwards, but I was still a little nervous. When you are in the set, talking to the girl and trying to read signals on the fly you often lack the clarity of the outside observer and tend to think things are more precarious than they really are. Taking no chances I hailed a cab, bundled her into it, and we were on our way. She knew what was happening. She didn't ask where we were going. There was no resistance but I still felt as though success balanced on the edge of a knife.

I started babbling. Knowing she was from Thailand and the national sport there is Muay-Thai kickboxing, that's the direction my babbling took. She humoured me, giggling in that hamster manner. I poured her a drink in my lounge and left for a minute to use the toilet. She sipped her drink and looked at the books on my coffee table.

I returned and we sat on the sofa with our drinks, I pulled her close to me and she immediately jumped me, straddling my lap. I grabbed handfuls of her ass, having had itchy fingers for it since Sunday. Then I reached my hands around her shorts and the very edges of my fingers ever so slightly touched her through her underwear. She started moaning, really moaning.

I'd underestimated this girl's horniness.

Tasanee didn't merely feel a Kantian inclination towards me. This was the full dialectic, critique and transcendental idealism all rolled up into one little brown hamster-shaped package. She wanted her epistemology good and hard.

All that time moving things tentatively forwards, overthinking, wondering if I was moving too fast, and now Tasanee was moaning and grinding better than a $1,000 lap-dancer. She'd probably been thinking of sex all evening. *Fuck it, this is so on*, I thought. I stood up and she wrapped her legs around me to hold her straddle position. I walked her into the bedroom, threw her onto the bed and undressed as she scurried out of her own clothes.

I moved her mouth towards my dick and she looked up nervously, "I don't know. I'm not very good at this."

"Oh, it's okay just go ahead and try it," I replied, ever the gentleman.

```
Very happy with a new
    Thai girlfriend
```

It was another tell that I'd missed, that hinted Tasanee was as keen to impress me as I was to impress her. It's comical when I think back. I wanted it so bad I couldn't see what was plainly evident in front of my nose. All the while she was thinking she needed to prove something to me.

Tasanee was a moaner. Everything I did to her brought squeaks and moans. I hadn't had sex for a couple of weeks so when I came on her face she was messed up like a plasterer's radio. We lay there together for a while then I did her again. It was even better the second time. Finally, we were both satiated, and I was so very pleased with myself. I was lying there thinking, "Oh my God I just fucked a twenty two year old!"

I wasn't sure why her age was such an important part of it. I could've just as reasonably been pleased because she was pretty, or Thai, or very likeable, or enthusiastic. But for some reason her youth was what fixed in my mind. I looked at her lying on my bed, and she looked so young. She could pass for seventeen or eighteen. Her skin was taut and perfectly smooth with the dewy freshness that women lose with age. The last time I had banged a girl in her prime — Ryoko from Okinawa notwithstanding — was when I was the same age myself. That had been Ioe, my ex-wife. As I'd aged, so had she. In itself that's no surprise, nature being as it is. Back then I didn't mind or even keep track of Ioe's subtle signs of ageing. The silky softness of women's skin dries out over time. Their springy stomachs go soft and the bloom comes off the rose. They even begin to smell a bit funny.

Being with Tasanee was like re-living my youth. That explained why I'd been so energised by her from the beginning, and why my mind fixated on it now.

"I've only dated one boy before you," she said, propping herself up on an elbow and softly tugging at my chest hair with her other hand. She looked blissfully happy, which raised my mood even higher. "My family is very traditional."

"How traditional?"

"I met this boy when I was eighteen. We dated only six months. We had sex, but I haven't been with a man in the four years since."

"No men in four years? You must've been climbing the walls," I said.

"Oh, I dated some boys but we didn't go far."

I hadn't expected that. Her clumsiness with blow jobs suggested some inexperience, or at least a straight-laced traditional attitude towards sex. Nonetheless, she'd been a Yes Girl from the beginning with me and followed me home in under three hours of the first date. I had to ask.

"So what was the difference with me? You just met me and here you are in my bed wiping my cum off your face with a tissue."

"I just knew… you were the one."

That tickled my vanity. Intellectually, I knew that her age and hormones were at least as important as my awesomeness. Four years of celibacy had caught up with her. Also Asian girls typically went for my type. It's common knowledge that if you see an Asian girl with a Western man, it's typically a white, nerdy kind of man like I was then. That's why so many white men go to Japan to teach English.

It's why I'd gone.

Sarge School night out

Tasanee stayed overnight and forgot her watch in the morning. I texted Jimmy. "Hey, guess what? I slept with a twenty-two year old girl last night. She's a lawyer, from Bangkok."

"Nice one. Twenty-two!"

I dated Tasanee for nine months, meeting once or twice a week, and enjoyed every moment of it. There wasn't any of the frostiness that sometimes crept in with Luminita. Tasanee was bubbly and agreeable, like Miwako had been years earlier. Knowing we'd see each other a lot, I knew there was a big question to resolve: do I tell her that I'm always chasing skirt? There was conflicting advice in the PUA community, with the shiftier elements suggesting I lie my ass off and pretend I'm an exclusive boyfriend. I didn't like that. I freely admitted to myself and others that my moral code could be flexibly self-serving, but I wasn't a liar.

One of the inner game products I'd begun studying was an audiobook, by an American commercial PUA called Hypnotica, designed to be played while sleeping, the theory being it would subliminally infuse strong inner game to the subconscious mind. That seemed like psycho-babble to me, but I tried it anyway. The first file began with the admonition, "you will resolve today, at this moment, to never tell lies." It had surprised me at first, as I then thought most old PUA advice was based on lying your ass off. Perhaps I'd gotten the wrong impression. Coupled with what I'd read in Brad Blanton's book *Radical Honesty*, I knew I'd have trouble squaring this circle. How do you tell a girl you want to date her, that she can't sleep around, but you want to keep chasing other girls? I seemed a tough sell.

I asked Jimmy.

"You can't lie, mate, that'll wreck your inner game. Just put it out there. You're a high-value man, you don't want to be tied down so soon after your marriage. She'll trust that, because it's true. She might squawk a bit, but she'll trust it."

A couple of weeks after first meeting Tasanee, I told her I wanted to date several girls. She accepted it without quibble, surprisingly. We did all the things a happily dating couple should do. She'd come around to cook for me and my friends, taking great pleasure from the childish smiles of satisfaction as we ate her Thai curries. We went to the cinema, for walks in the park, and hung out in my room. I banged her in several public locations, including the toilets at the Pizza Express where I'd ranted on at Luminita a couple of months earlier.

She's a full-fledged lawyer now, in Bangkok, and married to a man for Newcastle who looks a bit like me. I doubt that's a coincidence. She met him in London a year after we broke up, so they've been together seven years so far. I will never forget Tasanee nor the effect that she had on my life. Her pleasant demeanour helped me restore a favourable view of women that had been damaged through my divorce and 'red-pilling' from the Internet. My time with her was the first step in letting go of some of the bitterness that I still held on to, and moving to the next stage of the Kubler-Ross process. After that first date by the river, I was always calm and relaxed with Tasanee. I began to realise how complimentary a feminine girl's energy can be.

Fun in Malaga

Nightgame with Jackie Johnny and Fernando

With Jimmy and Lee

CHAPTER 22

YET MORE GRINDING

CHAPTER 22

YET MORE GRINDING

I'd begun making big changes to my style of daygame. The simple version Johnny had shown me only went so far, and really it was just an opener. What happened after that? There were still several minutes to chat with the girl, so surely there must be an optimal way of doing so.

I looked around for men who'd already built a name as daygamers. There weren't many of them. One man making waves in early 2010 was a chubby London-born Kurd called Yad. He was in his early twenties and all the forums were abuzz over an impressive in-field video of his on YouTube. He approached a cute young Russian girl on The Strand in London, chatted ten minutes, and then kissed her, right there on the street. I'd never seen this before, a "street kiss close". I didn't know it was even possible. It seemed so.... out there.

Nowadays, when I look back at the video it feels rather 'off' to me. I wouldn't say it's necessarily fake (i.e. that Yad hired an actress for the role) but *something* isn't right. Also, the video was produced with Richard La Ruina who has a rather mixed reputation for claiming things that never really happened. Let's say that it impressed me in 2010 and doesn't now, and leave it at that.

The famous Yad kiss close video

Inspiring though Yad's video was, so much so that even Roissy posted an extensive second-by-second analysis on his blog, that's not what interested me most about Yad. I am technically-minded and, with Roissy's help, I understood Yad had been innovating daygame technique.

That's what I wanted to learn. Better technique.

So far I'd only ever paid *Sarge School* for coaching, relying on wings, books, DVDs, and my own experience on the street to teach me. Yad cost £50 an hour in 2010 and I decided to book a four-hour one-on-one coaching session with him. Keen to extract the maximum value out of the session, I spent the preceding weekend recording my own approaches on a small 'gum' camera, a cheap Chinese-made spy camera that was shaped like a packet of chewing gum and clipped onto my breast pocket. It wasn't very convincing, but girls never seemed to notice. Fernando and I had spent several months experimenting with cameras bought from Ebay. We tried gum cams, pen cams, button cams.... anything and everything. I'd learned from my martial arts training that recording yourself is a valuable diagnostic tool. You only get to experience a round of sparring once, directly, and your mind is focuses on the fighting ebb and flow. If you record it, however, you can experience that same round dozens of times. You can pick it apart and deconstruct everything that's happening — good or bad.

Naturally, I brought the same attitude to my daygame. From the beginning, I conceived of pick-up as fundamentally similar to fighting and amenable to the same pedagogy. So, when I met Yad in his apartment behind Oxford Street, I had a USB drive with ten recent infields on it. We spent the first half hour watching through a couple of them so that he got a feel for what I was saying to girls. Then we hit the streets.

I was extremely curious about Yad. He'd been daygaming four years longer than me and had a reputation for going out every day, doing hundreds of sets per week. There wasn't a man alive more experienced than he. Additionally, that kiss-close video suggested he had some secret sauce to his game. What was he doing, and could I imitate it?

The sun was shining, girls were promenading in their short shorts and life felt good. Within two minutes Yad was talking to a pretty Austrian tourist. She'd passed by us so he'd tapped her arm and said hello. He was so smooth, like a crocodile slipping into the water without a splash. I stood quietly next to him, observing. He was unbelievably relaxed and within ten seconds of saying hello the girl was completely at ease, smiling, and contributing back to the conversation. Yad took her number, excused himself and we continued along the street. I opened six or seven girls and Yad did a few demonstration sets. I could feel his Zen vibe rubbing off on me as I slipped into the "daygame trance."

The trance is a flow state daygamers hit when all the social barriers dissolve and you feel at one with the energy of the streets. In this peak state you feel like you can talk to anybody in any situation and your mind automatically presents the right thing to do. It's the Holy Grail of game but, unlike history's real Crusader knights, a daygamer can actually find it once in a while. It's unnerving the first time it happens because it's the antithesis of the approach anxiety that I'd feel most of the time.

Every girl I spoke to stopped and responded well. It was addictive. Roughly speaking, men need three types of happiness in their lives: hedonism, flow and meaning. Daygame amply satisfies the hedonism through sex (eventually!) but so does every other type of Game, as does getting laid through non-game routes. By making daygame my mission and obsessing over every little technical detail, I'd imbued daygame with existential meaning too. The real special pleasure of daygame, however, is neither the sex nor the sense of purpose. It's actually those fleeting periods of trance-like flow. It is incredibly difficult to find flow in your life but an avid daygamer gets repeated fixes of it, losing himself in the skilful practice of a manly art. For me, those periods were a higher level of happiness than the eventual sex it can generate.

Good daygame tapped the same pleasure circuits in me as a good sparring session in kickboxing. I was reminded of my first fight in Japan, how it had felt like a peak self-actualisation.

By this point Yad had been daygaming for five years and was a confirmed pussy rat. The streets were his playground and it showed in his exuberance in chasing down girls without a trace of approach anxiety. As the afternoon progressed he'd drop in little snippets of advice here and there, fine-tuning my work. He said I was already competent at the basics so his input was more holistic and woolly, trying to refine my vibe. Midway through, he dragged me into a cafe on Regent Street so he could eat. Yad is famous for using one-on-ones as mealtimes. While sitting across from him at a rickety table in a French cafe, watching him stuff his face with some kind of beef pastrami, I could see he was trying to form the right words to articulate his thoughts to me. He had the look of a man who has glimpsed the answer to a puzzle but can't quite bring it into focus. Chewing a mouthful of bread, he looked dead in my eyes.

"Nick, your vibe is a bit off. You seem angry."

That's rather cutting, I thought.

I sat there with pursed lips and a stone-cold stare, trying not to let him know how prickly my ego was. Nonetheless, I knew he was right. Vibe is the special sauce of daygame. It's as elusive as nirvana. Yad let me ponder that in silence as he finished his sandwich.

"Right, we've got an hour left. Let's walk over to Covent Garden and try to get you an instant date," he said.

We did a couple more sets each. He held a group of three girls walking up by Seven Dials roundabout and brought me in to the chat. Finally, just as the session was winding down I fell into conversation with a Japanese girl and took her for coffee. Yad waved goodbye and went off, probably to a kebab shop.

I'd been very impressed with him. Everything he did was relaxed. He seemed extremely happy to be on the streets. I'd taken notes throughout and as I reviewed them back at my apartment in Kennington, I tried to make sense of why Yad was getting such good reactions from girls. He was just a chubby Turk (sorry, Kurd. I've heard there's a difference) with thick glasses, bad skin, and a messy haircut. He wasn't ugly but no one ever accused him of relying upon his looks. Despite this, he had an almost magical ability to get into long chats with hot young women. From the first moment, they'd immediately settle down and feel comfortable with him.

I believed in the power of daygame. I had my own personal experiences to sustain this belief, but in Yad I seemed to be glimpsing new levels of it.

Yad was a pivotal early figure in the development of what is now called the London Daygame Model. Before him, no-one really had a plan. His most famous innovation was the 'Yad Stop', being his way of jogging up behind a girl and then getting in front of her to make her stop. He'd seen Robert Downey Jnr do it in a movie called *The Pick Up Artist* and immediately recognised how powerful it was on a busy thoroughfare such as Oxford Street. I hadn't known it then, but he'd popularised it and a ginger PUA going by the moniker Keychain had copied it from him. It had been Keychain who had shown it to Johnny, who had shown me. The Seduction Community was just like the Brazilian Ju Jitsu community in that sense, the way hot new techniques would spread like wildfire through forums, sparring, and seminars.

I'd already added an innovation of my own. Roissy's blog gave many examples of funny teases to drop onto girls early in a bar-game set. His rationale was adapted from Mystery Method's 'negging'. Mystery postulated that there is an imbalance in sexual and social value early in a set, because a girl's SMV is immediately obvious from her youth and beauty, whereas a man's is opaque as it rests more on confidence and character. Until the man can display these positive traits (what Mystery called 'demonstrations of higher value') the girl has the upper hand and may lose interest early. To combat this, Mystery recommended throwing a 'neg', essentially a back-handed compliment, to make the girl's ears prick up.

"I like your nails. Are they real?"

"Your dress is great. It's very popular with girls this season."

These were example negs Mystery popularised. By giving a clear compliment wrapped up with a vague put-down, it catches a girls attention and possibly makes her a little self-conscious. An additional advantage is it suggests you like her but are not yet completely sold. Thus, unlike all the other men, you aren't a push-over. That makes you more interesting.

Mystery's negs were rather lame and tailored for bat-shit-crazy LA party girls. Roissy was on the American east coast, a different social milieu. He was also a hilarious writer, so his negs were often brilliant. I adapted the principle to daygame by pairing a compliment and a tease. For example, "I like how tall you are. Like a giraffe." It was meant to be playful, rather than insulting. I quickly found it worked well. Girls would easily absorb the compliment, as it was expected, but the tease would jar them, usually into laughing. But that's as far as it went. After that there wasn't any real structure to running the set. We couldn't simply follow Mystery's model because it was designed for indirect game, where you mask your intent until the girl has already displayed interest in you.

Yad used a structured but quite bland opening, which went as follows:

"Hi, sorry, can I just say something really quickly. I just noticed you walking by and I want to say you look nice. What I noticed about you was...." and then he'd drop in an observation, specific to her if he could and if not, drawn from a library of generic observations. So though the words weren't special, there were many subtle differences in his vibe and sub-communication that I picked up during the session and began to implement. I was interested in his less-is-more body language (he didn't move or gesture much) and his habit of verbally bamboozling girls with elaborate flights of fancy delivered in a soft steady voice. I got the impression he was spinning a web around them until they got confused and started babbling nonsense. Most of all, I liked his sense of calm. I saw how a relaxed vibe immediately relaxes girls.

I'd been too hyper.

"What you feel, she feels," said Yad. It's important to get a vibe conducive to meeting strangers. Try not to startle the horse. A major jigsaw piece had been inserted into the puzzle. I felt that while the jigsaw was incomplete, I now had all the corners and edges. I resolved to go back for more coaching with Yad in six months or so, for a refresher. I was still determined to learn primarily from my own experience. Fernando, Johnny and I were going out every week now, so we figured out a lot for ourselves. Occasionally, we'd even get Jimmy out.

Summer arrived.

More dates to nowhere

My Thai girlfriend Tasanee filled me with joy and a zest for life, and my new friends were excellent company. It didn't feel so tough on the streets any more. We'd still get blow-outs, awkward conversations, and sometimes spend over an hour walking around unable to find a girl we wanted to talk to. Despite all that, it was fun. I felt I was moving forwards.

Spending so much time on the streets often led to statistically improbable experiences. One such day was June 24, 2010. I had three dates in three hours. *Sarge School*'s British-Indian coach Shameem had called me so we went out together around Covent Garden. It was burning hot. I wore a baseball cap and sunglasses. My first few approaches went okay, just warm ups really. I complimented a stunning girl on her dress and got into a ten minute conversation with a songwriter who had written top-ten hits and recently signed to a major label to sing solo. It appeared to be going well but she got a call from her parents and had to go — suggesting she wasn't overly interested in me after all. We exchanged Facebook details and I saw from her Wikipedia page that she wasn't bullshitting about her career. She seemed to be on the verge of national stardom.

So, that was the first pop star that I never banged. In my first year of daygame I'd manage to not bang a whole range of interesting girls: singers, TV actresses, catwalk models, sports stars. I dare say I'd already gotten really good at *not* banging such girls. The next stage in that progression would be rather impressive, but it didn't seem very close.

Always experimenting with technique, I tried a new style based on the audio books of an American instructor called Gunwitch. He had pretty much invented modern daygame, ten years earlier. As befitting a pioneer, his style was raw, undeveloped and long-since surpassed but nonetheless there was real gold buried in those audio books. I'd come to believe (erroneously) that my technique and calibration were absolutely fine and thus I didn't need think about anything while in the interaction. I trusted my faculties to sort it out. The major missing link, I surmised, was my inner game. Specifically, I took a long slow route after the opener when I ought to be showing far more sexual intent. So having warmed up on this scorching hot June day, I decided to practise two principles.

First, to express strong sexual intent through sub-communication (but not verbally). I had a bad habit of opening with a masculine, direct come-on but would then ease up and fall into pointless chit-chat. I resolved to maintain sexual intensity throughout, but without being so overt as to talk sexually. Gunwitch recommended projecting sexual thoughts through eye contact, trusting the girl to notice and, if she likes you, reciprocate.

Secondly, I tended to end most sets by asking for a phone number even if the girl told me she was ambling around with no specific plan. This is a common beginner mistake. The ego is stroked by getting a phone number as it represents a 'win', however small. In contrast, asking a girl onto an instant date and getting rejected, is a 'loss' to the ego. I had a tendency to eject with a phone number, and such 'number collecting' felt good but didn't get me far. I was deceiving myself to earn an ego boost. So, I resolved to keep plowing all the way through to the Same Day Lay (or rejection).

Given my current level of success, I was expecting a rejection rate of 100%.

I was tired of long instant dates that ended without even a kiss

The point was to learn, and to develop my skill set. I reasoned that getting the skills was permanent whereas a lay was temporary. Something about giving a man a fish to feed him for a day, or teaching him how to fish to feed himself forever. If I was going to get sexual with girls, I'd need to develop my abilities in which girls, of the hundreds walking around Covent Garden, I should approach. I created these logistical filters to help.

1. Alone
2. Dressed in a sexually provocative manner (as opposed to merely pretty)
3. Showing some leg and/or cleavage
4. Not in any apparent rush
5. Get my blood tingling in an "Oh man, I'd love to fuck her" compatibility.

These were my early fumblings in what was to gradually coalesce into a clearly-defined teachable method. We were moving away from directly stating sexual intent to a girl (e.g."You're gorgeous") and instead towards what Roissy called "plausibly-deniable direct" game. This means to clearly convey sexual intent with eye contact, vocal tone, body language, and innuendo while keeping the content of the conversation completely innocent. I was also forming my initial ideas of a more sexualised presentation, to introduce myself as a potential casual sex partner rather than as a boyfriend. They were as yet only partially-formed ideas, rather than the precision-engineered tactics they'd eventually become.

My third interaction of the day hit well. She was a half English/half Indonesian girl ambling along Neal Street wearing a tight revealing black top and tight black leggings. Her large breasts were nearly falling out of the top. Aside from revealing much of her body shape, I was interested in what her fashion revealed about her disposition. Did her fashion express her mood? This was a girl who left the house at least intuitively wishing to be noticed by men, I reasoned. I got in front of her.

"Hi. I just have to ask. What's with the silly boots?"

She looked down self-consciously at her beige suede boots. She smiled, taken aback. That's the power of a playful push. So I continued, "Yeah, I was just back there when I noticed you ambling along–you have a very feminine manner, by the way, I like that–and you caught my eye. Then I noticed those boots!"

She hooked easily and quickly took up her side of the conversation. When a girl is talking animatedly to you for ten minutes it's a fair bet she fancies you, at least a little, so that's a good time to instant-date her in a nearby cafe. Remembering my learning points for the day, I tried to project sexual energy through my eyes. Hers opened wide.

"You should wear your hair down, I think. It'll look more sexy that way," I said, as I reached to touch it near her ear. I wanted the conversation to come alive, so these were intended to spark it. She responded well, flirting plenty. It was a long, long way from a same day lay but after the coffee I suggested a drink in the pub next door, nonetheless. She refused so I took her number. She left the UK two weeks later. It didn't go any further.

When I looked around, Shameem had disappeared. He had a tendency to wander off and forget about his wings. He wasn't rude, just a little weird, so it didn't bother me. I sent him a text then ambled along to Trafalgar Square. I found a twenty-three year old Korean tourist walking past, and I had my next instant date. She had lovely short-shorts, a tight top, and the general fertile springiness to her walk that screamed "Please open me, I'm receptive". She wasn't especially hot–perhaps a six on the universally agreed scale–but she got my blood a-tingling. She wore ludicrously bright Converse trainers so that gave me an opener.

"Hey, Korean girl. I love your style, it's cute. Except your silly shoes."

Silly boots, silly shoes. There seemed to be a theme today. Min-seo enjoyed chatting so I walked her to a grassy knoll by the National Gallery, and then to a pub. She was flirting strongly but also refused to come home with me. Considering we'd only spent an hour together, it's hardly a surprise. Like I said, I was just practising to see what was possible. Girls are swept up in the energy of the moment but tend to become suddenly clear-headed when you suggest going home together. For some, they don't like you enough to go that far. Others may really like you but it is simply too much too soon. Min-seo was situationally perfect for a quick pull, given she was travelling on her own in Europe, young, and something of an "outsider" in her own culture. Unfortunately, taking it slower wasn't an option. She left for the next leg of her Euro-tour a few days later and never met me for a date.

I checked my watch. Only two hours had passed since I'd opened the Indonesian girl, but it felt like yesterday. Busy daygame sessions warp one's perception of time. Back in Covent Garden I had a few forgettable sets. I opened a black girl and she was initially frosty but started to soften. As I was gearing up to suggest coffee, her friend arrived and cockblocked. The vibe hadn't been so strong so it was no great loss. I immediately stopped a lovely Asian in a summer dress and she hooked nicely but told me she had a boyfriend. There was also a tired dancer that chatted for a little while.

More meat fed into the grinder. Still, I was in a great mood.

I wasn't the only ambitious man chasing skirt that day. Outside Covent Garden station I saw a French daygamer who'd been working the same patch for the past month. We'd seen each other around and shared those I-know-what-you're-up-to looks before finally having a chat and making friends. He had a name I couldn't ever pronounce so I called him Clouseau, after the hapless detective from the *Pink Panther* movies. We were still chatting when a stunning Lithuanian strode past. Long legs, hot pants, sunglasses. Absolute stunner, a rare ten. Clousseau's face blanched in reaction to her hotness but that spurred me on and I gave chase. As I caught up I couldn't think of anything about her that interested me except that she was super hot and her bag was ugly.

"Hey, wait! Right. You are hot and your bag is shit."

That was the best I could manage and it came out wrong. Luckily, it sounded ballsy, especially on a girl so hot she probably had men kissing her ass 24/7. Surprisingly, she liked it and after a tough initial sixty-seconds where she was silent, and I had to keep talking, she softened. Whatever test she was giving me, I'd passed.

"I'm glad you stopped me. I'm Kamile," she said.

She was soon laughing and into the chat. I bounced her to the Starbucks across the road for a takeaway coffee, and then we sat outside chatting for nearly an hour. She was nice but seemed to be going through some sort of existential angst.

"I'm starting work in ten minutes," she finally said. "At a restaurant."

My chances of a same day lay dropped from 0.000001% right down to zero.

While she was asking me about my hobbies I dusted off an old NLP boxing routine that had her literally panting as her imagination became caught up in my descriptive narrative. Was I finally learning how to *Make Women Hot* through speech alone? She looked like a Victoria's Secret model, and I struggled to cope with her beauty. I simply wasn't used to being near girls of this calibre. Strange thoughts entered my mind.

"I don't deserve a girl this hot."

"She won't be interested in me."

"She's probably dating an actor or a footballer."

I could feel all those broken pieces inside jangling again. While my behaviour held together I suspected she could sense the sudden lack of conviction in my conversation. Nonetheless, I'd stumbled into a very hot girl who fancied me and was currently at a life crossroads. We swapped numbers and a couple of days later, during a good flow of texting, she wrote that her fortune teller had told her we'd been fated to meet.

Needless to say I messed up the date, a week later.

I was unable to escalate. Deep down, I didn't feel like a girl like that belonged with a man like me. I was somehow disturbing the natural balance of the universe. We had coffee in a colourful small courtyard in Neal Street. I literally didn't touch her once, not even her hands. I was very frustrated.

For about one year, from mid-2009 to mid-2010, I felt like a race driver who has fought his way to pole position in qualifying and then, when the race begins, turns the key and the engine won't start. And all the other cars race past me while I sit punching the steering wheel in frustration. That's how it felt to be on a date when invisible mental barriers stopped me from escalating. Kamile never came out for a second date.

Perhaps the fortune teller had told her we were not fated to have sex.

Back to my June 24th daygame session... After dropping Kamile off at her work following the initial takeaway coffee, I walked along the piazza and caught sight of a hot Bengali with dyed red hair.

She was sitting on a kerb. My blood was once more a-tingling and I noticed she was showing cleavage and thigh. She saw me coming from ten metres away and stared as I approached.

"C'mon, I have to know about the hair. It's brilliant," I said.

I was riding a wave of high vibe following Kamile, so it was a super-strong hook, and we chatted about twenty minutes. She was a stylist and her next client called, some rock star, she said, so I asked for her number and she practically thrust it onto me. My state was so good that I could do no wrong. Finally, I decided I had to pop by the office, as I was still on jury duty and thus unable to check my emails. I did a couple of light sets on the way. I gave a few compliments, got decent responses but my intent was gone now. Peak state burns your energy like a race car at top speed burns petrol. It was a great day and nice to be back on form.

I'd become a whole different person to a year ago. My days were now often action-packed.

Around this time, the London community had something new to get excited about. Yad had teamed up with another emerging name in daygame, Andy Yosha, to create a coaching company called Daygame.com. Initially, they had a simple colourful website presenting a happy vibe. This was in direct contrast to most night-game coaching companies who would plaster glamour photos of hot models wearing lingerie and pouting with come-hither expressions. Most PUA marketing was designed to appeal to the sleazy aspect of sex, so it was refreshing to see Andy appeal to normality: every young man's desire to get a girlfriend. He wanted his company to be clean-cut.

As a fledgling company, their pitch was all about Yad. Andy built up Yad's image as a mad genius of daygame and himself as the one man able to decode the magic and teach it. They offered two-on-one coaching initially, where both Yad and Andy would take a single student out infield. I'd have tried it, but they wanted £150 an hour. It was probably worth it, but I had men like Fernando, Johnny and Jimmy as wings, who were free. I passed on the coaching, but I kept my eye on Daygame.com. They'd develop into a major force — perhaps *the* major force — in establishing daygame as a 'thing' in the community.

Meanwhile, I kept grinding it out in relative obscurity.

Kamile wasn't my only missed opportunity with a stunner in June. Back in March I'd opened a Georgian dancer called Diana on the cobbles outside Covent Garden station. She liked me and we had a beer in the empty upstairs function room of the pub where *Sarge School* had been running boot camps.

"Georgia is a very traditional country," she told me. "Most girls are married young. I have known my boyfriend since I was seventeen."

That rather put a damper on things. "How old are you now?"

"Twenty-three."

"How many boyfriends have you had?"

"He is my only boyfriend. He is still at home. Georgian girls are traditional, we don't have many men. It is disappointing, we miss out on all the excitement."

Somehow, I missed this hint. Or perhaps I just couldn't believe she meant what she seemed to imply. Diana then began talking about her dancing background.

"I've been training many years."

"Are you flexible?"

"Yes! Watch!" She stood up and relaxed into a full front-splits. I missed that hint, too. Thinking back, it's a face-palm moment. Diana was making it as obvious as a girl can while sober and in the day time. The subtext was obvious: she was bored, looking for novelty, away from traditional obligations, and was demonstrating her physical abilities. She said she couldn't give her number, in case her boyfriend checked her phone. Instead, she took my number and promised to call.

She didn't call. No surprise there. That should've been the day I pushed for same day lays, evidently.

Two months later, while finishing up a boot camp in Covent Garden, I saw Diana walk past again. This time it was crazy-hot summer weather and the crazy-hot Georgian was wearing crazy-hot short shorts. Oh damn, I love dancers legs. She had beautiful supple thighs. I gave chase and called her name. She turned around. I stared, smirked, and then she recognised me. She beamed a huge smile, genuinely pleased to see me. Her eyes seemed as startled as a racoon's. The whole time we talked she swayed back and forth, gazing deep into my eyes.

"Let's have a drink, now," I said.

"I can't. I'm going to class. How about later this evening?"

"Okay."

We exchanged numbers and met up outside the station. I took her to the *Lamb & Flag* pub nearby. She'd had two months to think about our first date and reflect upon it. Evidently it was still 'on'. We bought pints and stood by the bar. It was busy and we were pressed up quite close together.

Again, I just couldn't find it within myself to escalate. All of my existing beliefs about myself, about women's sexuality, about what is possible in dating were hamstringing me. There was a little voice telling me she was in a serious relationship and it would be rude for me to push towards sex. Perhaps even immoral.

Immoral? Jesus, what a faggot!

So Diana stood at the bar in her hot pants and tight top, gazing into my eyes over the top of her drink while she got some "plausible deniability" alcohol into her system... and I just chatted like she was my grandmother. I didn't even try to kiss her. Diana was doing everything she could to make me bang her, and I knew it, yet I just couldn't take control. This was the second chance she'd given me, the poor girl. And she was a stunner too.

I was so frustrated with myself. Something, somewhere, was badly wrong.

Dating Tasanee

A date to nowhere

Back in Newcastle

CHAPTER 23

CRUSADER KING

CHAPTER 23

CRUSADER KING

Banging Tasanee had gotten the ball rolling. There were still many barriers between me and the success with women to which I aspired, but at least I was getting *something*. Though a full year had passed since my divorce, I still felt shaken. My old confidence and self-belief had gone AWOL. I couldn't figure out why. I'd long since gotten over the physical and emotional shock of divorce, and I hadn't the slightest interest in getting back with Ioe. Divorce wasn't the issue. That had merely been a catalyst. It was like finding a loose thread on a knitted sweater. If you keep pulling, the whole thing unravels. Something about Ioe leaving me had unearthed deeper problems, things I'd gone my whole life without addressing. A normal reaction would've been to grieve a few months, tentatively venture into dating once more, and then start a relationship with a new girlfriend.

What wasn't so normal was what I'd actually done: quit my job, get entirely new friends, re-evaluate all my ideas about the world, and to chase girls obsessively. While I was beginning to enjoy my new life (sometimes immensely so) there was no denying it was an extreme reaction. I was faced with quite an existential question: which version of me was closer to my authentic self, Daygame Nick, or Corporate Nick?

I'd long assumed that the real me was the straight-A student who worked in the financial services industry. The year living on a tropical island, the punk bands, the kickboxing, the porn filming.... those were just exceptions to the rule, weren't they? Just something I did as a break — a rebellion — from the real me.

I was beginning to reconsider that. I had been far happier telling the girls of Newcastle's *Barley Mow* pub that Punky Bear thought they dressed stupid, or teaching village kids English, or interviewing fighters at Tokyo MMA events. I'd never really enjoyed the office work. Sometimes I took professional pride in producing high quality work, but it always felt vacuous and pointless at its core. By contrast, even though daygame was incredibly stressful, I always felt myself while doing it. Not so much because it involved hitting on girls. What made daygame sing in my soul was the idea that I was living by my wits, solving problems, and bucking the system. I liked it for the same reason I liked pirates, hard-boiled detectives, and bounty hunters in adventure stories.

Still, for all this, I was an emotional wreck. I was unhappy most days and it often amazed me so many pretty women took an interest in me. Everything was in turmoil, a complex mix of hope, anxiety, depression, and joy.

My principle worry was, *will I ever get good at this?*

I'd quickly realised Tony Clink was full of shit, as was all the other PUA marketing. If there really was 'one secret trick' to banging hot women they'd kept it to themselves. Game was hard. Really, really hard. At times I seemed to be swept off the streets by a tidal wave of rejection. Faced with frequent self-doubt, I comforted myself with a patchwork emotional quilt stitched together from of a combination of hope, desperation, and various self-development theories. Each man manufactures his own custom quilt depending upon his specific worries and what materials he is exposed to. We each have our favourite mantras:

— Every rejection is a brick in my palace of awesomeness.
— She's not rejecting me, she's rejecting my approach.
— If it was easy, everyone would be awesome at it.

Yes, those are hokey, but a man will cling to them in times of need.

I was spending increasingly more time with Johnny. Fernando and I looked up to him following the *Sarge School* boot camps we'd both done. He was already dating a lovely Ukrainian girl so he lacked our desire to keep chasing skirt, but he seemed to miss the thrill so he'd sometimes accompany us and do the occasional set just to keep his hand in. His new passion was Neuro Linguistic Programming, a pseudo-science of psychological manipulation that was popular in the wider self-development community as a way to 'program' your own brain to better achieve success. While I think NLP has a shaky scientific foundation, that doesn't make it worthless. Most modern medicine is pseudo-science and there's a replication crisis in social science that suggests the whole thing is more scholarship than science. I'd used some NLP myself and found it helpful.

Johnny was really into it. He'd even earned the official Master Practitioner certificate. He now very conscientiously applied NLP principles in his life and was trying to create a small consulting business. What Johnny, a twenty-six year old Englishman, already possessed was a deep slow voice, good style, and solid eye contact. Girls liked him. He liked my determination and work ethic on the streets and had decided to draw me in to *Sarge School* in late 2009. We'd have long chats over coffee while I tried to soak up his self-development knowledge. I'd started hanging around on the edge of his daygame boot camps too, offering myself as an approach coach. So we became pretty good friends.

He'd come into the Community having been an extremely introverted, weedy little loser. His personal moment of truth — in Joseph Campbell's terms, his 'call to adventure' — came while driving his beaten-up Fiat Panda through the backstreets of Dubai on his way home from a shitty copywriting job. Something snapped, a "this can't go on" moment, and he'd thrown himself behind NLP as a way to take control of his life. He then drifted into Game about a year before me. Johnny spoke with conviction about the importance of facing your fears and building self-confidence as if it's a muscle. A mantra he'd frequently tell me was, "Sex comes first as a trickle, and then as a flood."

This makes sense. The two biggest problems all new players face are approach anxiety and attraction. They are so scared of cold-approach that they either can't talk to girls, or tie themselves in such mental knots that they make a terrible first impression. Compounding this is the harsh reality of the sexual market place, that most men are not attractive to most women. As a man begins handling approach anxiety and becomes more attractive, he will gradually surmount the threshold over which girls become increasingly likely to fancy him. So results come in at a trickle. If his upward trajectory continues, he rises above this threshold increasing often and should (theoretically at least) experience a flood of interest.

In theory, there's no difference between theory and practice. In practice, there is.

I was certainly getting a trickle now–Rakiya, Luminita, Tasanee—so I stitched the idea of an incoming biblical flood into my comfort blanket. Should I just rub my hands in glee while I wait the inevitable pussy shower? I decided to keep working the streets, just to be on the safe side.

Tasanee and I were still dating, though she knew that I saw other girls and that I was still in the game. She was accepting of the arrangement for now. Fortunately, she assumed I was way more successful that I actually was. I wasn't about to disillusion her. Girls like to know their man is in high demand, even when he's not.

One hot Saturday in June found me trawling Oxford Street as usual. Only the first generation daygamers like myself would be seen on the streets in those days. There were probably, in total, just ten men doing this regularly (of whom I knew six on a first-name basis) and you could go all weekend without seeing anyone but your own wings. Devak was winging with me. We'd been friends a couple of years due to our mutual interest in mixed martial arts fighting and the career of Ukrainian star Igor Vovchanchyn in particular. He'd joined me in bar game since I first began cold-approach and was now dabbling in daygame.

Oxford Street is Europe's busiest shopping street. Three hundred shops crammed together to service a torrent of cash-rich tourists and day-trippers. If you've never been there, you can only imagine the amount of foot traffic that the street gets on any given day, hence, its popularity for daygame. That day was especially crowded due to the lovely weather. It took some time to weed out all the girls that weren't in our desired demographic. There were the grandmas, the married girls, the girls holding onto a boyfriend's hand as they walked by, the fatties, and the blue-haired feminists.

After eliminating all of that chaff, there remained masses of women within our single-hot-solo demographic, so I'd done a few sets and gotten a few phone numbers.

I ducked into the large HMV music store, thinking about getting a horror film DVD to watch that night when Tasanee next came around. It was also a chance to get off the streets. Chasing girls made my head spin with the cocktail of adrenalin, anxiety, and dopamine. I needed a break.

As I browsed the DVD section, I noticed a young Arab girl also aimlessly browsing. She was slim and petite, in very good shape from what I could see, and clearly a tourist. Her eyeliner and lipstick were overdone in the Arab fashion, reminding me of a doe-eyed Japanese Anime character. Perhaps that's how Muslim girls over-compensate for having to cover their hair and wear drab colours. This girl was ever so slightly westernised, wearing tight blue jeans, no head scarf but carefully concealing most of her skin in the Arab fashion. She also wore a strange flat cap which gave me an easy opening tease.

I sidled up to her.

"Hi, I just noticed you while I was looking at the DVDs. I had to come over and tell you that I love your style."

She smiled brightly and said, "Thank you."

"Except the silly hat," I told her. "It looks like something my granddad would have worn to go greyhound racing."

She gasped, laughed, and got defensive—which was exactly the effect I wanted. The whole point of teasing a girl right away is to get her emotionally engaged. She experiences a pleasant cocktail of emotions within a few short seconds: flattery at being approached, respect for the man's boldness, vanity at being the subject of conversation, insecurity at being teased, surprise at being challenged, pleasure at having the tedium of her day broken. You can hit a girl hard with a good opener.

Mafalda was from Libya, on holiday, and leaving England in a day or two. A young Muslim girl out alone on holiday... *that can't be right*, I reasoned. *The goat-fuckers never let women out unsupervised.* Sure enough, just as the idea of a chaperone entered my mind, I felt the Earth shake underfoot. DVDs rattled in their racks and the lights swayed and flickered. It was like the scene in

Jurassic Park when the T-Rex first approaches and the cups of water ripple on the jeep dashboard. In seconds a huge fat Arab woman materialised, looming over me.

"Oh well, that's that," I grumbled, certain that this regrettably bad-looking woman was here to squash my game.

There's a standard operating procedure I'd learned for when a potentially cockblocking female interrupts a conversation. Once should immediately shower them with pleasant attention to bring them onto your side.

"I caught your friend shoplifting. She said she's very sorry and if I let her go she promises to be very good in future," I said. The behemoth cocked its head to one side and studied me with a suspicious eye.

"He's joking," helped Mafalda. We both smiled.

There was a brief moment when I thought I was going to be eaten, but the behemoth laughed and we introduced ourselves. I had her giggling (and jiggling) along in no time. She was quite a pleasant girl. They were two friends on holiday in their fantasy city, full of high spirits. I knew I couldn't peel Mafalda away from her protector so I took her Facebook details instead then walked away assuming I'd not hear from her again. *It's too bad*, I told myself, *I've never banged a Muslim. She's more than likely a virgin.*

Mafalda accepted my Facebook friend request two days later and the first time she came online I hit her up for a chat. She had a strange way of communicating. Every sentence was bookended with rows of smiley-faces, thumbs-ups, and the vowels we all veeeeeeeery drawn ooooouuuuttt!!!!! Her profile didn't have her own photo on it. That's a quite common ruse by Arab girls to circumvent the social pressure their local men subject them to. I asked her about it as my opener, as I wasn't even sure I'd gotten the right details.

"Hey, I just had a quick look through your photos. Is that really you? They look like you cut them out of a fashion magazine."

"Hiiiiii. Those are not my pics... Hehehe,"

"That's very naughty," I wrote, "and I thought you were a nice girl."

"Lol, I am a nice girl. You think putting other pictures than mine would be naughty of me?"

"Yes."

"But I'm not."

"Ha-ha. Okay, I believe you... this time. You can send me a real picture so I feel like I'm talking to the real Arab girl? Maybe you could wear your old man flat cap from the greyhound racing...?"

She didn't make any promises. Staying chaste is interchangeable with staying in the marriage market and not bringing shame on your family for a woman in the stricter Muslim cultures. It sounds like a problem for a would-be seducer but it's actually the opposite. Mafalda was already well-versed in living a double life before I met her. London represented her escape from the smothering social pressure back home. And lastly, her opportunities for amorous adventure were likely severely curtailed back in Tripoli so she might well be sexual dissatisfied. Chaste-looking Arab girls are often simmering pressure-cookers of sexual energy waiting for a discreet man who can supply her with adventure sex. I didn't know this at the time, but I was ever the optimist.

Mafalda's keen communication habits made her a hot lead despite her being on another continent. Going out day-after-day chasing girls inevitably leads to collecting flaky numbers and half-hearted text exchanges because most girls just aren't particularly enthusiastic. That's the harsh reality of cold approach pick-up. You have to flip a lot of stones to uncover a hot lead. But when you do, you can really feel the enthusiasm.

The next day I logged in to Facebook and almost immediately a chat window popped up. It was Mafalda opening me. She said hello and asked if I remembered her. "Ha-ha, I remember you. You're the pretty girl with the silly hat."

"You really thought the hat was silly?"

"Yeah, but it looked cute on you."

We flirted a bit but I wasn't particularly adept at messaging. We enjoyed the male-female polarity, then I probed a bit to see if there was any future in our talking. Was Mafalda planning a return visit to London?

"I don't know yet," she said, "Maybe in July or August, but I'm not sure."

"It'll be good weather then. I'll show you around if you promise not to be naughty and cause trouble."

I was trying it amp up the flirting. Either I would never see her again, and I may as well have some fun before it petered out, or, I'd get her excited for when we meet again, and perhaps she'd be ready to go.

"Hahaha, I am a good girl. I'm not a trouble-maker. But sometimes people get me involved..."

"Put up a real picture."

I'd never dated a Muslim or an Arab before. This daygame journey was already introducing me to new vistas and at this early stage I had no idea where it would lead. I let my imagination take hold picturing Mafalda's life, one part fantasy and one part empathy. I imagined her as we were Facebook chatting, sitting in her poky bedroom in a white-brick flat-roofed house while her traditional Muslim family went about their business downstairs. Mother in the kitchen cooking, father praying at a Mosque... and there she sat, stirring the sexual pot on Facebook. I found it all rather amusing and continued chuckling to myself as I sauntered off into the shower. Before long the thought experiment ended with me deflowering her on the rooftop while ISIS Jihadis fired AK-47s into the sky in impotent rage.

She went offline a few days, but she'd liked a few posts on my Facebook page which is a female way of keeping herself in the mix. Then she re-opened me, telling me what a great week she was having. It's a positive show of interest when a girl re-initiates contact with you. They are used to being The Pursued so if she breaks form to contact you first it's a sign she's been thinking about you a lot and can't quite hold herself back.

"That's nice, send me a picture," I insisted.

Finally, I got to see how she looked in a photo. She sent one of her on the street in London the day before we met, and she was not smiling at all.

"You look miserable in that picture," I told her. "You should have sent one from right after we met, then you'd have a huge grin on your face."

"I looked miserable because I hadn't met you," she said.

"Do you have one of you smiling?" I asked her.

"Maybe, let me check."

I waited for a while and then I messaged, "Waiting..." I wanted to be pushy and demanding.

"My Internet is slow," she said. "How's the weather there in London."

Much of seduction involves normal behaviour. It's not a set of swirly-twirly super-charged interactions, just as real football matches are not ninety minutes of non-stop goals and saves. It's enough to use everyday chit-chat to open the lines of communication then try to give the occasional steer towards a more sexual direction. PUAs called this "spiking", a way of lifting the chat out of the friend-zone trap so she always sees you as a sexual being.

"It's burning hot. I bought an old man's flat cap, similar to yours. We can wear them when you come and we can go greyhound racing together. We'll be like a cute old-age couple."

"Wow, that would be cool. Maybe in July."

"Hopefully not between the 1st and 11th?" I asked. Jimmy and Tony had scheduled a trip to Lithuania for that week, for all of us.

"No," she messaged back, "Probably towards the end."

"Cool. What else will you wear to the dog racing? Think carefully, we have to look really old or they won't let us in."

"Hahaha, did you get the pic yet?" she asked.

"Yes. In your room. No smile."

"You didn't like it?" she asked.

"It's a nice photo, but I asked for one with you smiling. I remember you having a cute, shy little smile."

"I haven't got many I'm smiling in," she told me, "but I'll tag one soon and send it to you, tomorrow."

"Too cool to smile?"

"Yeah."

I was trying to engage her emotionally, so she'd admit that she fancied me, at least indirectly. Her return to London would only be a couple of nights, so I couldn't afford to have her dance around pretending we were just friends. I still wasn't confident of my competence in escalating a girl on a first date. My weak escalation had been queering a lot of good opportunities, such as the Kamile and Diana. The further I could move Mafalda on Facebook, the more confident I'd feel on the date itself.

"You have a lot of nice pictures," she said. "My favourite is one of you in an old city. It's too far away though."

"Ah! Seville," I say, "Beautiful city. I went with my ex-girlfriend." That was Ioe.

"Yep, that's cool."

"I didn't put her in them."

"No pics of her, hahaha," was her reply. "I love the pics."

"Thank you," I told her before signing off for the night.

Over several weeks we had probably twelve long conversations. The first ten were light-hearted, like the exchanges above. I was interested in building comfort and rapport with her during that time, while just throwing in some light attraction. She talked about coming back to London in our tenth chat and I encouraged her. Once she booked the flights I amped up the sexuality to make my intentions clear before she arrived.

A few more weeks passed and my jury duty had ended. I was now unemployed and very happy with my newfound freedom. It was Friday, and Mafalda's arrival was just five days away. I took a walk into town at ten am, much earlier than usual, to see if any girls were out. It was summer and that typically brought women out earlier in the day. I ran across a young, slim, pretty Portuguese girl. I opened her to get the first set out the way ("the firstest is the worstest" I told myself) but she had to rush off to meet a friend.

I was in Trafalgar Square, the natural gateway to everywhere London, and it is always buzzing with life. The tourists love the massive statue of Horatio Nelson, architect of Britain's greatest military triumph, and the four giant stone lions that guard him from pesky Frenchmen. From the top of the steps there is a stunning view of Big Ben. Droves of people were already out, watching the street performers, feeding the pigeons, or just admiring the gorgeous fountains with the larger than life statues. I didn't know it then, but I was about to encounter another girl who would become key in softening my distrust of women.

A young French woman wandered past me, London guide book in hand and snapping pictures of the lions with a camera she wore around her neck. She had masses of light brown curls on her head, like Sideshow Bob from *The Simpsons*. I call the style "wop hair" because it's particularly common with girls from the Mediterranean. Her eyes were big and dark brown, wide-open to drink in the novel surroundings. She was slim and dressed very cute with a blue denim jacket and blue jeans and a colourful scarf. She had a European look about her. I got the familiar DNA-tug. I had to talk to her.

"Hi, do you speak English?"

She smiled and said, "I speak English, yes. A little." She actually spoke it very well.

"Cool," I said, "I just noticed you, and I had to come over and talk to you. I find you very attractive." She giggled at that, a pretty, shy little smile.

We talked for ten minutes. Her name was Adele, she was nineteen, and this was her first trip to London, after an adolescence pining for a chance to visit the city of her dreams. Her friend, Margo, lived here for a short internship, and Adele was visiting but only for the weekend. They had a lunch date for one o'clock so, it now being almost 11am, I had two hours to make a lasting impression.

"Do you want to go inside the gallery and see the paintings?" I asked her, pointing up the steps at the National Gallery.

"Sure," she said and off we went.

One thing about daygame is you spend so much time on the streets that you don't experience them like a normal person does. We daygamers never really live the life we appear to from the outside. We're like simulacrum. A normal psychologically-healthy person would wander around the National Gallery to absorb the atmosphere, pay attention to the detail in the paintings, and perhaps read some liner notes about his favourite pieces. A healthy person would use the gallery as it is intended—to look at art and perhaps drink a coffee afterwards to discuss the experience. In contrast, I was thinking, *this is an opportunity to bounce her from room to room, display some leading, initiate physical touch, and perhaps make some cheeky sexual comments about the pictures.* I didn't give a toss about the paintings. I just feigned interest as an excuse for all the other stuff. The beautiful parks, museums, and cafes of London were just a stage upon which to do the real performance of pick-up.

"Oh look at this one," I'd say and Adele would either come over, or I'd take her hand and pull her in. We played a game where we made up silly background stories about the paintings. I was, of course, picking out the pictures full of nudity. Anything to raise the sexual energy.

After ten minutes I said, "I'm bored, let's go."

"Okay," she agreed, readily.

"Hey," I asked her, trying to sound like the idea had only just occurred to me rather than it being a carefully-laid plan. "Do you like Sherlock Holmes?"

"Yes," she said, enthusiastically. She seemed to say *everything* enthusiastically. It was refreshing. Adele had a delightfully soft feminine manner.

I walked her over to the nearby Sherlock Holmes pub which has a nice outdoor square in front of it where you can sit on the steps. Adele was excited about this and during the next hour as we talked, I found out why. My little French friend was actually quite the Anglophile. She told me that she absolutely loved all things English: The Beatles, Shakespeare, Sherlock Holmes, and anything else that was specific to my country and culture. I was specific to England, I reasoned, so I was beginning to believe I had an excellent chance of showing my interest in all things French in the most physical of manners. Or at least my interest in this French citizen in particular.

Adele was born in Tunisia (hence her tanned colouring and wop hair) but had been raised in France since the age of three so everything about her manner was typically French. I tried being the nice guy, soft and gentle, listening to her talk and watching her take in all of the new sights and sounds that surrounded her. I was a good listener back then. I was afraid anything too direct so early would scare her away. I looked at my watch. She had to meet with her friend soon. Adele took my number and promised to text as soon as she'd finished lunch with her friend. It seemed solid and I went out and met up with Fernando while I waited for her.

An hour or so later my phone buzzed. She'd kept her promise. We met again near Trafalgar and I suggested we try Camden Market.

"Oh yes, let's!" she cooed. It had been on her tour list.

Adele gave me full compliance, letting me lead her around without a quibble. The bus to the market was standing room only, literally. She and I were standing belly-to-belly in a vestibule in the front part of the bus reserved for wheelchairs. I had been wondering how I was going to escalate and this seemed an opportune moment since we were pushed up against each other already. I kissed her very lightly, and she gave back fully, like she had been waiting for me to kiss her.

We strolled through Camden market for a bit, hand-in-hand, looking to all of the world like a normal couple. Camden Market is electric, alive, and pulsating with the sights, sounds and smells of so many things that it's practically a labyrinth. Adele loved it. The place is always filled with such a variety of people: beatniks, goths, emo-kids, plus the usual horde of tourists trying on the vintage clothing stores and often leaving with a new tattoo or piercing. The indoor and open air markets all have their own distinct flavour and on a weekend the air sizzles with a collage of food smells from the street food court. It is a beautiful place in the sunshine and we were soon sitting by the canal sipping a beer.

We whiled away a few hours peaceably, getting a drink and a bite to eat. The glee with which she lapped up her surroundings delighted me. Her energy was so positive that it seemed to radiate from her smile. I still wasn't really used to the company of truly feminine women. They don't really exist in England. I imagine my English readers immediately bristled at that and, if so, my advice is to take a trip to central Europe and just people watch. Look at how the girls dress, how they move, how they respond, how they hold the muscles of their faces. Everything just oozes a femininity that is lost in the Anglosphere. Having spent so much time around English women I'd come to believe they were normal—rather than the badly-raised, ill-mannered oafs that most of them actually are.

I took Adele on a stroll along the canal. I was becoming drunk on her feminine charm and wanted to kiss her again. The old paved canal-side path tucked under a bridge and we took some steps up to street level. We soon came upon a small church and graveyard next to Regents Park. It seemed empty, so I lifted her over the wall and we sneaked around canal-side to sit on a bench and make out privately. While my tongue was down her throat I heard a cheerful whistle. I broke off and craned my head around to see the church gardener approach. He was in the mood to chat so we engaged him for ten minutes or so. When we could finally break away, we continued on to Primrose Hill. That's a lovely place for a mid-afternoon date. Rolling green hills, old beautiful trees with benches underneath and a perfect view across Central London too.

We found a patch grass to lay down between all the other picnickers and teenagers drinking lager from cans. It was so sweet and romantic. I was lying back looking up at the cloud patterns through the gaps in the tree branches, following vapour trails from passing air planes, while this delightful girl snuggled up against me with her head on my chest.

Am I really living this?, I wondered. I'd only met Adele that morning.

We kissed again, and I could tell that she was already falling for me. She'd spent several years creating an idealised image of a romantic Englishman in her little girl-sized brain, and now I'd come along to be the screen upon which she projected that image. It was cute, and it made me want to live up to her image. Adele already had plans to see her friend Margo that night so we agreed to meet again the next day, a Saturday.

The next day I texted her. She replied, "I'm with Margo. Could she come along?"

Great, another cockblock.

Sarge School had now rebranded ourselves to *Rock Solid Game* and set up a new, much cooler website. We didn't like the way rival outfits were all trying to look like James Bond. We were rock'n'roll. Or, at least, Jimmy was rock'n'roll. So he suggested the change, had a friend create some style designs and we all agreed it was a great idea. That weekend we had a big boot-camp going on so all the RSG guys were busy assisting the nightgame session.

I had no one to wing me but it was as yet only the afternoon. The girls showed up at Leicester Square and we walked around Soho. Margo didn't talk much. She was suspicious of me, knowing full well I wanted to rattle Adele. She was probably also jealous of the attention, being very plain compared to her slimmer, prettier visitor. To her credit she didn't bitch and moan, but her miserable omnipresence soured any chance of moving things forwards. I'm sure she was only being protective of her friend, who was running around with a man literally twice her age but, at that point in my life, I wasn't in the mood to give her any points for being a good chaperone. I'd have rather she disappeared.

Alas, she followed us everywhere, stopping in a shop here and there, but never long enough that I was able to make any head-way with Adele. The only time we were truly alone that afternoon was for half an hour when we ditched her in a shop and ran off to a nearby park frequented by brazen homosexuals.

Finally, I accepted that there was no chance I was going to get Adele alone that afternoon, so I suggested we meet up later that evening. She agreed, but since it was her last night in town, she said that she couldn't leave Margo out. I forced a smile and, choking on my words, told her Margo was welcome to come along. Then I let them go off together to do whatever girls do.

It was now 4pm. Fernando called me after he finished up the boot camp daygame session without me. I walked into an HMV record shop at Piccadilly to get away from the street noise to take the call. I was still on the phone when I saw a slim, tall, olive-skinned Brazilian girl. Sweet. I opened her and we bought a takeaway coffee and sat drinking it in Leicester Square's small park. We flirted heavily and swapped numbers, but ultimately the experience was as transient as vapour.

I met Adele and Margo outside a tourist-trap club called On Anon (now Piccadilly Institute). It's a huge, crowded place, popular with a wide demographic of people, and it has dancing and music on four floors. Considering its location, it's surprisingly nice. Not too many of the brown immigrant animals you see in the other Piccadilly clubs. Fernando joined me.

We ditched the club after a couple of hours and headed down to Clapham. The old town is a mix of Georgian, Victorian, and Queen Anne architecture while there is a huge Common and a long High Street with plenty of vibrant places to spice up the night life. For as long as I can remember estate agents have called Clapham "up and coming" but I mostly thought it's full of try-hard twats. Fernando lived there and had offered to try an after-party extraction with the girls so I agreed to give it a chance.

Fernando had a Polish girl from his salsa class come meet him for a first date, and we all shared a cab to his favourite bar. Adele rode on my lap so that was at least a pleasant start to the evening. Margot pressed into the corner and looked out the window, hating the world.

Back then I hadn't settled on a visual style for my fashion so I was trying different clothes and combinations. I'd always liked Brad Pitt's fashion in *Fight Club*, especially the iconic burgundy jacket over a retro shirt. Ebay sold replicas and I bought one—unfortunately it was a far brighter red than in the movie. It looked good, but a little... attention grabbing. As soon as we walked into the bar a hot drunk Asian girl came out of nowhere to compliment me on it. Throughout

Hanging out with Adele
in Clapham

the night, this chick was everywhere, batting her eyes at me and openly flirting, even though she saw that I was obviously with Adele. It was my first chance to run a "jealousy plot-line" in a bar. That's an old Mystery Method technique of playing girls off against each other to stoke their competitive spirits. This opportunity fell into my lap so I milked it, giving the Asian cocky smirks and gestures from across the bar. Quite a few of Adele's sweet kisses that evening were designed to let the Asian chick know who had a claim on me. Which is exactly what I wanted.

I wasn't trying to get the Asian girl. It was all about getting Adele excited.

Fernando took his Polish girl home around midnight, and I taxied back into the West End with the two French girls. We ended up in my favourite private member's bar *Milk & Honey*. The entrance is literally an unmarked black door on the street. When you knock, they see you on the camera and buzz you in. Its décor is cool Prohibition-era and art deco. It has a bar level where they serve a lot of unique kinds of cocktails. The booths and stools are all a dark burgundy and the lighting is intimate. The upper floor is like a Gentleman's club (of the Victorian, not stripper variety) and has deep comfortable dark burgundy couches and chairs, where you can relax, talk, or whatever.

There'd be no 'whatever' because Margo was maintaining her vigil.

At one point, I thought that I had gotten a bit lucky in giving Adele "the tour" of the bar. I pulled her into one of the private toilets up on the third level while Margot waited a floor below. We kissed and groped and I tried to pull down her little hot pants to bang her there and then. Denied! I began feeling quite sorry for myself. Fernando was banging his Polish girl on the other side of London, but thanks to Margo's magnificent work, I slinked home unfulfilled.

We had a romantic send-off at the EuroStar terminal on Sunday afternoon, and before unpacking her suitcase in Paris, Adele was already messaging me on Facebook.

"So when should I come and see Paris?" I asked her. Jury service had ended two weeks earlier, and I was officially unemployed with nothing to do all day. I had plenty of free time, and plenty of money. That's the best combination a wannabe player can ask for.

"How about in a fortnight?" she said.

I had the EuroStar website up on another browser tab looking at the dates, times, and prices of train tickets. The hotel-combo prices looked fine, so I clicked through to the checkout. I did one last check before pulling the trigger, my dick going hard at future-projecting that I was just two short weeks from corrupting this delightfully innocent Parisian.

"Are you sure about the date, because I'm just about to book," I asked.

She typed out "yes", but then, "Wait! Oh Fuck! That's going to be the wrong time of the month. I'll be on my period and I won't be able to have sex."

I love how direct the French are about these things.

It was Sunday night, and I performed rapid mental arithmetic. Mafalda was due to arrive from Libya in three days, the coming Wednesday evening. Could I squeeze in a trip to Paris before that? How much would I enjoy being in Paris, shown around by a nineteen year old French girl who is down to fuck? Can you put a price on that experience?

The EuroStar website told me you can. £336 including three nights in a hotel.

I went for it, in for a penny in for a pound. "This may sound really fucking crazy but... do you want to meet tomorrow?"

"YES!"

So I confirmed my ticket reservation immediately, midnight on Sunday, and I was standing at Kings Cross EuroStar terminal 9am the next morning with a travel bag in my hand and a raging hard-on in my jeans. I wasn't nervous, because Adele had already laid it out on a plate for me. But I was really, really excited. It was another of those "only in Game" moments. On Friday morning I had been having breakfast at the local greasy-spoon cafe gathering my courage to go out daygaming in Trafalgar Square and now three days later I was on an express train to Paris to bang a delightful teenager.

CHAPTER 24

D DAY LANDINGS

CHAPTER 24

D DAY LANDINGS

The Eurostar train shuttled at high speed through the French countryside. I stared at the laptop open on the table in front of me, trying to focus my eyes on an RSD pick-up instructional video. A blur of trees, cows, and unionised farmers streamed past the windows. Be-suited businessmen conducted early morning power meetings at the tables nearby. I felt completely apart from the world around me, an increasingly common state. This was an early Monday morning train out of London so naturally it was full of commuters and business-trippers. Only a year ago I'd been one of them, taking my briefcase and IBM Thinkpad around Europe on visits to client offices. The smells, sounds and tastes were familiar to me: The crackle of an Uppercrust paper bag pulled open to reveal a re-heated BLT baguette, accompanied by the smell of a Caffè Nero latte bought at a terminal coffee stand and spilled slightly in the rush to board the train.

I looked around, taking in the lively scene in my carriage. Half-read copies of *The Economist* and *Financial Times* were tucked into the back pouch of a black canvas laptop bag. I saw a lightly-thumbed John Grisham paperback peek out between sheaves of report printouts on a middle-aged professional woman's seat. Oh, I was only too familiar with this world. I remembered a top investor telling me, "You know you're arrived in finance when you spend half of your life in airports and train stations."

That had been my life, but now I was on the outside looking in. I hadn't fully unplugged from the matrix, but I was seeing the glitches, not yet fully cognizant of the path I had already irrevocably committed myself to. Last time I'd boarded the EuroStar, two years earlier, I was leading a team of three young accountants for a short project in a regional office in Brussels. Now I was unemployed, possibly even unemployable. To me the endless rolling hills of the French countryside represented freedom, an adventure into the unknown. What awaited me in Paris? I knew sex was there, but what emotions would be stirred? How would I feel after knocking Adele over? Would sex with her reduce the aching sense of emptiness I'd had for the past eighteen months?

I fancied myself as Omar Shariff on the train in *Doctor Zhivago*. I hadn't even seen the movie, I just remembered the scene from YouTube. Daygame gives you something of an introspection fetish. Before long the train arrived at Gare Du Nord station and things became real again. It's the busiest train station in Europe, and outside of Japan, the busiest in the world. Hordes of cheese-eating Frenchmen clamoured on the platforms and I squeezed through them and to the Metro station steps. My hotel was to the south, between the city centre and suburbs. Adele was still working in her father's shop so I made the trip alone. I had a few hours to kill.

My hotel was situated in a pleasant area of patisseries, bakeries, and cafes. It had the air of a budget business lodge complete with sliding automatic doors, a uniformed receptionist, and English-language shows playing on wall-mounted televisions in the lobby. The hotel was okay. A mid-level business place, nice, and clean enough. Not that I'd have cared if it was a cockroach-infested shack with peeling wallpaper—I was in Paris on an adventure, I'd have slept in a park, if necessary. My prior life of routine, predictability, and creature-comforts was in the rear-view mirror.

My room was on the second floor overlooking a quiet road. I spent a while inspecting my room, making a mental checklist of objects I might bend Adele over whilst banging her: bed, sofa, rickety wooden chair, shower cubicle. Check. Could I open the window and push her head out while doing her from behind?

That remained to be confirmed. I couldn't get it to open more than twelve inches.

Adele had received a middle class suburban upbringing. Her father was an engineer and her mother a doctor. Incredibly, she'd told them all about me, including my age, and that I was coming to see her. They hadn't raised the expected furore. This wasn't a case of parental neglect, such as characterised my own parents' utter lack of concern in my love life, rather that the French have a laissez-faire attitude about a lot of things, and sex is at the top of that list.

I soaked in a deep hot bath and took a nap while I waited for time to tick on to four o'clock, the hour we'd chosen for the rendezvous. Adele rapped on my door in timely fashion. As the door creaked open I was treated to a beaming girl hopping softly up and down with a barely-suppressed giggle. She wore denim shorts, Converse shoes, a colourful scarf. Her make-up had that extra level of care to say she was dressed to impress. She had such a freshness about her, partly due to youth but also due to her character. I hadn't yet realized, but meeting Adele was going to be another step in my getting over the ugly bitterness that I was still trying to purge from my system.

I was rather excited myself. Things were very real.

We laid down on the bed side-by-side like friends, sipping tea. We talked at first but that didn't last long. So much sexual tension had built up after a weekend of Margo running interference that it now crackled between us. After ten minutes or so I took Adele's cup and set it on the sideboard, then I pulled her in for a kiss. That quickly turned passionate and soon clothes were flying off and thrown around the room. Within a half an hour of her arrival, we were both naked and having sex.

It was good sex, of the sweetly incompetent variety. Adele was inexperienced but enthusiastic and eager to please. I'll take that any day over the modern porn star sex where the girl is an empty and aggressive caricature of a sexual partner. Any time a girl shows high-level skill in bed I'm always moved to wonder, *how did she get that good?* Not so with Adele. She was sweet and it was all very romantic. Afterwards, while we laid there talking, she admitted to me that I was only the fourth man she had ever kissed and only the second she'd had sex with.

"Who was the first?"

"He was a bad boy at my school. We only did it twice."

She went on to tell me that she'd begin university in Australia in September so this was her last summer break before becoming a college student.

We watched episodes of *Fawlty Towers* on YouTube. Being an Anglophile, she quickly took to Basil and Cybil at each other's necks in the Torquay hotel. We took a break for a shower and more sex, then back to *Fawlty Towers*. The pressure was off, for both of us. I was no longer plotting and scheming back-up plans in case she'd been reluctant to have sex after all. Adele was calmed with the knowledge she'd gotten her man and not disappointed in bed. The tension dissipated, replaced by an aura of calm contentment. I was awash with positive just-fucked-a-teenager vibes. It was still only 7pm and light outside.

"Let's go into the centre. I'm still a tourist, you know," I said.

"Where would you like to go?"

"I dunno, somewhere French."

"It's all French. We are in Paris."

"Notre Dame Cathedral, then. That should look good."

We took a metro into St Michel. Adele knew an Indian restaurant near Notre Dame Cathedral so after I snapped off a few photos we went for dinner. I was still determined to practice the NLP nonsense I'd seen in *Make Women Hot*. For some reason, I found it greatly entertaining. We sat waiting for my chicken korma. I began with a little exposition of body language and the concept of IOIs—the indicators of interest a girl gives a man when she's sexually attracted.

"What do you mean?" asked Adele, intrigued. Birds always like talking about male-female relations.

"Well, if you don't mind me getting vulgar, have you heard of the Pussy Tingle?"

"No, what is it?" she asked, clearly amused, and perhaps surprised because I rarely swear.

"If a man gets a hard-on while wearing trousers it can be quite uncomfortable, especially if he's in polite company. He'd like to reach his hand down and readjust, but doesn't want to be obvious about it. Well, girls get the game thing. When a girl is attracted to man, and he says or does something that turns her on, she gets a certain feeling. Girls will typically try to say that it is like "butterflies" in her belly, when the feeling is really down lower."

Adele grinned and said, "And how would you know?"

"I can tell by watching. She's tingling, she wants to touch it, but she's in public so she can't. So she starts squirming around."

"Like this?" she asked, wriggling in her chair and laughing.

"Precisely. She'll squirm in her seat or cross her legs. I can give you a pussy tingle right now."

"Try me."

Challenge accepted. I laid on my best sex-eyes. My eyes bored into her with all the predatory menace I could muster as I softly and deeply told her how beautiful her eyes were. That they were so dark and deep that I wanted to "get lost in them" while I wanted to slip my hand between her legs and feel her wetness. This was all delivered in a deep, sexy tone of voice (so I'd like to think, at least). I moved on to rhapsodise on how full and sexy her lips were. I told her to close her eyes and think about her heartbeat and to feel it as she also felt her core getting warm.

She started to squirm, and crossed her legs. Then she laughed heartily. "Good," she said. "Very good. What else do you know?"

I smiled and looked at her first in one deep brown eye and then the other. Then I looked at her lips. It's another technique we use called 'triangle gazing'. It's designed to encourage a girl to think about kissing, as she follows your gaze. I saw Adele lick her lips.

"You're thinking about kissing, aren't you?" I said.

"How did you know?"

Back in my hotel room, I pushed her to her knees and stuck my dick in her mouth.

"Wait wait wait!" she gasped, drawing back and turning her head to one side. "I haven't done this before. Give me a moment.... Okay, ready."

I've taken some pleasure in being the first man to do a variety of sordid things to girls. I guess it's a similar feeling to being the first to walk across a field of fresh snow, or to pop the foil of a new jar of coffee. We had sex again then fell asleep. Adele left in the morning to go to work. What a great day I'd had!

I spent the afternoon in St Michel, killing time waiting for Adele to finish work. There was a Starbucks overlooking the town square. I bought coffee and settled into a sofa with the book I 'd brought with me, Ayn Rand's *The Fountainhead*. I felt very pleased with myself. Here I was in Paris, the third greatest city on earth (after London and Newcastle) and I had just spent the night banging a pretty nineteen year old French girl I'd only met a couple of days earlier. Not a bad life at all. I watched the people come and go outside.

I noticed a young Korean girl had been in Starbucks the whole time, sitting a few seats away to my left, studying. She was alone, and looked bored. She was a cute little thing, plump for a Korean but pleasantly curvy by European standards. She wore short shorts and a t-shirt that barely contained her ripe young breasts. Her skin shone with teenage vibrancy.

No, you can't! I thought.

Outside the Paris Opera

Everything about her made me want to go over, but I dithered. I was, at that very moment, completely sexually satiated. The night and the morning with Adele had been sweet, pleasing, and satisfying. *But there's a hot girl, sitting alone and bored,* whispered a voice in my head. I shook my head and tried to focus on my book. It didn't help. A voice I didn't recognise as my own kept egging me on to approach the Korean. This is a common problem for hardcore players, especially daygamers—you can never switch off. I knew how to talk to women anywhere, at any time, and now I always felt obliged to do so. Even though my sexual desire was near zero, I'd spent a year drilling myself into the approach habit. Like a hound dog catching a scent, I strained at the leash.

I considered my situation.

I had my steaming coffee and a book that I thoroughly enjoyed. Barring a natural disaster or horrible accident, I'd soon return to my hotel to have more sex with a beautiful young French girl who was my entire reason for being in Paris. Yet, as I watched this Korean sitting there, it was like her vibe was screaming out that she was looking for some excitement, almost desperate for it. It would be rude not to chance my hand, surely?

I knew I'd be disappointed in myself if I didn't at least open her. I had no idea if she spoke English and perhaps she'd already sensed me staring at her. I leaned over and waved my hand to get her attention.

Wandering around Paris with Ayn Rand

"Hello. How's your English?"

"Um, I speak a little bit."

It was much better than a little bit, but I wasn't here to argue the point. I needed to explain my reason for interrupting her, and to stack into a real conversation.

"I've just spent the past ten minutes trying to figure out what that book is you have there, and why you have it." This was meant to neutralise the weirdness of my having stared at her, by recognising and explicitly mentioning the fact.

She smiled, "It's my diary."

"Oh," I said, "I thought it was one of those old Reader's Digest books. When I was a little boy, my grandmother used to give them to me to help my reading. I'm Nick, and you are?"

"Kim," she said with another giggle. She liked me. It was going well.

"Do you mind if I sit with you a minute?"

"No, go ahead," she said and shuffled aside to make space.

I cracked silly jokes to make her laugh and she was increasingly comfortable with me. After about ten minutes I suggested we go for a walk. She was game. We walked along Paris side streets past little bistros, flower stalls and other local fauna. We soon arrived at a church garden. I climbed up and sat on a low ledge, pulling her up next to me. We were holding hands, and we start talking again.

"How old are you?" she asked.

"Too old for you."

A year ago, when reading Tony Clink's book and contemplating becoming a player, I'd held numerous self-defeating ideas, about being unsuitable for the life. One of them was my age. I'd recently turned thirty-five, much older than the girls I chased. Nobody I knew was dating girls fifteen years their junior, except Jimmy and Tony.

"Really, how old?" she asked.

"I'll tell you if you take one guess first." I replied.

She made a face, screwing up her nose, and said, "Twenty-seven?"

I smiled and said, "Higher."

"Thirty?"

"Closer, I'm thirty-five."

"How old do you think I am?" she asked.

"Twelve." She laughed at that and I said, "I don't know. It's hard to tell with you Asian women. There's that whole range between sixteen and thirty where you all look the same age. Let me have a look."

I looked her up and down, blatantly. I made a point of lingering my gaze on her breasts and then slowly let my eyes travel down her legs. "Turn around," I told her. She turned herself around and giggled self-consciously.

"Twenty-one?"

She gave me a proud smile. "No, I'm nineteen."

Instant boner.

This couldn't be true, could it? Would I be banging two teenagers, on consecutive days, in one trip to Paris? We walked towards a small park. I wanted to keep pushing the sexual theme, as Kim was soaking it all up.

"What's the craziest sexual experience that you've ever had?" I asked.

"Hmm, tough question. I once kissed a guy I didn't know in a nightclub. What's yours?"

Her naivety was cute and amusing at the same time. I tried not to laugh as I said, "You're not very original. You're only repeating my questions."

"Yes," she admitted, "but I want to know. What was your craziest sexual experience?"

"Wait, here's a church. It's better if I tell you inside the church, like a confessional."

She laughed, and then I launched into a story about fucking Ioe in a car on the streets of Seville. It was actually a hybrid story of two separate incidents, but it sounded way more exciting this way. Kim looked shocked but very interested, opening her slanty eyes as wide as a Korean can.

"Wow."

She was speechless for several minutes, mulling it over. Importantly, she wasn't showing the slightest sign of discomfort. Girls do like thinking about sex. I laid down in the grass at the park, and Kim sat upright next to me. I rested my hand on her thigh and, as we talked, she admitted that she was a virgin and had only been kissed by two boys. Soon she lay down next to me and put her head on my chest. I stroked her her soft hair and looked up at the clear blue sky with birds flying overhead.

"I want to find a strong, confident, dominant man someday."

"I should tell you," I said, "that I like you. I'm going to kiss you before we leave this park."

"How are you going to do that?"

"I'll dominate you," I told her.

She giggled again, and after five minutes of half-heartedly pushing me away she relented and I had my tongue down her throat. She was a hopeless kisser. It was obvious that she had no idea what she was doing at all. I liked that, a lot. I was Neil Armstrong taking man's first steps on the moon, corrupting something untouched and uncharted. Now I needed to plant my flag.

As we kissed, I felt up her tits.

"I'm going to fuck you," I said. I doubted that would be the case, but it doesn't hurt to try.

"That won't happen" she gasped, moaning as we rolled around in the grass.

Not something I'll easily forget

"I'm going to pull your clothes off and fuck you right here, in the park." Again, this was just talk. I'd already seen, out of the corner of my eye, a few pedestrians walk past and shoot us funny looks. A dog on a leash had wandered over to sniff my legs before his master yanked him back.

"It's never happened before. Why would it happen now with a guy I met met an hour ago?"

"Well look, it's only been an hour and here we are. I've already got my hands up your shirt."

"I know, I can't believe it," she said with a mischievous giggle. She was enjoying it, that was obvious, but she was also fighting it in her forebrain. "I have to go meet my dad," she said.

"Meet me back at Starbucks for lunch tomorrow," I told, more than asked, her.

"Okay," she said readily, with a smile. We swapped numbers and said goodbye.

I took the Metro back to the hotel, showered and cleaned the room of clutter. I was buzzing. Adele arrived shortly after four. We had sex again, almost immediately, and then talked about what to do for the rest of the evening.

"Let's go out sightseeing," I told her. "I want you to show me around."

Adele was, as always, passionate about that idea. We had a nice evening, a proper date, you might call it. She showed me around the city and I saw all the grand sights of Paris with a beautiful girl on my arm. We kissed in front of the Arc D'Triumph, a memory I will always cherish. We had dinner back to the hotel, and sex again. Everything with Adele somehow felt sweet and pure. I liked that. It never occurred to me that I was now a cad. I'd completely absorbed the values of the Seduction Community, foremost of which is that constantly chasing skirt is the most natural thing in the world. It's a self-serving ethos but given it was serving me so well, I never thought to question it.

Adele went to work and I went to St Michel to meet Kim at Starbucks for lunch. This time Kim was as keen for tomfoolery as I so, right from the beginning, we were kissing. She surrendered to it, letting my hands roam wherever they pleased. While we were talking I pulled out her t-shirt with my finger and looked down inside. "Nice tits," I told her. And it was true they were very nice. Big for an Asian girl and beautifully round. She responded with mock outrage but was clearly enjoying it. I was groping and mashing them in the middle of Starbucks and she still wasn't complaining. Fortunately, the few customers were at the other side of the room and paying us no attention.

We went for another walk and settled in another park, on some benches. I took her hand and put it on my dick, over the top of my jeans. She pulled away, but the second time left it there, looking down in fascination.

"Have you touched a dick before?"

"No."

"How is it?"

"Kinda weird."

I slipped a finger into her shorts and finger fucked her a bit. Her grip on my cock got less tentative and I sensed she wasn't finding things quite so weird any longer. I really should've dragged her into a public restroom and tried to bang her. The window of opportunity was open. Instead, we carried on this way a few minutes more before Kim suddenly stopped and checked her watch.

"I need to get back to my house. I sneaked out while my dad was sleeping. I need to get back before he wakes up."

That tore it. It was my last full day in Paris so I told her, "Come look me up in London sometime. We'll probably end up getting married, going to the Bahamas, and banging on the beach."

We exchanged Facebook details. We never did meet again, but that didn't bother me. The experience had been good for my inner game. I was getting a window into another world—that hidden world of fast adventure sex that most men never see and most women don't even believe in until it creeps up on them and they get swept along on the waves. Kim had literally sneaked out of the house while her dad was sleeping so that I could molest her near Notre Dame Cathedral.

How odd.

That night was to be my last with Adele, for a while. I was leaving Paris for London. She came over to my hotel and I came over her face.

"I haven't done that before, either" she said, wiping her face with tissues.

Score.

CHAPTER 25

RECONQUISTA

The clock was ticking.

My EuroStar arrived back in London on Thursday afternoon and Mafalda's visit to London was already half over. We chatted on Facebook messenger and agreed to meet the next day, Friday night. I needed to rustle up a wing for the double date so I pinged Fernando, my best friend at the time.

"Remember that Libyan bird I said was coming?"

"Yep."

"She's here. Her friend is with her, as a chaperone."

I could sense Fernando wincing on the other end of the phone. "The big fat lass?"

"I don't know. She didn't say if it was the same girl. Look, I need a wing tomorrow to take care of the obstacle. Can you help me out?"

"Sure, I'll take one for the team."

I made arrangements with Mafalda for the two girls to meet us at London Bridge. I met Fernando an hour earlier and we sat in a nearby pub. When 9pm came, I went out to meet them but they hadn't shown up. I gave it ten minutes and messaged.

"We're here. You?"

Ten minutes after that, Mafalda messaged. "Hiiiiiiii.... sorry..... we are late!"

I went back to the pub and explained to my Brazilian friend.

"Don't worry pal," he said. "We'll just get another drink. It's Friday night. No problems!"

Two hours passed and even Fernando's calm temperament was sorely tested. Fortunately, neither of us had anywhere else we needed to be. We were both angry at getting messed around, though while I was concerned I was losing a chance at sex, Fernando was likely relieved at precisely the same eventuality. Finally, close to 11pm, Mafalda messaged.

"Where are youuuuuu?"

I showed Fernando the message on my phone. "This is why women shouldn't vote or be elected to company Boards."

We finished our drinks and walked over to the station entrance where two girls were waiting. The "obstacle" was actually reasonably good-looking, a tall slim Libyan twenty-something called Azhar. I could see Fernando let out a low whistle of relief. She was worth a poke. As it was late and we were on the fringes of the night-life zone, most pubs were already calling last orders or shutting up shop for the night. We found one open by the river with a quiet room in the back. As the girls took off their coats and placed handbags on the cushioned booth seats, I stood over them.

"What will you drink?"

They looked at each other, shyly, as if each waited for the other to speak. Ah, Muslims!

"Will you drink alcohol?" I asked.

They looked askance at each other again. "We've never had alcohol before," said Mafalda.

"This is London, so it's English rules. Every tourist must drink alcohol. It's the law. Queen Elizabeth herself demands it."

Both girls nodded meekly. I bought them mojitos, while Fernando and I drank beer. "Start slowly" I admonished them. They sipped through straws and giggled like naughty schoolgirls. Both finished the cocktails quickly and demanded more.

"I feel funny.... so funny," said Mafalda.

The conversation flowed well and it seemed all four of us where playing to the same song-sheet. Mafalda and I were soon holding hands, and it was obvious Azhar liked Fernando. She kept whispering in Mafalda's ear, as if forgetting neither of us spoke Arabic. By one am the pub closed.

"Let's walk along the South Bank riverside," I suggested.

Mafalda and I walked ahead, hand-in-hand, while Fernando and Azhar dawdled behind maintaining a discreet distance of at least

Mafalda and Azhar break the first of many taboos

a hundred meters. We turned a corner, temporarily breaking line of site with the others, and I pushed Mafalda up against a wall and kissed her. She pushed up into me enthusiastically until she heard footsteps approaching. It was a safe bet that Azhar was doing the same thing with Fernando when Mafalda wasn't looking, but both girls seemed keen to preserve the formal appearance of modesty with each other. We disengaged and let the others catch up. I was pleased, having confirmed Mafalda knew the score. It was now only a question of how far she was willing to go.

We walked along the river for over an hour. The skyline is beautiful at night with all the office and landmark lights reflecting across the black water like a kaleidoscope. We stopped a few times to quietly gaze over the railings. It was a warm summer night. Every few hundred metres I'd drag Mafalda to one side for a little molestation while Azhar and Fernando affected not to notice. We crossed a bridge and walked up to Piccadilly Circus. It was late. Mafalda discussed something in Arabic with Azhar then told me they needed to take a bus to the hotel. It was clear Fernando and I were not invited. We hugged them goodbye and watched them leave.

"How was it with Azhar?" I asked.

"Good. We made out a bit. She likes me. You and Mafalda?"

"She let me finger her by the river. That time we ducked behind the hot dog kiosk she wanked me off a bit."

"Nice."

We made plans to meet the girls at *Milk & Honey* bar the next night, the girls' last before returning to Libya. They arrived almost two hours late again. This time Fernando was angry.

"Fucking idiots. We've already passed the bullshit stage."

"Hey, I would understand perfectly if you left right now. If I hadn't invested so much Facebook time with Mafalda, I'd leave right behind you."

"I'll give them one more chance."

Frustrated though we were at being made to wait, the silver lining was we were waiting in *Milk & Honey*, my favourite bar. The maître d' had given us a good booth in the basement, tucked into a corner. When Mafalda messaged to say they'd finally arrived I didn't even go out to the street to meet them.

"Come inside. Ask for Nick at reception. We're downstairs."

One of London's coolest secret bars

Churlish, perhaps, but we wanted to make them come to us. For the first ten minutes, Fernando and I gave the girls the cold shoulder, like they weren't even there, instead continuing our conversation with each other. In the seduction community it's called a "freeze out" whereby you withdraw attention from girls as punishment for their bad behaviour. It's much more effective than telling them off because, counter-intuitively, many girls enjoy being dressed down — it's attention. Some like to know they have stirred your emotions. So, if you give them the "reward" of a punishment they'll continue to act up to earn more such rewards. When you reward a behaviour you get more of it.

I find that kind of thing screwy but, I reasoned, they'd started it by being two hours late twice in succession. They were lucky we didn't throw them out and colonise their country again as payback. The girls talked with each other a while then tried to get onto our good sides. We relented.

"So," I asked Mafalda, "How about a tour?"

Yes, the famous *Milk & Honey* tour that always ends in the toilets on the second floor. She nodded, knowing full well that the tour was an artifice to give us all plausible deniability. We went through the motions of me showing Mafalda each room and her nodding and agreeing that yes, it really is very nice. Then, on the top floor, I pushed her into one of the cubicles. Her eyes spazzed out, going wide and bright. Arab girls usually have big heavily made-up eyes anyway, so now she looked like a startled raccoon. We kissed and, within moments, I slipped my fingers up her skirt and inside her. She pulled me in tight and bit my shoulder, so I pushed her head down towards my dick. To my surprise and delight she scooted down onto her knees and swallowed it up, sucking like a fat kid with a new ice lolly.

I grabbed a handful of hair and dragged her back to her feet, spun her round, and pulled her jeans buttons open. She batted my hand away.

"No!"

I tried a few more times but each time she refused.

So I pushed her back to her knees, grabbed her head tight and face-fucked her against the wall. I could hear little whimpers, moans, and gurgles but she didn't fight me off. Quite the opposite, in fact, she had both hands on my arse pulling me in harder. Dirty bitch. I pulled back a little, and she made up the difference, bobbing her pretty Arab head up and down on the end of my dick until I filled her mouth with infidel cum. She gagged and instinctively retreated, but I wasn't letting her go until the cum was dribbling out down her chin and she was batting me with her little fists in annoyance.

She got up and spat it all into the sink.

"I've never done that before," she said, flashing me a satisfied look.

I wiped my dick off and we re-joined Fernando and Azhar downstairs, catching them in the middle of a make-out.

"Azhar and I are going to a nightclub now," he said, and Azhar was hurriedly putting her coat on and eye-coding Mafalda. Evidently they'd agreed to separate. Fernando took Azhar's hand and led her out, turning to give me a wink. Mafalda stayed sat next to me on the sofa, her hands in her lap, looking down demurely. We both knew the 'nightclub' was actually 'Château Fernando'.

Mafalda was squirming around and breathing heavy. She seemed to have committed to stay the course tonight.

"Let's get out of here." I said and she nodded.

My Kennington flat was a short cab ride away. I continued to tease and tantalize Mafalda on the way home so as not to lose the sexual momentum but it wasn't really necessary. She wanted her holiday adventure and knew Azhar was getting her's. We arrived at the house and I marched her straight into the bedroom. We began undressing each other.

"I'm a virgin" she said, then knelt on the bed and began sucking me off. She had darkly tanned skin and white underwear, which made an attractive contrast. I turned her words over in my mind, wondering what she'd meant. Was she saying she couldn't have sex? Or was she going to let me deflower her? Suddenly I wondered if I was to have a disappointing end to this liaison.

"Is that a problem?" I asked.

"Yes. I'm engaged and will be married soon. I must be a virgin on my wedding night or I bring shame to my family."

"Ah," I croaked, disappointed.

Mafalda continued with her enthusiastic blowjob while I adjusted to my newfound failure. I'd spent almost two months chasing her and after all this build-up, I'd have just some fooling around and a blow job to show for it. Yet another disappointment to add to a long list of daygame disappointments. Perhaps I really wasn't cut out to be a player. This stuff was too dramatic.

Mafalda disengaged and looked up at me with her big eyes.

"But, I think.... perhaps you can have sex with my ass?"

I suppose it was obvious — her being from a strict Muslim country but keen to enjoy herself — but it took me by surprise nonetheless. I'd never had anal sex before, so it hadn't occurred to me as a possible workaround. Frankly, the thought disgusted me. I'd need to think about it. Anal sex was, technically, sodomy.

And who engages in sodomy? Homosexuals, that's who.

And Arabs.

I weighed up my mild disgust in the 'negative' column against the new notch as the 'positive'. Mafalda really was cute, and I was in the Game to get laid, wasn't I? How many chances would I ever get to bang a Libyan virgin in the ass? Fifty years hence, when lying on my deathbed, this could possibly be my greatest regret.

I couldn't let future-me rue a missed opportunity.

"Okay, in the ass it is," I said.

Mafalda lay back on my bed and I pulled her panties off. She seemed very nervous, though I forgot to ask if she'd done it before. It wasn't easy to squeeze it in, as I didn't really know the right approach and she seemed no more enlightened than I. We made the best of it, all the time I thought that I couldn't understand how gay men did this for pleasure. After some initial pain, Mafalda began to enjoy it. I turned her over and she ground her hips and ass back into me as I hammered her.

It was okay, I guess.

After ten minutes of unremarkable rutting I pulled out and deposited my cum all over her face. Unlike her gagging experience in the toilets an hour earlier, this time she took it like a trooper and didn't even flinch when I caught her in the eye. She was wrapped up in enjoying her basest fantasies. I left her on her knees, cum dripping onto her breasts and thighs, while she licked the last bits off the end of my dick. Then we took turns showering.

I went first. It was my house.

Mafalda spent the night. I fell asleep. I rarely bang a girl more than once a night. Usually I try to make the one time as good as possible rather than drag things out and lose a good night's sleep.

The next morning while Mafalda was in the shower, I got a call from Fernando.

"I'm in a taxi from Clapham with Azhar, pal. She wants to be dropped off at your place to collect her mate."

They arrived half an hour later, by which time Mafalda was back in her jeans and headscarf looking to all the world like a chaste Arab.

The girls greeted each other warmly as if nothing had happened, chuntering on in their language. It was funny, I was sure that they were both denying their respective adventures, although they both had to know.

"I hope you enjoyed your holiday in London," I said as I hugged Mafalda. She refused to kiss in public.

"Yes, it was great. Thank you."

We said goodbye and tucked them into the idling cab. As Fernando and I watched them drive away I asked him, "So, did you fuck her?"

He nodded, "Yeah, in the ass."

"Me too."

"It's shocking really. Late last night, when she was sucking me off, her phone rang. I assumed it was Mafalda, maybe cock-blocking or something. Azhar told me to be quiet and answered. She was talking in Arabic and got increasingly angry, telling off whoever had called, almost shouting at them. Then she hung up on them."

"Odd," I agreed. "She took a phone call during a blow job?"

"Yeah, she had my dick in one hand and the phone in the other. But that's not the shocking thing."

"Spill it."

"She looked angry, so I asked if she was okay. You'll never guess what she said. 'That's my fiancée, asking what I'm doing. He's jealous. I told him how dare he keep checking up on me.' Then she sucked me off again."

He was ashen-faced, remembering the scene. It really had shocked him.

"It's true what they say. You can't trust women."

"Snakes with tits, mate" I agreed. "Let's go over the road and get a fry-up breakfast in the greasy spoon cafe. Tasanee is coming over later so let's get some scoff first."

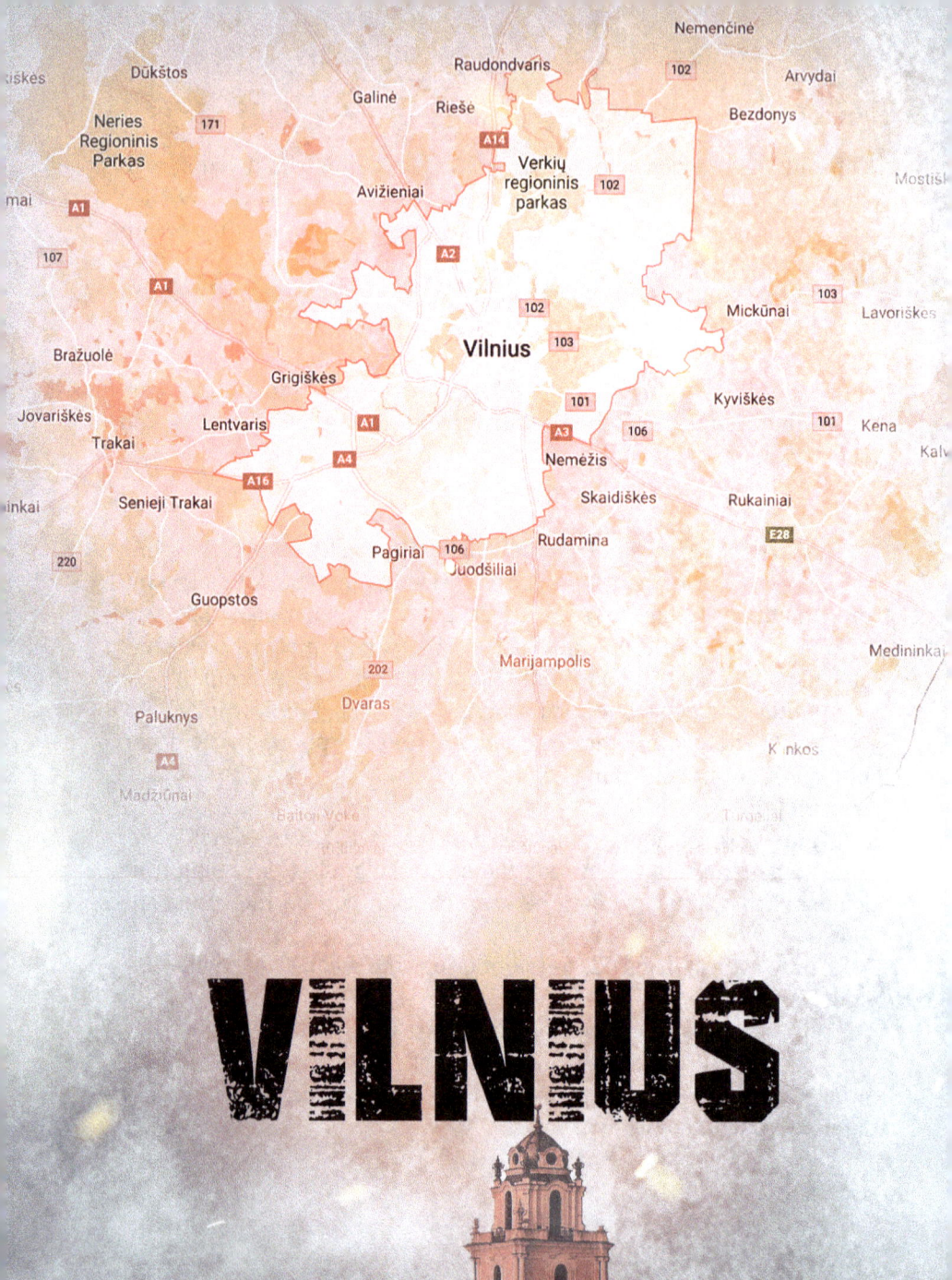

CHAPTER 26

LITHUANIA

CHAPTER 26

LITHUANIA

I'd shagged four birds. Three of them had made my all-time Top Five list in quality. I wasn't yet a world-class womanizer, but you could make a reasonable claim that the last six months were (statistically) the peak of my entire sex life so far. A Frank Sinatra or Warren Beatty may find it unimpressive but it felt like winning the lottery to me. I was racking up approaches in London and getting to know the guys at RSG better, making more new friends and learning a lot.

I'd say I was now happy about half of my waking hours. That was a one-hundred-percent improvement over a year earlier.

In May, RSG had been contacted by a Lithuanian man, Ignas, who ran a men's development meeting group based in Kaunas. He wanted to organise a PUA boot-camp for his group, in Vilnius. This was unusual. At that time, Pick Up Artists (in the tradition inherited from Ross Jeffries and Mystery) existed only in Anglophone countries, for the simple reason that Game is a male reaction to feminism. Feminism destroyed traditional gender roles and the social contract between the sexes, freeing up women to chase *hawt* dudes. A tiny group of good-looking or high-status men benefited hugely from the sudden mass availability of casual sex (before marriage) created by the ensuing chaos. Game represented an alternative strategy, whereby normal men could use skill and charisma to compete with the hawt dudes. Feminism is most deeply entrenched in the West and its aggressive expansion (especially via the United Nations and European Union) hadn't infected non-English-speaking countries as badly. Men from Central and Eastern Europe don't need game to get laid because the average quality of woman is so much higher there, traditional gender roles exist, and women are far more likely to want a monogamous relationship than bed-hop every alpha male. Every country has its slags, of course, but at a macro societal level such countries hadn't been destroyed by feminism and thus Game wasn't so necessary.

Now, we didn't know this at the time. I didn't even know what Lithuania was. It sounded like a type of cheese.

Jimmy called a meeting.

"What do you lads think we should do with this Ignas character?"

It was a risk to take him up on his offer. All we had was an exploratory email from a stranger, located in the arse-end of the world.

"Do we know his bona fides?" I asked. Tony turned his laptop around so everyone could see. He'd brought up the website of Ignas' self-development group. There were a few photos of him on stage speaking to a small crowd in a seminar environment. Jimmy peered closer. He wasn't wearing his glasses so I doubt he saw much.

"Well, that's all just nonsense written in his silly country's silly language, isn't it? We can't rely on that. All it tells us is he once stood on a stage somewhere saying something to somebody. I don't know about you lads, but Jimmy doesn't leave London for that."

"I've never been to Lithuania," said Mick, our resident adventurer. "I visited Estonia a couple of times. The cruise ship I dealt cards on often docked in Tallinn on the way to St Petersburg. I like the Baltics."

"If Ignas pays, I'll go," said Tony. "I'll check it out, report back."

We all agreed there was no harm in sounding out Ignas further. Jimmy swapped a few emails and Ignas explained our London prices were very high for Lithuanians so we'd need to help him promote the event. Until then, he didn't have the budget to make reservations for the flights, hotel, and seminar rooms. Could one of us visit and help test the market? Mick and Tony were keen, so it was agreed they'd visit for a weekend, speak at one of his monthly events, and then demonstrate some night game in the bars afterwards. If the sales pitch flopped, Mick and Tony would still have a fun trip, and Ignas would only be out of pocket by a small amount.

Two weeks later, the two-man RSG expeditionary force flew to Lithuania. They returned on Sunday evening and reported back to Jimmy. It had been a success. The crowd had eaten up the talk and been impressed with their bar game. Ignas said there seemed to be market demand for an event and offered a one-week all-expense paid trip for ten of us. We would be expected to teach for three days, and the rest of the time we would be "lads on holiday" in Eastern Europe.

Diamond couldn't get time off work, and Perry wasn't interested. The rest of us agreed, so it would be Mick, Tony, Jimmy, Fernando, Johnny, Lee, Ace, Becky, and myself. We all arranged for our flights and hotel rooms and headed out to Luton airport with enthusiasm. We all met in the departures lobby and, after check-in, I noticed their were only eight of us.

"Where's Jimmy?"

"Not coming," said Tony.

"Why?"

"He didn't say. Just told me he wasn't coming and hung up."

Coming just six months after the Malaga trip, it was another fantastic venture abroad. The quality of the women in Lithuania was outrageously high compared to England. Stepping off the bus in central Vilnius felt weird at first, and we couldn't quite figure it.

"It's as if everyone is younger here," I said. "The country feels young, demographically."

"Birds are miles hotter," said Mick. "In London you have to fight your way past four or five fatties to get to the one slim girl. Here, the average is slim."

This was somewhat ironic coming from Mick because that summer he was outrageously fat himself, looking like a beach ball with little arms and legs sticking out. He'd been far slimmer the prior year, and would soon become extremely fit. But in 2010 he was, as Jimmy never tired of saying out loud, "a fat Aussie bastard."

"Something about the energy here feels different," I said. "The last time I felt this was in Japan. It feels.... like high social trust. It feels safe."

Gradually it dawned on us. No fatties. No third-world immigrants. No feminists. No degenerates. This was a country that had mostly escaped infection by the disease of modern Western culture. It was full of normal people who spoke the same language, shared similar values, and didn't eat like hippos. It was so refreshing. In London, one wrong turn could land you in Islamabad or Lagos. My further travels in Eastern Europe would be eye-opening, seeing what England would've looked like if we'd avoided the lunatic social engineering of the post-war years.

The boot camp hadn't sold well, with just five students paying up. It meant Ignas would lose money, but the students had a good time. I taught the daygame with Fernando and Johnny, and left the nightgame to Mick and Tony who were far better at it than us. Ace and Becky helped out a bit, to justify their presence. Our teaching responsibilities were discharged by the first weekend, and then we had another seven days to take in the Baltic architecture, cheap beer and the astonishing young women. Ignas had booked us into a budget business hotel on the edge of the Old Town where we shared rooms along the same corridor. The other rooms were full of Erasmus students on a university trip. It created a lively party atmosphere though none of those girls were hot enough to inspire action on our behalf.

We attracted a lot of attention on the streets and in bars. Vilnius is a small city of half a million people in an isolated country that has no world-famous tourist sites. So, although many Lithuanians worked abroad, especially in England, they weren't so used to seeing foreigners in their own land. Our dress, speech and mannerisms were different, and we were also high on the vibe of being on holiday in a strange land. The weather was sunny all week, which helped draw the young women onto the streets. We had a great time. It was eye-opening.

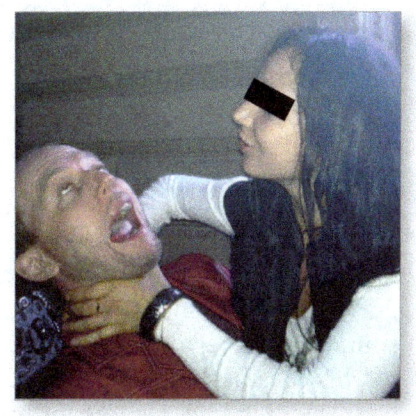

Catching attention outside nightclub 3OI

The football World Cup was reaching it's climax that week and Brazil had gotten to the semi-finals against Holland. There was a bar at the top of the Old Town, a cobbled street leading from the old medieval cathedral at its base up to the old Town Hall at the crest of a hill. A long thin park led off to the right, and at this junction was the bar's massive open-air beer garden. They'd decked out a dozen wooden A-frame benches and hoisted up a projector screen at the end to show the World Cup games. We arrived just before kick-off, and it was jam-packed.

"You nervous?" I asked Fernando.

"Yeah, Brazil aren't so good this year and it's a strong Dutch side."

We found a spot sitting on a grass bank atop a brick wall near the entrance, which gave a clear view of the game. I noticed a few cute girls in the crowd. Two in particular drew my eye, a tall model-esque blonde and her friend, a shorter cuter girl possessed of ass-length thick black hair, olive skin, and dark features. She looked like the love-child of Borat and Cheryl Cole. Fernando didn't look at anything but the football, barely pulling his eyes away to say thanks when I brought the drinks over. At half time, he finally relaxed.

"See those girls?" I said, indicating the blonde and brunette.

"Yep, I like 'em. Let's go over."

Fernando opened, so he got to choose which girl he wanted. Fortunately, he liked the blonde who was, by objective standards, a point or two hotter than the brunette. The latter, Martina, was more my type so I didn't feel like I got a raw deal. Martina gave me a cute, shy smile. She was timid, demure, and I liked her right away.

We stood by the wall, leaning up against a wooden pillar and sipping the local Utenos beer from flimsy plastic glasses. Conversation flowed well. Soon we'd dragged them across to our pitch up on the grassy bank for more teasing and chat. Then the referee's whistle sounded the beginning of the second half and Fernando switched off, his eyes back on the game. It was obvious that his target, Illona, was watching him, waiting for him to pay attention to her. Fernando was aware of that but intent upon the game and, so long as I held the attention of both girls, it would work in his favour by showing him to be somewhat distant and inscrutable. Brazil lost the game, so it took a disappointed Fernando a quarter hour to get back into a playful vibe.

By now, Martina and I were holding hands. The four of us swapped numbers and planned for a double date on Sunday.

Saturday was spent daygame coaching. I met a few more girls, got some more numbers and Facebooks, two of which ended up leading somewhere. I found one of these girls walking across the park by the aforementioned pub. I complimented her flowing summer dress, saying it had a nice swish and she reminded me of Audrey Hepburn. She was a pretty twenty-two year old girl with big anime eyes named Justina. We sat together on a park bench for half an hour, exchanged numbers, and she met me later that evening for a short drink in the Old Town.

"I've just broken up with my boyfriend. I feel fragile," she said.

She sat across from me under a darkening sky, and many revellers walked past taking in the Old Town sights, the restaurants with outdoor dining areas, and the two nightclubs further up the bank. We talked for an hour. We'd already swapped Facebook details so, when she made it plain things weren't going to progress, I made my excuses and met my friends a few streets further away at a small nightclub called 301 Club.

The final day of coaching was on Sunday morning. One of the students asked me about some technical point so I looked around for a girl I could demonstrate with. A curvy blonde turned the corner, headed down the pavement towards the cathedral. She wore tight blue jeans and strode quickly with purpose. She was wearing headphones.

"Watch this," I commanded then went over and stopped her with gestures, motioning for her to take out the headphones,

"Hi, I just wanted to say I really like your walk, it has a purposeful stride to it."

She responded well, and we spent the next ten minutes talking. Well, I was talking and she was giggling inanely—which, it would turn out, was a habit of hers. She was called Danute, a half-Finnish, half-Kazahk air hostess. She liked me and I walked away with her number.

First date with Martina, in Shooters bar

That evening Fernando and I had our double date with Martina and her friend Illona. There was also a third girl, a dark-haired Russian, who we hadn't expected. We met by the Town Hall and Martina soon paired up with me, walking arm-in-arm. Fernando had a more difficult time. Illona was extremely pretty and wouldn't look out of place in a fashion magazine. She was also a silly bitch. As I got to know Martina better, I'd find out more about Illona's inane lifestyle and her deep-rooted troubles. For now, the second time we'd met, she was simply a silly bitch. We walked them to a bar at the top of the cobbled street. Martina and I chatted between ourselves, entirely happy. Fernando had Illona on one side disagreeing with everything he said, and on the other the Russian girl interjecting every time she felt ignored. I felt sorry for him and knew he was only tolerating it so as not to ruin things between Martina and I. And, of course, men tend to be tolerant in direct proportion to how hot a girl is.

We switched venues for the second drink, to a burlesque-style bar called Shooters. It was virtually empty so we had the entire basement rooms ourselves. Martina and I sat on one of the soft sofas and sipped our drinks.

"Let's have a look upstairs," I said. She agreed and we were alone for the first time. We kissed for ten minutes then joined the disharmonious group downstairs once more. Martina worked shifts at the airport so she soon told me she needed to go home to change, then on to work. Though she was sitting on my lap purring like a kitten, her job responsibilities cockblocked me and she took a taxi home. It was 10pm and I could now turn my attention towards helping dig Fernando out of his hole. I saw off Martina into the taxi and returned to the bar.

"Nick, I'm going up to the look-out point with Illona now. She said it's worth seeing."

"What's that?"

"It's a park on top of a hill. There are three big crucifixes. You can see the whole city and she says it's beautiful at night."

Translated into clear English, I heard these words as, "I need to isolate Illona because her Russian friend is cockblocking me."

"I don't want to go! We go dance!" insisted the Russian, pawing at Illona's arm. Fernando's girl obviously wanted to go with him and the two girls argued about it, in Lithuanian. Never underestimate the tenacity of a single girl to stop her friend getting laid. I'd have to take one for the team. The Russian, Aliza, was a hot girl but absolutely not within my reach to pull at that time of my life. The whole situation was wrong anyway—how could I hit on a girl who I'd met through Martina? Surely word would get back to her, and likely Aliza was of the type who might deliberately come onto me just so I'd try it on, so she could tell Martina. I wasn't yet good at covertly pinging girls for interest without tipping my hand.

"Aliza, let's go to a club. My friends are at 301. We can join them."

She was reluctant to leave Illona but the latter shooed her away and raced off with Fernando. It took Aliza twenty minutes to recover from her pique and she said little as we walked to 301. I showered her with the attention that she hadn't been getting all afternoon, and she finally came around and turned out to be quite a sweet girl. We arrived early so we had the basement dance floor all to ourselves. We started doing silly dancing, and I now made her work for her attention, which she did. Eventually the rest of my friends showed up and we were soon in full party mode.

My phone buzzed with a message from Fernando. "Coming to 301 now."

Taking one for the team with Aliza

A minute later, he followed it up with another. "Kissed her, but she's difficult."

I pulled Tony to one side and explained the situation. He leant back against the wall and took a deep breath, nodding his head in a pose of deep thought. Finally, he turned back to me.

"It sounds like Illona is a superficial woman, and she responds to social status. Thus, we must raise Fernando's social status. We must act like he is our leader."

We spread the word, so when Fernando walked in with Illona he got a big cheer from Tony, Mick, Ace, Becky and myself. We'd practised this kind of routine before so Fernando immediately recognised the plan. We shifted to make space for him against the bar. He smoothly locked into the power position of the group, with us all facing him like a large horseshoe. I bought him a whiskey and we all allowed him to be the conversational anchor. Illona ate it up, feeling like she was dating the king. After an hour of princess behaviour, she became a queen, and gave no more trouble.

Earlier that evening, before the double date, I began engaging Danute, the giggly blonde, over SMS. "Hey Miss Fashionable, guess we're text buddies now, Nick."

She texted me a big smile and said, "How's your evening? I don't like the rain."

"We're all having a hotel party, listening to the thunder, drinking a white Russian. You?"

This routine texting continued all evening. She said, "Which hotel," with a smiley face.

"I'm at home still, relax." I told her the name of the hotel and said, "If the rain stops, we'll go out. Want to come join me?"

"I would like to meet with you tomorrow for a coffee?" she floated.

Fernando couldn't make any headway with Illona that night but we all had a great time. The next afternoon I met Danute and walked her to a bar. There was a lively playful vibe between us and by the time we left she was poking, teasing, and prodding right along with me. We went to Shooters walking arm-in-arm. It was early in the evening and, the previous evening with Martina, I'd made a note of how good the sofas were for dates. It was empty.

Danute was comfortable with my touching her and she was fully invested in the conversation, often qualifying to me. She seemed like she wanted to kiss, but she just wouldn't. Perhaps she was hyper-sensitive to public displays of affection? I thought. I stood her up and pushed her against the wall and went in, caveman style, for a kiss. She turned her head to one side , giggling, and refusing the kiss. I tried again and she turned to the other side, still giggling and still refusing to kiss. At no point did she try to push me away or move her feet.

It was fun, but I became impatient. I checked my watch and remember I had a second date with Justina coming up in less than an hour. So, I sat back in the sofa with Danute, chatted for another drink, and said goodbye. I texted her later that evening. "It was fun today, you're weird, but I like you."

"I think you are drunk. Just not like the others," she replied.

The date with Justina was short, just one drink, as she was meeting friends for dinner. It didn't go anywhere.

A short date with Justina

Martina and I met again before trip's end, on our second-to-last night in town. My friends were all in an open-air temporary drinking area set up in the middle of the same cobbled street. Martina joined us, alone, wearing short shorts and tight, plunging top. She nestled up against me with a big smile. *Looks on*, I thought. By 11pm it was getting cold in the beer garden. We headed back to the hotel en masse to mix cocktails with the many bottles of spirits we'd bought at the Maxi supermarket the previous day. We began drinking in the room I shared with Fernando. After an hour, everyone left discreetly so it was just Martina and I remaining. I doubt it was an accident. Finally I had her alone and on my bed. She looked great.

I played around with her, slapping her ass, rag-dolling her over my shoulder, and she whooped and laughed like an excited toddler. Before long I threw her back onto the bed and leant over to kiss her. She wrapped her legs around me, pulling me closer and pressing hard against my body. I tugged her vest loose and pulled it off over her head. She smiled and laid back, her arms limp at her sides in a posture of final surrender.

Brilliant! Game lay number five!

I reached down to the brass buttons of her shorts and fumbled to undo them. It wasn't easy so I instead gripped the denim on either side of the top button and ripped the buttons apart. Martina squealed and giggled. At that moment the door crashed open, making a startling bang against the wall. Fernando lunged him, very drunk.

"Niiiiick! We are...... oh....... sorry!" He quickly realized his mistake but the damage was done. Martina scuttled backwards and quickly put her shirt back on. Fernando left without another word, closing the door behind him. Martina and I continued making out, and she was obviously soaking wet, but the window of opportunity had slammed shut. Whatever courage she'd built up to have sex had now gone. Her resolve had dissolved. I put her in a taxi a couple of hours later because she had another early shift at work.

I went to bed feeling miffed.

Fernando apologised the next morning but I couldn't really blame him. Though it was unwise of him to intrude in that situation, he had no way of knowing things had escalated so quickly. Martina texted me the next morning, "Hey, I woke up with a nest in my hair, thanks to you! You're definitely gonna pay for that!"

"What's my punishment?"

"Still deciding, but I warn you, I'll be pitiless."

I tried to bully her to come out one last time before I left. She resisted, claiming work, but eventually folded and agreed. So on the last night we had another drink. The fast sex vibe had gone, and I could feel ourselves slipping into a more patient track. I didn't mind that because I was still dating Tasanee and Adele so I didn't need to rush it with Martina. I knew she'd be visiting London by the end of the month because her brother lived in Essex. Additionally, I'd resolved to come back to Lithuania. I'd had a great time and had several leads to chase down. So, I chose the patient route. Martina and I met for an hour, had a drink, engaged in some light kissing, and I got her a taxi home.

A day trip to Niida island

I ended that trip with lots of numbers and Facebook details, but I didn't get laid once. Fernando managed to bang a girl from a club, as did Lee. It was bittersweet for me because I'd worked hard but was still having big problems in seeing things through to the finish. We were all exhausted by the time we touched down in Luton airport and took the shuttle bus back into London. The next afternoon I called round to see Jimmy.

"Why didn't you come?" I asked him. "We haven't heard from you all week."

He grumbled something unintelligible, then explained, in vague terms, that he'd had a temporary emergency situation with a robbery. It was clear he didn't want to go into detail. Something about an expensive guitar and not being fully insured.

"So, how was Vilnus?" he asked.

"Fucking awesome, mate. The boot camp was a bit shit, but you wouldn't believe how high the quality is compared to London. We are shiny over there. Literally, the girls haven't been daygamed before. It's like shooting fish in a barrel."

Jimmy grumbled some more. "I should've gone, shouldn't I?"

I pulled out my phone and opened Facebook, then showed him profile photos of Danute, Martina, and Justina. "I had dates with these three. Nearly banged the little one. I'm going back as soon as I can."

"So you think there's something in travelling to Eastern Europe? The English level is okay, and the girls are amenable?"

I enthusiastically explained that it was completely different to traipsing around London. We'd experienced an excitable holiday vibe, been impressed with the novelty of new locations and unknown streets, and of course the far higher average quality of woman.

"But are there stunners in Lithuania, Nick? Jimmy isn't in the Game for average birds. No, not at all. Jimmy wants stunners."

I assured him there were. He canvassed opinion from the rest of *Rock Solid Game* and it was clear we all wanted to test out more trips and other countries. Lithuania was merely a taster. Up until that moment it had never crossed our minds to travel Europe chasing skirt. London had seemed just fine. A new world of possibility had opened up. Literally. For now, in London, I needed to figure out a way to keep the Lithuanian girls interested in me until my next trip. I'd had some success with Mafalda using Facebook messenger so I experimented with that. I called it 'long game' due to the potentially long time scale. I couldn't find any advice online on how to do it so my messaging style was primitive. For example, this is how I spoke to Danute.

"Hey! I'm back in London now. Palanga/Nida were amazing. I'm so burned now that I look like a tomato. It's unlucky we couldn't meet on Saturday but we had to decide as a group where to go and we agreed on Nida."

"Hello, Nick. You are lucky tomato :) :) Because I spend my Saturday at office... I'm happy because Spain won! :) I wish to see you one day... Maybe you'll come again to Vln?"

"Yeah, I'm glad that Spain won. Before the match, I didn't care but when I saw how the Dutch team were fouling I wanted Spain to beat them. I'll be returning to Lithuania. Possibly October — we might have a long seminar then. We'll definitely meet. Let's stay in touch on Facebook for now—Keep your chat window open."

We'd taken lots of photos in Lithuania, including a day trip to the beach resort of Palanga and the isolated island of Nida. Some of them showed me with really hot girls so I posted them to my Facebook account. It showed the new, more outgoing, popular side of my life. The one I'd only recently developed. PUA theory told me those photos would demonstrate pre-selection and DHV my social status. Or something. I was sitting and having coffee on Tuesday when my phone vibrated. It was a text from Danute:

"Hey Nick :) How are you? I saw your pictures from Palanga-a lot of girls ;) Today is too rainy, I'm almost sleeping." I guess the preselection took effect.

I shot back, "Sleeping at work, or in your bed?"

"At work. I wish to sleep at my bed (not alone)"

Was that a proposition?

Surely not? Danute had blocked my ten-minute-long attempt to kiss her in person and now over text messaging she was intimating she wants to be in my bed? Had I misread the nuance of her message or was there a valuable lesson to be learned about not making myself too available? Had my leaving Lithuania had the unintended effect of making Danute notice my absence and thus fear future loss of my attention? Or was it a reaction to seeing me with lots of other girls on Facebook, that it had raised her competitive spirits?

I didn't know, but whatever the answer, it looked like a good omen. Smiling from ear to ear I replied, "I know the feeling. When are you coming to London? I want to show you around."

"Are you invite me? Actually, I'll have one week in August free, so... who knows," with another smiley. "I wish to see London and... you."

"Great, let's do it! I look forward to seeing you."

"That's nice, you are very kind," and a wink.

"We're gonna have fun. I'll show you my favourite places—give you a dream holiday."

"When I will know the dates, I will inform you. Thank you."

"Cool."

Yes, Nick, this state of affairs does indeed look cool, I thought. The pre-selection of my Palanga photos had dovetailed with the meta-level takeaway of leaving the country. Danute was now very keen. When we were in Lithuania, I had run my game as tight as I could manage but it had been only a solo approach and a solo date. She had seen nothing of my life except what I showed her there. Having taken the time to scroll through my Facebook photos she had a better idea of my life and seemed to like it. I began looking forward to August.

London was fun and the weather held. I continued my work on the streets, increasingly with Fernando as my main wing, but sometimes joined by Johnny, Jimmy, or Mick. We'd frequently experience things, or notice patterns, that we couldn't find explanations for online. We began to invent our own jargon to describe what we saw. One term I coined was 'The Russian Minute'.

We'd notice some girls would allow you to approach but barely responded. They stood still with a stony expression, exuding haughty arrogance. They seemed to be thinking: "Out with it, little man! What do you want?" It could be quite unnerving. It tended to be the tallest and most beautiful girls who did this, and there were a disproportionate number of Russians among such girls. The girl's near-silence tended to last for a minute or so, before she'd either walk off or suddenly relax and become friendly. Hence the term, 'The Russian Minute'.

That is a long difficult minute to withstand the withering scorn of a stunning girl. Perhaps that's why they did it. We affluent Londoners presumed life in the Former Soviet Union is direct, harsh, and without the soft beating-around-the-bush much loved by indecisive

Western men. Perhaps she required us to withstand that minute to earn her respect and only then she'd soften up. I realised the need to put hairs on my chest and testosterone in my bloodstream if I was to convey the kind of masculine, self-assured dominance these Siberian ice-queens required. I had one minute to take control, or she walks away. It felt like staring down a wolf, looking into each other's eyes for the first flicker of weakness.

Were Russian girls really so different? Were there cultural, or genetic, differences that made so many of them cold and unresponsive? Or did we simply have a small sample size and had, coincidently, encountered a statistically improbable run of ice-queens?

I suspect deep in the frozen wastes of Arkangel lies an old Stalin-era factory, with red brickwork and steaming furnaces. The lights never go off as the factory groans, creaks, bangs, and rings with the sounds of industrious cloth-capped workers toiling away at chunky machinery like otters damning a stream before winter. Miles of thick pipelines criss-cross the arid landscapes of the Arctic like tendrils, drawing natural gas and oil to feed this monstrous factory. Locals still respect the KGB-era blackout, banned from revealing the factory's true purpose to outsiders.

It's the darkest, most compelling secret of the post-Stalin era.

This is the factory where Russia produces its hotties. Every three minutes, around the clock, a new smoking-hot Slavic Princess emerges from the conveyor belt ready for stringent quality control testing. She is checked for long legs, pert breasts, and a pouty mouth. Should she emerge with the slightest flaw, she is consigned to the junkyard and shipped off to Siberia. But, should the woman pass inspection she's packed up in a crate and sent by railcar to the Moscow transit hub and her eventual release into the wild.

Having not yet been to Russia, or indeed any of its neighbouring countries, it wasn't hard to sustain an unrealistic fantasy image of the women there. Russian girls were the Holy Grail of Game. They were the Batman, He-Man, and Superman of the female sex. I knew this because if you typed "Hot Russian Girl" into Google images all the girls were hot. And Russian.

I thought back to the girl who'd first made me intrigued by Russia.

It was a scorching hot August day, in 2009, almost a year earlier. I was out solo again, starting at Borough Market. After my first two sets I began to lose my voice. Perhaps I'd been drinking too much alcohol lately, or the warm weather had dehydrated me, but my voice dropped to a low barely-perceptible croak. I felt like a stereo having the volume gradually faded down to zero. It never crossed my mind to stop daygaming until my voice recovered. The streets were one massive chocolate box where I could pick and choose delicacies for a nibble. Damned if I was giving up due to the trivial matter of being unable to speak above a gravely whisper. So I soldiered on.

Borough Market was slow.

There were few girls of the right demographic, but it was a beautiful day for a riverside stroll. There's a section along the Thames that is completely pedestrianized, a beautiful place for a walk. Lots of tourists, joggers, and dog-walkers file along the riverside. This day, plenty of people were out, the weather was gorgeous, but the problem was that I was just not running across a lot of girls. There were groups of men hanging out in beer gardens watching cricket, long jabbering straggling mobs of Portuguese junior high school students and their teachers on excursion, and then the random one or two girls walking solo. I approached a few. One told me she had just left her boyfriend who played in a nearby busker band. A couple of others, an Italian and a Chinese girl, said they didn't speak English. I was getting discouraged and with my voice dying I was seriously contemplating calling it a day.

Then an odd scene developed.

The crowd of pedestrians in front of me seemed to part, as though making way for royalty. Both men and women shuffled to either side as though something ominous approached that they wanted no part of. It was subtle, and took only a few seconds, but it felt like Moses standing at the Red Sea watching the waves part.

Then I saw her, one of the most beautiful girls I had ever seen in real life. She was six feet tall with legs that went upwards forever. Silky brown hair was pulled back into a long, straight pony tail that fell down her back, a light tan and a pair of big, intimidating sunglasses. She was jaw-droppingly hot. Men and women alike got out of her path, the men's heads creaking around to follow her with their eyes, tongues hanging out. Ordinary men rarely see never mind get a shot at this calibre of female physical perfection.

She was walking my way. I hadn't, as yet, been laid in nearly a year and I certainly wasn't having any luck today. I was already at the rock bottom "this day can't get any worse" stage that encourages bold opening. From ten metres away I could feel her aura and my mouth went dry. I veered across her path to intercept and at first she tried to walk around me, swatting me aside like a badly-told joke. Not having it, I stepped in front of her again. This time she stopped, took out her earphones, and gave me the Russian Minute. The look that clearly said, "State your business and move on." She didn't say it out loud. In fact, she hadn't said anything, yet.

But, she was still standing in front of me so I croaked out in my weak voice, "I like the way you walk. It's very aggressive-looking,"

She looked at me, without expression, and saying nothing. If I tried to form long sentences my voice went completely silent, so I made short statements with long pauses in between. It sounded very odd.

"It's a beautiful day. I like it. I like you. I'm English. Hello."

Those words took perhaps thirty seconds to get out.

Imperceptibly, and against her better judgement, her expression softened. Bright afternoon sun was shining directly into my eyes. Squinting like Clint Eastwood I continued on, "Hey, let's move. Out of the sun" I croaked as I turned her around. And just like that, I had control of the situation with the hottest girl I had ever approached. I was croaking out my words like a grumpy frog and she listened. She didn't walk away, and after about a minute, she was even smiling. I doubt she understood my words at first. Many times since I've verbally bamboozled girls where they give the look of, "I have no idea what you're saying but I love how you're doing it!"

I'd heard about instant dates so I was trying for them. I looked around for a pretext. Sitting parked up on the pavement by the river was a colourful little ice-cream van, its motor chugging away and a short line of tourists queueing up.

"There. Ice cream."

"Yes."

She followed me to the van and I couldn't believe it was happening. My stomach rattled and I became dreadfully nervous. That would've made me babble quickly but today, fortuitously, my vocal problem was forcing me to speak slowly and sparingly. It allowed me to think through what I was going to say before I blurted it out. So through no skill of my own I was limited to the kind of short sentences and long silences that can convey high value. I was an Accidental Alpha. My thoughtless behaviours coincidentally turned out to be the correct action to create attraction.

She told me she was Russian, from St. Petersburg, and day-tripping to London from Norwich, her train home leaving in a few hours. *She's leaving today, so I have to fuck her... today*, I thought. It hardly seemed likely, especially as I hadn't banged a new girl in nearly ten years, much less the hottest girl I'd ever seen in my life. With penetrating clarity I knew there was no option but to gun for the same day lay and again the Accidental Alpha came out as I began fearlessly leading. She didn't know my boldness was because every other option had been taken away from me.

After the ice cream I suggested that we go to the National Gallery at Trafalgar, just five minutes walk across the river. She was game for that as well so my confidence rose. The adrenaline surged through my body, giving me a warm, powerful feeling. It seemed to be going very well. Perhaps she just liked bald Englishmen with quiet Newcastle accents? We walked around the museum and looked at some art. It was boring. I could tell she wasn't impressed with the art (telling me the Winter Palace in her home-town was far bigger and better), but she didn't leave. She was there because she'd rather be with me than whatever else she had going on. That boosted my confidence further. We went back outside to walk some more and we played a questions game. She still wasn't bubbly and giggly like some other girls may have been at this point, but she answered my questions and smiled, definitely coming around. Finally, thinking we needed some alcohol I whispered, "Do you like Sherlock Holmes?"

"Yes."

"Come on, I'll show you something."

I took her to the Sherlock Holmes pub a few hundred metres away. It was crowded downstairs with the usual fauna of tourists, locals, and Conan Doyle pilgrims so we went to the beer garden upstairs. It was a small place, and not too impressive, but we were alone and I was getting some alcohol inside her, so it was all good. Her manner remained cool, not rude. We hadn't touched beyond light socially polite contact now and then.

I asked her about her dreams, so I could gauge her personality a bit from the snippets she gave and then fed it back to her. That was a standard PUA routine I'd read about online. I told her a few stories and she seemed at ease and warmed up. She began smiling, laughing, and sitting knee-to-knee with me.

That's it, I'm going for the kiss. I think it's on, I thought.

Just as I leant forwards to make my move, a group of loud Italian tourists tumbled into the beer garden, jabbering on in their silly wop language. They sat down just behind my back, facing her. The moment was lost but not entirely gone. They left fifteen minutes later and we were alone again.

This time, another chance!

Another group of tourists piled in and spoiled the moment, again.

I was at a loss as to what to do. The clock was ticking for her train, and I couldn't talk much. So far we'd been able to skirt around the lack of verbal communication by using props in the environment: the ice cream, the walk, the gallery.... it all eased the pressure of long silences. Given my inability to advance the seductive quality of the mood (it was still bright daylight too) I resolved to advance the seductive quality of the location. I'd try to get her to my apartment in Kennington.

And I'd do it without letting her know that was the plan.

Back in those early days I hadn't yet realized it was better to make clear we were going to my place and smooth it by offering a pretext. It really doesn't matter what the pretext is so long as she knows the subtext to the interaction. Instead, on this occasion, I went by a more roundabout route.

"Why don't we go for a walk in the park? There's a really nice one only a five minute train ride away."

"Yes."

Technically, I hadn't lied. Kennington did have a lovely park by the station, and I'd frequently jogged circuits around it earlier in the year. I did intend to take her there. I merely omitted the part about my house being two hundred metres away. We got onto a crowded train and stood nose-to-nose in the vestibule. Everyone, and I mean *everyone,* was looking at her. She was the hottest girl on the street that day with her short denim pants and tight pink vest. The train edged closer to my house as I tried to convince myself I was going to shag this girl within two hours of meeting her on the street. Every man on the train was jealous that I got to stand so close to her. My legs were trembling.

We got off the train at Kennington and I had a big decision to make: apartment or park? The latter would be a smoother transition but there was the pressing time issue. I didn't know exactly when her train was but she'd implied it was very soon. I had to figure out how to spring the surprise that I was trying to get her back to my house. My palms sweated and my brain spun. The stakes were high. Nothing clever came to mind,

"I live there. I need to stop by my house for a few minutes."

"Okay."

I still didn't know where I was regarding the progress of the interaction. There seemed to be two completely different possible interpretations. Interpretation One was that she was killing time before the train, amused by my antics, and entirely confident she could 'handle me' should I be bold enough to try to bang her. Her vibe suggested this wasn't the case. The way she looked at me, dumbly followed me, and had responded in the pub each gave a crackle of electricity to the air between us. I'd been friend-zoned many times before and in those cases the energy always felt flat. With this Russian, whose name I'd forgotten since she told me before the ice cream, it felt anything but flat. Why on earth would she follow me around for her last two hours in London unless she liked me?

That left the second interpretation: she liked me. She knew what I was up to and followed me to my apartment because she liked the idea. Could that really be true? Game is often like that—you are waiting for some kind of signal from her that she likes you, perhaps some hair twirling or a light touch on your forearm, but nothing happens. And then you realise that she's been following you without protest for a long time. That's the signal, right there.

Compliance is everything. So long as she's complying, it's going well.

My apartment was on the ground floor of a Victorian block built with sturdy brick walls. So sturdy that it was impossible to get mobile phone service inside unless I stood my phone on the window ledge inside the street-facing window. We arrived at the front door. I took my key out and placed it in the lock. The Russian stood back, in the short hallway between street and door, ready to come in. She looked completely comfortable, just waiting for the door to open.

Her phone rang, she looked at it, and answered.

Fuck.

My old street in Kennington

She barked something in Russian as I opened the door and stepped inside. She had now stopped and didn't come inside. For five minutes or so I busied myself in the doorway of the flat while she spoke into the phone. If only we'd arrived ten seconds earlier, she'd have been inside and the call wouldn't have connected through the thick brick walls. As I watched her talk, I could see the sexual energy draining out of her like a pot coming off the boil. The pink flush left her cheeks and the sparkle faded from her eyes. She was looking at me differently.

She hung up the phone and I said, "Okay, come on in."

"No, I catch my train soon."

The bubble had burst. I was instantly deflated.

"Come on in. Five minutes."

"No."

I tried to kiss her.

"No, I go train now."

I walked her back to Kennington station and on the way she explained the call was her boyfriend. He was here with her from Russia and staying in Norwich. I said good-bye to her at the station and didn't take her number. There was no point. I walked back home with the wind knocked out of my sails, but also with a feeling of amplified confidence. I had approached the kind of woman usually seen only on Pirelli calendars, and beyond that, I had spent two hours with her and almost got her home.

I pondered over those events for days. How close had I been? If I'd gotten her inside before the phone call, would I have shagged her? Would I have squandered the chance regardless, due to my poor escalation skills? Was she disappointed? Or had the whole thing been a gigantic waste of time and she'd never had any interest in me at all? I would never find out the answer, but as the years went by and my game improved I would have experiences which suggested to me that this had indeed been a near miss.

It seemed my Game was cursed with near misses.

Palanga gutter game

Double date with Mick

Fun in Palanga with Mick

CHAPTER 27

TURKISH DELIGHTS

I was increasingly enjoying London summer time. For several years I'd spent most of it sitting in an office looking out the window. I might as well have been watching it on television, for all I actually experienced sunshine and warmth. That had all changed, and I increasingly spent most of the daytime outside. Prior to daygame, I might catch the sun by walking through St James Park and sitting in a deck chair by the lake, reading a paperback novel while ducks quacked and squirrels rustled leaves overhead. By August of 2010, the rolling hills and grassy plains of London's parks were still full of picnicking friends and packs of tourists, but my deck chair was long since vacated. Now I was an urban hiker, covering perhaps ten miles a day performing laps of the Oxford Street-Piccadilly-Covent Garden daygame triangle.

My decision to quit work was pivotal. Initially, I'd intended to simply reduce my working week to three days. I walked into Amir's office in spring and explained my intentions.

"I like working here, but for personal reasons I think it's taking up too much of my time. I think I can carry my share of the work load in three days, and I'm willing to do full-time for business trips, but I must get more free time."

Amir was pleasantly surprised. He'd noticed my change in attitude over the past twelve months and two of my team-members had already resigned due to rising dissatisfaction with the post-merger restructuring of our department. He'd expected me to quit entirely.

"That works for me," he said, "but I have to run it past Head Office in the US. They are micro-managing personnel now."

We both resented their interference. Amir had spent six years building up a solid team and work-flow but the new attitude flowing from the Board was forcing everyone into a restrictive code of practice. We'd lost our independence and discretion, and with it our interest in the work. Predictably, Head Office refused my request.

I resigned.

I handed in my ninety-day notice on April 1st. In a stroke of luck, just two days later I received an official letter from Her Majesty's court calling me up for jury duty. A quick call with Human Resources informed me that company policy was to treat jury duty as additional paid leave. So, every day I went to court was a day I worked off my notice period at full pay. Luckier still, the case I was assigned lasted almost three months. The upshot of which was that my last day in the office was April 9th. Court began at 10:30am, had a one-hour lunch break, then finished at 4pm. It was like gardening leave and I took full advantage. There are few better feelings like walking around in the sunshine being paid a corporate salary in order to chase skirt.

I enjoyed the full British summer. I loved it.

For all the free time and great weather, just getting onto the streets each day required me to fight off negative self-talk buzzing in my head. The dates were coming through for me but most of the time I faced a wall of rejection and time-wasting. It was particularly difficult to get the first few approaches done each day.

One such August afternoon I'd been losing the battle with approach anxiety. I couldn't shake myself out of avoidance so I instead sat in my favourite Covent Garden Caffè Nero with Ayn Rand's *The Fountainhead*, which I'd almost finished. I was on a relentless self-improvement drive on all fronts so my "to read" list was piling high. I ordered a cup of coffee, found a table at the back of the cafe, and decided to skip daygame. I was emotionally spent. The rejections often astronomically outweighed the small successes. That was hard on my ego.

I found my concentration wandering from the page and towards daydreams. Before long I was staring into space as my imagination crafted a fantastical hypothetical scenario. I pictured myself rummaging through my parent's loft back in early 2009, searching for old comic books. I stumble upon a dusty old lamp tucked at the bottom of a battered old suitcase. I breathe onto it and wipe away the dust, to bring out a shine... and a fat genie pops out in a cloud of purple smoke.

"Who are you? You can't be the genie of Aladdin's lamp, surely? This is Gateshead. We don't have Muslims here," I say.

"You are perceptive, young Nicholas. Aladdin's Three-Wish genie is busy today. He has asked me to take his place."

"So who are you? Do I get three wishes from you?"

"No, you do not. I am the Faustian genie. I offer you a simple trade," says the fat jolly apparition.

"Sounds legit," I reply. "What's the trade?"

"It is simple, Nicholas. For the next eighteen months you will walk alone through purgatory. It is a journey of many miles, racked with grief, stress and self-doubt. You will stumble and fall many times. Your friends will mock you but you'll continue walking forwards. On the final day, you will emerge into the light. Your feet will ache, your emotions scarred, your ego destroyed. At this moment, I'll give you a hot twenty-two year old Thai girl and a hot nineteen year old French girl to bang as often as your wicked heart desires."

Fantasy Daygame Me considers his trade for mere seconds.

"Deal!" I cry, and the Faustian pact is agreed.

Silliness aside, imagine such a trade were possible in the real world: a set amount of pain and/or wealth in return for a quantifiable and guaranteed reward in hot young skirt. Of course, the real world isn't like that, but play along with the thought experiment. What is it worth to you? If you're female, switch out the details for the equivalent result of romantic fulfilment. We all make a version of this trade. Men devote their lives to their careers, personal fitness, education, and whatever else they estimate will bring success in the dating market. For their part, girls dedicate themselves to punishing diet regimes, grooming skills, and fashion. Well, English girls don't, but most others do.

I once put the question to my friend John Bodi. If that Faustian genie had materialised one day before he made his first ever daygame approach, would he have accepted the bargain?

"Of course," he replied. "I'd have snatched up the pen and signed the contract, drooling frantically over the paper in my excitement.

I wouldn't have let the genie back into the lamp until he pretty-promised with a cherry on top. Even if he *was* a Muslim."

"What are the minimum terms you'd have accepted? How big a reward in girls for how much pain?"

"Give me a minute, this is complicated."

John pulled over a beer mat and scribbled some numbers on it, then computed sums in his head. He crossed out some lines and wrote some more. I took the pause as an opportunity to buy a new round of drinks from the bar. When I got back to the table he was ready.

"Okay, these are my terms. I will give the genie my entire life savings and the proceeds from selling my father's house. In return, he has to give me three 'sevens', each under thirty years old, per year, for the next ten years."

"So, that's about £200k for thirty girls?"

"Oh, it's a lot more than that. I considered throwing in my He-Man action figures collection too, but those are irreplaceable."

Herein lies the irony of politics in modern Western society. The central division in politics is between the socialists of the Left, and the capitalists of the Right. To take their arguments at face value, the Left is deeply concerned about inequalities in the distribution of wealth. They rail against "the 1%", or the "ruling class", or whoever else is above them in the economic hierarchy, concentrating wealth in their hands. This strikes me has having the wrong priorities. The Left isn't at all concerned about the concentration of *sex* into too few males. Their economic and social policies actually create that problem. Their priorities are misguided because, as most men would agree, it is better to be poor but with lots of quality skirt than to be rich and celibate.

Hence, an injustice all around.

Socialism has the effect of levelling personal incomes downward. In contrast, a capitalist society creates a strong causal link between the wealth a person creates and how personally rich he himself becomes. That's the whole point of it — being rich is a better life than being poor, so it motivates you to put in the work and take some risks. An enterprising young man with a smart head on his shoulders can work hard at school, crack open the textbooks at night, and pour his energies into his career. Before long this effort pays off and he's a valued employee with a high salary, and all the benefits that confers to his quality of life. Take for example an experienced industrial engineer. He can design a bridge that spans valleys. That bridge links two settlements, bringing incalculable value in trade and culture to those populations whose lives are transformed. Such technical expertise is rare and difficult to attain. Capitalism will reward him, his salary likely forty times higher than unskilled work such as baby-sitting or street-cleaning. That's not to say those other jobs have no value, but they help less people and create less wealth, per employee.

Good luck to the engineers, I say. If you get rich, put your feet up and light a cigar. Give yourself a pat on the back, mate, you earned it. It's social justice in action.

Socialism destroys this causal link. My South African surfer friend Bruce, who you'll remember as my training partner at the media firm, quit London and took a highly-skilled job in Denmark. His career is somewhat comparable to our fictional engineer. Yet, his net take-home salary in Denmark, he told me, was only 2.5 times higher than his teenage baby-sitter's salary. That is the destruction socialism wreaks upon society: social injustice magnified. When a society is organised "from each according to ability, to each according to need", it quickly finds out nobody has ability and everyone has need.

It's evil. Pure evil.

Such a train of thought is a standard position within political debate, and by reading Ayn Rand I was getting it good and hard on the anti-socialism front. What was new to the manosphere, and I hadn't even considered until reading Roissy, was socialism's chilling effect on the sexual market place.

The modern man in Western socialist democracies is increasingly unable to effectively distinguish himself through a career. His struggles may win him a higher headline salary but once the pernicious poisons of socialism are factored in (high taxes, welfare payments, housing benefits, socialised education and healthcare) the net result on his life isn't so different than the lower salary would have been. Perhaps his house is a bit nicer than the baby-sitter's, in a nicer area, and he has nicer hotels on his holidays. But it's a vast amount of risk and effort for precious little incremental reward.

I had a striking example of this living upstairs from me in Kennington: a work-shy, low-IQ African immigrant whose apartment, after all the free council improvements, was actually nicer than my own. It was topsy-turvy. The key skill to getting ahead in a socialist economy is not talent, nor hard-work, nor risk-taking. It's graft. You get ahead by being craftier and more shameless in milking the welfare system. Honest men refuse to do that, knowing how graft corrupts your soul and destroys civilisation. Yet they must stand by and watch Leftists doing precisely that. It made me furious just on economic grounds, so imagine my feeling when Roissy postulated it's affect on getting laid. If you read classic fiction, a common theme is of an adventuring male seeking to make something of himself. He goes into the world, takes chances, and raises his station. Society was designed to reward that by better marriage prospects. Men made themselves eligible through real-world success. That's gone now. Women see a vast ocean of similar worker-drone males with similar incomes and similar lifestyles. There's no economic reason to choose one man over the other. A man has less scope to differentiate himself through ambition.

It gets worse.

Feminism has completely restructured Western economies. Drives to push women into the workforce, equal pay scams, and massive transfer payments through the Welfare State has freed women from reliance upon male economic providers. An ambitious woman can easily find a job with a living wage, and a lazy woman can survive on welfare without giving up cable television, mobile phones, or indoor plumbing. Women no longer need individual men for security, because the West has the rule of law, police, military, and border control (provided by men en masse). There used to be a social contract: men provide security (economic and physical) and women bring fertility. Now, the government has taken over that role — paid by men's taxes, and the difficult jobs still all done by men.

At a societal level, men have been cuckolded.

In a socialist country, women don't need a man. So, how do they choose their sexual partners?

Naturally, they chase the most *sexually attractive* men. Whether a woman is attracted to his looks, his fame, or his charisma the end result is the same: the tiny group of most attractive men monopolise the hot young women while the vast majority of men go thirsty. Socialism's dubious success in levelling personal incomes (at a cost of great social injustice and wealth destruction) has spawned the additional pernicious effect of creating vast inequalities in the distribution of hot tight skirt.

The eighty/twenty rule is in effect.

Given that pretty much every man would rather live in a tent and bang a procession of hotties than live in a palace and masturbate to Internet porn, I'd say society is on the wrong track. The socialism of Soviet Russia created gulags of political prisoners, millions of wretches condemned to hard labour in the salt mines of Siberia. The socialism of modern Britain created virtual gulags of sexual outcasts, millions of wretches condemned to video games, porn, and the occasional fat ugly woman from Tinder.

I paint an exaggeratedly dystopian image, but I think the point holds on a less extreme scale. These are the thoughts that occupied me as I poured semi-skimmed milk into my Americano in Caffe Nero and cast my eyes for a comfortable sofa to collapse into. My whole world view was changing and *The Fountainhead* was to continue that process. I was determined not to disappear into a virtual gulag, like my university friend Tony had with his scuba-diving and real ale tours. A prisoner, such as Edmund Dantes of *The Count Of Monte Cristo*, may spend months chipping away underground to build an escape tunnel. I considered my work on the streets to be the modern equivalent.

My flights of fancy reached a natural end and I returned to my book. An hour into my reading I'd hit a nice flow, the pages turning fast as the story whipped along. The paperback felt comfortingly substantial in my hands and the dense type filling every page made me feel intellectual. Perhaps a wry smile turned up the corner of my mouth as my eyes focus intently. And then I needed a piss. The coffee had gone right through me. I got up and joined the toilet queue at the back of the cafe.

As I walked there I noticed a hot dusky girl, sitting at the table nearest the toilet, reading. She had long dark hair and, though seated, appeared to be tall and slim. Her clothes were colourful and accessorised in the style of an "outsider". A cute Turkish proto-hippy, but without the tattoos and piercings that usually go along with the beatnik crowd. I tried weaselling out of the approach. *You already decided not to open today*, I reminded myself, but my spider sense had irreversibly triggered. The girl let out a heavy sigh as she turned a page. That seemed an opportune moment to act.

I walked over to her table

"Hi, is that book really so boring?"

She looked up and smiled at me. "Well, sort of."

"I was just standing in the queue over there for the bathroom when I looked over and saw your eyelids drooping. Then you let out this massive sigh. What are you reading?"

She laughed and told me the name of it, but I don't remember now. Some sort of physiotherapy textbook. I was sure it was pretty dry, and she seemed happy to take a break from it to talk to me.

"It sounds really boring, I sympathize," I told her, briefly placing my hand on her shoulder in an exaggerated display of reassurance.

Approaching in a café is different than on the street because it's akin to an ambush. On the street, the woman is free to leave at any time without incurring any cost. Thus many will smile, say thank you, and keep walking. In the café, she is tied to whatever she is doing there, i.e. drinking the half cup of coffee in front of her. If she doesn't like you, it's not so easy for her to leave. Perhaps it's her favourite seat and she's comfortable there. Thus a player must be sensitive to how she responds to his intrusion. The simple rule of thumb is to look for subtle signs of disengagement. Does she look back at whatever she's doing, give short closed answers, and only respond to direct questions? If so, she's trying to give you the polite brush-off and you should take the hint. In contrast, if she stops what she's doing, gives you full attention, and continues the conversation then she's happy to talk. This Turkish girl closed her book, set it aside, and looked at me with a big smile. I guess I'm just *that* charming. After about a minute, I asked her if she minded if I sit down.

I sat down, and we chatted briefly. I was mindful not to say anything overtly sexual. I complimented her outfit, which was mostly black with nice flashes of purple and blue, and her thick black hair.

I didn't trust my calibration to try it on any stronger than that lest I come across creepy.

"I'm Nick."

"I'm Baharak."

"Interesting name. It sounds like what you'd call in Orc in *The Lord Of The Rings*. I wonder if there's a connection. I remember reading an analysis that said J.R.R. Tolkien used Turkey as his inspiration for Mordor."

"Oh I hope not! Istanbul is a very beautiful city."

"I've never been to Constanti.... Istanbul. I'd like to see it sometime."

I teased her a little more, then we swapped numbers, until the rising pressure in my bladder forced me to re-join the toilet queue at the back. True to my plan, I didn't do any more daygame and instead slipped out of the cafe and had an easy night at home. That same evening I texted Baharak.

"You're from Istanbul, right?" I asked. I figured that's something Roissy would approve of — standoffish and cool.

Her text back was a simple, "Yep."

"Cool."

That was the extent of that conversation. I waited two days before I texted her again, not because I wanted to but because the Internet told me it was tighter game that way.

"Hey, little Miss Mordor. I'm going to be in Covent Garden this afternoon. What are you doing?"

She replied quickly.

"Hey! I just left Covent Garden. I had some plans with friends today. Have a great day."

I'd been practising minimising my text chats, using as few words as possible to avoid gushing with over-investment. I texted back simply.

"Aye."

It was One Word Game, something I'd read on Roissy's blog.

"Is it an Irish way?" she asked.

"That's almost exactly... the opposite."

We continued a back-and-forth and twice she seemed to be fishing for a date invitation, so I asked her out for a coffee near

Soho. The conversation went well. She was a very intelligent girl but, unfortunately, a bit of a Leftist. She was part-timing as a waitress and had been in London on her own for a while. She was "pushing thirty" by her own admission, but refused to ever really tell me her real age. I would guess twenty-eight or nine.

I liked her, but her Leftism was a sore point. For years, I'd never cared about a woman's political persuasion. Frankly, I didn't even listen to them much on *any* topic. I figured that if I wanted an interesting conversation, I'd talk to a man. But now I was all hopped up on Ayn Rand, the manosphere, and blaming Leftism for all the world's ills.

And for my ills in particular.

I guess I was spoiling for an ideological showdown. That's tear gas for seduction, but I wondered if I couldn't somehow twist a political debate into a seductive process. Escalation was still a problem for me, especially when I opened girls indirectly like I'd done with Baharak, and I remembered that as a teenager most of my sex came after arguing with a girl. Perhaps this would be a good time to take some risks. My inner game remained fragile and I hadn't internalised the correct mind sets. Everything I'd read, and discussed with Jimmy and Johnny, suggested that I needed to believe — really believe, on a deep instinctive level — several principles that were counter-intuitive to what I'd been socialised into. Specifically:

- I am a sexually attractive man.
- Women like sex for its own sake.
- Women want men to hit on them.
- When a girl meets a man for a date, she is hoping he seduces her.

I still struggled with these. Intellectually it wasn't a problem. I knew it. The problem was that I didn't *feel* it. It hadn't bedded down emotionally. I merely *wanted* to believe it. That caused problems on dates, when the light-hearted joking of the street and text messages gave way to really getting to know the other person. I'd turn up on dates thinking I still needed to attract the girl, which put pressure on me to perform. Deep down I thought I needed to convince girls to have sex, and that her doing so was somehow taking something from her, chipping away at her value. That was the manosphere meddling with my mind again—it's full of self-righteous thirsty men who are convinced the solution to their love-life is to find the one Good Girl who has barely had any sex. A grand myth had developed on the forums and blogs that girls "lower their value" by having casual sex and, thus, when you hit on a girl you are, fundamentally, taking something away from her.

Tricking her into lowering her value by sleeping with you.... that's an awful self-defeating frame that completely misunderstands women's sexual schema. For all the helpful techniques and theories I was absorbing in my online research, I also took on my fair share of faulty ideas. So much of it was new that I lacked the overall view, and judgement, to properly organise my thoughts. Too much information, too fast. There were errors. Now that I was friends with Jimmy, I frequently called him to clarify key theory for me. He was always keen to help, enjoying the mentor role.

"Nick, you're overthinking this. If a woman comes on a date with you — assuming you actually hit on her when taking the number — then she already likes you. It doesn't mean she's sold, or isn't juggling better options. But it does mean you can assume attraction. She's going to co-operate with you on the date. She's hoping you'll win her over."

"I've been friend-zoned plenty. Those times didn't feel very co-operative."

"Ah well, I didn't say she's going to make it easy for you. She'll still be kicking the tires and getting a good look at you."

This swirling confusion of contradictory ideas and deeply-buried assumptions from my earlier life had conspired to create my escalation problems. Escalation requires courage and conviction, a strong belief that what you are doing is the right thing to do. If you don't feel attractive, don't feel she likes sex, don't feel sex is good for her, and don't feel she's come to fuck... that's going to hamstring you.

Generally, the man must lead the girl towards sex. Each girl presents a slightly different puzzle based on her individual preferences, horniness, other options, cultural upbringing and so on. There are always quirks. You may "solve" one woman and bang her, thinking triumphantly, "I've cracked it," and then the next girl does something to blind-side you and you fail. Effective escalation is one part playing the percentages, one part inspiration, and one part blind luck. I didn't yet have enough experience in solving puzzles to be confident I could solve the next one. Yet a man must escalate. Be it his body language or conversation, he must do something to up the ante, polarise the interaction, and create a clear Man-Woman vibe.

A man who always lets girls come to him is a man who is happy with dregs.

Baharak and I sat next to each other on a Caffe Nero sofa, upstairs and across from Leicester Square station. I noticed she was reluctant about letting me get closer to her. I crossed my ankle over my knee, then I let the bent knee drop a few inches so it touched her thigh. This was a mild compliance test, to test her reaction. She didn't immediately jerk away from the contact but after a respectable minute she moved her thigh.

Hmmmm... what did that mean?

At this time, 2010, most of the PUA dating advice concerned the use of 'routines' on first dates. The theory was as follows: unfocused boring chit-chat gets you nowhere. At best it builds Comfort, but does nothing for Attraction or Seduction. Rather than blather on aimlessly, a player should build a store of 'routines'- short canned stories or playful games- that are each purposely designed to move elements of the seduction forwards. For example, find a story from childhood which effectively conveys some attractive character traits and fleshes out your personality. Recast this story to include 'attraction triggers' and polish it to be interesting and dramatic. This story should keep a girl's interest and temporarily free her from whatever stresses and worries weigh down her mood. A player can lead her mind on a more interesting journey, while building rapport. She'll enjoy herself and form an impression of you as an interesting man.

I had three routines that I'd rehearsed and was comfortable telling. One about when I was a child in church, one about walking on the beach in Okinawa when I lived there, and one about boxing. They were more interesting than those brief summaries suggest. These days I can ad-lib any topic and my verbal style is so well-drilled the resulting story is naturally compelling. However, in 2010

I was still methodically and laboriously putting each brick into place. I told Baharak the boxing story, just as I had Kamile a year earlier.

It's a ten minute description of the preparation and lead-up to my first boxing match in Japan heavily laden with evocative details. Recall the earlier chapter about it in this book, but imagine it retold with vivid sensory details: how it felt to be in the ring with my adrenaline pumping and sweat dripping off my brow into my eyes, the smell of leather and canvas, the dull roar of the crowd, and the inner battle against fear. As my storytelling progressed Baharak began to lean over towards me, fiddled with her hands, and her eyes opened wide as she listened intently. I'd talked her into a heightened state of emotion. That is the correct time to sexually spike.

"Sorry, I just have to say, can you keep a secret?"

She leaned in towards me and said, "Yes."

"Don't look now," I said, "but that Italian couple behind you, she's totally into him. She's a really slim petite girl, but look..... she has absolutely massive tits."

Baharak laughed and, after a few seconds, discreetly turned to take a look. With a look of astonishment she turned back around and said, "Yes, she does! I used to know someone at school like that."

I wasn't in a rush to have her thinking about me sexually — not overtly at least. My intention was to raise her "buying temperate".

I wanted to *Make Baharak Hot*.

A most wonderful pub

We drained our coffee cups and I took her to a pub nearby, *The Cross Keys* in Covent Garden. The sun had disappeared and the clouds opened with a light drizzle. Baharak let me take her hand as we walked through the rain huddled under her umbrella. *The Cross Keys* is a traditional English pub with the concomitant brass fittings, hunting pictures, and farm implements on the walls. The landlord was proud to have hosted many celebrities over the years, as the numerous framed photographs on the walls showed. The music was soft and non-intrusive. It's a good place for making conversation.

We sat there, still holding hands and talking. Baharak said, "This is romantic."

"What is?"

"Sitting here, holding hands like this."

I heard the sound of a window of opportunity opening.

"How about this?" I asked, then leaned in and kissed her. She was warm and receptive, so we necked on for a while then she had to leave to go to work. It was a good date.

Our second date was a few days later, at Piccadilly Circus in mid-afternoon. She looked really nice. I took her to another Caffé Nero, since it was nearby, and I only needed two more stamps on my loyalty card to earn a free coffee. We took the drinks downstairs and found a table in the corner. After the light playful conversation of the first date, Baharak began telling me more about herself, things closer to heart.

"When I came to England, I left all my good friends behind. After a while, I realised lots of the things I took for granted as normal are actually peculiar to Turkey, and to my social group."

I'd felt the same after four years in Japan. Newcastle no longer felt like the centre of the world, with styles and customs the rest of the world ought to adopt for itself.

"For example?" I pressed.

"I'm almost thirty years old. I've seen some of the world now. I'm changing my mind about many things. My old beliefs are being shaken." I could relate to that. She continued, "Since I was a teenager, I passionately believed in counter-culture. I think the English word — I read it recently — is 'beatnik'. My friends and I, we all had the same ideas about the government. The government should give us everything. I suppose I was a socialist. It seemed absolutely normal."

"And now?"

"And now I've been working as a waitress, and my new friends are mostly ambitious or risk-taking people from many different countries and backgrounds. They want to work, and improve themselves. The things I believed in before..... it's like being a parasite."

"For the government to give something to someone, it must first take it from someone else," I added. I had almost finished *The Fountainhead*, and it was having as profound an effect on me as *Atlas Shrugged* had back in the Intercontinental Hotel in Santiago, Chile, a year before I'd begun Game. My unplugging was still in process as I'd quit my job, reduced my expenses, and was now casting around for intellectual resources to fill in the missing pieces of my new world view.

"I understand," I said. "I've always been somewhat iconoclastic and I never really let go of the anarchist ideas I'd passionately believed in as a teenager. It took years, several jobs, living around the world, and new friends, until I really let go."

"Yes!" said Baharak, the word's bursting forth. She was gripping my hands.

I have the personality type — Introvert Intuitive Thinker Judge (INTJ) per the Myers-Briggs classification — that needs always build and maintain a holistic world-view. Many people are happy to pick up snippets of information here and there, holding each in isolation from the others. I call this the 'pub quiz' attitude, that life is full of interesting trivia. It is akin to buying books for your mind's library but never organising them into topics, nor creating a registry. It's just 'books' piled up haphazardly around the mental 'room'. Certain personality types feel no anxiety at this, believing the world to be a rich tapestry of compartmentalised knowledge.

I hated it. It created anxiety.

Such mindsets guarantee you'll hold mutually-exclusive ideas and have a mind rife with internal contradictions. It's tough enough to limit hypocrisy and inconsistency caused by ego pressures. It struck me as madness to introduce extra contradictions simply because your mind is disorganised and you can't be bothered to clean it up. So, any time I learned something new I'd play around with it, twisting, shaping, turning and positioning it until it would fit into the current version of my mental map of the world. That map was dynamic, reorganising to incorporate new learning. Sometimes, a paradigm shift was required. Several times in my life I'd entirely switched positions on the key concerns of philosophy, politics, and psychology. I was inspired by a famous quote attributed to economist John Maynard Keynes, "when the facts change, I change my mind. What do you do, sir?"

I don't mean to posture as some kind of independent free-thinker who made all his decisions rationally and based upon the best available evidence. I was often muddle-headed and wrong about things. Nonetheless, I believed strongly in Karl Popper's theory of falsification and I also believed knowledge advances more through the elimination of bad ideas than the creation of good ones. I figured Popper's was a system that at least gave the potential to gradually approximate the truth, like an artillery observer gradually placing the shells onto target. I considered a man's process of seeking, acquiring, and organising knowledge to be more important than the factual content in his head at any given point.

Being a good fisherman is a more valuable predictor of future wealth than however many fish happen to be in your larder on any given day.

Baharak had hit on a tension in my world-view that I'd not yet resolved. Since first discovering radical Leftist politics as a teenager, I'd struggled to reconcile two competing ideological positions within the movement. On the one hand, most of the theory I was exposed to in pamphlets and meeting groups was what Ayn Rand termed 'collectivist' and 'equalist' (solidarity, federalism, mass action etc.) so in that sense I was "anti-capitalist" and followed standard Leftist group-think. I grew out of that as soon as I got a job and paid taxes. On the other hand, unlike the socialists and communists in our midst (who we hated), my teenage punk friends were anarchists. We strongly believed that the individual is sovereign and that the primary problem with government is that it takes away your freedom. Such anarchism is diametrically opposed to the collectivism and equalism of the traditional Left.

We were just kids then, so this distinction wasn't clear to us. I'd held both positions simultaneously, never able to figure it out.

At the time I met Baharak my worldview was undergoing extensive renovations. I saw a swirl of possibilities and *The Fountainhead* was bringing some of it into clearer focus. In the People's Republic of Northern Britain you become a pariah if you let slip that you don't believe it's okay for the government to tax you into penury, in order to fund free food, board, education and healthcare for lazy slobs and foreign invaders. As both Yad and Luminita had sensed, I still held residual anger over this. My reaction had been to become strident, to provide me with the impetus to completely break the chains that bound my mind and lifestyle. I'd now openly declare my opposition to nonsense around people to whom I'd have previously bit my tongue.

Baharak had surprised me by expounding on her own shifting ideas. She was openly soliciting my opinion. So, I launched into a theory I'd pulled from Ayn Rand.

"There are, at the simplest level of approximation, two types of people in the world. The Hosts, who work hard and are responsible for meeting their own needs, and the Parasites who are riding their coattails with a sense of righteous entitlement. Everything in political theory comes down to this. On the one side are the Hosts becoming aware of their exploitation and then struggling to free themselves. We call this 'the Right'. On the other are the Parasites, struggling to stay attached to the Hosts. We call them 'the Left'."

I liked that. It didn't mince words about which side better aligned with Good, and which with Evil. I'd been taught my entire life that things were the other way around, and resented having been lied to for so long. Like I said, I was strident and still harbouring considerable anger.

"The funny thing is that the Left has so effectively taken control of culture that few in England call themselves Marxists, even though they believe almost every tenet of *The Communist Manifesto*."

"The what?" asked Baharak.

"*The Communist Manifesto*, the popular book written by Karl Marx and Fredrich Engels. Quite ironic really, that the core book of the 'worker's party' was written by two men who never had a real job their whole lives."

"Ah yes, I know that book, but we call it something different in Turkish."

I really laid it on thick, unrolling the sum total of my last three months of intellectual research. Somewhere during my exposition of Ludwig Von Mises' book *Socialism*, I saw the change in Baharak's eyes. She crossed her legs and leaned forward—it was turning her on. I was spouting off because it was a topic close to my heart at that time, but I'd stumbled upon something unexpected. I was heating her up through monologuing on intellectual debates. It was a form of dominance via intellect, reaching out into the woman's mind to take control of her world view. I knew most women love being told what to do, but did they also love being told how to think? They are attracted to a man who is sure of himself in both deed and thought. At this moment, in Caffe Nero talking about Marxism, I'd reached a temporary peak in just that and Baharak responded.

It was exciting to me as well, to meet a woman to whom I could talk to about these things. I was stating the truth about something I feel very strongly about and in the process possibly curing a Leftist and seducing a hot chick.

"Come here," I said and I pulled her up onto my lap and kissed her. Then I discreetly, in the room full of other coffee drinkers, slipped my hand under her skirt and rubbed her through her panties.

She tried to protest a bit saying, "What are you doing? Stop it, I'll melt," but she was making no move to get off my lap, and as I continued to finger her pussy, she leaned back into me and made very soft, quiet moaning noises. I kept it up until she came and soaked her underwear. Then she needed to go to work, so I put her on the Tube and got ready for my next date, with a different girl.

The third date with Baharak was on the following Sunday. I told her to meet me at Kennington station which is right by my house (a detail she didn't yet know). She arrived at 9pm and, as we walked, we agreed that we were starving. I walked her to Tesco and on the way I told her, "there's my house right over there."

"Your house? That's sneaky. I didn't know we were having dinner at your house," she said.

I kept walking and she followed me into the supermarket. I handed her a shopping basket and began dumping groceries into it. She looked at me with mock outrage. I call this "parody brute" in playfully exaggerating chauvinistic behaviour. Baharak took a double thrill of indignation and submission which spiked up their sexual state. Her eyes blazed. I did my weekly shopping, all the while with Baharak lugging around the basket as it filled up. Though quiet, I could tell by her face she couldn't believe my audacity in having her do this. Nevertheless, she continued to follow me around until we checked out, and then she followed me home and watched as I made pasta.

We filled our bellies at the dining room table and retired to the lounge for a drink. When we sat on the couch, I pulled her in for a kiss. She was okay with that, but as I tried to pull her up to straddle me, she resisted. I kept after her until she finally relented, and then she got really into it. When breathing turned to panting, I stood up, with her legs still attached around my waist, and carried her to the bedroom. As we reached the lounge door, however, she slammed it shut ahead of us so we couldn't leave.

Damn. Another unexpected problem to solve.

Nonchalantly, I set her up against the wall, watching her, looking into her eyes poker-faced while I sipped my White Russian cocktail still in my hand. I didn't kiss or touch her at all, content to rape her with my eyes. Baharak quivered and downed her drink in one gulp. I didn't say a word, and I still didn't kiss her. Instead I wrapped my arm around her waist and walked her into the bedroom.

Some touching ensured. Lots of touching. A half hour later she lay back, naked, staring at the ceiling. "I can't believe you got me to have sex," she said.

We continued to see each other. After about a month, I told her about Game. I was too enthused with it to keep it to myself. She was fascinated as I explained it, as most women are. That day, we were walking with Fernando on Oxford Street.

"Does it really work? I mean, the way you describe it sounds like how you spoke to me, but I was sitting in a cafe." That sounded like a challenge.

"Watch, and I'll show you."

She seemed to like the idea. It took me a while to find a woman that I had any interest in, but eventually I saw a tall, leggy Russian girl walking past Leicester Square station. I told Baharak and Fernando to wait and I ran across the street.

I did my usual opener about noticing how lovely she was, and that I couldn't just let her walk by without telling her. The Russian smiled and bit deep onto the hook. Her name was Victoria and she was exceptionally pretty. That put me into a quandry: how far should I push the interaction, knowing Baharak and Fernando were watching from across the road. I wanted this Russian and it was going surprisingly well. It would be a shame to let the opportunity go to waste. *Ah well, you did ask for this, Baharak,* I said to myself.

We happened to be standing in front of a coffee shop, so I invited Victoria in for a coffee, as Baharak stood watching. Knowing I may be a little while, Fernando walked her around the corner and they had a cup of coffee in a different shop while they waited for me to finish. I kept the idate short, feeling a bit guilty, and fifteen minutes later, I walked in with a big grin on my face. I had Victoria's number. Baharak looked at me with disbelief, and something else, admiration. "I can't believe it; you can have any woman you want, just like that," she spluttered. How I wished that really were true, but I liked the fact Baharak saw me as a superhero.

Another month went by, and I had begun to lose interest in her. She knew this, sensed it, and we were embroiled in a passionate texting session where she suggested that I didn't need her since I could have any woman I wanted. I responded to that like a dickhead, asking her if she'd like me to pass her off to one of my friends. I didn't see her again for two months. We ran into each other in a pub, and it ended with us having sex. I bumped into her one more time about a year later. That night I had a Lithuanian girl Dovile on my arm. Baharak gave me an amused knowing look, and we both went on our way.

CHAPTER 28

BLACK MAMBA

CHAPTER 28

BLACK MAMBA

To say I tended to over-think Game is an understatement. I suppose it's the double-edge sword that is the INTJ personality type. On the positive side, I see patterns everywhere. They often emerging suddenly before my eyes with Gestalt-like clarity. As these patterns become integrated into my mental map of the world I become increasingly accurate in my predictions, and increasingly comfortable in understanding my place within it. It's rare for an INTJ to feel lost, or adrift. He is usually anchored at the centre of a predictable, comprehensible world-view. The negative side is that my analytical mind doesn't ever want to switch off. I don't like to take things at face value. Whenever I see something new, I begin rifling through my mental archives to compare and contrast it with the closest matches from my experience and education.

I bring this up now because I've come to compare a man's 'player' career trajectory with that of a prospect in boxing. Say a young lad wins some amateur titles, signs with a well-connected manager, and turns professional. His career will need to be carefully managed if he is to make the big time and rise to championship calibre. If he's thrown in early against veterans he'll be out of his depth. The ring is an unforgiving place to learn your craft. Wily veterans have a whole arsenal of tricks to befuddle, frustrate, and ultimately knock out an inexperienced young talent. Thus smart managers move their prospects along slowly, against gradually stiffening opposition. They let him see a variety of styles from fighters who can test him but are unlikely to beat him. Thus he'll fight crafty southpaws, face-first brawlers, volume punchers, flighty jabbers and so on. After a few years of that the prospect has seen most of what there is to see in the ring. Now he can step up in class without getting tooled.

Sometimes the management errs and throws him in too deep too fast. He gets exposed, beaten up, and knocked out. That's how I felt when I met a busty long-legged black girl called Aisha. Game has many parallels to boxing and once of them is seasoning. Girls can be likened to opponents in the ring. Each brings a unique set of challenges, a box of tricks, that can befuddle you the first few times you encounter them. So long as you keep putting yourself in there you'll gradually see the patterns and begin to dominate. I tended to jump into the deep end and expose myself.

Not literally expose myself. That would come later.

I found some girls too much to handle at my current level of experience. Failure is a better teacher than success, so I learned a lot from each experience. With Aisha I stepped aboard a wild ride with a girl more savvy than I could cope with, and hotter than I'd ever assumed it possible for me to get. She was a 'bad-ass bitch'. She knew her sexual power and expected a lot from her men.

It all began on a Saturday morning in summer. RSG had a boot-camp so I locked up my Kennington flat and walked to the Tube station feeling pretty good. That station is where the single Northbound line splits into left- and right-sided sub-branches to continue through Central London, joining up once again at Euston in the North. That means trains often wait at Kennington for the signals to change, which happened in this case. There was a train waiting for five minutes at the platform. The carriage was about half full when I walked on. I saw an extremely hot black girl already seated. There were no empty berths opposite her, so I sat alongside and tried to figure out the best opener. Nothing immediately came to mind and I started to wonder. Her look intimidated me. She appeared very fly and unapproachable, causing me to stall and second-guess myself.

What should I do? I wondered. *Can I open her?*

Less than twenty seconds had passed since I saw her and I was already on the defensive. Lacking any better ideas, I regulated my body posture to be as 'alpha' as possible, leaning back in my seat, opening my legs, and stretching out as far as possible without being impolite. Then I completely ignored her, not looking her way at all, as if I had weighty issues to ponder. This was intended to calm my mind ('physiology determines psychology' the books called it) but that self-composure evaporated when I caught a glimpse of her knockers. They were impossibly good, straining to escape her too-tight t-shirt. They were massive for such a tall, slim girl, as if she'd put two balloons under her shirt and challenged a car mechanic to inflate them with an automatic pump.

I wanted my hands on those knockers. I couldn't think of a single thing in the world I'd ever wanted more.

The train pulled out. The driver announced over the loudspeaker that it would terminate in a few stops, at Charing Cross, to be taken out of service. I looked again at the girl, scanning for anything at all about her that was comment-worthy. The only thing that stood out, aside from her physical charms, was her leopard print handbag. I was nervous, wondering what the other passengers were likely to think. I assumed she'd blow me out anyway, so I resolved to go down dramatically, burning like the Hindenburg Zeppelin.

"Excuse me," I said as I gestured for her to pull out her headphones. She did, and waited with in inscrutable expression. "Okay. There's no way to say this without it sounding weird so I'm just gonna say it."

She was intrigued. "Uh-huh" she nodded. Waiting. So I took a deep breath and stepped off the cliff.

"That handbag of yours. Do women realise that when men see anything in leopard print; shoes, skirt, whatever, we think of... prostitutes?"

Now, she didn't expect that. She gasped, eyes wide.

"Did you just call me a prostitute?"

Across the carriage from me a few passengers were stifling chuckles. I was emboldened. I knew I'd hit pay dirt. "Um, I guess I did. I didn't mean to." I didn't apologise, and she let out a laugh. She seemed relieved, as if thinking, *finally! A man with balls!*

We got off together two stations later, chatting about inane stuff as we went up the escalators. She was initially reserved, absorbing my banter and saying little. By the time we reached the ticket barriers she was laughing and having fun. I deliberately didn't ask for her number and motioned as if to leave.

"Can you help me a minute?" she asked, quickly. "I'm going to my boss's barbecue in Morden but I've got to get to Maida Vale first. I'm not sure the best route."

"Let's ask him," I said, pointing at a uniformed assistant. He was currently advising a tourist so we waited, standing close together.

"Oh, I'm so tired" she said, and put her head on my shoulder.
STOP!!!!
ALARM

Girls *never* initiate touch by accident. Not ever.

Every single early touch a girl gives you is a calculated signal that you should read. This girl was awfully forward here. Why? Was it because she's a dominant forceful woman and therefore she hoped to snatch control of the interaction? If that was true and she succeeded, she'd lose interest in me. I ran the options through my mind. I settled on playing hard to get. I pushed her away to arm's length.

"Hang on, if you're gonna hug me I have to check you out first." Then I cast a slow appraising glance over her figure while she giggled. I got her to spin then said, "yeah, you're hot. Come here," and pulled her back in. "You're a cute spirited girl. I especially like your tits."

She loved that. Presumably she was used to men wilting under her predatory manner. The Tube assistant finished with the tourist and gave us directions to Maida Vale. I was conscious of the RSG boot-camp starting soon.

"Okay crazy girl, it was nice to meet you. But I have to meet my friends in five minutes. You've probably already made me late."

Again, I deliberately didn't ask for her number. That seemed to rattle her a bit. She didn't want to let me go so easily so she threw herself into a big hug on me, pushing her tits up hard into my chest. It wasn't the subtlest of come-ons but I'd be lying if I told you I didn't thoroughly enjoy it. I pushed her off.

"Woah, steady on! I'm getting a boner."

She laughed mischievously, and I made a show of checking my dick by thumbing my jeans open at the belt-line and looking down inside my boxer shorts.

"Yes, definitely a boner. Stop that, I don't want this when I show up to meet my friends."

"It will help you remember me until we meet again."

"About that. I'm Nick. Give me your number."

"I'm Aisha. Let's meet tomorrow. I'm free on Sundays."

"I'm busy."

That little push prompted another big hug from her. I tilted her chin up with my finger and lightly kissed her. She made a game jiggling her tits up. "This will help extend your boner," she explained, laughing. "God, I'll be so tired after this barbecue. I'll sleep all evening."

I walked away thinking, *what just happened?*

It had been far too easy. I checked my pockets to ensure my wallet was still there. My mind remained fogged all the way to Covent Garden where Fernando and Johnny were waiting for me outside the pub. Was that really me who had done those ballsy moves on such a fly chick? Everything I'd done had been pitch perfect. Was I really capable of that?

Aisha would tell me later that she'd seen me get on the tube at Kennington and thought, "He's cute, I'd do him" and had checked my hands to see if I was married, stared full-on for ten seconds checking me out while I was looking the other way, and begun jostling me to attract attention. Did girls really make decisions on who they'd like to shag so quickly? In my case, Aisha had. Her overt flirting had been fuelled by the certainty in her mind that she wanted to catch me, rather than a general super-flyness of character.

I thought she was scary hot. Her face was good but her body was a perfect ten, probably combining for an overall score on the eight/nine border, depending how much you like black chicks. She sported a tight round arse springy to the touch like a rubber ball, long shapely legs and a flat toned gym stomach. Whoever her tit-surgeon was, he deserved a Medal of Honor.

When the boot-camp finished, we began texting. "Woken up yet darlin' ? ;)"

"Yeah lol, where are you now? x"

"Back home. Making myself beautiful for a night on the razz. You?"

I'd already made plans with Fernando, who had two Brazilian girls lined up, friends of friends, that he'd promised to show a good time. I wanted to hold back on inviting Aisha out, as I was following the principle, *if a girl starts chasing, keep her chasing.*

"At my boss's house in Morden for a barbecue... where are you going tonight?? X"

"Clubbing at Funky Buddha. Might be able to squeeze you on the guest list for the birthday party I'm going to there."

"Really... only if you'd want me with you?"

"Yeah, sure. I like you :P Full name needed."

She confirmed with an estimated arrival of 11pm. I already had a Japanese girl, Eiko, scheduled for a first date at 8pm. My plan was to have them both in the club and see if I couldn't stoke a little rivalry. Eiko showed up late and wasn't much fun on the date. We met Fernando outside the club. He had three Brazilian girls with him and we were soon at the front of the queue. The doorman waved us in, but then stopped Eiko.

"No casual shoes." Eiko wore Converse deck shoes.

I was almost pleased. The two hour date had been a pain, with Eiko blocking all of my escalation attempts. It was an easy decision, to keep my promise to Fernando and bail on the miserable Jap. I pointed her towards the station and said goodbye.

The Brazilian girls weren't hot, two sixes and a seven, but they were dolled-up and full of life. Having them with us created the magic of pre-selection and before long I got strong come-ons from two different girls, each wearing similar red dresses. The first was a tall black chick and the other a slightly porky white girl. Both looked about twenty years old. They each tried to catch my eye but I refused to give it. Fernando and I talked like nothing else in the club mattered but us and the three Brazilians dancing next to us. I figured this might encourage the girls to chase harder, and if not, well, I'd already spotted two warm targets I could approach later. I walked outside with Fernando when he went to smoke. As I passed the tall black chick on the way out she made a big effort to catch my eye and I blanked her again. This time she probably knew I was dicking with her, because I gave a self-satisfied smile, which is what I wanted. It's the subtle I-know-that-you-know-that-I-know dance.

Just before reaching the doors to the street I told Fernando to hold still a moment and sure enough both girls were following me out. I hadn't realised they were friends.

"Hey girls, I see you used the same pair of curtains to make your dresses. Are you twins?"

They lapped it up and joined us on the smoking break. The first ten minutes went well with light touching and deep eye contact with the black girl, Neera. Fernando was handling the white girl but she was a typical pain-in-the-arse bolshie Northern English idiot who managed to kill the vibe and cockblock me. Just as it looked like the black girl had lost interest entirely, Aisha turned up.

"Nick!" she screeched, excitedly, and came rushing over. She was alone.

I turned my back on the too-cool-for-school black girl and embraced the friendly black girl. I could feel daggers directed at my back, and smirked. Aisha had noticed Neera, which made it easy to play the girls off against each other. The fact they were physically and demographically similar made their rivalry particularly acute. This may sound Machiavellian but consider my previous life's experience in nightclubs: standing on the edge of the fun, not part of it, struggling to even get a girl to look at me. Girls are ruthless in clubs, and this pair looked of that type. Now I had three Brazilian girls in my group (thanks to Fernando), a smoking hot black girl for a date, and another hot black girl who was interested. None of them knew the score, which I planned to take advantage of.

Neera soon came back inside to order a drink, at the opposite side of the bar. Knowing I was in full view of her, I leant back with a beer in my hand while Aisha draped herself over me. Aisha had picked up on Neera's interest, sparking her jealousy. It was on! Both girls briefly locked eyes, obviously noticing they are almost twins, and it began. Girls always pick up on a nightclub's invisible alliances, so Fernando and I were now so massively preselected that we could pull in a nearby cute Colombian girl to further bolster our numbers. Aisha knew she had the upper hand over Neera by way of being my actual date, so she pressed that advantage by grabbing my cock and kissing me hard.

Neera accepted the challenge. She threaded her way through the bar to conspicuously brush past me, grabbing my arm with a smile, then danced six feet in front of me, staring at me continuously. It was as blatant a come on as possible. I was like a fat kid in a cake shop. The smart move (and fair play) was to stay with Aisha all night, but was it possible to get Neera's number without blowing it with Aisha? I saw Neera go outside for a smoke and figured it was worth a shot, so I discreetly followed her out and re-engaged her.

Aisha presses her advantage. Both of them

Neera didn't seem at all interested. Was it a test? Had she really lost interest? Had she just been leading me on for ego reasons, to beat Aisha? Had I been in with a good chance and simply failed to maintain my temporary status as the in-demand social guy? I didn't know and with Aisha likely to interrupt at any moment, I didn't dare risk persevering. I wished Neera a good evening and turned my attention back to Aisha, who was swatting away a line of thirsty hopefuls hitting on her the moment my back was turned.

Over the next five hours with her I'd learn more about game than with any other girl so far.

"Let's go outside," she said. "I need to go to the ATM."

"Why didn't you go on the way. I saw you walk past it when you arrived."

"Very astute, Nicky, but my friend hadn't yet texted telling me she'd successfully procured a hundred pounds' worth of cocaine."

We went out and Aisha was soon bitching about her high heels being painful. I didn't need cocaine to maintain my high, as earlier events had my spirits soaring. I threw her against a wall and molested her.

She kept pushing me away. "Get off me, you oaf!"

"Shut your mouth."

I knew she wanted to fight it out, so she soon began biting my lip and wrapping her long legs around me, getting increasingly horny. She got her money and we went back into the club. I started to feel it was boring there, and there wasn't any need to have Aisha inside, with all those thirsty men pawing at her.

"Let's go somewhere better. I'll get us a table at *Milk & Honey*," I said, pulling out my phone and dialling.

"Is it good?"

"Yes. Now shut it, I'm on the phone."

While I was talking to reception, Aisha stumbled around, fiddling with her high heels. I clicked my fingers and indicated her to come over. She did, loving the dominance. I grabbed her by the throat, pushed her up against a wall, and in between sentences with the *Milk & Honey* receptionist, we made out. Aisha loved it, fire in her eyes.

Men really underestimate the power of dominance on a woman's mind. I was developing a suite of moves to test a girl's willingness to be pushed around. The most effective one I'd found is done when kissing—gently cup her cheek in one hand and then let your hand drag softly down to her neck. Watch for her reaction. Some girls will flinch a little so you ease off—no harm no foul. Other girls will moan a little to encourage you, so bring your thumb across her windpipe so you have a very gentle one-handed rapist choke. She shouldn't feel any pressure against her neck, just a soft skin-on-skin contact so she knows your hand is around her throat. It's very delicate. Now watch her reaction again—is she encouraging you? If so, gradually increase the pressure, alternating between gripping her throat and then releasing the pressure completely. That's more fractionation— on and off. Never press her windpipe because that's uncomfortable for her. Instead focus on the muscles either side. If you get to this stage, and she's still moaning in pleasure, then you've won. She loves dominance, and you've smoothly demonstrated that you "get it". She's very much looking forward to getting into your bed.

I said goodbye to Fernando and we hailed a taxi to the bar. Aisha draped herself over me on the back seat, kissing, then suddenly pulled away.

"You're a loser, Nick."

That seemed to be an obvious challenge. I'd long since learned how to deal with such tests: either shrug them off like it's a fly biting an elephant, or agree and amplify the insult.

"Yes, I'm a loser," I replied.

"You're probably shit in bed. I'm amazing in bed, the best."

"You're right. I've got a tiny dick and I cum in five seconds."

She grabbed my dick and for several moments was carried away rubbing it, before recovering her princess attitude. "It's tiny. That's not getting inside me."

"I guess today is my lucky day. Now shut your fucking mouth."

I'd come to term these spats as 'the rub', named after when a cat rubs itself up against your legs to enjoy the physical sensation against its fur. I'd noticed some girls deliberately tried to provoke me *specifically* so that I'd slap them down. They seemed to get an adrenalin rush from being put back into their place. I'd first noticed this with Emily back at university, and again with Ioe at the very beginning of our relationship. Strong-willed girls, especially if they are eye-catchingly hot, are often like this because they spend all day every day watching men roll over like obedient dogs. I imagine they sometimes feel starved of masculine strength.

Aisha had her hands down my pants now. I guess my dick suited her tastes after all.

We arrived at *Milk & Honey* ten minutes later and were shown upstairs to the Red Room. Soft low ambient light bathed the room, failing to penetrate the dark corners. Jazz floated across the air while a pair of cocktail waiters waited discreetly behind a velvet curtain in the tucked-away bar area. Aisha and I sat together on a leather sofa. It was surprisingly quiet for Saturday night, perhaps because it had only just chimed midnight and *Milk & Honey* was often used for after-parties. We chatted, and Aisha flitted between being sweet and pleasant, then occasionally confrontational and difficult. I don't think she meant anything by it, she probably considered it a fun game for both of us. Still, I felt on edge at times, encountering tests I hadn't seen before.

"Are you free tomorrow?" she asked.

"Yeah, I'll have time."

"Ha! In the station when we first met, you said you were busy!"

"Just busy on the evening with my Turk girl who I'm gonna fuck. We can meet in the afternoon"

A normal girl might've slapped me and walked out, but I was gambling that I'd read Aisha's personality correctly. Sure enough, her competitiveness was spiked again. Not to be outdone, Aisha pulled out her iPhone and scrolled through her text messages.

"Look! Here are messages from three guys. This one is my ex-boyfriend, here's another ex, and this one is my fuck buddy. I shagged them all this week."

"Well done." I tipped an imaginary hat.

"You wouldn't know. My breasts cost four thousand pounds. They are perfect, look!" She had grabbed her low-cut vest and stretched it away to show her magnificent cleavage. She seemed completely earnest, genuinely wanting me to appreciate them. I reached my hand down her shirt and gave them a squeeze, like checking the ripeness of melons at a farmer's market.

"Yes, very good," I agreed, trying to sound underwhelmed despite them being the best pair of tits I'd touched in my life.

"My pussy tastes the best. It's so sweet and juicy."

"I'm sure it is."

"Men go wild for it. They can't stop licking me out. They get addicted. Black girls have the sweetest pussies and mine is the sweetest of all."

"That may well be true, and if so I congratulate you, but I'm not interested in going down on a girl. Your sweetness or lack thereof really isn't here nor there to me."

That was true. What I really care about is that a girl knows how to hold her body in visually appealing poses and is enthusiastic in her actions. I told her as much.

"I can do all that," she said, preening. "I know how to look great, and I'd scream your name all night."

I took that as a good sign. Nonetheless, I felt like I was on a tightrope in high winds because Aisha kept probing for weakness, sniffing for any excuse to triumphantly rule me out. All I wanted to do was pull her in, make out, and then go home and have sex. My instinct told me Aisha wasn't ready and had plenty of games left to play before deciding I could have her. Why can't girls be more straight forward?

I like you, you like me, let's have sex. How hard can it be?

Her phone rang and she beamed in excitement at the caller ID. She answered and rushed downstairs, returning a few minutes later.

"Got the coke. Where's the bathroom in here?"

"Upstairs."

"Back in a minute."

Aisha was even more provocative on her return, having snorted some Colombian marching powder. As she came through the door, still standing, she scanned the whole room. "Where's everybody gone? There's no-one here."

The legendary Red Room

I'd noticed patrons gradually filtering out until no-one was left. The two waiters always retired behind the velvet curtain, no doubt taking advantage of quiet periods to check their smart phones. A mischievous smile crossed her face. She got her massive hooters out, in the middle of the bar.

"Look at these. Four thousands pounds of perfection," she boasted.

"Those are going in my mouth right now," I said and dragged her upstairs to the toilet and locked the door shut.

I figured on a few minutes foreplay and then I'd try to do her from behind in the toilet. I buried my face into her bare breasts and she leaned back, bracing herself with a hand on each wall. She fiddled with the bolt, not knowing I'd already locked it, and accidentally opened the door wide. At that moment another man and woman mistakenly burst in on us, evidently with the same idea, and we all started laughing. Aisha ran downstairs to The Red Room, laughing.

"God that made me even hornier," she said breathlessly. Sadly, the window of opportunity, of being alone in a locked toilet, had now closed. The momentum seemed good, so I figured we should get the bill and take a taxi to Kennington. The waiter soon came over and laid the bill on our table. I looked through it, totting up our totals.

"You pay, you're the man," she said.

Another test. If she'd been a broke-ass student and behaving well, I'd have happily paid. However, Aisha had a professional City job and had been a pain in the ass. So, no dice.

"No. We're splitting it. You were rich enough to buy a bag of coke."

"This is outrageous. You're a cheapskate. A nobody."

"Be that as it may, we're still splitting it."

"You'll never get your dick inside me like that. You have no idea how to treat a woman. Pay the bill!"

"I guess I'm destined to die alone. Now, I'm paying my half cash. Are you doing cash or card?"

She reached into her bag to pull out her purse, making a production out of flipping through all her ten and twenty pound notes. Finally she gave up trying to look angry and started laughing. We left enough cash to include a generous tip.

"I've still got lots of coke left. Let's go up and do some lines," she said.

The toilet cubicle was tiny, so narrow as to have only six inches of space either side of the toilet bowl. Aisha leaned over the cistern and began sorting out some lines on the ceramic lid. Her ass was too good a treasure to leave unplundered so I slipped my fingers up her dress and began fingering her. She was soaking wet.

"Get off! You're disturbing my work."

I slapped her ass and kept fingering her.

"Really, Nick! I'm trying to cut the lines but I can't get them straight with you doing that. Fuck off! You'll never get near this pussy again." She said all this between moans of pleasure.

It was at this juncture that I made my first, and perhaps only, mistake of the entire interaction. I should've just lifted her skirt and stuck my dick in her. She would've almost certainly squawked, told me to fuck off, and then gotten well into the shagging. However, I was overflowing with confidence, thoroughly enjoying the back-and-forth, and sure Aisha was already a done deal. So I stopped fingering her and we took turns snorting a line.

The cocaine stretched out my skeleton and I felt myself growing to reach the sky. It felt sensational. Aisha wiped her nose and looked at me with wild eyes, also feeling the rush. I pushed her up against the wall, held her wrists firmly by her sides and stared into her eyes, our lips almost touching, for five minutes as we got the rush. The cubicle seemed to throb with massive sexual energy.

I was enjoying myself too much, over-complicating it. That was the perfect moment to fuck her and I let it pass.

"Let's go downstairs," she said.

We went back to our sofas, still the only patrons in the room. She shuffled up next to me and I reached my hand behind her, sunk it deep into the cushion, so as to get the correct angle to slip two fingers inside her. It looked like she was simply sitting next to me with my hand on her arse. The waiter came to collect the tip.

"Excuse mate," I asked. "I wanted to ask you something about the cocktails here."

I engaged him in low energy conversation for five minutes while continuing to finger Aisha knuckle deep. She didn't say a word, holding her head in her hands trying not to make a sound or show the ecstasy on her face. If the waiter noticed, he hid it well. When he finally went away she hugged me.

"Oh my fucking God. That was so sexy!" she gasped.

"Let's get a taxi."

"Where?"

"To my place."

"No, I don't want to leave yet. I'm having fun. I'm still high."

We ordered another drink, and now it was really late on, perhaps 3am. Aisha hadn't yet finished trying to snatch the frame, to show me she was the prize and that I was the lucky one here. She stood up. The sofa was pushed into a corner so that it was slightly behind the entrance door, partially shielded by a protruding wall of a couple feet in width. She leant back against this wall and hiked her right leg up onto the sofa arm rest.

"Look at this," she said, pulling up her dress to show her panties, her legs three-quarters spread. "Isn't this the most beautiful pussy in the world?"

She pulled her panties aside, then pulled her labia apart.

"I taste like honey. The world's sweetest honey."

I'd have liked to agree but every single time Aisha had tested me this way, I'd pushed her away. Each and every time she'd rewarded me by getting more (not less) horny. So, I hid my rising excitement. I could feel the pressure of all this testing. It was thrilling, but tiring. Surely at some point I'd do the wrong thing, lose the game, and Aisha would lose interest.

"It's alright. I only go down on a girl if it's her birthday. Is it your birthday?"

"No."

"There you go."

She was smiling as she sat back on the sofa, feeling her point proven. I pointed up at the ceiling directly above us. There was a tough plastic dome like half a basketball attached to the ceiling.

"That's the security camera," I noted.

Aisha drew a sharp breath in shock. Her face blushed as red as a black girl's can. Then she broke into belly-laughs and waved at it. If I was to soberly tot up all the evidence I'd accumulated since meeting her on the Tube, I'd say my original tease about her being a prostitute wasn't far off the mark. Aisha was a cocaine user, a club girl, a shameless cock-tease, and if not promiscuous in her total number of men (she claimed the ex-boyfriends had been around a few years, rather than that she went through lots of new men) then she was at least uninhibited in her bed-hopping. By any objective standards, she was quite the little whore. And a total pain in the ass. But she was also endearingly fun and direct. I was having a great time with her.

Finally, we drained our glasses. I assumed it would be a simple matter to hail a cab back to my flat. We'd had our fun, played the games, but the mutually-acknowledged truth was we fancied each other and now the mating dance had finished, we'd stop the dancing and proceed directly to the mating.

Apparently not. "I'm so tired. I have to go home," she said.

We picked our way through the cobbled backstreets of Soho, past Dean, Frith and Greek Street towards Charing Cross road. Aisha's heels clicked loudly, echoing along the silent alleyways. Barely another soul was around.

"You're a boring loser," she said. "I know you want to fuck me. Never gonna happen. Never. Gonna. Happen."

"You're a whore and a pain in the ass."

She snorted — in the normal way, not the cocaine way. She spun around, flaunting her rear curves. "It's an ass you won't tap."

It was all a game but it seemed convincingly serious at times. Outside *Revolution* bar, in a narrow back alley, I pushed her into an alcove and we made out. As before, she exhibited extreme passion suddenly flipped into mouthy bullshit.

"Don't bother, you won't ever fuck me."

"Shut your mouth, you stupid bitch."

"Get your hands off me. Don't try to..... Have you ever cum in a girl's mouth?"

I grabbed her throat and pinned her to the wall while I took out my smartphone with my spare hand. I browsed through to the Gallery files and found a video I'd recorded a week earlier, of cumming on Tasanee's face. I turned the screen to face her and her eyes sparkled as she watched Tasanee suck me off and then tilt her face upward to present a good target.

"You like taking videos, do you?" she asked, breathlessly.

Without answering, I pushed her head down. She dropped to her knees and sucked me off enthusiastically. It was an amazing blow job.

"Don't make me cum. I'm saving it for the Turkish girl tomorrow."

She kept going for a few minutes, both of us thoroughly enjoying it, until we heard footsteps coming down the alley. She jumped to her feet and I reorganised myself, so we just looked like a couple kissing against the wall. We walked on to the corner of Shaftesbury Avenue and Charing Cross Road where she hailed a cab. She wouldn't let me get in.

"No, I'm serious. I need to go home and sleep."

Disappointed but no longer surprised, I took a night bus home. Half an hour later Aisha sent me a nice text saying she'd had a great time and wishing me good night. It seemed to confirm my conclusion that all her princess behaviour had been part of the game, intended to be fun.

Phew! What a day!

I learned so much in just one night that by the time I collapsed onto my bed fully-clothed my brain was melting. Aisha was a self-confessed sex addict and ball-buster. The way she talked about her exes (and the texts she showed me) it was obvious she completely dominated the men in her life. They were gushing with compliments and letting her push them around. She'd told me they were all rich and good-looking. I'd never been tested so hard and in so many different ways. It was an education. I think the only mistake I'd made was in not trying to bang her in the toilet cubicle the time we did the lines of coke. In every other respect, I think Aisha was in full control of herself and sticking to some kind of resolution to fool around but not have sex.

I really couldn't think what I could've done better. I'd been at the absolute top of my game. Aisha was just a mountain too high at that point in my life. I could feel my inner game strengthen. As recently as two months earlier I'd have been unable to handle her at all. Two years ago I'd have been no more to her than a fly to be dismissively swatted away. So many of the obstructions men feel when dealing with women are in their own minds, mental constructions that bear little resemblance to reality. Girls only have the power you give them, and they sometimes love to play the game. Aisha had a brilliant time with me. It emboldened me that I could be the source of such value for a smoking hot girl who had lots of rich good-looking men sniffing around her. I had a dick in my pants, testosterone in my blood, and some basic social savvy. That's enough to make some girls very happy indeed.

For all this, I wasn't sure if I'd see her again. She was massively attracted to me, but she'd often skirted the line with me rather than cross it. Obviously she had lots of options already set up and wasn't lacking sex nor the wherewithal to go out and find it. Somewhere along the line I must've dropped the ball, if only a little. I should've fucked her and yet I didn't so, ergo, something had gone wrong.

We continued to text over the next fortnight. Twice she agreed to and then flaked on a second date. Frame control was a huge problem. Aisha constantly tried to put me through her hoops in the text messages. I thought about what I had to offer her that all the other men in her life didn't. What was it that she'd responded to best? I staked my strategy on the insight that she craved a man who won't put up with her bullshit and would instead slap her down. Every time I'd done that, she'd liked me more. Aisha and I finally got back together on a Monday night in early September. We were supposed to meet 8pm but she kept pushing it back. Here are the texts:

Her 8:41pm: Running behind, 9:30???
Me 8:44pm: Ok, I've not left the house yet. I hope this extra time was spent on looking good...
Her 8:50pm: Lmao, spend time on looking good?? Don't make me laugh! I have a baseball cap on, vest & ripped jeans lol... now why would I go to the bother of even trying to impress you?? lol!! Too funny x
Me 8:51pm: That's exactly what I wanted you to wear. Well done.

The RMT driver's union had called industrial action so there was an Underground strike and thus no trains. This was memorable if only because I seemed to encounter every possible type of cockblock from every possible angle. Aisha called up to say she needed to get a replacement bus service, and she sounded quite agitated. For all her bluster she was still just a girl who was keen to have a date. She arrived on a replacement bus a ten minute walk away and called me, giving a play-by-play as she walked towards our meeting point in Piccadilly. Upon arrival she gave me a beaming smile and huge hug. Despite all her phone tag, her vibe was excellent in person. We went to O'Neils Irish pub just before a folk band started playing.

Having already had my dick in her mouth the last time we'd met, it was easy for me to begin by holding a strong frame. She willingly submitted, after a quick test.

"I'll have a glass of wine," she said, looking at the pub food menu on our table. "And get me a beefburger, without fries."

"I'm not buying your food."

"Well, it's like that is it?" she pouted. "I'll just go order at the bar myself."

I slapped her arse as she walked off, which made her laugh, confirming my guess that the pout was an act. I waited until I saw her head through the crowd, at the front of the bar, and sent a text to rub it in.

"If they've got Doom beer, I'll have that. Otherwise any pint of bitter. Thanks x"

She came back with only her own drink. "I left yours at the bar."

I went over and was surprised to find she had actually bought my drink and had told the barman I'd come collect it (it was amazing to see how easily she twisted men around her fingers). I came back and she scooted her chair next to mine and wrapped herself around me, straining for attention. It was a great vibe. I caught all the other men ogling her and giving me envious looks. My mind went off on a flight of fancy as I imagined what they must have been thinking. Something like: 'Woah, she's hot!!! Look at those tits! And that arse! She's so sexual! Who is that guy she's with? He's just a normal dude. Eh? He must be rich and all over her... but hang on... he's not. He's totally ignoring her. She's so gonna dump him. I'd treat her much better. Hang on, is she trying to wank him off in the middle of the bar?! Did he just tell her to stop it, turn away, fold his arms and start watching the band? She's gonna go mental... Hang on, she's pulling down her top and trying to show him her tits. Now she's licking his ear. What's going on?

brain explodes

She had indeed tried to wank me off in the bar.

Aisha loved chasing and didn't respect a man who was easily swayed by her charms. I dirty talked her and after we finished the food we went out to the taxi rank. We were in the taxi and things looked good.

"Kennington please," I told the driver.
"No, no. Canary Wharf. I have to wake up early tomorrow."
"Okay, we'll go to yours."
"No, that's not what I mean. You can't stay. Anyway, I'm on my period."

I agreed I'd accompany her there, then get the taxi on to my place. Of course I was hoping she'd relent once we got to Canary Wharf, but if not I'd only lose fifteen minutes and perhaps twenty pounds through the diversion. Given how hard it had been to get her out again, I thought I might as well risk it.

Predictably, her coldness quickly turned to heat.

"Do you still like these?" she asked, pulling her tits out in the back seat of the taxi. The driver, a middled-aged black man with tired resigned movements, briefly glanced in the rear-view mirror to get an eyeful, then turned his eyes back to the road. Aisha began rubbing my dick through my jeans.

"Have you ever had a blow job in a taxi?"

She looked uncertain. I could see in her eyes she'd never done this before. She looked very excited, waiting for encouragement.

"Not for a few years." That may not have been a lie, because I have a vague recollection that Ioe did it once in Tokyo, but I figured it was the right thing to say. "Do it."

She started unzipping me, stopping to look up into my eyes to see if I was serious. We were like children doing dares. I didn't flinch.

"Get on with it," I ordered. She did

Aisha bent all the way over and gently took my dick into her mouth. She bobbed up and down for about thirty seconds, then came up, tucked my dick away, and smiled. She beamed with the satisfaction of a child who has just won a gold star in the maths test. She seemed to be checking whether I was embarrassed. I wasn't.

"Do it again, but properly this time."

She did. This time she went for it, so obvious and noisy that the taxi driver seemed to flinch several times, affecting not to notice. Finally we arrived at her Canary Wharf apartment. I'd been sure to test whether she was telling the truth about being on her period. I'd fingered her through her jeans but she hadn't let me put my hand inside. Seeing how little resistance she'd offered to skin-on-skin contact the previous date, I took this as confirmation that her timing was against me.

We said our goodbyes. Our text chat continued after midnight:

Me: Now I have to decide whether to have a wank or go straight to bed

Her: Oh, choices choices huh, well if you're nice to me upon your return, I might wank you myself?? Then let you taste me??

Me: So you're trying to get me to wank while thinking about you? Not very subtle. Sheeeesh!

Her: Well treat me nice then you'll see ucker!!

Me: Btw, the taxi driver said he expected to see a longer blow job. I told him it was fairly enjoyable as is, but he disagreed.

Her: Lmao, yeah right!! Tell him I'm glad he enjoyed the show, I always aim to please!!

Me: Ok, I'm gonna wank over you. Just this once. Gonna try and find a porno girl who looks like you on the interwebs. This is me being romantic

Her: Really? You're being romantic?? Now that's a major turn on!! Chicks don't dig brutes! Give me yr email address & I'll send some naughty pics!

I sent the email address.

Me: Sweet. Do it now, I haven't settled in.

Her: Sent, check now x

She'd sent me three photos, all naked. One was of her bending over with a Christmas tree in the background

Me: Nice Christmas tree ;) got any with your legs at quarter-to-three?

Her: How about that one? Gosh nothing gets by you, & u certainly cannot say you're not demanding!!! Go on, where are pics for moi??

Me: I like 'em. Good work!

Her: Merci beacoup!!

Me: I've only got videos with me, not pics, and they are mostly of the girls with just a stunt-cock appearance by me...

Me: Btw, any of you sucking cock or with cum on your face?

Her: None of me like that. I've sent more though x

I noticed that the file name on one of the new photos was numbered seventy-two.
Me: Ok, I think I've got enough to get started. Gonna enjoy tapping your ass. Feel free to send the other 71 photos over the next week — if you wanna keep my mind off the Lithuanians
Her: Lol!!! Have a safe trip!!

If Aisha was one end of the spectrum, my adorable little French girl Adele was at the other. She was due to begin her University in Australia in the fall. She came to London once more, before heading down under, staying with me in Kennington. We had an amazing time. She was so enthusiastic, energetic, and eager that she was a joy to be around. The Anime costumes that had been tucked away in my wardrobe since Ioe left got another try-out.

She would be the last girl to sleep in my old apartment. I was about to move house.

Jimmy and Tony were full of schemes. Jimmy was a dreamer, always plotting a new way to find girls or find a laugh with his friends. Tony was more financially motived. He wanted to live well without having to work for it. The combination of the two led to some frequently ingenious ideas. Most never came to fruition but this one did.

Tony had heard about property guardianship, a system whereby agencies placed short-term tenants into vacant buildings, as a service to the landlords, to keep squatters out. Jimmy's lease with Perry was ending on their Kennington apartment so when Tony was registered at an agency and given a room in a dilapidated old care home in Essex, Jimmy joined him. Within a couple of weeks, they'd persuaded the agency to upgrade them. They were offered rooms in a massive retirement care home that now stood empty. It needed cleaning and decorating but was otherwise quite serviceable. There were twenty bedrooms, each with en-suite toilet, and an additional three large common rooms on the ground floor. Its big glass windows fronted onto a leafy garden the size of a tennis court fully enclosed on all sides by thick high hedgerows and trees. Better still, it was located in Hampstead — the safest, nicest and whitest district of London.

It was perfect.

Jimmy clinched the deal with the agency, that they'd let him move in with ten of his own hand-picked friends, rather than have the agency choose from its own register. He called me one morning to explain.

"It's Project Hollywood, mate," he said, referring to the legendary mansion Mystery and Neil Strauss had lived in, as told in the latter's bestselling book *The Game*. "Cheap as chips, perfect location, and I'm telling you.... Me and Tony went to see it today. We're standing in the garden now. It's unbelievable. You want to live here Nick. I'm telling you — you want to live here."

"Okay, I'll come and have a look."

"No time, no time. The agency guy is here now. He's locking up and going back to the office. He's told us we must sign by the end of business, at 4pm. That's it. If you want in, you better get your boots on and meet us at the office. Tony and I are signing up right now. Lee and Becky are in. Johnny too. Do not miss this opportunity."

I guess I'd become something of a risk-taker. I agreed. I found my passport, some proof of address, and recent bank statements. I put them in a bag and took the Tube to Old Street, to the agency office. I signed up and took my keys. I was supposed to move in straight away but I didn't really need to. There was a week to run on my current apartment before incurring the following month's rent. I called up Derrick.

"Mate, I found a new apartment. I want to move out."

"Sure, when?"

"As soon as possible. I've got a week left at your bird's place. But I appreciate it's short notice so I don't mind paying one more month's rent."

"Don't worry about it Nick. A week is fine. Good luck!"

I moved in the same weekend Adele was visiting me from Paris. We walked through the doors for the first time, me dragging my suitcase and Adele fluttering around behind me with her little French nose sniffing the piss-sodden old-people-air curiously.

"Zees house, eet smells of piss," she said.

Unlocking the door to my room, on the first floor next door to Jimmy, I was overcome by the bad smell. Old women's clothes hung in the closest and a pair of false teeth were in the sink in

The team moves in together in Hampstead

my en-suite toilet. The bed was a hospital-style contraption that electronically rises and falls. We dropped off our bags and explored. Lee and Jimmy were in the garden downstairs, drinking cans of beer, but no-one else had yet moved in. There were three floors and many little nooks and crannies. We found a small hair salon on the top floor with special sinks for rinsing hair. The potential of the place was amazing.

Also on the top floor, we found an office. It was the one room that didn't smell of old people. I pushed the door closed behind us and bent Adele over the desk. Then I did her from behind.

"Nick!" she gasped. "People may come."

"I'll come, and I hope you come. That's two people who will come."

My new room needed a severe clean and also a paint job. I called my regular house cleaner and offered him a good price and Tony offered to redecorate my room for a small fee before I moved in my stuff. Great.

I spent the next few nights back in Kennington, saw Adele off onto the Eurostar and then moved in for good. The mansion was gradually redecorated and re-purposed into an amazing place. For three years we lived like kings on a pauper's budget. It was the beginning of the *Rock Solid Game* golden age.

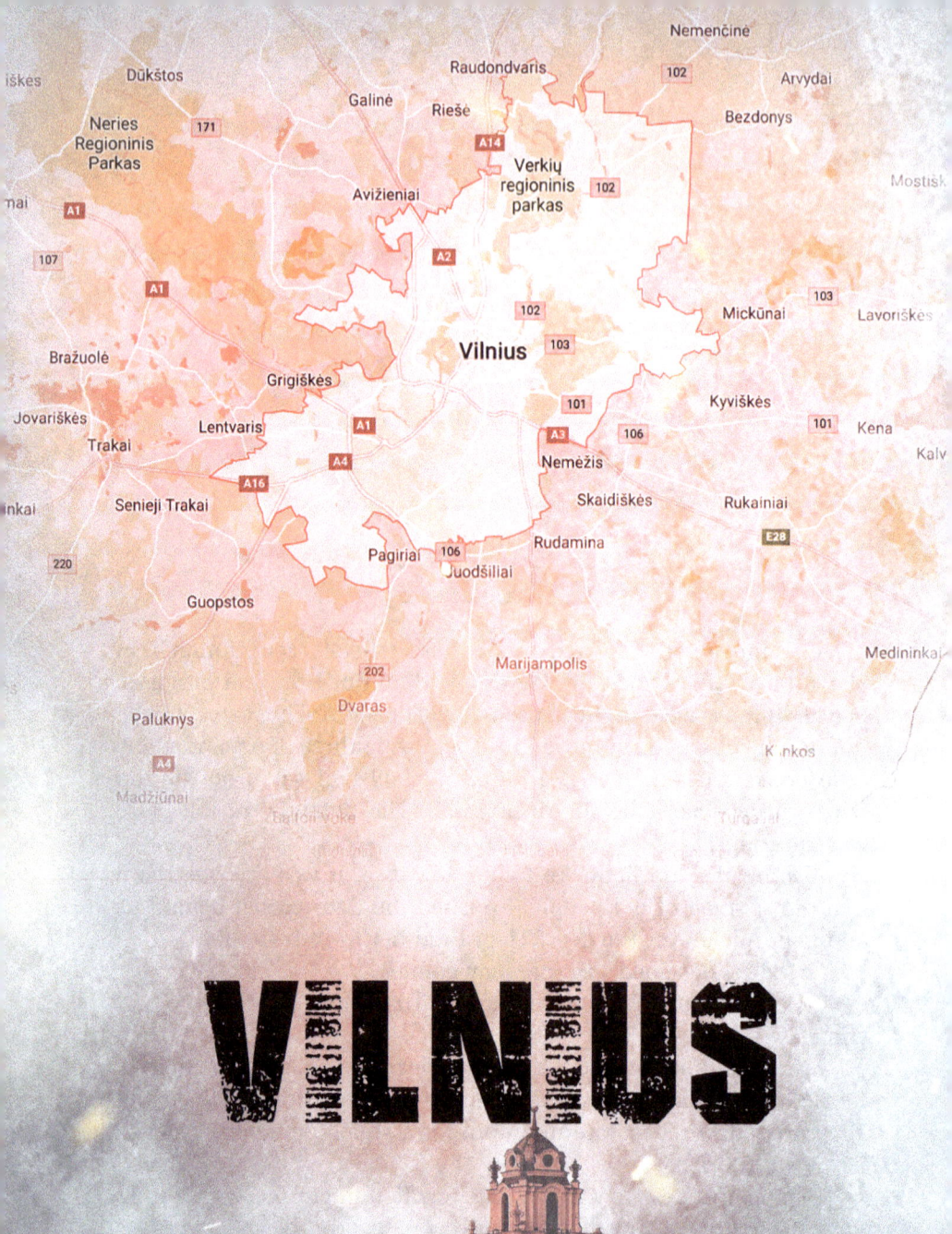

CHAPTER 29

BALTIC CAMPAIGN

CHAPTER 29

BALTIC CAMPAIGN

Life in the new 'Chateau RSG' in Hampstead was fantastic. We'd signed contracts that required the agency to give us only two weeks' notice of eviction, and the manager said he expected we'd have six months at the most. It turned out to be much longer, but we didn't know that yet.

We all loved it. It was like one big holiday, ten friends hanging out together every day in the lounge or garden. It reminded me of my student years, especially as now I didn't need to go to work. Jimmy's room was next-door to mine, Johnny's next one along. Fernando was upstairs. We set up an Xbox360 in the lounge and had marathon multiplayer sessions playing the *Left4Dead* zombie shooting game. It wasn't long before our eyes turned East.

Yes Jimmy, it really was that good

"So you really reckon Lithuania is that good?" asked Jimmy.

"Yes. Just ask Fernando."

"I will." He went upstairs, returning minutes later. Evidently Fernando supported my assessment. "Right then, I've got a week's holiday due from work. Do you fancy going back to Vilnius?"

"Danute is my hottest lead and she couldn't quite make it here in August as planned. So yeah, I want to see her, Martina, Justina, and any other interest I can drum up on the streets."

The three of us agreed a week-long trip in September. We shared a rental apartment across the road from the old Varpine cathedral on the edge of the Old Town, by Gedimino shopping boulevard. The apartment was above a restaurant and had one big bedroom and another smaller one with two beds. We made a pact that whomever came back with a girl got to claim the big bedroom for the night. Any other nights we'd rotate it between us.

On the first afternoon I showed Jimmy around, up the main shopping street and then winding through the back alleys of the entertainment district before emerging into the Old Town and down my favourite cobbled street, Pilies St, to the cathedral. It was one big loop. He was favourably impressed.

"Lots of classy skirt here, mate. I reckon I'll find a few Audreys slinking around."

To call a girl "an Audrey" was the highest compliment Jimmy could pay, as it suggested she was of the type and quality of Audrey Hepburn, his personification of the feminine ideal. We alternated between chatting up a few girls each and sitting in cafes feeling like sophisticated world travellers. I'd let Danute know I was coming as soon as we'd booked flights, and we arranged to meet at the 301 nightclub on the second night. Fernando was on a date. Jimmy and I found good sofa seats in the basement and when Danute arrived at 9pm, the club had begun to fill up a little. As expected she was very giggly, perhaps more so because Jimmy was also present so she may have been a little nervous at meeting a new person.

She was drinking and laughing and seemed to be letting go a little. We'd been Facebook flirting for two months, so she was warmed up before my plane had even touched down. She told me a little more about her life, born in Kazakhstan, growing up in Poland, and then coming to Lithuania at a young age. Jimmy did a fantastic job bigging me up, dropping subtle references to the cool things I'd done in life, and being slightly deferential towards me without losing his own aura of laconic charm. He noticed her turning to face me with her hands pressed tightly between her knees and a big eager smile on his face.

"Nick, I'm going upstairs to buy a drink. What are you having?"
"Whiskey."

"You need ice?"

"Yes."

'Ice' was a codeword used in RSG, as a shortening of 'isolation'. Jimmy had sensed Danute was ready to be kissed so he'd offered to leave us alone — that is, give us isolation — for several minutes and had let me know he thought I should act soon. I agreed.

As soon as he turned away and walked up the stairs, I pulled Danute closer and we kissed.

Jimmy returned with the drinks and Danute was blushing like a naughty schoolgirl. We settled back into light-hearted chat until our drinks were finished. It was getting late. Jimmy wanted to go home so we walked that way. I was hoping Danute would come inside but didn't expect it. As we were walking down the old cobblestone roads, I dirty-talked her. Jimmy pulled ahead, giving us some privacy. There was a wide arch in the building to my right leading into a deserted courtyard, so I pushed Danute inside, up against the wall, and started grabbing her tits.

Danute seemed to like it

She seemed to like that. Jimmy had kept walking, affecting to be studiously unaware of whatever was happening behind him. I unzipped my jeans, took Danute's hand and put it on my dick. She liked that too, and started wanking me off.

"Turn around."

"No."
"Turn around."
"No."
"I'm going to fuck you right here."
"No."

That's an abbreviated version of the actual conversation, which went on for five minutes in bursts of speech between lots of groping. Finally, it was clear Danute was adamant not to have sex. I took her to the bus stop and we agreed to meet the following evening. Then I went home and Jimmy and I sat in the lounge/bedroom chatting.

"She's nice, Danute is," he said. "Pleasant girl. Pretty."

I felt the same way.

The next afternoon I met Justina again. We'd kept up some occasional Facebook chat since our two short uneventful dates in July. Jimmy and I sat a patio café on Gedminos Avenue, the seats right out on the pavement. Justina approached, wearing a lightweight cardigan, thin blouse, and discreet skirt. She clipped along in heels, one leg in front of the other like a catwalk model.

Jimmy raised his eyebrows. "She's a bit of an Audrey, this one."

I reminded him that's exactly what I'd told her when first meeting two months earlier. Justina gave us a smile and sat down. The waiter brought us all a coffee and we chatted.

"What are you doing in Vilnius this time?" she asked, a few minutes into the conversation.

I was still experimenting with radical honesty, and Jimmy let me field the question because it was my date and thus my privilege to determine the frame.

"We want to see the city, drink coffee, and chat up some girls."

"I thought so."

I'd long since learned girls usually know what you're up to, in general if not in specifics. At that precise moment a girl who was exactly Jimmy's type crossed the road and began walking in our direction. His eyesight isn't good and his head was down, as he carefully unwrapped a small chocolate on his saucer. I tapped his arm.

"That's a Jimmy Girl, no?"

She was drawing closer now. It was a tall blonde girl dressed like a surfer chick. She was very pretty, an eight. Her figure lacked the buxom curves of Justina's but she had a prettier face and in sum was a point hotter. Jimmy took a close look.

"Yep, she's nice."

"Open her."

He looked at me, at the girl, at Justina, at me again. I think he was more concerned about the impropriety of chasing fresh skirt while in the presence of my skirt, than with any approach anxiety.

"Go on!" I encouraged.

"Yes, talk to her," said Justina.

By now the blonde had reached the end of Gedimino street and turned up a side road. Jimmy loped off towards her with long strides and disappeared around the corner. Five minutes later he returned with her.

"Nick, Justina, this is Alyona."

We exchanged introductions and now four of us crowded around the tiny table sipping coffee. Jimmy's stunt had a magical effect on Justina, wiping away her previous aloofness. She was now very keen, her eyes glittering. After settling the check it was a good time to split up so we left Jimmy and Alyona and walked through the nearby park outside the cathedral. We sat down on a bench and watched the world go by.

I could feel it was on.

We kissed, for the first time. I checked my watch. It was almost five o'clock and I had a date lined up with Martina at five-thirty, and Danute had agreed to the general principle of meeting though we'd not yet fixed a time. I wanted to stay with Justina and press my advantage but I couldn't bring myself to cancel Martina at such short notice.

"I have to go in ten minutes," I said.

"Why? We're just getting comfortable."

"Well.... um.... I have another date."

"Oh, I see."

Justina didn't seem at all piqued, and I watched her carefully for any sign of indignation. Another piece of the seduction jigsaw slotted into place. I didn't quite know what it meant, but I'd read several theories that offered potential explanations. When you're a Provider Guy, said a theory expounded by manosphere blogger

Rollo Tomassi of *The Rational Male* website, women will go ballistic if they suspect you are even open to the idea of dating other girls, much less *actually dating* them. A provider is useful to a woman because he supplies attention and resources. That is a divisible quantity, a zero-sum game. If you date two women, your provision is halved, and thus the first woman loses when you add a second. In contrast, the Lover (the 'hawt guy') is useful because of his sex appeal and high-value DNA. That is literally unlimited and adding new girls to a man's rotation doesn't reduce the value given to each existing girl. Girls may not *like* it (though some get a thrill) but they are considerably more understanding of the Lover sleeping around than the Provider doing so. I wondered if this explanation fit Justina's extremely understanding attitude towards me.

We said goodbye and I walked into Tres Mexicanos restaurant, across the road from our apartment, ten minutes late. Martina was sat at a table looking cute as a button with her little hamster cheeks and flowing shampoo-commercial hair. Conflicting emotions stirred in my gut. On the one hand I felt extremely guilty at having just disengaged from Justina, while on the other I felt like I was closer to the Tony Clink dream of banging a different hot girl every night.

There was a limit on just how much radical honesty I was comfortable with. The theory had a habit of vanishing from my mind when it was unhelpful to my sexual strategy. Martina and I ate dinner and drank cocktails. We laughed, kissed, and I had a thoroughly enjoyable time. After a few hours I invited her back to my apartment but she refused. She took a taxi home and we planned to meet again within a couple of days.

Martina visits London

I finally returned home after a long day. My stomach sloshed with coffee and cocktails. Jimmy was still out with Aldona so I stripped down to my boxer shorts and flopped onto my bed, watching YouTube. My brain felt fried so I barely moved for a few hours. I messaged Danute but she replied only briefly to say she was still at work. I tried Justina, keen to see how our little afternoon's adventure had affected her. She was online and replied quickly.

"I'm at a house party. It's boring."

"Is it big? Lots of people?"

"No, just a few friends. There's a guy here I dated a couple of times. He's been trying to sleep with me for months."

"Tell him to fuck off and come see me."

To my surprise, she replied, "okay, where?"

I hadn't thought that far ahead. It was past midnight and everywhere I knew was closed. Additionally, it didn't seem awfully likely that she would be willing to come directly to my apartment. "Outside Tres Mexicanos restaurant," I wrote.

"Okay. I'll be there in ten minutes."

I hurriedly threw on my clothes and cleaned my teeth. When I looked out of the hall window it was 1am and Justina has just arrived. I went out to meet her, kissed, and we walked straight back to my place and to the bedroom. It seemed too easy. We sat on the bed and took turns choosing YouTube videos. I tried to escalate.

Justina wouldn't let me undress her but was happy for us to roll around on the bed pawing at each other. Things gradually heated up until I got her shirt off, then the bra, then her trousers. That trio took twenty minutes of trying, hearing objections, trying again, and finally succeeding at removing the item of clothing. By the end of the first hour, she was finally completely naked.

It felt like shovelling coal into a furnace. Back-breaking labour.

Nevertheless, Justina looked fantastic naked. She was careful in her diet, liked sport, and was naturally blessed with firm medium-sized breasts and a solid bubble ass. I was half-drunk, which made her even sexier. She lay at full stretch on her back and I fingered her a while. She tried to keep her self control but eventually decided better of it and turned her head towards me and sucked me off. All these years later I still have that mental image fresh in my mind, of Justina lying naked in front of me with her legs wide, while I kneel near her head as she's sucking me off. I'm surprised time and the interference effect of later sexual adventures hasn't dimmed the memory. I suppose she just looked *that* good naked. Sadly, she wouldn't let me fuck her.

She was coy about it, trying to walk the tightrope between having lots of fun with me but not losing any further self control and doing what she may later regret. I tried everything. While I dirty-talked her she seemed especially close to surrendering but I just couldn't quite manage to get my dick into her. She did give me another fantastic blow job, though.

So, not all bad.

I wanted her to stay overnight, figuring I'd eventually wear her down. Perhaps knowing this, she left around 3am. I lay back in bed, defeated but mostly satisfied. Twelve hours earlier, waiting at the pavement cafe with Jimmy, I hadn't expected I'd come so close with Justina. It had been a good day.

My eyes began to close. I was tired.

My phone buzzed.

"Heyyyyy! What are you doing?" It was Danute. In all the action, I'd forgotten about her.

"I'm in bed."

"Can I come over?"

Exhausted though I was, there could only be one answer. Danute had finished work late and been out with friends. She was close by, with her car, and wanted to pop by to say hello. She hadn't been drinking. Fifteen minutes later she parked outside my apartment and I led her upstairs. Perhaps it was my own pent-up sexual frustration, perhaps she'd fully intended to do the dirty. Who knows which? Nonetheless, we soon began rolling around and before long Danute was naked underneath me. She too looked great. She had a fuller, wider figure than Justina but still sported a tight waist and pleasing shape. She lay back and I banged her. We got quite into it, I dare say, trying several positions, stopping for a breather, and getting back on it. Finally she knelt on the carpet by the bed and I came on her face. She stayed overnight.

It had been quite an eventful day. Jimmy had come back alone but told me the date with Aldona had gone very well.

The whole trip was action-packed, at least in terms of cold-approach, idates, and dates. I opened a strikingly good-looking brunette on Gedimino street outside a clothes boutique and she joined me for a coffee right away. Up close, I could tell she was pushing thirty, but this woman was photogenic to the extreme. She said she worked as a television newscaster, which explained it. Our coffee became a beer and then, in less than two hours, I tried to take her home. She refused, politely.

Later that day I met a smoking hot blonde called Raimonda. She was all long hair, slim legs, and rock'n'roll fashion. We met outside a bookshop on Gedimino street and I bounced her to a cafe for an instant date further up the road at Double Coffee. We sat in a corner on some comfortable sofa chairs and chatted for an hour. She was very talkative but rather screwy, talking in-depth about psychology, her hopes and dreams, and her bad experiences with men. Rather than take control of the conversation and direct it to more useful topics, I let her spin on with it until she was unburdening all her problems onto me. It killed any possible seductive vibe and made it even harder for me to escalate. So, I just sat there nodding my head, trying to get a word in edgeways. We swapped numbers and separated.

I found Jimmy again, wandering around a nearby park, and we explored further up Gedimino. I saw a very attractive tall brunette come out of a cake shop so I stopped her. She was called Laura, a student, and an exceedingly attractive girl. We chatted ten minutes and swapped numbers. It seemed like every girl in Vilnius liked me. Socially, at least.

We walked through a small town square by the theatre. I saw a pretty young brunette sitting on a bench. She was wrapped in a big purple coat so I couldn't ascertain the quality of her figure, but her face was pretty enough. I pretended to do a double take, giving me a careless pretext to approach. She smiled up at me nervously and I told her that her coat was nice and the colour reminded me of my favourite raspberry yoghurt that I ate as a child. She laughed and talked in faltering English for a minute or so, telling me she was waiting for her sister. She refused to give her number, mentioning a boyfriend, so I persisted until I walked away with her Facebook details. She was called Dovile. Just more grist for the daygame mill and no reason to suppose it would go anywhere.

More memorable was a date with a younger girl I had met on the same street, Zusane. She was seventeen, had told me she had a 'pretty serious' boyfriend, but she was very chatty and agreed to meet the next night for drinks if she could bring her friend. I said sure and brought Jimmy along. Her friend was named Saule and she was a tall attractive blonde.

In the pub, Jimmy was in his element. Not having opened Saule, he could run the set completely indirectly, using the Mystery Method that he so loved. He leant back, acted aloof and unloaded a series of strategically-placed DHV bombs into the conversation. Saule very quickly swallowed the bait and became fascinated with him. While that was going on, I was floundering with Zusane as it appeared she really did mean her boyfriend was a serious one.

So, the set took on an ironical turn. My girl was only socially interested in me, while our respective friends seemed to be brimming with sexual attraction for each other. I couldn't blame Jimmy, as he hadn't foisted the boyfriend onto Zusane, had he? He'd done me a good turn with Danute a couple of days earlier, so I wanted to follow his example and keep Zusane engaged long enough to allow Jimmy and Saule to make their little magic acquaintance.

The first bar wouldn't serve the girls alcohol. We took them to the beer garden at the top of the Old Town where Fernando and I had met Martina and Illona during the World Cup game. By now, after booze, I sensed Zusana warming to me and hope flickered that perhaps I could get things going. Alas, I couldn't quite make myself escalate. Somehow, escalation conflicted with my deep-rooted feeling that it would be ungentlemanly in this case. It was nice weather, there were lots of people around, and I saw out of the corner of my eye that Jimmy had begun kissing Saule. Good on him, but I felt disappointment keener than I should have. It got my goat that I'd done all the work in the set, and now Jimmy was raking in the full pot. He hadn't done anything wrong, so really I was just shaking my fist at the sky. Saule was beside herself with glee, as if she'd met her own personal rock star. Soon after the two girls shared a word and Jimmy took Saule home.

I'd pretty much lost the will to live, so when I finished my drink ten minutes later, I said goodbye to Zusane and slipped into our apartment quietly, so as not to disturb Jimmy in case he was having trouble sealing the deal. I saw four pairs of shoes under the clothes horse. The door to the big bedroom at the end of the hall was closed with a beam of light visible around the edges. I could hear Jimmy talking. Fernando was in the small bedroom. He'd spent all this time with the girl he'd picked up from the club in July, so we'd barely seen him. It appeared that now she was staying over.

Both bedrooms taken, that left me to sleep on the small sofa in the lobby. It was tiny, with ragged cushions, and there were no blankets. I shook off my shoes, stretched out as best I could on the sofa, and pulled my coat across me for warmth. Within minutes my back ached.

"Uuuuh.... uhhhhh.... uhhhh." came sounds from the end of the hall. It sounded like Saule was getting into it. She was soon screaming, "oh God! Yes! Jimmy.... Yes!"

The creaking of bed springs slowed and softened. Just as I thought I'd be able to sleep, I heard rhythmic thudding from the small bedroom, and now grunting I recognised as Fernando's voice. It was joined by squeaky feminine moans. Just as they settled down, Jimmy had started up again at the end of the hall. This went on at least twenty minutes, taking turns with Fernando it seemed. I wasn't at all happy about it.

The next morning, Raimonda surprised me by texting to say she wanted to meet that evening. I had already lined up a date with Laura. Jimmy and I discussed how we'd plan our day.

"Saule wants to meet me again tonight, and she wants to bring Zusane," he said.

"That's fine, but I doubt there's much in it for me with Zusane. She showed a little interest towards the end, but it didn't feel strong at all."

"Fair enough, but it might be worth a try. It's at least worth poking your head in. For all we know, Zusane is jealous Saule got laid and now she wants hers. Jimmy-boy here may be able to get baldy Nick laid."

A series of postponements and misunderstandings meant that by 8pm all of our dates had merged into one. I sat in a large curved booth around a table in an American style diner. Raimonda showed up first and slid in alongside me on my right. She had a mischievous look in her eye, like perhaps she was interested in me after all. We ordered drinks and ten minutes later Jimmy came steaming in making a commotion. He had Saule on one arm and Zusane on the other. He sat on my left with a big thud, and stretched his legs out. Saule sat on one side and Zusane on the other. Both girls were giggling like excitable idiots. I immediately saw Raimonda's eyes light up as her attraction switched from me to Jimmy. He'd just blown me out by his powerful preselection. I wasn't at all happy about it. He should've known better.

I'd created the phrase 'value-tap' to name a process by which one player steals all the social value from another, like a bloodsucking leech. There are many ways to do this, some subtle and some obvious. For example, if you talk louder than your friend it can subtly dominate him. Another way is to encourage your friend to talk a lot, carrying the weight of conversation, while you lean back laconically, like the cool guy, and occasionally contribute carefully-crafted witty statements.

Jimmy was very, very good at value-tapping. He always claimed he didn't know he was doing it.

He was doing it now, drawing all the room's energy and attention towards him as he teased and play-fought with Saule and Zusane. They lapped it up. Saule because she was besotted with him, and Zusane because it fit in with the energy of the moment. I'd opened the latter and had him introduced to the former, whom he'd banged. Now he was pawning them off to look good in front of Raimonda. She was of the superficial type who assesses all situations according to who has social value, and then attaches herself to the highest-ranked male. That was clearly Jimmy.

It gave me a horrible sinking feeling.

Saule and Zusane were so enthralled with Jimmy's comedy hour that they almost ignored me. Whenever I'd turn to engage Raimonda I'd hear loud guffaws behind me and watch her eyes immediately distracted his direction. He was the warm end of the pool.

Around that time, Laura walked in.

She was at the opposite side of the personality spectrum. Where Raimonda was vacuous and calculating, Laura was sincere and wholehearted. She walked to our table, blinking in surprise, too polite to express her disapproval any stronger than that. Raimonda made space and Laura squeezed in next to me. I'd already decided to give up on Raimonda as she'd clearly lost interest in me and that seemed extremely rude, considering she'd come to meet me and immediately begun fighting for Jimmy's attention. So, I talked to Laura.

It went well, for a while. Every time Jimmy's end of the table collapsed into giggles, Laura's eyes would flash with disapproval, then she'd turn back to me with a big smile. I should've made excuses and taken her to another bar, alone, but the situation had snowballed out of control so fast that I was dizzy.

Fernando now arrived. Raimonda took an immediate liking to him. Unlike Jimmy, he was steadfast in his adherence to wing rules and didn't flirt at all. This was around the time Fernando had made a major leap upwards in his game and he now presented an aura of effortless cool. I was outgunned on both sides. It was horrible.

Jimmy went to the toilet and Raimonda followed him down the stairs, giving him a blatant come-on. He turned her down, and I think that's when he became consciously aware of how badly he'd messed up my date. After about two hours of total clusterfuck, all the girls left. Back at the flat, I was furious. Jimmy agreed he'd stolen the play and we'd never have that problem again. Live and learn. We were always looking to fine-tune our game and learn from our mistakes.

We while away the night in a small kitchen, at a table by the window. Jimmy was brewing a pot of tea and sheepishly handed me a mug, clearly feeling a little guilty about the evening's shenanigans. Fernando was snoring in the next room. While we talked, Jimmy started texting a few girls, showing me the exchanges. I absorbed every snippet of advice from him that I could. My text game was still lame and followed the standard PUA community advice. By contrast, Jimmy's texting was outrageously creative and on-point. For half an hour we deconstructed what he was doing and why. That chat over the cramped kitchen table was the genesis of my entire text game method.

My laptop was open and I noticed Dovile, the girl in the purple coat waiting for her sister that afternoon, had immediately accepted my friend request on Facebook. She was online so I experimented with what Jimmy and I had discussed. He looked over my shoulder as I typed the first message.

"I know what you're thinking," I wrote, without preamble.

"What?"

"You're thinking, 'If I had realized he was this cool, I would have given him my number.'"

We went back and forth like that for about a half an hour. I decided then that whatever she had with her boyfriend had to be at least a little shaky for her to show so much interest in me. It was getting late and Dovile said she needed to wake up early the next morning, so we said goodnight. Raimonda too continued to send me occasional messages on Facebook. She soon moved to the south of Spain, to work as a stripper. She seemed ideally suited for the job, physically and psychologically.

The next day, bleary eyed and with a throbbing headache due to an uncomfortable night, I went on yet another date with Martina. It was long, romantic, and great fun. I was still getting used to receiving such high-quality affection from pretty young women so it felt great. I took her to dinner and to the cinema to see *Inception*, and then we had a long walk through the park as the evening lights twinkled. It was going great. The whole time, my phone kept buzzing with texts from other girls. Rather than set my phone to silent and ignore them, I began replying. Martina wasn't so enthused by that.

We walked back to my apartment and she came inside, along to the big bedroom I'd reclaimed from Jimmy. We began rolling around, kissing, when suddenly she sat up straight.

"No, I shouldn't."

"Yes, you should. Come here."

She pushed me away. "No. You are a player. I don't feel right about this." Emotion was suffusing her face, and she looked close to tears. "I want a proper relationship."

That sucked, because I didn't. I suppose my thoughtless returning of the earlier text messages had made things too obvious, and denied her the plausible deniability necessary for her to just pretend things were normal. I got angry and told her that she was wasting my time. I had spent all that time talking with her on

Facebook and texting her, and the long date and rearranging things around her busy schedule.

"You knew where this was going. You led me on, teasing me."

I'd invested a lot of effort and emotion into Martina only to be told "no" at the crucial moment. My disappointment overruled my good judgement and blinded me from seeing how it was entirely my own fault. I'd brought it on to myself. Fernando blundering into my room two months earlier had been the first strike. Letting her put me on the boyfriend track had been strike two when I should've been more explicit about my intentions. Strike three had been rubbing her nose in it by answering all those texts during our date.

Yes, I'd been very stupid. Not wishing too admit that, I blamed her.

Martina was upset but wouldn't relent. Nor would I. So we went back outside to Tres Mexicanos. She called for a taxi but the booking service told her we'd need to wait twenty minutes. Obviously I couldn't leave her standing by herself in such circumstances so we waited together.

"This isn't fair. I want to be with you," she sniffed, tears filling her eyes. "But I can't. Not like this. Not with you chasing other girls all the time."

I was sad too, as I'd liked Martina from the beginning and that feeling had only grown through all the late-night Facebook chats and several dates. I was deeply conflicted. On the one hand I wanted to date her, but on the other I was on a mission. Nothing would stop me in my quest to become 'good with women'.

I didn't feel especially good with women at that moment. It looked like I'd be saying goodbye to Martina forever. I pulled her to me and we hugged. Martina buried her face into my shoulder and cried, her shoulders heaving with sobs. I felt awful, and not just from disappointment in not banging her. I felt like a scumbag.

As we stood there on the street, both of us tearing up, I heard a voice behind me.

"Nicky Nicky Nick Niiiiiiccckkkk!!!!"

It was Jimmy, his voice booming. I turned to see he'd come around the corner with Aldona on his arm. She didn't seem especially committed to hanging onto him. Jimmy blundered over sporting a stupid grin and lolling gait. It wasn't until he drew close that he picked up on our sour vibe.

"Ah," he stammered. "You alright mate? Had a good night?"

Forgetting my own predicament for a second, I could tell things were a little awkward between him and Aldona. It was subtle, but it seemed clear he was trying to take her back to the apartment and she hadn't quite made up her mind. Seeing Martina's sniffling and me ashen-faced didn't help matters.

"Is anywhere open that we can get a drink?" he muttered. I took that as a cue and played my part of helpful wingman.

"There's a bottle of vodka open up at the flat."

That was the push Aldona needed, the plausible deniability for entering the apartment. He looked at her and she nodded. They walked off to the front door and let themselves in while I waited in the cold for fifteen minutes until Martina's taxi arrived. I said goodbye to the little Azeri and returned to the apartment. I opened the door and crept quietly up the stairs. Once more I was consigned to the terribly uncomfortable sofa in the coldest part of the house. I lay down and imagined I was going to rest in my own tomb. I was desperately upset.

Just as had happened a couple of nights earlier, I was forced to listen to Jimmy bang a girl he'd have never met without my urging. The irony was biting. I was cold in the miserable apartment, my feet sticking out under the mangy little blanket and the sofa cushion buttons digging into my back. The knockback from Martina had shaken me, especially because I'd grown very fond of her. I couldn't sleep because of Jimmy's grunting and Aldona's moaning. Enough! I wanted to go home. I had a mini-breakdown that night. There was still a small lingering pain from my divorce, I still didn't feel attractive to women, and I doubted I'd ever get good at seducing them.

I wanted to give up. It was my lowest point in the Game so far.

CHAPTER 30

LAST EXIT TO CAMDEN

I was drawing tremendous ego-validation from having a small rotation of girls. I could have sex any time I wanted in London just by booty-calling one of my regulars. For the first time in my life I was living something approximating the life promised by Tony Clink's book—a different girl each night of the week.

So, naturally, I became an insufferable cunt.

Here is a sample of text/Facebook messages I received in one day, in October 2010. Baharak wrote, "You are God-like. you can get any girl or anything you want and I simply can't bear this. Offering me to your friends was so ridiculous and hurtful cos you know it very well that I was melting in your arms, so don't knock my door again with your sick ideas." For all that anger, she came around to see me soon afterwards.

I had a short exchange with Tasanee beginning with me writing, "and I just thought about fucking you now. In a toilet in Starbucks." She replied, "Haha, don't talk like this cos I won't stop myself from going to Starbucks to suck your cock ;)"

"I won't stop you :D"

"When you are free :P"

Danute wrote, "I hope nothing is change in your plans about my visit =)"

"No change," I replied. "We meet, we date, we fuck. It'll be a good week ;)"

"I coming to London not just to fuck with you, I really like you Nick …"

Adele was now going through her first university term in Australia and had a few weak men orbiting her there. She wrote, "Oh no, that's terrible... You were right. I'm extremely attracted to impossible relationships with bad boys, especially if it's an English pick up artist who could never fall in love with anyone... and I find quite boring to date a nice Australian guy who is still a virgin... :(that's not fair. I miss you. Anyway, now I do understand why some people need to be taught how to become... more like you. Sleep well."

Soraya at Trafalgar Square

There was also a hot Brazilian girl, Soraya, I'd dated a couple of times and she messaged me a lot during her trip back home to see family. "I can't survive without you! :(" she said, simply.

My phone was blowing up with female attention and my instinctive reaction was to puff up my ego. I'd started from such a lowly position, and endured so much rejection over the past eighteen months, that the dramatic up-tick in my sex life threw me out of equilibrium. Every evening I'd have six or seven chat windows open in Facebook as I juggled girls and tried to get more of them into bed. Game had become an obsession and it worked on me like a pendulum—in the beginning I was too far in one direction (too soft, too timid, too needy) so I over-corrected to the opposite side by becoming too hard, too bold, and too aloof.

Whereas earlier I'd lost girls by moving too slowly and failing to escalate, now I'd lose them by pushing too hard and being a dick. It often started well, the girls extremely attracted to my outrageous confidence and asshole game (which was really just well-disguised bravado). Then they'd expect me to turn the volume down a little and show more warmth, which never happened. Most girls tired of it, and like U.V. and Martina, they'd eventually bolt. It frustrated them because they were still attracted to me. Here are three examples of how needlessly sexual I'd get, just during the initial street approach:

I met a Spanish girl mid-afternoon by Covent Garden station, a young student at an English school. About three minutes into the chat I said, "You're very curvy aren't you. Look at this nice slim waist," and put my hands on each side, above her belt. She liked that so I kept pushing. "You've got a good pair of breasts too, let me have a feel," and I lightly squeezed her tits. She just laughed. This was in the middle on a busy shopping street, with hundreds of people walking past. Another time I met a French teenager on Oxford Street and took her for coffee at Carnaby Street around the corner. She told me she was visiting London to see her boyfriend and expected to meet him in around ten minutes. Undaunted, I dirty-talked her until her eyes were glazed over and she fiddled nervously with her cigarettes and lighter, her mind full of sexual thoughts. I met a Romanian blonde outside Primark and took her for a beer, sitting outside at a table on the pavement. We played a questions game which I rapidly sexualised until she was telling me she wanted anal sex but was afraid to try, and she likes men to cum on her face. I'd met her perhaps half an hour before that disclosure. It was 3pm.

All three of those examples were captured on video with the little gum camera I used to analyse and run diagnostics on my technique. I was dramatically overcooking everything, flush with excitement at how far I could push girls so soon after meeting them. None of those three slept with me, but I didn't care because I was cycling through so many new phone numbers that losing any one girl was no big deal. The street was my laboratory. My enthusiasm to break through personal barriers now outweighed my enthusiasm to actually get laid. Whatever happened, I had Tasanee and Baharak to sleep with on demand, and Danute and Adele occasionally visiting too.

Though dedicated to daygame, living at Chateau RSG with the lads meant I was sometimes dragged out to join them in nightgame. Usually I'd only dabble a little, opening the occasional girl. Other times, I'd be fired up with alcohol and act outrageously. Here is one memorable example.

Lee had joined *Sarge School/RSG* the same time as myself and moved into the mansion with us. Although a good person and still a close friend, he was the worst possible wing for my nightgame. He stood six foot three, was jacked from the gym, well dressed, and twenty-four years old. He stood out. In additional he was so good-looking facially that he worked a few years as a catwalk and photo model. So, standing next to him in a bar or nightclub was like being Hillary Clinton next to Melania Trump. He soaked up all the attention from girls. As far as personalities go, Lee and I were opposites. Whereas I relied heavily on my verbal dexterity, humour, and wide-reading (essentially seducing a girl with my brain) Lee was almost one-hundred percent physical. He was socially awkward but disguised it well with a cheerful happy-go-lucky vibe. You'd have to talk with him for a while before you realize that there are some issues.

Our polar opposite strengths and weaknesses dictated that our pickup styles would differ. I went through the process of choosing the girls, suffering a formidable attrition rate, and then carefully strategising those that remained interested. It was an uphill struggle from the first moment and remained that way. Lee would more or less let the women choose him. He'd walk into a club or bar, stand with his drink, and scan the room to see who was checking him out. As the best-looking and best-dressed man there he'd start getting IOIs. If that didn't work, he danced a few songs and re-scanned the room. Having identified some warm leads, he went over and said hello.

I was jealous, of course. He was playing the Game on easy mode. Despite this, he was frustrated. The reason was simple — quality. Relying entirely upon your looks guarantees a low quality ceiling. The reasons had already been amply understood in Pick Up theory. Allow me to explain.

The hard-wired dynamic of the sexual market place is that *the man chases the woman*. To put it sequentially the process is thus, (i) woman makes herself pretty and puts herself in the shop window, (ii) man chooses woman and makes a pass, (iii) woman accepts or rebuffs the pass, (iv) if accepted, the man pushes towards sex while the woman resists at a pace of her choosing, (v) sex. Women are absolutely loathe to make the first approach, and to escalate the man towards sex.

This dynamic breaks apart when there is a severe imbalance between the relative SMVs of the man and woman. The lower-SMV side feels lucky to be there. If they are two points below, they'll be an embarrassing push-over. If three points below they completely lose their minds. This is why men relying entirely upon their looks always pull below their class: only women far below will humiliate themselves by being so forward, and so easy. This put Lee in a quandary: as a male nine it was easy for him to take home sloppy sixes for one-night-stands. If he wanted an eight he suddenly needed Game, and faced all kinds of new challenges. If he wanted a nine, he was out of luck. They don't really exist in London. You might only see one once a month in a normal bar or club, and a bit more often in daygame.

Watch for this dynamic next time you're out. Spend an evening people-watching at a nightclub. Note those cases when a girl throws herself at the man, or conversely when a man lets a woman shamelessly disrespect him. There'll usually be a two or three disparity in their SMV.

For all this, I was intensely jealous of Lee's success because I had to drag myself across broken glass to get laid while he just needed to show up and wait. It didn't feel fair. As time passed I got a better look into his sex life and realised the quantity wasn't making up for the lack of quality. He was as frustrated as me, but for different reasons. I was an average-looking thirty-five year old man hitting on hot girls in their early twenties. It's not *supposed* to be easy. Life had dealt me a hand so that's what I must play. Thank God female sexuality responds to a wide range of masculine traits beyond just height, youth, and good looks.

This particular night in October we went to *The World's End* pub on Camden High Street, on the edge of the famous market. The basement held a five hundred capacity live venue called Underworld but we always stayed in the ground floor bar. It got crowded on a Saturday night with a lot of the beatnik crowd, but also with a mixture of other types as well like Goth, Indie, and Rock. There are a lot of drugs in the area; it was a favourite hangout of Amy Winehouse in her day.

In rolled Lee and I.

"Remember," I admonished, as we walked to the bar. "No kissing girls in the first hour. I'm not having half a drink and then standing on my ronson for the rest of the night just because you cop off with a bird straight away."

"Yes, agreed. Let's just have fun ourselves first."

Lee was always positive and upbeat, and it's one of the things I liked best about him. That night, he was buzzing with energy.

I bought two pints of beer from the central bar then walked back to Lee who'd taken up position in a space against the wall. I noticed three girls, in their early twenties, standing around a high table a few metres way. Two of them were quite good-looking. I tapped one on the shoulder and threw out a simple situational opener, I don't remember what, and the girls chatted with me. Two were Czech and one Polish, all three in London for work. Conversation was going well until a Czech happened to glance over my shoulder and see Lee. Her eyes went wide then blank, as her frontal cortex seemed to switch off. Her jaw slackened, conversation ceased, and she eyeballed Lee with her tongue hanging out. I saw one of her friends equally stricken.

I knew what would happen next. Having absorbed the initial blast of Lee's good looks, their brains rebooted. They then each performed the same rapid calculation, *this Nick guy is friends with that hot guy, so we can step on him to get to his hot friend.* It was hardly subtle.

"Say..." said the red-headed Czech, giving me her sweetest smile, "your friend looks really bored. You should help him out."

Snakes with tits, mate, snakes with tits. I remembered what I'd told Fernando after we'd gazed into the abyss with the two Libyan tourists.

Before I knew it, Lee had the good-looking red-head up against a wall, making out with her in this really lively bar. I continued talking to her friends but they seemed resentful that I wasn't as hot as Lee, as if it was unfair that the red-head got all the fun. I got a little pissed off with them and with Lee. We'd had an agreement and he had broken it, but that wasn't really what bothered me. The issue was envy. I had prepared myself to handle the envy all night, but we'd agreed to at least have an hour's truce before he hit his stride. We'd had some Jagermeister before leaving Chateau RSG for Camden, so I was already a little drunk. The combination of factors made me angry.

I walked over to Lee, who had his tongue down the girl's throat, and physically pulled him off.

"Lee, what the fuck are you doing? You promised no kissing in the first hour and yet here you are making out with this girl."

"Uh, yeah. Sorry. You're right."

Meanwhile, the girl stood there confused, listening to all of this. It was surreal because we both just assumed she was gagging for it and didn't have any place in these deliberations.

"Look, you made a promise. It's too early; we're supposed to be having fun. Get rid of this girl." He looked at her, then at me, then at his drink. There was no question he'd take my side in this, but he looked ruefully at leaving the red-head behind. She was quite pretty, and kissing girls is a lot of fun. I realised I was being excessively harsh, so I endeavoured to pose a reasonable proposition.

"Either take her into the toilets and fuck her now, or take her number and let's move on."

Her eyes opened wide at that but she remained quiet, clearly understanding that the only way she'd win the genetic lottery and have sex with Lee was if I gave him permission to bang her. She looked at me like a dog begging scraps from the table. The toilets at *The World's End* were a pissed-drenched mess. Exactly what you'd expect in a pub full of alcoholic beatniks and Occupy Wall Street types.

Lee gave her his number, "Nick, can she call me in, like, an hour?"

"Yes. After an hour is okay."

We walked out and along Camden High Street towards another regular haunt of ours, *The Camden Head*. It was lively, with a few pretty girls, but nothing great. We had a couple of pints. I checked my watch and saw it was precisely one hour since we'd left *The World's End*. Lee's phone rang, on cue. He looked at me.

"Has it been long enough? Can I have her come over now?"

"No problem."

She rushed over as fast as her whore legs could carry her. I was throwing down shots of whiskey with wild abandon, anaesthetising myself against the pang of envy I'd feel when Lee took this girl home, who'd piggy-backed my own open to throw herself at him. I was in a boisterous mood. I turned to the bar and ordered another slug, Lee was on the street outside, waiting for the Czech girl so as to lead her inside.

I spotted a blonde queuing next to me. Perhaps she was giving me a proximity IOI, pushing through the bar to present herself to my gaze so that I'd talk to her. Perhaps not. I was too drunk for subtleties. Glimpsing her through my drunken haze, I decided she was styled a lot like Jennifer Jason Leigh's character in the movie *Last Exit to Brooklyn* with blonde Marilyn Monroe type curls and heavy red lipstick and dark eye make-up.

"You look just like that actress from *Last Exit to Brooklyn*," I told her.

"What's that?" she said, confused and a little vacant-looking.

"It's not as important as what's this," I said, indicating my whiskey glass. I snapped off the shot, gulping it down in one. "Whiskey. Brilliant."

She was still confused and vacant-looking, but now she was smiling too. I propped myself up against the bar. By wild coincidence she was called Marilyn, and I must admit that I suddenly became very sexually aggressive.

"You've got nice tits."

"Oooh, thanks!"

"I want to touch them."

I did. She didn't object, remaining fixed to the spot in front of me, transfixed, giggling, and staring wide-eyed. After touching her up a few seconds, I continued, "I want to do naughty things to you."

Her lips were caked with scarlet gloss, like it needed to be scraped off with paint thinners and sandpaper, so I didn't want to kiss her yet. She pressed up against me and I could feel her crotch push against mine.

"Yes, that's my dick," I told her. "I'm going to ram it into your pussy so hard that it'll take surgery to remove." I mashed her tits some more and bit her neck. She was oozing sex, giving me The Look. I continued in this vein until Lee arrived with the Czech.

"Nick, we're heading straight back to the mansion. Gonna get a taxi. Do you want to come?"

"Right-ho," I agreed. I indicated Marilyn, who I hadn't yet introduced. "I'm gonna bring this girl back and fuck her. Come on, woman."

Marilyn agreed readily. I don't think the possibility of defying me entered her head. She was completely cowed and gagging for sex. Despite my belligerence in the bar, I'd remained self-possessed and quite aware of what I was saying. The moment we stepped outside and the cool night air hit my head, the whiskey took hold. I was suddenly shit-faced drunk. Dizzy, off-balance, and completely out of control.

We tried to hail a taxi but every single one whizzed by, already engaged.

"There's a mini-cab office up the road by *The Hawley Arms*, let's try that," said Lee and we struck off deeper into the market. I forgot about the lipstick problem and kissed Marilyn. Lee stopped until we caught up and then burst out laughing.

"You look like killer clowns! It's hilarious."

We continued walking, with Marilyn and I stopping for brief moments to kiss. Several times passers-by gave us rude looks which struck me as unreasonable. We were only kissing. It was not until an hour later, looking into a mirror, that I saw Marilyn's lipstick smeared all over my face like I was a toddler eating birthday cake. That explained the disgusted looks.

I'm at a loss to explain this now, but all of a sudden on that walk to the taxi rank, I wanted to be a dickhead.

"Hurry up," called Lee, as we'd once more fallen behind.

"Wait up Lee, my slut and I are coming," I shouted. Then I turned to Marilyn and said, "hurry up, slut."

She was still in a daze and didn't immediately register my words.

"What did you say?" shouted Lee, more in disbelief than because he hadn't heard me.

"I said wait a minute, me and my slut are going as fast as we can."

All girls must balance their passion for sex with the muzzling counter-weight of not feeling that they are too easy. Thus, most seductions involve carefully leading a girl so she can get laid and not feel bad about it later. I know many ways of delicately handling this problem. Repeatedly calling a girl a slut to her face, in public, is not one of them. There were a few more such exchanges and Marilyn responded badly.

"Come along, slut," I hollered and she stopped, feet rooted to the spot.

"No, I shouldn't do this. I'm just going to go home," she protested.

I realised she wasn't enjoying this as much as I. It was time to pour on comfort. I apologised, pressing her shoulders, looking sincerely into her eyes.

"Look, I'm sorry. I'm just being drunk and stupid. I don't really think you're a slut. You're a nice girl and I like you. I promise I won't say it again."

She smiled timidly and nodded her head. "Oh, okay then," she murmured as she fiddled absent-mindedly with the lapels of my motorbike jacket. She gave me another smile. I motioned with a head tilt to see if she was happy to continue walking. She gave another cute nod.

I turned around and yelled at Lee, who was now fifty metres further up the road with the Czech redhead, "Hold up Lee, my slut and I are coming."

Marilyn stopped again and tried to turn around. Again, I profusely apologized. She really wanted to follow me but felt compelled to refuse because of the way I was talking to her. She accepted my apology again, and then, just as she was going to start coming along again I said, "Hang on Lee, my slut's giving me trouble."

That was it for her. She shouted, "Fuck off," and stormed off in the opposite direction. I never saw her again.

Our remaining trio got to the mini-cab office and took a taxi home. When we finally arrived, Lee raced through the door and to the toilet, having almost wet himself during the journey. That left me with the Czech red-head. She looked at me and said, "I swear, I never do this. I'm not a slut. I promise you, I never do this."

I assured her that I didn't think she was a slut, even though she was. I went to bed alone, while Lee banged the slut. I woke up the next day will a helacious hangover and walked downstairs for my morning shower, chuckling to myself as I recalled the evening's events. Whatever dreadful mistakes I'd made in the set, one thing I couldn't be accused of was under-escalating.

I met Aisha again late September. I was in Brick Lane with Jimmy when she called and though circumstances weren't opportune, I didn't dare risk refusing her offer to join us in case she disappeared for another few months. We sat in the upstairs room of a nice pub and chatted. Jimmy tried his best to big me up, as an apology for his antics in Vilnius, but Aisha wouldn't bite. Something had changed, probably in her life circumstances rather than her attitude towards me. The energy was flat. Jimmy found an excuse to leave, in the hope that it was only social pressure holding her back, but Aisha still wouldn't let me kiss her. I was puzzled. It was like I was dating her fictional twin sister, the one who went to church and never kissed boys.

We walked back to the station and I decided to raise the issue overtly.

"How come you're so boring today?"

"I promised myself I wouldn't kiss you or suck your cock on this date,"

"Why?"

"I don't know. I just know I shouldn't."

Normally in these situations it means there's another man in the background, one she's either dating or hopes to. Girls like to "monkey branch" by keeping men on back-up while they resolve the uncertainty surrounding their top choice. I guessed Aisha was going through a rocky period with her boyfriend, or perhaps not sure if she was able to lock-down the man she really wanted, so she wanted to keep me around as Plan B. I was pretty confused, so I threw something else at the wall to see if it'd stick.

I told her, "You know, I've been trying to get a read on you for a long time. You're complicated, but I think I've figured you out. You present yourself as a sexually aggressive man-eater. It's all blow job this and eat my pussy that. But I think that's just a role you like playing. I think that really, underneath the act, you're just a sweet little girl. I see flashes of her. That's who I want to get to know. That's why I stick around."

"Oh, you're so sweet!" she gushed and gave me a strong tits-first hug. Then she snuggled under my arm as we continued on towards the station. She told me she split her time between an ex-boyfriend in Maida Vale (presumably who she'd visited the day I met her) and her own apartment in Canary Wharf. A week later, having not heard from her, I sent out a feeler text. "Maida Vale or Canary Wharf?" I wrote.

"Neither, just woke up, sorry... autumn has barely begun & I'm dying from an awful sore throat!!! Feel as rough as a badgers arse!! :("

"Charming image. Maybe it's cos you talk too much." I replied.

"*sigh* empathy only Nick style eh?? It's overwhelming!! Or maybe it's because I 'blow' too much?? Takes a toll on a gals throat, gag reflexes & all ;)"

"Classy. Very classy. With all that blow job practice, I'd have expected you to be good at it by now :P Presumably your fucking skills are equally overrated... Lucky you have a winning personality..."

"Lmao lmao lmao!!!!"

I knew I was wasting my time. I texted more because I enjoyed it, than thinking it would go anywhere. Two days later, she messaged me at 9am. I was in bed with Tasanee. "Call me, I'm dying been bed ridden since Friday!!!" she wrote.

"Just woke up. Give me a little while so I can get rid of my girl."

We talked on the phone, mostly comfort, and she was all sweetness and light. As I mentioned, for all the rampant sexual aggression, she had her sweet side. A few days later I was walking back across Blackfriars bridge after a date with a black girl who looked similar to Aisha, though not as hot.

"Just walking past a [her former company] building and thought of you. Is that sweet or creepy?" I wrote.

She called me half an hour later and gushed over how she loved the text. We talked for a long time as she regaled me with stories about how she'd stayed in all day relaxing by watching Internet porn and masturbating every few hours. She described with open-eyed wonder all the fetish sites she'd found for dwarves, grannies, and animals. This type of contact continued for several weeks, of friendly intimate chat but never going anywhere meaningful. Twice she agreed to dates and cancelled them. I was running out of ideas and trying anything to get her out. I tried a Hail Mary pass.

"The girl I fucked tonight has bigger tits than you. Not better, but definitely bigger."

This was a complete fabrication. I'd spent the evening playing *Call of Duty Black Ops* with Mick. He'd begun losing weight so his man-boobs were considerably smaller than Aisha's now. Had I sent the text in July, it may have been half-true.

"Gosh yr senses r good!! I literally just got back from Madrid, Spain just now!!! Bigger is definitely not a winner if it's not aesthetically pleasing ;) x"

"Madrid, Spain, she says, like I never got an educashun."

I'd accepted the inevitable, that I'd never bang her. Aisha had settled in with her boyfriend and we never met again. Within a few months her Facebook pictures showed a bumpy stomach and eventually a baby boy. It wasn't obvious who the father was, but the baby was considerably lighter skinned than her so I could guess. That filled in the details for the "something going on in the background" that had caused her flighty behaviour. Between our first meeting and her showing a visible bump, only five months had passed. I'm grateful for the game education she gave me. The whole time I felt like I was one mis-step from detonating the whole set. It was like staying on a rodeo bull and I hung on as long as I could. Fortunately, very few girls exhibit this level of bad ass bitchery so I'm ready for them now.

God bless Aisha and her £4k knockers!

Fun though London was, we'd all developed the itch to travel. Lithuania had been our gateway drug, opening our eyes to the possibility of chasing skirt throughout Europe. We had no idea where to try next, so the first cities that came to mind were the popular bachelor party destinations, such as Prague, Riga, and Krakow. I'd been to the latter for my university friend Tim's bachelor party the previous year and knew it would be fun. Jimmy was still tied to work, but Fernando and Shameem were available. The three of us booked flights to Krakow and a three-bedroom apartment just outside the Old Town for a long weekend.

Krakow is a beautiful old city with the kind of medieval Old Town that draws summer tourists and international students in droves. There's a wide-open cobbled square bracketed with a church at one side (with a guided tour of the high steeple and tower) and a line of traditional restaurants at the other side. There are also tours out to the salt mines and the Auschwitz concentration camp. If not for the packs of drunken stag-do Englishmen stumbling around the streets, and the ecosystem of tarts and touts to rip them off, then it would be a perfect skirt-chasing location.

We had a great time, running around the streets chasing girls and then drinking in the bars each night. Fernando got laid very quickly, pulling a rat-faced brunette out of a nightclub and banging her the same night. The next morning, over breakfast, I asked him, "what's with all her screaming and your slapping?"

"Did her in the ass," he said.

"Oh! I understand that with the Libyan girl — Muslims and all — but this is Poland. You don't have to."

"I'm Brazilian, mate. As we always say, if you're not fucking your girl in the ass, someone else is."

I'll admit I hadn't thought of it that way. I wasn't convinced. Anal sex struck me as rather unappealing. I still believed it was just a porno thing: something done for porn, to try to squeeze more schlock out of the scene, rather than something couples did for fun in private. Why would anyone want to stick their dick into a girl's brown-eye? I'd read about Sodom and Gomorrah. God had levelled entire cities in punishment for that abomination. Maybe that explained why Brazil was such a shithole: punishment from God because of people like Fernando.

I didn't believe in God, so I parked the thought and finished my breakfast.

"Daygame again, lads?" I asked, receiving the affirmative from both Fernando and Shameem.

The previous day I'd had a few good interactions but I'd ruined the best one. A cute girl studying French had hooked really strongly for fifteen minutes but five minutes later she'd caught me talking to another girl. She stood ten metres behind, arms folded, in a comical display of indignation. The second girl hadn't especially liked me, so the whole episode was a disaster, losing the bird in the hand while chasing a second in the bush.

With Fernando in Krakow

After breakfast, the second day was my worst daygame session in months. I opened six girls around the Old Town square and every single one blew me out without even breaking stride. It was a humbling experience. My two friends did only slightly better.

"Well, that wasn't fun," I said as we shuffled along the park path, walking back towards our apartment. It was still just four in the afternoon and we'd already given up.

"Tonight we'll get our wind back, just you wait," said Fernando. "There's a bar at the opposite end of the square that serves flaming cocktails. It's got a club on two floors."

My mind turned over the prospect, and I looked forward to it. We came out of the park and crossed a busy road behind a tram, then turned into our apartment's street. I saw a girl walking towards us wearing a vibrant summer dress. She was cute. *One more set,* I thought, trying to lift my spirits to open her. I was tired, cold, and dispirited. Already I'd mentally switched off until the evening. Still, I forced myself to act.

"Hi. I have to say something... I love your dress... everyone here is dressed in dull greys and browns, but you're so colourful."

"Oh, that's so nice of you to say!"

"I'm Nick."

"I'm Charlotte. It's nice to meet you."

My vibe roared into the stratosphere like a rocket launch. She was hooked strong and wouldn't stop talking. When she wasn't talking she was smiling. We chatted a couple of minutes before I decided to go in hard. Fernando and Shameem stood off at a discreet distance.

"Have you ever kissed an English man in the street?" I asked.

She looked at me coyly, and blushed. Then her eyes flicked to my lips. "Noooooo.... I haven't."

"Would you like to?"

"You are so bold! No! It's so public."

We chatted a bit more, by which time Fernando and Shameem had wandered off into the house. I was faced with joining them for an afternoon nap, or seeing what I could do with this extremely promising situation with Charlotte.

"Let's get a drink. Do you know anywhere good?" I asked.

She did. There was a grotty dive bar back on the side of the park we'd just left. Charlotte led the way and we were soon sat at a table. Polish rock music played on a little TV hanging off a wall bracket. All the leather seats were torn, and wallpaper hung off in places. I liked it. It reminded me of the metal bars I'd first started drinking in as a teenager. The pub was empty but for us, the barman, and two teenage boys playing pool in the next room.

I felt sex in the air, so I pushed that vibe.

"Tell me about your sexual fantasy. How would you like to be fucked?"

"I think..... hmmmm..... there are different things. One thing I like is sex on the floor, instead of the bed. It's more, how do you say, primal?"

I looked in her eyes and said, "I really want to kiss you right now."

She smiled and said, "Really?"

"Yes, like this."

We kissed briefly then I pushed her away. "You're not so good at it," I said.

She laughed and kissed me again. "There, that's better?"

Sexual tension crackled between us, while a few metres behind us the barman sat on a stool at the end of the bar reading a newspaper, oblivious to us. We both felt a warm glow of having found something lucky, against our expectations for the day. I pulled Charlotte's legs over mine, pulled her in, and rested her head on my shoulder while I scratched the hair on her temple.

I lowered my vocal tone, and growled into her ear.

"When I fuck you, it'll be violent at first. Very rough. You'll feel my power. My strength. My cock will be hard and you feel it, inside you, hard, fast, powerful. In and out. Your heart will be beating fast. Crazy fast..."

I felt her heart pounding fast as she leant against me. Her leg muscles quivered.

Then her phone rang.

She took the call, scooting away from me and standing up. She babbled on in Polish so I had no idea what she was saying. To my ear it sounded like white noise. She got off the line as soon as she could .

"It's my friend. We are meeting soon."
"How soon?"
"Maybe forty minutes."
"Okay, come here."

I took her hand and walked her towards the toilets. She resisted, pulling her hand free and scurrying back to the table. "My phone!" she said, picking it up, then grabbed my hand again.

The two boys were still playing pool and didn't even look up as I led Charlotte past them, to the toilet in the corner. My legs trembled because I was about to get my first ever same day lay. Even better, I was about to bang a girl in a public restroom. Can't get more 'player' than that, can you? I pushed the cubicle door open and dragged her in. She stumbled inside the stall, giggling quietly. As I slid the bolt, I could hear her breathing heavily, stood with her back against the wall. Her eyes were wide and hungry. I walked over and kissed her hard. Then I turned her around, pulled her skirt up, and did her from behind.

It was fast and dirty. Within fifteen minutes, probably less, we were back at our table finishing our drinks. My heart still beat fast at the sheer audacity of what we'd done. Charlotte's eyes were wide in disbelief. She kept grinning.

"How old are you?" I asked.
"Nineteen. You?"
"Thirty-five."
"Nice."

We chatted some more, reliving the drama of the event, and swapped Facebook details. Then Charlotte needed to meet her friend so we said goodbye. We never saw each other again.

Krakow main square

Danute comes to visit London

Third date with Soraya

CHAPTER 31

PORNALIKES

Spoken language is a recent evolutionary development. Humans have been mating since long before the first grammatically-correct sentences were ever uttered (and indeed in Scotland, they still are). If shagging happens before chatting, the necessary logical conclusion is that words don't mean much. The Seduction Community agrees, and postulates that sub-communication is the make-or-break of a successful pick-up. It's the *how* you say, not the *what*.

Actions speak louder than words.

Given this, the typical man's anxiety over figuring out 'the right thing to say' is misplaced. Whatever SMV bracket you're in (looks remain the single most important factor), the biggest determinant on results is vibe. In the beginning, on the street, a good vibe will express itself this way: solid eye contact, low and slow vocal tone, a cheeky smirk, underlying sexual intensity, and a dominant command presence. The words are mostly bullshit, greasing the wheels. The common daygame opener I'd been using for so long was effective because of how it could convey vibe, rather than any magical properties of the words themselves.

I often compare the opener to the first service in men's tennis. It is both a carefully-designed combination of mechanical actions, and also a deep psychological play aimed at misdirecting your opponent. The service only takes a couple of seconds to deliver, yet tennis professionals spend hours a week, year-after-year, attempting to perfect it. Why? Because strong first serves dominate points and thus matches. The daygame opener is like that. A good player will fine-tune the technique while also working in the background on all the inner game, vibe, and mindset factors which coalesce into those crucial opening seconds.

You deliver the opener and the girl gives her instinctive response. She asks herself questions about you. How do you carry yourself? What kind of intonation do you have in your voice? Do you sound sincere or full of shit? She assesses your body language, the angle of your head, the look in your eyes, and the sum total impresses itself upon her emotional decision-making. Then she eye-rolls and tells you to fuck off, or stops dead with a huge excited smile, or any one of hundreds of variations in between these extremes.

Be glad seduction isn't reliant upon the informational content of your words because this is what makes it possible to seduce girls who don't speak your language. Now with that being said, 'possible' does not mean 'easy'. It's hard work to seduce a girl whose first language is Gibberish. Nonetheless, if your vibe is on, a girl who might've given you the no-speaky-English routine suddenly becomes extremely conscientious in understanding you, making the most of her limited vocabulary, and creatively employing gestures to convey her meaning.

October of 2010 delivered a good example of this. Yet again, I was out in Covent Garden. I'd just finished teaching the daygame session of an RSG boot camp with Fernando and Jimmy. I was still keenly aware of my failings in the mid-to-late game with girls, so I only ever coached students on the street opening. I was good at getting hook points, numbers, and idates. Jimmy and I were exhausted. We'd been drinking the night before on the night game session in Old Street and then woken up early for the daygame session.

"I'm glad that's over. A good bunch of lads, those students, but it was like tear gas trying to stay awake and do demo sets," said Jimmy.

"I want to lie down somewhere warm and sleep all week."

We walked down Longacre, back towards Leicester Square station, with our minds drifting towards relaxation and repose. Coaching felt productive so despite fatigue I usually had a satisfied glow after each boot camp. Jimmy suddenly perked up, "What do you reckon, *Left4Dead* when we get back? Lee and Mick are coaching tonight, but Perry will be around. Could get some three-way action in on the

One of the cuter JAV stars, Chihiro Aoi

old Xbox." We still spent hours shooting zombies together, sat in a line on a long couch in our dining room. There was a revolving door of drop-in / drop-out players with sessions going on twelve hour stretches. Living together in a big house, most of us not working, it was just so easy to become wops. And it was fun.

"Sounds good. I'm looking for-....... woah, wait! What have we here, James? Look at that, across the road."

We'd reached a cross-roads near Leicester Square station, on the opposite corner was a Pret A Manger sandwich shop and in front of that was a cute little Japanese girl, crossing the road towards us. She looked really nice. My first thought was she could be a doppelgänger for the JAV porno actress Chihiro Aoi, who I liked. She stood five-two with long, silky straight black hair. Her body was petite, but curvy, with nice hips and ass and breasts pushing out against her coat. She was the kind of soft feminine-looking girl that made me want to corrupt something innocent. She wore a long funky green woollen coat with wide sleeves and thick wrist cuffs. Those cuffs looked like cheerleader's pom-poms, inspiring an obvious opener. I waited on my side of the road for her to reach us.

"Hi.... hello... yes. Stop! You look like a cheerleader walking down the street with her pom-poms in that coat."

"Pom pom?" The girl gave me a bemused look, but a shy smile had crept onto her face. Ah, she barely spoke English. Probably fresh off the boat.

"These," I said, lightly grabbing her cuffs and gently raising her arm. "Cheerleader. I like."

She had stopped easily enough (a positive sign) so I simplified my language and concentrated more on my sub-communication as we engaged in a stilted but pleasant ten minute conversation. I dropped in occasional Japanese words whenever I struggled to convey my intentions in English, and from that I was able to gauge she was shy even in her own language.

"I'm Nick, from England."

"I Makiko. Japan."

Her eyes held the tell-tale sparkle. As non-threateningly as I could, so she didn't bound off like a scared rabbit, I pivoted her shoulder with one hand and pointed to the Pret A Manger with the other. "Let's have coffee." I said.

"Yes."

There was a late-afternoon bustle of shoppers and tourists, as usual, but Pret was well-equipped to handle them. A half-dozen lines of customers holding plastic-wrapped sandwiches and baguettes milled around the counters, while seven or eight staff rushed around dealing with them. We had our takeaway coffees in minutes and took them over to a high table further inside the shop. For ten minutes Makiko and I sat across from each other and communicated with our eyes. Usually when I first meet a girl I'll keep things chugging along with words: telling stories, joking, laughing and letting her tell me more about herself. Girls often enjoy the sense of anonymity brought by daygame and open up, knowing they can say anything and it's not going to get back to her friends or family, who I am unlikely to ever meet. When it's going well, daygame makes connections that are pure and discreet. A one-on-one interaction entirely cocooned from the rest of her life.

With Makiko, the language barrier hamstrung all of that. All of the subtlety and finesse that can be communicated verbally was rendered useless so I needed to get creative. I found a picture of a hamster on my smartphone browser, to tease her. Mostly I used eye contact and playful movements with her, all of which she seemed to be enjoying, but I was getting bored quickly. I was still exhausted and my energy was crashing.

What to do? I was rapidly losing my momentum.

I walked Makiko across the street to a pub. We each ordered pint of Guinness. While the silky goodness of black silver oiled my gullet,

I kept the sub-communication open. Our silences crackled with energy. We held hands and she seemed to be liking that too. I was boring into her with my eyes, imagining her bent over the table, her long hair wrapped around my fist as I yanked her head back while I smashed her balls-deep from behind. I doubted I had the energy to stay awake another drink or two. It took us an hour to get past all the get-to-know-you chit-chat.

"I from Sapporo. I study English in London," she explained.

We finished our beers and we kissed on the street corner. She gave me her number and I took the Tube home to West Hampstead then walked up the bank feeling good about myself. As anticipated, the roar of gunfire cutting down zombie hordes emanated from the lounge. I could hear Jimmy talking trash at the television and Lee belly-laughing in response.

"Oh right, think you can sneak behind me round that parked car, do you?" Jimmy inquired of a video-game zombie. "I'm gonna stave your head in. Bash!" Jimmy liked to do his own sound-effects in *Left4Dead*. "Not so sneaky now that I've bounced the shovel off your head, are you?"

"You hit him! On the head! With a shovel!" gasped Lee, as though experiencing the peak of world comedy. "Hahahaahahahahahahahahahaha!"

I poked my head through the door. Lee was sitting in his coat, with a hat on, dressed for outdoors. "Lee. Are you coaching tonight?"

"Oh SHIT!!!!! Yes. Gotta go. Gotta go!" then he dropped the controller on the table and rushed out. I picked it up and smoothly continued the game alongside Jimmy and when I felt tired, I passed it along to Johnny who had just come back from grocery shopping. I slept well.

I sent out a feeler text the next morning. "Hey, is this Makiko? The cute little squirrel from Sapporo?"

Half an hour later my phone buzzed, "Hi Nick. How are you? Do I look like a squirrel? ;/"

Great, that meant she'd slept on it, cooled off, and still wanted to stay in touch. A good sign. The idate had been sudden, and perhaps high pressure for her because of the language problems.

Many times girls will allow themselves to be led (even to the extent of making out) but reconsider their options overnight. Makiko had gotten back to me quickly and invested a little. So, she was definitely keen.

"Or maybe a hamster... but you are definitely cute. Are you at school?"

After a short back-and-forth we arranged a date for later that same afternoon. I don't put any faith in tourists or newcomers to navigate their way across London, so I kept it simple–meet in more or less the same place again. After rendezvousing at Covent Garden, I walked her to nearby China Town for a snack. We didn't talk much but we both knew the score and the sexual energy was palpable. I continued using physical momentum as a crutch to prevent things becoming awkward.

Drinking in Camden

"Let's go to Camden Market."
"Yes."

At the market, I found all sorts of things to keep it moving and fill the conversational silences with action. We acted silly, trying on hats and looking through stalls, and then I took her to *The Lock Tavern* pub. It's a hip little Indie bar, really nice place. Towards the back were some leather corner sofas which encouraged intimacy. It was dark both outdoors and in our corner, and Makiko seemed to adjust to the more seductive mood. She leant into me, touching my hand. While discussing hobbies earlier, she told me she liked to play the piano. This seemed like a good pretext to get her home.

"I have a piano at my house. I'd love to hear you play." It wasn't a lie — the first part anyway — I did have a piano there.

"Yes. I do."

It was that easy. Makiko had made her mind up and thus didn't present the slightest obstacle. Sometimes girls just want to fuck, make the decision, and then let you lead them home without fuss. Frankly, I wish they'd do it more often. I was getting tired with pushing the boulder up the hill all the time. Still, I fumbled things a little.

"Jimmy, that Jap is coming back with me. Have the lads talk me up when I show her around," I texted. It was completely unnecessary, a symptom of my over-thinking everything.

We alighted the bus and bought a few beers at the Turkish grocery store on my street, the owners of which were likely now harbouring suspicions of all those lads living in that mansion, who brought a never-ending stream of different girls into their shop to buy wine and beer. Back at my place, I gave Makiko a thoroughly unnecessary tour of the house. I even knocked on doors, introducing her to my friends.

I cringe, writing that now.

Makiko followed me around like a loyal puppy, obviously just waiting for me stop with the preamble and bang her. It was eight pm. I put on some music in my room, opened the beers, and sat on my leather cube stool, facing Makiko who sat on the edge of bed. It happened fast. Makiko stood, walked to me and gestured me to take her drink, which I did. She then sat down heavily on my thigh, pushing herself into me. I felt her breath on my face and her wide eyes filled my vision. The girl was on fire. We kissed passionately and I needed apply just the slightest pressure to the top of her head before she slipped down to her knees, unzipped my jeans, and sucked my dick.

She really did look like Chihiro Aoi now. It was uncanny. I had another out-of-body experience.

I looked down at her head bobbing up and down in my lap. *This is so weird*, I thought. While married I'd been unable to indulge in sexual novelty, being unwilling to cheat on Ioe (and possibly even unable to, anyway). So like any red-blooded man I'd look at hot models on advertisements or discuss with friends who was the hottest bird in Hollywood. It was psychological release, a harmless displacement of the male impulse towards sexual novelty into a societally-approved outlet. In Japan, I'd sometimes wander into a store selling porno DVDs. I'd look at the various DVD covers and carelessly decide which actresses were sexiest. The Japanese porn industry takes great pains to present most actresses as cute 'girl next door' types, so I'd wonder how the movie producers enticed such young, cute girls to have sex on video. I mean, obviously I knew the girls did it for the money. Perhaps many also did it due to their high levels of exhibitionism and bi-polar disorder. Nonetheless, being a normal chodey male, it seemed unreal to me.

Looking down at Makiko, who'd now taken off her clothes and knelt fully naked as she continued to busy herself down there, I reflected on this. She had a good body. Being just twenty years old, her skin was smooth and fresh. She looked just like one of those actresses in particular — Chihiro Aoi. I liked that. A couple of years ago I took what vicarious thrills I could from looking at Aoi on a poster or DVD box, whereas now I was banging a girl who looked just like her. Even better, Makiko had those cute looks without being a whore.

I suppose if you're going to be judgemental about it, you may say "sleeping with a stranger one day after meeting him makes her a whore, too" but I'd beg to differ.

At such moments of indulging in sex acts my mind was sometimes at a meta-level wondering what it all meant to my life. I'd become so accustomed to sexual poverty (in terms of novelty) that I'd count my blessings for every moment of sexual abundance. I guess it's how Eddie Murphy's character felt in *Trading Places*, the movie about a homeless bum who switches places with an Ivy League investment banker.

My ruminations soon expired and I pushed Makiko over to the bed, pushed her again onto all fours then banged her hard from behind. She squeaked, moaned, and gasped like Japanese girls always do. I was reminded of a children's toy, those brightly coloured plastic hammers which squeak when you hit people over the head with them. After twenty minutes of positional variety I dragged her to her knees and came in her mouth.

Brilliant. Well done Nick!

We lay in bed a while. After some pillow-talk I began probing for more information, figuring that after sex is about as good a time as there'll ever be for an man and a woman to be honest with each other. Those vague, ill-defined thoughts about Japanese porno actresses still nagged at me. I wanted to know more about Makiko's sexual history and why she'd decided to have sex with me. She was coy, but was insistent she'd never done "this" before.

"I only sex boyfriend before," she explained.

The PUA community had told me that *all* girls will have fast casual sex if they really like you (or if you are appropriately "alpha"). Per the theory, if you failed to bang a girl quickly, it meant there was something wrong with you or your game. My own experience suggested this was muddleheaded. While I agreed with Rollo Tomassi in his concept of alpha-fucks/beta-bucks at a high level, the PUA community advice was misleading. It was written mostly by Americans living in coastal cities who went to trashy bars and clubs, filtering girls down until they found one trashy enough to go home with them. Such a lifestyle, by its nature, filters out all the girls who *don't* engage in regular casual sex. If you base your world-view on the skewed sample of sluts who do like regular one-night-stands, it'll give an inaccurate impression of women as a whole.

Many women didn't sleep with me because I wasn't cool enough, or my game not tight enough, or they were already taken by another man. But that was only part of the story. It seemed to me, based on experience and discussions with the RSG gang, that the alpha-fucks/beta-bucks thesis was wildly over-stated. I was coming to believe that normal women have a limited number of fast-sex 'indiscretions', or 'flings'. Each woman's propensity differs. Chaste girls may have only one fling in their whole lives while a cheap slag might have over a hundred. Makiko was only twenty years old and it seemed I was the first of hers. She hadn't slept with me because she was easy, but rather because the right confluence of factors had come together to persuade her into her first indiscretion. Would it be her last? Who knows? It didn't matter, anyway. I'd earned my little win and was already running a mental victory lap.

We had more sex and Makiko spent the night. She came around a couple of days later for more of the same. After that, she fluttered away. Maybe she was looking for a boyfriend and decided I wasn't it, or perhaps she was finished with her adventure. I ran into her again, a year later, in Camden Market. Devak and I were walking under the old arches by the Stables market when I recognized her face in the crowd, by the food court.

Her body had changed. Dramatically.

She was at least ten kilos heavier, on her small frame. I didn't want to point her out to Devak in case he laughed at me for having banged her. *Thank God I banged her when I did*, I thought. I was shocked at how quickly she'd destroyed her SMV. I turned my face away as she waddled past, worried she'd talk to me, or perhaps even eat me.

I wasn't to know it at the time but this was only the first in a series of girls I'd have sex with who reminded me of porno actresses I'd liked from my pre-Game days. It's not like I tried searching for look-a-likes. But any time I noticed a resemblance, I'd make a mental note. It pleased me. It represented progress, to move from ogling girls in videos to banging their twins. To date I've banged lookalikes of Tabatha Cash, Gabriella Bond, Aliza, Tania Russof, Maia Ginger, Lenka Gabarova, Vanda Vitus, Tera Bond, Joy Love, Anita Gyongy, Demia Moore, Myrka, and a few others. Look them up. Very pretty ladies. Just remember to have 'safe search' enabled on your browser.

CHAPTER 32

DUTCH UNCLE

P ick-up artists like their jargon. When I first encountered the community I was bewildered by it all. Having spent time in the worlds of politics, academia, martial arts, and finance I was quite well acquainted with the utility of jargon as a short-hand to communicate specific ideas. I was equally familiar with people's tendency to overuse jargon in order to look clever.

Some PUA jargon is completely redundant, as everyday words already exist with the same meanings. Thus a PUA's "day 2" is a normal person's "first date". A "time-bridge" is really just "an agreement to meet later". The nerdy beginnings of PUA often leaks out of the old terminology. The community was originally created by dorks. In contrast, some jargon beautifully encapsulates key concepts that I haven't ever heard better expressed elsewhere, such as approach anxiety, anti-slut defence, last minute resistance, qualification, and push-pull. It's not all dorky nonsense.

Jimmy and I were discussing this, one cold afternoon. He was sitting on his bed, a bass guitar on his lap, as he fiddled with his small home studio system. Jimmy often dabbled in making music.

"What other PUA terms are ridiculous, then Nick?"

"How about 'sarge'? That sounds retarded." It was a term coined by Ross Jeffries to mean cold-approaching girls. If you hit on a girl, you were 'sarging' her. He'd had a randy pet cat called Sarge who bothered female cats, and the term stuck.

Jimmy grimaced. "Yeah, what were we thinking calling ourselves *Sarge School*? It has a catchy ring but..... yeah, *Rock Solid Game* is way better."

We had an unlimited appetite to talk about game. It's all we really cared about. Jimmy was driven by dreams, picturing himself as a modern day adventurer. The details varied but were usually inspired by a Carey Grant or Audrey Hepburn movie. "You know what we could do, Nick," he'd say. "We'll throw our ready cash together and buy a classic BMW convertible from a garage here. We'll drive it down through the south of France, stopping off for a few days in each of the small towns. Get lunch on the Riviera, overlooking the Mediterranean, then go chase some local French skirt. Before long we'll have a skirt each, sitting in the back seats with their hair blowing in the wind as we drive through the mountains."

He loved to expostulate about Game theory and tie it in to one of the dozens of girls he'd known over the years. He'd always come back to the same conclusion, "everything is in *Mystery Method*, Nick. He figured it all out." I was like the precocious student, soaking it all up and asking thoughtful questions that would inspire new theoretical excavations.

"I don't agree with the normal concept of the 1-10 scale of female hotness," I said. "It's too static, and tries to be objective. That could be true, given it's all biologically determined, but it's not so helpful in pick-up."

"What do you mean?"

"Well, the first problem is girls ranked from one to five. Nobody is chasing them, so why have them in the scale at all?"

"Dunno, man. You haven't seen some of the skirt the LSS guys chase. But okay, point noted for the RSG gang."

"But let's start the scale at six, and I'll tell you how I think of it. So, a six is a bird who you'd want to bang, if you didn't have to work hard for it. Maybe you're at a club, a bit drunk, and you fall into a conversation. She's got curves, isn't overweight, okay face. You notice she's keen and seems up for it. You start thinking to yourself, *actually I think I'd like to bang her.* So you look around to make sure your friends can't see, and take her home. That's a six. Bangable, you enjoy it and don't regret it, but everything is tinged with a sense of shame. Like eating a McDonald's after midnight."

"A Mick Girl, then," laughed Jimmy. That was a bit unfair on our Aussie friend because he did get some very pretty girls. But he'd been doing online dating lately so his quality had dipped.

"A seven is simple: no pride, no shame. She's a pretty girl with nothing wrong with her. If her personality is good you'd date her. Take her to the pub to meet your friends, eat in restaurants together, sign both your names on the same birthday cards. People would say, Jimmy's got a nice bird, he has."

"I notice you link me to the sevens there. I'm watching you."

"An eight is a head-turner. She walks past and men go, 'fucking hell, have you seen her?' If you clack one of these birds, you high-five yourself in the mirror afterwards and start thinking up pretexts to be seen with her in public. There's pride."

"Right then, so we'll call them Jimmy Girls. We've already got Krauser Girls for fives and below." He couldn't help laughing at his own joke. The bass guitar slipped off his lap and fell heavily on the floor.

"Nines are astonishing, like super-heroes. They light up the room and you can't believe you're even talking to one. It's like meeting a tiger in the wild. No-one would ever believe you could bang one. If people see you together they assume you're her gay best friend, or personal shopper. Now, here is where it gets subtle: the difference between nines and tens. You could, theoretically, think of ways that a nine could be hotter. Bigger tits, longer legs, wider hips, different hair colour, or whatever. A nine can have a flaw. A ten can't. If you can't think of a single thing to change that wouldn't risk upsetting her perfect balance, you're talking about a ten."

"So, Kelly Le Brock in *Weird Science*, then?"

That was a movie everyone our generation had seen as teenagers. It was a comedy about two science geeks who build a Frankenstein machine in their

If you grew up in the 1980s, you remember Weird Science

bedroom and create the perfect woman. Everyone remembers the scene when that woman, played by actress Kelly Le Brock, first emerges from the smoke-covered machine, in tight underwear.

Jimmy had picked up his bass and was thumbing through some notes on a song he'd written. "So, what other jargon or theory needs to go before our PUA Adjudication Committee?"

"None for now, but I'm sure something will come up."

At that moment, Fernando knocked on the door. He was wrapped up in a black military-style coat and grey scarf. "I'm headed into Covent Garden for a bit daygame. Either of you coming?"

"Nah, working on my music."

"Yeah, give me a minute to put my shoes on," I said. "Actually, I'll take my camera. I want to try shooting a promo video for our site. We can find some good background shots there. Maybe even record a few sets."

"Sure, I'll wait downstairs."

We took the number thirteen bus all the way to Trafalgar Square then had a walkabout. The day was a bust. Our vibe was weak and things weren't going well. The camera ran out of battery before we'd recorded anything of consequence, and the day was turning into another cold, bleak London afternoon.

"I'm cold and knackered, mate," I said.

"Me too. I've only got one number to show for it all. Let's pop in the *Punch & Judy* for a pint. Warm ourselves up a bit."

The famous old market-place stands in the centre of a massive cobbled square. It is lined with Greek columns and a triangular roof. Inside is a rabbit warren of market stalls and boutiques. Street performers caroused the crowds for spare change. As we walked in there was a small crowd around a man currently extricating himself from a strait-jacket while giving entertaining stage patter on a microphone fastened to his ear. On the other side of the cobbled square a juggler sat atop a high unicycle threw several batons into the air. Cafés and restaurants buzzed with tourists.

In the middle of all of this, before we had reached the pub, I felt a tap on my arm. I turned to see a young blonde woman.

"Excuse me," she said in a foreign accent. "Do you know where the London Transport Museum is?"

She wasn't especially attractive, though far from ugly. Somewhat chubby and a little horse-faced, but with beautiful long blonde hair and nice eyes and lips. Her apparent youth meant she carried the weight fine and her face was fresh. A six, per the scale Jimmy and I had discussed.

"You're really close. Take this exit, right past the guy in the strait jacket, then turn right. It's the building at the end of the cobbles." I pointed the way, helpfully.

"Thank you, that's very clear."

My spider-sense tingled. The girl was looking at me strangely, and lingered. I got a sense that she was up to something. Perhaps she'd used the directions as a pretext for her to talk to me? Men do that *all* the time.

"I can't place your accent. Where are you from?" I asked.

"I'm from the Netherlands. You're English aren't you?"

She seemed pleased I'd continued the conversation. Yes, she fancied me. My game automatically switched back on. We chatted for a few minutes.

"I'm in London for four days on a school trip."

"When do you go back?"

"The day after tomorrow. The teacher left us alone for a couple of hours to look around, so I want to see the museum." Fernando was looking at a boutique not far away, keeping a discreet distance. She continued, "But I'm not too bothered about it. Why don't we get a drink?"

Now there's a first: a girl opening me, then inviting me to an instant date. The *Punch & Judy* pub was only twenty metres away so we walked there. She seemed hesitant. "I'm too young to be served alcohol."

"How old are you?"

"Seventeen. And my name is Mieke."

"Okay, you go sit over there in the corner and I'll get the drinks. Don't worry, you don't look underage."

Mieke had surprised me. While ordering the drinks, I wondered whether I was doing something immoral. Sixteen is legal age in the UK, I think, so seventeen was well within the bounds of legality, but seemed perhaps close to the border. I should clarify that. I mean, I wondered about if it was immoral to buy her alcohol. *Of course* I was going to try to fuck her.

The more Mieke talked, and the more light-touching that passed between us, I could tell she was horny and wanted this to happen. I used the age dilemma to fuel my desire, letting it make me feel like a bad man and telling myself that it was fun to 'push the envelope.' Not every middle-aged man would bang a seventeen year old girl, but I guarantee every one of them gets a hard-on thinking about the possibility. Mieke told me more about her school trip. I never found out if it was high school or college. She was travelling with a group of twenty students. The following day, a Sunday, being her last full day and night in London.

"We are staying with host families. My family is in a suburb, in the south. I'm with two other girls."

"Why aren't you looking around Covent Garden with them now?"

She smiled naughtily. "That would be boring, wouldn't it? I like to explore by myself."

What were Mieke's words and situation telling me about this girl, and what she was looking for? She had willingly separated herself from the herd. Women cluster together like a herd of bison for collective security, security being their primary emotional need. This herd behaviour encourages celibacy, as the women are always in some kind of competition with one another. A woman only becomes vulnerable to (male) predators if she falls behind. Some fall accidentally, while many shuffle to the edge of the herd, put a foot outside, and then scurry off before the other women can drag her back in. Women looking for sex will find a way to put themselves into a 'vulnerable' position to encourage men to hit on them.

I said at the beginning of this book that most of what I'd thought about women was wrong. Many men struggle to understand the subtext of female rivalry and deception, as women try to stop each other getting laid while trying to do so themselves. They are like bank robbers in a fragile alliance, co-operating to make The Score but each harbouring plans to double-cross their fellows for the loot while distrusting the others for holding the same plan. That sounds pessimistic, but once you've seen it happen enough times, you'll come to accept it.

Mieke had gone so far as to put her head into the lion's mouth. We sat in a dark corner of the *Punch & Judy* holding hands. We talked and kissed across the table. She checked her watch.

"I have to go now, or the teacher will come looking for me. Give me your number and we can meet tomorrow, after the tour."

I did. Then I kissed her goodbye and found Fernando. I'd only been gone an hour and he was talking to a cute Greek girl sitting on a kerb outside the Apple Store. He took her number, then we had a pint of beer in *The Nags Head* across from the station. Mieke and I exchanged some texts that night.

I met her by Leicester Square station shortly before five the next afternoon. It was Mieke's last night here so I had to move quickly. My vibe was full-on dirty mode from the start. We walked to a traditional English pub around the corner from the Pret where I'd taken Makiko. I bought drinks and we carried them to a table where we sat side-by-side in a booth. It was busy.

"I've only got an hour before the teacher wants us all back." Oh, I'd rather hoped we'd have longer than that. I guess I'd have to move *really* quickly. "My host family house live in zone five. After I make attendance with the teacher I must catch an overland train by six to get home on time."

We talked and occasionally kissed. Viewed from above the table, we were a normal couple enjoying a romantic drink. Below the table, I slid my hand up her skirt and fingered her. She was soaking wet. She squirmed, alternating between closing her eyes and biting her lip, and with looking around the pub like she was afraid we'd get caught. I was horny as a dog with two cocks.

"Let's go into the disabled toilets," I said, grabbing her hand and pulling.

Mieke's eyes glistened, her cheeks pinked and an agonised look of frustrated desire set her face. "No! I can't."

I tried a few times but she wouldn't be dragged away. The clock ticked on relentlessly and we ran out of time. At six, Mieke had to go. It was evident sex was very high on her mind. "My host grandmother and the other two students will be out for the evening. You should come out to the house. We'll have it to ourselves."

It was six o'clock when she left for her train. I rushed home, showered and changed. It still seemed in the balance whether she'd stay in contact, considering she was young and it was a novel high-pressure situation. A half hour later, she sent me the train details. Now

I must decide if this adventure was worth the effort. The arithmetic was simple: one hour on a train to get there, ten pounds on tickets, and a slim chance that I would bang her before her host family returned. It was a reckless gamble. Jimmy picked that moment to begin strumming on his bass next door, suggesting to me I'd have his music thumping through our shared partition wall if I stayed home.

Fortune favours the bold. I took a bus to West Hampstead train station.

What I was getting myself into? The train arrived and I took a seat in the corner, looking vacantly through the window as London speed past in a blur. It took an hour, during which my mind sifted through all the possible permutations of what the evening may hold. Nothing felt real. Other passengers came on board, sat down, then got off again. The whole time I was oblivious to the world around me. Finally the train pulled into the station Mieke had told me about, which seemed to be the middle of nowhere. It was already 9pm and dark. I got off the train and walked up the long grey platform, alone, to the ticket barriers. We were so far outside London that the ticket office was closed and the barriers left open.

Mieke stood waiting for me, bright-smiled and nervous. She seemed unsteady on her legs, like a boxer walking back to his corner after having been battered pillar to post. However wild and fantastical the situation felt to me, it must have been doubly so to Mieke: far younger, and in a foreign country. She wanted it, but she seemed very afraid of getting caught.

We walked for ten minutes through a quiet leafy suburb, exactly where I'd expect a middle class grandmother to host foreign students. This was the land of Enid Blyton novels, tea-cakes, and ballroom dancing. Parked cars lined the streets, the pavements empty but for a dog-walker or two. Flowers and hedges surrounded the front of each house and, once inside Mieke's place, I felt like I was a child again. Old memories of going to my own grandmother's house for lunch flooded my mind — of sitting on a rickety wooden chair at her sideboard eating fish and chips, watching *Rainbow* and *Let's Pretend* on her black and white television. We made sure the house was empty, then I didn't waste time. I pushed her up against the paisley wallpaper, next to the shelves filled with brass knick-knacks, and underneath photographs of fly fishing. Out of the corner of my eye I saw an interesting painting of Horatio Nelson on his flagship at the Battle of Trafalgar.

I began to kiss her and take off her pants.

"No, no," she gasped, batting my hands away from the buttons on her jeans. I bit her neck. "Yes, yes," she moaned, and then "no, no" as I tried again to unbutton her. She wanted it but had no experience of these situations. No doubt her last sexual adventure had been kissing behind the school bike sheds with a classmate. She rubbed against me in the heat of passion and grabbed at my dick through my pants.

Thus encouraged, I kept at it.

I had just gotten my pants undone and my dick out when we heard the rattle of a key in the front door lock.

"Oh no!" gasped Mieke. "They shouldn't be back so soon."

Scrambling, I pulled my pants up just in time, while Mieke launched herself towards the sofa, sat upright and composed herself.

"..... so, Newcastle actually has the world's first house lit entirely by gas," I rambled, standing by the mantelpiece and attempting to look respectable. If I'd had a pipe, I'd have puffed on it. Grandma and two other young student girls came in.

"Oh, hello. Mieke, I didn't know you had friends in England," said the wrinkly old lady. Her hair was white and curled. She struggled out of her heavy wool coat. "I won't be a minute," she said to me, "it's lovely to meet you."

The students, two young Dutch girls curious about the male stranger, introduced themselves and then Granny came back from the hallway. She was a lovely lady and soon took a shine to me. We chatted about Blackpool and Whitley Bay resorts, the weather, and the whole time I was struck by the comical weirdness of the situation. Moments earlier I'd been practically raping her young charge, whereas now we all sat like extras in a 1930s Agatha Christie murder mystery, passing around a small tray of After Eight mint chocolates and minding our p's and q's. There were lace doilies on the table and flowers on the frilly curtains. I felt like I was in my own grandmother's house.

Mieke's eyes blazed in suppressed passion. She sat behind Granny, staring intently at me. Finally she plucked up some resolve and said, "Do you want to come out to the garden with me and have a smoke?"

"Sure."

"Would you like a cup of tea?" asked Granny. "I'm about to brew a pot. It's a lovely Indian blend." I paused, processing the two different offers I'd received simultaneously. Perhaps mistaking my momentary confusion for reluctance, Granny applied her persuasion skills. "I have custard cream biscuits!"

"Yes, I'd very much like one, thanks," I replied, sneakily pinching Mieke's ass on the way out of the sliding lounge door. Granny went through to the kitchen to brew the refreshments while I followed Mieke out, hoping to bang her under the stars.

The back garden was long and narrow, stretching fifty metres. It ended at an old wooden shed and fence. Beyond that lay a school football field. Mieke walked languidly to the very end, as far from the house as possible, before lighting her smoke. We stood silently in the dark as I waited for her to finish, and then I pulled her in, kissing and groping her once more. She tensed and let out a pleased whimper.

I pushed her down to her knees and told her to suck my dick.

"I've never done that before," she said, fumbling awkwardly with my zipper. "I'll be bad at it. I don't know if I'll like it." My dick popped out and she wrapped her hands around it, looking at it uncertainly.

I grabbed a handful of hair to steady her position and then pushed my dick into her mouth. Her instinct took over. A minute of that and I was so horny that I lifted her back to her feet and spun her around. I pulled down her jeans and bent her over against the garden shed. The familiar smell of woodstain and lawnmower oil wafted across the air. She was surprised at my roughness.

"I haven't done it this way before," she said, but didn't stop me. I believed her, because she didn't know how to push her ass backwards into position. I moved her hips, pushed her lower back down, then stuck my dick in her. She gave a little cry of pain as I pushed my way in. I got off two strokes before she scooted away from me.

"I can't do this, it hurts. I can't do it like this."

I didn't think it possible, in the circumstances, to bang in normal missionary style. The grass was damp from recent rain and squelched under our step. The narrow path of paving slabs by the shed were also damp, and covered in assorted junk. We'd be so obvious if we went back for our cup of tea with mud smeared over our knees, ass, and back.

I kissed Mieke again, said everything was okay, and then pushed her back down on her knees. There was no lack of passion. She was just an inexperienced girl struggling to handle an intense situation. She sat on her haunches and sucked my cock. While her little blonde head bobbed up and down, I let my head rise to take in the atmosphere. I glanced over towards the house. Granny was busy in the kitchen, bustling around opening cupboards and setting out cups and saucers. She didn't look outside. It was a different story at the bedroom window above the kitchen. The light was on and both of the other student girls seemed to be looking right at us. Perhaps they too were staring out at the night, but I doubt it. The garden was dark but the girls seemed to be looking in our direction. Thankfully, Mieke didn't notice them looking. No telling what they said to her later.

I came in Mieke's mouth and she swallowed. Then she lit up another cigarette to calm her nerves. The lounge patio door slid open again. "Tea's ready," called Granny. Mieke stubbed her cigarette out on the lawnmower and we went back inside.

Granny was perched on the edge of her high-backed easy chair. On the low table was an elegant china teapot with a pattern commemorating one of Queen Elizabeth II's many jubilees. Three cups and saucers were laid out. Granny poured my tea and pushed it over to my side of the table. She then pulled the top off a biscuit tin and fished out two custard cream biscuits and placed them on my saucer.

"This looks lovely!" I enthused. "And I love custard creams."

I drank my tea and nibbled the biscuits while chatting with Granny. I could feel the cum-drippings on my boxer shorts beginning to dry,

"You remind me of my grandson Thomas," she said. "Look, I'll show you. We've got the photo album in the sideboard. Wait a moment."

She pulled out the album and showed me pictures of Thomas graduating university, at his wedding, and at a christening of who I assume was his child. Mieke sat silently in the corner with flushed cheeks and a smile. I don't know if she felt guilt, excitement, or something else. At last I realized how late it was and I needed to catch the last train home.

"Another cup?" asked Granny, gesturing to the teapot.

"I really need to get going. It was very kind of you to make me tea. I've had a lovely time here."

"Oh, you're welcome! It's always nice to meet strong young men," said Granny, and fussed around in her biscuit tin again. She pressed a Blue Riband chocolate bar into my hand and put a finger to her lips and winked, as though it was a big secret. Mieke walked me to the station, and I kissed her goodnight.

"Are you okay?" I asked. "It was all a bit dramatic. I hope I didn't hurt you."

"I'm fine. Tonight was wonderful. It's just, I've only sex one time previously, a couple of months ago. I'm sorry I wasn't better."

"I enjoyed my time with you. This was a good adventure. I'll always remember it."

"Me too."

I was equally spaced out on the train back as I'd been on the way out. I arrived home after ten and immediately walked a circuit of the house, banging on all the bedroom doors. "House meeting!" I called. Johnny and Fernando were already in Jimmy's room. Lee joined us.

"What's going on, potato head?" asked Jimmy.

"You asked me earlier if there was any issue that needed to go before the PUA Adjudication Committee. I've got one. I just banged a bird tonight. Or, I think I did. The thing is, it didn't last long so I don't know if it counts, officially, as a notch."

"You better explain the story," said Johnny, amused.

I described the evening's date with Mieke from beginning to end then we held a vote on whether my two strokes were enough in-out action to constitute sex. The motion carried. Thus the two-stroke rule was born. As long as you got two strokes in, you could consider yourself laid. Mieke went back to Holland the next day, and we talked on Facebook for a while. Nothing more ever came of it. She wasn't returning to London, and I wasn't sufficiently interested in her to go to Holland.

ZAGREB

CHAPTER 33

EURO JAUNTS

CHAPTER 33

EURO JAUNTS

It was November 2010, the bright summer days having been overcome by the bleak greyness of the onrushing English winter. The initial promise of daygame was coming true. I'd banged a new girl in each of the past six months. I didn't know which I liked more: the sex with pretty young women, or the adventurous context in which it occurred. Our travels abroad gave us the sense that the world had opened up in front of us, our horizons broadening. London has some hot women but their social value is inflated by their relative scarcity and that they are grossly outnumbered by the city's abundance of attractive men. The type of effort we were expending in London had served us better in a place like Lithuania where *we* were the cool guys and hot girls were everywhere. Now winter approached, London became bleaker and even less conducive to daygame.

Jimmy and I sat in my bedroom, a bottle of whiskey between us.

"Where shall we go next?" he wondered aloud. "The Baltics are good but we've done that now, or at least one of them."

"There's no point doing Western Europe, it'll just be the same as London. I had two days sniffing around Paris with Adele and it's not much good. Malaga was too quiet and, thinking back on when Ioe and I were in Seville, I don't remember it having the right kind of footfall. It might be okay, being a tourist site, but it's the wrong season now."

I rose and poured another slug of Johnnie Walker Double Black, then sat at my laptop and opened my browser. "Let's do some research. Name a possible country."

"Denmark."

I typed 'hot Danish women' into the search engine and clicked to display by images. Google brought up rows of photos of tall blonde women. They looked nice, but I've never been moved by blondes, perhaps due to having blonde hair myself.

"Try German. I can speak German, I love the country," said Jimmy. I typed in 'hot German women' and was again underwhelmed. That's not to say there aren't a lot of very attractive squareheads, but we were aiming high.

"I like wops. Dark hair, big lashes, brown eyes, olive skin. When I think of my perfect woman I think of someone like Tabatha Cash or Nicolette Faluudi," I said.

"They are porn stars, Nick. You can't be dating slags."

"No, no. I only mean physically. It's the darker sultry look I like. The Penelope Cruz type. I'll try Italian."

"She's Spanish."

"That's not the point. They are all wops. Same country really."

"Bollocks to all that," said Jimmy, rising purposefully from his slouch and sitting on the edge of my bed. "I'll tell you where the proper hot skirt is. I'm talking the real class."

"Okay, spill it."

"Dubrovnik. A little fort town at arse end of Croatia on the Adriatic coast. Me and Bazza went there back in... oh when was it? About six years ago. There's this long tourist street in the middle of the town, the bit inside the walls, and I'm telling you. The wine bars there, you would not believe the quality of the skirt. Knock-outs, mate. Absolute knock-outs. Me and Bazza said to ourselves, we said these are *the hottest women in the world*." He looked wistfully out of the window, then added, "and Sarajevo. Same thing."

I'd never been to the former Yugoslavia. I knew almost nothing about it, except the newspaper and television reporting of their various civil wars. There was something in the early nineties, when it seemed everyone was fighting everyone else. I dimly remembered the BBC making a big deal of the siege of Sarajevo. I'd heard more about that when reading of the Rwandan genocide in April 1994. The couple of books I'd read suggested that the UN Security Council had not approved peacekeepers for Rwanda because they'd been so chastened

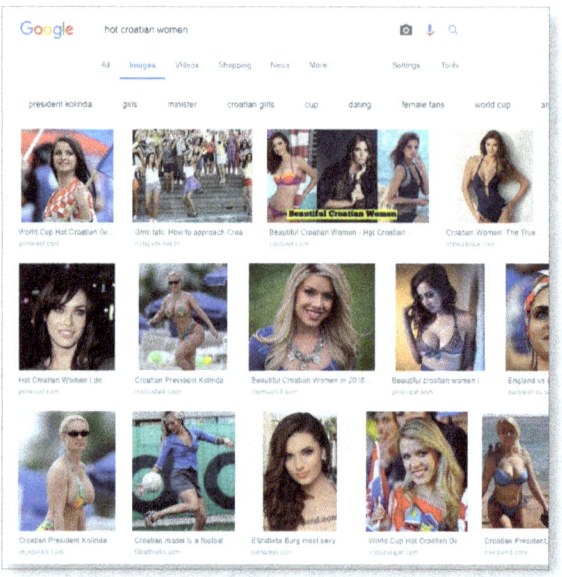

A decision is made

by the Sarajevo experience. The BBC had also made a big song and dance about massacres in Srebrenica. Serbs killing Muslims, I think.

"Jimmy, it's a war zone down there. Loads of psychopaths shooting their neighbours at the drop of a hat. I'm not going there."

"Trust me, baldy. Just type the magic words into your little search engine."

I did. My eyes popped out of my head.

"Bloody hell, I like the look of these Bosnian birds. But I'm still not sure. Remember in 1999 there was another war, that's when NATO bombed Serbia to help the jihadis in Kosovo. I'm not going to a country full of goat-fucking head-choppers. It's probably dangerous enough just going there to drink their wine and take photos of churches. Imagine what they'll do if they catch us stealing their women."

Jimmy adopted a philosophical air. "Nick, are we or are we not skirt-chasers? Right then, are we not also ambitious men? Do we not wish to chase the highest of high-end skirt? Agreed. Then we must go to Yugoslavia."

I reluctantly agreed. I racked my mind for any Balkan girls I'd met in London and came up blank. There'd been Romanians, Turks, and Greeks but it seemed Yugoslavs never came to London. Odd that. It made the region seem even more like the heart of darkness. I opened up the Skyscanner and Kayak flight comparison websites then we began comparing prices to each of the former-Yugoslavia capital cities. There was a clear winner: Zagreb. The budget airline EasyJet flew there every other day. Sarajevo and Belgrade were both over three times the price. Jimmy continued to swear that Sarajevo had the hottest women but it appeared we'd have almost as much difficulty getting into that city as the Serbian army had done in 1992.

"Here's a lucky coincidence. I've got a mate living in Zagreb, my partner in that tech start-up I did five years ago. He's American, Clint, he's called," he said.

A plan quickly formed. Jimmy called Clint, who offered him a stay in his loft conversion in the Old Town centre, while I would find a hostel around the corner. Return flights cost only seventy pounds. The day soon arrived and Jimmy and I drank a few beers in Stansted Airport lounge before boarding. I felt like I was taking a ride into oblivion. My nerves settled immediately upon arriving in Zagreb airport. We stepped off the plane and it was noticeably warmer than London. Everyone around us looked normal and no-one tried to slit our throats. We rolled our suitcases out through Arrivals and sat at a small cafe by sliding automatic doors leading outside.

"Let's get ourselves a coffee and figure out the best way into the city centre," said Jimmy. We stretched out in our flimsy chairs and looked around the airport lobby. There were hot women everywhere. Not in the sense like we'd stumbled into a Victoria Secrets after-party, but our skirt radar noted that the overall average quality far surpassed London. Even the middle-aged women had mostly shapely figures and good poise.

"Here's my prediction," I said. "The type of women who become fives in London are sevens here. I'll bet the default, median hotness of a university-aged bird is low-seven. Just the average, the sort the local men don't even say 'she's hot she is'."

"Wait till we hit the classy bars, mate. They'll be full of Audreys."

Adventure was in the air. I felt my book of life turn over a new page. We took a bus, then a tram into the centre. I checked into a four-bed dorm room above Noktorno restaurant on what appeared to be the main street for nightlife. Jimmy was only fifty metres away, on the other side of that main street. We had a week in town and the weather held the whole time, raining only once. Clint came out to show us around, pointing out his favourite cafes and bars. He knew Jimmy was a ladies man but probably underestimated the extent, having not met him since he'd consciously turned to Game.

Our biggest surprise was the unusual niceness of the Old Town. Unlike the litter-strewn streets and graffiti-spoiled walls of London, central Zagreb was clean. Lovely little outdoor cafés dotted every street, each full of locals passing the day with coffee and conversation. They all looked so happy. We continued walking around, taking in the architecture and orienting ourselves to which streets looked good for daygaming. My head spun. It was like Vilnius, but better in every way that mattered to us. After a while, I began to develop an odd feeling.

"Jimmy, have you noticed something? It feels very safe doesn't it? No dodginess."

"Yeah, now you mention it. It's all very orderly isn't it? People holding doors open for each other, petting each other's dogs. Kids running around."

"I can't imagine it kicking off here. On the telly in the nineties, I got the impression Croatia was like Beirut or Gaza. It's not. This is the most civilised place I've seen since Tokyo. I half expect to come across Nikola Tesla playing chess with Albert Einstein."

Clint piped in, "Zagreb is very safe. I've never had any trouble here. They are traditional people."

We sat at a table under an awning, sipping coffee from small ceramic cups, looking out over a small square. Jimmy and Clint caught up on gossip while I gazed out, people-watching. After twenty minutes, the penny dropped. I'd figured out why Zagreb was so nice, and why I already felt so at home there.

"There's no diversity."

"What?" said Jimmy.

"What's missing from Zagreb? What is it London has, which makes it an utter shit-hole, and Zagreb doesn't have?

Jimmy looked around and comprehension lit up his eyes. "You're right! There's no black people. No Arabs. No Pakistanis. I'll bet there aren't even any Serbs. This place is wall-to-wall Croatians."

"That's why Japan is so beautiful. It's a monoculture. Where I lived in Ogikubo, you could go all day without seeing anyone but Japs and the occasional white."

Monocultures exude a sense of social capital. Everyone has a shared background, shared language, and shared understanding about life and the way things should be. Your nation is your great extended family. In England, since the 1950s, the globalists had been deliberately conflating the State (a political entity) with the Nation (a people), while ramming immigrants down our throats. Croatia was like England should be, when you remove all the people who have no business being there.

My love affair for London was ending one minute at a time.

Clint was forty-five years old and ran a head-hunting recruitment business out of his apartment. He had his phone, Skype, and email accounts which were all he needed. His clients dialled a local number from the United States and it routed through to him and he worked the regular hours that a typical American business would be open. So he was earning a New York income while spending according to Zagreb expenses, a dodge that we immediately saw as a potential route for us. Jimmy and I began floating ideas of financial and geographical independence, looking for ways to avoid the office-mortgage-wife gulag of modern English life. Clint was already living that dream.

Well, except for the female end. Clint was horrendous with women. Think of whoever in your friendship group is the worst at seducing women, then imagine him on a bad day. That was Clint's whole life. At the time we arrived in Zagreb, he had a local girlfriend, a thirty-nine year old career woman. We met her and while she was a nice enough woman, she was so far below what Jimmy and I dated that she may as well have been sexually invisible. Clint, however, had lived in a world of sexual scarcity so long that it had become the norm — the sexual equivalent of growing up in a North Korean labour camp. He had once admitted to Jimmy to having a five year dry spell before moving to Croatia.

Clint took us to a lovely steak restaurant after the cafe, then moved the topic onto his accumulated knowledge of Croatian women. "You won't have much success here, I'm afraid. Women are different here. Your game stuff won't work on them. They don't easily give up sex. They don't even agree to date without first having you meet their friends and family and obtaining approval from them."

Jimmy and I shared a discreet knowing look. Clint was going to get the shock of his life.

No, not this shock

"It's the Seven Dates Seven Friends rule here," he continued. "That's what it takes to get a Croatian girl."

We weren't at all surprised or discouraged to hear this. We'd heard it all before from men in other places. Everyone seems to think that their town is "different" and that their girls are tougher. It can be quite comical to read on Internet forums. Americans will argue that American girls are the toughest, and Russian girls are easy. All you need do is flash the US passport, and those poor oppressed Slavic girls will jump into bed. Five minutes later a Russian man will explain how no, actually, it's the Russian girls who are hardest because they are so demanding and traditional, whereas American girls are so slutty you just need to pour a few tequilas down their necks to get a blow-job in the bar rest-room. Of course, both positions are equally untrue. The grass is always greener on the other side.

Jimmy and I listened to Clint explain how we ought to go about meeting women, while I ate my steak and drank a glass of red wine. I'd noticed many pretty girls walk past us but so far hadn't quite gotten my motor started. Clint had thrown down the gauntlet so I felt I ought to present my side of the argument.

A beautiful girl walked past.

"Excuse me a moment, lads." I said, getting to my feet and wiping my mouth with a napkin. Then I caught up to the girl and did my usual stop. Over her shoulder, I could see both men watching me, Jimmy slouched with his arms folded, legs stretched out, and a grin on his face. Clint was leaning forwards eagerly, elbows on the table.

The girl was a nineteen year old student and a solid eight. She cooed, giggled, and gave me her number. It didn't feel solid and did indeed turn out to be a flake, but I'd wanted to make the point that we didn't need a social circle, a dance class, a book-reading club, or any other artifice to meet women. I'd gotten the number of the very first girl I'd spoken to, a very hot young kitten. I returned to our table.

"I'm not so sure these girls will be different. I dare say I'm optimistic."

Poor Clint sat there shell-shocked, caught somewhere between fascination and fear. I knew, thinking back to watching Johnny do his first demonstration on the *Sarge School* boot-camp, that daygame can be impressive. Hadn't famous science-fiction writer Arthur C. Clarke once postulated his Third Law thus: "Any sufficiently tight daygame is indistinguishable from magic"? Clint had built an entire world-view around Croatia being 'hard' and that world-view was crumbling. His rationalisation for the dry spell withered in the harsh glare of an in-field demonstration. We didn't labour the point. Clint was a good guy.

Jimmy and I took our leave and then turned our minds towards rustling up some leads. We found the girls almost uniformly friendly, as if they'd never been daygamed before, which they probably hadn't. By the end of the day I had gotten three phone numbers. I sympathised with Clint. The pre-game Nick had always assumed you have to wait for opportunities to fall into your lap, and then carefully nurture a lead with a girl over perhaps weeks or months until you dated her. When I'd first seen Johnny just stroll up to a girl and complete the process in mere minutes I'd been blown away too.

We benefited from being in a new country. It made us shiny and interesting, both for our obvious foreignness and also because we were full of the excited holiday mood. Our vibe was great. We were on holiday, having a great time, eating good food all in a beautiful city. I was talking to a lot of hot twenty-year-old girls. There was nothing to complain about at all. Most of my leads went nowhere, and I had less action than the Vilnius trips, but it was so much fun I didn't care. Zagreb Old Town is a compact little place so over the course of the week I ran into Clint several times. One particular day I bumped into him three times, each time with a different girl on my arm. One was a seventeen year old wild child who told me she was bisexual. We had an idate and kissed, but after messing around a little in a park, she left. The other two leads ultimately petered out without fanfare but Clint was still fascinated how much interest we were able to drum up so quickly. He was good natured about it, and we didn't rub his face in it. I wasn't trying to parade girls in front of him.

As much as we enjoyed running around after girls, we weren't getting laid. I hadn't expected to, as I'd only managed one notch per month in London and worked very hard to get that much. Spending a quarter of the time (and chasing hotter skirt) in Zagreb set a high bar.

For our fourth night, Jimmy and I went to a busy beatnik bar with a live soft-rock band just off the main Jelacic square. We stood propped up against the bar with bottles of beer in our hands, taking in the scene. Two squirrely girls walked by and threw us a look. They weren't stunning, I'd say one was a seven and the other a low six, but they'd shot us a look so I opened them and pulled them over to the bar. While they cooed and giggled like schoolchildren we leaned back against the bar so they faced us. It's a subtle trick from *Mystery Method* — any time you talk to a girl, try to manoeuvre so you have your back against something. Other girls will see the contrasting body language and interpret it as the girls appearing to chase you, and thus assume pre-selection.

Sure enough, a brunette drifted over and hung around on Jimmy's left, just inside his peripheral vision. She stood against the bar looking around, down, and up towards where the band was playing. This is something girls do when they are looking to give a man a chance to hit on her, what Mystery called a 'proximity IOI'. They'll usually have their backs to you, looking studiously away.

"Jimmy, did you catch the proximity IOI on your left?"

"Yeah."

"Are you gonna open?"

"Dunno, she's not an Audrey." She was a seven, and dressed casually.

Jimmy looked over at her, shrugged, and immediately slid into his groove. He's always been at his best when he can laconically post up and make the girl come to him. Jelena was a thirty year old journalist and keen to give out her number. I was faintly envious because he'd gotten the strongest lead. Again.

The band finished and the two little squirrels wanted to show us a hidden dive bar. At first it seemed a little menacing, filled with shifty looking middle-aged men with battle-scarred faces who likely listed 'ethnic cleanser' on their resumes to cover the period 1992-94. It turned out to be a fun, safe place. I was able to sneak the six back to my hostel and she stayed overnight, but for whatever reason refused to have sex.

Jimmy went out on a date with the journalist the next day, went back to her place and banged her. That was our day five in Croatia. I met up with them later for drinks. We walked down a pretty little cobblestone street to a piazza where liquid fuel lamps lit the way. The crowd seemed more sophisticated than at the beatnik bar. I was in a phenomenally good mood. Imagine a comedian on the best night of his world tour- that was me this night. The three of us sat on sofas in a sidewalk café and, since Jimmy had already rattled Jelena, I didn't have to worry about the consequences of making jokes at Jimmy's expense. So, I held court. I fired off jokes one after the other, cracking up both my companions with laughter. Two girls at the next table seemed to be feeding off our energy, noticing the glowing aura coming from our table. That's how bar game works — people notice the warm end of the pool and drift towards it. Sadly, I rarely have such a mood when out doing night game.

The girls introduced themselves and invited us to another bar. We followed as they clip-clopped their high heels down the street like racehorses. We hung back slightly to admire their fine forms. Over to the right, we saw a compact European-style bar that looked great. The thrum of laughter and merrymaking was loud, and we saw through the windows that it was busy.

"Let's go there," said Jimmy.

The two new girls weren't having it and made excuses to leave, so we left them to it and went on inside. There was a horseshoe-shaped bar in the middle of the room, akin to a blackjack table, with the bartenders placed as the blackjack dealer and the patrons fanned out on the outside curve. We were literally around the corner from Clint's apartment so Jimmy invited him to join us. The four of us stood at the bar drinking beer and looking around, soaking up the positive energy. The bar was filled with mixed groups and some girl-only groups. It was a hottie-free zone but some were pretty enough to raise our mood. I was still buzzing.

Jimmy was always at the top of his game when parading a woman on his arm. He was excellent at what Mystery called "pawning", named after the chess piece. That's when you use the girl you're with to get attention from other girls. He would tease and push away his girl, playfully, and then a little while later, pull her back. He'd tell her stories meant to be overheard, or lean back and let her talk excitedly to him. It worked great. The target girls would see this and frequently conclude Jimmy was interesting. Then he could open them indirectly, which rarely failed due to the disarming of suspicions that comes with already being with a girl. Jimmy could open sixes in a bar and then pawn them up to meet the eights. His strategy suffered less attrition than going directly to the eights.

At a table a few feet from us, a group of four mid-twenties girls were celebrating a birthday. They kept looking over, drawn to our energy. One was a tipsy six-foot-tall blonde who couldn't keep her eyes off Jimmy. He saw that and subtly sent her an eye-code invitation that she jumped on, coming over and flagrantly hitting on him right in front of Jelena. Seeing this, I distracted Jelena for a while to give Jimmy a chance to work the blonde. For about an hour Jelena bought me shots and I became increasingly loud and belligerent in telling her wild and flagrant sex stories. She ate it all up.

"You are very sexual," she said, approvingly, looking over the top of her drink at me.

"If you saw the movies I filmed on my phone, you'd think I'm a bad man."

"Show me! Now you've told me, you have to show me."

I feigned reluctance because of course I'd dropped the bait precisely so she'd ask. Then I pulled out my smartphone and showed her short clips of me with Tasanee. That video was coming in unexpectedly useful, I discovered. Jelena was very horny. Jimmy had seen what I was doing and laughed along. He'd had his jollies and was generous to his friends. He'd already told me he wasn't especially fussed about Jelena. "Nice girl, but I'm in this for the Audreys. She ain't no Audrey."

Soon after, Jimmy sidled up to me and whispered into my ear, "you can have this blonde. I think she's trying to get laid tonight. I'm not that into her, and I reckon I'll just bang Jelena again."

He commandeered Jelena to talk to him and she jumped on it, blocking off the blonde girl. The latter girl stood back and shot daggers at them both. I turned towards her, next to me.

"Aw! She's all jealous now that she lost."

The blonde gave me priceless look, one part indignation and one part embarrassment at being so obvious in her mood. I was drunk and loving it, so off I went, as belligerent as I'd been with Marilyn in Camden. The blonde, called Maria, was surprisingly up to the challenge so we bantered back and forth. Memory fails me, due to the alcohol, but I remember her repeatedly calling me an asshole and once she punched me in the stomach.

I don't know why so many girls punch me, but every time it's happened I've ended up banging them. So, I took Maria's abuse as a major indicator of interest. She'd switched her sights to me. I was starting to like her. Clint looked anxious to try his game so I decided it would be a fun to give him a run with Maria to see what he could do. What followed was a stark contrast to Jimmy and I. Clint was all 'pull' and no 'push'. He leaned in close talking to her, kept constant eye contact, talked a lot, agreed with everything she said, and showed himself already sold on her.

Maria quickly became bored.

The first thing a man must learn is 'pull', that is to demonstrate sexual intent and try to get the girl. Most men are terrified of showing intent and thus opening themselves up to rejection, hence why they fortify themselves with alcohol before opening. Granted that a man does 'pull', as Clint was in this case, the next thing he must learn is to 'push'. That can mean anything from literally, physically, pushing the girl away to a metaphorical push such as teasing, challenging, or withdrawing attention. Mystery was the first to formalise the concept, initially called "cat string theory." He said if you dangle a string of wool in front of a cat it might look at it or even swat at it for a minute but if you just leave the string hanging there the cat will eventually get bored and walk away. In contrast, if you shake it, pull it up and down, or move it side-to-side, you've created a game and the cat can't help trying to grab at it. Cats are enticed by the push-pull game with the string.

Push-pull is most effective in the initial attention-winning phase of making a girl attracted to you. It continues throughout the seduction with a delicate balance of pushes and pulls so the girl is frequently off-balance and always keen. The modern analogy for this, the one I prefer, is hooking and reeling in a fish. When you throw out your line you need a lure to draw the fish into biting. Once she bites, the hook is set, and you can start reeling her in. The difficulties arise when the fish tries to wriggle off the hook and, in the beginning, has lots of energy with which to do so. The fisherman must apply the optimal tension to the line. Too much "pull" (i.e. reeling in) will snap the line and too little "push" (i.e. letting out slack) will cause the hook to slip and the fish wriggles free. By maintaining the appropriate amount of tension while reeling in, relaxing and tightening, the fish gets tired and eventually gives up. Then you can reel it all the way in.

Clint didn't have an ounce of push in him, so Maria instinctively began tooling him. She sat back on a high stool with one leg underneath her and her arms pulling the knee of her other leg up to her chest, her hands clasped. She had created a physical barrier between them. Clint was unaware she had already wriggled off his weak hook. He plowed on trying to recapture her interest but that made it worse, pulling even harder when what he needed to do was push.

Maria snatched furtive glances at me.

Finally, she walked away from him, and over to me. I was steaming drunk and still a brash, playful asshole.

"Don't come near me. You're drunk. Clear off!" I said, pushing her away.

She forced herself onto me.

"You're such an asshole, I'll never let you fuck me," she said, the taunt losing its effectiveness because she was pressed up so close I could feel the heat of her breath. Deep down, I thanked Aisha for the clinic she'd given. Maria was fun but a rank amateur at this role compared to Aisha. We continued in a confrontational vein for another twenty minutes and finally Maria's friends left without her. I was surprised at that, but she must have given them a signal to the effect of *leave me to it*.

Seeing them leave, she licked the tip of her finger, placed it on my lips and said, "I'm going to the toilet. Wait."

She came back a few minutes later having obviously resolved to become more proactive. I was sitting on a high stool and she jumped into my lap and leaned in to kiss me. I turned my head to the side in refusal.

"Get off me, you crazy woman!"

She bit my ear. It really hurt.

We kissed.

I was high time I pulled the trigger and took her back to my hostel. She came willingly. I been harbouring hopes of pulling the receptionist girl at the front desk so I didn't want her to see me with Maria. It was against the rules to have guests so we needed to get to the common room, rather than my shared dorm room. We sneaked past the reception desk by crawling on our hands and knees. Maria found it all hilarious, struggling not to giggle aloud and give us away to the receptionist, who was half asleep in her chair.

Fortunately, the common room was empty. It was around midnight. The door to the hallway wouldn't lock, but at that point neither of us cared. It would make the sex more dangerous and exciting. I stole a few cans of beer from the communal fridge and we gulped at those while I pulled Maria's skirt up and panties down. She dropped back onto the sofa and I banged her there. It wasn't mind-blowing, but the thought of getting caught made it that much better.

Afterwards, she opened the big window and leaned out to have a smoke. We had sex a second time. She'd barely made herself decent after that when two drunk Italian backpackers stumbled in and put an end to further jollies. It was late and we were both tired.

```
Saying goodbye to Maria
```

I walked Maria to her tram in Jelacic Square and on the way she told me that she was a single mother having had a child when she was twenty-three. She was twenty-eight now. This was the first time I'd empathised with her, having been so wrapped up in the belligerent interplay between us in the bar. She seemed suddenly vulnerable and morose. I didn't feel guilty but it gave me a sense of melancholy about her situation. Maria had wanted an adventure. It had been in her blood since the birthday party with friends. She'd found that adventure that with me, but now she seemed to be feeling regret that it was all so fleeting. Her tram trundled up to the station and I kissed her and said good-bye. There was no pretence on either side that it was anything more than it was: a one night stand.

Opposite Hemingway Cafe

Remaking the Krakow photo

CHAPTER 34
OLD WINE, NEW BOTTLES

Now that I was living with my new *Rock Solid Game* friends, and hitting the streets with them, I didn't have much time for my old friends from university. We hadn't really fallen out but we had so little in common. They represented my past, of life in the Matrix. Their life was working Monday to Friday and if you're lucky, and the missus allows it, having a few drinks on the weekend and maybe a late-night curry. It was a life of waking up in the same bed every morning, with the same woman, when the alarm buzzes. Putting on a suit, taking a one-hour train into The City, to slog through a nine-hour work day in the office. It was a life where watching Netflix was a highlight of the week.

Dull, boring routine. Stressful jobs, unattractive wives, and high taxes.

No thanks.

That's not to say my old friends were unhappy. I think even lifers in San Quentin grow to enjoy being caged animals. I knew from experience that the corporate life sucks you in. The free newspapers, in London they were *The Metro* and *City AM*, begin the drip-feed of propaganda on the morning commute. They are full of the usual stories: a politician who said something that some grievance-monger has found racist, or sexist so now they must resign. Then there's a feature about the new must-have Apple gadget, or the new paperback novel *everybody* is reading. On the middle pages is the showbiz gossip of degenerate celebrities going to parties you're not invited to, and then a travel report on the hip alpine ski resort for this year.

Even when I worked as a corporate drone, this trash repelled me. I'd sit on the Tube watching a stream of commuters board the train, find an empty seat, and pick up the same copy of *The Metro* that the seat's previous occupant had left behind. They'd put their headphones in, shut off from their surroundings, and download today's approved opinions from the paper. I hated it. London has an entire culture designed to suck you in to soulless corporate striving and conspicuous consumption. While still part of the hive-mind, I'd considered myself a free-thinking radical. By the standards of my office, I was. It wasn't until I yanked myself out of it that I realised just how deeply the insidious corporate Globohomo frame had sunk its tentacles into my mind.

Refugees Welcome! Gender Pay Gap! Transexual Tolerance! Unite Against Racism!

FUCK.

ALL.

THAT.

I'd made considerable progress in moving past my anger. I no longer wanted to nuke the entire city, though if the big red nuclear button was placed in front of me, my finger would've still wavered. Perversely, I'd enjoyed my life as a drone. Most of my office colleagues had been good people and I was reminded that they weren't really drones. Many were just like me: adapting to fit into the system without quite buying into it intellectually.

I wasn't so special. It would behove me to remember that.

So I kept in touch with my old friends and tried to accept them as they were. I tried not to evangelise about my new life and new ideas. We conversed on the same old subjects we always had: politics, careers, football, television shows. In some respects it was a nice change of pace from the pressures of Game. I was still mildly resentful that they'd shut me out of their lives a year earlier. My guess, unconfirmed due to lack of evidence either way, was that their wives and girlfriends considered me a bad influence and a behind-the-scenes female consensus was reached to exclude me from dinner parties, nights out, and other social events. I can't say I missed them, because I found such gatherings interminably boring, but I suspected my friends had just dick-tucked and allowed their women to rule them.

That much I was sure of. Tim, Yasin, Des, and Warren were absolutely under the thumb. It disgusted me because they were good company on the rare occasions they were allowed out. I understood where they were coming from. I had become a different person than the one who had been there at the parties with his own wife.

Tim, Yasin, and Des were allowed out one Friday night in November of 2010. I hadn't seen the inside of an office since April, but as they were still working I adjusted to their schedule. We met in the financial district immediately after work, in *The Counting House*, a favourite pub from my old life.

Des used to be a player, before we knew what the term really meant. He was fun, outgoing and chased skirt in the bars each weekend. He always seemed to go cop off with a girl on the dance floor, and occasionally took one home. He had a good run of several years, taking Yasin around as his wing-man, and the few times I saw him at work with my own pre-Game eyes, it was like watching magic. Sadly, Des was doing this before the Internet erupted and thus he never heard of the Red Pill. He got sucked into a relationship with a thoroughly unlikeable Vietnamese lawyer and she crushed his spirit. By the time he came out with us in November 2010, Des was a beaten-down, hen-pecked shadow of his former self. He looked like Bill Clinton after a lifetime married to Hillary.

The Counting House is a traditional English pub behind the Bank of England, of a type common throughout the City. It's richly decorated, in impeccable condition, and expertly preserves the sense of Victorian England. The beer selection was good, with plenty of Midlands ales. As usual for Friday night, it was filled with professional men in suits, relaxing after a hard week's work. They stood around drinking, talking about politics, business, and skiing in the Alps. It missed only one thing: women. It wasn't a pick-up bar, nor a dance club. It was a getaway for the men to have some peace and quiet to wind down in before going home to the family. The women who did go there were usually masculine business women and not sexually relevant at all. I didn't care about that this night, however. I was there to drink with old friends and catch up.

"Ho ho ho! It's the lads! On the razz!" I called out as I walked in. We all shook hands. There was a fourth guy waiting, a muscular young Asian man.

"This is Guac," said Yasin, introducing him. "He'd been reading your blog and getting into Game."

"Nice one," I said, shaking his hand too. "I'm getting my drink in. Anyone?"

"Nah, we just got ours," said Tim, raising his full pint glass. I bought a drink, joined the group, and we caught up. It was refreshing. I hadn't seen them in a few months.

An hour passed and it came to my round again. I stood at the bar five minutes and ordered four pints and some salted peanuts. It was a challenge bringing them to the group in one run, so I gripped the nuts in my teeth, pushed the glasses into a diamond formation and wedged them precariously between my hands and chest.

"Lads, help me out," I hissed through my teeth, not daring to unclench them lest the nuts fall into the beer. Yasin rushed forward to carefully relieve me of two pints. As he did so, I noticed a small quartet of young people come in. They were completely out of place, like conservatives in Silicon Valley. Two girls spearheaded the group, one chubby and the other tall and slim enough to be a head turner. My head turned, anyway. She had a catwalk model figure but her face was only slightly above average. Nonetheless it made her the hottest girl in the bar by far, possibly even in the entire Financial District. Two skinny emo kids brought up the rear, following meekly.

"Is that a tranny?" asked Yasin, pointing at the girl I fancied.

"She's high-testosterone, I'll grant you that," I said. She was half-caste with quite a strong jawline.

We were all several pints to the good so although I considered myself off the clock I thought perhaps I'll show off a little in front of my friends. They'd never really seen me do any game before. The tall girl and her chubby friend stood with the two boys in a loose circle just in front of us so I deliberately used a hokey *Mystery Method* opener. Mystery had an overly-complicated, intellectual approach to gaming, but it could be interesting, like putting together a puzzle. I'd become quite good at it, winging with Jimmy all these months. The main thing with a Mystery-style set is to remember: *never start with the hot girl*. Give her the opposite of what she expects, by ignoring her. I affected to look back over my shoulder, as if just having thought to ask for someone's opinion, and threw out a question.

"Excuse me," I said to the chubby girl. "Maybe you can settled a disagreement we are having. This place, it's called *The Counting House*. My friend says that's because it used to be bank. I say it was a house for counting commodities. I don't suppose you know?"

That was long-winded, which was the point. I was trying to open badly, just for fun. I had my back to the hot girl, as if she didn't interest me in the slightest. The chubby chick knew I was just making carefree conversation and that I wasn't trying to bang her, so she let her guard down and gave me a considered answer.

"Well, I don't really know this pub. It's only my second time here. But now that I think of it, I remember something in high-school History class about the Corn Laws. There were counting houses all over the country in the 1800s. I think it is about commodities."

The tall girl evidently wasn't used to being ignored and she tried to butt in with her opinion. "I think it's because-"

I glanced over my shoulder at her and playfully interrupted, "Hang on Missy. I'm not talking to you."

Her mouth fell open with indignation. Bang! Ordnance dropped on target! She was now emotionally engaged and up for the challenge. She kept trying to interject as I feigned further interest in the chubby girl. I shushed the tall one a few times.

"Be quiet, I'm talking to your mate. You'll get your turn."

I brought the other two boys into the conversation. So, here we were three males and her friend, almost completely excluding her from the conversation. Eventually we let her fight her way in, but I made her work for it. The whole time, Tim and Yasin watched in fascination while Guac, who'd been reading about Game theory, gave them snippets of what he understood to be going on. I suspect Des had an instinctive read on my game. After about fifteen minutes I rolled off and went back to my friends. For the next hour or so, I switched between the two groups, chatting back and forth. After a while, the tall girl pulled me to one side.

"Sit at the bar with me and I'll buy you a drink." she said. "I'm Harriet."

"I'm Nick. Thanks, I'll sit with you, but I buy my own drinks."

Harriet began testing me immediately, a clear sign she was sexually interested. She wanted me to go outside with her for a smoke and while we were out there, she flirted with the other old office men smoking. I expressed my disinterest by walking back inside the bar, leaving her with them. She came back inside. I was talking to my friends and she began flirting with another couple of mid-thirties businessmen on the next table, carefully chosen to be within my line of sight. The men were knocked completely off balance, unable to handle a pretty twenty-two year old girl flitting around them. They went bright red and laughed at everything she said.

I heard "Oh cool! Awesome! Wow!" over and over again.

This is why *Mystery Method* is such a good book—he patiently outlined the tactics women utilise naturally to trigger competitiveness and anger in men. They are toying with you, probing for weakness and trying to establish how thirsty you are. After Aisha, this was all child's play. Harriet was transparent in her games. I liked it though. Harriet was a sassy girl and not willing to roll over without a fight.

She tapped Tim on the arm. "Let's have a smoke outside. Do you have a lighter?"

Tim looked at me in confusion, having barely spoken to any women in the six years he'd been dating his now-wife. I'd known him since university and he'd never banged a girl as hot as Harriet. He followed her out, sweating with nerves. Harriet made conversation and flirted by squeezing his arms and punching his shoulder as she laughed. Tim physically resembled the comedian Hugh Laurie, who made his name on UK television playing the fool. That's how Tim looked now, nodding his head and flashing a gormless grin; enjoying the attention, somewhat confused, but not interested in cheating on his wife. Observing this from the corner of my eye, I affected disinterest.

Of course I *was* interested. I wanted to bang Harriet. But this was a test, so I had to play the game and pass the test. She came back in and appeared to give me an approving nod. Her mind made up, she dropped the games and we chatted normally for a while. She ignored her friends.

"I need another tab," she said. "Let's go outside so I can light up." Once outside she took the lead. "Let's go somewhere else, me and you. I like *Abacus* bar."

"No, we're going to *Milk & Honey*."

"What's that?"

"A good member's bar in Soho. Look, here's a few taxis with the lights on. Let's get one."

She stubbed her half-finished cigarette out on the brick wall as I flagged the cab. It pulled up and we jumped in. My tongue was down her throat before we'd reached the first traffic lights. Belatedly, I sent Yasin a text that I wouldn't be back. There hadn't been time to finish my drink or say goodbye.

```
Halloween party
with the RSG gang
```

We alighted the cab in Poland Street, directly outside the big, black unmarked entrance door of *Milk & Honey*. I was buzzed in and the receptionist showed us upstairs to the Red Room. Harriet and I sat facing each other on soft leather chairs, and perused the menu. Somehow, Harriet talked me into buying a bottle of cheap champagne. The vibe still felt a little confrontational but perhaps that was a figment of my imagination. I still felt intimidated by tall leggy girls.

My conversation wasn't so good and I seemed to pick all the wrong topics. I told her I was a player and banged lots of girls. I thought it was helping my game to push the pendulum all the way towards extreme douche-bag. Harriet didn't seem to mind but she preferred the deeper hopes 'n' dreams talk. We talked about ourselves for a while. Harriet was mixed race, half-black and half-English, and worked in an office job she didn't much care for. Her eyes began to fill with tears. She didn't even seem to be sharing anything especially vulnerable, so I was surprised that she cried.

We shook out the last drops out of the champagne and by then we had a mutual unspoken understanding. We settled the bill and took a taxi to her flat-share in Shepherd's Bush, close to the Westfield mall where I'd met Luminita. Harriet's bedroom was in the attic and sported nice skylights. I tried to bang her but she wasn't having it. I was drunk and tired (champagne always goes to my head) so I didn't really care. We fell asleep.

I woke up the next morning with cotton mouth, dehydrated. I stared at the ceiling with aches throughout my body, too tired to get up but too hungover to sleep. I desperately needed the toilet but couldn't make myself get up. Harriet seemed equally immobile. So we lay in bed touching and messing around. She soon grabbed my dick, the biggest single signal a girl will ever give you that it's time to pull the trigger. She was very horny.

"I want to fuck you now," I said, simply.

"Okay."

Technically speaking, this was our second day together, and in her mind that made it okay. The sex was unsatisfying. I took my notch, showered, took my leave, and then scoffed a full English breakfast at the nearest cafe. Harriet was a nice enough girl, albeit a little strange, but I had no plans on seeing her again. Easy come, easy go. A week went by, or maybe two, then she messaged me.

"What are you doing?"

"Call Of Duty," I wrote. A minute later I realised that was rather abrupt so I sent a follow-up message, "Black Ops, multiplayer."

She replied moments later. "I'm in a taxi, and I don't have any money. Can you come and get me?"

"No."

Who was she kidding? What a stupid, childish thing to do. This was a twenty-two year old adult with a job and the right to vote. I was definitely taken aback.

"Well then, can I come to you?"

"Yes, if you pay for your taxi. I'm not paying for it."

She was currently in Acton, at the western extremity of London while I was in Hampstead in the north-west. We weren't close and I dreaded to think how much a taxi would cost over that distance. I would guess about fifty pounds — approximately forty-nine pounds more than I was willing to pay to bang her again. I tossed my phone onto the bed and un-paused *Call of Duty*. Twenty minutes later, during a kill-streak in the game, I could hear a taxi pull up onto the driveway outside.

I didn't feel the slightest sexual desire. If Harriet had messaged with positive sweet things, like Tasanee always did, I'd have felt good about her coming. Instead, I braced myself for some kind of scam. Harriet was both tall and feisty, a combination that frequently wraps men around a girl's finger, a temptation to tool men that not all of them resist. I was wearing crappy boxer shorts and a Hulk Hogan yellow vest. I pushed my feet into some slippers and shuffled downstairs to the front door. Harriet was waiting, anxiously.

"Hello."

"Hi. I've got no money. The taxi driver is mad."

She looked quite hot and I started to think maybe I would quite like to fuck her again.

"You think so?"

I looked over her shoulder where a battered Hyundai was idling. The driver was a slim Indian man with a bad moustache. He looked like the industrious type who pulls twelve-hour shifts. I felt bad for him, standing non-threateningly by his car wondering if this stupid girl was going to rip him off. I gave him twenty pounds, for his sake rather than Harriet's. She could freeze to death on Hampstead Heath for all I cared, the silly bitch. I was reminded why I try not to talk to English girls. The driver took my money, muttering thanks to me and flashing an indignant look at Harriet. I couldn't imagine the bullshit he was forced to endure on any given weekend driving fares home from bars and clubs.

"I suppose you'd better come in," I told her.

"Thanks," she said, brushing against me and laying a kiss on my cheek. I didn't like it.

Château RSG was actually two separate buildings side-by-side and connected by an enclosed passageway. In the right-hand building lived ten random tenants who weren't a part of our gang. This held the main entrance that Harriet and I came through. It was squalid due to the low value of its tenants and we called it the "crack house". In stark contrast we'd already redecorated our side, moved in lots of good furniture, and created special purpose rooms such as a home cinema room and a top-floor "gentleman's club" inspired by the Red Room in *Milk & Honey* which we called The Hemingway Suite.

Harriett and I walked through to the back of the crack house. As we passed the lounge, two hipster types sitting on wooden chairs smoking out a bong noticed us.

"Hey, man" they called, so I paused a moment.

Unbelievably, they started hitting on Harriet, trying to flirt and chat with her right in front of me. She wasn't interested, but that wasn't really the point. They were hitting on my girl, a blatant challenge.

"Piss off, lads" I said, and ushered Harriet on. I marked their cards accordingly. We continued on through to my house and up to my room. Harriet wanted sex and jumped me without preamble, so I fucked her and she stayed the night. We had sex again the next morning and I saw her off at the bus stop.

Now I definitely had no further interest in meeting her again.

CHAPTER 35

WIZARD AND OZ

Christmas was coming and RSG was resplendent in its golden age. We usually charged three hundred notes for the boot camp weekend and we'd loaded it up to deliver as much value as we could. The December 2010 boot camp was unusual in that six friends had block-booked us. They were their own pick-up rat pack. Our favourite seminar venue in Old Street, *The East Rooms*, had recently burned down so we held the seminars in the cinema room of Château RSG.

We missed *The East Rooms*. It was a classy members bar, restaurant and private rooms on the same membership account as *Milk & Honey*. We'd reserve a room and everyone piled onto the wall-to-wall leather sofas and dipped into ice buckets full of beer bottles, creating a friendly lounge-lizard atmosphere. A large screen television overhead showed the slides we taught from. Usually Diamond did the first presentation, on opening in bars and building attraction, the same lad who'd taught me on my first ever boot camp. Then Jimmy and Mick would alternate presentations on how to show personality and charisma. The program was finely-honed, with slick graphics and a rock star vibe. After three hours the students would be fired up to hit a busy loud bar in the West End or around Old Street itself. I'd often hang around to absorb the rat pack vibe but I never taught night game — it wasn't my thing and my results were far too erratic for me to be a good approach coach.

The next day, late Saturday morning, the daygame gang took over the reins. Johnny would give his talk about confidence and approach anxiety, then I gave mine on beginners daygame. We still liked to run it Covent Garden and experimented with several pub function rooms for the talks. By lunchtime, the students were paired up with instructors and we took them out and pushed them into opening.

I'd noticed students were usually more nervous in the daygame than at night, probably because the latter allowed them to drink alcohol to loosen up socially. I found that strange, as it was the opposite for me. It was bars and especially clubs where I got nervous. Usually we'd all regroup over a beer around four o'clock and encourage the students to swap war stories. We thoroughly enjoyed coaching.

On this particular December boot camp, the Saturday nightgame session was held in the hipster-junkie-tourist haven of Camden, at *The World's End* pub where I'd had that night of drunken idiocy with Lee and Marilyn a few months earlier. I tagged along, off the clock, to enjoy a night out. The place was packed, standing room only. I sat on high stools chatting to Fernando while watching Jimmy and Mick go through some learning points with the students. At some point I looked over and noticed two girls standing against a pillar at the next table, within arm's reach of me. The nearest girl was fairly hot and wore a short skirt and outrageously colourful long rainbow socks pulled up to just below her knees. Her friend wasn't pretty, but she was wearing such a funny-looking cardigan that a self-amusing opener immediately came to mind.

I tapped a student, Martin, and told him to watch the demonstration.

"Hey," I told her. "I like your cardigan. It looks like exactly what my grandma would wear."

The hotter girl laughed at her friend's expense and gave me an easy hook point. I was drunk and loud, being the same playful dickhead that had worked so well in Zagreb. I made jokes and kept the pair intrigued with push-pull.

"Where are you from, woman? I can't place the accent," I asked the hotter one.

"Australia, Sydney."

"Ah. I went to Australia once. They stopped me at passport control, suspicious I think. The border guard says 'do you have a criminal record?' I says, 'no, do I still need one?'"

I threw my head back and cackled while she punched my arm. She was called Zoe. I guessed she was in her early twenties and rated her a six. She had decent tits, wide hips and, seeing as I was drunk, that was good enough for me.

"Anyway, nice meeting you girls," I said and rolled off.

The principle purpose of the roll-off, according to Mystery who coined the term, is to demonstrate to a girl that you are not needy. Usually men will latch onto any girl who returns their attention, which can quickly become cloying. Rolling off relieves the pressure and prevents you coming across as a push-over. Additionally, it introduces some uncertainty into the girl's mind — it's not clear if you'll come back to her. This fear of loss will make her value your attention more highly, assuming she likes you in the first place. Thus a roll-off fits into the standard schema of push-pull: talking to her is the pull, and leaving her is the push.

I figured ten minutes would do the trick.

"My round, mate," I said to Fernando. "What are you having?"

"Whiskey cola."

I walked to the bar, shared a few words with Lee, then waited to get served. Mick was talking to a girl next to me, spinning a yarn about working in a ski resort. Things felt good — a warm buzz from alcohol, a lively night, my friends around me, and a good set to return to.

Rolling off is not without its risks. The biggest is that some other man will swoop in to engage the girl, trying to steal her from you. It's not such a big risk. Realistically, most men don't approach and even the Don Juans of any given venue don't open a lot, and tend to stay in conversation with the first girl to return some interest. There's no guarantee such a man will achieve hook point if he does open, and even should he do so, you can still go right back and blow him out the set. Ultimately, girls choose to talk to the men they like most. If that man is you, the interlopers are easily dealt with.

The worst you'll experience is inconvenience.

The World's End pub
in Camden

While I was at the bar talking to Lee, the student Martin, maybe thinking I had left the set cold, moved in. It pissed me off more than it should have, because I'd built up a drunken head of steam. I returned with the drinks.

"Excuse me," I said, stepping between Martin and Zoe. "Here's your drink, Fernando." Then I turned to the Aussie girl and blocked Martin out with my shoulder. He lingered a few seconds and, not getting encouragement from any of us, he wandered off to do another set. I wouldn't have done it had I been coaching that night.

"So, Zoe, are the rumours true?"

"What rumours?"

"That Aussie birds have tight asses?"

Her jaw dropped in a playfully exaggerated show of surprise. I reached around and slapped her ass. "Not bad, that," I said. "I like your ass."

"You can't do that!" she gasped, though her body language very clearly suggested she wanted me to do it again.

"I've been doing my research on your shitbox country, you know. I read. I'm not as dumb as I look. Of course everyone knows Australia is one massive desert with kangaroos, Fosters beer, and *Home & Away* on the telly. But!" I said, holding my finger in the air for emphasis, as if about to drop an interesting fact.

Zoe and her friend waited, expectantly.

I turned to Fernando and said to him, "did you know that, statistically speaking, Aussie girls are more likely to have great tits than any other former British colony?"

"Is that true?" asked Fernando, not believing a word of it but playing along as my wing. I turned to the girls.

"I'm scientifically minded. Let's conduct an experiment."

Then I reached my hand down the front of Zoe's top and fondled her breasts. She let out a splutter of shock, but let me do it and seemed greatly amused. We all started laughing. I must've been on quite a roll because it was very much out of character for me to be so bold in a bar. For the next twenty minutes we had a more normal chat, and people came and went. I went to the bathroom, chatted to Mick, and the time flew by. It was getting on to midnight, so the bar would call time soon.

"Let's get a last drink in," I said to Zoe and walked her to the bar. I sat on a stool while she stood next to me, and the barman brought us each a beer. The sexual beast built up inside me again, having been dormant for a quarter hour.

"I'm going to fuck you in the ass," I told her. Her expression was no different to if I'd told her I was going to buy her a pretty pair of socks. "After I fuck you in the ass, I'll pull my dick out and put it in your mouth. And then, I'll cum over your face."

Zoe squirmed a little. I heard the bartender call last orders.

"I think I'd better find my friend," she said, edging away from me.

"Why?" I asked, sensitive to the suddenly serious energy between us. It would appear I'd finally overreached myself. Playtime was over.

Zoe rested her hand softly on my forearm and said, "because I need to tell her I'm leaving with you."

Score.

I leaned back on the stool and watched her slink away. It felt good knowing the work was done, and within half an hour I'd be balls-deep in the ass of a new nationality. Zoe came back a few minutes later. I downed my drink, slid off the stool, and then she hung onto my arm and followed me outside. We jumped into the first taxi to pass by. There was none of the usual tension or drama. It was oddly anti-climactic for me to be heading home with a girl who had already explicitly agreed to sex. There was no dramatic will-she/won't-she tension. Zoe didn't put up the slightest resistance nor pretence. She knew exactly what was going on, and she wanted it as much as I did.

We arrived at Chateau RSG and I paid off the taxi driver.

In my bedroom, I put some music on, poured a shot of rum for each of us, and then pulled Zoe in to begin kissing. I pulled off all her clothes except the rainbow socks, which looked good on her. Then we tumbled onto the bed.

I did in fact fuck her in the ass and cum on her face.

It was dominant, dirty sex, which was precisely the squalid adventure she was looking for. I still have an image burned into my memory of Zoe on my bed, on her hands and knees while I drilled her in the ass and she screamed "Fuck me! Fuck me!" while I looked on in puzzlement at her long rainbow socks, trying to count how many individual colours were represented but struggling to do so in the low light conditions.

It was proper grot-sex, like eating two McDonald's cheeseburgers in a row.

For some bizarre reason, after we finished, I told her about *Rock Solid Game*.

"I could see it happening, in the bar," she said.

"So it's obvious?" I asked her.

"There's a big group of guys and some are teaching and some are watching. Yeah, it's obvious."

I showed her a few of my hidden-camera street videos before we fell asleep. She liked them. We didn't have sex again that night nor in the morning. She woke up and showered while I had a lie-in. Then we sat in the lounge drinking tea, not talking much but with a comfortable atmosphere between us. We both knew it for what it was, a one night stand. She was fine with it. I didn't make her feel bad or dirty about it, I just didn't give her any indication that it was anything else.

"Right, I need to go home now, I've got some homework to do," she said, picking her handbag off the sofa and straightening her shirt. I walked her to the front door and pointed to the bus stop directly outside.

"You can take any bus. The 82 and 13 both go to Oxford Street."

She reached up and gave me a peck on the cheek. "I had a good time. Good bye!"

"Goodbye," I returned. Not 'see you later'.

Zoe smiled and walked away, re-enforcing my idea that sometimes girls just want a one night stand too. My last look at her was of that firm Aussie ass that I'd done bad things to. An hour later the six students came over for the last day of boot camp. We'd set it aside for de-briefing and a long Q&A. I also presented an early version of my Long Game ideas, on how to draw a girl in when she's living in another country.

While Zoe had told me she'd go back to Australia for Christmas, Adele was coming back in the opposite direction. She'd finished her first university term in Sydney and thoroughly enjoyed it. I was keen to see her. I really liked her.

"Can you visit me in Paris again?" she'd asked over Facebook messenger, a couple of weeks earlier.

"Yes, I'd love to see Paris again. But I'll need to check prices. I imagine accommodation is expensive."

"Oh, don't worry about that. My dad has a small rental apartment in the centre, near the Opera house. It's been rented to a Japanese man, but he moved out a week ago. My dad said it'll be vacant over Christmas and you can stay there, for free."

"Brilliant, thanks!"

"My dad and I will need day to clean it, and prepare it for your arrival. Then we can both stay there."

I genuinely could not imagine anything I'd rather do over Christmas then be tucked up in a Paris apartment with nineteen-year-old Adele. That her father was offering (and even cleaning) the apartment in which I'd bang his daughter seemed a little odd. I'll never understand the French. I booked onto the Eurostar again and arrived in Paris when a light blanket of snow covered the streets and buildings.

It felt like I was living the dream, my life having opened up to reveal new vistas. It brought to mind television and magazine advertisements about The Good Life I'd seen when first working in London. When flicking through *The Economist* magazine I'd see pages of ads showing distinguished gentlemen wearing a Patek Phillipe watch, or sipping a fine wine on a balcony overlooking the Sagrada Familia cathedral in Barcelona. Perhaps these distinguished men drove an Audi, dined in Marseilles with a dusky young beauty, then hopped aboard a ferry boat to Italy and took a walk through Rome. It's all a bit silly, but that's how I felt to be walking arm-in-arm with Adele past the Paris Opera House then sampling buttered croissants in a pavement cafe outside the Louvre, while she wittered on musically in her cute French accent.

I was living the good life. No doubt about it.

It felt even sweeter because I'd worked so hard to reach this position.

We had sex within minutes of arriving at the apartment. There was a double mattress on the floor, without a bed frame, and a long sofa against the wall. It was clean, functional, and not especially roomy. We didn't care. Adele had been waiting three months to see me and my enthusiasm almost matched hers.

We lay in each other's arms for an hour and then, as it was still early evening, we made plans. She took me out to the Eiffel tower. An ice rink had been installed between two of the tower's massive steel legs, sixty metres above street level. It felt like having Paris at my feet. That was a magical night with mulled cider and pastries, ice skating, and Adele. We walked back to the apartment arm-in-arm, Adele smiling with joy. I wondered how I could make the night even more special. As we shook the snow off our shoes and hung up our coats, I had a good idea.

"I'm going to do you in the ass," I said.

"Okay." I'd expected resistance. "But go easy. I've never done it."

We make out, undressed, and had regular sex. Then I moved her to the sofa and instructed her to rest on her elbows and knees, with her ass pushing back towards me. She looked very sexy. I stood upright, awkwardly getting into position, then began pushing my dick into her ass.

"Owwwwwwww!" she moaned. I paused. She took a few deep breaths, then said, "Okay, more."

It took a minute but finally I was banging her in the ass. She closed her eyes tight, wincing, and bit her lip. I wasn't sure she was enjoying it. "Are you okay?" I asked.

"Yes. It hurts, but don't stop!"

Perhaps I'm just an old-time romantic, but there was something very sweet about that. After five minutes, I said, "I'm going to cum on your face." And I did.

I only stayed three nights in Paris then two weeks later Adele came to London for a week, staying with me in Château RSG. It started great but my mood soured in the last two days as it seemed increasingly clear that I've have to dump her. If she'd lived in Paris I'd have tried to manage a distance relationship — Eurostar was so fast and convenient that it wasn't at all unfeasible to date between London and Paris. But...... Australia? That was different.

It was a self-interested decision of mine, but I knew also that it was good for her to be free of me. She was growing increasingly attached, and I honestly feared that if I had told her not to go back to school in Australia that she would have stayed with me and given up her education. I wouldn't want to be responsible for that. She cried when I told her, though she understood, logically, that our relationship was doomed. I'd told her months ago that I dated other women.

"But will you still write to me?" she asked.

"Yes."

Adele went back to school, messaged me for a month or so, and then met a French student in Sydney named Alain. She sent me a picture of him and told me that he was a "nice guy with a bit of an edge."

"I'm thinking of dating him," she said.

"Give it a try."

We talked a bit off-and-on through Facebook for a while longer before she finally faded away, and then un-friended me. I went to her page two years later and saw that she was still with Alain, both having moved back to Paris. Judging from their pictures, it seemed like she was happy. I'm happy for her. Adele will always be special to me and one of the four most important girls out of the two-thousand-plus I'd meet over the two-year period covered in this volume.

CHAPTER 36
MASTER OF THE UNIVERSE

CHAPTER 36

MASTER OF THE UNIVERSE

I'd been plateauing of late. It was mostly expressed through a lack of motivation for approaching and dating. Fernando would knock on my door asking if I'd join him on Oxford Street and I'd decline.

"Nah, man. I'm playing *God Of War 3*."

I fancied I looked a bit like the hero, Kratos. He was a heavily-muscled, aggressive skinhead engaged in a one-man vendetta against the gods of Olympus. I too had a skinhead. That was close enough. My door was open and the screams of harpies echoed down the first floor hallway as I stabbed them to death with my twin blades. Fernando stepped inside my room. He wore his faded blue jeans, brown leather boots, and a black waxed jacket. He looked extremely cool. Cooler than me or Kratos.

"Come on, Nick. You've been slacking for a month now. In fact, now I think of it you haven't been the same since Poland. Where's the old fire?"

I was tapping the shoulder buttons on my controller, following on-screen prompts. There was a ripping noise and I pulled the head off Icarus. Now Kratos held it up, to taunt Zeus. Blood drenched the combat arena. Explosions rocked the background, as Titans battled.

"Mate, I'm having way more fun here, smashing up Ancient Greece."

"Have it your way," he said, without rancour. "But I'm getting a few hours on the streets before it gets dark."

I settled back into the video game, not feeling the slightest sexual intent.

He does look a little like me

The last four girls — Zoe, Harriet, Maria, Mieke — had been good stories but not especially hot. Definitely a step down from earlier in the year. I was now hitting on girls mostly because I felt compelled to do so. *I'm the guy who hits on girls*, I told myself. A year earlier, my self-image had been consistent with my reality: not good with girls. I'd set myself rational, logical targets (e.g. approach twenty girls per week) that I stuck to come hell or high water. Thus was born cognitive dissonance. My logical forebrain dragged me toward a new identity while my emotional hindbrain fought back, kicking, screaming and holding its breath until blue in the face. The consistently positive reference experiences had eventually trickled in. My hindbrain was now accepting of the new identity, that of "player". Change is rarely free. Two years of sustained effort had burned me out. It was tempting to take my foot off the pedal and snuggle into my new comfort zone.

All afternoon I ran amok amongst the gods, smiting left and right in blood-curdling fury until a trail of shattered corpses littered Mount Olympus. The whole time, I ruminated on my progress so far. I broke the seal on a bottle of Johnnie Walker Double Black and tossed off a few slugs of whiskey. I continued to ruminate under a long hot shower. All these ruminations led me in the same direction.

My inner game needed work.

Beginner's Hell was behind me. I'd normalised the act of approaching and banked the attendant experiences. I'd devoured the

PUA ebooks and DVD box-sets. I'd mechanically applied their lessons time after time in-field. All those days of feeling nausea before the first approach, of getting blown out in seconds, of robotic and fake lines, of dates-to-nowhere: they were a gradually receding memory. For the past few months, the basics had been second nature. I'd picked up Zoe, Harriet and Maria while drunk and on autopilot. It hadn't even felt like game any more. I was in a transitional phase. A plateau. I needed something new to kick me forwards.

I had an idea where to go. *The London Seduction Society* board was still active and one of the senior members, Colin (who posted under the moniker Skeletor) had recently announced he was accepting consultation clients again. Colin interested me because of the quality and insight of his forum posts. He'd regularly drop five-hundred-word essays addressing formerly-vague concepts in the most precise and illuminating terms. Everyone called him "the Yoda of game", after Luke Skywalker's mentor in *Star Wars*. When I saw him speak at Curran's 'Game for over-35s' talk a year earlier I'd been impressed with the sophistication of his inner game model. He had command of the topic and a concise manner of delivery. So it was fortuitous timing that just as I was recognising my new plateau, Colin happened to advertise a new commercial venture called *Alchemy 42*. He'd pulled together a group of pick-up instructors and also some therapists to teach his version of game — the Harmony Model. He was now available for 1-on-1 consultations.

He wasn't cheap, at £50 per hour. I had savings but I was also unemployed and reluctant to run down my nest egg further. Still, I couldn't think of a better person to consult. I sent him a mail, explaining a little about myself, my progress, and what I wanted. I wasn't quite sold on him, so I was interested to see how he'd respond. The mentor-student relationship concerns more than just cash. If we went ahead, I'd be letting Colin dig deep into my inner game. He'd require me to reveal a lot about myself, things even my parents didn't know. Confronting those demons privately is hard enough but confiding in another person even harder. I still didn't like to admit my flaws and my ego didn't want someone poking around in my head telling me I'm weird.

Later that evening, I canvassed opinion in the Château.

"Waste of time. Just read *Mystery Method* and figure out the rest for yourself," said Jimmy.

"Sounds good," said Johnny. "It's good to get a third-person perspective. We all have blind spots."

Tony breathed deeply, sighed, and slowly nodded his head. "Yes, good," he said.

"Awesome, bro! BOOM!" said Lee.

Mick had a girl in his room and wasn't available for comment.

I presumed I'd be an interesting case study for Colin, so I hoped my mail would pique his interest and he'd agree to take me on. His reply dropped into my message box the next day and we set up a one-hour free consultation in a Caffe Nero off Charing Cross road. The night before, I spent two hours preparing. It seemed important to verbalise exactly what I wanted. I had four specific goals:

- Believe 10s are lucky to meet me.
- Reduce my envy of other men's success.
- Balance my desire to open girls with my reactive need to feel like I should.
- Project solidity and certainty in my interactions.

I'll break these down further.

Currently, I could walk up to a pretty girl and feel — deep in my core — that she is lucky I chose her. There was a large element of delusion in this belief, but I'd mostly convinced myself. Of course, that didn't necessarily mean she'd fall over backwards with her legs in the air. Generally, though, such girls got a warm glow from me hitting on them and some dated me. Even the rejections were polite, girls often thanking me for giving it a try and brightening their day. There wasn't any mystery to it. Girls are overwhelmed by male attention. Most of it is so low-quality as to be an annoyance. They prize high-quality attention. They'll doll themselves up and promenade in public in the hope a high-value man will notice and approach them. Most of the time they go home disappointed. So when I actually do hit on her, she feels lucky.

Knowing this made my manner increasingly relaxed and confident. I could talk the way I wanted, expressing myself authentically. That's how I'd picked up the last few girls so easily—I felt entitled to that class of female beauty. Such confidence wavered when I stepped up to the next tier. For example, in Zagreb I'd street-opened a handful of 'perfect tens' and though I'd run ostensibly good game, there were flickers of doubt in my manner. It was very subtle but enough for the girl to sense, *he doesn't date girls like me.*

Jimmy wasn't the only one of us in it for the Audreys.

The second problem was that despite having already achieved far more success than I'd ever thought possible, I still reacted badly to other people's success stories. I'd gotten my knickers in a twist over Jimmy's success in Lithuania three months earlier. Two weeks after that, RSG did a boot camp in Dublin with Mick and Lee coaching. They had a great time. Mick pulled a girl out of a bar and banged her in an alleyway. The boys came piling back into Château RSG on a massive high that Sunday evening, full of stories of sexual adventure. Intellectually, I was genuinely pleased for them. Emotionally, I envied it. It wasn't rational but I was so competitive that I couldn't bear other people succeeding.

Clearly, not a healthy mindset.

Third, I'd come to feel "daygamer guilt". I'd become so accustomed to approaching that it was now a Pavlovian response, approaching because my identity was *the man who approaches*. My head snapped up like a hunting dog catching a scent any time a hot girl ambled by, then I'd be off on the hunt. Clearly, it isn't feasible to open every single hot girl I saw, so I'd let many go by unmolested and then suffer a pang of guilt, like I'd let myself down. Ultimately, this was caused by a scarcity mentality — my ingrained belief that I will never have enough girls and therefore I need to be taking every single opportunity I get. Again, that's not logical. The streets are full of hot girls every day of the year including Christmas. There's no reason not to take days off.

Daygamer guilt is really a novel transformation of approach anxiety. As a beginner, AA froze me and blocked all my lofty self-improvement goals. Over time I learned to push through and develop a long-term momentum to keep going out week-after-week. However, it always felt fragile, like one bad run could shake me off the cliff-face before I reached the summit. It's worrying, to have climbed halfway up the mountain and then look down at how far you could yet fall. Hence daygamer guilt is an expression of the constant worry that if you stop climbing up, you'll eventually tire and fall.

My aspiration was simple: to live my life and, should I wish to meet a new woman, go out and get one. The basic daygame skills were already there. I didn't want to be trawling Covent Garden every weekend. It was too early to think about my end-game but I certainly didn't want to be grinding it out forever.

Lastly, I wanted to improve my masculine vibe. When I spoke to Tony it was like talking to a statue on Mount Olympus, such was the solidity and certainty in his sub-communication. Kratos would have more trouble bundling him over than he had with Poseidon, Athena, and Icarus. Studying body language and non-verbal micro communication wasn't the answer, as I'd already done all that with only a modicum of success. Rather, I needed to organise my frame internally and then let the sub-communication take care of itself.

It was with these thoughts in mind, summarised on a page in my moleskin notebook, that I met Colin in Caffe Nero. I was in the queue ordering a latte and chocolate cake when he walked in. He was tall and thin, very noticeably so. He wore a flat cap, wool duffel coat, and simple trainers.

"Hey Nick, I thought I'd probably recognise you," he said, shaking my hand with his right while fumbling to unfasten his coat with his left. "You said you were at my talk at Curran's event last year. I think that's why."

"Do you want a coffee?"

"Tea, if that's okay. An Earl Grey. I'll go find a table downstairs and we'll get cracking."

I walked down the basement stairs with my coffee and Colin's tea sloshing around, threatening to spill over into the saucers. I set them down then sat back in a battered tan-coloured leather sofa while Colin sat across from me. We made a little small-talk and got down to it.

"Tell me more about your childhood. What sort of kid were you?" he asked.

I launched into a recollection of key childhood memories, of being a star pupil throughout school, of getting into mischief when I became bored, and of being very proud of going to a good university after growing up on a council estate.

"How is the relationship between your parents?"

"My mother is dominant. She's very aggressive, psychologically, and terrorises everyone around her if she doesn't get her way. My dad goes along to get along. He's an ideological pacifist and a loner. They rarely have friends around. I remember two of my mother's friends. One was a quiet little woman called Norma whose husband used to beat her up. One time, when I was about twelve, she and both her daughters stayed at our house for a week because the husband had been drinking and become violent. Another friend was Arlene. She was fat and always on crutches, moaning about her health problems. I hated both of them."

Colin raised his eyebrows, seemed about to say something, thought better of it and sipped his tea. He nodded, appreciatively. "Lovely tea! How about your brother?"

"He takes more after my dad. He's gentle, passive. People say he's like me, but nice. We are very close and share many hobbies, such as fighting, reading, and many political opinions. I take more after my mother. Growing up, my mother was always squabbling with us, the neighbours, and random people in restaurants and shops. My brother finally adopted my dad's strategy, of keeping his head down and letting her run wild. He moved out as soon as he could, when he was sixteen. Since then he's remained in Newcastle, bought a house, and had a steady girlfriend since he was twenty, who he's now married."

"And you?"

"I rejected my mother's frame, I think. I'd look at my dad curled up in a fetal position — metaphorically — while my mother ran the house and I swore, *I'll never be like that*. Most men want a wife like their mother. I want one as different to my mother as possible. I absolutely reject the dominant female / submissive male dynamic. I'd rather die."

"Do you love your parents?"

"I think so. Hard to tell. I'd certainly be very upset if they died."

"Do you feel they love you?"

"Yes. They aren't unloving, just really weird. They try their best with what they know."

Colin sipped more tea. He'd certainly become intrigued by my case.

Ultimately, meeting Colin would require addressing the single biggest issue, the one I'd been avoiding for almost two years: why did my marriage fail? That's a long involved question. There's the version my wife gave me and then there's another version, that which I really think. Crudely put, Ioe told me I was too mean, didn't show enough interest in her, had become dull, and that she eventually fell out of love.

That's half-true. I told Colin what I then believed was actually the reason.

"I lost most of the qualities that had attracted her to me in the first place," I said. "I used to be self-absorbed and rebellious. She loved that side of me for years. I used to follow my whims, strive for interesting new experiences, and I was impossible to control. Ioe was from a broken home with her father pushed out of the house by her mum. Her younger sister became fat and depressive, never dating at all. Ioe doubled-down on her dancing. On the face of it, I thought Ioe was very stable but looking back, I think she had some daddy issues. It was precisely my frequent emotional and physical unavailability that intoxicated her, on the attraction side."

He was sipping the tea again, looking at me keenly. I wondered if he was judging me harshly. "Go on," he said.

"Then I decided to get married. I turned my back on the old me and tried to become a good husband. I dusted off my suit, got a corporate job, and we moved in together. After two good years things went rapidly downhill. I cared too much about making the marriage work without really understanding why we'd done so well before marriage. She was right that I became boring. I cared deeply for her but my family just doesn't express that kind of thing, so she probably thought I didn't feel it."

"You make it sound like it's all your fault. I know you don't believe that. What did she get wrong?" I knew Colin was trying to draw me out. That was the whole point of our consultation — to explore what was buried and unaddressed. What resentments, fears, and passions was I hiding from myself?

"She got old and masculine," I said, simply. "She was no longer the sweet feminine flower I'd dated. I think I could've handled her ageing, as that's natural and I still saw her as a composite of how she looked now, and how she looked aged twenty-three when we first met. She was a beautiful girl. But her masculine shift was horrible. I hated it. It was like all her smooth edges rubbed off and it was jagged steel underneath. She became bitchy, rebellious, and distant."

"If you were to sum it up, how did you feel when you got divorced?"

"Betrayed."

God, it felt good getting that out! I'd been holding onto resentment for a long time, not willing to unburden myself onto my friends. I sat back, breathing deeply, and fiddling with my chocolate cake. I've always despised weakness. Admitting I felt betrayed was admitting I'd been weak enough to allow someone to betray me. That's why I'd kept my own counsel so long.

Colin let me relax a few minutes in silence as he scribbled some notes into his exercise book. So far he hadn't offered any explanations or theory. It had been entirely about him interviewing me, pumping me for information. He changed tack.

"Tell me about your history with girls."

"I think I did pretty well, for a normal man. I banged fifteen girls up to and including my wife. At college I got lots of make-outs and I'd go to house parties in Newcastle just assuming I'd kiss the prettiest girl there, which I usually did. In my third year at university, I'd play the football video game *Sensible World Of Soccer*. You could customise your teams, so I created a Nick's Girls team of all the girls I'd kissed, as a log. Eventually, I had four teams of twenty players each. Just kisses, mind. Didn't bang many of them."

Colin looked intrigued again, probably by my odd record-keeping habits.

"How about now?"

"My first year of game was horrendous. I didn't get a kiss until six months in, and laid nine months in with a chubby black lass. This year something clicked. For the first half of 2010 I was getting lots of dates, lots of attraction, and lots of *almost* lays. Then suddenly in June the lays came in and I've banged a new bird every month since."

"Why is that, do you think?"

"There have been lots of outliers, outcomes that couldn't be explained by my lacking a confident and dominant mind-set. I've had a dozen girls crazily attracted to me over the past year, to the point where they'd say things like, 'Before I come out to meet you my heart is beating fast and I'm short of breath,' and they'd be super horny. Yet, I failed to bang them and they drifted away, much to my bemusement." I summarised the Aisha and U.V. stories as two memorable examples. "Then in May I met a Libyan bird and I've never looked back. I think I got my alpha shit together."

"Libyan?"

"Yeah, did her in the ass."

"Did you like it?"

"No. It was icky. Only did it for the notch."

Colin gave me a sly grin. "You should try more anal sex. It grows on you. Anyway, that's off topic for now. Why the sudden change to, as you say, becoming more alpha?"

"I think it's my new friends, the *Rock Solid Game* lads. We all moved in together around that time. They say you are the average of your five best friends. Suddenly I'd spend all day every day with Jimmy, Fernando, Johnny, Mick, and Lee. They are all cool. In fact, I remember one specific moment that really stuck in my mind. It was a couple of months ago in Poland. One of our old friends, Ace, returned to his home-town Lodz to attend university and he invited us to visit while we were in Krakow. We took a train one afternoon, he took us to a nightclub called *The Bedrooms*, and then we left the next day. But it was quite a night. Fernando and Ace pulled a pair of girls from the club, and went back to their separate apartments. I nearly got laid too, getting a street kiss close with a pretty blonde student in the afternoon and then meeting her again late after the nightclub and almost getting her home."

"So? What was special that stuck in your mind?"

"It was in *The Bedrooms*. I was sitting in a booth with Lee's mate Samir, a young Polish lad we knew from London. We were drinking, chatting, having a good time when I looked over towards the bar where Fernando was locked in, leaning back, while one of the girls giggled with him. I remember thinking, *he looks really cool now!* I'd first met Fernando a year earlier, when daygaming in Covent Garden and he came up and said hello, as he'd started the same thing a week earlier. I liked him, but he was just a regular lad. Now, in that Lodz club, he was *the* guy. The coolest guy in the club. He'd transformed and I'd seen it happen in real time. It hit me, and I realised I was headed the same direction, just a little behind him."

The hour ticked by and Colin continued scribbling into his exercise book. Finally, he indicated his watch and began packing up. "I think I know what the problem is," he said, then shook my hand and wished me a good afternoon. "Let's talk by text and set up the first proper session."

A week later, we had a three-hour sit down in a casino cafe overlooking Leicester Square. "Free coffee and tea," he said by way of explanation. The casino comped the gamblers with simple drinks and weren't too rigorous in weeding out freeloaders. Colin continued to pump me with questions delving deep into my attitudes on men and women, on sexuality, the relationship my parents have, whether I was popular at school and so on. That took an hour.

"I think I've got enough now. I'm going outside for a cigarette break, to compose my thoughts. Chill out here for ten minutes, then I'll feed back. We'll begin the task of identifying and fixing your problems."

"I'm hungry. Want a cheeseburger? I'm going to Burger King across the square."

"Yeah. And fries."

We put on our coats and walked down the winding stairs into the fresh breeze. Colin sparked up in a doorway while I collected our food. He was stubbing out his second cigarette when I returned and handed him a brown paper bag of junk food.

"Thanks, mate."

We ate quickly in silence then tramped back up the stairs and resumed our seats in the empty casino bar. The waiter gave us a fresh pot of tea to share. Colin and I had hit it off well so I felt relaxed in his presence, but I tensed up waiting for him to unload his feedback onto me. Would it help? Was he any good at this?

I didn't know it at the time, but my sessions with Colin had a long half-life. His initial feedback that cold winter day was helpful but he was also sowing seeds in my mind, like the movie *Inception*, that wouldn't bloom until months and years later. He began with an outline of the Sexual Market Place according to his Harmony Model. It was freakishly similar to my own understanding despite him not knowing about any of the blogs I read, such as *Roissy In DC* or *The Rational Male*. We had different models and different priorities but we essentially agreed about what Game is and how to go about acquiring it. That told me I was on the right track. I wasn't missing a trick. All the theoretical knowledge I'd picked up from eighteen months voracious reading, all the worldly wisdom I've picked up in the past thirty-five years, was consistent with what Colin told me.

I felt enormous relief.

Theory was all well and good but I was most interested in direct feedback about my own unique idiosyncrasies and issues. I'd given Colin a direct unfiltered look into my character, as best as I could, to enable him to do his work properly. There'd been no point holding back or intentionally re-framing facts to impress him. Just as a defendant shouldn't hide things from his lawyer, I had determined not to hide anything from Colin. I handed him full disclosure in a way no-one but my brother had ever seen before and hoped he could work some magic. We had three sessions that month in order to fully investigate, process, and distil Colin's feedback.

"It comes down to two main character traits," he said, once more sipping tea. It seemed all he ever did was smoke cigarettes, scribble notes, and sip tea. "There's a lot going on, and lots of detail to work through, but at a high level you have two main issues. You lack soft dominance, and you look to the world for external validation of yourself as a worthy man."

It was my turn to sip. I looked at him from over my mug, nodding in encouragement for him to continue. He went on.

"A woman looks to her man to lead her safely through the dangers of a hostile world. Men have the ability to impress their will upon the world, to build (symbolically speaking) an impregnable fortress within which she will be safe. We call this capacity his 'hard dominance'. She feels protected both physically and in her social status, which becomes attached to the man's. You can do this very well, Nick. You are strong-willed, capable, belligerent, and certain in your mind how the world works. Bad boys have hard dominance, but they also have fleeting attractiveness that eventually turns the girls away. Why is this? Because hard dominance is not enough. This is why those girls — the black chick and the jungle girl — were so excited by you but ultimately refused to submit."

Okay, I liked how this was going. I kept up my sipping and nodding routine.

"Girls also crave a garden paradise within the walls of the fortress. A warm beautiful space to express their true character without risk of judgement, and to let all their love flow. They need to feel cherished, needed, and to experience a romantic connection with their protector. Otherwise, the fortress becomes a prison and the girl feels trapped in her relationship. Think of it like a motorcycle helmet during a crash. If there is no hard shell, the force of impact upon the road kills the rider. If there is *only* a hard shell, with no interior padding, then the unabsorbed impact goes through the shell and the helmet itself kills the rider."

We talked about my attitudes and it became clear that I lacked soft dominance. My father lacked hard dominance, choosing instead to let my mother run roughshod over him. I'd rejected this, vowing to develop hard dominance before I had the language within which to express it. I vowed to never let a woman dominate me like my mother dominated my father. In addition, my family isn't a warm one. We never developed the habit of hugging, smiling, or overtly expressing kind emotions such as saying "I love you." I mean, we *sometimes* did, but far less than a typical family. I felt just plain awkward expressing such emotions directly to family members. There was narcissism on my mother's side and Asperger's on my father's. Both my brother and I were lucky to emerge mostly unscathed, so we were both considerably more social and popular with others than our parents were.

Still, we weren't completely unscathed. I could be rather cold-blooded.

"Okay, that's the first thing," I said. "You said there were two."

"Hang on a minute, we haven't reached the end of the soft dominance."

I'd grown up as an intellectually exceptional but athletically unimpressive student. I was always drawn towards the bookish hobbies that played to my strengths. That made me extremely sure of myself in all things intellectual, sometimes overbearingly so. Sadly, I hovered around mediocrity in sports and all things physical until I reached university. I then began an over-compensatory quest to become physically competent that led me into boxing, Brazilian ju-jitsu, and Muay Thai.

Having been a bit of a wuss for years, and overcome it, it was now a matter of pride that I was no longer a soft bag o'shite. I rightly credited much of the success of my relationship with my wife as due to my being strongly masculine, aloof, and (hopefully) bad-ass. I rightly blamed much of the relationship's subsequent collapse upon us losing this complimentary male-female polarity. Since beginning my game journey I'd become determined not to be a wuss. Hence so many interactions with girls where I pushed hard with the douchebag game, often to a ludicrously crass extent such as with Marilyn, Maria and Zoe.

"This explains your wife's complaints during the marriage about you being cold. They stemmed from real unmet needs," said Colin, "it's all well and good being a devilish arsehole during the Attraction phase, but you can't sustain a relationship on it. You do attraction well but are piss poor at comfort. Probably, your wife tolerated the lack of comfort precisely because your attraction was so good. But, like you said, once you hit a tough period at work and lost your mojo, that attraction fell away. Suddenly the lack of comfort became a big problem, because there wasn't anything to compensate for its absence."

Colin went on to outline his Harmony Model and how to build soft dominance. He explained 'hypnotic scanning', a phase that usually occurs on a date, while in deep rapport, where a man and woman look at each other intently, as though trying to solve a puzzle. The man is scanning the girl for genetic fit, while the woman is scanning him for identity fit. She is hard-wired to detect the subtlest of weaknesses in his self-image. Is he wearing a mask to hide his identity and frustrate her scan? This is why old-style Game based on scripted routines and fake avatars ultimately fails with high-esteem women. It's why in my first year I'd get girls onto dates and they'd consistently lose interest in me. I'd been able to show an attractive mask for the ten minutes I needed to on the street to take her number but when the date rolled around, when we had to actually get to know each other, I would either keep the mask on, or let it slip and show her the broken pieces jangling around from my divorce. Either way, the girl didn't make an emotional connection with me.

"You need to clean up and strengthen your identity," said Colin, "bring it into alignment with your masculine core. Once that process is complete, you won't need the technical outer game. Focus on removing all the barriers that prevent your identity showing through in your interactions with girls. You've already got enough outer game. Now we can move on to the second issue, your external referencing."

He fed back to me much of my life's achievements. There are many positive things I've been able to internalise in my life. I always came top of the class in every subject, literally from my first year as a little five year old playing in the sandpit between classes, right up to my school leaving exams. Always the best, in everything. But I went to a shitty school so I wondered if I could still be top at college. I was. But it was a shitty college. Finally I went to a top university and it took a full academic year before I realised I was smarter than everyone else. Then I went into business for a top consulting firm and, again, I wasn't sure I'd rise to the top of my peer group but I did. In the face of such consistent positive feedback over literally two decades I had fully internalised that I am among the top one percent of men intellectually. I projected as such with serene confidence.

"But have you noticed, Nick, that you talk about these things as though they are outside of you."

"What do you mean?"

"You talk about certificates on your wall, of test scores, of a top university and a top consulting firm. These are all external to you. They are outside, not inside. You draw your self-esteem from two sources. First, by competing against others and winning. Second, by membership to certain clubs. These are not internally-generated. They are not elements of your personality, they are success markers. This is what I mean by external referencing. You go into the world and act, so as to provoke feedback from it that reinforces your self-image as a successful man. You use the world as a mirror to reflect back your self image."

I rebelled at that. "Surely that's not a bad thing. Who wants to be a loser?"

"It's certainly not a bad thing, in moderation. Competence and capability are attractive to women, and women love winners. The problem is that it makes you vulnerable. When your self-esteem is tied to feedback from others, you become dependent upon them. It's volatile. If you can make the shift toward generating your feedback internally, of judging your self-worth according to how well you live up to your own values, then you are in control. That's more attractive still."

I didn't like to hear that. Colin made it sound like I was one of those vacuous normal people who buy the things television commercials tell them to. Buy this new car, this new watch, and wear the aftershave that Calvin Klein or Paco Rabanne tells you is cool. Surely not. I told him so.

"I'm not one of those fashion fags. I go my own way."

"More than most people, yes, but not as much as you think. Look, there are levels to this. Compared to the average man, you are more confident, more dominant, more attractive, and objectively-speaking more intelligent and more successful." I was starting to enjoy this session again. "But I assume you're not here to be simply above average. You told me you want the very best women. Well, we need to get you closer to your ultimate potential."

"How do I do that?"

"I recommend Zen. I'll email you links to some good speeches from Alan Watts. He's a crusty old hippy who popularised many Eastern concepts on Buddhism and Daoism. It'll help."

"Help how? I hate hippies."

Colin chuckled, shaking his head like I was an especially difficult case. "You won't let go of the safety rope. Alan Watts has a good talk on this, called 'fear of enlightenment'. Nick, you just don't appreciate your own value. I've taught hundreds of people over the past five years, I've met everyone in the London community, plus all the normal people when I lived overseas. Believe me, you are not average. Not even close. You talk like you are still a stumbling amateur, as if you have all kinds of self-doubt and confusion. Nothing could be further from the truth. You are so hyper-focused on the little things you do wrong that you are oblivious to all the things you do extremely well."

"Oh."

"It's like watching an Olympic swimmer who won't take his inflatable arm bands off. I'm sure that, to you, it's very real and problematic. To me, as an outsider, it was obvious within the first few minutes we met that nearly everything is already in place. You just need to believe it. Your lack of belief is, ironically, what's making you unattractive. Be more Zen."

When not feeding back on my concerns directly, Colin outlined his own Harmony Model. I think he enjoyed having a client who could really understand its subtleties. He'd developed an abstract schema to explain how different types of men and women tended to pair up. He ranked men from one-to-four according to their confidence and competence. A top-tier male possessed both qualities. Women were ranked according to beauty and self-esteem thus together creating a dual hierarchy of four types each, male and female. Durable relationships, said Colin, occur when the man and woman are from matching types, so 1s match with 1s and 2s with 2s and so forth.

Colin's intellectual approach appealed to me. He wasn't an armchair philosopher. His reputation in the London community was a man who'd already proven himself (before I entered it) with cold approach and lay reports of his own. I was never good at taking advice but I was considerably more amenable to instruction when a man both talked the talk and walked the walk. I was deep into reading. Having finished with Ayn Rand I'd recently moved on to Ludwig Von Mises, the godfather of Austrian economics. Colin recommended I read about Karl Jung, especially the book *King Warrior Magician Lover* by Robert Moore and

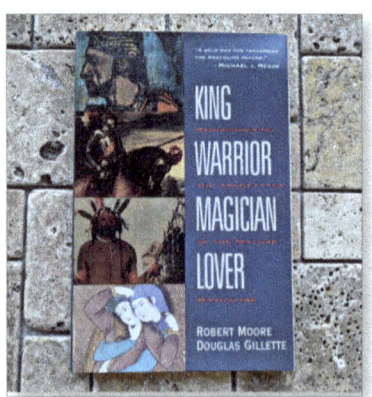

Continuing to introspect and unpick my inner game issues

Douglas Gillette, two disciples of Jung's. That was my homework assignment, which I dutifully read in the week between sessions.

Moore & Gillette contended that modern society is undergoing a crisis of masculinity in which boys are not being inducted into manhood due to an absence of coming of age rituals. This leads men to remain locked in 'boy psychology'. I'd already noticed this when working out in weightlifting gyms — a certain portion (certainly not all) of gym rats were huge men completely lacking maturity or confidence. My brother and I used to call them "little boys in gorilla costumes" and later "gymcels" (a contraction of gym and incel). I saw the same thing expressed on the intellectual plane throughout university, when many highly-regarded academics where just building walls and fences of impenetrable jargon and bullshit to protect a vulnerable core of intellectual incompetence. But due to their socially elevated position and the huge barriers to entry in getting to their ideas, they were able to sit atop Mount Olympus and pretend to be gods. I used to call them "a dwarf on a mountain".

King Warrior Magician Lover offered more examples of men with stunted development: "The drug dealer, the ducking and diving political leader, the wife beater, the chronically crabby boss, the hot shot junior executive, the unfaithful husband, the company yes man, the indifferent graduate school advisor, the holier than thou minister, the gang member" and interestingly the therapist who attacks his clients' efforts to shine and achieve so he can impose upon them a grey mediocrity. These are all boys pretending to be men. Within the seduction community were further examples of stunted development: I'd add the perpetual-SNLing pick-up artist, and the manosphere "big baller troll" who posts comments about how awesome he is just to belittle the guys trying to improve.

Karl Jung had set out a schema of male archetypes, each channelling one of four types of masculine energy. The *king* can lead and impose order upon the world, telling people the way things are and should be. A modern example would be Donald Trump. The *warrior* seeks single-minded mastery of a skill in order to act directly upon the world. The *lover* possesses a carefree and joyful love for the pleasures of life. Lastly, the *magician* harbours a fascination for the hidden patterns that determine the subtext of the world. Jung had claimed each is a mature male archetype that is attractive to women. Moore & Gillette were contending that the natural process of boys maturing into these archetypes was disrupted by a lack of coming-of-age rituals.

I was, of course, fascinated.

"Jimmy, you should check out this book on Jung. It's really applicable to Game," I said, waving it in my hand as I stepped into his room. He was playing on an Xbox 360 he'd only just bought.

"What's it called?"

"*King Warrior Lover Magician.*"

"So it's not called *Mystery Method*?"

"No."

"Not interested. Everything is in *Mystery Method*."

I went back to my room, put some suitably cultured ambient music on YouTube, and continued exploring this fascinating world of Jungian psychology. Being scientifically-minded, I didn't take the book at face value. To me, it was a world of symbolism and metaphor. That, however, was what I wanted. I wanted meaning and context above cold hard facts. I'd read enough cognitive psychology at university and already binned it as pseudo-scientific bullshit.

Each of Jung's four adult male archetypes has a preceding 'boy' archetype that determines the final make-up of the mature male, should he make the ego-killing transition to 'man psychology'. In this sense the boy is the father of the man. The archetypes are:

- King: The Divine Child
- Warrior: The Hero
- Lover: The Oedipal Child
- Magician: The Precocious Child

These boy archetypes represent a balance between two extremes, or shadow sides, which boys need to tread carefully between. For example, the *Divine Child* is the baby of unlimited potential who is both almighty and vulnerable at the same time (such as the young Jesus). He is the source of life, energy and boyish wonderment at the world, producing our sense of well-being and enthusiasm for life. However when out of balance, he can become the *High Chair Tyrant*, sitting at the table banging his spoon and demanding the universe revolve around him and his insatiable desires. If the adults around him enable this dysfunctional behaviour it leads to inflation through pride, hubris, and narcissism. When such a tyrant is set loose upon the world as an immature adult we end up with Hitler, Stalin, or Obama. Less murderously, we get the *Wolf Of Wall Street* characters who would rather bankrupt a brokerage than deal with their own hubris and grandiosity. The seduction community is full of such boy tyrants, usually very good-looking men who attract women so easily they can mess them around and get laid without ever facing real-world consequences. At least until they hit thirty and a life of dissipation catches up with them.

The opposite extreme for the Divine Child is the *Weakling Prince*, a pathetic little boy with no personality, initiative or enthusiasm for life. This boy plays the act of sickly child who needs mollycoddled throughout life lest he break. It's all a false posture, as shown when he attacks those around him with sarcasm and passive-aggressiveness. He's exemplified by the liberal male feminist, the cuckservative, and the soyboy.

"You have strong King and Warrior energy," Colin told me, when I was still halfway through reading the book. "Not so much Lover or Magician though."

"I've always distrusted magicians," I replied. "As a kid reading *The Lord Of The Rings* I didn't like sorcerers. I didn't even trust Gandalf."

"And let me guess, you thought Lovers are big pufters?"

"Yep."

I was thus keen to read more into what Jung said about warriors. I liked the idea of being one of them. Hadn't I just thoroughly enjoyed myself with *God Of War 3* playing the role of Kratos, an avenging warrior? Now I came to think of it, he was killing all the gods in that game. If the game had been called *God of Love* or *God of Magic* I'd have never picked it off the shelf.

The balanced child archetype of the warrior is the *Hero*. He is bursting with the desire to achieve, to impress, and to become great. He provides the means to tap into our masculine energies and propel us from boyhood to adulthood. The book notes, "...ours is not the age for heroes. Ours is an age of envy, in which laziness and self-involvement are the rule. Anyone who tries to shine... is dragged back down by his lacklustre and self-appointed peers". As modern Western society shifts further into socialism and woe-is-me-ism the space for a hero to shine is cut down. This was helping me make sense of my own frustrated ambitions, at feeling like I wasn't allowed to spread my wings and pursue excellence, and conversely why I took so gladly to daygame and its intrinsic freedom. Daygame really suits the man who wants to wander free through the world and hone his skills.

My favourite novel during my twenties was Eiji Yoshikawa's *Mushashi*, about a lone swordsman wandering Japan seeking challenge and enlightenment in order to hone his craft and understand Bushido. My favourite short stories featured *Conan*, a warrior barbarian, freebooter, and pirate. Now I knew why they appealed to me so strongly.

When out of balance, the child of the warrior is commonly a *Grandstander Bully* who believes the centre stage belongs to him and he's going to rattle off display-after-display of unnecessary attention-whoring so everyone will applaud his brilliance. Think of Tom Cruise in *Top Gun*, or Muhammad Ali in everything. He's the jingoistic officer throwing his men into peril to earn his own Victoria Cross. The hero thinks himself invulnerable and chases the impossible dream. But once the hero has slain the dragon and rescued the princess he doesn't know how to live with her. At the other extreme is the *Coward*, a self-explanatory category.

I read up on lover and magician archetypes too, but they didn't apply so closely so I needn't labour the point with them here.

Working through Colin's homework list was teaching me a lot about myself. I'd sit with a highlighter pen, marking up passages that seemed to describe my worst excesses or greatest hidden potential. I'd already scored myself on the Myers-Briggs test as an INTJ, a self-identification that made it easier to direct my game efforts into avenues consistent with my personal disposition. The definition of INTJ seemed to explain exactly why I was drawn to daygame—It was solitary, one-on-one with the girl, and suffered few distractions. It allowed me to walk around alone with my thoughts until I met a girl and made a strong personal connection with her, using mostly words. Learning about Jung's male archetypes was furthering this self-knowledge. I'd been misdirecting my energies. My lack of lover energy explained why I was neither warm nor brimming with passion for life's hedonistic pleasures. My lack of magician energy explained why I was repelled by much of the manipulative side of game theory.

I possessed a very clear sense of what is, what should be, and a drive to perfect my skill in imposing this vision onto the word. I somewhat flattered myself that I was a Warrior King. I guessed that attitude would soon eliminate my fear of enlightenment.

Life sometimes throws you opportunities at the most fortuitous of times. At precisely the time I was sitting with Colin for these sessions, I'd begun to date a Russian catwalk model who was very firmly in the top tier of beautiful women. Our first date was immediately after our very first consultation. Let's turn our attention to how I met Zaria.

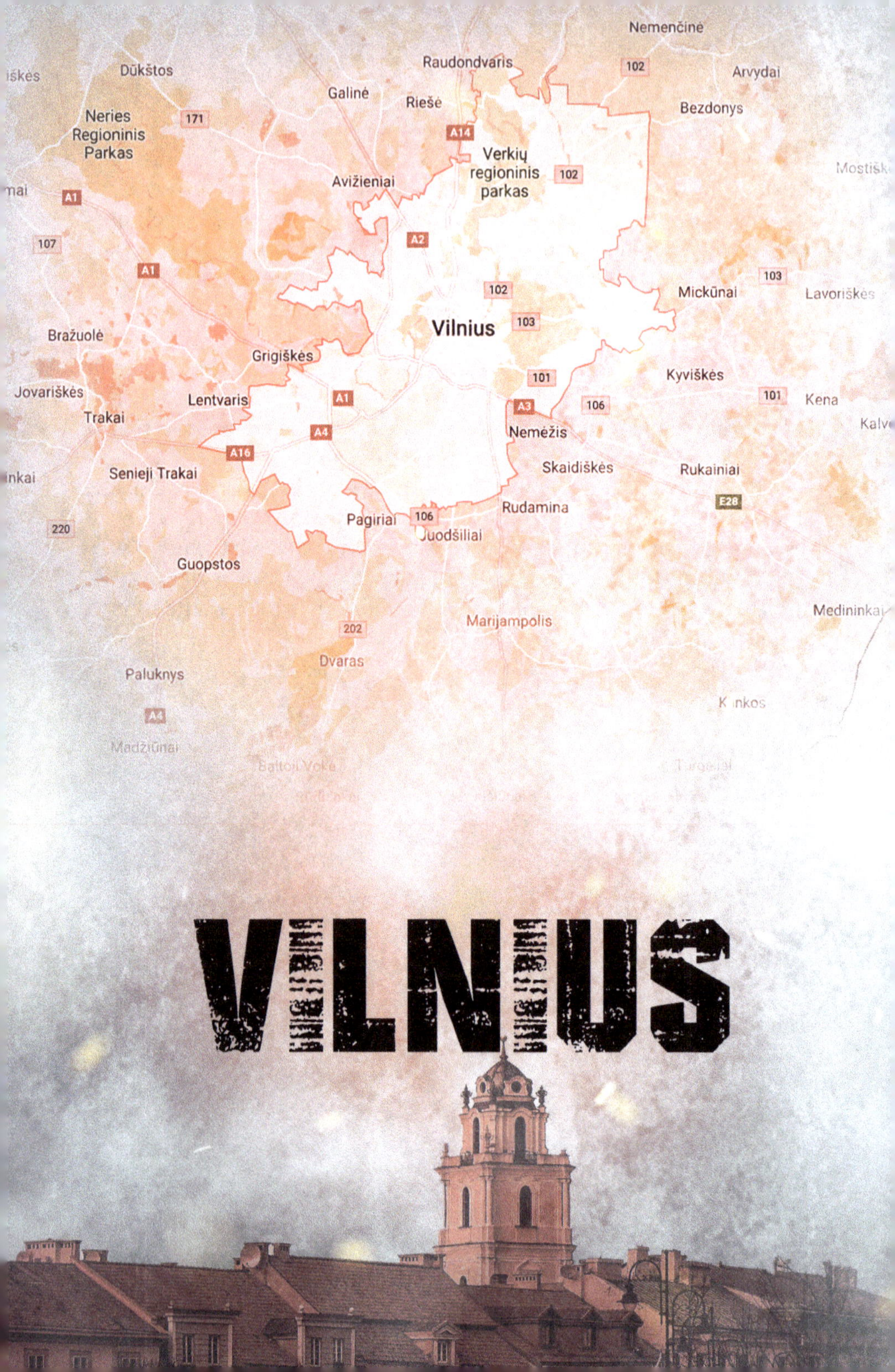

Nemenčinė
Dūkštos
Raudondvaris
102
Arvydai
Galinė
Riešė
Bezdonys
Neries Regioninis Parkas
171
A14
Verkių regioninis parkas
102
Avižieniai
A1
A2
107
A1
103
102
Mickūnai
Lavoriškės
Vilnius
103
Bražuolė
Grigiškės
101
Kyviškės
Jovariškės
A1
101
Kena
Lentvaris
A3
106
Trakai
A4
Nemėžis
A16
Skaidiškės
Senieji Trakai
Rukainiai
E28
Rudamina
220
Pagiriai
106
Juodšiliai
Guopstos
202
Marijampolis
Medininkai
Dvaras
Paluknys
A4
VILNIUS

CHAPTER 37

OPERATION BARBAROSSA

In October 2010, I was out at Piccadilly Circus with Jimmy and Fernando to record some infield videos for marketing purposes. Not much was going on all morning and the highlight was having some PR girls outside Thornton's thrust some free samples of strawberry chocolate into our hands. As we came to the big pedestrian crossing at Trocadero, I saw a Russian woman standing on the other side of the busy street. The familiar DNA-tug hit me. She was beautiful, like a gazelle. Tall and slim with super long legs. She was fashionably dressed in a short skirt and leather boots over black tights. She was the kind of girl who at that time I thought I didn't even have a chance with. A proper trophy girl with a truly imperious look. A genuine ten, I thought. I had never had anyone of her quality before and didn't believe myself worthy of it. She was at the top tier of "head-turner", a type of figure and manner that can't help but attract attention.

Sigh. I wanted her.

My first problem was a logistical one. She stood waiting on the opposite side of a busy crossing. Cars whizzed dangerously between us. If I waited for the traffic light to change then she would walk by as we crossed paths. If I opened her in the middle of the street while crossing, we'd be stranded before a building cavalcade of traffic. Waiting for her to come to be would be stalker-like. Hmmmm. What to do?

My spy camera was clipped to my t-shirt, from the day's earlier aborted attempts at filming. I had to make a fast decision, given that I wanted to talk to this girl. So, I handed Fernando the handheld camera and set off across the street dodging traffic. A few fast-moving cars came close to clipping me. The bystanders stood waiting to cross noticed and gave me quite an audience. The girl, however, was still not paying attention. She looked blankly into space in another direction. Upon reaching her I stepped up and mumbled some nonsense about her jumper being the same colour pink as the chocolate Fernando had been eating. She was a little taken-aback but would admit later to feeling an instinctive liking for me. We chatted for five minutes at the crossing. I remember being so nervous that a lot of my chatter was just babble, but Russian women do like directness, so that worked in my favour. It ended with me getting her Facebook information. I was proud of myself for approaching the type of girl that still intimidated me, although I still didn't think anything would come of it.

Her name was Zaria and she was twenty-nine years old. Originally from Tashkent, Uzbekistan, she had been picked by a talent scout and moved to Moscow at age fourteen to begin a career on the fashion runway. She'd spent quite a few years as a top-tier model in Russia and she identified as Russian. I was scheduled to go to Croatia for the first time that week and while I was there, I added her to Facebook and we messaged.

I was surprised when she answered me. I was timid in my messages because I didn't want to risk blowing it by being too pushy–precisely the wrong attitude. So I talked about things like travel and architecture in Croatia. Fortunately, that seemed to peak her interest. She told me that she loved architecture and waxed lyrical about her trips around the world. We didn't get sexual or intimate over the exchanges, but after eight long messages each she seemed interested enough for me to invite her onto a date. She agreed. That too was a surprise.

I distinctly remember the first date was immediately after my first session with Colin in late November. I told him on the way out, "I'm on my way to meet my first legit ten. I'm sure I'll fuck it up and complain about it to you in our next session."

Over the course of the first date Zaria opened up and told me a lot about herself. As you can imagine, working full-time at a high level of modelling she quickly drew rich admirers. At age eighteen she met a hot-shot politician and businessman from Italy with a lot of power, money, and prestige. He was fit and good-looking and he flew her First Class all over the world. She dated him for eight years, making him wait a full year before they had sex. He was her first lover. When she was in her mid-twenties she had tired of modelling and took a job teaching at a specialist catwalk finishing school in Moscow. Looking to set up a life after modelling, she'd then dumped the Italian and come to London to enrol in a Business Administration degree while taking photo-shoot work to cover the bills. Although a lovely girl, she had that top-model expectation that the world is her oyster.

She met another man in London, a hotel receptionist. Zaria told me later she found him really good-looking and something clicked for her right away. They dated for six months then broke up. He was her second lover. By the time I met her, she had been with precisely two men in her ten years since becoming sexually active, and had been without sex for three years. Looking at her, it was hard to believe. She had demonstrably high IQ, good classical education and high self-esteem. She read Russian literature, listened to classical music and always made time to spend with her family. She didn't fit the coke-snorting party girl archetype like a lot of young models. Quite the opposite, she was introverted and liked knitting and reading. It just seemed impossible to me that she wasn't already snapped up by a movie producer or hedge fund manager.

Within a few dates I figured out the reason. Zaria was what John would later term a "supply problem girl." This theory is based on the way evolution has hard-wired men and women for sex. Men will fuck anything, as long as a girl is at least average-looking and not too crazy. Women are more choosey for the simple reason that they have a limited number of big juicy eggs whereas men have literally billions of sperm to fertilize them. A woman's half of the reproduction puzzle is scarce, and the man's half is abundant. This central fact, extrapolated into various contexts, explains the entire history of sexual dimorphism and the structure of modern society. A woman's evolutionary job is to carefully marshal her limited fertility resources whereas a man's job is to spread the seed wide. If women mated indiscriminately, the human species would weaken until ultimately dying out. On the flip side of the coin, men are hard-wired to leave their DNA every chance they get. They set out to go forth and multiply. They can leave their DNA anywhere and walk away with a notch on their belt, moving on to the next conquest leaving the woman to endure the risks of pregnancy.

A woman is most fertile when she's young and this is when she's looking for a mate with perfect DNA. When women do get pregnant it puts them in a vulnerable state and makes them more dependent upon men. She's typically not going to put herself in this position, and take on these risks, unless she deems that the man's DNA is worthy. That's where the "No" mechanism comes in.

All women have a "No" mechanism. It's a lock that only certain keys can open. It's her default response, her fail-safe so she doesn't get impregnated with less-than-prime DNA. Men have a default "Yes" response of "if she offers it, I'm saying yes." As soon as a woman sexually matures in puberty, men start looking at her, hitting on her, and trying to fuck her. By the time she's in her early twenties she's already dealt with five or six years of subtle glances, direct looks and blatant come-ons. It's like a laptop coming under constant assault by viruses, or an email account attacked by spam. Each man develops his own strategy, his own attempt to breach the anti-virus defence. A university professor might attack by being her gentle teacher or intellectual mentor, pulling her mind into his world. Her neighbour might offer to move things for her or fix things around the house. She might meet the "bad boy" who's going to be a dick and try to get into her pants by being exciting and dangerous. The boss may offer a promotion with strings attached. The bottom line is always the same: men scheme and plot their way into a girl's panties while women try to rebuff everything until their filter allows the right man through.

The woman is like the immune system, fighting off all of these viruses attacking her at once. This is where the societal double standard comes in. If a woman says "Yes" to any and every offer she is branded a slut. If a man has sex and leaves his seed every chance he gets, the younger and more fertile women he fucks the better, he's done his job. He's deposited his DNA as he was meant to. So, technically, it is not a "double standard". It is the standard that nature intended for the perpetuation of the species.

There are three types of women, when it comes to the "No" mechanism. There are those with mechanisms that any key will open, meaning she doesn't say no often enough. These sexually-incontinent women are sluts. There are the women in the middle (most women), and then there are the women at the chaste end of the spectrum whose "No" mechanism is too tight and thus she rarely has sex.

The "No" mechanism complements a woman's need to be dominated. Women have an inherent need to be dominated by men, as the international success of *Fifty Shades Of Grey* proves, and Olivia made clear in an earlier chapter. The level of dominance needed varies across women and races. So Asian women will typically take fright at high dominance whereas black girls such as Aisha demand it as the entry requirement for her attention. The women with the broken "No" mechanisms that say no too often are usually either feminists, or girls like Zaria.

A charismatic and dominant male has a similar SMP position to a hot young girl: a scarce commodity in high demand from the opposite sex. Some women have a personality that requires high dominance but they are too fat or ugly to play at that level of the sexual market place. This creates a huge problem for them. The dominant man has no interest in these women, and the men lower down the totem pole who would date them lack the requisite dominance to turn them on. So the woman has an unfulfilled dominance need. It's not in her nature to lower her threshold of what she'll accept, because the whole reason she needs dominance is she's a wild horse that requires breaking. So these women go crazy. They'll often try to get attention by acting out, getting piercings or tattoos, or colouring and cutting their hair in weird ways. They are trying to signal to dominant men "come and break me" but the price of dominance they set is far higher than the market is willing to pay for their goods. Typically they retreat into feminism as an exhaust valve to let out all the pent-up sexual frustration, thrashing around wildly in an anger at something they can't understand. This simple mechanism explains why young feminists are universally bratty, rage-filled crazies with lots of self-inflicted damage to their bodies, and the older feminists are crazy cat ladies who've never held a marriage together.

That explains the unattractive girls with an excessively strong No mechanism. But what about the hot ones?

There are also girls like Zaria who are beautiful and well-balanced. She was tall, hot, intelligent, and fashionable. She had a stable family and high self-esteem. She was well-educated, well-travelled, and had already, in a sense, been with the perfect man at least once. Sometimes she'd been hired to sit in the background at billionaire yacht parties just to make the scenery look good. Zaria's problem was raw hypergamy — from her mid-teens she'd become intensely aware of her own value and required a man who was "above" her that she could thus look up to. When you're six feet tall, high IQ, affluent, and well-educated that pool of eligible men is very shallow indeed. She'd rather go without than to settle for anything less than a man meeting her precise specifications.

Zaria would tell me later what was going through her head the day we met.

"When you stopped me I just wanted the ground to swallow me up. I was late for a meeting and you were totally not the type of guy I like. I never like guys with pendant chains and rings. You seemed dumb."

Although she would also tell me I had a strong effect on her and that she was sexually attracted to me from the beginning, at that time she was ready to say no because of all of the above and that was how she approached men and sex. She'd say no first and never be around to ask questions later.

So, when I returned to London from Croatia, I went out for our date in front of Top Shop trembling with anticipation. I didn't really expect her to show up. I thought she would blow me off at the last minute. But show up she did and I despite wearing very little make-up, and bland clothes, she looked great. I took her to the Argyle Arms, an old English pub. We stood by the bar chatting over the first drink. Honestly and directly, she told me, "Your Facebook mails showed another side to you, when you spoke about travelling and how you enjoy the culture of Croatia. I thought maybe you are different to how you first looked. I wasn't really interested in having a date with you but it was a strange time in my life and I'd just decided to give up on a guy I liked a few days earlier."

I could feel her testing me. I was on the edge of failing. A few times she mentioned how nervous I seemed (very true) but I was trying hard not to show it. I suggested *Milk & Honey*, thinking this would impress her, obviously not thinking she had already spent a big part of her life living a high life that was stratospheric compared to what I could offer. It wasn't until two years later I'd really understand the importance of not mixing up lover and provider signals. I was trying to convey to her that I had a good job and a successful lifestyle.

That I was worthy.

We went upstairs to the Red Room lounge and sat on the sofa sipping drinks. I tried to kiss her a few times but she wasn't having it. She was still testing me, saying things like, "It seems like you're trying hard to impress me. I wish you could be yourself, you don't really seem happy with your life, and you seem to be trying to convey that you're more confident than you are." She told me I should stop putting on an act. Everything she said was freakishly accurate at that moment in my life. By the end of the night I thought I'd blown it, and would never see her again. Despondent, I walked her back to the station and tried one last roll of the dice. We stopped on the street outside a shuttered up Foot Locker store and I went in for a kiss, expecting her to resist again. Surprisingly she let it happen and after a grudging first few seconds her mood changed and she really went for it. She'd tell me later that she had already decided not to see me any more and my kiss had completely reversed her.

Zaria had many conflicting thoughts spinning in her head during the date. In later Skype chats she'd say, "I wasn't sexually attracted to you on the date. When you were touching me you seemed like all the other guys I've dated. I decided I was never going to see you again... When you showed me that private room upstairs in the jazz bar I wondered what it would be like to have sex with you there... When you kissed me at the end on Oxford Street something changed. I saw a different side to you, in your eyes. I've never felt that way before when I've been kissed. It was an incredible experience. In those six hours I feel we got to know each other better than people I've known for years. When I got home my friend asked me about the date and I said, "I want to have him.""

Of course, I didn't know any of this the first morning after the date. I told Colin the next day, "I fucked it up."

Fortunately, Zaria replied to my subsequent texts and agreed to a second date. This is why you should never over-think the success or failure of a date — you really have no idea what's in a girl's mind or what's going on in her life that impacts on her options. So long as the girl stays in contact and comes out on the next date, assume she's up for it. The medium is the message — you could even disregard her words and focus entirely upon the central fact that if she's responding to you, it's still on. We met again mid-afternoon, about a week later, at Caffé Nero in Covent Garden. I was still nervous and feeling unworthy even after I'd kissed her. I was again thinking she wasn't going to show... But she did.

Following the initial testing ground with Baharak, Zaria would be the girl with whom I discovered the potential of using my world-view as a seductive weapon. She hadn't liked the push-pull high energy approach that I typically used with other girls so I was running low on ideas, grasping at straws to maintain her interest. I happened to be reading Ludwig Von Mises' classic 1922 economics text *Socialism*. It was a critique of the intellectual apparatus that accompanies Marxism, a book without peer in intellectual achievement or prescience.

Zaria sat opposite me at a high table by the windows as we set upon our coffees. There was the usual how-was-your-day chit chat and then I went off on a tangent about the book. I was enthusiastic about it, the type of book where every page has a new idea I wanted to fix into my memory lest I forget it. My monologue began slowly at first, a few thoughts on enjoying old books for the difference in perspective to modern writers and how it's important to understand the prevailing conditions in which a book was written to understand why the author writes as he does. In Mises' case he began the book two years after the Bolshevik Revolution, when there was no historical record of socialism in action and reports out of the new Russia were unreliable. Thus he'd been forced to do a theoretical analysis and make predictions, rather than interpret an observable historical record. Zaria was engaged so I went off into talking about Aristotle and John Locke, biology and universal Darwinism, cultural meme theory and the evolution of mixed martial arts, weaving them into a seamless narrative. I was on fire and for about fifteen or twenty minutes I talked passionately about it all.

Ten minutes into my monologue I saw a moment, as clear as day, when Zaria decided she wanted to have sex with me. I could actually see the change in her eyes and body language. She was fascinated, leaning forward, eyes wide, stroking her coffee cup with her fingers while she listened to me. She would later confirm to me it was at that point that I had her. We kissed more that evening, and I left that date feeling so much better than the last one. I didn't doubt this time that I would see her again.

We walked around Camden market for our third date and as the sky darkened she invite her to a nightcap. It wasn't easy persuading her

"I want you to come back to my place," I said.

"I'm not having sex with you."

That seemed a rather abrupt re-interpretation of my words, though not inaccurate.

"Don't worry about that, I want you to see how I live."

"OK, but I'm not having sex."

"You don't have to do anything you're uncomfortable with."

She agreed, finally. It was already late and we arrived at Château Hampstead shortly before eleven o'clock at night, After a quick house tour I took her to my bedroom. I dimmed the lights and we drank wine and listened to music.

Despite her token protestations, Zaria was there for the taking. However, I still wasn't sharp in separating signal from noise. Her explicit statement to only accompany me home if we agreed not to have sex weighed heavily in my deliberations on how to proceed now that she was sitting on the edge of my bed.

I kept my distance, honouring our deal. Hardly my wisest escalation decision.

We stood up again while I poured wine. I put out my hand, grabbed her throat, and pushed her up against my wardrobe. Staring forcefully into her eyes, I reached over and picked up my wine glass. I took a long drink, like I was pondering what to do with her. Zaria's eyes took on the deer-in-headlight look. She gasped for breath–from excitement, not from the strength of my grip. I was intoxicated by the very fact she was there, in my bedroom. I kissed her hard and we ended up tumbling onto the bed. While fumbling around I managed to get my hand down her pants, fingering her as she lay on my bed moaning, squirming, and clawing at my shoulders. Looking at her, head thrown back, eyes-shut and mouth open in ecstasy, it felt surreal. I never thought I could get a girl like this, and here I was in my bedroom with my fingers knuckle-deep in her pussy.

I still didn't get to fuck her that night, though, failing to escalate smoothly. She took a taxi home an hour later.

Her student visa ran out in December 2010 and she went back to Uzbekistan for Christmas to see her family and to reapply for a new working visa. She had already told me she loved to sit and knit for hours at her family home in front of the fire, surrounded by the animals they raised. So, in keeping with the idea that if she's making something for you, she has to be thinking about you, I told her to knit me a sweater. She knitted me a really nice burgundy sweater. I still have it, wearing it on the colder winter days in Newcastle. We frequently chatted on Skype, and even had Skype sex. I got her masturbating and talking dirty to me. They were not video chats, but it was keeping the connection alive.

Colin had noticed I was still quite antagonistic towards women and tended to treat seduction more like a fight I had to win than a dance both sides could revel in. I'd built up thirty-four years of reference experiences that (a few minor hot streaks aside) I wasn't particularly good with women. My fifteen pre-game successes were more like lottery wins than hard-earned victories. I felt separate and apart from the world of hot women. They were something to be looked upon from afar, no closer to my grasp than the moon and stars. It hadn't really bothered me until now. Starting with my lifelong assumption that hot girls were unicorns, appearing in perfume advertisements or on the arms of a famous actors, it never occurred to me that I should have one in my life. I was just a teenager who went to the pub with his mates, got drunk, cracked on with reasonably pretty student girls and, once in a blue moon, banged one. It was Leonardo DiCaprio who got the Victoria Secrets models, not me. I was okay with that.

I wasn't ambitious. I wasn't aware ambition was even relevant with women. I assumed they just showed up willingly once you were rich and famous, and not until then.

Some lucky men, the so-called "naturals", have an opposite life experience. From an early age, they build up continuous positive reference experiences with girls. *Someone* gets to date the head cheerleader in college, after all. Even the smoking hot models who go on to date celebrities will begin their dating life with the cool kid in their school. A small band of men are those cool kids and thus their formative years forge an unbreakable connection in their minds between women and happiness. Naturals struggle to even conceive what life is like for a normal man. They can't imagine being invisible to women, fearing a bad reaction, being tooled by them, or to invest huge amounts of time and emotional energy only for a girl to say, "I'm not looking for a relationship right now" then immediately jump into the bed of a cool good-looking bad boy. Normal men see the bad side of women that naturals are oblivious to, because women never showed the natural that face — they were to busy trying to impress him and playing nice.

For the vast majority of men, university graduation changes everything. They are no longer even within the proximity of pretty women. University demographics and extended social circles keep young men and women around each other. Getting a real job destroys that. Most men progress through young adulthood with progressively smaller and less attractive social scenes.

If a boy reaching sexual maturity goes his next twenty years with merely intermittent and unremarkable success with women he will solidify and fossilise a web of unhelpful mindsets. I'd been lucky. I'd at least had one long happy relationship with a very hot girl, so I knew what it was like to win the love of a woman desired by other men. But, I'd never developed the natural's careless optimism that the next hot girl is always just around the next corner. When I got divorced, I thought that was the end of a satisfactory sex life.

I'd felt betrayed, lost and fearful. I transformed those emotions into anger.

Once I'd decided to 'get good with girls', I knew reading books about it, or to sitting on a therapist's couch, were not the answer.

The only way to really shake off bad experiences is to replace them with positive experiences. The streets were my therapy. Four girls in particular gave me priceless experiences that eventually dissolved my lingering antagonism and freed me to pursue women from a light, carefree love for them. Tasanee and Adele got the ball rolling. Both were adorably sweet. From them, I learned to enjoy basking in sweet young feminine energy. I realised I really could date girls in their sexual prime. Two other girls would reinforce the trend. Zaria helped a lot, but before continuing her story let's return to Dovile. She was the student I'd met in Vilnius in September, who'd been sitting waiting for her sister when I approached. We'd had a short chat on Facebook the same evening. For the next eight weeks, we chatted almost every night. I found her to be introverted and thoughtful, and that made for interesting conversations. Nonetheless, my primary motivation came from perusing her Facebook photos.

She was twenty years old and had amazing tits.

My long discussions with Dovile would dive deeper than the kind of superficial claptrap I'd had with Mafalda. We got to know each other. Dovile told me her hopes and worries. I realised much of my misunderstanding of women had come from projecting my own thoughts onto them, assuming they saw the world as I did. For example, I tended to only see a girl when she was in public, usually in bars and clubs. She may be dolled up, dressed to kill, and putting on her best front.

"She's well hot," I might comment to a friend, her high SMV obvious to all.

"Indeed. I'd love to fuck her," my friend might agree.

Looking around the bar, many other men may be eyeing her up. Should she choose to dance, several may attempt to show off and attract her attention. This would all confirm the working hypothesis: *she's a hot girl and everyone wants to fuck her*. That's obvious, and true, but it was my subsequent leap of logic that created misunderstanding.

"Her whole life must be awesome. She's probably dating the coolest man and going to the best parties," I'd instinctively assume. Why wouldn't she? She's in demand. There are all kinds of mistakes in this surmise. Let's consider a handful of them.

First, it ignores the big difference in sexual preferences between men and women. I could look at a girl and immediately know I wanted to bang her, and that banging is my highest priority. Every town has its sluts who think the same way, but I wasn't interested in *them*. Normal girls (the ones I wanted) usually prioritise emotional connection and stability over the hedonistic pleasure of casual sex. They want a boyfriend and usually feel bad if they succumb to temptation for a quick knee-trembler. Thus being in a nightclub full of men wanting to bang them wasn't anywhere near as valuable to a young woman as the equivalent in-demand scenario would be to a man, of having a club full of girls wanting to bang him. To think so is to project male priorities onto women.

Second, a young man's primary problem with women is to generate initial sexual interest. Most of the time, most girls aren't the slightest bit interested in him. Thus when he does have a couple of girls sniffing around, he's mightily pleased. By contrast, a young woman's primary problem is being overwhelmed by masses of low-quality interest she must fend off, while attempting to filter for the considerably rarer high-quality interest. That woman in the club might have thirty men eyeing her up but she says to her friend, sincerely, "there are no men in here."

Third, as bright as young women shine in their peak, the bloom soon comes off the rose. It is as though every girl, on her sixteenth birthday, is given ten million dollars. She must carefully manage it to set herself up for life. No-one advises her how to invest it. For years she's swarmed with grifters attempting to steal it, and once it's gone it is gone forever. A normal man standing at the bar, invisible to girls, may grumble that "girls have it easy." That's true, they do — for about eight years. Then it grows increasingly difficult for them. So long as we men only look at the hot girls in their prime, we are oblivious to all the *formerly*-hot girls who now struggle.

Until talking to Dovile, I didn't much think about these things. I looked at girls and thought life was still a little unfair that sex came to them but didn't come to me.

Hot though Dovile was, she did not live in a penthouse apartment over-looking the sea, nor did she party all weekend at the hippest joints — like the internet told me hot girls did. She lived in a grotty Soviet-era studio apartment with her family. There was one real bed where her parents slept, and a pull-out couch she shared with her older sister. There was also a tiny kitchen and shower. From a male perspective, Dovile was very high value: young, buxom, and kind-hearted. From her own perspective, however, she was a regular girl with a boring life. She'd write later, "I lived a tedious life and Nick was the one shining glitters across the river. And step-by-step I'm running into the river trying to reach out and find out if it is really what it seems when viewed from a distance." She had been dating the same boy since she was fifteen, studied hard at university, and didn't know what she wanted to do after graduation. Her only foreign trip was a school excursion to Italy.

"How old are you?" she asked, on Facebook messenger.

"I'm too old for you. Or maybe you're too young for me. Will you have to order juice to my wine when I take you out?"

I hammered the frame that she was just a kid which seemed to spur her on to convince me that she wasn't. Much later she'd tell me our late night chats had become the highlight of her day. It had given her something to look forward to, and a glimmer of excitement she had been lacking. I really underestimated how quickly and strongly she'd hooked. I still couldn't believe such a hot girl in her prime would develop sexual interest in me so easily. The thing is, girls can sit on the fence forever, soaking up free attention. I was investing lots of my time in these late-night chats so I wanted to know they held at least some potential. That meant I needed to express my intention and escalate.

"Your photos on Facebook are nice. I like them. But I prefer sexy to nice."

"What do you mean?"

"I want to see a sexy photo of you."

"Oh my! I don't have any. I'm shy." This was not a censure, I noted.

"I'd like to see you naked. I'm sure you look good."

"No!"

A week later she sent me a few tame topless shots with her face cropped out. Her body was incredible. Back in Vilnius the day we met, she'd been sitting down and wrapped up in a thick coat and muffler. I'd never had a good chance to check her out. When these new photos arrived, I saw her full firm tits, flat stomach, and amazing ass. It would be a contravention of my human rights if I never got to bang her.

"Oh, I like them," I said.

"Thank you. I'm not so special, I think."

She'd taken them just for me, in the main living room, when her family was out. It was obvious to me she was hot, so it surprised me she couldn't just look in the mirror and reach the same conclusion.

Importantly, she'd gotten off the fence. There was now no doubt which direction our interaction was leading. The suspense was in whether it would get all the way to the end of that line. Dovile was fully invested in our chats and over the next month she sent a dozen tasteful-but-topless photos of her from three different selfie-sessions, clearly enjoying the salacious secret we shared. Logistics were the next bridge to cross.

"Come to London," I said. "It's the greatest city on earth."

That was a lie- Newcastle is. I try not to lie to women but this is a special case.

"I can't. My parents won't let me. And my boyfriend will want to know why I'm going."

"Don't tell them."

"No, it's not possible. I'm interested to see you, but I'm too frightened."

It seemed another milestone had been passed — a tacit agreement to meet at some time in the near future, on a romantic basis. She wasn't blocking my advance, merely slowing it. I rose from my chair and knocked on Jimmy's door.

"Enter!" he shouted. I walked in. He was still playing on the Xbox360, *Red Dead Redemption*.

"Do you fancy going back to Vilnius after Christmas?"

"Sure. I like it. A city full of Audreys. I'm in." He hadn't even paused to think about it.

I returned to my laptop and sat down. Then I got up again, poured myself a double whiskey, and sat down once again. "Jimmy and I will visit Vilnius in January." It was now mid-December.

"Oh," she said. I'd expected a bit more than that.

"I tell you I'm coming all the way back to Lithuania and all you say is, "Oh?"
"I just didn't realize you were coming so soon,"
It was a lot of pressure for her. She still had a boyfriend and before I had come along her entire life had been mapped out before her — graduate, marry, half-assed job, get pregnant, turn into her mother. Now things were becoming real. I was no longer just a mysterious stranger at a safe distance on the other end of a text chat. I didn't press her for an answer. We moved onto other topics.

"What do you think a woman wants in a man?" she asked me.

I parroted back Colin's Harmony Model, explaining hard and soft dominance. Then I pulled Aubrey Andelin's *Man Of Steel And Velvet* from my bookshelf and typed some quotes from that. Dovile was fascinated and probed me all night with questions, sharing her thoughts.

"I don't want to start to feel anything more than I feel now. I don't want to suffer afterwards," she wrote.

It was the first time she had overtly mentioned her feelings for me. My goal had always been *get her interested enough that she'll bang, at least one time*. Dovile was well past that stage and imagining how she'd feel afterwards.

"I'm not going to let you fall in love with me. I'm just going to show you a very good time, lots of fantastic memories and teach you about yourself and the world. I want to help you learn about men so that you avoid the mistakes most girls make."

That learning would, however, require her making one mistake — with me.

I future-projected what we could do while I was in Vilnius. "If you cook for me and I like it I'll give you a kiss."

She soon agreed we'd meet. "I think we cannot go out to cafes or bars. Vilnius is a small city. People may see us."

"Jimmy and I rent an apartment with a good lounge."

Dovile had her normal public face and stable boyfriend but evidently felt constrained. I'd driven a splinter into her brain, a sense that she was missing out. Her resistance was weakening. The urge for adventure can be sublimated, into reading *Fifty Shades Of Grey* or dancing like a tart in a nightclub one night, but young adults eventually want some of the real thing. Everyone finds a way to indulge their dark side. It had taken me a couple of months to nurture Dovile's adventurous side, by small increments. Discretion was key. When the cost to a girl of cheating with you drops to zero, the odds of her doing so shoot up. She'd later show me a diary entry discussing her anticipation: "So day after day was coming to our meeting... I could not stop thinking about it. My thoughts constantly revolved around it and my boyfriend was only the background. I had never been embroiled in any such intrigues. It was our secret mission."

I dare say I was equally excited.

Jimmy and I arrived in Lithuania around noon, scheduled for a week's stay in a comfortable apartment in the Old Town, in a street behind Salento nightclub. Snow piled up on the roadside, right up to the windowsills of nearby houses. Dovile agreed to come around to the flat at seven that first evening. Jimmy and I were unprepared for the cold winter. Temperatures reached as low as minus ten. Initially, Jimmy wore his coat, gloves and woolly hat indoors as we struggled with the thermostat, rejoicing when the familiar whoosh of the boiler firing up told us hot water was flowing into the radiators. Frost patterned the outer windows and as I peered onto the streets, they were deserted. An occasional car skidded slowly along the black ice.

The intercom buzzed at half past six, while I was showering. Dovile's husky voice announced her early arrival. It was thrilling to hear. Up until she arrived, I hadn't been sure the trip would be worth the effort. Certainly there'd be few opportunities for daygame on the deserted streets.

It was too cold to leave her on the door step while I dressed, so I buzzed her up and answered the door with a towel around my waist. It was still holiday season and she had been out with her friends for a beer to fortify her nerves before coming over. Nervousness was apparent in her tightly-controlled facial expression and careful timid movements. Twenty years old and alone in a strange foreign man's apartment (a man she had only met once face-to-face), that had to provoke anxiety, so I admired her determination.

"It's nice to see you again," I said, and gave way to let her into the hallway, where she struggled out of her boots and long coat.

"Hello," she said, shyly.

"Eh up, hello there!" Jimmy shouted from the kitchen, where he was eating a packet of chocolate biscuits and warming his hands over the hob.

"Take a seat in the lounge and I'll be dressed in a couple of minutes," I said.

Five minutes later I rejoined her in the lounge. Tension crackled, but of the awkward, not sexual, kind. Dovile showed me a bag full of food. Cooking gave us a shared activity to busy ourselves with as a distraction from the lack of spoken communication, a dodge I'd learned with Makiko the Japanese girl. Dovile's English was poor and conversation remained stilted even after she'd visibly relaxed. I remained on the fringe of her cooking activity, saying the occasional word, peering over her shoulder into the pot, and having a chat with Jimmy who sat at the kitchen table.

He'd gone through the whole packet of biscuits already and crumbs were strewn everywhere.

"Couldn't help it," he lamented. "I knew you're cooking but this cold makes a man hungry."

We sat together around the small square table and ate meat stew over boiled potatoes then I helped Dovile wash up. We repaired to the lounge and Jimmy made himself scarce. There was now real tension in the air. Just the two of us, alone, standing a few inches apart in the middle of the lounge. She was waiting to see what I'd do next. Electricity crackled.

"Remember I told you, what I'd do if I liked your cooking?" I asked.

Dovile rocked backwards slightly, her legs shaking with anticipation, "Yes, did you like it?"

"I did, it was very good."

Then I tilted her chin up and kissed her. It was a symbolic affirmation of our burgeoning illicit affair. I didn't push her hard, and disengaged after a few seconds. We lay on the sofa watching movies on my laptop, intermittently kissing and making out. It was slow going, due to Dovile's reticence. By the time she left an hour later, I'd done little more than grope her tits. I saw her to the door and she walked off to the bus-stop. I'd have accompanied her but we were both mindful of discretion, to not be seen together in public. I wasn't worried by the slow pace. Just having her show up, cook, and kiss meant the plan was coming along very nicely.

Her tits had felt just as good as they looked.

"I'm friggin' knackered, I am," said Jimmy as he heard the front door close and wandered out of his bedroom. "That travel and cold has knocked me out."

"Let's have an early night. I won't see Dovile 'till tomorrow evening and we'd best recover for a walkabout tomorrow afternoon."

That plan was soon scuppered when Dovile texted at midnight to invite us to Salento nightclub, mere minutes away from our apartment. She'd returned to her friends and they planned to go on to the club and dance.

"What do you think?" I asked Jimmy, showing him the message.

"I'm shagged out but we are on holiday, aren't we? Can always sleep in tomorrow morning."

"But what about the game aspect? What's the smart play?"

"Nothing to lose, I'd say. She's inviting you out. She wants to see you again. So soon after the meal, that's a good thing. It's likely she wants her friends to see you and pass judgement."

Rock Solid Game practised a type of "rat pack" nightgame that works well for coordinated groups. We'd roll in as a team, ignore everyone else, and make a big noise amongst ourselves for long enough that all the girls noticed we're more lively than the other thirsty, unhappy men there. Then we'd gradually draw girls in, pawning off the less attractive ones, and get everyone reacting to us. Done properly over the course of an hour or two, we'd be the buzzing centre of attention in the club and the girls wanted in on the party-within-a-party. Jimmy had been doing that since university: make a splash, see who is up for it, take her home.

In reality, it was hit and miss. What I liked was even that the misses were fun nights.

Despite lacking a full-strength gang, Jimmy and I were not to be daunted. We rolled in to Salento and down the main stairs, cut right through the dance floor between dancing girls, and posted up at the centre of the bar. We talked amongst ourselves, pulled nearby girls into the conversation, guffawed and gestured like the happily self-absorbed buffoons we pretended to be. I had already spotted Dovile out of the corner of my eye, dancing with a friend near the edge of the dance floor. Jimmy and I became increasingly jolly, loud, and buzzing with fun energy. That's magnetic in a club because almost every other man is having a bad time.

At first, I didn't let on to Dovile that I'd noticed her but eventually we shared some eye-coding that let her know I was watching but understood discretion. A couple of drinks later, Dovile came over and said hello, before skipping off back to her friends. That confirmed in my mind she was either proudly showing us off, or seeking a second opinion. Jimmy and I soon tired and went home to crash out. I'd not exchanged more than a brief hello with Dovile all night, which was precisely the right way of building the larger-than-life narrative. I knew how important mystery and excitement was for her, so I played along.

The next evening, Dovile and I watched another movie in the lounge. We made out more, and after some coaxing she stripped to her panties. My eyes almost popped out of my head. Raw animal lust coursed through my veins as I ran my hands along her youthful curves, totally intoxicated. I felt like Jimmy Saville in a kid's hospital. The rest of the world disappeared. There was hot nubile flesh writhing in front of me and nothing else mattered. I hooked my thumbs into her waistband and began pulling her panties down. There was the tell-tale lift as she pushed her hips up to create space between her ass and the sofa cushion. She wanted it. Then her phone rang. It was her boyfriend and, as she sat almost naked in my lap, she talked to him in her silly language for a few minutes. The bubble had popped and her panties went back on.

A pattern was developing. Jimmy and I would wake up late, then sit next to the radiators all morning until hunger drove us out to lunch. We'd make a half-assed attempt to daygame. I got a few numbers and idates, the most memorable with a nineteen year old art student called Auguste. Then the sky would darken and Dovile would come around again. On day three the canoodling got as far as my hands down her panties before I hit the next roadblock. It was slow going but I didn't doubt the eventual conclusion and, frustration and impatience aside, it made the whole experience quite sweet.

Dovile was busy the next two days for a family gathering, a birthday party for her aunt. Her whole family would be there. Her boyfriend had driven into town so I can only guess the cocktail of emotions that stirred up. It's tempting for aspiring players to misunderstand the nature of the Secret Society. Girls have the hard-wired capacity (need, even) to cheat but that doesn't mean they feel good about doing it. Listen carefully to how girls describe their sexual responses. They'll often talk about being drawn to the bad boys against their better judgement. They'll express regret at their illicit affairs like a fatty does after scoffing a bucket of Ben & Jerry's ice cream. These are not simply rationalisations for bad behaviour. Their conscious mind — the "me" that forms their identity — is like a monkey riding an elephant. The rider can nudge and direct but it's never in control of their base impulses in the way Ayrton Senna was of his McClaren race car. The whole point of Game is to hijack those impulses and coax her along towards sex.

I was beginning to appreciate women's sexual dilemma. All is fair in love and war.

On the evening of day six, Dovile brought her best friend Austeja as a cooking buddy. Jimmy was licking his lips eagerly at more free food and tried it on a bit with Austeja but her stilted English made it a slog to get rapport going. She obviously fancied him and enjoyed the attention, but it was practically impossible to surmount the language barrier and we suspected she probably wasn't amenable to casual sex. Jimmy never got his jollies but he stayed on-point with the mission of Get Nick Laid. Austeja went home after dinner, willingly leaving Dovile in my grubby sweaty hands, so I knew something was going to happen. Describing that night later in her diary, Dovile wrote, "The hour has come when I am left with Nick and the two of us we knew what will happen tonight or not."

I took her hand and led her, without resistance, up the spiral staircase from the lounge to my room. At the top of the stairs I pushed her against the wardrobe, forcefully and dominant, and kissed her. It was another memory that would stick with me, and Dovile, too, as she wrote about it, "A climb, it brings me to nail down the wall and pressed a passionate kiss. The strong hands held me tight, I felt his masculine energy, I felt that he was not afraid to be the one it is, I felt safe, like what Hercules embrace. I have never before been to me nothing so powerfully embraced, I could even say that it was quite rude, but... gently rude."

We laid on my bed and undressed, slowly. Dovile had plenty of time to back out but, nerves be damned, she was determined to stay. Sensing her mind made up, I laid on my back with my arm around her and waited, wanting her to come to me. Her face was a picture, like a child struggling with a difficult maths problem. At one point she sat up with a pensive look. She was quiet and thoughtful for a minute and then said, "I'm such a bad girl."

"Why?" I asked. She didn't respond. "Tell me."

"I left my boyfriend at home with my parents. They're watching television together now. He's angry. He doesn't know where I went." I didn't say anything to that. She continued, "I also forgot to log out of my Facebook. I hope he doesn't see our messages."

"So are you staying the night?"

She didn't really answer that. After an hour of fooling around under the duvet she finally overcame her doubts and let me fuck her. She was tense throughout and never completely relaxed but it was good sex simply because she was so hot and the tension had been building for so long. We lay back, satisfied.

A few minutes passed as Dovile stared at the ceiling. Finally, she spoke. "Okay, you got me."

"What?" I said, taken aback.

"I'm another one of your victories."

At first I had thought she said *victims*, but it was her accent confusing me. She spent the night and we had sex again before she left. There was nothing slutty or dishonest about Dovile. I was only the second man to fuck her. She would write later on about her decision to move forward with me: "Here and there I remembered the well-known saying-better to regret what I've done than the fact that I did not."

I certainly didn't regret what I'd done.

Jimmy and I flew back to London that afternoon and I continued to chat with Dovile on Facebook. I wanted to see her often, but that would mean returning to Lithuania or persuading her to visit London. One morning, she opened our regular chat by pasting a link to my blog. In particular, to the lay report, *I Bang My First 21 Year Old Lithuanian Painter*. It had her photo on it, as this was before I stripped all such pictures from my blog and instead posted look-a-likes. It was a jarring lesson in the need for discretion and to respect privacy.

When the realisation first dawned that she'd discovered my PUA identity, I felt cold sweats. How should I reply? The clock was ticking because the longer I waited to reply, the more obvious it would look that I was spinning a yarn. I reasoned that I should hold my frame and let the steam come out of her ears.

"Oh sorry!" I wrote. "I thought I'd taken down the photo."

I held the frame on being a pick up artist and blogger, not allowing any chink in my armour on that. It was brass-necking, but what else was there to say? I conceded ground on the photos and took them down, and apologised for the indiscretion. Dovile didn't seem particularly annoyed, beyond the first moments. When she finally calmed down we returned to our regular late night chats.

She began sending more sexy and increasingly bold photos. I was the canvas upon which she painted the new direction of her life, evaluating her limited horizons and deciding she wanted them broadened. In February she explained the Erasmus Program at her university would give her a chance to visit London. Erasmus is a European Union student exchange program that allows students from poorer EU countries to do internships with a business in another country while also attending school. Like all EU programs, its primary goal is to dilute the identity of the European nations and thus reduce opposition to a satanic totalitarian global government. Aleister Crowley, famed Satanist, proclaimed "do what they wilt shall be the whole of the law." I could live with that, so the EU and myself entered into a temporary truce. They'd cover Dovile's costs to stay in London, and thus help me bang her more.

One program requirements is to find an employer willing to sign on as a sponsor and host for the internship. Erasmus paid all of the expenses and provided a monthly stipend, so the employer got three months of free labour, a sweet deal. I asked Perry, the RSG guy also living in Château Hampstead. He worked as a hairdresser to high class fashion industry clients and was looking to open his own salon with his friend Bogdan. I told them Dovile and her friend Ugne were looking for any chance to get to London and they'd be willing to help set up the salon in return for official sponsorship. Perry was enthusiastic about getting something for nothing and swiftly agreed. I handled all the documents until Erasmus gave the girls the all-important confirmation letter. So it was on. The girls would arrive in April.

Dovile moves to London

Ugne added me to her Facebook. I think she wanted to get to know me and give me a stamp of approval before they came out. Dovile told me later she'd told Ugne we'd had a little affair but denied we'd had sex. Ugne and I chatted so I could ease her nerves, but there was no flirting. I dislike men who use provider-type schemes to meet and attract women, such as Couchsurfing or offering girls jobs. I kept as far away from the Erasmus program and salon business as possible, merely facilitating the paperwork. It turned my stomach to position myself as a provider chump trying to weasel into a girl's panties through cash transfers. I'd already banged Dovile for free. I wanted her to continue to see me as the Lover. However, I had no problem providing a little help to a girl I'd already banged for free. It just showed Dovile I liked her.

I really did like Dovile. She inspired in me the kind of noble feelings I hadn't had since dating Tasanee and Adele. I looked forward to spending time doing normal relationship things — walking in the park, going out for dinner, sharing a bond of affection as well as of lust.

Lust was the main thing, though.

Château Hampstead had five spare guest rooms and we typically had friends visiting for days at a time. I spent two days redecorating a large double room on the ground floor, outfitting it with new curtains, bed sheets, and wall art to match the new lick of paint. I told the girls they could stay there for two weeks while they house-hunted in London. After that, it became a waiting game, crossing off the days in my calendar until April.

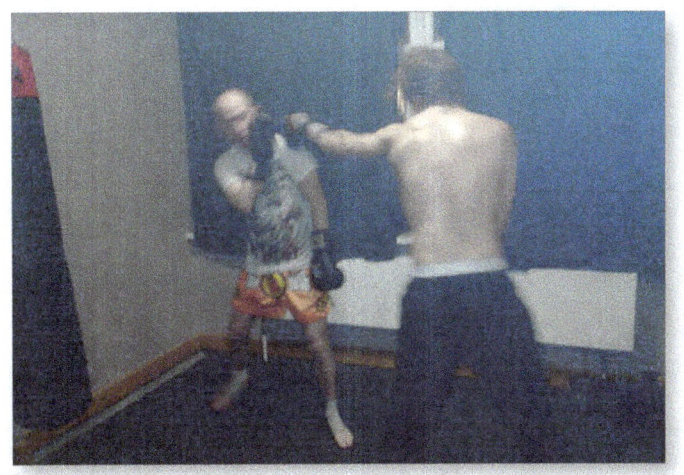

Sparring Lee in the Chateau gym

Visiting Vilnius again

CHAPTER 38

DEPRAVED

CHAPTER 38

DEPRAVED

While my time with Dovile made me feel like the hero in a Disney cartoon, I was still furiously plowing the sordid and squalid furrows of the sexual market place. In late 2010, I was walking near Trafalgar Square when I noticed a hot twenty-year old English girl walk by quickly as she ate a sandwich. She had flowing brown tresses with a light curl, and wore tight black leggings. I rushed up and got in front of her as she crossed the street to a traffic island.

"Excuse me, woman."

That stopped her, and she gave an expression suggestive of both pleasure and shock.

"Right then, you speak English?"

"I am English," she retorted, still not quite sure what game was afoot.

"Great. Then I can be very clear. I like your ass." Her eyes opened wide. "But you eat that sandwich like a savage."

"You just said you like my ass! Like, almost the first thing you said!"

"I was going to say you walk slutty, so I think I picked the more gentlemanly compliment of the two."

We shared a nice ten minutes of banter, and she responded well, but it never quite seemed to be going anywhere. Nonetheless, she gave me her number and I followed up the next day.

"So is this Olivia? The kinda cute but kinda feisty girl who owes Nick a coffee (white Americano, no sugar)"

"Do I look like a girl who buys men drinks?"

"No. Just mine."

"You are so insane." I took that as a good sign.

"Uh-huh. I'm on my way out now. Talk soon. I'm thinking Saturday afternoon, about 5pm. Be a good girl and say "yay!""

"I'm not a good girl and maybe I'll discuss with my boyfriend then see. ur outrageous."

"Cool."

That was in keeping with the tenor of our previous conversation on the street, where she liked me but wasn't willing to let things go anywhere. Nothing happened and she didn't respond to my next two messages. I dropped it, and focused on likelier leads. In late January 2011, after returning from Lithuania, I'd had a moment of inspiration to create a new "recovery text", meaning a generic message to spam all the dead leads in my phone. I browsed through the contacts of my phone and sent it to a half-dozen girls. Olivia was the only girl to respond.

"You just invaded my dream. I can't even remember what you look like. That's totally not fair," I wrote.

"Sorry who is this? I don't have this number saved…"

That was not an auspicious start. I didn't reply for two hours, to let her stew in the off-chance she was intrigued. Surprisingly, she followed it up.

"?? Come on I am so curious now I don't have this number in my phone."

"Don't worry about it, you barely know me ;)"

"It doesn't matter if I barely know you then how do you have my number?"

"You liked me so you gave it to me. I don't think you do that often to strangers."

"I don't… So where did I meet u? If u have forgotten my face it had to have been long ago right?"

"Just a few weeks ago. We were both stone cold sober. I might not remember your face, but I do remember meeting. Dunno your excuse…"

I was having fun, stringing it out and playing with her curiosity. I figured that as soon as she connected the chat to me, she'd lose interest again.

"It would be helpful if u gave me your name or where we met and then I will remember... come on if u waited 2 weeks to text or something what do you expect? I am fairly sure I remember you but I changed phones so my sim lost you... are you the sandwich compliment man who chased me down outside costa?"

I didn't especially like the label she'd pinned to me. Sandwich Compliment Man seemed only one rank above being the Drinking Own Piss Man or some-such.

"Not sure about a sandwich. I think I complimented your arse or your walk."

"Sandwich complimenting! U complimented them in an offensive way!"

"Offensive? Yeah right... Little Miss Innocent now, are you?"

"Of course! I was raised Catholic ;) I think using the word slutty was a bit much..."

I was beginning to sense that Olivia enjoyed chatting to me, and perhaps there was more than met the eye. "So should I apologise and do some Hail Mary's?"

"I could def use some form of grovelling right now... bad dayyy. Maybe explain what I was doing in ur dream"

Okay, I definitely felt a hook point. I had to think this one through, trying to decide whether to make the non-existent dream tame, sexual, or fantastical. I wanted to interest her but didn't want to spin my wheels entertaining a girl in the friend-zone. Perhaps piquing her indignation would help, as she'd responded well to that strategy previously.

"It wasn't sexual. Well, not very... You were sort of a cameo character in the background. I don't remember the details—you know how dreams are—but somehow it was definitely you."

"How... flattering?"

"Oh, I like you Olivia. But I don't control my subconscious. Why's your day so bad?"

There, I'd put my intent out. The ball was in Olivia's court, to friend-zone me or to give me space to work.

"Oh god its an old cliche to be honest... 'my boyfriend and I broke up' blah blah blah. But you know... new day, new start"

"Boo, that sucks :/ Does your breakup recovery plan involve chocolate and wine?"

"No because that will lead to weight gain and me feeling even worse!! My breakup plan involves fruit and cocktails. Lol I don't know I don't have a breakup plan I am not organized enough."

"If I was proper shifty, I'd be looking to pounce during your window of emotional vulnerability right now...."

"'If'??!! Anyway sadly for anyone thinking that, break ups make me toughen up."

"Ok, I'm shifty.... Unburden yourself on your girl friends for a few days (I'm a bad listener), then we'll do something together"

"Hahahahahahahahahahaah ok"

I figured I'd given a good account of myself, considering how tenuous a lead Olivia was. Perhaps I'd simply caught her at the right time to chat to a stranger. She wouldn't quite commit to a date so by February 2011 I was once more resigned to writing her off as a no-go. It was snowing outside and I hadn't gotten any new leads that week. Having nothing to do all evening, I texted her out of the blue late one night, the first time in a fortnight.

"Haven't been drunk in two weeks. You must be missing the texts"

"Drunk now I take it?" she responded, quickly.

"Nope. Just being filthy on Facebook chat and I thought of you." I wanted to get to the point quickly, so didn't mind if I over-escalated. To me, anything happening with Olivia was just found money anyways.

"Wonderful! :) how r u anyway?"

So far she was cheerful and engaging. I persevered. By now I was lying flat on a sofa in the Château cinema room, with a can of beer at my feet. "Doing great. Been back in the gym so I'm fit as a fiddle. How come your Facebook updates always make you look like a nutjob?"

"Lolllllll because I am a nutjob!!!!!!!"

"I'm now officially wary of you."

"Why what in particular freaked u out?"

"*Sex and the City*. I always screen girls out on that. Doesn't matter how tight their ass is." She'd posted a quote from the popular TV show, denigrating men, and expressed approval of it.

"I do hate sex and the city for many reasons. I abhor the films. But sometimes when I hate men, it cheers me up."

"Ok, you've earned a reprieve. While we're on the subject, is your ass actually tight? (I mean, the butt-cheeks, not the anal sex fit) I only got a glimpse, after all....."

This was quite far beyond my usual escalation, and of quite the opposite tone I'd used on Facebook when first messaging Dovile. My appetite for boldness came entirely from the fact I expected nothing to ever happen with Olivia. The opportunity cost of pushing the envelope was zero.

"It's a beautiful ass. Of course. But then again I am biased."

"How about the tits? They showed promise, but again I've not really had a good look"

"You are terrible. I will tell you that I have been blessed in the three areas men care about most — legs, ass, breasts, but anyway, moving on.... how are tricks?"

"I'm a man talking to a woman. It's the most natural thing in the world. Anyway, about me.... I'm off to Latvia next week with friends. Starting to get excited. You strike me as a vacation skier." I said that because it was clear she was from a posh upper-middle class family.

"I totally am! U keep jet setting around!"

"Since June 2010 I decided I will do only those things that interest me and not give a fuck. Grab every opportunity. Make my life a hell of a story for when I'm aged seventy as a washed up drunk in a Jamaican beach-front dive bar."

An hour passed. I was now sitting upright in the cinema room, half watching a James Bond movie while picking at a plate of pasta. It was dark and most of my housemates had gone to bed. I was horny and in the mood for pushing things. Damn the consequences. My phone vibrated and I saw Olivia was back.

"Why did u suddenly decide that? What happened to u?"

"Oh, you're alive again?" I wanted to keep pushing her, showing backbone.

"Was on the phone to an admirer..."

"Sorry to interrupt you princess. Are you cadging free meals and rides from the office boys?"

"Absolutely not! And I can't believe u used the word cadge! Ha!! Anyway answer my question"

"I don't believe you. You totally have the airs and graces of a girl who tools the beta boys to get a little army of orbiters to validate the princesses ego. You dirty dog you."

"I used to be like that! But since I had my heart broken repeatedly by the same cunt and had it smashed around and then began to piece it back together only for him to swoop in a slide it around on the floor again.... well, I kind of stopped being a girl with an ego and became someone a little fragile and cynical. Oopsies. I also never used to drop the c-bomb. But I am sorry, he does not deserve any other word."

"Is this where the "I hate men" thing came from?" I asked, realising the inspiration for her *Sex And The City* Facebook post. "Actually, I can relate to that but usually I was the heartbreaker. I'm not bragging in some power trip, I'm actually quite ashamed of it. C-bomb indeed. I try not to use the F-word, the B-word, or cunt."

"Lol yes, I am usually the heartbreaker too!!! I understand. And now it has happened to me I am a bit more contrite about my horrific abusive behaviour. Yes, the I hate men came up when that cunt and I tried to maintain a friendship when the dust settled and he felt the need to brag about shagging hookers. Cunt. I enjoy swearing. Used to never ever do it, but now it amuses me."

"Shagging hookers is so lame. That's what losers do when they can't get it for free. Ugh. I hope you were disgusted, rather than jealous. Swear away, but try to keep it thematically relevant, well timed, and above all creative. I have standards."

She was replying so fast now that her follow-up messages would come in while I was still typing my replies. We'd gotten quite a momentum going, which I wanted to ride. I couldn't quite believe she was being so candid with me, and enjoying my more vulgar suggestions.

"Ha ha ha! A man with standards?! Nevaaaaah! Well I was both disgusted and jealous. He and I are not speaking any longer. I hope he contracts a painful sexual disease and his penis falls off. And people see it happen and laugh. Am I mean? I don't think that's mean...."

"Oh dear, you just lost me. A girl jealous of hookers has a few screws loose. Are you a better lay when you're angry and wrathful? I suspect you are."

"I am a good lay at all times. Always. I'm not jealous of hookers I just don't like the thought of him with anyone but me! But I kind of just hate him too much right now to care. Why do we always discuss me anyway? Tell me something about u mr judgemental."

So Olivia was angry and dissatisfied with her current options, alone in the house, and thus as close to being taken at the flood as I was ever likely to find her. I wasn't used to talking dirty over text messages and still felt pretty uncomfortable with the idea of sexting. Without any real idea of what one is supposed to do in such situations I free-wheeled and wrote whatever seemed fun. She was expressing curiosity in asking me questions, so I wanted to make the most of her temporary interest.

"You have three questions. I promise to tell the whole truth. Don't waste them. The window will snap shut after and I'll be the cocky arsehole again."

"One, what was the worst moment in ur whole entire life? Two, what is ur penis size, DONT LIE ABOUT IT! Three, how many times have you honestly been in love? And bonus question number 4 if u care to answer, how often do you follow girls down the road to sandwich compliment them?"

"Oh, she's firing both barrels!! +10 points for Olivia. Lemmee see….."

"Hell yehhhhhhhh"

"1. My divorce. Very unpleasant for three months and not a whole load of laughs another year longer. 2. Not measured since I was an adult. Bang on average, the girls tell me (they say above average but I think they're just being nice). If big dicks are your thing, look elsewhere. 3. Once. My ex-wife. Not any more. If you want the fourth, you gotta take a question or two."

"I want to hear about that. When did u get married, when did u get divorced and why? I don't need some essay just some concise facts. Am tres curious ma cherie. I will answer anything come on u can ask me three"

Bingo. This was really heating up. I think I probably should've lied and said I had a big dick, now I think of it. I mean, by the time she had a chance to find out otherwise, it would no longer matter.

"Met 1999, married 2006, divorced 2009. Three questions. Cool. Gimme a moment."

"Why did u divorce?"

"We changed. Long story. I'll tell you if you feed me vodka long enough"

"Maybe I dont want to know lol"

"1. How many men have stuck their he-rocket in your she-pocket? Real number, I don't wanna be multiplying by three. 2. Feminist ideology aside, do you enjoy being dominated in bed? 3. What's the sexual thing you most thought about but haven't had the courage to try? Heh! Answer THOSE badboys"

I expected her to equivocate and dissemble over such direct questions, but Olivia surprised me. I guess the anonymity across a text message connection is a powerful lure.

"Real number, and its something I am not proud of at all... oh my god... ok its nine! I have held off men for ages because I don't wanna reach double figures. Three were long term relationships and the rest were friends of mine who it seemed like a good idea to sleep with... potential relationships etc etc Oh dear. You are the only person I ever told that to... Love being dominated. I'm horrifically kinky, especially dirty talk. its something I miss about my ex, our disgustingly filthy texting."

"I appreciate your candour. Really. I know what you mean though, it can take a long, long time to find someone who'll do the right things and get into a position to do it. The shit I used to do to my wife. Christ, it's probably illegal in many countries."

That wasn't entirely fabrication, mind. We did some things that seemed outrageous to my naïve pre-game self. Olivia continued, "I have tried every real fantasy of mine. The only thing I have considered is letting a girl... pleasure me. But I wouldn't do it in real life, some things are better left in the imagination, everything else I have at least attempted. mostly they are just nice to talk about or think about but are not as good to do. Same question back to you, as well as how many girls u have... With and also how many times a day on average you play with your... 'he rocket'.. was it?"

"If I do these three, I'm getting another three. No freebies. Deal?"

"Deal!"

Sometimes with a girl you read her correctly and the right thing to say comes to mind. Other times you're playing the percentages based on previous experiences, making the best move in conditions of incomplete information. Other times it's just a shot in the dark that hits. I was about to fire the gun blindly.

"Ok. 1. I have recently become enormously interested in fucking girls in the ass while telling them they are dirty bitches. Only got to do it twice so far. Kinda liked it. Would like to do it again, but with the girl giving me some backchat so I have to slap her around a bit."

"Definitely enjoy being slapped around....." She replied. Oh! I noticed the sudden tonal shift. This had become co-operatively sexual, or at least hinted towards that direction. "Makes me worry for myself to be honest lol the things I enjoy in the bedroom… anyway good honest answer."

"Girls. Remember I've been coupled up for most of my adult life. Thirty-five in total I think. I feel like I should be upping the count as a matter of urgency. Masturbation. No regularity at all. Depends on how I'm doing with girls, hobbies, and how rapey I'm feeling. If I was to keep a spreadsheet (which I don't) I'd estimate a weekly average of four."

"Rapey?!"

"Not literally rape-y. A synonym for horny. Though my wife used to enjoy the occasional simulated rape." I was playing the middle ground, having noted she'd revealed herself as kinky and then picked out that one particular word as a focus. "My questions. I'm gonna totally do you on these :D 1. How many times have you masturbated in 2011 (and if it counts as the same question, what were you thinking about). 2. How do you feel when a man comes on your face? 3. did you / would you enjoy having a man fuck your face while he sticks a dildo up you and grabs a handful of that nice long hair?"

I was into pure dirty talk now, trying to heat her up as much as possible until she began blocking my escalation.

"Fucking hell… over a hundred. I like to do it around ten times a day sometimes. Usually I think about being raped or I guess fucked in a harsh way, being called names… everything dirty and kinky you can think of. I'm not a massive fan of someone coming on my face.

I don't dislike it, I just like my face to be clean so I immediately want to wash it off. I have been told I look beautiful like that though LOLLLLLL"

"+25 points. I think I've just fallen in love. Your honesty is quite compelling."

"Lollllll well I have had my face fucked... its not bad. Never had a dildo inside me. I kind of prefer the real thing, not that I know the difference, and I don't know how a man could really use a dildo whilst fucking my face."

"Btw, shooting on a girl's face is a major kink of mine. So I guess we won't get on after all...."

"Hahahahahahahahahahaahahahahaha what honesty? why should I lie? I love that I am so honest with u, u now know everything about me that no one else knows. Looooool. All men like it."

"On that latter point, girls describe the feeling as "full""

Written out in full like this, the chat looks like I was driving it with a modicum of self-possession but the reality is my fingers trembled as I typed. I'd only banged thirty girls in my life and only recently had what might be considered *sordid* encounters. Despite my best endeavours I hadn't internalised the Secret Society mind-sets about quick sex and women's feral sexual desires. I still wanted to believe there were Good Girls and Bad Girls, and that I dated the former. I was still often timid in how I escalated girls. The wilder of my recent encounters had been exceptions to the rule, rare cases of forcing myself to push the envelope and the girls responding well to it. Many times, such as with Aisha, my lack of conviction had ultimately sunk me. Everything I was writing to Olivia was a kernel of truth wrapped up in experimental bad-boy clothes. And yet it was working. She was absolutely on the hook for filthy talk and despite her youth and innocent look, her mind was as dirty as a porn set fluffer.

"So you have done that before then??" she asked.

"And got the videos. Heh! I like the idea of stuffing a girl so full she just squeaks."

"Hahaha. Oh my god why are u so honest as well? U do seem to share a fair few fantasies with me."

"I love sex. I think it's the most natural thing in the world. I don't care what society says — I just wanna fuck my girl like it's the last night on earth. C'mon, raise the stakes. Ask me something challenging."

"Lollll I am running out of questions. Ever had a threesome?"

"No. Several near misses. It's on my 'will try, would enjoy, but not gonna bust a nut finding it' list. Would like it at least once for my memoirs. You?"

I little knew how prophetic that statement would be, as you'll see in *A Deplorable Cad,* the next volume.

"Nope, never. What is it u like about fucking a girl in the ass?"

"Owning her body and soul. I'm big on the masculine dominance. It's not the physical tightness — don't care about that. I do like the visual image because the ass looks more round and peachy than in normal sex. But mostly I like to see her biting the pillow, panting and squealing in that peculiar mix of pleasure and pain. If that makes me a bad man, then so be it. Obviously I'm gonna reverse the question. What do YOU like about being nailed in the ass?"

"Oh my god. Marry me."

"Haha. Answer the question Olivia darlin'"

"Oooooooo u assume I've been nailed in there??? I have tried it, twice. And i cudnt do it for more than a minute. I absolutely pleasure myself to it… its a massive fantasy of mine and I loved my ex to talk dirty to me, it's particularly hot to imagine a man kind of raping me in there because I KNOW how much it would hurt. I'm also massive on male dominance. Being slapped, dick slapped… everything like that."

"Dear lord, whatever kept us apart so long :D Quick question (doesn't count as a real one). Are you thinking of rubbing one out right now?"

"I absolutely am lol. It's not a maybe its a certainty. Are u?"

"Not yet, but it's a dead cert before I go to bed. I'm well up for fucking you right now. Teaching you a lesson. And that includes slapping, grunting and punishing that tight ass of yours."

"I think some texting when the time comes is in order…."

"Facebook chat please. It's far more dynamic. And if I'm gonna wank over you, I expect some encouragement

"My Internet is rubbish but I'll give it a go later. such as?"

"A couple of filthy photos. Crop your head out if you're shy"

"I am not sending u photos!! Totally not!"

"Then you gotta rub one out while I masturbate. I don't do solo sex. Deal?" I had absolutely no intention of doing so, as I don't get off on sexting at all. Viewed hedonistically, sexting strikes me as pointless. It's merely a way of drawing a girl in, as I was attempting to do with Olivia.

"I thought that was the plan anyway?"

"I wasn't sure you were gonna wait :P"

"Of course"

"Ok, we'll park that till bedtime. Tell me something filthy you want me to do to you"

"I'll tell u later..."

"Short answers. Your brain is shutting down. I think the tingle is getting the better of you"

"the tingle?? U crack me up!"

"Haha. I'm in my room now. Log on to FB whenever you're ready"

"Won't be for a while"

"You're not at home?"

"I am but supposed to be consoling flatmate whose boyfriend cheated on her..."

"Boo! I'm going to bed imminently. Let's do some more back and forth. Describe a sex act you like. Shock me."

I'd made the decision to push as hard as was possible, to get her horny, and then see what happened. There's always a spark of excitement when a lead you've given up for dead resuscitates itself. Olivia was a very hot young girl, right on the threshold of the top tier and above what I was used to. And English too — a rare case of a local girl I liked and who liked me.

After such a frantic back-and-forth there were longer gaps in messages, as evidently Olivia was typing out long pieces. Fifteen minutes later, she sent this one.

"Contrary to popular belief I really, really enjoy giving blowjobs. And not just the usual mundane shit. There is something called a lingham massage which involves getting a man to lie comfortably, naked on his back with his legs apart. then the idea is to massage all the area around his cock, then gently massage his balls and perineum and finally the head of his dick. But its not like a handjob its some crazy penis massage I don't know… usually ends with the man exploding everywhere but personally I don't like men to come from that. I prefer to do that until they are well and truly aroused and then start using my tongue to gently lick from the base of the cock up to the tip, before just licking around the head whilst playing with the balls in one hand until the man gets so excited he forces my head onto his dick until I am deep-throating and choking and he pushes me up and down on it by my hair. Shocking? No. Fun? very. Your turn."

"Not shocking. Just very impressive. I love a girl who loves sucking my cock. I like her to treat it like her favourite toy in the whole world. You can really tell the difference between an enthusiastic blowjob and a dutiful one. Btw, another kink of mine is I like forcing a girl into surprise blowjobs — in restaurant restrooms, elevators, ferris wheels etc. Ok, now mine. Gimme a minute."

"Public sex is a massive turn on… and yes I agree there is a big difference between someone who likes doing it and someone who just does it"

"I like to tie girls up in a carelessly aggressive manner. I just grab them from the kitchen or whatever they were doing, drag them into the bedroom, chuck them on the bed then handcuff their hands above their head to the bedpost. Usually without saying a word — just an intense "I'm gonna do you now" look. I'll do a bit of foreplay, not much in this scenario, mainly sticking my cock in her mouth and face-fucking her till she's gasping, slap her face, slap my dick against her cheeks and nose. Mash her tits a little, then without much preamble, start fucking her hard with no real concern for her opinion in the matter. Shall I continue?"

"Please, I am intrigued… Don't you care if she's wet?"

"She will be. I'll be eye-fucking her for five minutes before I first grab her."

"ok,,, and then what?"

I must admit going into such graphic details felt vaguely embarrassing in the same sense as overly explaining a joke can be after it falls flat. Perhaps I'm just too much of a gentleman. Nevertheless, Olivia persisted in drawing me out, so I played along.

I wasn't the slightest bit turned on, rather I was simply excited at the dawning prospect of getting into Olivia's pants for real.

"Ok, so I'll fuck her, make her feel all my weight, pull her head into my chest and get some moaning and screaming out of her. Then flip her over, still handcuffed, and do her so hard she's scared she'll get smashed into the wall. Maybe in the ass too, maybe not. Depends on my mood. Then I'll pull out, put my cock in front of her mouth and wait for her to hungrily reach for it and suck me off till she's draining every last drop of cum out of me."

I paused for comedic effect, then texted the punchline, "then I'll put the cricket on television."

"Lad points!"

"Heh! I actually do all the tender romantic stuff as well, but I'm a big fan of variety in mood / location / acts. Give it a score out of ten and tell me how you'd feel"

"I completely agree with u, depends on the mood. I score it maybe a seven. I prefer something random like me going downstairs to the bathroom in a bar but on the way in the stairwell being followed, skirt pulled up to reveal I'm not wearing underwear and then being fucked against the wall with my face pushed against it and a couple of his fingers in my mouth. And being called a bitch and a slut... then people are coming so I'm dragged by the hair down into a cubicle, forced onto my knees, fucked in the mouth then turned and bent over so I'm touching my toes and fucked in whichever hole he wants whilst he slaps my ass and then pulls out and comes all over it."

I dare say I'd have never guessed any of that based on our first meeting in Trafalgar Square.

"That's like you are describing one of my favourites," I continued, "I like a quick knee-trembler especially with the girl standing while I fuck her from behind. Did that in Poland a few months ago in a pub toilet one afternoon with a local I'd just met. Very happy memory."

"I also enjoy begging him to stop so he becomes angry and slaps me and tells me to shut the fuck up, or forces my head into a pillow to drown out moaning and screaming."

"Good lord woman! Have you any idea how much I wanna fuck you now????"

"Oh my gosh I'm so horny. Tell me something else you like… like something really, really rough or kinky"

"You got work tomorrow?"

"I haven't been fucked for over half a year… I need it. Big time"

Right there she was signalling she was ready to be taken at the flood. I inwardly groaned that she wasn't saying this while sitting across the table from me on a date. She was bubbling in her love juices, gagging for sex, and *somebody* was likely to come along and take her. Damn! How could I make sure that somebody was me?

"Get a taxi here. Literally, just book the fucking thing. I wanna make you scream."

"I have to go out of London during the day and then to the ballet :("

"Pack your ballet bag and come suck my cock woman."

"I really, really want that too.. but I cant I'm still with my fucking flatmate and I gotta be up in six hours, the best I can suggest until I'm free next week is some texting so at least when I'm alone later on I can come thinking of u fucking my brains out. What wud u do to me if I was there now?"

Imagine my frustration. Too many sure-fire plans had fallen through over the past year for me to have any faith in Olivia and I doing the dirty a week later.

"Something really fucking outrageous"

"Liiike….? Details….."

I hadn't a clue. This would require making it up as I went along. "I hope you like costumes and sexy clothes. I got a wardrobe full of that stuff. Lots of… ahem… japanese imports…."

"Me too."

"Ok, here we go…."

"Make it super super dirty and rough. I can already feel that I'm wet without touching myself."

"First thing I do when you get out the taxi is tell you you're a dumb fucking whore for being so late and walk off so you have to meekly follow like a naughty child. I walk you through the lounge where all my friends are. I announce 'this is Olivia. She looks cute but I'm gonna take her upstairs and fuck her in the ass'. You blush.

Then I apologise in advance to them for the noise you're gonna make. I expect dynamic feedback on this, bitch"

Reviewing that message after sending, I felt I'd quite surpassed myself. What would my mum think?

"Well what am I supposed to say? Ur pretty much just telling me what ur going to do, which I like seeing as ur in control and ur pretty clear about that"

"Yup, but tell me how horny you get. Don't bother protesting though. Talk to the hand on that one."

"well I'm aroused but ur dick isn't out yet so it's only mild. Bearing in mind I'm not able to have my fingers on my clit right now...."

There were two learning points in Olivia's reply that I logged for future reference.

"So I decided you're gonna suck me off in a few different rooms first. First we go into my boxing gym. I tell you to play with yourself while I hit the bag a little. You rub yourself while you watch me whacking the bag around. You know I'm not gonna actually punch you, but you are turned on by the thought that I could, if you are disobedient."

"Still no dick out/rape/forcing me into things...."

"Wait your fucking turn woman. I'm boxing."

"Yessir!"

"So I just grab you, push you to your knees and wait. You look up at me, pretending to be all innocent. Totally unconvincing. I pull my dick out and then watch myself in the full length mirror, while you go to work."

"Nice involving the mirror."

"I see your reflection in the mirror, full body, trying to cram my dick in your mouth. I tire of this so I grab a handful of your hair and drag you out into the garden."

"Very very horny now fuck."

"You bitch about it being cold. I tell you to shut the fuck up and suck my cock. You do. I see one of my friends happen to glance out of the window. He gives me a knowing wink like I'm the Man. He assumes you are some cheap street whore I just ordered online."

"I want ur dick in me"

Grrrrrrrrrrrrr! *Then why did you refuse the taxi invitation?* Girls never ceased to frustrate me.

"I'm tempted to just cum in your eyes and leave you outside till a taxi comes, but I'm selfish. I wanna fuck your ass till you squeal. I stand you up and roughly finger fuck you for a minute or two, then pull your shirt and bra off. Throw them on the grass and hair drag you past my friends on up to the bedroom. You are totally fucking humiliated but it just turns you on more. Wait. You don't get my dick in you till I say so."

"Oh my god... fucking hell."

"Fucking presumptuous bitch! As if having a job and some qualifications is gonna make me listen to you about bedroom matters...."

"Am actually gonna have to go into the bathroom and finger myself I'm so turned on"

"Haven't even stuck my dick in your ass yet. Horny slut. Make sure you get a good handful of your tits, cos I'll be mashing them up good and proper when I see you for real."

"Ok keep going...."

"So I finally give you the honour of sharing my bed. Which, frankly, is more than a cheap whore like you deserves. But I find you physically stunning, so I do you this one single favour. You are just begging for my cock now. I slap you a couple of times. No reason. Ok, there is a reason. I want to see your cheeks pinken and a flash of submissive fear in your eyes. Then I rip your clothes off so you are naked and vulnerable."

"Just so u know I have two fingers inside my fucking wet pussy and my thumb on my clit and I want u so fucking much u cant imagine to fuck me."

Grrrrrrrrrrrrr.

"Then I stick my dick in you. You quiver, gasp and grab me. I fuck you good. In and out, over and over again. You feel me aggressively pushing into you Believe me Olivia, if you didn't have that annoying friend and stupid trip, you'd be getting it fucking big time for real right now. You are scratching my back, biting my shoulder and screaming all kinds of filthy shit while I rail you"

"Not dirty or painful enough...."

Learning point logged.

"I keep telling you to watch your fucking mouth when you're in my house but you can't control yourself. So I slap you around a bit. Not because I expect it to quieten you. Just because I'm an aggressive arsehole and I know I can treat you like some worthless street whore. I draw some blood from your lip and nose. I wasn't trying to, you just wouldn't take a telling. You gasp and get off on it. So I yank your hair and cuff you around." It would appear my drunken outbursts calling Marilyn a slut in Camden weren't so out of character after all. What stores of filth had I yet to uncover inside me? "I'm gonna silence that yapping for a while so I grab your throat and squeeze. I'm not trying to kill you, but I do want your face to go purple so you learn your lesson. The look of fear in your eyes is priceless and almost makes me come. You can't believe you are getting nailed so hard off someone who seems to have so little respect for you and your body. You feel ashamed it makes you so horny."

"I meant more sexual violence..." she wrote.

I wasn't really sure how to up the ante. This was already far beyond what I ever fantasised about women, never-mind had ever actually done to one. I dimly remembered hearing about Nancy Friday's book *Secret Garden* which some PUAs had as recommended reading. It is an anthology of lurid female fantasises. The book's introduction had impressed me just how depraved the contributors were.

"I flip you over. I pull your head down onto my cock so you can feel it bashing against your throat, and inside your cheek. You nearly retch it feels so deep. While I'm doing that I pull a huge dildo out from under the bed. Your eyes go crazy-wide. You are terrified of having that inside you. But you've got no choice. I thrust it up you from behind. It's so big your pussy tightens and resists at first, then gives up"

"I am extremely close to coming btw, hence lack of textage."

"As I ram it home, it feels so deep you think it's gonna touch my cock at the other end. You feel thoroughly spit roasted and cheap as hell. I spit in your hair and laugh. I face-fuck the shit out of you, while ramming the dildo in and out violently. You aren't even thinking human thoughts now. You are just gurgling and moaning, your spit running out your lips onto my cock, and your hot pussy juice streaming down your legs"

"Are you touching yourself too???"

"It's the closest feeling to dying, but it's so fucking good you want more. You feel like you're gonna rip in half. Not yet, gotta type fast ;)"

That was a blatant lie. The thought had never even occurred to me. This entire chat was a technical experiment for me and I approached it the same as I would a maths problem.

"You can vaguely hear me shouting at you, calling you a whore and names worse than shit. You are past humiliation. Your whole world is reduced to my cock pumping in your mouth and a fucking massive dildo nearly tearing your pussy apart. For a moment you get random thoughts. What the hell would your workmates think of you if they knew what a slutty little whore you really are."

"Well I just came. A lot. And I think it is horrifically obvious from the noises I was making what I was doing :/ so ... u must be pretty horny by now...?"

"*bows*"

"You are an absolute hero of this genre. I take it u have a lot of practice... can't wait til u fuck me for real..."

Grrrrrrrrrrrrrrr.

"Yeah. I well wanna fuck you. I'll knock one out before I go to bed. Type me a short story to think about while I do it. Something to make sure I'm thinking of you and only you, bypassing all my porn. Yup, I'm a horrible pervert ;)"

"Ok hold on..."

"Cool. Btw, +100 points for frigging yourself stupid while I wrote that. We can add 'Nick watches while Olivia masturbates' to our shopping list of future depravity. I like that."

I was quite proud of that story, probably the first time I'd got a girl masturbating over sex chat without having already made out with her in person. I'd come to realise that while Olivia was an outlier in how readily she confessed her extreme fantasies, the actual content of them was nothing out of the ordinary. She was telling me she loved it fast, hard, squalid, and in the ass. The point was noted, and I'd test this hypothesis out with other girls over the next few months to confirm it as a generalisable principle. It helped me make the mental leap over to Lover territory, able to rapidly sub-communicate to girls that I was the man with whom they could explore their fantasies in person, guilt-free.

Still, my primary feeling throughout the chat had been one of frustration, that Olivia was completely in the mood to fuck but wouldn't shift her lazy arse over to my place. I never really believed her promise to meet in a week or so. My gut told me this was an unlikely aligning of time and place, a sexual adventure encased in a bubble that would burst the moment she went to sleep. Olivia replied twenty minutes later with a long sexual fantasy for my benefit. Good though it was, I didn't give a shit. All that mattered was the fact that she had written it, and what that meant for my increased likelihood of banging her.

"I'll do this all in one text, its easier for u to read that way. Imagine u come to my place of work one day, unannounced and its a total surprise but ur horrifically horny and u were in the neighbourhood and u knew that if u needed a little slut to fuck then I was the one to visit. So u come in and ask me to excuse myself. I start complaining so u subtley grab my nipple. Hard. No one else sees u do it but I have to bite my lip to stop from calling out. You want a blowjob. Immediately. You force me into a corner and onto my knees so that ur facing the walls but its obvious what we are doing. u put ur hands behind ur head and start rocking ur pelvis a bit so that whilst ur cock is in my mouth and I'm licking it at the same time as sucking it, it is going in and out of my throat. Like ur gently fucking my face. after a while I try to get up, I take ur cock out of my mouth and explain to u that I have to work, but u force me back onto my knees with a thud and slap my face with your dick, still wet from my mouth. You tell me to shut the fuck up before u make me, and before I can talk again u put ur cock back in, but this time roughly, fucking my face so that with every thrust my head bangs against the wall. You want to come but you want to be inside my tight pussy first, want to hear me call out ur name and moan so you drag me up by my hair and tell me to go into the back room where there is a table. You lie me out flat on my back with my pussy at the edge of the table and my legs in the air and you ram your cock deep inside me. The shock of the first time you enter me makes me yell so loudly that someone knocks at the door. You tell her to shut the fuck up because ur fucking a little bitch to teach her a lesson and unless she wants the same treatment she will fuck off. You continue fucking me so hard that I am moaning so loudly and touching my clit at the same time. U grab my breasts roughly, hurting me so I moan louder in pleasure and pain and you watch my face contorted in ecstasy. But ur bored. I'm enjoying it too much so you yank me up and put me on all fours on the ground. Doggy style. I wait, my pussy wet and open for you to come into it, but instead and without warning you shove your hard dick into my unprepared ass. I cry out in pain so you stick some of your fingers in my mouth, a few more thrusts then you move to my pussy again, and soon I'm calling out your name in pleasure, asking you to fuck me harder, which you do, but then go back to my ass, repeating this, every time changing so I go from pleasure to pain until u feel I am enjoying ur cock in my ass too much and my pussy is dripping onto the floor so u turn me around and command I suck your cock until you explode onto my face and at the same time as you do, you make me finger myself so as I suck it I'm also moaning in enjoyment. Then you pull out of ur mouth and the hot come runs down my face and I lick the remainder of it off ur dick."

"Thanks. Gonna take me a while to read it. Gonna cheat and look at one of your photos too. My dick's in my hand now."

It wasn't.

"Which photo of mine"

"Profile 8 of 43. You'll be in this position when I fuck that slutty mouth of yours."

"Lollll! Ok well lets say night night. Talk tomorrow x enjoy urself'"

"Good gosh woman, you do have a way with words there! good story and certainly one I can buy into. Good night. if you rub out any more for me, be sure to send a text to confirm the deed. I don't mind waking up to read that."

":) I will be doing that btw. U can count on it. At least twice more."

"Heh! That's my girl ;)"

I never did bang Olivia. We set up a date for the next week but in the interim her boyfriend came begging and she took him back. Two months later it blew up in her face but the momentum between us had gone and her six-month sexual starvation had ended. We stayed in touch, had a couple of weird friend-zone dates where she deftly avoided my escalation, and then I refused to slip into orbiter status. Nonetheless I'd learned some valuable lessons about female sexuality and how to sex chat that would serve me well over the next few years.

Olivia got married six years later, and we occasionally share memes or congratulations on life events. Most recently, I congratulated her on the birth of her young son.

CHAPTER 39

LIVING THE DREAM

By February 2011 I'd been laying at least one new girl a month for nearly a year. Tasanee was my regular London girl and Adele and I had traded visits during her winter holiday from university. This was a pleasant situation. I'd been to Lithuania, Croatia, and Poland, developing an itch for foreign exploration. I'd come to firmly believe this journey into Game was paying off handsomely, far better than I'd ever expected it to.

Sitting in the lounge of Château Hampstead one cold afternoon with the heating turned up full and frost forming on the bay windows, we all felt winter blues. Our garden was blanketed in snow and the couple of times we'd been outside for game there'd been nothing to shoot at. Jimmy was in his dressing gown at 3pm, his gangly long legs stretched out so he could put his feet on the table. Lee hunched over his laptop halfway through his day's plan to watch all three *Twilight* movies back-to-back. Mick had strung out a hammock across his bedroom and spent all day lying there watching snowboarding documentaries and *Family Guy* re-runs. Johnny would occasionally come out of his room to boil the kettle then quickly shuffle back with his cup of tea, shutting himself in to plow through an online Ayn Rand positivism study course.

We were getting cabin fever. Something had to change. Talk drifted towards another European adventure.

Lithuania had gone well for us all so it seemed wise to stick with what we knew and try a fellow Baltic state, Latvia. Flights were cheap and one of our recent students, Simon, had recommended we go with him because he owned rental properties there. It never crossed our mind that the weather might be worse than London.

Simon was a difficult character. Everyone who comes into the community has something wrong with them, the symptom of which is failure with women. Simon's major fault was he burned with an entitlement that he was owed the best of everything without having to go through the inconvenience of actually earning it. He wasn't brought up rich and by the time we met him in his mid-thirties he'd developed a chip on his shoulder about becoming the "local boy done good." He was obsessed with money and various get-rich-quick schemes, His self-esteem was tied to his bank account and external markers of having "made it" such as his sports convertible car and some Latvian buy-to-let properties he'd gotten during the UK lending bubble by leveraging up on easy credit and off-plan condo sales. Simon wasn't a bad guy but this external referencing and something-for-nothing attitude oozed out of him and could be quite repellent.

He came into the Seduction Community for the same reason he did everything else: he thought it was a short cut. On the positive side, Simon was a brawny, masculine man with decent looks, an intense presence, and he did have occasional candid moments that inspired real empathy. I could see some girls would find him attractive. Girls with the social acuity to see deeply tended to fade away but he was more interested in trophy girls anyway, particularly Chelsea girls at the high-end bars.

"He likes Latvia and wants us to coach him there. We could sell him a residential training course," said Jimmy, "that'll cover some of our costs."

We took Simon up on his Latvia offer and scheduled in one week of coaching. The 'residential' format is better than the two-day boot camp. The student gets a longer time to bed down new ideas and instructors get to know him better to tailor the one-on-one advice. A week with a man is ample time to find his sticking points and craft solutions (nowadays, it takes me less than an afternoon). For the instructors it is less pressured and higher paid: than the boot camp: we get paid to go on vacation. It's win/win. I hadn't liked Simon at all when we first flew out to Riga but by the end of the week we got on fairly well and I'd begun to see far more of his positive character traits previously hidden under his rough outer shell. But before heading out, I wasn't sure of him.

"How's that John character?" Jimmy asked me. As usual, he was still in his dressing gown.

"Who's John?" interrupted Lee.

"You weren't on the boot camp we did. It was the middle of last year. He's a lad from Newcastle. Same age as me. He really got into it and did some night game coaching with Fernando and Johnny. Since then he did a bit more daygame coaching with me."

"Oh wait! Wait!" cried Lee, punching a fist into his open palm. "I know him. Short black guy."

"No. Tall, white guy."

"Oh."

I explained that John and I often bumped into each other around Covent Garden and on the South Bank of the river, where he daygamed. I wouldn't find out until much later (when John wrote about his experiences in his *Death By A Thousand Sluts* memoir) that he was sufferingh intense approach anxiety and rarely opened. Still, Jimmy, Fernando, Johnny and myself had all gotten onto friendly terms with him.

"I'm thinking of inviting him to Latvia," said Jimmy. "What do you think?"

"By all means," I agreed. "No need to charge him. Invite him as a friend."

Perhaps lured by Simon's filthy lucre and desire to escape London, we weren't really using our heads. It was February and Latvia is one of the coldest countries in Europe. We'd just frozen our asses off in what was considered one of Lithuania's milder winters, but for some reason we never joined the dots until we stepped off the flight in Riga into a snowstorm.

Lee and I arrived a day early, on a Friday night. He almost missed the plane, requiring me to sweet-talk the cabin crew into holding the gate open while he frantically sprinted across the airport and boarded at literally the last second. Lee's a good friend but harder to wrangle than a wayward toddler. So, we found ourselves in a picturesque winter wonderland. Wonderful if you were indoors sitting next to a radiator, that is. The cobbled streets were sprinkled with snow. The quaint little Old Town shops and houses looked cute with pointy tiled roofs and thick timber door-frames. Imagine a Disney movie and you're halfway to describing the beauty.

It was Friday night, so we wanted a look-about.

Much too cold for daygame

"Let's hit a night club," enthused Lee. There's only ever one man who ever enjoys a nightclub — the best-looking man in there that night. Usually Lee was that man, so he was always enthusiastic about them. I, rather less so.

"I suppose."

"Come on, Nick! We can do rapid escalation. It's been working great for me. You should try it."

This was a game-plan he'd picked up from a man writing under the odd pen name of 'Sixty Years Of Challenge'. I had never tried rapid escalation, but we were in a new environment and I was full of lads' abroad holiday spirit, something I'd not likely find myself feeling again anytime soon.

"Okay, I'll do it. Treat me like a student."

Lee warmed to the task, explaining the system over a warm-up drink from our duty-free vodka bottle. "The idea of rapid escalation is to go in right away with strong sexual energy and momentum. Escalate everything quickly. No numbers. No Facebooks. No dates. Gun for the fast lay with purity of purpose. No distractions, no temptation to back off and escape with a number."

After an hour, alcohol buzzed through our veins and we headed onto the snowbound streets to find a club Lee had researched online.

"We're gonna rapid escalate every hot girl in the club! Push 'em all until they either blow us out or come home with us!" Lee said, laughing to himself to raise his mood.

Looking as I do, I fully expected to get a never-ending stream of horrendous rejections. I was willing to eat that. I could burn the whole town and not care because I wouldn't be back. Occasionally I slip into a mood were nothing knocks me off course, and that night I was in such a mood.

The club was on a pleasant side-street just off from the main Old Town thoroughfare at the end towards the river. We'd only gotten as far as the coat check and already our eyes were popping out of our heads. The club seemed filled with gorgeous women, bursting out of every door, booth, and room. Unlike the brutally competitive London nightclubs, the men here were mostly either with girls as their boyfriends, or stood around gawking at the girls, not sure what to do with them. It was still early, maybe 10pm, and there had to be at least a hundred people in the club, over half of them women.

Lee bought a vodka at the bar in the chill-out room and before taking a first sip he walked straight up to the nearest hot girl and shook her hand. He looked into her eyes, caressed her hand, leant in close until he was almost breathing on her, talking close and intimate. *That's textbook rapid escalation*, I mused. It is intended for you to overwhelm a girl with your confidence and sexual energy, forcing her to filter you into either "yes" or "no". If she pulls away or blows you off you immediately drop her and move on to the next girl. Conversely, if she likes you she'll stay there and caress your hand back. Either way you've quickly flipped the stone and prevented a girl from sitting on the fence, tooling you for drinks and attention. Any girl returning the caress is showing herself to be horny and into you.

The lynchpin of this system is to show a massive amount of confidence. It's basically "good-looking guy game" on fast-forward, but Sixty had claimed that even average-looking men can have success. He argued that harsh rapid-fire initial rejections are liberating, like a splash of cold water to the face. By stepping so far out of your comfort zone initially, it builds up physical freedom that stays with you as you retract your ambitions a little. Your vibe shoots through the roof and compensates for any lack of good looks.

I intended to put Sixty to the test.

I was nervous. Nightclubs were tough for me and I had to be in a really good mood to enjoy them. I braced myself for some brutal blow-outs. That comes with the territory for this approach style, and I was brand new at it. So we began. My only opener for the whole night was to show seductive sexual eye contact and a playful smirk as I walked directly to a girl and shook her hand. "Hi. I'm Nick" I said, then pulled the girl in.

I did it twenty-five times, maybe more, over the course of four hours.

The results were astonishing. Only two girls blew me out entirely but I easily laughed off their rejections. There was something liberating about being so blatantly on the prowl and so obvious in my intentions. Soon, every patron of the club knew it. Rather than feel embarrassed, I thoroughly enjoyed the buzz. Nearly every girl hooked at least long enough to talk. Two hot girls let me kiss them and several others reciprocated amorous touch, pawing at my forearms and shoulders. Lee and I were owning the club, a whirling dervish whipping the whole place up into a dust cloud. Between us, Lee and I must have escalated every hot girl in the club.

I received more good reactions than I did bad. Even the girls who were blowing me off were being polite about it. Often I went back for a second and third try and eventually got them to hook. As the night progressed, I felt a ball of fire building in my gut, urging me on. That was about the time I saw two hot Turkish girls standing off to one side of the upstairs dance floor. Dusky Turks are a one hundred percent match for me — thick glossy black hair, heavy eyebrows, fiery eyes, tanned skin — just perfect. I tried it on with the first Turkish stunner. She hooked on the hand-holding but when I pushed it further she slid away out of reach. An hour later, I went after her friend stood on the fringe of the dance floor. She hooked strong, returning my hand caress. Her eyes sparkled and her nostrils flared in excitement. I walked her backwards to the wall and then, standing forehead-to-forehead, eye-fucked her while breathing hard on her face through my nose. My arms were behind my back. It felt intense. She returned my look, neither of us moving at all.

Then we kissed.

She was well into it, so I thought perhaps I'd found my girl. The main wall where we stood turned into a corner a few feet away, leading to a dark alcove. I manoeuvred her there. I dirty-talked her and pulled one of her breasts out of her vest. She checked her phone a few times, as her friend was texting incessantly.

"I must go find friend," she said, looking quite sad about it, and rushed away.

I left it for ten minutes, found her again, then dragged her back. We were just about to get it on again when the friend stormed over and pulled her out the club. Damn. Shrugging my shoulders and mildly disappointed I marched right through to the middle of the dance floor and pulled another girl in, led her off to the bar. She'd smiled knowingly as I approached, having no doubt seen me pull the same stunt over and over. I felt bulletproof. She wrapped herself around me, her crotch pushing into my thigh and her arms draped around me. Later, her boyfriend came over and peeled her off.

It was never-ending, four hours of madness. I remember eye-fucking and hand-holding a girl on the dance floor then another random girl, a hottie, interrupted her by grabbing my neck chain and literally dragging me away so I could eye-fuck her instead. How was this even happening? It was completely outside of my prior nightclub experiences. Another girl did a faux stripper dance for me to which I exaggerated a yawn and back-turned so she upped the ante by grinding and kissing her female friend in front of me. Later she tooled three local men into dancing like monkeys around her at the same time while we eye-coded each other across the bar.

Every half hour Lee and I would bump into each other and give each other looks of "fuck me, this is awesome". So many girls responded well, swept up in our energy. We were literally opening every hot girl, one after another, and after Lee opened I'd open the same girl. Counter-intuitively, we lost no social value chasing like this. Our intent was so strong. It didn't take long for the other men to notice, staring slack-jawed in disbelief.

For all the fun, neither Lee nor I got laid that first night. The downside of rapid escalation is that it's 'flash game', being all sizzle and no steak. You can sometimes turn up a Yes Girl but usually you get false positives of girls wanting a bit of excitement around the dance floor and nothing more. Nonetheless, we had a great time. I've only had a couple of nightclub nights like it since. Something special was in the air.

We left the club around 3am and walked back to the flat in biting cold.

"So you like rapid escalation now?" asked Lee.

"Yeah, but I don't think I can sustain that kind of energy more than once a year. I felt bulletproof and that's very unusual for me in a nightclub."

Jimmy, John, and Simon arrived the following afternoon. They joined us in an Old Town coffee shop, *Double Coffee*, like a Latvian version of Starbucks only nicer. We sat there scoffing pancakes and talked about our night out, not daring to venture out into the snow. It was too cold and bleak for any girls to venture out either, so there was no daygame to be had. We spent several hours dodging from cafe to cafe, chancing only a few minutes on the streets at a time. The lack of daygame didn't dent our holiday mood.

As a 4pm dusk descended we fought our way through knee-deep snow back to our squalid little apartment and spent the rest of the day sitting in our underwear with the heat turned up, talking online and playing video games. Five of us were crammed into an apartment with two bedrooms. The larger room had two double beds and the room next to it was more like a closet and held three single beds stacked up like the Auschwitz budget rooms. We decided beforehand that whoever was able to bring a girl back for sex could claim the good bedroom for themselves for the night.

When I first heard about Game I had preconceptions. I think everyone does. I looked at the cover of Neil Strauss's famous book, *The Game*, with its idealised cartoon image of the "player" and took it at face value. His image is the cool, well-dressed lounge lizard who cocks his head and winks slyly at the camera while in repose at the VIP table in a top-end club, lots of club bunnies around him. There is the tinkle of girl's laughter above the music. Perhaps on the weekend he'll drive his Ferrari into the hills for a date at an obscure châteaux restaurant. The Player has an expensive flowing haircut, like an Argentinian footballer (or Johnny Wisdom), and a neatly-trimmed stubble. His shirt is loose, open and from the most expensive salon. Perhaps you can smell Old Spice aftershave on his collar. That describes most aspiring player's first conception of "living the dream", I think. Two years in, my epiphany was quite a shock.

Players are nothing like this. It's as close to reality as James Bond movies are to espionage.

In Roissy's terms, this Straussian player archetype is actually a beta male. He's the man mainstream media would have you believe is "the guy who bangs hot girls", rather than the guy who *actually does* bang the hot girls. He's really *the guy who tries too hard*. He's the man of Gillette razor commercials and GQ magazine feature articles. He's deeply enmeshed in the matrix.

"I actually believed Neil Strauss and Mystery were banging the hottest girls in the world," Jimmy confided, years later. "It never crossed my mind they were lying, to big themselves up. I was banging sevens at university and afterwards, then I read Mystery and looked up to him. *That's what I need to do to get the tens*, I thought. But it was all a big joke, wasn't it? Here was me banging girls like that Aldona biker chick in Vilnius. She was an eight and I was actually a bit embarrassed because I've been doing game for years and I thought that's all I'm doing while Mystery is banging tens. Oh, how wrong we were!"

As I got further into game I began to see through the James Bond front so many well-known PUA coaches put on. My calibration was so well-honed that I could see men the way women do. I could look into their eyes and see fear, and the need to please others. I could see how brittle their self-esteem was, giving themselves away with little ticks and tells a keen-eyed observer can spot. Such men do often attract girls but I lost count of how many times I saw them look "in" during a bar conversation or dance floor grind and then an hour later I'd see the girl had transferred her attention elsewhere. The charisma simply wasn't there. They were like little boys who hadn't developed killer instinct and didn't really now their place in the world.

"If I'd known the big-name PUAs like David DeAngelo, Mystery, Strauss, Hypnotica, and all that lot... If I'd known they were liars who barely got laid, I don't think I'd have persevered. I'd have given up in my first year, when I wasn't getting laid. My naivete helped me. It gave me the delusional confidence to keep plugging away," I replied to Jimmy.

This growing realisation first crept up on me as we sat in our cold damp Latvian apartment. The men who bang lots of hot women are nothing like the urban player myth. What they actually do is sit around in their underwear trolling online dating sites such as Plenty of Fish. They hustle in Covent Garden through wind and rain. They get shit-faced drunk in Hoxton bars and tool big sets until one of the girls chooses him. They rapidly-escalate in nightclubs and bundle girls into taxis at 2am. They get £30 Ryanair flights to foreign cities and then hole up in shithole apartments like ours plotting their next move.

Real players are semi-employed because getting laid a lot is a part-time job. There's no time or energy left over for being successful in normal pursuits.

All real players have personality flaws that drive them into mastering the skill-set of seducing girls, at the exclusion of most other goals. Sometimes they bang fatties or MILFs just to get a good story. Sometimes their sex drive is so high that they masturbate ten times a day and still stick it into an ugly woman just to satiate the hunger. What they don't do–ever–is spend hundreds of pounds on fashionable clothes and grooming products, two hours getting ready, and then swan around a top-end club looking like Ryan Gosling.

About ten that evening we dressed and went back out. We'd been recommended a club a taxi ride away so we all piled into a single cab. John sat in the front while the rest of us tried to fit along the back seat, Simon lying stretched out across our knees. The driver took offense at that so Simon ended up sitting in the boot, like the opening murder scene of *Goodfellas*. Living the dream indeed.

It was Saturday night and, before we got to the club, we resolved to go in with Rat Pack mentality. That's when we go in and prop ourselves up in a central location, in this case it was in the middle of the bar, ignore everyone around us while we had our drinks. We did a lot of high-fiving and back slapping, talking loudly and attracting a lot of attention. The idea of this approach is that it separates you from the other men in the club who are actively chasing girls or standing back scanning the room for them. Jimmy and I had done it in Lithuania the previous month but it was far more effective now there were five of us combining together.

After a while the girls began checking us out. The hot ones kept their own council behind stoic facial expressions but the sixes and sevens looked over and tried to attract our attention. They would go out of their way to bump into us while getting to the bar to order a drink and we would draw them in. Sometimes we would literally reach out and pull them in — an old PUA move called "the claw."

We'd push-pull, chat for a while, and then push them away and ignore them again. As this went on we seemed to glow with energy. Girls throughout the club threw us looks and drifted closer by as they danced. Then, finally, the hot girls entered the game. Jimmy had taught us a lot about pawning in small environments and now the concept was writ large across the entire club. Once I felt sufficiently fired up I began rapid escalating with mixed results. Without moving from my perch against the bar I was able to fix the claw on seven consecutive girls, drawing each into a full body press against me. They'd enjoy brushing up against me like little kittens and then each flit softly away when I tried to kiss them.

I'd learned the previous evening to expect false positives. Nightclubs are a fantasy land, like the floating world paintings of feudal Japan. I couldn't find a girl who both liked me and was up for it. I began to suspect there were many semi-pros in the club — Riga is notorious for scammer girls. Jimmy ended up drawing in a nice, tall blonde girl who fawned over him but for unknown reasons he turned her over to Lee. She and Lee hit it off and, needless to say, Lee got the big room that night when he brought her home to fuck her. He also got the coveted F-Town ring.

What is the F-Town ring? Well, I'm so glad you asked.

Since the first group trip in Lithuania the previous July we'd taken a special metal ring that I'd engraved with the words *F-Town*. We treated it like a boxer's championship belt. Whoever banged a new girl in a foreign country won possession of the ring and kept it until he was dethroned by somebody getting a newer lay. The holder of F-town had bragging rights: he was allowed to shut down any banter by simply waving the ring around. Over the next year there'd be some real shenanigans as we jostled for the right to wear the ring, culminating in Jimmy taking a girl from London to Paris on the Eurostar just so he could notch her in a hotel outside of UK territory and thus claim F-town.

Sunday night we went walking out through the beautiful Old Town. It was still horrifically cold but a few revellers were out. Simon opened a mixed group of three girls and two men. They told us they were on their way to a nice bar and that we should come along. The bar was perfect for game. Lively but not too crowded. It was perhaps half capacity. We propped ourselves conspicuously at the bar and ordered our drinks. Scanning the room I noticed a brunette and a blonde sitting at the bar ten feet away, nursing cocktails. The brunette was really cute, a white band in her hair like a schoolgirl from the 1960s.

I stood next to her while ordering a beer and said off-handed, "Hey, can I just say something? When I was a little boy and learning to read at school, we had these books called *Peter and Jane*. The girl Jane was really clumsy and naughty. She had a white hair-band exactly like that."

They laughed and the brunette flashed me a receptive look. Two minutes of chat later and I took my drink and change then rolled-off so as not to appear too keen. Interest piqued, they looked over a lot after that, whispering and giggling. Eventually, and for no apparent reason, the girls walked past us, close. I reached out the claw and dragged the brunette in. She was named Regina and had just turned twenty-one. They chatted with us and recommended a nightclub they were going to, inviting us along.

Mid-conversation I glanced out the window and saw a tussle break out in the street. Nobody else seemed to have noticed. I turned to Jimmy, unable to resist the opportunity to use a hackneyed Mystery Method line.

"Hey, Jimmy. Did you see the fight outside?"
"Fuck off."

"No, really. Look!"

His glasses had steamed up so he had to wiped them on his Stone Roses t-shirt. "Fucking hell, pal. You weren't kidding. This we have to see." We left our beers on the bar and rushed to the windows.

Two young lads, no older then their early twenties, were biffing each other around while a crowd of over a dozen of their friends watched. Weirdly, both men fought like trained MMA fighters and there seemed to be a referee. They circled with high guards, poking out jabs and feinting heavier punches. I recognized Brazilian jujitsu moves as one man hit a takedown and the other pulled him into guard, lying on the cobbled street. It must've been below zero, but both combatants had stripped to their t-shirts.

It was a real fight.

For whatever reason, they didn't like each other. However, instead of a sloppy, drunken bar brawl they had agreed ground rules. We watched out the window for a while then went outside for a closer look. After five minutes the cops showed up. At the first flash of police lights the men separated and everyone scattered. One of the combatants rushed past us so I pulled him into our group and made him part of the conversation. That was my second use of the claw in ten minutes. He gratefully blended in and the police did a quick scan and didn't notice him. That probably saved him a night cooling off in jail and was our way of thanking him for the entertainment.

The bar wound down towards midnight so we necked our drinks and moved on to a nightclub. We had no idea where to find the one recommended by the girls but coincidently we ended up there anyway. From street level it was marked by a narrow wooden door with chipped red paint and lots of graffiti on the walls. I'd have never risked going down the stairs had I not seen a flock of tarted-up local girls go inside ahead of us. Down a winding staircase we found a basement club with walls painted black and a warren-like arrangement of small rooms branching off from two dance floors separated by a long partition.

It was the kind of dank, dark basement you'd expect below a Washington DC pizza parlor, the kind internet message boards accuse of satanic child sacrifice rituals. It wasn't busy. I'd estimate about fifty patrons, all around university age or slightly older.

While scoping out the club I saw Regina and gave her a hip bump as I walked past. She smiled enthusiastically. I returned to John and Simon in the next room while she danced with her blonde friend. As usually happens, girls started noticing Lee. Blondie decided her friend's "in" with me was her in with him. Lee wasn't interested. She wasn't hot and he hadn't gotten drunk enough to drop his standards. He politely brushed her off.

Did she not like that!

I was near the bar and they were on the dance floor. I couldn't really hear what was going on, but I could see her shouting at Lee with considerable vigour. Finally, red-faced and hyperventilating, she grabbed Regina and stormed off towards the coat check, about ten meters away from where I stood. I raised an eyebrow at John and Simon while inwardly thinking, "Oh fuck, there goes a good chance."

I caught blondie's eye and mouthed, "What's going on?"

Those readers who still believe women should be allowed to vote, drive cars, and hold positions of authority in the boardroom would do well to watch a woman scorned. Blondie was determined to burn the city to the ground. Twisting her face into an angry mask she sent as withering a look as she could put forth and flipped me the bird. I was appalled. I hadn't done anything to her. All my behaviour had been completely appropriate and friendly. I thought her behaviour outrageous.

I said to John, "I'm not having that!"

I stormed over and got into blondie's face. "How dare you? Who do you think you are? You're acting like a stupid cunt," I roared.

I grabbed Regina's arm and dragged her back out on the dance floor as blondie stood there temporarily frozen. We danced thirty seconds. Regina got into into it, showing me physically that she was still up for it, then I pushed her against the wall and made out with her. I whispered dirty talk into her ear, hearing her breath quicken and feeling her crotch pushing up against me.

Extraction time!

However, blondie was recovering from her aneurysm and remained a threat. Jimmy was already on it, without a word from me, sidling up and cracking a few jokes with her. The sudden male attention defused her but she continued to eye me suspiciously.

There wouldn't be a right time to pull the trigger, I'd have to just pick a moment and roll the dice, trusting to Jimmy to cover me.

"Come back to my place," I told Regina.

She nodded.

I walked her to the coat check then outside into the freezing night, now twelve below zero. So far, so good. Seeing me move, Jimmy spun blondie around to face the wall and ad-libbed nonsense about flying dinosaurs and fairy monsters to keep her pea-sized brain distracted. We'd made our escape. Despite my leather fur-lined gloves, I still felt like one of my thumbs would fall off from frostbite. It was the most physical pain I've ever been in from mere cold weather. Fortunately our apartment was only two hundred meters away and it would be roasting hot from having left the heater on all day.

"I'll come but I must tell my friend," said Regina.

"Lets walk now. You can send her a text."

"No, I must tell her."

Regina disappeared back down the stairs so I walked after her and waited by the coat check until she returned. Surprisingly, blondie didn't give her any trouble but she did want us to see her onto the tram first. So we walked down to the tram stop. Blondie was now all sweetness and light, the foul venom-spewing monster from five minutes earlier now a mere mirage of a faulty memory.

Lee had indeed gotten drunk and lost what slim sliver of judgement he'd previously possessed. In the fifteen minutes the tram detour had cost me, he had found a girl and brought her back to the apartment. Her entourage had joined her, two men and another woman. They were shifty characters. The blonde girl who sat on the sofa with Lee looked strung out on drugs. He was oblivious to it all, laughing at everything and nothing, while John sat in the corner watching everyone carefully.

The blonde crack whore tooled Lee mercilessly while he tried to caress her and escalate, his eyes unfocussed and his jaw slack. She continued playing him for attention. Her weird friends drank our beer and tried to engage us in weird conversation about nonsense. At one point, the two men disappeared into the bathroom together and shot up heroin. Our patience wearing thin, we encouraged Lee to take the crack whore into the tiny bedroom where she'd be out of our sight. I took Regina into the big bedroom.

Now I started thinking about F-town.

The rules were clear: the ring changes hands upon every new notch in a foreign country. Currently Lee wore the ring. With both Lee and myself in adjoining bedrooms with new girls, timing was crucial. I needed him to fuck his skank first otherwise I'd win and lose the ring within minutes. Regina was crawling all over me, tugging at my trousers, while I pressed my ear against the wall for any tell-tale sounds of thumping and moaning.

As much as I wanted the notch, I wanted F-Town more.

To my surprise, the bedroom next door shook with uproar.

"Get out, you fucking bitch!" Lee shouted, quickly followed by the slam of a door crashing open. I have no idea what precipitated the outburst but the girl left without quibble and the rest of her gang meekly followed her out.

Great!

I turned around and threw Regina onto the bed, stripped down to my Mr Potato Head boxer shorts, and undressed her. She lay back and thought of Latvia.

It was okay drunken sex. We both enjoyed it. Afterwards, she told me that she had never done 'this' before, which I doubted but who knows? I left her in bed while I checked in next door. Huddled in the tiny bedroom with a broken radiator were Jimmy, Lee, Simon and John. Jimmy's long legs stuck out from under a threadbare fleece blanket and he'd kept his clothes on to better endure the cold. The other three had their faces popping out of zipped-up sleeping bags. It was a shameful sight, like I imagine what greeted the first Allied soldiers to liberate Buchenwald.

I slowly unzipped Lee's sleeping bag, reached in, and took the F-town ring off his finger.

"Thanks pal," I gloated, then I went back to the big bedroom and spent the rest of the night fucking Regina.

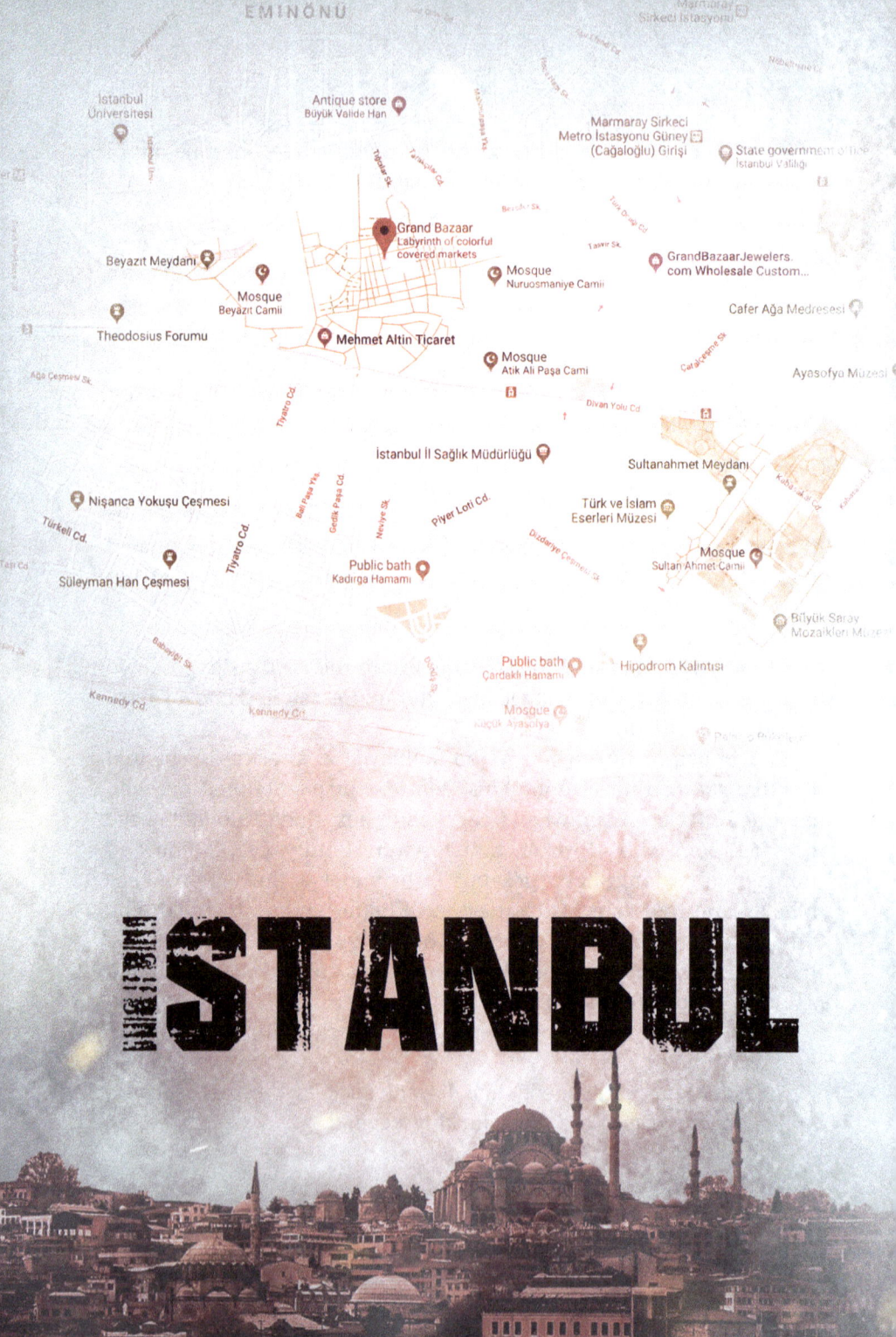

CHAPTER 40

THE SUMMIT

Zaria had maintained Skype conversation with me throughout the trip to Latvia. She clearly wanted to fuck as badly as I did and was starting to fall in love with me. In one of our chats she told me: "You do not believe in yourself and you put on an act. I'm not impressed with that… When you told me about your mother visiting and then your going to Latvia, I got really worried, and I cried all night thinking you were losing interest in me."

I reassured her that I was still very much interested, and looking forward to her imminent return to London on a more permanent basis. It struck me as a solid platform for building a relationship. With the hottest girl I'd ever dated, at that.

Early one February morning I was back in London and sleeping off the Latvian excesses. I was woken by the buzz of my phone. Snow was ankle-deep outside and my windows frosted over. I didn't even want to extend my arm out from under the duvet, so delightfully cocooned was I. Before noon I am like a grumpy bear disturbed in his hibernation. But I could hear the buzz of several rapid fire text messages incoming. Bleary-eyed, I picked up the phone. It was Zaria, completely distraught.

The British government had denied her visa.

She was upset, telling me that she was falling for me, and she wanted to see me and now she couldn't come back. I too was distraught. I wanted Zaria, badly. I didn't just want her to fuck. I wanted to properly date her. Again, I had to double-take on the surreal nature of events compared to where my life stood just two years earlier. Here was a beautiful Russian catwalk model tucked away in Uzbekistan knitting me a sweater, dreaming of dating me, and now absolutely crushed that she couldn't come back to England to have sex with me.

"Send me a scan of the letter the British Embassy sent you. I'll take a look at it."

"I don't understand. I meet all of the visa conditions," she wailed.

"I believe you. Let me see the letter and see the specifics of why they refused."

We subsequently found out that after the recent election, that threw out Labour and installed a Conservative government, it had become standard policy to automatically deny visas from certain countries the first time they were presented. It was an attempt to regulate immigration without incurring the wrath of the liberal media. I wholeheartedly support this policy in principle, but in practice it was severely cock-blocking me.

I read the British Embassy's letter. It was a form letter making no reference to any specifics. It was obvious they hadn't considered her case at all. That gave me hope.

"I'm sure its a petty bureaucrat trying to meet a quota," I reassured Zaria. "If we push back, politely but firmly, they'll take the path of least resistance and approve the visa."

My personal conviction wasn't so strong as I presented to Zaria but it was the only play. I drafted a letter to the Embassy which methodically and concisely explained how Zaria met all of their criteria and that the visa rejection had not followed their own rules. It was a very professional letter. Zaria had been so emotional she wanted to storm the Embassy and shout at everyone, until I took charge of her re-application. She sent off my letter and then the wait began. There was no reply for the next week and February came to an end.

"What happens if they refuse again? I'll be lost! I want to see you. I need to see you," said Zaria.

"Me too. London isn't the only place to meet. If necessary, we can fly to a third country. Make a holiday of it."

That might not solve the relationship issue but at least we'd get the sex. Plan B formed—a holiday in Istanbul. Neither of us would need a visa for Turkey and if her UK application was approved before then we could simply cancel the trip. Zaria agreed.

The British Embassy didn't move fast. I wondered if they still sent the Embassy's mail around the Cape of Good Hope. So, in early March 2011, I boarded a flight out of Heathrow to Istanbul with the anticipation of seeing Zaria hot on my mind.

I didn't yet realize it, but I had screwed with my own psyche while we had been apart, planting the seeds that would sour our relationship. I had been running Long Game, a key concept of which is "anchoring". Falling in love is like learning a new skill–it can't be taught, it can only be learned. The active agent is the person doing the loving/learning, and they do it to themselves. Falling in love is something you do to yourself while the other person is absent. Girls fall in love by daydreaming of their man while in maths class, by looking at a souvenir in a gift shop window and imagining his smile when they present him with the gift, by clicking through all his old Facebook albums to piece together his back-story. And, of course, by sitting by the fire a few hours every night knitting him a sweater.

It had worked. Zaria had fallen in love with me remotely, before we'd even had sex. What I wasn't ready for is the fact that anchoring works both ways. I'd been investing equally hard and constantly thinking about how I was going to close her. Because of her beauty and status I'd pinned my self-esteem and self-image as a seducer upon getting girls like her. Notching Zaria would be the real-world proof that I was the seducer I wanted to be and had endured two years of hard graft to become.

My ego needed Zaria.

During this time I had been looking at Zaria's modelling photos and built up an expectancy of her as the "Russian catwalk model ten." Three months of looking at only her portfolio pictures had warped my image of who she really was. She'd ceased to be a flesh-and-blood person and instead come to embody a concept. I'd anchored myself to a mirage.

I got off the plane in Istanbul, paid thirty dollars at immigration for a visa, then collected my suitcase from the baggage claim. The customs officers let me through without inspection and I rounded the hallway of the security area and into the Arrivals lobby. Zaria stood in the crowd waiting, easy to spot from her height. She

I arrive in Constantinople

wore plain clothes and no make-up. Her hair was pulled back into a simply pony tail.

I was sorely disappointed. Fantasy crashed headlong into reality. I looked at Zaria and thought, *I don't fancy you at all.* A chill climbed my spine.

Zaria had no such reservations. She bobbed up and down with excitement. We bought coffee at the airport cafe and while we chatted, I was relieved to find myself once more seeing all of the things I fancied about her. Nonetheless, I couldn't help but focus upon minor faults: a mild heat rash she had inside both elbows. Her airbrushed portfolio photos showed perfect skin, not rashes.

We took a two hour bus and train ride to our hotel. It was a crappy little hole-in-the-wall place with a shitty bed and one window, a hundred metres downhill from the famous Grand Bizarre. We didn't mind the grottiness. It was further proof that women aren't about the money. Zaria was accustomed to princess treatment and staying in five star hotels. She didn't care what this room looked like. She wanted to fuck me and that was all that was on her mind. So we stripped and started fucking.

I tried my best to keep it slow and gentle. I had previously asked her in one of our Skype chats if she liked rough sex and she had said no. So for ten minutes or so I fucked her gently and then, feeling underwhelmed at the energy level, decided to go for it in my usual style. I pulled her hair and slapped her ass. I held her throat and flipped her over, doing her from behind. She wasn't upset or complaining, to put it mildly. Rather, she gasped, clawed, moaned, and generally went crazy over it. She had a look of wonderment in her eyes, and I knew she had loved it. Perhaps she was not as kinky as Olivia professed to be, but that sordid text exchange had certainly emboldened me on matters of violent sex.

Zaria realized for the first time that she had a desire to be dominated. The rough sex had cemented it. Lying in bed twenty minutes after the first sex she told me, "Nick, now I understand why my friends go crazy for sex. I'd never had good sex before and thought they are just silly girls. But now I understand. I feel insatiable."

After I'd shot my muck down Zaria's throat, I was still conflicted and for the rest of the holiday I acted a little sullen. I knew deep down that she wasn't the girl for me, but I thought there must be something wrong with me for feeling that way. Zaria was exactly everything I had ever wanted but thought I could never have, since those days as a teenager seeing glamorous models on perfume advertisements. Now that I had her, I no longer wanted her. Each day, walking through the Grand Bizarre, taking the ferry to the Prince's Islands, sitting in rooftop restaurants eating gozleme and fried fish, I would go hot and cold on her. I was fractionating, doing an accidental push-pull. Naturally, that made her want me more. She had spent her entire adult life having her ass kissed and being fawned over by provider males who wanted to do anything for her to be with her, and here I was pushing her away. It messed with her head.

It wasn't going quite how I'd hoped

After a week of my childish bullshit, she decided we wouldn't see each other again and told me, "I'm euphoric. After you pushed me away like that I feel free.

I don't need you. My feelings have changed completely and we'll not see each other again so let's just enjoy this holiday"

I wasn't the only one blowing hot and cold. Some minutes later, she added, "I want you to teach me sexually, use me however you want. I want you to rape me in London... I don't know how you have this effect on me. I've never enjoyed sex before but now I'm becoming a sex maniac and I want to experience everything. It's like you are dragging me into a swamp and the further I sink the harder it is to get out."

She was conflicted, genuinely not knowing what she wanted or where she stood with me. I'd have liked to have provided her with some certainty but I didn't have any myself. I had no idea what to do. We ended the holiday with a mutual tacit agreement not to see each other again.

A month later, she called me.

"My visa was approved!"

By this time, after a month of absence, I had once more built up an idea of her in my head, struggling with my own strange emotions. Zaria had become a touchstone. If I could succeed in a relationship with her it would prove to myself I wasn't a broken man. It would prove all those jangling pieces had once more repaired themselves.

So, I willed myself to make it work. I agreed to meet Zaria at the airport. It was now mid-April and there was an incoming complication. Two complications.

Dovile and Ugne arrived late evening. I met them at the bus stop outside my house. It was really awkward, much more so than anticipated. I had to be careful mixing lover and provider signals at this point. I didn't want to feel sleazy by taking away from the purity of the romance by becoing a sponsor instead of a boyfriend. So although I'd let them stay in the spare room, which was bigger than Dovile's entire family flat at home, I hoped the two week limitation softened the provider signal and made them feel less obligated to me. They only stayed a week, until finding another flat down the street. It was really small and they had to share a bed, but having their own place suited us all.

Awkward though it was, the real source of discord was the uncertainty over just what relationship Dovile and I were to have.

Since having sex in Vilnius, Dovile had learned about my PUA identity and constant skirt chasing. If she was reading my blog (I had to assume she was, and she admitted later she read every post as I uploaded them) she'd know about Zaria. She might have even seen the street approach video I'd uploaded to my YouTube channel. From my perspective, the best possible scenario was I'd have Dovile as a regular girlfriend, but it would be an open relationship on my side to chase other girls. It wasn't likely she'd be happy with that.

The girls began their Erasmus internship for Perry and Bodgan, fully intending to meet the conditions of their maintenance grant. The new hair salon had only recently been refurbished. The girls cleaned, decorated, and did some light advertising for the grand opening party.

Something felt really off.

Dovile knew about my attempted juggling act and no doubt felt uncertain about her position in my affections. It would be reasonable for her to feel resentful. In fairness, she hadn't yet broken up with her long-time boyfriend. Nonetheless, things quickly came to a head.

A week after the Lithuanian girls arrived in London, and while still staying at the Château, Zaria Skyped to ask if she could stay in another of the guest rooms for a fortnight. She was flying in from Uzbekistan on her newly-acquired working visa but her apartment rental had fallen through. I dreaded the fireworks that would ensue if both Zaria and Dovile were living in adjoining rooms and sharing the same facilities. The life of a player sounded great in theory, but sometimes the rubber hit the road at uncomfortably high speeds. Making matters worse, Mick and I were booked up to fly to Estonia a week later to teach a residential course. That would leave the Lithuanians alone with the Uzbek. My private life was becoming complicated.

I refused Zaria's request.

Of course, Dovile read my blog. She had uprooted herself to come to London and it would be uncomfortable for her, to say the least, to read about my Estonia escapades just a week after she arrived. Foolishly engaging in subterfuge, I posted the week's events, including a squalid lay report, on Mick's blog. Dovile found it.

Returning to London, I knew right away that things had changed. Dovile was cold and frosty towards me. The grand opening at Perry's salon was that weekend. Dovile and Ugne worked the bar they'd set up behind the reception counter. I noticed an odd vibe vibe between Dovile and Bogdan. They exchanged looks. When I introduced her to people as my girlfriend she went silent.

Jimmy noticed it all too.

"Something is up with Dovile," he said. "I don't like how she's acting around Bogdan."

"Yeah, I see it. He's chasing her, and she seems happy about it."

Bogdan had been openly flirting with Dovile from the moment they were introduced. Never underestimate a thirsty man's willingness to betray the people who have done him a good turn. I've since learned that you can never ever trust a man who isn't getting laid. The male urge to fuck pretty women is so strong, and so usually frustrated, that given the slightest sniff of hot pussy the typical man will burn everything around him. That's the main reason I don't believe the internet blow-hards of the MGTOW movement and also why an aspiring player should be careful in choosing his wingmen.

I'd set the tinder in a heap. It needed only a spark to catch alight. Bogdan was Dovile's boss, ordering her around every day, which inevitably pulls a girl into the man's frame. I don't know if she made a conscious decision to get even with me, if she'd turned to him out of emotional vulnerability, or if it was even simpler still and she just fancied him and wanted to jump his bones for the sheer pleasure of it. Whatever her motivation it seemed to be moving in that direction and I had to face it. Confirmation trickled in from various sources. First, Lee came to me one afternoon while I was cooking in the Château Hampstead kitchen

"I need to tell you something. Perry was laughing about it, but I think you'd want to know."

"Okay..."

"Perry says that Bogdan is going around saying that he's trying for a threesome with Dovile and Ugne. He says that he's had them both over to his flat, kissed them both, and he thinks next time he can fuck them."

That froze me.

I know it's hypocritical to demand Dovile be monogamous while I juggled a couple of girls and travelled abroad to chase more. Nonetheless I was angry. I thought of her as my girl, and I didn't want to think she had been with Bogdan. For the first twenty-four hours after Lee's news I was shocked.

My ego was hardest hit. I didn't have the "pimp hand" over Dovile that I'd wanted. Mixed into this was sadness that I'd created a bond of affection with her above what I'd had with other girls and then let it sour. The next day, I had a chat with Mick as we daygamed Oxford Street (yes, hypocrisy!).

"She's already fucked him, mate."

"Who told you?"

"Nobody, but it's obvious. I don't know if they are an item, but I'll bet money she's fucked him at least once."

I know how this sounds, but I felt betrayed. I felt like she had been betrayed as well by Bogdan who was supposed to be in a position of helping her along in her career and her studies and instead had taken advantage of her. That was the ego talking. I didn't like the idea that I might lose a girl simply because she liked another man more than me. So my ego cast around for alternate explanations, no matter how spurious. I preferred to believe she'd been ensorceled by some wicked Bogdan magic. Despite my gleefully taking advantage of women's hard-wiring to enjoy adventure sex I didn't enjoy being on the other end of that smoking gun.

Daygame teaches you many things, often with tough love.

By this time, the salon was open and running so there wasn't much work left for the girls to do there. Dovile and I were still seeing each other but we were like cyphers. I was fucking her but she always seemed inhibited and non-compliant, somewhat mechanical. It didn't help that Zaria was coming around twice a week too.

Ugne had found a waitressing job in a bar near their house. Dovile and I were out at the Starbucks in Golders Green one day when she began spinning a yarn about how Ugne's bar manager was coming on to her and creating discomfort. The story didn't ring true and I increasingly came to the opinion Dovile was trying to tell me something about herself. I took that as a segue into asking for the straight truth about Bogdan, something we'd been avoiding.

She didn't know anything of what I'd discussed with Lee, Mick, and Jimmy. She didn't know I suspected she'd slept with him.

I wanted her to tell me if he was coaxing her. Bogdan was a good-looking young man. Dovile was spending a lot more time with him at work than with me outside of it, but I wanted to believe she was being coaxed. Once I moved the topic from Ugne's manager to Bodgan, Dovile clammed up and wouldn't tell me anything mmore over the coffee. We separated for the day and later that evening we messaged on Facebook.

The trickle truth seeped out.

I told her what Lee had told me. It was obvious she was having a difficult time holding all her emotions together and making sense of her situation. She wanted to tell me the truth but feared what I'd do with it. It took her an hour of vacillation until she admitted he'd kissed both her and Ugne one night. The story she told was they'd passed a major milestone preparing the salon so Bogdan had bought a crate of beers and invited them back for a little celebration. They'd got drunk, danced to music, he'd made his move and after initially going along with it they'd had second thoughts and backed out, hurriedly making excuses and leaving his flat. Ugne had since been cold to Bogdan, deciding it was a big mistake and refusing to return to the salon at all. That's why she'd taken another job at the bar.

Dovile had accepted Bogdan's invitation to his flat the next night, by herself, and she'd let him put his hands down her pants. This rocked me but I was determined to face it and find out the full story. I pressed her for details about how long his hand was in there and how far she let him go. After about an hour of that, she asked me to wait half an hour. So I knocked back a few glasses of whiskey in the interim.

Eventually, a long email landed in my inbox, from Dovile. It was carefully written, and it was, finally, the truth. She admitted that she'd had sex with him and spent the night. She said it was crappy, terrible sex and she'd felt terrible as soon as it happened. She'd left as soon as she could, regretted it and didn't want to go back to work at the salon.

Her confession hit me hard. For the first time in well over a year, I realised how white knights feel. I instinctively believed her explanation and cast Bogdan as some kind of black-hearted rogue. My first reaction was to swallow down the sense of betrayal, go to the salon, and break Bogdan's legs. Such emotionalism would not do. I held my metaphorical tongue, took some deep breaths, and tried to logically apply my own knowledge of women to the situation.

The first unwelcome, but highly likely, conclusion was that Dovile's story was probably a load of shit. It was far more likely that she'd enjoyed the sex and had been entirely willing to be swept along on the tide of alcohol and passion. She'd been resentful of my skirt-chasing so that would've been both her motivation and exculpatory evidence. I believed she regretted it but not for the reasons stated. I suspect the sex itself was fine. It was the inevitable fallout at the salon and Château Hampstead that she feared. She regretted getting found out more than the act itself. This of course didn't mean Dovile was a bad person—consider the situation I'd placed her in—but women instinctively tell men whatever will calm them down. So I dismissed her sob story.

She'd cheated on me. I'd walked her into it.

Although my gut had already known the truth it was a shock to read about in black and white, my ego unable to deny or finesse its hard edges. I went next door and disturbed Jimmy in the middle of his Skyrim game, telling him the story and showing him Dovile's messages. He saw it for what it was but there wasn't much to say. He offered a few platitudes about taking the rough with the smooth, about don't hate the player, hate the game. He suggested that if I want to keep her around I needed to dismiss Bogdan with a subtle put-down and then just ride out the emotions and stop being such a woman about it.

I didn't respond for half an hour. Dovile worriedly messaged me, asking if I'd received the email. Finally I composed a reply, "Yes. I got it. He's a loser and you lowered your value by sleeping with him." I was so angry I wanted to burn everything. "It's amazing you slept with him. He tells people he needs to use Couchsurfing to get laid. We think of him as a bit of a clown." This was all true but not really the point. She apologised profusely.

I replied, "You're dead to me" then logged off and went to bed.

She started texting me on my phone and I ignored her. She then showed up on my doorstep at 6am. I was still angry, but she looked so sad and lost that I felt bad and let her in.

"I've got nothing to say to you but I'm willing to hear you out," I said coldly as we walked up to my room. I lay on my bed while she sat timidly in the far corner and tried to explain herself and begged for a second chance. Pumped up with my pompous and self-righteous indignation, I had no desire to hear any of it. Finally I told her she needed to go, and that I would think about it for the next forty-eight hours and let her know what I decided. As I let her out the front door I said, "At this point, I don't want to ever see you again. However, I may be over-reacting. I'll think about it for a while."

My natural reaction to pain, betrayal, or disappointment is to burn every bridge and build new ones elsewhere. I don't like to repair damaged friendships nor make the best of a bad situation. As an introverted and self-reliant man my instinct is to turn my back on the problem and walk away. Dump the girl, quit the job, bin the friend. I'm instinctively cold and ruthless when someone crosses me. I don't get vindictive and hunt them down. I just pull up the drawbridge and shut them out. Forever.

In this case, I distrusted my instincts. I was feeling so bad I needed to talk to someone to help figure this all out. I messaged Colin. He was painfully honest, and slapped me with a heavy dose of reality. He told me it was my fault entirely. I'd taken an idealistic, inexperienced young girl and seduced her. She'd given me everything she had to give, and in return I gave her nothing. Instead, I was still out fucking other girls, not seeing her much after she left her life behind to be with me in London. I had put her into the situation where Bogdan would be her boss, and spend more time with her than I did. He told me I was a stupid cunt and had only gotten what I deserved.

I checked that analysis with my housemates.

"Yes, you're a stupid cunt who got what he deserved," said Mick.

"I agree with Mick," said Jimmy.

They said that the fact I put her in the salon job wasn't so bad, since it was necessary to get her into London, but I'd taken my eye off the ball. My anger receded and I accepted that it was my fault. Dovile had two months remaining in London and I wanted her with me. The most painful periods of the player's journey are not the endless approaches nor even the rejections. The real pain comes when your success puts you into situations that are at odds with your ego and the truth forces you to humble yourself. I never was good at humility.

The forty-eight-hour thinking window closed. I called Dovile and asked her to come over to talk. She rushed up, sat down on my bed, and softly quivered in fear. I started talking. I was dramatic about it, telling her how hurt and betrayed I had felt, and that instinctively I didn't think she deserved another chance. Then I softened a little and I told her what Colin and the others had said, and how I'd reluctantly agreed. I told her we could have a formal relationship until she went home. Then when she was back in Lithuania we could still see each other but we'd have to figure out some different ground rules. I also told her that while in London there would be some "strict rules" for her.

"What are the rules?" she'd asked, barely able to contain her joy at getting a second chance but also a little apprehensive.

"First, you have to give yourself to me completely. No nervousness or anxiety or holding back in bed any more." She nodded enthusiastic agreement and then I told her, "Second, I'm going to do you in the ass right now."

She agreed to that as well, without argument. She threw herself onto me, hugging my waist tightly and sobbing happily on my chest. I was relieved too. We had a nice time reconciling, and she completely surrendered herself to me. The next hour was like a scene from Pornhub as I did her in the ass, face-fucked her, threw her around and then made her swallow my cum. She loved every moment of it. Finally those strange barriers were broken and we had a real uninhibited connection. In the years since, I'd have sex that was technically better, or more primal, or with hotter girls, but I haven't since slept with a girl where there was such a purity of affection and connection as I'd found with Dovile. There was something very welcoming and comforting about sticking my dick in her, no matter how outwardly sordid the act.

The next two months were great. We went out on real dates, talked a lot and developed a strong bond. We also had a lot of good sex. I almost had a threesome with her and Ugne one night when we'd come back from clubbing. Both girls were dolled up nice and Tom Torero (more on him in the next volume) had signed us in to one of the nightclubs he'd been running entourage game at. A strange sexual vibe had been in the air. I knew Ugne fancied me but she was a very straight-laced and inexperienced girl. Dovile confided that she thought Ugne might still be a virgin. I'd come to feel quite paternal with both girls. They did everything together like sisters, so I'd never hit on Ugne and instead limited myself to light teasing and flirting. This particular night I'd noticed Ugne looking at me hungrily — subtle but there was definitely something there. The three of us had an after party in my bedroom, drinking gin. Before long I was lying on my bed with a girl on each side snuggled up to me. I'd lean to one side to kiss Dovile then the other to kiss Ugne. They were playing along and giggling but it never quite had the threesome vibe. With the benefit of hindsight and experience I think it was there to be had but I just didn't feel comfortable pushing for it. I guess I didn't want to mess with Dovile any more than I already had and fucking Ugne in front of her was a real wild card considering the girls were room mates and inseparable.

I regret it. It would've been a great threesome. So, I contented myself with kissing them both, making some jokes, then letting it fizzle. The next week Dovile formally dumped her boyfriend. Poor guy. He flew into London the next day to try to win her back but her heart belonged to me. After her initial pain of empathising with him dissipated (she clearly felt terrible letting him down) she was lifted up by her newly-gained buoyant freedom.

A fantastic holiday in Barcelona

Their London adventure was winding down and the girls wanted to go on holiday to Barcelona. I joined them. We had a great time eating out, sightseeing, and relaxing. We shared a twin room so I'd be fucking Dovile while Ugne pretended to sleep. Again, I'm sure the threesome was there for the taking, but I never really wanted it. Well, obviously I wanted it, but I had concluded it carried too much risk of queering the pitch between us all. Dovile said the trip was the best week of her life. We had a tearful farewell at the Golders Green bus stop as I put the two girls onto a National Express bus to the airport. It was the end of a golden two month period, the best I'd ever had with a woman.

It was not yet the end of our relationship.

I brought her back to London a few more times and also visited her in Lithuania. A year after their first trip, the Erasmus season rolled around again and this time both girls found a placement in Greece. Her horizons were well and truly broadened. While her character was still the cute conscientious small-town girl, she'd developed a lot of self-confidence and now followed her dreams, determined to live life to the full. We stayed in touch on Facebook and she gave me a blow-by-blow account over the month of meeting a Spanish guy on her Erasmus program named Felipo who had been a professional football player in his teens. She was thinking about dating him, but hadn't done anything about it yet. She always ran her life choices by me, trusting my judgement. We had an open relationship now but she hadn't activated her privileges and wanted my approval first.

Ugne's birthday was in spring of 2012 and between them the girls hatched a plan to spend a week on a Greek island for sun, fun, and wine. It had been a couple of months since we'd last met so they asked Jimmy and I to join them. Felipo was also coming, as was his friend Jose who was chasing Ugne. Quite a strange situation but it felt completely fine to me. I wanted to check out Dovile's prospective boyfriend and, of course, wanted to fuck her too. Jimmy and I shared a two-bedroom apartment and a few buildings further down the same resort complex the girls had theirs, sharing a bedroom. The two Spanish boys shared another.

These were young, good-looking boys with no game. They'd been patiently investing in the two girls for a month the way men normally do when part of the same social circle or university residence. We all chatted a bit, and I quite liked them, but they were obviously subdued, having to endure the daily routine of spending all day entertaining the girls at the swimming pool and harbour only to see Ugne go to bed alone and Dovile sneak off at nightfall to spend the night in my apartment being fucked by me.

Towards the end of the holiday Dovile told me that she was deliberately testing Felipo to see how he would handle the situation. She wanted to date him, and I experienced conflicting emotions over it. I couldn't say no, I didn't have

Now that things were good, they were very good

the moral right. I had her for a year, and I wouldn't be able to give her the life she wanted — a proper monogamous boyfriend who carried the potential of becoming a serious marriage prospect. We had several emotional talks about it and I told her to just do as she felt right and see where it led. She dated him the remaining two months of the Erasmus scheme and stayed in close contact when each returned to their home countries.

I visited Vilnius for a couple of days in summer 2012 and fucked her again, and finally saw the family home where she grew up. It was cute because she had a framed picture of us together that her art student friend had drawn from a photograph of us in Barcelona. Again, I felt Dovile pulling away from me and as we talked it over she said she wanted to go with only Felipo. I gave her my blessing and we didn't talk much for the next few months. It didn't work out for them and she was back in the loop by Autumn.

She came over to visit me again in London in early 2013 and in May, on my way to Belarus, I stopped off in Lithuania and we met up and fucked more. A month later I stopped on the return trip home and after we fucked she told me that she'd met a new Spanish boy named Enrique. She really liked him and wanted to date him, so she had to stop sleeping with me. Again I left her with my blessing.

Dovile eventually received another Erasmus offer for the summer of 2013. We were still talking on Facebook and she told me all about it, asking for direction on another big life decision. The scheme was in Chisinau, Moldova and they were funding students one thousand Euros a month for a master's degree in marketing. It was for a two-year commitment. For the region, that's a great deal of money — considerably more than the median family income. A person could live in luxury on that in Moldova. She said that her parents had told her to "follow her dreams" but that her friends didn't want her to go.

"What do you want?" I asked her.

"I don't know," she said.

"What does Enrique say?"

"He says I should follow my dreams as well."

"Do you want to be with Enrique?" I asked her.

"Yes," she said. "I like him a lot."

"Do you want to go to Moldova?" I asked her.

"Not necessarily," she said. "Not really, no."

"Does the Master's in marketing interest you? Will it help you?" I asked her.

"Not really, no." she said again.

"So you want to go somewhere you don't care about to do something you don't care about. For two years?"

I patiently explained that she was being lured by the money and travel but at some point a girl has to resist. People, and moving your life in the right direction, is what matters. I future-projected the most likely outcomes, bearing in mind she told me she didn't want to marry a Moldovan and didn't really want a career in marketing. I told her the relationship with Enrique wouldn't survive two years at long distance. She was now twenty-two years old, and two years passes fast for a girl in her sexual market prime. She'd party for two years, living an exciting but transient lifestyle. Then she'd return to Vilnius two years older, a little fatter, a little more jaded, with a few more dicks on her resume. I advised that if she really liked Enrique, she should go to Spain and explore that. Get to know him better and see if he is what she wants.

Knowing Dovile was a great experience in understanding the challenges and worries that young girls face. She confided everything and I felt a strong protective urge to look after her and guide her as best as my wisdom could. Like Adele, Tasanee and Zaria, my time with Dovile helped me empathise with women and understand why they act how they do. Dovile took my advice and followed her heart to Spain instead of the money and adventure in Moldova. Enrique took her on a one-month road trip throughout the Spanish hinterlands which I saw on her Facebook updates. A year later she was still dating him, having moved to Madrid so they could live together. Recently, they married and started a family. It is a textbook example of a successful relationship.

Overall, I dated Dovile for over two years — longer than I had any other girl except for my ex-wife. I was closer to her than any of the other girls, and I learned a lot about myself and women because of it. Dovile learned from me that there was a whole new world outside of her comfort zone and she compared herself to the Disney character Pocahontas in her writing as she stepped outside of it: "Pocahontas in my opinion, reflects the high level of a woman who is not afraid to take risky decisions, seek what you want, even if most are opposed." Šis personažas gan tiksliai atitinka mano asmenybę, taigi nuo šios dienos Internetinėje erdvėje būsiu Pocahonta.

I'm glad to say I was a part of helping her discover that. It was a rare case of the PUA maxim "leave them better than you found them", despite some rocky roads getting there. Even now, years later, we sometimes chat online.

Winding our clocks all the way back to April 2011, I didn't yet know what the future held for Dovile and I. We'd found a good thing after the Bogdan situation, but there remained the question of what to do with Zaria.

I'd kept my promise to greet her at Heathrow Airport upon her return from Uzbekistan. We took a taxi to her friend Diana's apartment in Chiswick, where she had arranged to stay in the guest room. We chatted with Diana and her boyfriend for a bit, it was a bit awkward, and we agreed Zaria would leave her suitcase there but spend her first night in England at Château Hampstead.

We fucked. The sex was brilliant.

I still saw her off-and-on for a while after that. Things got really messy between her and Dovile and I didn't handle it well. Zaria used to call her "that Latvanian whore" and truly believed that every girl I slept with was a cheap whore, except for Zaria herself, of course. Her princess complex simply couldn't handle the fact I was spinning plates, dating a few women, rather than committing to her. Admittedly, it's not an easy reality to acclimate to for a girl, so I don't blame her.

Zaria had decided that she liked sex. She even told me that she felt like she had "wasted her twenties" by holding out. She ended up going on to fuck three more guys that year—more men that year than she had in the previous twelve. Finally having made up for lost time with a little adventure, she went back to the rich Italian guy.

I took stock of my life. It had been two years since I started this journey. I had achieved the dream. I had been dating Tasanee and Adele off-and-on. I was in a fantastic relationship with Dovile. I had fucked Zaria, my first trophy girl and, to top that, she had fallen in love with me. Within two years I had succeeded beyond my wildest expectations. All I had really wanted when I started was a girlfriend. I would have settled for a mediocre-looking thirty year old lawyer or whoever else was willing to have me. But instead, I had gotten so much more. The boy from Newcastle had caught the Unicorn.

So I had to ask myself, *why was I still so often miserable?*

Why was I on an endless emotional roller-coaster? Running my game and banging girls was tremendously satisfying but my emotional baseline was still stuck somewhere down at the bottom of the trough and I didn't know why. I was no happier than I was before. I had peeled back the layers of my mind like an onion but still didn't know who I really was or what I really wanted from life.

I was in several unconventional relationships. Despite the different girls I juggled I'd finally met two girls who inspired me to date, connect, and do all the normal boyfriend-girlfriend things. Zaria and Dovile both knew about the other girls and weren't too enthused by it. Both said they understood why and that it's okay but I'd need to disband the rotation eventually. I was certain both girls were fronting and would take whatever I offered them but that wasn't the point.

I was genuinely thinking I should take my leave from the Game.

I stopped approaching girls while I decided what to do. In the sessions with Colin I speculated about getting out, that perhaps I should choose one of them and call time on my player experiment. I'd gotten as good a girl as I would ever get and should hang on to one of them.

EPILOGUE

So ends the first volume of my story, almost two years to the day since my first cold approach. Looking back now, the entire journey began with a simple first step. It was a decision made while lying on my sofa, depressed, listlessly playing my Xbox360: I would dedicate six months of my life in attempting to become a pick up artist. That experiment expanded and mushroomed into two years of hard work, constant introspection, self-examination, and literally thousands of rejections on the street. I clawed my way up the mountain, sometimes with joyful leaps and other times struggling on my hands and knees. In just two years, my life transformed. The slightly overweight cubicle drone living alone and unhappy, wondering if he'd ever find another girlfriend he liked, became an international traveller tasting true freedom for the first time. I had a circle of cool friends and dated a genuine Russian catwalk model.

And yet I was still unhappy.

My life was unimaginably better than it had been, but my expectations had sky-rocketed. I'd escaped the gulag of office-mortgage-wife but was now ranging across strange uncharted territory looking for answers to questions I couldn't yet formulate. I knew with absolute certainty what I *didn't* want—my previous life (and for my old friends, their current life). That life is a gilded cage. A velvet prison. I could no longer imagine living with such restricted options and limited horizons. I wondered if Dante had a special circle of hell in his Inferno, where men were condemned to bang the same woman every week for the rest of their natural lives. Worse — *as she continued to age.*

Ghastly!

Knowing what I didn't want represented a measure of clarity. However, I didn't really know what I *did* want. For now I could only think to keep plodding forwards—more approaches, tighter game, and more notches.

I'd unplugged from the Matrix and tasted the fruits of freedom but I still carried with me a lot of emotional wreckage. I was only now beginning to look deeply into my identity to better understand who I was, what I wanted, and what had been wrong with me all of these years. The old life had ended, but my new life hadn't quite begun. So it's at this point that I leave you, dear reader. Standing atop the summit of Mount Improbable and realising with trepidation that there was at least one bigger mountain still left to climb, Mount Awesome.

I was a long way from the finish line. Perhaps there wasn't a finishing line at all.

Continue your Player's Journey with Nick Krauser's other resources!

The Model

Everything you need to know about street pick-up is packed into these cutting-edge textbooks. Each volume is written to match your own progress in learning the art form. *Daygame Nitro* introduces the basics of street pick-up and inner game in a simple, easy-to-follow guide. *Daygame Mastery* breaks apart the model into minute detail to help you fine-tune your method. *Daygame Infinite* unlocks your potential with extensive vibe and calibration advice.

  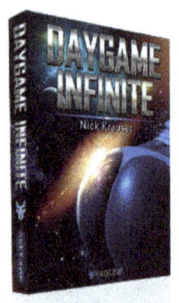

The Journey

Dive deep into the Player's lifestyle with the most detailed and most insightful Game memoir ever written. Four massive volumes take you through every stage from zero to hero as Nick tells you his story. Higher level knowledge seeps out of every page. Live the life!

THE DEMONSTRATION

It's one thing to understand the theory but another to watch, on video, how to run street game and master dating. *Daygame Overkill* provides a play-by-play breakdown of Nick's infield videos, showing you how to get Adventure Sex. *Black Book* explains the dating model in detail, and *Womanizers Bible* provides high-level theory on the Player's World.

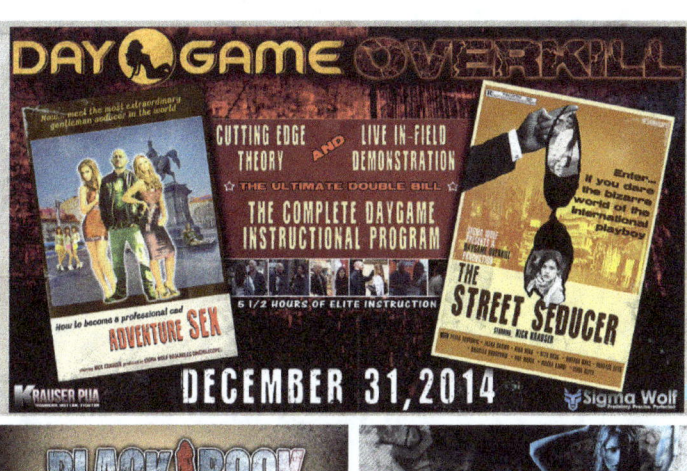

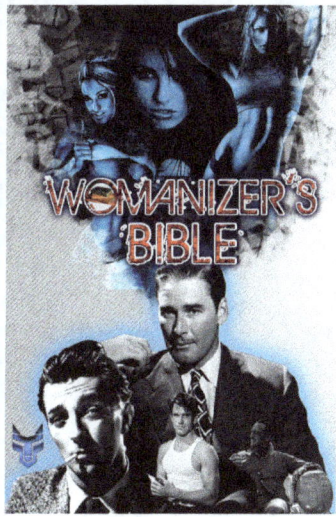

Check out **sigmawolf.com** *and* **daygameoverkill.com**
to access these amazing resources.

www.ingramcontent.com/pod-product-compliance
Lightning Source LLC
Chambersburg PA
CBHW071327080526
44587CB00017B/2751